Take One's
Essential Guide to
Canadian Film

Edited by Wyndham Wise

UNIVERSITY OF TORONTO PRESS
Toronto Buffalo London

© University of Toronto Press Incorporated 2001
Toronto Buffalo London

Printed in Canada

ISBN 0-8020-3512-4 (cloth)
ISBN 0-8020-8398-6 (paper)

Printed on acid-free paper

National Library of Canada Cataloguing in Publication Data

Main entry under title:
Take One's essential guide to Canadian film

ISBN 0-8020-3512-4 (bound)   ISBN 0-8020-8398-6 (pbk.)

1. Motion pictures – Canada.   2. Motion picture actors and
actresses – Canada – Biography – Dictionaries.   3. Motion
picture producers and directors – Canada – Biography –
Dictionaries.   4. Screenwriters – Canada – Biography –
Dictionaries.   5. Motion pictures – Canada – Awards.   I. Wise,
Wyndham, 1947–   II. Title: Essential guide to Canadian film.

PN1993.5.C3T34 2001   791.43'0971   C2001-901387-6

University of Toronto Press acknowledges the financial assistance to its publishing
program of the Canada Council for the Arts and the Ontario Arts Council.

University of Toronto Press acknowledges the financial support for its
publishing activities of the Government of Canada through the
Book Publishing Industry Development Program (BPIDP).

Take One's Essential Guide to Canadian Film

Edited by Wyndham Wise

Take One's Essential Guide to Canadian Film is the most exhaustive and up-to-date reference book on Canadian film and filmmakers, combining over 700 reviews and biographical listings with a detailed chronology of major events in Canadian film and television history. Compiled by Wyndham Wise, the publisher and editor of *Take One*, Canada's most respected film magazine, and with a foreword by Canadian director Patricia Rozema, this is the only reference book of its kind published in English.

Each film title is listed with credits, a mini review, and significant awards. Biographical listings of directors, producers, actors, writers, animators, cinematographers, distributors, exhibitors, and independent filmmakers are accompanied by date and place of birth, date of death if applicable, a brief career overview, and a filmography. Wise celebrates Canadian achievement on both a national and an international scale, and juxtaposes the distinctly Canadian with Canada's exports to Hollywood: Maury Chaykin and Jim Carrey, John Candy and William Shatner, *Mon Oncle Antoine* and *Porky's*, *Highway 61* and *Meatballs*, *The Red Violin* and *The Art of War*.

From great early Hollywood stars such as Walter Huston, Fay Wray, Mary Pickford, Norma Shearer, and Marie Dressler, to our current crop of star directors – including Patricia Rozema, Atom Egoyan, David Cronenberg, Denys Arcand, Peter Mettler, Guy Maddin, and Robert Lepage – Canadians have made an important but largely unrecorded contribution to the history of world cinema. Impressive for its breadth of coverage, refreshing in its opinionated informality, this comprehensive and lively look at Canadian film culture at the start of the twenty-first century admirably fills the gap.

WYNDHAM WISE is the publisher and editor-in-chief of *Take One: Film & Television in Canada*, published five times annually.

For my daughters Sarah-Jane and Tessa

Contents

Foreword by PATRICIA ROZEMA   ix

Preface   xi

Abbreviations   xii

Take One's Essential Guide to Canadian Film   3

Appendix 1: A Chronology of Canadian Film and Television   229

Appendix 2: Awards   259

Foreword

ON TRUDEAU, THE NATION, AND CANADIAN CINEMA

Pierre Elliott Trudeau sat a few rows ahead of me at the first screening in Canada of my English-made, American-paid, very Canadian adaptation of Jane Austen's *Mansfield Park* at the opening of the Montreal Film Festival, in August 1999. I almost asked a festival official to introduce me, but then suddenly feared appearing like another hustler with an agenda – even though I had no agenda. Trudeau died recently. I now wish I had made contact. He was our leading man for so many important years. He was our star. And we never once worried that he'd move to Los Angeles.

We choose our stars. Who we pick speaks volumes about us. I think it might be useful to consider what our nation's selection of Trudeau tells us about ourselves. As members of the collective writing and directing team of the 'Late Twentieth Century Canadian History Movie,' what type of central character did we choose? Well, we thought, let's pick one who is cosmopolitan and undeniably intelligent. His journey must call forth the language of justice, pride, and finely spun philosophy. Of course, if he's going to be interesting to just about everybody, he'll have to be good-looking, yet not too good looking. Just the proper blend of the individual with the classic; the

random – that odd little slant of the eye – woven into the eternally right.

Our star needs to be an original. One with an aristocratic sense of entitlement, along with the greatness of vision to worry about the vulnerable among us. He must be straight but not narrow; let him declare that the state has no place in the bedrooms of the nation. He should be unquestionably comfortable in the world's great cities, and at home alone in the wilds. We'll need a few gags, and some pirouettes. Let him flip the bird (this is not a character desperate for our approval) and have a rocky, splashy love life. In his later years let's give him an alternative family structure. And he *must* know the value of a rose.

Trudeau. The collaborative imagination of our country couldn't have constructed a more alluring and admirable character. We can be proud of our creation – he was a character of range, subtlety, and quiet authority, and beneath this stillness he had an inexplicable boisterous life force that unsettled the surface of any description. Yes. This is a leading man worth watching. But why have we not tried to fabricate someone this spectacular in our movies? He is not a recognizable protagonist we find as we flip through the directory of our cinema. Why do we continue with modest people leading modest lives?

Perhaps the most enlightening question is not what leading character we chose, but what *type* of film we made. If Trudeau were this movie, what sort of movie would he be? It seems we created an art film – certainly no blockbuster this one. Not pandering to the Americans, we designed a truthful creation that played well in festivals, but not necessarily in malls. The narrative was dense, and perhaps even erratic – no clear career-building narrative thrust in this number. Ours is a work of fairly elevated culture without tremendous mass marketable appeal (much to the distress of our industry types).

We sense that originality and success are strangers to each other. 'Success' in the mass market is often forgotten. Originality, however, has children. It is felt. The money comes later. Something within us, within our nation, cries out for the original. We must, like our favoured leading films, speak to the new. So it was for Pierre Trudeau and so it is for all our finest cultural expressions, whether they be in collaborative nation building or in creating our own national cinema. As we survey the contents of *Take One's Essential Guide to Canadian Film* and consider the films we have funded, shot, and fêted, we see a portrait of a nation – a nation that carries a conviction deep within itself that we are most ourselves when we try to be new, to be different from what has gone before. We are a country and a film industry as yet unimagined with purpose far beyond survival.

PATRICIA ROZEMA

Preface

Take One's Essential Guide to Canadian Film began as an issue of *Take One* published in the summer of 1996 in celebration of the hundredth anniversary of film in Canada. This issue, which featured 100 of the most famous Canadians who made a living in film, whether at home, in Hollywood, or abroad, engendered a shock of recognition. From the stars of silent movies, such as Fay Wray, Walter Huston, Mary Pickford, Norma Shearer, and Marie Dressler, to our current crop of star directors, including Robert Lepage, Patricia Rozema, Atom Egoyan, David Cronenberg, and Denys Arcand, Canadians have made an important but largely unrecorded contribution to the history of cinema.

There are a number of earlier reference guides to Canadian film. My goal, with *Take One's Essential Guide to Canadian Film*, is to continue the process of charting our national cinema that was begun almost thirty years ago by Eleanor Beatty in *The Handbook of Canadian Film* (1973, 2nd ed. 1977) and Canadian film history professor Peter Morris in *The Film Companion* (1984). Both of these volumes are now out of print, and the paradigm of Canadian feature filmmaking has changed dynamically since 1984. English-speaking Canadian cinema is no longer an under-appreciated cousin of Quebec cinema. With the

emergence of the Toronto new wave in the 1980s, and the corresponding growth of independent features from Newfoundland, the Maritimes, Quebec, the Prairies, and British Columbia, Canadian films now take their place with the best the world has to offer.

The more than 700 entries in *Take One's Essential Guide to Canadian Film* identify Canadians who have made a contribution to the world of cinema and important, award-winning Canadian films that have made an impact on our national culture. However, this guide is by no means complete. It is a start, a work in progress, that will grow with each new edition. A number of individuals and films have been omitted due both to space constraints and to the availability of the films to be viewed (always a problem when it comes to Canadian film). It is my intention that these will be included in future editions.

This guide would not have been possible without reference to the following publications: Eleanor Beattie, *The Handbook of Canadian Film*, 2nd ed. (Toronto: Peter Martin and Associates, 1977); Peter Morris, *Embattled Shadows: A History of Canadian Cinema, 1895–1939* (Montreal: McGill-Queen's University Press, 1978); Peter Morris, *The Film Companion* (Toronto: Irwin, 1984); D. John Turner, *The Canadian Feature Film Index, 1913–1985 /*

Index des film canadiens de long métage, 1913–1985, French text by Micheline Morisset (Ottawa: Public Archives of Canada, 1987); Donald Bidd, ed., *The NFB Film Guide, 1939–1989* (Montreal: National Film Board of Canada, 1991); Michel Coulombe and Marcel Jean, eds, *Le Dictionnaire du cinéma québécois*, 3rd ed., rev. and enlarged (Montreal: Editions du Boréal, 1999); *Who's Who in Canadian Film and Television / Qui est qui au cinéma et à la télévision au Canada*, 2000 ed. (Toronto: Academy of Canadian Cinema and Television, 1999); Maria Topalovich, *And the Genie Goes To ...: Celebrating 50 Years of the Canadian Film Awards* (Don Mills, ON: Stoddart, 2000).

Take One's Essential Guide to Canadian Film would not have been published without the helpful assistance and encouragement of Eve Goldin, senior library technician at The Film Reference Library, Toronto, and members of the *Take One* editorial board including: Tom McSorley, the executive director of the Canadian Film Institute in Ottawa; Maurie Alioff, a film journalist and screenwriter who teaches screenwriting at Vanier College; Cynthia Amsden, editor-in-chief of Canadian Weeklies Syndicate; and Matthew Hays, the associate editor of the weekly *Montreal Mirror*. I would also like to thank the following *Take One* writers for their contributions: Angela Baldassarre, Pamela Cuthbert, Paul Eichhorn, Tim Foley, Marc Glassman, Barbara Goslawski, Laurence Green, Lee Parpart, and Isa Tousignant. And finally, I would like to offer my deepest gratitude to Ruth Pincoe, Geri Savits-Fine, and Susan Tolusso, who helped with the difficult task of copy editing and cross-referencing the entries, and Jill McConkey of the University of Toronto Press, whose enthusiasm and support made *Take One's Essential Guide* possible.

Organization

Cross-references to other entries in the *Guide* are indicated by an asterisk. Films are listed by year of release both in the entries and in the Chronology (Appendix 1). Films in the Awards section (Appendix 2) are listed according to the year the award was given.

Wyndham Wise
publisher and editor-in-chief, *Take One*

Abbreviations

General

a	actor/actress
ad	art director
an	animator
ap	associate producer
assist. ed	assistant editor
B+W	black and white
CCA	capital cost allowance
d	director
ed	editor
exp	executive producer
m	minutes
mus	music
narr	narrator
p	producer
ph	cinematographer
prod	production company
sc	screenplay
sr	sound recording
V	available on video

BBG	Board of Broadcast Governors
CBC	Canadian Broadcasting Corporation
CFDC	Canadian Film Development Corporation
CGMPB	Canadian Government Motion Picture Bureau
CMPDA	Canadian Motion Picture Distributors Association
CRBC	Canadian Radio Broadcasting Commission
CRTC	Canadian Radio-Television and Telecommunications Commission
FPCC	Famous Players Canadian Corporation
NFB	National Film Board of Canada
SRC	Société Radio-Canada
TVO	TV Ontario

Organizations

ACPAV	Association coopérative de productions audio-visuelles
ACTRA	Alliance of Canadian Cinema and Radio Artists (after 1984, Alliance of Canadian Cinema, Television, and Radio Artists)
ASN	Associated Screen News

Canadian Film Awards

CFA-A	Actor/Actress
CFA-AE	Arts and Experimental
CFA-AS	Animated Short
CFA-ASC	Adapted Screenplay
CFA-D	Director
CFA-E	Editing
CFA-FD	Feature Documentary
CFA-FF	Feature Film
CFA-FY	Film of the Year

Abbreviations

CFA-M	Musical Score	PJ-D	Director
CFA-NTS	Non-Theatrical Short	PJ-E	Editing
CFA-PH	Cinematography	PJ-FD	Feature Documentary
CFA-S	Song	PJ-M	Musical Score
CFA-SA	Supporting Actor/Actress	PJ-P	Picture
CFA-SPA	Special Award	PJ-PH	Cinematography
CFA-SC	Original Screenplay	PJ-S	Short
CFA-SD	Short Documentary	PJ-SA	Supporting Actor/Actress
CFA-TD	Theatrical Documentary	PJ-SC	Screenplay
CFA-TS	Theatrical Short		

Academy Awards

AA-A	Actor/Actress
AA-AD	Art Direction
AA-AS	Animated Short
AA-D	Director
AA-E	Editing
AA-FD	Feature Documentary
AA-LAS	Live-Action Short
AA-P	Picture
AA-S	Short
AA-SR	Sound Recording

Genie Awards

GA-A	Actor/Actress
GA-AS	Animated Short
GA-ASC	Adapted Screenplay
GA-D	Director
GA-E	Editing
GA-FD	Feature Documentary
GA-LAS	Live-Action Short
GA-M	Musical Score
GA-P	Picture
GA-PH	Cinematography
GA-S	Song
GA-SA	Supporting Actor/Actress
GA-SC	Original Screenplay
GA-SD	Short Documentary

Special awards presented at the Genie Awards ceremony

CJA — Claude Jutra Award
GRA — Golden Reel Award

Academy Award Nominations

AAN-A	Actor / Actress
AAN-AD	Art Direction
AAN-AS	Animated Short
AAN-ASC	Adapted Screenplay
AAN-D	Director
AAN-FLF	Foreign-Language Film
AAN-LAS	Live-Action Short
AAN-P	Picture
AAN-S	Short
AAN-SA	Supporting Actor
AAN-SC	Original Screenplay
AAN-SD	Short Documentary
AAN-SE	Special Effects

Prix Jutra

PJ-A	Actor/Actress
PJ-AS	Animated Short

Take One's Essential Guide to Canadian Film

A

Acadie, l'Acadie?!?, L'
1971 118m *prod* NFB, *p* Guy L. Coté, Paul Larose, *d* Michel Brault, Pierre Perrault, *ph* Michel Brault, *ed* Monique Fortier, *mus* Majorique Duguay, Valère Blais. This important direct-cinema documentary – much admired in Quebec, but less so by Acadians – covers the protests in 1968 and 1969 at l'Université de Moncton in support of French-speaking students in New Brunswick. The film, which focuses on the street marches and sit-ins, includes interviews with students as they discuss what it means to be Acadian. The protests ultimately failed to move the university establishment, and the conclusion seems to be that the French fact is safe only within the borders of Quebec. (V)

Acker, Sharon
Actor; b. Toronto, 1935. A leading lady seen mostly on American television (she played Perry Mason's loyal secretary Della Street in the last season of the long-running series) who occasionally appeared in films. Acker began her career as a model and joined the Stratford Festival company in 1956. A brief acting stint in England led to a part in the comedy *Lucky Jim* with Terry Thomas. Ten years later she was in John Boorman's cult classic *Point Blank* with fellow Canadians John Vernon* and Lloyd Bochner.* She also appeared in Paul Almond's *The Act of the Heart.* **Films and television include:** *Lucky Jim* 1957; *1+1: Exploring the Kinsey Reports* 1961; *Waiting for Caroline* 1967; *Point Blank* 1967; *The First Time* 1969; *Don't Let the Angels Fall* 1969; *The Act of the Heart* 1970; *The Senator* 1970–1 (series, one of three rotating elements from *The Bold Ones*); *The New Perry Mason* 1973–4 (series); *Executive Suite* 1976–7 (series); *Happy Birthday to Me* 1981; *Off Your Rocker* 1982; *Threshold* 1982.

Across the Border
1938 54m *prod* Central Films, *p* Kenneth Bishop, *d* Leon Barsha, *sc* Edgar Edwards, *ph* George Meehan, *ed* William Austin, *mus* Morris Stoloff; *with* Charles Quigley, Rita Hayworth, George McKay, Edgar Edwards. This 'quota quickie' was one of a dozen B movies featuring lumberjacks and mounties that were made for the British market during the late 1930s on Vancouver Island with minor Hollywood talent. *Across the Border* was shot back-to-back with *Convicted* in the winter of 1937, and released in London, England, two months later. Both films show glimpses of a future Hollywood screen goddess – Rita Hayworth, age nineteen, had been in the movies for only two years.

Action: The October Crisis of 1970
1974 87m *prod* NFB, *p* Tom Daly, Normand Cloutier, Robin Spry, *d/narr* Robin Spry, *ed* Shelagh MacKenzie, Joan Henson. A thoughtful look at the October Crisis, when FLQ terrorists kidnapped a British diplomat and killed Quebec cabinet minister Pierre Laporte. Compiled from news footage and other films, *Action* portrays past and contemporary independence moments, the rise of the separatist movement in Quebec following the death of Maurice Duplessis, and the confusion and dismay when the Canadian army was ordered out to patrol the streets of Montreal. The 'stars' of the film are Pierre Trudeau, René Lévesque, Robert Bourassa, Jean Drapeau, and of course, the terrorists themselves. See also *Reaction: A Portrait of a Society in Crisis.* (V)

Act of the Heart, The
1970 103m *prod* Quest Film Productions,

p/d/sc Paul Almond, *ph* Jean Boffety, *ed* James D. Mitchell, *mus* Harry Freedman, Gilles Vigneault; *with* Geneviève Bujold, Donald Sutherland, Monique Leyrac, Gilles Vigneault, Bill Mitchell, Sharon Acker. The second of three films by Paul Almond* featuring his wife at the time, Geneviève Bujold* (see also *Isabel* and *Journey*). Martha (Bujold), a religious young girl from the Quebec North Shore, arrives in Montreal to serve as a nanny to a widowed business woman (Leyrac) and her son Russell (Mitchell). She joins a local church where she becomes infatuated with the priest (Sutherland*). When Russell dies in an accident, Martha temporarily loses her faith and declares her love for the priest. They live together, but she is consumed by guilt over her moment of weakness and commits suicide. The film split critical opinion: some called it pretentious while others found it had rich, deep subject matter. It won six Canadian Film Awards but was a box-office failure. **Awards include**: CFA: Director, Actress (Bujold), Art Direction, Overall Sound, Sound Editing, Musical Score.

Adams, Beverly

Actor; b. Vancouver, 1945. Adams, a lovely, sensual actress who appeared in 1960s kitch classics such as *How to Stuff a Wild Bikini* (with Annette Funicello and Frankie Avalon), also played the recurring character of Lovey Kravezit in the series of Matt Helm spy-comedy films starring Dean Martin. She retired from acting after her marriage to hair stylist Vidal Sasson. **Films include:** *The New Interns* 1964; *How to Stuff a Wild Bikini* 1965; *Murderers' Row* 1966; *Kiss the Girls and Make Them Die* 1966; *The Silencers* 1966; *Birds Do It* 1966; *The Ambushers* 1967; *Torture Garden* 1967; *Hammerhead* 1968; *Mind Games* 1996.

Adjuster, The

1991 102m *prod* Ego Film Arts, Family Viewing Productions, *p* Camelia Frieberg, Atom Egoyan, *d/sc* Atom Egoyan, *ph* Paul Sarossy, *ed* Susan Shipton, *mus* Mychael Danna; *with* Maury Chaykin, Jennifer Dale, Patricia Collins, David Hemblen, Arsinée Khanjian, Elias Koteas, Don McKellar, Gabrielle Rose. Insurance adjuster Noah Render (Koteas*) attempts to restore the damaged lives of his clients. His methods are unorthodox. He sleeps with most of them, puts them up in a designated hotel, and quotes his profession's code to them like a mantra: 'You may not know it yet, but you're in shock.' This amoral yet compassionate protagonist who lives with his film-censor wife (Khanjian*) in a barren, unfinished suburban development is one of Egoyan's* most strangely compelling creations. Egoyan's effective use of wide screen portrays the terrifying abyss that separates Noah from everyone he encounters. *The Adjuster* – a haunting drama of disconnection and desire – is a searching re-interpretation of Luis Buñuel's *Nazarin*, with distant echoes of Andrei Tarkovsky's *The Sacrifice*. (V)

Adventure of Faustus Bidgood, The

1986 110m *prod* Faustus Bidgood Productions, *p/d/sc* Andy Jones, Michael Jones, *ph/ed* Michael Jones; *with* Andy Jones, Greg Malone, Robert Joy, Maisie Rillie, Mary Walsh, Cathy Jones. This film was created by what was essentially the core of the Newfoundland comedy group Codco. The legend of *The Adventures of Faustus Bigood* is its ten years in the making. Once completed, however, it received little commercial distribution and remains difficult to find. Crammed with gags, off-the-wall ideas, and freewheeling experiments in form, the film chronicles the final days in office of Faustus Bidgood, an obsequious little bureaucrat (played with winning numbness by Andy Jones*) who, after a decidedly lachrymose revolution, becomes the first ruler of the People's Republic of Newfoundland – a twisted take on Canadian documentaries mixed with a large dash of Monty Python: very bizarre and very funny.

Affaire Bronswik, L'
1978 24m *prod* NFB, *p* René Jodoin, *d/sc* Robert Awad, André Leduc, *an* André Leduc, Robet Awad, Jean-Michel Labrosse, *ed* Robert Awad, *narr* Ian De Voy. A clever satire of conspicuous consumption and the documentary genre. Directors Robert Awad and André Leduc combine live action with animation to 'document' stories about unfortunate consumers whose psyches are invaded by subliminal waves emanating from their Bronswik TV sets. The victims are 'forced' to buy things they don't really need, and then interviewed by the filmmakers in a realistic manner. The film's humorous, tongue-in-cheek style masks a disturbing message about media manipulation and the power of the steady flow of television commercials. **Awards include:** CFA: Theatrical Short.

Afterlife
1978 7m12s *prod* NFB, *p* Derek Lamb, *d/an* Ishu Patel, *mus* Herbie Mann. This animated short from the Indian-born Ishu Patel* uses innovative techniques with back-lit plasticine to offer impressionistic and visionary views of the eternal question: Is there life after death? The film, based partially on case histories that provide some evidence of an afterlife, blends modern and ancient beliefs with transcultural myths. (V) **Awards include:** CFA: Animated Short.

After the Axe
1981 56m *prod* NFB, *exp* Arthur Hammond, *p* Sturla Gunnarsson, Steve Lucas, *d* Sturla Gunnarsson, *sc* Steve Lucas, *ph* Andreas Poulsson, *ed/narr* Roger Mattiussi, *mus* Patricia Cullen, Sharon Smith; *with* James Douglas, Janine Manatis, Anne Christison. This docudrama examines executive terminations and the growth industry of relocation counsellors. Biff Wilson (Douglas), a senior marketing executive, is let go from a major food company after fifteen years of solid service. His fall from security and status to dependent house-husband, as his children come to resent him and his former colleagues avoid him, is detailed with the use of non-actors and real-life situations and locations. The film, a damning account of a corporate culture that stresses success over compassion, received an Academy Award nomination for Short Documentary. (V)

Agnes of God
1985 98m *prod* Albion Films, *p* Norman Jewison, Patrick Palmer, *d* Norman Jewison, *sc/play* John Pielmeier, *ph* Sven Nykvist, *ed* Antony Gibbs, *mus* Georges Delerue; *with* Jane Fonda, Anne Bancroft, Meg Tilly, Janine Fluet, Deborah Grover, Michele George. *Agnes of God*, Norman Jewison's* only Canadian film, is based on the popular play by John Pielmeier. The plot concerns a young nun (Tilly) who is accused of giving birth to an illegitimate baby and then killing the child. This heavy, even hysterical, melodrama with no clear moral solution provides a field day for its two American leads, Fonda and Bancroft. It was shot by Ingmar Bergman's ace cinematographer, Sven Nykvist. (V)

Ahô ... au coeur du monde primitif
1975 91m *prod* Les Productions Via la Monde Canada, *p/d/sc* Daniel Bertolino, François Floquet, *ph* François Boucher, Daniel Bertolino, François Floquet, *ed* François Arnaud, Pierre Larocque, *mus*

Pat Prilly. A visually arresting documentary about the last surviving primitive tribes around the world. The filmmakers travelled to the island of Sumatra in Indonesia, the jungles of Brazil, and the Congo River basin to record this fascinating study of a world rarely captured on film. Perhaps the most successful section is on the pygmy tribes of the Congo and their relationship with the jungle that surrounds them. Scenes of filing teeth and ritual circumcision are not sensationalized, but rather portrayed as an integral part of the tribal ethos. The closing scenes – showing tribal women doing exercises directed by a gramophone-toting white woman and men working with giant forest-clearing machines – are devastating. **Awards include:** CFA: Feature Documentary.

Air Bud

1997 97m *prod* Keystone Entertainment, Walt Disney Pictures (U.S.), *exp* Michael Strange, Michael Vince, Bob Weinstein, Harvey Weinstein, *p* Robert Vince, William Vince, *d* Charles Martin Smith, *sc* Paul Tamsay, Aaron Mendelsohn, *ph* Mike Southon, *ed* Alison Grace, *mus* Brahm Wenger; *with* Michael Jeter, Kevin Zegers, Wendy Makkena, Bill Cobbs, Eric Christmas, Nicola Cavendish. *Air Bud*, a modest boy-and-his-dog Disney knockoff, tells the sentimental and mostly clichéd tale of Buddy, a lovable basketball-scoring stray, and Kevin (Zegers), a lonely, inward boy. Buddy escapes the clutches of a bad-tempered clown (Jeter) and is befriended by Kevin, who discovers his hoop abilities. Through a series of improbable events, Buddy becomes the star of the local high school basketball team. When the misanthropic clown returns to reclaim his dog, events culminate in a climatic chase. Warm performances, especially by Zegers, Makkena (as the mother),

and Cobbs (as an ex-pro coach), enliven an otherwise paint-by-numbers script. (V) **Awards include:** Golden Reel Award.

À la croisée des chemins

1943 93m *prod* La Société des Missions Étrangères de la Province de Québec, *d* Jean-Marie Poitevin, Paul Guèvremont, *sc/ed* Jean-Marie Poitevin, *ph* Paul Morin, *mus* Fernand Gaudry, *narr* René Lévesque; *with* Paul Guèvremont, Denise Pelletier, Rose Rey-Duzil, Jean Fontaine, Camélienne Séguin, Denis Drouin. The first dramatic feature film produced by a Quebec religious community tells the story of a young man's struggle to leave his wealthy life of comfort for a missionary calling – forceful but dated propaganda for the Catholic Church narrated by René Lévesque, the future Quebec premier.

Aldon, Mari

Actor; b. Toronto, 1927. During the 1950s, Aldon was a minor leading lady with Canadian stage and radio experience who managed to appear in a few good movies (*The Barefoot Contessa, Summertime*). She retired in 1955 after her marriage to Hollywood director Tay Garnett. **Films include:** *Distant Drums* 1951; *This Woman Is Dangerous* 1952; *Tangier Incident* 1953; *The Barefoot Contessa* 1954; *Summertime* 1955.

Alexis Tremblay: Habitant

1943 35m *prod* NFB, *p/d/sc/ed* Jane Marsh Bevridge, *ph* Judith Crawley, *mus* Louis Applebaum, Maurice Blackburn. One of the first NFB films to be produced, directed, written (Jane Marsh Bevridge*), and shot (Judith Crawley*) by women. *Alexis Tremblay* is an idyllic portrait of life of a rural Quebec family who live in the Charlevoix region along the St Lawrence River. Each season has its traditions and rituals (spring planting, fall harvest, winter chores, etc.) overseen by the Catholic Church. For years this was one the NFB's most popular films, although today its view of 'happy peasants' in the bosom of a benevolent church seems rather quaint and outdated.

Alias Will James
1988 83m *prod* NFB, *p* Eric Michel, *d/sc* Jacques Godbout, *ph* Jean-Pierre Lachapelle, *ed* Monique Fortier, *mus* Robert M. Lepage, Ian Tyson. A poetic and loving look at the life of Ernest Dufault, a Québécois who claimed to be a cowboy from Montana. During the 1920s, under the name of Will James, he became known in Hollywood as a writer and illustrator of westerns. The film explores Dufault's contribution to the myth of the Old West and parallels his life with modern Québécois pursuing cowboy aspirations on the American rodeo circuit. A quest for a Québécois hero and an examination of the subconscious framework of the human imagination form the basis for one of Jacques Godbout's* best films, with particularly evocative songs by Ian Tyson. (V)

Allan, Ted
Writer; b. Alan Herman, Montreal, 1916; d. 1995. Ted Allan was Canada's leading left-wing writer of books, screenplays, and radio, television, and live drama. His life was defined by an obsession with Dr Norman Bethune, his comrade-in-arms during the Spanish Civil War. Allan co-wrote a biography of Bethune – *The Scalpel, The Sword* (1952) – and battled for nearly fifty years to make a movie about the Canadian surgeon who became a hero of the Chinese revolution. After an arduous production, Phillip Borsos's *Bethune: The Making of a Hero,** based on Allan's script and starring

Donald Sutherland,* was released in 1990 to almost universal critical condemnation. In 1976, Allan's autobiographical screenplay for Ján Kadár's *Lies My Father Told Me** won a Golden Globe Award and was nominated for an Academy Award. **Films and television include:** *Son copain* 1950 (sc); *The Money Makers* 1952 (sc, TV); *The Webster Boy* 1962 (sc); *7 fois ... (par jour)* 1971 (sc); *Lies My Father Told Me* 1975 (sc/a, CFA-ASC, AAN-SC); *Lies* 1976 (a); *It Rained All Night the Day I Left* 1980 (sc); *Falling in Love Again* 1980 (co-sc); *Love Streams* 1984 (sc with John Cassavetes); *I'm Almost Not Crazy ... John Cassavetes: The Man and His Work* 1984 (a); *Bethune: The Making of a Hero* 1990 (sc).

Allen, Jule and Jay
Exhibitors; **Jule:** b. Bradford, Pa., 1888; d. 1964; **Jay:** b. Bradford, Pa., 1890; d. 1942. The Allen brothers, along with their father Bernard, opened their first 'Theatorium' in 1906 in Brantford, Ontario, and formed one of Canada's first distribution companies, the Allen Amusement Corporation. They built their first luxury theatre in Calgary in 1912 and by 1918 owned the largest chain in Canada. In 1922, after losing a fierce bidding war for first-run features, they went bankrupt and sold all of their fifty-three theatres to the American-owned Famous Players Canadian Corporation. This would be the last time Canadians made a significant impact through ownership of a national exhibition chain until Garth Drabinsky* built up Cineplex Odeon in the 1980s. The Allens continued to exhibit films, and they operated Ontario's largest independent theatrical circuit prior to the Second World War.

Alligator Shoes
1981 98m *exp* Don Haig, Barry Shapiro,

p Clay Borris, John F. Phillips, *d/sc* Clay Borris, *ph* John F. Phillips, *ed* Gordon McClellan, *mus* Murray McLauchlan; *with* Garry Borris, Ronalda Jones, Clay Borris, Rose Maltais-Borris, Len Perry, Simone Champagne. A slice of *cinéma-vérité* set in Toronto's working-class Cabbagetown. Two brothers (played by real-life brothers Garry and Clay Borris) drink, carouse, and make trouble while holding close to 'down home' family values of the Maritimes. Their life is changed forever when a mentally unhinged aunt (Jones) comes to stay. Clay Borris's intensely personal drama drew a great deal of critical attention and was invited to the Cannes Film Festival, but the film received only limited distribution and Borris's promising career never materialized.

Almond, Paul

Producer, director, and writer; b. Montreal, 1931. From the mid-1950s into the 1960s, the Oxford-educated Almond directed more than 100 dramas for CBC-TV and British television. When he turned to feature filmmaking, he attracted domestic and international attention with a trilogy of understated, highly interiorized explorations of mind and spirit, starring his then wife, Geneviève Bujold.* In the title role of *Isabel*,* she almost drowns in a flood of threatening memories. In *The Act of the Heart*,* Bujold plays a troubled woman who falls in love with a priest (Donald Sutherland*) who is living through his own spiritual crisis. In *Journey*,* Almond cast Bujold again as his destabilized protagonist, along with John Vernon.* Almond's attempt to establish an art cinema met with critical resistance and only modest commercial success, leading to his absence from filmmaking for nearly ten years. He returned in 1980 with *Final Assignment*, again starring Bujold, but the film was a critical and box-office disap-

pointment. **Films and television include:** *Night Watch* 1954 (p/d, TV); *The Hill* 1956 (p/d/sc, TV); *Wuthering Heights* 1957 (p/d, TV); *Under Milkwood* 1959 (p/d, TV); *The Watchers* 1960 (p/d, TV); *The Dumb Waiter* 1961 (d, TV); *Backfire* 1961 (d, TV); *Forest Rangers* 1963–5 (d, series); *Journey to the Centre* 1963 (p/d/sc, TV); *Seven Up* 1964 (p/d/sc, TV); *The Birthday Party* 1965 (p/d, TV); *Romeo and Jeannette* 1965 (p/d, TV); *A Doll's House* 1966 (p/d, TV); *Isabel* 1968 (p/d/sc); *The Act of the Heart* 1970 (p/d/sc, CFA-D); *Journey* 1972 (p/d/sc); *Every Person Is Crazy* 1979 (d, TV); *Final Assignment* 1980 (d); *Ups and Downs* 1983 (p/d/sc); *Captive Hearts* 1987 (d); *The Dance Goes On* 1991 (p/d/sc).

Anderson Lee, Pamela

Actor; b. Ladysmith, B.C., 1967. Pamela Denise Anderson was the first baby born in Canada on 1 July 1967; she received the title of Centennial Baby, and her parents won several cash prizes and awards. She moved to Vancouver in 1988, and her career was launched when a cameraman noticed her at a B.C. Lions football game and put her up on the stadium screen. She found work on the sitcom *Home Improvement* and was cast as a regular on *Baywatch*. Anderson has had a rocky marriage to Motley Crüe drummer Tommy Lee, and her first attempt at a movie lead in *Barb Wire* proved to be less of a box-office hit than anticipated. However, due to the unparalleled worldwide success of *Baywatch* and *V.I.P.*, Anderson remains one of the most recognizable women on television today. **Films and television include:** *Home Improvement* 1991–3 (series); *Baywatch* 1992–5 (series); *Barb Wire* 1996; *V.I.P.* 1998–present (series).

Animation

The roots of animation in Canada lie in Great Britain. John Grierson* and Norman McLaren,* both from Scotland, transformed filmmaking in Canada in the early 1940s. Grierson, the founder of the NFB, always claimed that his finest discovery was McLaren, whom he persuaded to come to Canada to make animated films. When he arrived in Ottawa in 1941, McLaren was immediately put to work creating propaganda pieces for the war effort, and within a year, he was asked to create an animation unit for the Board. The crack team he assembled included Jim McKay, George Dunning* and René Jodoin.

McLaren's interest was in formal experiments, particularly drawing directly on celulloid. His animated works were not character or plot driven; in conscious opposition to Hollywood cartoons, his films were abstract, operating on principles of rhythm, melody, and colour. His style and philosophy influenced Canadian animation both at the NFB and in the private sector, which began to grow with the establishment of Dunning and McKay's Graphic Associates in Toronto in 1949.

With Colin Low's *The Romance of Transportation in Canada** (1953), a sense of character and incident entered animation at the NFB. As McLaren's successor as head of the animation department, Low* helped to foster the new generation of artists who entered the Board in the late 1950s. Among them were Derek Lamb,* Kaj Pindal,* Arthur Lipsett,* and Gerald Potterton.* McLaren gave informal animation classes to these youngsters, but the films they produced were quite different from his stylized works. Humorous shorts such as Pindal's *What on Earth!** (1966) and Potterton's *My Financial Career** (1963) told tales in a manner that communicated directly to Canadian and international audiences.

In the 1960s, Wolf Koenig* replaced his collaborator Colin Low as the head of the NFB animation department, and

more importantly, René Jodoin was made executive producer of a new French department of animation. Jodoin's unit produced both abstract pieces and simple stories with limited dialogue. Foreign talent such as Co Hoedeman* and Bretislav Pojar were brought in to augment a talented crew that included Québécois pin-screen wizard Jacques Drouin and experimentalist Pierre Hébert. By contrast, the English department, spearheaded by Derek Lamb, contributed well-plotted, often sardonic pieces by such talents as Caroline Leaf,* John Weldon,* and Eugene Fedorenko. Many of their films were multi-award winners. Frédéric Back,* the German-born animator who spent his career in McLaren-like freedom at SRC, also won two Academy Awards: for *Crac!* (1982) and for *The Man Who Planted Trees* (1987).

The 1970s saw the growth of private animation houses as commercial work in television became plentiful. Such companies as Nelvana* in Toronto, Cinar in Montreal, International Rocketship in Vancouver, and Crawley Films and Lacewood Productions in Ottawa became important players in the North American marketplace. Community colleges established credit courses, and graduates, especially from Sheridan College in Oakville, Ontario, continued the high standards set by the NFB. More recently, Canadian animators have infiltrated Disney and Industrial Light and Magic, contributing to the success of such megahits as *Aladdin*, *Who Framed Roger Rabbit*, *Jurassic Park*, *The Mask*, *Terminator 2: Judgment Day*, often with the use of groundbreaking Canadian software programs created by Alias/Wavefront, Side Effects, and Softimage.

With the NFB's tenth Academy Award (for *Bob's Birthday**) in 1995 and Alias/Wavefront's Academy Award nomination for its experimental short, *the end*, in 1996, Canadian animators continue a proud tradition of producing some of the best work in the world.

Anne Trister
1986 102m *prod* Les Films Vision 4, NFB *exp* Roger Frappier, *p* Roger Frappier, Claude Bonin, *d* Léa Pool, *sc* Léa Pool, Marcel Beaulieu, *ph* Pierre Mignot, *ed* Michel Arcand, *mus* René Dupéré, Daniel Deshaime; *with* Albane Guilhe, Louise Marleau, Hugues Quester, Lucie Laurier, Nuvit Ozdogru. The title character, Anne Trister (Guilhe), is a young Swiss-Jewish artist who is profoundly affected by the death of her father. She leaves Switzerland for Quebec to visit her friend Alix (Marleau), a psychologist to whom she becomes attracted. Through her work, Alix has developed an emotional bond with Sarah (Laurier), a rebellious child with an enormous need to be loved. Detached from the world around her, Anne takes over a vacant studio to paint a gigantic fresco and throws herself into a series of impulsive affairs. In this feminist, abstract drama with an emphasis on the characters' emotions rather than on plot, director Léa Pool* delicately creates an overlapping world where Anne, Alix, and Sarah explore the many improbable forms of love and dependency. **Awards include:** GA: Cinematography.

Anniversary
1963 19m8s *prod* NFB, *exp* Nicolas Balla, *p/sc* William Weintraub, *an* Pierre L'Amare, Kenneth Horn, *ed* Tony Lower, *mus* Norman Bigras; *with* Walter Pigeon. This compilation film features clips of early Canadian actors who made big it in Hollywood – Marie Dressler,* Mary Pickford,* Norma Shearer,* Walter Huston* – with host Walter Pidgeon.* **Awards include:** CFA: Theatrical Short.

Applebaum, Louis
Composer; b. Toronto, 1918; d. 2000. Louis Applebaum was perhaps Canada's most prolific composer of film music. He studied at the University of Toronto before moving to New York to further his education. There he fell in love with the worlds of theatre and movies. He wrote over 250 scores for the NFB (including *Alexis Tremblay: Habitant,* Around Is Around,* The Fight: Science against Cancer,* Royal Journey,* The Stratford Adventure,* Paddle to the Sea**), and his score for *The G.I. Joe Story* earned an Academy Award nomination in 1947. He also composed music for dozens of plays at the Stratford Festival, which he helped launch with Tyrone Guthrie in 1953. During the 1980s he fronted the Applebaum-Hebert advisory committe on federal cultural policy.

Apprenticeship of Duddy Kravitz, The
1974 121m *prod* International Cinemedia Center, *exp* Gerald Schneider, *p* John Kemeny, *d* Ted Kotcheff, *sc* Mordecai Richler, Lionel Chetwynd, *novel* Mordecai Richler, *ph* Brian West, *ed* Thom Noble, *mus* Stanley Myers; *with* Richard Dreyfuss, Micheline Lanctôt, Jack Warden, Randy Quaid, Joseph Wiseman, Denholm Elliott, Joe Silver. If Canadian cinema is in some way defined by Norman McLaren's* pristine animation, Ted Kotcheff's* version of Mordecai Richler's* novel comes across like a burp at a society ball. *Duddy* is an early Canadian feature that's not afraid to get its hands dirty in the material world. A young Jewish hustler grasps for success and breaks the hearts of everyone around him. Despite the fact that Duddy Kravitz is a louse, you can't stop yourself from responding to his naively hopeful, crackling energy. It may be in bad taste, but it jumps at you in Dreyfuss's career-

making performance. All Kotcheff had to do was keep up with the pace. (V) **Awards include:** CFA: Film of the Year, Sound Recording; AAN: Adapted Screenplay; Berlin Film Festival: Golden Bear.

Arcand, Denys

Director and writer; b. Deschambault, Que., 1941, brother of Gabriel Arcand. Denys Arcand is now firmly established as one of Canada's handful of star directors, but not too long ago, he was worried about ending up in the Salvation Army hostel he could see from the room where he was writing *Le Déclin de l'empire américain*.* Before the huge success of this breakthrough film, Arcand had been labelled an unbankable troublemaker, the kind of filmmaker who made politically explosive documentaries such as *On est au coton*.* In the mid-1980s, although he had won acclaim for a string of irreverent fiction features and a couple of mainstream hits in Quebec, this so-called agent provocateur found it hard to make a living in the movie business.

Arcand's films portray a world so irredeemably corrupt that he has been accused of being a cynic and a nihilist. However, his movies also convey inherent values expressed with wit and insight. 'I can't bear people who don't want to see what appears, to me, to be reality,' Arcand once told *Cinema Canada*. 'I don't know why. I've always been that way ... it seems to me that the first attribute of humanity is intelligence.'

Arcand spent his childhood in a riverside village, then moved to Montreal, where he attended a Jesuit school. In 1962, after an apprenticeship in the University of Montreal's theatre groups, he and some friends (including Denis Héroux* and Stéphane Venne, with the assistance of established NFBers, Michel Brault,* Gilles Groulx,* and Bernard Gosselin*) made a film about student life, *Seul ou avec d'autres*. Then, like most budding filmmakers, Arcand went to work for the NFB. The commissioned documentaries he shot didn't cause much of a stir until the Board refused to release *On est au coton*, a gritty, angry exposé of Quebec's textile industry. Although copies of the film were circulated clandestinely, the ban lasted six years.

When Arcand turned to fiction, his work began to modulate outrage with the amused disdain of a sophisticated observer. In *Réjeanne Padovani*,* a sleazy construction mogul has his unfaithful wife murdered during a party and entombs her under the asphalt of a just-completed highway. Arcand expresses shock at the depravity of his characters but he is aware of the layer of comedy they provide.

By the time he directed *Le Déclin* – which picked up the International Film Critics' Award at Cannes, nine Genies, and an Academy Award nomination, and remains one of the most profitable Canadian movies ever made – Arcand admitted that he felt affection as well as amusement for his self-deceptive, philandering characters. In fact, his biting humour can turn on a dime into passionate intensity.

Jésus de Montréal,* released in 1989, is perhaps Arcand's richest, most rewarding creation. In it he orchestrates perfectly timed mood swings between reverence and irreverence, detached irony and dark tragedy. In *Le Déclin* and *Jésus*, Arcand mastered the unobtrusive visual style and rapid pacing that he admires in classic American moviemaking. No matter how bizarre the content, his approach to filmmaking is straightforward, understated, and laconic. In this, Arcand resembles the Spanish master,

Luis Buñuel, another cool, witty minimalist who swam through powerful currents. **Films and television include:** *Seul ou avec d'autres* 1962 (d/sc with Denis Héroux and Stéphane Venne); *Samuel de Champlain* 1964 (d/sc); *Ville-Marie* 1965 (d); *Volleyball* 1966 (d/ed); *Atlantic Parks* 1967 (d/ed); *Entre la mer et l'eau douce* 1968 (co-sc); *La Maudite Galette* 1972 (d); *Québec: Duplessis et après ...* 1972 (d/ed); *Réjeanne Padovani* 1973 (d/co-sc/co-ed, CFA-SC); *Gina* 1975 (d/sc/ed); *On est au coton* 1976 (d/ed); *Le Confort et l'indifférence* 1982 (d); *Empire Inc.* 1983 (co-d, TV); *Le Crime d'Ovide Plouffe* 1984 (d/co-sc); *Le Déclin de l'empire américain* 1986 (d/sc, GA-D, GA-SC, AAN-FLF); *Jésus de Montréal* 1989 (d/sc, GA-D, GA-SC, AAN-FLF); *Montréal vu par ...* 1991 (co-d); *Love and Human Remains* 1994 (d); *Joyeux calvaire* 1997 (d/sc, TV); *Stardom* 2000 (d/co-sc).

Arcand, Gabriel

Actor; b. Deschambault, Que., 1949; brother of Denys Arcand. In spite of an impressive list of film and stage credits, Gabriel Arcand still considers himself an apprentice in his craft. He spent his formative years – professionally speaking – at the Centre national dramatique de Marseilles in France, and in Poland, where he studied theatre. Since his screen debut in Denys Arcand's *La Maudite Galette*, he has become established as Quebec's iconic strong, silent type, and has given subtle but powerful performances in a wide range of films, including *Réjeanne Padovani*,* *Les Plouffe*,* *Le Crime d'Ovide Plouffe*, *Le Déclin de l'empire américain*,* and *Post Mortem*.* **Films include:** *La Maudite Galette* 1972 (a/mus); *Réjeanne Padovani* 1973; *Gina* 1975 (a/mus); *Les Vautours* 1975; *Ti-Cul Tougas* 1976; *Parlez-nous d'amour* 1976; *Panique* 1977; *Au revoir ... à lundi* 1979; *Suzanne* 1980; *L'Affaire coffin* 1980; *Les Plouffe* 1981; *Mémoire battante* 1983; *Le Crime d'Ovide Plouffe* 1984 (GA-A); *Agnes of God* 1985; *Le Déclin de l'empire américain* 1986 (GA-SA); *La Ligne de chaleur* 1987; *Les Portes tournantes* 1988; *Les Matins infidèles* 1989; *Nelligan* 1991; *Le Sang du chasseur* 1995; *Post Mortem* 1999 (PJ-A); *Le Grand Serpent du monde* 1999.

Archangel

1990 82m *prod* Ordnance Motion Pictures, *exp* André Bennett, *p* Greg Klymkiw, *d/ph/ed* Guy Maddin, *sc* Guy Maddin, George Toles; *with* Kyle McCulloch, Kathy Marykuca, Ari Cohen, Sarah Neville, Michael Gotti. Set in the remote northern Russian town of Archangel at the end of the First World War, *Archangel* is the story of Lieut. John Boles (McCulloch), a one-legged amnesiac Canadian soldier. As he fights courageously in a strategically suspect set of battles that are made more vague by the general amnesia afflicting most of those around him, Boles searches for his beloved, Iris. This trouble, as we know and as Boles has forgotten, is that Iris is dead. Shot in sumptuous black and white worthy of Josef von Sternberg, and filled with slices of the surreal and the cruel, Guy Maddin's second feature is a masterpiece – a wistful, luminous conflation of absurdity, high romance, and heroic delusion. Buster Keaton would have approved. Buñuel, too.

Around Is Around

1951 10m *prod* NFB, British Film Institute, *p/d* Norman McLaren, *an* Norman McLaren, Evelyn Lambart, *mus* Louis Applebaum. *Around Is Around*, an early NFB experimentation in 3-D by Norman McLaren* and Evelyn Lambart,* is one of two films (see also *Now Is the Time*) commissioned by the British Film Institute for the Festival of Britain in 1951. The film features moving patterns that are given stereoscopic form through the control of different left-eye/right-eye image postions. (V) **Awards include:** CFA: Special Award.

Artie Shaw: Time Is All You've Got
1985 114m *prod* Bridge Film Productions, *p/d/sc* Brigitte Berman, *ap* Don Haig, *ph* Mark Irwin, Jim Aquila, *ed* Brigitte Berman, Barry Backus; *with* Artie Shaw, Polly Haynes, Evelyn Keyes, Mel Tormé, Buddy Rich. Constructed from interviews with Shaw, the legendary American band leader who was controversial for hiring the black singer Billie Holliday in 1938. *Artie Shaw: Time Is All You've Got* is an entertaining portrait of not only the man but also the musician, who was determined to acquire fame and wealth only to put them aside. Interviews also include Buddy Rich, Mel Tormé, and Evelyn Keyes, Shaw's wife of fifteen years. (V) **Awards include:** AA: Feature Documentary.

Art of War, The
2000 100m *prod* Filmline International, *exp* Elie Samaha, Dan Halsted, Wesley Snipes, *p* Nicolas Clermont, *d* Christian Duguay, *sc* Wayne Beach, Simon Davis Barry, *ph* Pierre Gill, *ed* Michel Arcand, *mus* Norman Corbeil; *with* Wesley Snipes, Ann Archer, Maury Chaykin, Donald Sutherland, Marie Matiko, Cary-Hiroyuki Tagawa, Michael Biehn. Not since *Porky's** and *The Changeling** in the 1980s has a Canadian genre film performed so well at the box office. This James Bond–style action flick has super agent Snipes working for the United Nations in pursuit of a high-level diplomatic assassin. He jumps off high buildings and kung-fus his way through fancy receptions, working for a duplicitious boss (Archer) who, in turn, works for the Canadian Secretary General (Sutherland*). Director Duguay* (*Screamers**) has an original visual style and is a master of long tracking shots

with a Steadicam, but he is less successful in staging large action sequences. He keeps pulling his punches, and Snipes fails to bring any life or humour to what is essentially a cartoon character.

Atlantic City
1980 105m *prod* International Cinema Corporation, Selta Films (France), *exp* Joseph F. Beaubien, Gabriel Boustani, *p* Denis Héroux, John Kemeny, *d* Louis Malle, *sc* John Guare, *ph* Richard Ciupka, *ed* Suzanne Baron, *mus* Michel Legrand; *with* Burt Lancaster, Susan Sarandon, Kate Reid, Michel Piccoli, Hollis McLaren, Robert Joy, Al Waxman. The most stylish and cinematically satisfying co-production made to date, this French-American-Canadian hybrid stars Lancaster in one of the finest performances of his long career as Lou, an over-the-hill, two-bit hood still on the make. His relationship with Sally (Sarandon), a small-town girl from Moose Jaw, Saskatchewan, who works at an Atlantic City casino clam bar but dreams of becoming a Monte Carlo croupier, leads to an unexpected windfall when her sleazy, dope-dealing ex-husband (Joy*) arrives in town with her pregnant sister (McLaren). Lancaster's subtle performance, combined with Guare's almost flawless script and Malle's elegant direction, earned *Atlantic City* five Academy Award nominations, and is the only Canadian dramatic to feature to date to be nominated for Best Picture. The film also made Sarandon a star. (V) **Awards include:** GA: Foreign Actress (Sarandon), Supporting Actress (Reid), Art Direction; AAN: Picture, Director, Screenplay, Actor (Lancaster), Actress (Sarandon).

À tout prendre
1964 99m *prod* Les Films Cassiopée, Orion Films, *p/d/sc/ed* Claude Jutra, *ph* Michel Brault, Jean-Claude Labrecque, Bernard Gosselin, *mus* Maurice Black-

burn, Jean Cousineau, Serge Garant; *with* Johanne Harrelle, Claude Jutra, Victor Désy, Tania Fédor, Guy Hoffmann, Monique Mercure. In his debut feature, Claude Jutra* takes the viewer on a virtually plotless excursion into his own psyche at a decisive moment in his life. As the film's restless young hero, Jutra chases around Montreal, searching for personal, political, and sexual identity. He says yes to his homosexuality, and ends a real-life affair with a Haitian woman (Harrelle). As director, Jutra discovers a relentlessly jittery, ad libbing style that is an ideal match for the slap-happy turmoil that the picture aims to evoke. Today, the classic French New Wave moves of this film are being revived, not only by directors ranging from Wong Kar-Wai to Oliver Stone, but also in mainstream television series such as *NYPD Blue*. *À tout prendre* can be loosely translated as 'Everything's Up for Grabs.' **Awards include:** CFA: Feature Film.

Au clair de la lune

1983 90m *prod* Les Productions Albinie, NFB, *p* Bernard Lalonde, Louise Laverdière, *d* André Forcier, *sc* André Forcier, Jacques Marcotte, Michel Pratt, Guy L'Ecuyer, Michel Côté, Bernard Lalonde, *ph* François Gill, André Gagnon, *ed* François Gill, *mus* Joël Bienvenue; *with* Guy L'Ecuyer, Michel Côté, Pierre Girard, Marcel Fournier, Gilles Lafleur, Yvon Lecompte. When Quebec cabinet minister Pierre Laporte was murdered in November 1970, his separatist killers stuffed his body into the trunk of a green Chevrolet sedan. In André Forcier's* characteristically loopy *Au clair de la lune*, the same model car is home to the two marginalized protagonists. Bert (L'Ecuyer) tries to make the snowbound car more homey and dreams of regaining his title as the neighbourhood's top bowler. François

(Côté) is a buckskin-dressed albino who can literally walk on air. *Au Clair de la lune* is about abandoned people yearning for miracles, and is as much historical allegory as it is surreal slapstick comedy. (V)

Avec tambours et trompettes

1967 28m *prod* NFB, *p* Robert Forget, *d* Marcel Carrière, *ph* Alain Dostie, Bernard Gosselin, *ed* Werner Nold, *mus* Donald Douglas. In 1867, when Pope Pius IX called for volunteers to defend the papacy against invading armies intent on uniting Italy, Quebec duly sent a contingent of 503 men. The NFB's centenary coverage of this event is less than respectful, and the comic-opera depiction of the 'soldiers of the Pope' was seen by some as an insult to a revered Quebec tradition. (V) **Awards include:** CFA: Short Documentary.

Aykroyd, Dan

Actor and writer; b. Ottawa, 1952. Invoking the obvious connection between Ottawa and comedy is a popular Canadian tradition. Beyond Parliament Hill, however, the capital connection to hilarity must have deeper roots. After all, Dan Aykroyd, the multi-talented comic, impressionist, actor, and writer is only the latest incarnation of Ottawa humour – his generation's successor to Rich Little. Aykroyd studied criminology at Carleton University before embarking on a career that has included stints with Second City and *Saturday Night Live*. He's also had considerable success in such Hollywood films as *The Blues Brothers*, *Ghostbusters*, and *Driving Miss Daisy*, for which he earned an Academy Award nomination. In 1996, he launched the television series *Psi Factor: Chronicles of the Paranormal*, on which he serves as host. Aykroyd is a strong believer in the existence of extraterrestrials. **Films and television include:** *Saturday Night Live*

1975–9 (TV); *Love at First Sight* 1977; *The Rutles* 1978 (TV); *Dallas* 1978 (series); *1941* 1979; *Mr Mike's Mondo Video* 1979; *The Blues Brothers* 1980 (co-sc/a); *Neighbors* 1981; *Doctor Detroit* 1982; *It Came from Hollywood* 1982; *Trading Places* 1983; *Twilight Zone – The Movie* 1983; *Ghostbusters* 1984 (co-sc/a); *Indiana Jones and the Temple of Doom* 1984; *Into the Night* 1985; *Spies like Us* 1985 (co-sc/a); *Dragnet* 1987 (co-sc/a); *The Great Outdoors* 1988; *My Stepmother Is an Alien* 1988; *The Couch Trip* 1988; *Driving Miss Daisy* 1989 (AAN-SA); *Ghostbusters II* 1989 (co-sc/a); *Loose Cannons* 1989; *Nothing but Trouble* 1991 (d/sc/a); *My Girl* 1991; *Chaplin* 1992 (as Mack Sennett); *This Is My Life* 1992; *Sneakers* 1992; *Coneheads* 1993; *My Girl 2* 1994; *North* 1994; *Tommy Boy* 1995; *Casper* 1995 (voice); *Canadian Bacon* 1995; *Feeling Minnesota* 1996; *Sgt. Bilko* 1996; *Celtic Pride* 1996; *My Fellow Americans* 1996; *Grosse Point Blank* 1996; *The Arrow* 1996 (TV); *Psi Factor: Chronicles of the Paranormal* 1996–present (host, series); *Blues Brothers 2000* 1998; *Antz* 1998 (voice); *Diamonds* 2000; *Stardom* 2000; *The House of Mirth* 2000; *Evolution* 2001.

B

Back-Breaking Leaf, The
1959 29m *prod* NFB, *exp* Tom Daly, *p* Wolf Koenig, Roman Kroitor, *d* Terence Macartney-Filgate, *sc* Stanley Jackson, *ph* Terence Macartney-Filgate, Giles Gascon, *ed* John Spotton, *mus* Eldon Rathburn. One of the best documentaries from the *Candid Eye** series, which stressed a direct approach to the subject at hand. *The Back-Breaking Leaf* paints a graphic picture of the tobacco harvest in southwestern Ontario from the point of view of transient field workers. (V)

Back, Frédéric
Animator; b. Saarbruecken, Germany,

1924. It is a measure of Back's extraordinary abilities as an artist that his legitimate concerns for ecology, nuclear peace, and animal rights have not overwhelmed his films. Two Academy Awards and numerous international jury prizes testify to this animator's skill in dramatizing his ideals. Soon after his arrival in Montreal in 1948, Back found permanent employment at SRC, first in its graphics department and since 1970 as a full-scale animator. *Crac!*, his first Academy Award winner, is a subtle, political, pro-provincial tribute to folk art in Quebec. Back received his second Academy Award for *The Man Who Planted Trees*, an elegiac portrait of a French-Canadian Johnny Appleseed. Back's impressionist and painterly work typifies the strengths he brought to bear on his acclaimed stained glass in Montreal's Place des Arts subway station. **Films include:** *Inon ou la conquête du feu* 1971; *La Création des oiseaux* 1973; *Illusion?* 1974; *Taratata* 1977; *Tout rien* 1978 (AAN-AS); *Crac!* 1982 (AA-AS); *The Man Who Planted Trees* 1987 (AA-AS); *The Mighty River* 1994.

Back to God's Country
1919 79m *prod* Canadian Photoplays, Curwood-Carver Productions (U.S.), *exp* Ernest Shipman, *d* David M. Hartford, *sc* Nell Shipman, James Oliver Curwood, *short story* James Oliver Curwood, *ph* Joseph B. Walker, Dal Clawson, *ed* Cyril Gardner; *with* Nell Shipman, Charles Arling, Wheeler Oakman, Wellington Playter. *Back to God's Country*, Canada's most successful silent feature film, is an overwrought and at times unintentionally funny melodramatic tale featuring Nell Shipman* as a plucky heroine who possesses a remarkable natural affinity with wild animals. It is particularly memorable not only for the scenes of Shipman interacting with a bear in its natural habitat, but also for the first

nude scene in Canadian cinema. Recently, the film has been revived by feminists because of its strong female lead and the significant role played by Shipman in the film's script and production.

Badgley, Frank

Administrator and director; b. Ottawa, 1895; d. 1955. Frank Badgley joined the CGMPB in 1921 and was responsible for directing many of its films. In 1927 he was appointed director of the Bureau, a job he held until its absorption into the NFB in 1941. He wrote, directed, and edited *Lest We Forget* (1935), a film about Canada's participation in the First World War, and perhaps the Bureau's most notable film.

Baillargeon, Paule

Actor and director; b. Rouyn-Noranda, Que., 1945. After leaving the National Theatre School of Canada in 1969, Baillargeon co-founded the experimental theatre group Le Grande Cirque ordinaire. Her key 1980 film, *La Cuisine rouge* (co-directed with Frédérique Collin), brought the Cirque's Brechtian style to a fractured narrative about sexual role typing. An established performer with roles in some twenty films (including *La Femme de l'hôtel,** *Réjeanne Padovani,** and *Jésus de Montréal**), Baillargeon is best known in English Canada as the curator in Patricia Rozema's *I've Heard the Mermaids Singing.** **Films include:** *Le Grand Film ordinaire* 1970; *Montréal blues* 1972; *Réjeanne Padovani* 1973; *Les Vautours* 1974; *Le Temps de l'avant* 1975; *Gina* 1975; *Le Soleil se lève en retard* 1976; *East End Hustle* 1976; *Anastasie, oh ma chérie* 1977 (d); *Panique* 1977; *Vie d'ange* 1979; *La Cuisine rouge* 1980 (co-d); *La Femme de l'hôtel* 1984; *La Dame en couleurs* 1984; *Passion: A Letter in 16mm* 1985; *Sonia* 1986; *I've Heard the Mermaids Singing* 1987 (GA-SA); *Trois pommes à côté du sommeil* 1989;

Jésus de Montréal 1989; *L'Assassin jouait du trombone* 1991; *Love-moi* 1991; *Bulle* 1991 (d); *Montréal vu par ...* 1991 (co-sc); *Solo* 1991 (d); *Le Sexe des étoiles* 1993 (d); *Un 32 août sur terre* 1998.

Bain, Conrad

Actor; b. Lethbridge, Alta., 1923. Bain is best known as Maude's next door neighbour in the popular 1970s television sitcom *Maude* and as Gary Coleman's wealthy benefactor in the series *Diff'rent Strokes*. He has performed mostly on and off Broadway and at the Stratford Festival. He was a member of the Lincoln Center Repertory Company, where he appeared in Chekhov's *Uncle Vanya* directed by Mike Nichols. His film work includes appearances in Woody Allen's *Bananas* and Nichols's *Postcards from the Edge*. **Films and television include:** *Madigan* 1968; *A Lovely Way to Die* 1968; *Coogan's Bluff* 1968; *Last Summer* 1969; *I Never Sang for My Father* 1970; *Bananas* 1971; *The Anderson Tapes* 1971; *Up the Sandbox* 1972; *A Fan's Notes* 1972; *Maude* 1972–8 (series); *Diff'rent Strokes* 1978–86 (series); *Child Bride of Short Creek* 1981 (TV); *Postcards from the Edge* 1990.

Bairstow, David

Director and producer; b. Toronto, 1921. As one of the most profilic of the many producer-directors at the NFB during its glory years, Bairstow oversaw the production of more than 200 films from 1944 to 1974. His *Royal Journey,** an account of the five-week visit of the young Princess Elizabeth to Canada and the United States in the fall of 1951, proved to be a hit with its theatrical release and became the most successful NFB film to that time. In 1969, Bairstow spent a year with the Australian Commonwealth Film Unit. **Films include:** *Royal Journey* 1951 (co-d, CFA-FF); *Road to Iran* 1955 (p); *Men against the Ice* 1960 (p/d); *The*

Inquiring Mind 1960 (p/d); *River with a Problem* 1961 (p); *Morning on the Lièvre* 1961 (p/d/ed, CFA-TS); *Music from Montreal* 1962 (p); *First Mile Up* 1963 (p); *Arctic Circle* series 1963 (four films, p/d); *Max in the Morning* 1965 (p/d); *Twenty-Four Hours in Czechoslovakia* 1968 (p); *Grierson* 1973 (exp, CFA-SD); *Tomorrow Is Too Late* 1974 (p); *Blackout* 1978 (a).

Bar salon
1975 84m *prod* Les Ateliers du Cinéma Québécois, Les Films André Forcier, *exp* Jean Dansereau, *d* André Forcier, *sc* André Forcier, Jacques Marcotte, *ph/ed* François Gill, *mus* André Duchesne, Michel McLean, Jean Pierre Bouchard, Jean-Pierre Tremblay, *with* Guy L'Ecuyer, Lucille Bélair, Madeleine Chartrand, Jacques Marcotte, Gélinas Fortin, Louise Gagnon. *Bar salon*, a simple, effective story shot with a kind of poetry, is about a saloon owner in his fifties who is about to lose his bar, but manages to buy another only to lose it as well after an affair with a topless dancer. This downbeat, 'neo-realistic' film established André Forcier* as major talent in Quebec cinema at the age of twenty-five. He showed a great deal of insight into his characters and their working-class background. He didn't hesitate to take sides with the people in his film, who seem neither resigned to nor overjoyed about their lot in life and show no particular desire to improve it.

Battle of the Long Sault, The
1913 2 reels *prod* British American Film Co., *p* Frank Beresford, *d* Frank Crane; *with* Frank Crane and the Indians of the Caughnawaga (now Kahnawake) reserve. This early Canadian fiction film, produced by Americans with a Canadian registered company, portrays the story of the Iroquois expedition against the French in Montreal in 1660 and the resistance by seventeen colonists led by Adam Dollard des Ormeaux.

Bay Boy, The
1984 100m *prod* International Cinema Corporation, Hachette-Fox Productions (France), *exp* Susan Cavan, Frank Jacobs, *p* John Kemeny, Denis Héroux, *d/sc* Daniel Petrie, *ph* Claude Agostini, *ed* Susan Shanks, *mus* Claude Bolling; *with* Kiefer Sutherland, Liv Ullmann, Peter Donat, Alan Scarfe, Chris Wiggins, Leah Pinsent. *The Bay Boy*, which was adapted from a screenplay by Daniel Petrie,* follows the passage through adolescence of Donald Campbell (Sutherland*), a Cape Breton teenager whose family is struggling during the Great Depression. Donald is expected by his mother (Ullmann) and the nuns at his school to enter the priesthood, but instead is driven by his lust for the daughter (Pinsent) of a local police officer (Scarfe). However, complications arise when he witnesses the death of an elderly Jewish couple. The film launched Sutherland's career. (V) **Awards include:** GA: Picture, Original Screenplay, Supporting Actor (Scarfe), Art Direction, Costumes, Sound Editing.

Bead Game
1977 5m35s *prod* NFB, *p* Derek Lamb, *d/an/ed* Ishu Patel, *mus* J.P. Ghosh. In this beautiful, innovative animated film, thousands of beads are painstakingly arranged and manipulated into shapes of creatures, both mythical and real, that continually devour, merge, and absorb one another in explosions of colour. The film received an Academy Award nomination for Animated Short. (V)

Beatty, Robert
Actor; b. Hamilton, Ont., 1909; d. 1992. Beatty, a rugged character actor and occasional lead, studied at the Royal Acad-

emy of Dramatic Arts in London. He made his debut on the English stage and in films in 1938. His only Canadian film was *The Amateur* in 1981. **Films and television include:** *Mein Kampf: My Crimes* 1940; *One of Our Aircraft Is Missing* 1942; *San Demetrio, London* 1943; *Appointment with Crime* 1945; *Odd Man Out* 1947; *The Magic Box* 1951; *Calling Bulldog Drummond* 1951; *Captain Horatio Hornblower* 1951; *The Gentle Gunman* 1952; *Man on a Tightrope* 1953; *Albert R.N.* 1953; *Tarzan and the Lost Safari* 1957; *Something of Value* 1957; *The Shakedown* 1959; *The Amorous Prawn* 1962; *Where Eagles Dare* 1969; *2001: A Space Odyssey* 1968; *Sitting Target* 1972; *Pope Joan* 1972; *The Spikes Gang* 1974; *The Pink Panther Strikes Again* 1976; *Jesus of Nazareth* 1977 (TV); *Unidentified Flying Oddball* 1979; *The Martian Chronicles* 1980 (TV); *The Amateur* 1981; *Superman III* 1983; *Superman IV: The Quest for Peace* 1987.

Beaudin, Jean

Director, writer, and editor; b. Montreal, 1939. Although Beaudin has taken a few shots at wild and visionary moviemaking, he will be best remembered for the restrained performances and fastidious visuals of pictures such as his 1977 success, *J.A. Martin photographe,** which has been consistently nominated by critics as one of the best Canadian features ever made. At Cannes the film won a Best Actress Award for star Monique Mercure* and attracted Robert Altman to the cinematography of Pierre Mignot. Since *J.A. Martin*, Beaudin's career has been focused in Quebec with the film version of *Being at Home with Claude** and the hit mini-series, *Les Filles de Caleb*. Beaudin has complained on many occasions that Canada's inadequate feature-film budgets severely restrict the imagination. **Films and television include:** *Vertige* 1969 (d); *Stop* 1971 (d); *Le Diable*

est parmi nous 1972 (d/sc); *Par une belle nuit d'hiver* 1974 (d/ed); *Cher Théo* 1975 (d/ed); *Jeux de la XXIe Olympiade* 1976 (co-d); *J.A. Martin photographe* 1977 (d/co-sc/co-ed, CFA-D, CFA-FF, CFA-E); *Cordélia* 1980 (d/co-sc/ed); *Mario* 1984 (d/co-sc); *Le Matou* 1985 (d); *L'Or et le papier* 1990 (d, series); *Les Filles de Caleb* 1990–1 (d, series); *Being at Home with Claude* 1992 (d); *Shehaweh* 1992 (d, series); *Ces enfants d'ailleurs* 1997 (d, series); *Souvenirs intimes* 1999 (d).

Beaver People, The

1928 786ft. *prod* National Parks of Canada, *d/ph/ed* Bill Oliver; *with* Grey Owl. The first of several films featuring Grey Owl (Archie Belaney), the extraordinary Englishman who claimed Indian descent. The Grey Owl films, made during the late 1920s and 1930s for the National Parks of Canada, dealt with wildlife ways and conservation of the wilderness.

Begone Dull Care

1949 7m4s *prod* NFB, *p* Norman McLaren, *d/an/ed* Norman McLaren, Evelyn Lambart, *mus* Oscar Peterson Trio. *Begone Dull Care*, the quintessential jazz film, is a visual expression of music performed by the Oscar Peterson Trio. Norman McLaren* and Peterson developed the music together – two master soloists echoing and challenging one another in a complex interactive improvisation. McLaren deftly displays his full range of cameraless animation techniques, indulging a particular interest in texture that expands the film's already complex rhythms. *Begone Dull Care*, one of his most intricately detailed films, features spectacular shifts of mood and style that still impress today. (V) **Awards include:** CFA: Special Award.

Being at Home with Claude

1992 85m *prod* Les Productions du Cerf,

NFB, *p* Louise Gendron, Doris Girard, *d/sc* Jean Beaudin, *play* René-Daniel Dubois, *ph* Thomas Vamos, *ed* André Corriveau, *mus* Richard Grégoire; *with* Roy Dupuis, Jacques Godin, Jean-François Pichette, Gaston Lepage. Jean Beaudin's* film is a fine example of successful stage-to-screen adaptation, relying on the original eponymous theatrical work by René-Daniel Dubois. Set in Montreal, the film opens with a graphic sex scene between two men that ends in murder. Through the remainder of the film, Roy Dupuis,* the hustler/lover/murderer, attempts to explain his motivations for the killing to the police. Beaudin's intelligent handling of the material and Dupuis's chilling performance enhance the film's overall impact. (V)

Berman, Brigitte
Director; b. Frankfurt am Main, Germany, 1951. After studying film at Queen's University, Berman worked at the CBC for nine years before directing her first independent documentary, *Bix: Ain't None of Them Play like Him Yet.* Her next documentary, *Artie Shaw: Time Is All You've Got,** about the legendary New York jazz great, captured an Academy Award in 1987, and is one of only three Canadian feature documentaries to do so. Berman's weak foray into fiction, *The Circle Game,* included an amazing soundtrack but fumbled the conflicts between a musician and her estranged mother. **Films include:** *Bix: Ain't None of Them Play like Him Yet* 1981; *Artie Shaw: Time Is All You've Got* 1985 (AA-FD); *The Circle Game* 1994.

Best Damn Fiddler from Calabogie to Kaladar, The
1968 49m *prod* NFB, *p* Barrie Howells, John Kemeny, *d* Peter Pearson, *sc* Joan Finnegan, *ph* Tony Ianzelo, *ed* Michael McKennirey, *mus* Robert Fleming; *with* Chris Wiggins, Kate Reid, Margot Kidder. One of the best English-Canadian docudramas to come out of the 1960s, produced by the NFB for broadcast on CBC-TV. *The Best Damn Fiddler* is a realistic account of an itinerant bush worker (Wiggins) living in the rural area of the Ottawa valley who can't make enough money to feed his large family but nevertheless rejects government handouts. His tough self-reliance and hard-drinking lifestyle is viewed with compassion as his family ekes out an existence in a life of isolation and deprivation. The oldest daughter (Kidder*) eventually leaves home to find work and a better future. (V) **Awards include:** CFA: Film of the Year, Director, Original Screenplay, Actor (Wiggins), Cinematography (B+W), Editing, Art Direction.

Bête lumineuse, La
1982 127m *prod* NFB, *p* Jacques Bobet, *d* Pierre Perrault, *ph* Martin Leclerc, *ed* Suzanne Allard; *with* Louis-Philippe Lécuyer, Philippe Cross, Stéphane-Albert Boulais, Maurice Chaillot. A group of men depart for a weekend hunting trip in rural Quebec. One man among them – an earnest, philosophical teacher and poet – is so out of place that he soon becomes an even more pathetic victim of hormonal persecution than the moose the men have come to kill. Directed by Pierre Perrault,* the near-legendary Québécois poet, filmmaker, and anthropologist, *La Bête lumineuse* suggests there is a fundamentally ugly component in male bonding – something that makes sport of attacking anyone who refuses to play by the rules. (V)

Bethune
1964 59m *prod* NFB, *exp* Guy Glover, *p/sc* Donald Brittain, John Kemeny, *d* Donald Brittain, *ph* Robert Humble, François

Séguillon, Murray Fallen, *ed* John Kemeny, *narr* Lister Sinclair. *Bethune* is a biography of Norman Bethune, the Canadian doctor who served first with the loyalist forces against the fascists during the Spanish Civil War and later with the Mao's Red Army in China, where he died operating under fire. Subsequently he was hailed as a hero of the revolution. The film, created from photographs and interviews with surviving friends and collegues, is held together with Donald Brittain's* marvellous commentary, which takes the view that Bethune – a committed communist – was a 'great man.' This approach made the NFB nervous. Because of its political implications, the film never received official approval. In spite of the controversy, *Bethune* was a great success in Canada and the United States. (V)

Bethune: The Making of a Hero
1990 117m *prod* Filmline International, August First Film Studio (China), Parmentier/Belstar Productions (France), *p* Nicolas Clermont, Pieter Kroonenburg, Wang Xingang, Jacques Dorfmann, *d* Phillip Borsos, *sc* Ted Allan, *ph* Mike Molloy, Raoul Coutard, *ed* Yves Langlois, Angelo Corrao, *mus* Alan Reeves; *with* Donald Sutherland, Helen Mirren, Helen Shaver Colm Feore, James Pax, Guo Da, Anouk Aimée. A rare Canadian epic, *Bethune: The Making of a Hero* is more famous for its lengthy, arduous production and the bickering between the star and the writer than for anything else. Right from the start Donald Sutherland* and Ted Allan* clashed over the interpretation of Bethune's legacy. Sutherland (who is a dead ringer for Bethune) passionately believed that despite his drinking and womanizing, Bethune became a saintly hero in China, whereas Allan (who had served with Bethune in Spain) equally passionately believed he

remained a deeply flawed man until the end. Director Phillip Borsos* was caught in the middle of these conflicting visions and it shows. Despite its subject matter, the film lacks dramatic focus. With a budget of $20 million, it was the most expensive Canadian feature of its time, but it was universally panned and became a major box-office disappointment. (V) **Awards include:** GA: Costumes.

Between Friends
1973 90m *prod* Clearwater Films, *exp* Chalmers Adams, *d* Donald Shebib, *sc* Claude Harz, *ph* Richard Leiterman, *ed* Tony Lower, Donald Shebib, *mus* Matthew McCauley; *with* Michael Parks, Bonnie Bedelia, Chuck Shamata, Henry Beckman, Hugh Webster. In spite of the mythic resonance and justified fame of *Goin' down the Road,** *Between Friends* is really Shebib's* finest effort. This tale of a botched mine robbery in Northern Ontario involves the troubled quartet of Chino (Shamata), his American surfing buddy Toby (Parks), his girlfriend's father Will (Beckman), and Coker (Webster). While the robbery is being planned, Chino's girlfriend Ellie (Bedelia) becomes attracted to Toby. It is a taut, serious dramatic study of loyalty, Canada–U.S. relations and the limitations of male bonding. *Between Friends* is also distinguished for its intelligent, suggestive use of desolate Northern Ontario landscapes and its failed heist sequence that rivals any film noir you can name.

Beveridge, Jane Marsh
Director, editor, and producer; b. Ottawa, 1915. Although she was one of about a dozen women at the NFB during the Second World War, Beveridge was the only woman to direct and produce war films. She served as de facto producer of the *Canada Carries On** series, helming six films in two years, but

she quit over conflicts with John Grierson,* who refused to promote her. Although its overtly feminist script was watered down, *Women Are Warriors* stands out as one of the few wartime films to argue that women were not leisurely idlers before the conflict. Beveridge's *Alexis Tremblay: Habitant*,* shot by the legendary Judith Crawley,* was one of the most popular shorts in NFB history. Beveridge abandoned filmmaking in the early 1950s to become a teacher and sculptor. **Films include:** *Women Are Warriors* 1942; *Inside Fighting Canada* 1942; *Proudly She Marches* 1943; *Wings on Her Shoulders* 1943; *Alexis Tremblay: Habitant* 1943; *Air Cadets* 1944.

Big Snit, The

1985 9m49s *prod* NFB, *exp* Michael Scott, *p* Richard Condie, Michael Scott, *d/sc/an* Richard Condie, *ph* Gordon Manson, *mus* Patrick Godfrey. From the wacky imagination of Winnipeg animator Richard Condie* comes this tale of a middle-age and decidedly odd couple who play a game of scrabble, while the world literally blows up around them. They cheat, scheme, and chew on the furniture, blissfully unaware that global nuclear war has broken out. They only realize what's going on when the game is over and they go outside. This very funny and unexpectedly off-the-wall film received an Academy Award nomination for Animated Short. (V)

Binamé, Charles

Director, writer, and actor; b. Herve, Belgium, 1949. Blessed with a golden touch, Binamé has pursued a career in documentary film, advertising, acting, and screenwriting. He has directed two of Quebec's most popular television series of all time: *Blanche* (the sequel to *Les Filles de Caleb*) and *Marguerite Volant*. The latter won him seven Gémeaux and

a Fipa d'or at Cannes for Best Drama Series. Binamé has also directed a number of feature-length films, the best-known of which is *Eldorado*,* a ground-breaking film in the history of Quebec cinema created through a process of improvisation. His most recent feature is *La Beauté de Pandore*. **Films and television include:** *Juste pour partir le monde* 1974 (d, TV); *Les Fils de la liberté* 1980 (a, TV); *Maia Fauve* 1980 (d); *Un Autre Homme* 1991 (d); *Blanche* 1993 (d, series); *C'était le 12 du 12 et Chili avait les blues* 1994 (d); *Eldorado* 1995 (d/sc); *Marguerite Volant* 1996 (d, series); *Le Coeur au poing* 1998 (d/sc); *La Beauté de Pandore* 2000 (d/sc).

Bitter Ash, The

1963 80m *prod* Larry Kent Productions, *p/d/sc* Larry Kent, *ph* Richard Bellamy, *ed* Larry Kent, Richard Bellamy, *mus* Jack Dale, Clinton Solomom, Jimmy Thomas, Wilf Manz; *with* Alan Scarfe, Lynn Stewart, Philip Brown, Diane Griffith. This independently produced, semi-improvised drama from Larry Kent,* one of the original English-Canadian auteurs of the 1960s, is about the sexual shenanigans of a self-involved young playwright (Scarfe) who throws away his marriage and his last hope for spiritual integrity for the sake of an ego-gratifying fling.

Black Christmas

1974 98m *prod* August Films, Vision IV Productions, *exp* Findlay J. Quinn, *p/d* Bob Clark, *sc* Roy Moore, *ph* Reginald H. Morris, *ed* Stan Cole, *mus* Carl Zittrer; *with* Olivia Hussey, Keir Dullea, Margot Kidder, John Saxon, Andrea Martin, Art Hindle. As the holiday season approaches, a college town is terrorized by a psychopathic killer. One by one the residents of a sorority house are brutally slain by a heavy-breathing maniac armed with plastic wrap and some serious childhood traumas. The film acts as a somewhat less-than-graphic precursor to the impending run of slasher films in the later 1970s and 1980s (such as *Prom Night** and *Halloween*), and offers a preview of such horror conventions as the prowling, subjective camera, the slaughter of sexy but dumb young women, and the uncertain death of the killer at the end. (V) **Awards include:** CFA: Actress (Kidder), Editing, Sound Editing.

Black Robe
1991 102m *prod* Alliance Communications, Samson (Australia), *exp* Jake Eberts, Brian Moore, Denis Héroux, *p* Robert Lantos, Stéphane Reichel, Sue Milliken, *d* Bruce Beresford, *sc/novel* Brian Moore, *ph* Peter James, *ed* Tim Wellburn, *mus* Georges Delerue; *with* Lothaire Bluteau, Aden Young, Sandrine Holt, August Schellenberg, Harrison Liu, Billy Two Rivers. The hostile wilderness of seventeenth-century New France is the setting for this compelling examination of the clash between the differing belief systems of the French settlers and the Algonquin natives. Based on Brian Moore's* acclaimed novel, the film tells the story of Father Laforgue (Bluteau*), a young, idealistic Jesuit whose mission is to save the souls of the native 'savages.' Laforgue's physical and spiritual journey deep into northern Quebec, accompanied by Algonquin guides and a French carpenter, culminates in a deeper understanding of and a new-found respect for the people he set out to convert. (V) **Awards include:** GA: Picture, Director, Adapted Screenplay, Supporting Actor (Schellenberg), Cinematography, Art Direction; Golden Reel Award.

Blackwood
1976 28m *prod* NFB, *exp* Colin Low, *p* Tom Daly, *d* Tony Ianzelo, Andy Thomson, *ph* Tony Ianzelo, *ed* Les Halman, *mus* Ben Low, *narr* Gordon Pinsent. A poetic documentary about Newfoundland-born David Blackwood, one of Canada's foremost etchers. Blackwood takes the viewer through a step-by-step explanation of the etching process, while the filmmakers present scenes of his outport home and tales from an old mariner about the seal hunts and a way of life that has vanished. The film received an Academy Award nomination for Short Documentary. (V)

Blake
1969 19m *prod* NFB, *p* Douglas Jackson, *d/ph/ed* Bill Mason, *mus* Blake James, Laurent Coderre; *with* Blake James. James was an NFB filmmaker who spent his spare time flying solo across the countryside as an expression of personal freedom. *Blake*, shot by his friend Bill Mason,* is a loving tribute to a time gone by when career pressures could easily be set aside for the pursuit of spiritual values. (V) **Awards include:** CFA: Short; AAN: Short Drama.

Blinkity Blank
1955 5m15s *prod* NFB, *p/d/an* Norman McLaren, *mus* Maurice Blackburn. Norman McLaren,* compulsive innovator that he was, put aside his paints to make *Blinkity Blank*, a work composed entirely of images carved directly on to the film strip. With characteristic panache, McLaren used this rather simplistic methodology to create a remarkable experiment. Brief glints of imagery – scrawling and primitive – flash on the screen just long enough to register before morphing into the next shape. In his capable hands, the film becomes an hypnotic, dizzying experience – a perfect expression of his penchant for rhythmic interplay. (V) **Awards include:** Cannes: Palme d'or for animation.

Blood Relatives

1978 101m *prod* Cinévideo, Classic Films Industries, Filmel (France), *exp* Julian Melzack, *p* Denis Héroux, Eugène Lepicier, *d* Claude Chabrol, *sc* Sydney Banks, Claude Chabrol, *book* Ed McBain, *ph* Jean Rabier, *ed* Yves Lagnois, *mus* Pierre Jansen; *with* Donald Sutherland, Stéphane Audran, Micheline Lanctôt, Donald Pleasence, Aude Landry. This minor whodunit, one of three films that the French master Claude Chabrol directed in Canada, is based on a book by American detective novelist Ed McBain. *Blood Relatives* involves the brutal murder of a teenage girl and the subsequent investigation led by Sutherland,* reprising his low-key cop role from *Klute*. Various suspects come and go, but Chabrol can't seem to get a handle on the material, and the film never really gets out of first gear. However, Chabrol and his regular cinematographer Jean Rabier do manage to create an unsettling mood, effectively using the streets of Old Montreal to create an atmosphere of doom and gloom.

Bloomfield, George

Director and writer; b. Montreal, 1930. Bloomfield wrote, directed, and produced some of the best dramas for the CBC from 1963 to 1968 for the prestigious *Festival* series. Since then he has directed for virtually every television series produced in Canada, from *SCTV* in the early 1980s to *Emily of New Moon* in the late 1990s, including *Due South* (where he was a regular), *Road to Avonlea*, *E.N.G.*, *Outer Limits*, and *La Femme Nikita*. He shot his first feature, *Jenny*, in the United States, and he worked steadily during the height of the tax-shelter era.* His most recent feature is the remake of Mordecai Richler's* children's story, *Jacob Two-Two Meets the Hooded Fang*. **Films and television include:** *Jenny* 1969 (d/sc); *To Kill a Clown* 1972 (d/sc); *Child under a Leaf* 1974 (d/sc/ed); *Nellie McClung* 1978 (d, TV); *Riel* 1979 (d, TV); *Nothing Personal* 1980 (d); *Double Negative* 1982 (d); *Spasms* 1983 (a); *The Park Is Mine* 1984 (a); *The Argon Quest* 1990 (sc); *The Awakening* 1993 (d, TV); *Due South* 1994–8 (d, series); *Jacob Two-Two Meets the Hooded Fang* 1999 (d).

Blue, Ben

Actor; b. Benjamin Bernstein, Montreal, 1901; d. 1975. Blue, a superb, sad-faced, rubber-limbed mine and dancer on the New York stage from the age 15, stuck mostly to the stage and nightclub circuit, but his character cameos were the highlight of many features made during the 1930s and 1940s. Later in his career he appeared regularly on television. **Films include:** *College Rhythm* 1934; *Top of the Town* 1937; *Artists and Models* 1937; *The Big Broadcast of 1938* 1938; *For Me and My Gal* 1942; *Broadway Rhythm* 1944; *Two Girls and a Sailor* 1944; *My Wild Irish Rose* 1947; *It's a Mad, Mad, Mad World* 1963; *The Russians Are Coming, the Russians Are Coming* 1966; *A Guide for the Married Man* 1967; *The Busy Body* 1967.

Bluteau, Lothaire

Actor; b. Montreal, 1957. Bluteau, an intense and talented actor, has worked in theatre, film, and television throughout Canada and internationally. He was first noticed for his riveting performance in Yves Simoneau's *Les Fous de bassan*. After receiving great acclaim for the lead in the stage version of *Being at Home with Claude*,* he won a Best Actor Genie for his performance in Denys Arcand's* masterpiece *Jésus de Montréal*.* He has since appeared in the award-winning *Black Robe*<i>*</i> and *Le Confessionnal*.* His diverse international credits include *Orlando* and *I Shot Andy Warhol*. **Films and television include:** *Les Années de rêves* 1984; *Les Fous de bassan* 1987; *La*

Nuit avec Hortense 1988; Jésus de Montréal 1989 (GA-A); Bonjour monsieur Gauguin 1989; The Persistence of Memory 1991; Black Robe 1991; Orlando 1992; The Silent Touch 1992; Le Confessionnal 1995; Nostromo 1996 (TV); I Shot Andy Warhol 1996; Bent 1997; Other Voices, Other Rooms 1997; Conquest 1999; Dead Aviators 1999 (TV); Urbania 2000.

Bobet, Jacques

Producer; b. Saumur, France, 1919; d. 1996. After a brief stint as a teacher, Bobet joined the NFB in 1947 as a writer, and became a senior producer. As head of the French unit, he oversaw the production of some of the most important films ever made in Canada: Calude Jutra's (and others) La Lutte,* Gilles Groulx's Le Chat dans la sac,* and Pierre Perrault's Ile-aux-Coudres triology, Pour la suite du monde,* Le Règne du jour,* and Les Voitures d'eau.* He became a mentor to a whole generation of Québécois filmmakers, and went on to produce the official film of the 1976 Olympics in Montreal. He retired in 1984 but continued to teach. He once said his role as a producer was 'to do all those little things that you don't see in bringing a movie to the screen.' **Films include:** La Lutte 1961; Dimanche d'Amérique 1961; 30 Minutes Mr Plummer 1962; Natation 1963; Pattes mouillées 1963; Pour la suite du monde 1963 (CFA-FY, CFA-SPA); Percé on the Rocks 1964; 60 Cycles 1964; Le Chat dans le sac 1964; La Vie heureuse de Léopold Z. 1965; Volleyball 1966; Le Règne du jour 1967; Les Voitures d'eau 1969; Le Beau Plaisir 1969; La Dernière Neige 1973; Cher Théo 1975; Jeux de la xxie Olympiade 1977 (exp); L'Age de la machine 1978; Deux épisodes dans la vie d'Hubert Aquin 1978; Going the Distance 1979 (exp, AAN-FD); Le Pays de la terre sans arbre 1980; La Bête lumineuse 1982; Le Crime d'Ovide Plouffe 1984 (exp); Mario 1984 (exp); The Tadpole and the Whale 1988 (co-sc).

Bob's Birthday

1995 12m18s prod NFB, exp Barrie McLean, p Alison Snowden, David Fine, David Verrall, d/sc Alison Snowden, David Fine, an Alison Snowden, David Fine, Janet Perlman, mus Patrick Godfrey. Bob the dentist is reeling from birthday vertigo and searches for meaning in his life: his career seems pointless, his patients annoy him, and his friendships seem empty and boring. His wife, Margaret, has planned a surprise party, but as she welcomes the guests, Bob appears unexpectedly in his birthday suit. This funny piece of fluff was the pilot for the animated TV series Bob and Margaret. (V) **Awards include:** AA: Animated Short.

Bochner, Hart

Actor and director; b. Toronto, 1956, son of Lloyd Bochner. Hart Bochner had his screen debut in 1976 in Islands in the Stream. By the time he landed the lead in the 1984 television mini-series The Sun Also Rises, he was labelled a heart-throb. Later, he was cast effectively as the weasel executive in Bruce Willis's megahit, Die Hard. Hart has since become more interested in directing than acting. His first feature, the National Lampoonish PCU, was followed by High School High. **Films and television include:** Islands in the Stream 1976; Breaking Away 1979; Terror Train 1980; East of Eden 1981 (TV); Rich and Famous 1981; Supergirl 1984; The Wild Life 1984; The Sun Also Rises 1984 (TV); Making Mr Right 1987; Apartment Zero 1988; Die Hard 1988; War and Rememberance 1989 (TV); Fellow Traveller 1990; Mr. Destiny 1990; The Innocent 1993; PCU 1994 (d); High School High 1996 (d); Anywhere But Here 1999; Urban Legends: Final Cut 2000.

Bochner, Lloyd

Actor; b. Toronto, 1924; father of Hart Bochner. Lloyd Bochner has worked mostly in supporting roles and is perhaps best known as Cecil Colby in the television series *Dynasty*. His more notable films include *Tony Rome* (with Frank Sinatra) and John Boorman's cult classic *Point Blank*. **Films and television include:** *The Night Walker* 1964; *Harlow* 1965; *Point Blank* 1967; *Tony Rome* 1967; *The Detective* 1968; *The Horse in the Gray Flannel Suit* 1969; *The Dunwich Horror* 1970; *Ulzana's Raid* 1972; *It Seemed like a Good Idea at the Time* 1975; *The Man in the Glass Booth* 1975; *Riel* 1979 (TV); *Dynasty* 1981–2 (series); *Hot Touch* 1982; *The Lonely Lady* 1982; *Louisiana* 1984; *Race for the Bomb* 1986 (TV); *Millennium* 1988; *Naked Gun 2½: The Smell of Fear* 1991; *Batman: The Animated Series* 1992 (voice, series); *Morning Glory* 1993; *Legend of the Mummy* 1997; *Loyal Opposition: Terror in the White House* 1998 (TV).

Bones of the Forest

1995 80m *prod* Tansparent Film, *p* Velcrow Ripper, *d/ph/ed* Heather Frise, Velcrow Ripper, *mus* Hardkiss, Einsturzende Nuebauten, Jean-Luc Perron, and others. A poetic documentary about the environmental devastation caused by clearcutting in British Columbia, combined with politically correct coverage of the protests against the 500th anniversary of the discovery of the Americas by Europeans. Utilizing a host of cinematic techniques, from time-lapse photography to animation and an evocative soundscape, the film builds a case for the significance of the land to First Nations people and provides a platform for all involved – loggers, native elders, protesters, company flaks – to have their say. **Awards include:** GA: Feature Documentary.

Bons Débarras, Les

1980 114m *prod* Les Productions Prisma, *p* Marcia Couëlle, Claude Godbout, *d* Francis Mankiewicz, *sc* Réjean Ducharme,

ph Michel Brault, *ed* André Corriveau, *mus* Bernard Buisson; *with* Charlotte Laurier, Marie Tifo, Germain Houde, Louise Marleau, Roger Lebel, Gilbert Sicotte. The late Frank Mankiewicz's* best picture, made during a period when Québécois filmmakers were fascinated by dysfunctional losers (rather than by today's snappily dressed, gloomy yuppies), is saturated with a deep and satisfying melancholy. Set during a cold, grey autumn in the Laurentian mountains, the movie presents a fallen world seen through the eyes of an obsessive young girl who won't let her mother (Tifo) have a life. This child, created by the reclusive writer Réjean Ducharme, and played by Charlotte Laurier, is a dangerously compelling seductress who wreaks havoc out of a need to control those she loves. Mankiewicz was one of the most emotionally powerful and yet subtle Canadian filmmakers. It's hard to understand why he is also one of the most overlooked. **Awards include:** GA: Picture, Director, Original Screenplay, Actress (Tifo), Supporting Actor (Houde), Cinematography, Editing, Overall Sound.

Borradaile, Osmond

Cinematographer; b. Winnipeg, 1898; d. 1999. After studying at the University of British Columbia, Borradaile went to Hollywood and began work with Jesse Lasky Productions. He joined the Canadian Expeditionary Forces during the First World War, and then returned to Hollywood, where he was hired by Paramont's camera department. In 1930 he left for England where he worked for producer Alexandra Korda. A specialist in exterior photography, Borradaile shot the outdoor sequences for such classics as *Elephant Boy*, *The Four Feathers*, and *The Thief of Baghdad*. He travelled the world and worked in England, Ireland, Australia, and South Africa. In 1951 he shot *Royal Journey** for the NFB. **Films**

Borsos, Phillip

include: *The Private Life of Henry VIII* 1933
(2nd unit); *The Scarlet Pimpernel* 1934
(2nd unit); *Elephant Boy* 1937 (2nd unit);
The Four Feathers 1939 (co-ph); *The Thief
of Baghdad* 1940 (co-ph); *The Macomber
Affair* 1947; *Bonnie Prince Charlie* 1948;
Scott of the Antarctic 1948; *The Winslow
Boy* 1948; *I Was a Male War Bride* 1949;
Royal Journey 1951.

Borsos, Phillip
Director; b. Hobart, Australia, 1953; d.
1995. Borsos, a gifted filmmaker who
was once pursued by Marlon Brando to
direct a project, started out as a lab technician in Vancouver. He established
himself in the late 1970s with formally
assured short documentaries (his *Nails*
earned an Academy Award nomination
in 1979), and in 1982, emerged as a major talent with his feature debut, *The
Grey Fox.** This dramatic dissection of
the Canadian West is an understated,
finely nuanced essay on heroism and
technology. Its quiet, fatalist poetics
were extended in Borsos's four other
features, most notably the sprawling,
awkward grandeur of *Bethune: The Making of a Hero.** Cancer claimed Borsos
just weeks after the release of *Far from
Home: The Adventures of Yellow Dog*.
Films include: *Cooperage* 1976 (CFA-TS);
Spartree 1977 (CFA-TS); *Nails* 1979 (GA-
LAS, AAN-SD); *The Grey Fox* 1983 (GA-
D); *The Mean Season* 1985; *One Magic
Christmas* 1985; *Bethune: The Making of a
Hero* 1990; *Far from Home: The Adventures
of Yellow Dog* 1995.

Boys, Les
1997 107m *prod* Melenny Productions,
p Richard Goudreau, *d* Louis Saïa, *sc*
Christian Fournier, *ph* Sylvain Brault, *ed*
Yvann Thibaudeau, *mus* Normand Corbeil; *with* Marc Messier, Rémy Girard,
Patick Huard, Serge Thériault, Michel

Barrette, Paul Houde. A simple story
about some Québécois fellas who get together every Monday night for an amateur game of hockey. *Les Boys* was released in Quebec to an overwhelmingly
negative response from critics and a
massive public acclaim unprecedented
in the history of Canadian cinema.
Clearly, its home-grown sensibility and
endless jokes about Québécois identity
struck a collective nerve among the
province's moviegoers. There are plenty
of crude jokes and slapstick along with a
bit of suspense created when the hockey
team's coach (Girard*) places a massive
bet on the success of his motley crew
with a Mafioso who threatens his life.
Les Boys evokes the charm and camaraderie themes of such sport films as *Slap
Shot* and *The Bad News Bears*. (V) **Awards
include:** Golden Reel Award.

Boys and Girls
1983 25m *prod* Atlantis Films, CBC,
p Janice Platt, Michael MacMillan,
Seaton McLean, *d* Don McBrearty, *sc* Joe
Wiesenfield, *short story* Alice Munro,
ph Alar Kiriol, *ed* Seaton McLean, *mus*
Louis Natak; *with* Megan Fellows, Ian
Heath, Clare Coulter, David Fox. Set in
the 1940s, *Boys and Girls* (which was produced for the CBC-TV anthology series
Sons and Daughters) explores the critical
period in a young girl's (Fellows) life
when she first realizes the implications
of traditional sex-role stereotyping. At
thirteen, she enjoys helping with the labour on her parents' farm but soon discovers that they consider her only as
temporary help until her brother is old
enough to take over. An effective, well-
produced short with strong performances that surprised everyone, including
the producers, by winning an Academy
Award. (V) **Awards include:** AA: Live-
Action Short.

Boys II, Les

1998 120m *prod* Melenny Productions, *exp* Jeffrey Tinnell, *p* Richard Goudreau, *d* Louis Saïa, *sc* René Brisebois, François Camirand, Louis Saïa, *ph* Georges Archambault, *ed* Maxime Chalifoux, Gaétan Huot, *mus* Normand Corbeil; *with* Marc Messier, Rémy Girard, Patrick Huard, Serge Thériault, Paul Houde, Luc Guérin. The gang's all here once more. This sequel, released but a year after the success of the original, proved equally popular with Quebec filmgoers. This time the crew heads to France, allowing for a string of gags about cultural differences between the Québécois and their European counterparts. Again, the film was almost universally dismissed by critics, but in fairness, the crew manages a certain undeniable down-home charm. (V) **Awards include:** Golden Reel Award.

Boys of St Vincent, The

1992 92m *prod* Les Productions Télé-Action, NFB, CBC, *exp* Claudio Luca, Colin Neale, *p* Sam Grana, Claudio Luca, *d* John N. Smith, *sc* Des Walsh, John N. Smith, Sam Grana, *ph* Pierre Letarte, *ed* Werner Nold, *mus* Neil Smolar; *with* Henry Czerny, Sebastian Spence, Philip Dinn, Brian Dooley, Greg Thomey, Michael Wade. Originally aired on CBC-TV in two parts and screened as a film abroad, John N. Smith's* dramatization of how the children at a Catholic orphanage in Newfoundland suffered physical and sexual abuse is based on the real-life Mount Cashel orphanage case. The film was intensely controversial and was banned from airing in Ontario for a time during 1992 by the Ontario Court of Appeals on the grounds that the film would prejudice the trial of the Christian Brothers, which was still in progress. The first part deals with the actual abuse at the hands of pedophiliac priests; the second picks up the story fifteen years later when an inquiry into the events was launched and the victims must face their abusers and the awful past once again. Henry Czerny's* vivid and shocking stand-out performance as a sadistic perpetrator and Smith's effective direction led to subsequent work on Hollywood productions. (V)

Brault, Michel

Cinematographer, director, and writer; b. Montreal, 1928. Brault, Canada's most gifted and influential cinematographer, has been a seminal figure in Quebec cinema since the 1950s. His early work with Gilles Groulx* (*Les Raquetteurs**), Claude Jutra* (*À tout prendre,** *Mon oncle Antoine**) and Pierre Perrault* (*Pour la suite du monde**) virtually defines the look of classic Quebec cinema. Brault joined the NFB in 1956 and worked on the *Candid Eye** series. In 1960–1 he was in France, where he worked with Jean Rouch and Mario Ruspoli. There he is considered an originator and one of the purist practitioners of *cinéma-vérité*. His cinematography ranges from the gritty *cinéma-vérité* style of *À tout prendre** to the lyricism of *Kamouraska,** and his directorial work from the terse documentary of *La Lutte** to smoothly proficient television dramas such as *Les Noces du papier*. His masterpiece, *Les Ordres,** won him the Best Director Award at Cannes in 1975. This film seamlessly fuses documentary and fiction styles while dramatizing the trauma of innocent people caught up in the October Crisis of 1970. Since the mid-1980s Brault has worked mainly in television. His son, Sylvain, has become one of Quebec's top cameramen. **Films include:** *Les Raquetteurs* 1958 (co-d/ph); *Chronique d'un été* 1961 (co-ph); *Golden Gloves* 1961 (co-ph); *La Lutte* 1961 (co-d/co-ph/co-ed); *Seul ou avec d'autres* 1962 (ph); *Québec-USA ou l'invas-*

ion pacifique 1962 (d/ph with Bernard Gosselin); *Pour la suite du monde* 1963 (co-d/co-ph, CFA-FY, CFA-SPA); *À tout prendre* 1964 (ph with Gosselin and Jean-Claude Labrecque); *Les Temps perdu* 1964 (d/ph); *La Fleur de l'âge: Geneviève* 1965 (d/ph); *Visite du général de Gaulle au Québec* 1967 (ph); *Entre la mer et l'eau douce* 1968 (d/co-sc/co-ph/co-ed); *Le Beau Plaisir* 1968 (co-d); *Un Pays sans bons sens!* 1970 (ph with Gosselin); *Mon oncle Antoine* 1971 (ph, CFA-PH); *L'Acadia, l'Acadia?!?* 1971 (co-d/ph); *Le Temps d'une chasse* 1972 (ph, CFA-PH); *Kamouraska* 1973 (ph); *Les Ordres* 1974 (d/ph, CFA-FF, CFA-FY, CFA-D); *La Tête de Normande St-Onge* 1975 (ph); *Le Temps de l'avant* 1975 (ph); *Eliza's Horoscope* 1976 (co-ph); *Jules le magnifique* 1977 (ph); *Mourir à tue tête* 1979 (ph); *Les Bons Débarras* 1980 (ph, GA-PH); *Threshold* 1982 (ph, GA-PH); *La Quarantaine* 1982 (ph); *Louisiana* 1984 (ph); *No Mercy* 1986 (ph); *The Great Land of Small* 1987 (ph); *Salut Victor!* 1988 (ph); *Des Amis pour la vie* 1988 (ph); *Bye Bye Love* 1989 (d/ph); *Les Noces de papier* 1990 (d/ph, TV); *Montréal vu par ...* 1991 (co-d/co-sc); *Mon ami Max* 1993 (d/ph); *Quand je serai parti ... vous vivrez encore* 1999 (d/sc).

Breathing Together: The Revolution of the Electric Family

1971 84m *prod* Morley Markson and Assoc., *p/d/sc/ph* Morley Markson, *ed* Morley Markson, John N. Smith; *with* Allen Ginsberg, Jerry Rubin, Abbie Hoffman, R. Buckminster Fuller, Fred Hampton, Timothy Leary. *Breathing Together*, one of the few independent feature-length documentaries made during the 1960s, is perhaps the best film made about the hippies. For a very brief period of time, the 'system' seemed close to collapse. Director Morley Markson based his film on the Chicago Seven trial following the police riot at the 1968

Democratic Party convention, and combined newsreel footage of the riot with effects, television images, and interviews with such luminaries of the movement as Allen Ginsberg, Abbie Hoffman, Jerry Rubin, Fred Hampton, John Lennon, and Timothy Leary. It was a time of struggle: hippies against straights, and the forces of life against the culture of death in America.

Breen, Bobby

Actor; b. Toronto, 1927. Breen, a child actor and singer on stage from the age of seven, achieved American fame at age nine when he became a regular on Eddie Cantor's weekly radio show in 1936. That same year he became RKO's leading child star, and over the next three years, until his voice began to change, he appeared in half-a-dozen popular but slight films. Later he made a living as a tenor in nightclubs and musicals. **Films include:** *Let's Sing Again* 1936; *Rainbow on the River* 1936; *Make a Wish* 1937; *Hawaii Calls* 1938; *Fisherman's Wharf* 1939; *Johnny Doughboy* 1942.

Brittain, Donald

Director and writer; b. Ottawa, 1928; d. 1989. After an education at Queen's University and a stint as a journalist with the *Ottawa Journal*, Canada's greatest documentary filmmaker began his cinematic career by making sponsored films. At the NFB, which he joined in 1954, Brittain proceeded to illuminate obscure areas of Canadian life and to fashion witty and often withering portraits of Canada's famous and infamous. As director, writer, and most memorably, narrator of his own films, Brittain is arguably the most comprehensive chronicler of post–Second World War Canada. His filmography contains some of the best documentaries and docudramas ever made. Films such as *Vol-*

cano: *An Inquiry into the Life and Death of Malcolm Lowry** and *Canada's Sweetheart: The Saga of Hal C. Banks** constitute an incisive and passionate victory over Canadian cultural amnesia. **Films and television include:** *Sight Unseen* 1958 (d/sc); *Setting Fires for Science* 1958 (d/sc); *Winter Construction? It Can Be Done* 1958 (d/sc); *A Day in the Life of Jonathan Mole* 1959 (d/sc); *Everybody's Prejudiced* 1961 (d/sc); *Canada at War* series 1962 (d/sc, thirteen films); *Willie Catches On* 1962 (sc); *The Fields of Sacrifice* 1964 (p/d/sc); *Bethune* 1964 (co-p/d/co-sc); *The Changing City* 1964 (sc); *Return Reservation* 1964 (d/sc); *Summerhill* 1964 (p/d/sc); *Buster Keaton Rides Again* 1965 (sc); *Memorandum* 1965 (sc/co-d with John Spotton); *Ladies and Gentlemen ... Mr Leonard Cohen* 1965 (sc/co-d with Don Owen); *A Trip down Memory Lane* 1965 (p); *Stravinsky* 1965 (sc); *Helicopter Canada* 1966 (sc); *What on Earth!* 1966 (narr); *Never a Backward Step* 1966 (sc/co-d with Spotton, TV, CFA-FD); *Labyrinth* 1967 (co-sc); *Juggernaut* 1967 (sc); *Saul Alinsky Went to War* 1968 (d with Peter Pearson); *Tiger Child* 1970 (d); *The Apprentice* 1971 (p); *Tiki Tiki* 1971 (co-sc); *Death of a Legend* 1971(narr); *Grierson* 1973 (sc/narr); *Dreamland* 1974 (d/sc); *The Players* 1974 (d/sc); *Whistling Smith* 1975 (sc); *Volcano: An Inquiry into the Life and Death of Malcolm Lowry* 1976 (co-p/d/sc/narr, TV, CFA-FD, AAN-FD); *The Tar Sands* 1977 (narr, TV); *Henry Ford's America* 1977 (p/d/sc, TV); *The Champions,* Parts I and II 1978 (d/sc, TV, CFA-FD); *The Dionne Quintuplets* 1978 (d/co-p, TV); *Paperland: The Bureaucrat Observed* 1979 (co-p/d/co-sc, TV, GA-FD); *Running Man* 1981 (d, TV); *An Honourable Member* 1982 (d, TV); *Canada's Sweetheart: The Saga of Hal C. Banks* 1985 (p/d/sc, TV); *The Champions,* Part III: *The Final Battle* 1986 (d/sc, TV); *The King Chronicles* 1988 (d/sc, three films, TV).

Bûcherons de la Manouane

1962 28m *prod* NFB, *p* Fernand Dansereau, Victor Jobin *d* Arthur Lamothe, *ph* Bernard Gosselin, Guy Borremans, *ed* Jean Dansereau, Arthur Lamothe, *mus* Maurice Blackburn, Pierre Lemelin. *Bûcherons de la Manouane* was one of the most important documentaries from the period and had a considerable influence on Québécois filmmakers. Arthur Lamothe's* first film for the NFB took him back to a life he knew well as a young man in the lumberjack camps of the Quebec interior. The left-leaning point of view of this revealing direct-cinema look at the life and working conditions in the camps upset the NFB management, who were more accustomed to a folkloric approach to rural Quebec. (V)

Bujold, Geneviève

Actor; b. Montreal, 1942. Bujold, who arguably has had a higher-profile American career than any other Canadian actress since Norma Shearer,* began as a theatre usherette. Intense, sensual, and intelligent, she made three prestigious 'art' films with her husband, Paul Almond,* in the early 1970s. She gained international recognition in Philippe de Broca's cult classic *King of Hearts,* and received an Academy Award nomination for her performance in *Anne of the Thousand Days* opposite Richard Burton. Later, she joined Alan Rudolf's informal stock company and gave fine, cryptic performances in *Choose Me* and *The Moderns.* She is also memorable as the love interest of Jeremy Irons's twins in David Cronenberg's *Dead Ringers.** **Films and television include:** *Amanita Pestilens* 1962; *La Fleur de l'âge: Geneviève* 1964; *Romeo and Jeannette* 1965 (TV); *La Guerre est finie* 1966; *King of Hearts* 1966; *Saint Joan* 1967 (TV, as Joan of Arc); *The Thief of Paris* 1967; *Isabel* 1968 (CFA-A); *Entre la mer et l'eau douce* 1968; *Anne of* the Thousand Days 1969 (AAN-A); The Act of the Heart 1970 (CFA-A); The Trojan Women 1971; Journey 1972; Antigone 1973 (TV); Kamouraska 1973 (CFA-A); Earthquake 1974; Alex and the Gypsy 1976; Obsession 1976; Swashbuckler 1976; Another Man, Another Chance 1977; Coma 1978; Murder by Decree 1979 (GA-SA); Final Assignment 1980; The Last Flight of Noah's Ark 1980; Monsignor 1982; Choose Me 1984; Tightrope 1984; Trouble in Mind 1985; Dead Ringers 1988; The Moderns 1988; Bye Bye Love 1989; Les Noces de papier 1990 (TV); The Dance Goes On 1991; Oh, What a Night 1992; Mon amie Max 1993; The Adventures of Pinocchio 1995; Dead Innocent 1996; Last Night 1998; Eye of the Beholder 1999; The Bookfair Murders 2000 (TV).

Burns, Gary
Director and writer; b. Calgary, 1960. Burns graduated from Concordia's film study program in 1992 and has quickly risen to become Alberta's bright hope for independent films. His first feature – The Suburbanators, an artful, uneventful, ultra-low-budget, laser-precise study of twenty-something suburban male boredom – was a critical and festival success in 1995 and received limited distribution. Kitchen Party, released in 1998, was less successful, but his third feature, waydowntown,* made a major breakthrough with a wide U.S. and Canadian release. Burns is an original, emerging talent with a wry eye for the absurdities of our contemporary, throwaway society. **Films include:** Happy Valley 1992 (d); Turtle Heads 1993 (d); Beer Land 1993 (d); The Suburbanators 1996 (co-p/d/sc); Kitchen Party 1998 (d/sc); waydowntown 2000 (co-p/d/co-sc).

Burr, Raymond
Actor; b. New Westminster, B.C., 1917; d. 1993. Raymond Burr, the heavy in more than fifty low-budget thrillers, slimmed down for his starring role in the television series Perry Mason (1957–66). As the courtroom attorney who never lost a case, he was a huge hit, winning an Emmy twice. On film, he is remembered mainly as the murderer threatening Grace Kelly in Hitchcock's Rear Window, and as the lawyer in A Place in the Sun. He later found himself as a detective confined to a wheelchair in the television series Ironside. Burr closed out his career by reprising his role as Perry Mason in many television movies. **Films and television include:** San Quentin 1946; Desperate 1947; Adventures of Don Juan 1948; Raw Deal 1948; Walk a Crooked Mile 1948; Love Happy 1949; M 1951; A Place in the Sun 1951; The Blue Gardenia 1953; Fort Algiers 1953; Tarzan and the She-Devil 1953; Godzilla 1954; Casanova's Big Night 1954; Rear Window 1954; Perry Mason 1957–66 (series); Ironside 1967–74 (series); Tomorrow Never Comes 1978; Out of the Blue 1981; Airplane II: The Sequel 1982; Delirious 1991; The Legend of Kootenai Brown 1991.

Burroughs, Jackie
Actor; b. Southport, U.K., 1942. The career of Jackie Burroughs runs an on-screen gamut from the multi-Gemini-winning role of the prim and proper Aunt Hetty in the long-running Road to Avonlea series to the drug-addled tourist 'taking a vacation from feminism' in A Winter Tan,* for which she won a Genie in 1989. She made her stage debut in director Herbert Whittaker's production of A Resounding Tinkle at the University of Toronto's Hart House Theatre, and has since starred in countless plays, including Uncle Vanya and Present Laughter opposite Peter O'Toole. On film she won back-to-back Genies for her supporting performances in Phillip Borsos's The Grey Fox* and Robin Phillips's The Wars.* **Films and television include:** Notes for a Film about Donna and Gail 1966; The Ernie Game 1968; Dulcima 1968

(TV, CFA-A); *A Fan's Notes* 1972; *Monkeys in the Attic* 1974; *125 Rooms of Comfort* 1974; *Rameau's Nephew by Diderot (Thanx to Dennis Young) by Wilma Schoen* 1974; *My Pleasure Is My Business* 1975; *Running Time* 1976; *The Kidnapping of the President* 1979; *Heavy Metal* 1980 (voice); *The Grey Fox* 1983 (GA-SA); *The Wars* 1983 (GA-SA); *Dead Zone* 1983; *The Surrogate* 1984; *The Care Bears Movie* 1985 (voice); *Overdrawn at the Memory Bank* 1985 (TV); *Anne of Green Gables* 1985 (TV); *John and the Missus* 1986; *A Winter Tan* 1988 (co-p/co-d/sc/a, GA-A); *Midday Sun* 1989; *Road to Avonlea* 1989–96 (series); *Elizabeth Smart: On the Side of Angels* 1991 (TV); *Careful* 1992; *How Dinosaurs Learned to Fly* 1996 (voice); *Platinum* 1997 (TV); *Last Night* 1998; *More Tales of the City* 1998 (TV); *Happy Christmas, Miss King* 1999 (TV); *Further Tales of the City* 2001 (TV); *Lost and Delerious* 2001.

Bush Pilot

1947 60m *prod* Dominion Productions, *p* Larry L. Cromien, *ap/ed* Jack W. Ogilvie, *d* Sterling Campbell, *sc* W. Scott Darling, *ph* Edward Hyland, *mus* Samuel Hersenhoren; *with* Rochelle Hudson, Jack La Rue, Austin Willis, Frank Perry, Joe Carr. *Bush Pilot*, a long forgotten, low-level melodrama only recently restored by the National Archives of Canada and the TMN/Moviepix television network, is a curiosity – one of the few Canadian features made outside of Quebec during the 1940s. It was filmed in the Muskoka district of Ontario, and tells the story of two quarrelling bush pilot brothers (La Rue and Willis) – one good, the other bad – who fight over both the affections of a pretty girl (Hudson) and the territory for their separate charter operations.

Bussières, Pascale

Actor; b. Montreal, 1968. Bussières first attracted attention as a suicidal teenager in Micheline Lanctôt's* rigorously dark film, *Sonatine*,* but it was *Blanche*, a television series directed by Charles Binamé,* that gave her *étoile* status in Quebec. After playing the heroine in that series, and more recently the rollerblading cokehead in Binamé's Generation X picture *Eldorado*,* Bussières became the 1990s heir of Geneviève Bujold* and Carole Laure,* the most charismatic actress of her generation. It is a measure of Bussières's range that her follow-up to *Eldorado* was the role of a prim theology student who uncovers her desire for women in Patricia Rozema's *When Night Is Falling*.* **Films and television include:** *Sonatine* 1984; *La Vie fantôme* 1992; *Blanche* 1993 (series); *Deux actrices* 1993; *Eldorado* 1995; *When Night Is Falling* 1995; *The Whole of the Moon* 1996; *Les Mille Merveilles de l'univers* 1997; *Twilight of the Ice Nymphs* 1997; *L'Âge de braise* 1997; *Platinum* 1997 (TV); *Thunder Point* 1997 (CTV); *Le Coeur au poing* 1997; *Un 32 août sur terre* 1998; *Emporte-moi* 1999 (PJ-SA); *The Five Senses* 1999; *Souvenirs intimes* 1999; *La Beauté de Pandore* 2000; *La Bouteille* 2000; *Les Jeunes Filles ne savent pas nager* 2000; *Des chiens dans la neige* 2000; *Between the Moon and Montevideo* 2001.

Buttignol, Rudy

Producer, director, and writer; b. Pordenone, Italy, 1951. Buttignol came to Canada in 1955. After his graduation from York University, he worked primarily in the documentary genre, producing a number of films on Canada's contribution to space exploration. In 1983 he founded the Canadian Independent Film Caucus, a lobby group for point-of-view documentaries, and in 1993 he joined TVO to launch its documentary series, *The View from Here*. At TVO he has commissioned a number of distinctive Canadian documentaries, including *The Champagne Safari** (1995), *Hitman Hart: Wrestling with Shadows* (1998), and the Emmy Award-winning *Let It Come Down: The Life of Paul Bowles.* (1999). **Films and television include:** *Jack Bush* 1979 (p); *Shipyard* 1980 (p/d); *Inward Passage* 1983 (p/d); *Neon, an Electric Memoir* 1984 (p/d/ed); *The Space Experience* 1987 (d/sc, series); *Space Pioneers: A Canadian Story* 1988 (p/d/sc); *Alan Bean: Art off This Earth* 1990 (p); *The Spacewatch Club* 1991(p/sc, series); *Soviet Space: The Secret Designer* 1992 (p/d/sc); *Too Good To Be True* 1993 (p/sc); *Elwy: The Man Who Loved the Movies* 1995 (exp, TV); *Before Their Time* 1998 (exp, TV); *In Time's Shadow* 1999 (p, TV).

Bye Bye Blues

1989 117m *prod* True Blue Films, *exp* Tony Allard, Jerry Krepakevich, *p* Anne Wheeler, Arvi Liimatainen, *d/sc* Anne Wheeler, *ph* Vic Sarin, *ed* Christopher Tate, *mus* George Blondheim; *with* Rebecca Jenkins, Luke Reilly, Stuart Margolin, Wayne Robson, Robyn Stevan, Michael Ontkean. Director Anne Wheeler's* Second World War period film has Rebecca Jenkins (in a fine performance) playing a woman left alone and pregnant when her husband is sent off to battle. Finding herself in need of work, Jenkins is soon singing with a Prairie swing band for a few extra dollars. She's also drawn to one of the boys in the band (Reilly), leaving her loyalties seriously strained. Wheeler's delicate melodrama, beautifully shot by Vic Sarin,* is bittersweet and poignant – an unapologetically old-fashioned weepie. The film was inspired by the story of her mother's wartime experiences. (V) **Awards include:** GA: Actress (Jenkins), Supporting Actress (Stevan).

C

Calendar

1993 75m *prod* Ego Film Arts, *p* Doris Hepp, Arsinée Khanjian, *d/sc/ed* Atom Egoyan, *ph* Norayr Kasper; *with* Arsinée Khanjian, Ashot Adamian, Atom Egoyan. Egoyan* and Khanjian* took the opportunity to return to their Armenian roots to tell this oddly humorous tale. Accompanied by a local driver, an insipid Canadian photographer (Egoyan) and his lively wife (Khanjian) tour their Armenian homeland, photographing twelve historic churches for a calendar. As the project progresses, the photographer realizes that he is documenting the disintegration of his marriage as his wife becomes attracted to their guide (Adamian). Back in Toronto, the heartbroken photographer tries to come to terms with his loss by recreating the situation through a string of scripted, lifeless dinner dates with exotic women. The two narratives are told simultaneously, as scenes from both are interwoven throughout the film. It is Egoyan's most light-hearted work since *Next of Kin*, and was the result of a cash prize he won at the Moscow Film Festival. (V)

Cameron, James

Director, producer, and writer; b. Kapuskasing, Ont., 1954. Perhaps it's that stifling Canadian realist documentary tradition; perhaps it's our peculiar affinity for developing new image-making technology. For Hollywood-based Canadian expatriate Cameron, perhaps it's both. Indeed, while rejecting one cultural tradition outright and running away with the other, Cameron is making decidedly un-Canadian fantasy films (*The Abyss, The Terminator, Aliens, Terminator 2: Judgment Day, True Lies*) with the latest image-making pyrotechnics. Before alien life forms sent his career skyrocketing, Cameron studied physics at California State University, designed sets for Roger Corman, and cut his directorial teeth, so to speak, on *Piranha II: Flying Killers*. His *Titanic* is the biggest box-office hit of all time and one of the most popular films in recent American film history. It also provided Cameron with an Academy Award for Best Director – the first time in the history of the awards that a Canadian-born director has been so honoured. **Films include:** *Piranha II: Flying Killers* 1981; *The Terminator* 1984 (d/sc); *Rambo: First Blood Part II* 1985 (co-sc); *Aliens* 1986 (d/sc); *The Abyss* 1989 (d/sc); *Terminator 2: Judgment Day* 1991 (co-p/d/sc); *True Lies* 1994 (co-p/d/sc); *Strange Days* 1995 (p); *Titanic* 1997 (co-p/d/sc/co-ed, AA-D, AA-P, AA-E).

Cameron, Rod
Actor; b. Nathan Roderick Cox, Calgary, 1910; d. 1983. This handsome, lanky star of over ninety low-budget westerns and serials began his career as a stuntman and stand-in for Fred MacMurray before moving up to bit parts and leading roles in the 1940s. At one point there was even a Rod Cameron comic book. He continued working in Europe and America well into the 1970s, and caused a sensation in 1960 when he divorced his wife to marry her mother. **Films and television include:** *North West Mounted Police* 1940; *Wake Island* 1942; *The Remarkable Andrew* 1942; *The Forest Rangers* 1942; *The Fleet's In* 1942; *The Commandos Strike at Dawn* 1942; *G-Men vs the Black Dragon* 1943 (serial); *Secret Service in Darkest Aftrica* 1943 (serial); *Riding High* 1943; *Mrs Parkington* 1944; *Swing Out Sister* 1945; *Belle Starr's Daughter* 1948; *Ride the Man Down* 1952; *City Detective* 1953–5 (series); *State Trooper* 1956–9 (series); *Requiem for a Gunfighter* 1965; *Evel Knievel* 1971; *The Last Movie* 1971.

Campbell, Neve
Actor; b. Guelph, Ont., 1964. Campbell's career has been rocket fuelled. At nine she was accepted in the National Ballet School of Canada; at fourteen she joined the Toronto production of *The Phantom*

of the Opera; at twenty she moved to Los Angeles, where she was cast in the popular teen drama *Party of Five*. Wes Craven's horror megahit *Scream* made her a star, and by the age of twenty-four she was on the cover of *Time* magazine. Campbell's sexy physical beauty combined with a touch of vulnerability make her a top box-office draw. **Films and television include:** *Catwalk* 1992–3 (series); *Paint Cans* 1994; *Party of Five* 1994–2000 (series); *The Craft* 1996; *Scream* 1996; *Scream 2* 1997; *Wild Things* 1998; *54* 1998; *Three to Tango* 1999; *The Lion King II: Simba's Pride* 1999 (voice); *Scream 3* 2000; *Drowning Mona* 2000.

Canada Carries On
1940–59 series *prod* NFB. The NFB's first and longest continuing theatrical series was launched by Board founder John Grierson* and his hand-picked director, Stuart Legg.* During the Second World War its purpose was to show positive, uplifting images in order to encourage the war effort; one 10- to 20-minute film was released each month. *Churchill's Island* (1941) won an Academy Award and two others – *Warclouds in the Pacific* (1941) and *High over the Borders* (1942) – were nominated. When the war ended, the series was continued under producer Sydney Newman* with a mandate to 'interpret Canada.' Most of these films are unremarkable, but a handful stand out, including *After Prison What?* (1950), *The Herring Hunt* (1953), and *Farewell, Oak Street* (1953). *Canada Carries On* was cancelled in 1959 after the release of some 200 films.

Canada's Sweetheart: The Saga of Hal C. Banks
1985 115m *prod* NFB, CBC, *exp* Paul Wright, Andy Thomson, *p* Adam Symansky, Donald Brittain, *d/narr* Donald Brittain, *sc* Donald Brittain, Richard Nielsen, *ph* Andreas Poulsson, *ed* Rita Roy, Rich-

33

ard Todd, *mus* Eldon Rathburn; *with* Maury Chaykin, R.H. Thomson, Gary Reineke, Sean McCann, Colin Fox, Chuck Shamata. *Canada's Sweetheart* is the story of Hal Banks, an American thug imported into Canada to crush the communist-controlled Canadian Seaman's Union. With guns, baseball bats, and government complicity, Banks succeeded in bringing about a more compliant union. In the process, he destroyed the careers of over 6,000 seamen. Apart from Banks, the real villain of this story is the Canadian government, which imported Banks, quietly condoned his brutality, and for twenty-five years, protected him from prosecution. One of Donald Brittain's* most effective docudramas with a chilling performance by Chaykin* as the ruthless union boss. (V)

Canadian Cooperation Project
1948–58. The name associated with an initiative put forward by the Motion Picture Association of America, and agreed to by the federal government, to prevent the taxation of profits of the American distribution and exhibition cartel and the imposition of a quota system. In return, Hollywood producers promised to film some features in Canada, to insert favourable references to Canada in scripts in order to promote tourism, and to encourage the distribution of more NFB films in the United States. The whole project was a boondoggle that was hypocritically sold to the public as a boost to film production in Canada when it was nothing of the sort. It was, instead, a blatant – and successful – attempt to prevent the growth of a Canadian film industry. The initiative was officially (and quietly) dropped in 1958.

Canadian Pacific
1974 11m *p/d/ph/ed* David Rimmer. With classic precision and simplicity, Rim-

mer* turns a structuralist landscape study into an insightful comment on cinematic illusion, using one of his signature techniques: placement of a stationary camera in a single location to record the subtle changes that occur over time. In *Canadian Pacific*, Rimmer set his camera at a window of his studio, through which he could see the sky, mountains, water, and the Canadian Pacific Railway. These four elements become fields of play, where changes in one or more create an illusion of three-dimensional space. This film is more than just an exercise in depth perception; the fluid dissolves through time are nothing short of poetry.

Candid Eye
1958–61 series *prod* NFB. The NFB's famed direct-cinema series of fourteen films made for CBC-TV during the late 1950s. The key filmmakers – Terence Macartney-Filgate,* Wolf Koenig,* and Roman Kroitor* – were overseen by executive producer Tom Daly.* The films were observational; shot on location using new lightweight equipment, with an emphasis on ordinary daily events. **Films:** *The Days before Christmas* 1958; *Blood and Fire* 1958; *Country Threshing* 1958; *A Foreign Language* 1958; *Memory of Summer* 1958; *Pilgrimage* 1958; *Police* 1958; *The Back-Breaking Leaf* 1959; *Emergency Ward* 1959; *End of the Line* 1959; *Glenn Gould – On the Record* 1959; *Glenn Gould – Off the Record* 1959; *Cars in Your Life* 1960; *Festival in Puerto Rico* 1961.

Candy, John
Actor; b. Toronto, 1950; d. 1994. Given the funhouse gallery of characters he created, it's fitting that Candy was born on Halloween. From *SCTV*'s Tommy Shanks and Johnny LaRue, to *Uncle Buck* and the twisted Louisiana hood in Oliver Stone's *JFK*, Candy's affable and

malleable personality made him one of the most popular performers to emerge out of the comedy scene in Toronto in the late 1970s. After studying journalism at Centennial College, Candy became a co-founder of the Canadian chapter of Chicago's Second City comedy troupe. He went on to star in the fabled *SCTV* series until he found fame on the big screen with a succession of hits in the 1980s, including *Splash* with Tom Hanks, *Planes, Trains and Automobiles* with Steve Martin, and *Only the Lonely* with Maureen O'Hara. Before his death at age forty-four, John Candy played out a boyhood dream by being a part-owner of the Toronto Argonauts football club. **Films and television include:** *It Seemed like a Good Idea at the Time* 1975; *The Clown Murders* 1976; *Find the Lady* 1976; *SCTV* 1977–84 (series); *The Silent Partner* 1978; *1941* 1979; *Lost and Found* 1979; *The Blues Brothers* 1980; *Heavy Metal* 1981 (voice); *Stripes* 1981; *It Came from Hollywood* 1982; *Going Berserk* 1983; *Splash* 1984; *Brewster's Millions* 1985; *Sesame Street Presents: Follow That Bird* 1985; *Summer Rental* 1985; *The Last Polka* 1985 (TV); *Volunteers* 1985; *The Canadian Conspiracy* 1986 (TV); *Little Shop of Horrors* 1986; *Armed and Dangerous* 1986; *Planes, Trains and Automobiles* 1987; *Spaceballs* 1987; *The Great Outdoors* 1988; *Uncle Buck* 1989; *Who's Harry Crumb?* 1989 (exp/a); *Home Alone* 1990; *The Rescuers Down Under* 1990 (voice); *Nothing but Trouble* 1991; *Only the Lonely* 1991; *JFK* 1991; *Delirious* 1991; *Once upon a Crime* 1992; *Cool Runnings* 1993; *Rookie of the Year* 1993; *Wagons East* 1995; *Canadian Bacon* 1995.

Candy Mountain

1987 92m *prod* Les Films Vision 4, Les Films Plain-Chant (France), Xanadu Film (Switzerland), *exp* Gerald B. Dearing, *p* Ruth Waldburger, *d* Robert Frank, Rudy Wurlitzer, *sc* Rudy Wurlit-

zer, *ph* Pio Corradi, *ed* Jennifer Augé, *mus* Dr. John, Tom Waits, Joe Strummer, and others; *with* Kevin O'Connor, Harris Yulin, Tom Waits, Bulle Oglier, Robert Blossom, Leon Redbone, Rita MacNeil, Tantoo Cardinal, Joe Strummer. In tone, *Candy Mountain* is an odd throwback to the restless road cinema of the late 1960s and early 1970s; in narrative terms, it is a reversal of the east-west trajectory of *Goin' down the Road.** The plot follows the adventures of a callow young musician (O'Connor) from New York who is determined to track down a reclusive guitar maker (Yulin), who lives somewhere in Nova Scotia. On the way the musician encounters a variety of odd sorts – the film includes cameos by Tom Waits, Dr. John, Leon Redbone, and Joe Strummer (of The Clash). As usual with such fare, the destination is less significant than the journey, and the trip is accompanied by great music from a stellar cast. One of the best (unseen) Canadian movies from the 1980s.

Cardinal, Tantoo

Actor; b. Tantoo Martin, Anzac, Alta., 1951. Cardinal has been shot in the neck with an arrow in Bruce Beresford's *Black Robe,** has played Cupid to Kevin Costner's and Mary McDonnell's characters in *Dances with Wolves,* and has helped hold together the passionately dysfunctional family in *Legends of the Fall* with Anthony Hopkins and Brad Pitt. She is one of the most successful native actors of her generation and had a recurring role in the popular Canadian television series *North of 60.* **Films and television include:** *Marie-Anne* 1978; *Death Hunt* 1981; *Running Brave* 1983; *Loyalties* 1986; *Gunsmoke: Return to Dodge* 1987 (TV); *Candy Mountain* 1987; *Divided Loyalties* 1989 (TV); *War Party* 1989; *Dances with Wolves* 1990; *Black Robe* 1991; *Silent Tongue* 1993; *Spirit Rider* 1993 (TV); *Dr*

Quinn, Medicine Woman 1993–5 (series); *Mustard Bath* 1994; *Legends of the Fall* 1994; *Lakota Woman: Siege at Wounded Knee* 1994 (TV); *North of 60* 1994–8 (series); *Tecumseh: The Last Warrior* 1995 (TV); *Lewis and Clark: The Journey of the Corps of Discovery* 1997 (voice, TV); *The Education of Little Tree* 1998; *Smoke Signals* 1998; *Big Bear* 1999 (TV).

Care Bears Movie, The
1985 76m *prod* Nelvana, *exp* Carole MacGillvray, Robert Unkel, Jack Chojnacki, Lou Gioia, *p* Michael Hirsh, Patrick Loubert, Clive Smith, *d* Arna Selznick, *sc* Peter Sauder, *ph* David Altman, Jim Christianson, Barbra Sachs, *ed* John Broughton, Rob Kirkpatrick, *mus* Patricia Cullen, Carole King, John Sebastian; *voices* Mickey Rooney, Jackie Burroughs, Georgia Engel, Harry Dean Stanton, Sunny Besen Thrasher. Nelvana's* most successful animated feature is no more than a seventy-six-minute commercial for the heavily merchandised characters from the American Greetings Company and the General Mills Toy Group, the stated intention of which is to teach children to express their feelings. The plot has the Bears – each with a symbol on its chest representing a human emotion – saving the world from an evil spirit intent on removing the last shreds of caring from all children. The film, definitely aimed at the toddler set with limited adult appeal, nevertheless scored big in the United States and on video, virtually saving the floundering Nelvana at a time when their previous feature, the far more ambitious *Rock and Rule*, died at the box office. (V) **Awards include:** Golden Reel Award.

Careful
1992 110m *prod* Careful Pictures, *exp* André Bennett, *p* Greg Klymkiw, Tracy Traeger, *d/ph/ed* Guy Maddin, *sc* Guy

Maddin, George Toles, *mus* John McCulloch; *with* Kyle McCulloch, Gosia Dobrowolska, Sarah Neville, Brent Neale, Paul Cox, Victor Cowie. Maddin's third feature tells the story of the tiny fictitious town of Tolzbad, which is situated precariously somewhere in the Alps. The inhabitants of this nineteenth-century community must speak in hushed tones to avoid provoking avalanches. In this extremely repressive environment, the villagers find themselves in an array of obsessive and incestuous relationships in a story of love, duels, and suicide told in an expressionistic style reminiscent of the German mountain films of the 1920s. (V)

Carle, Gilles
Director and writer; b. Maniwaki, Que., 1929. Carle, a key figure in Quebec cinema, worked as a graphic artist and writer before he shot his first film in 1961. His innovative debut feature, *La Vie heureuse de Léopold Z,** tracked the adventures of a snowplow operator during a madcap Christmas Eve. The quirkily paced, proto-feminist *La Vraie Nature de Bernadette*, starring Micheline Lanctôt,* and *Le Mort d'un bûcheron*, with Carole Laure,* led eventually to the more mainstream but graceful *Les Plouffe** and the epic love story *Maria Chapdelaine** – both classics of Quebec cinema. Named in 1995 to France's Legion d'honneur, Carle continues his peripatetic career with theatrical and television films. Effervescent and optimistic, he once said about Canadian moviemaking: 'We're condemned to originality.' **Films include:** *Dimanche d'amérique* 1961 (d); *Manger* 1961 (co-d); *Patinoire* 1962 (d); *Natation* 1963 (d); *Patte mouillée* 1963 (d/ed); *Un Air de famille* 1964 (d); *Solange dans nos campagnes* 1964 (d/sc); *Percé on the Rocks* 1964 (d); *La Vie heureuse de Léopold Z* 1965 (d/sc); *Place à*

Olivier Guimond 1966 (d/sc); *Place aux Jérolas* 1967 (d/ed); *Le Québec à l'heure de l'Expo* 1967 (d/narr); *Le Viol d'une fille douce* 1968 (d/sc); *Red* 1970 (d/co-sc); *Stéréo* 1970 (d/sc); *Les Mâles* 1971 (d/sc/ed); *Un Hiver brûlant* 1971 (d/ed); *La Vraie Nature de Bernadette* 1972 (d/sc/ed, CFA-D, CFA-SC); *Les Corps célestes* 1973 (d/co-sc); *La Mort d'un bûcheron* 1973 (d/co-sc/ed); *La Tête de Normande St-Onge* 1975 (d/co-sc/co-ed); *Les Chevaux ont-ils des ailes?* 1975 (d); *A Thousand Moons* 1976 (d, TV); *L'Ange et la femme* 1977 (d/sc); *L'Âge de la machine* 1978 (d/sc); *Homecoming* 1979 (d, TV); *Fantastica* 1980 (d/sc); *Les Plouffe* 1981 (d/co-sc, GA-D, GA-ASC); *Jouer sa vie* 1982 (co-d); *Maria Chapdelaine* 1983 (d/co-sc); *Le Crime d'Ovide Plouffe* 1984 (d); *O Picasso* 1985 (co-d/sc); *Equinoxe* 1986 (co-sc); *La Guêpe* 1986 (d/sc); *Le Diable d' amérique* 1990 (d/sc); *La Postière* 1992 (d/sc); *Le Sang du chasseur* 1995 (d/sc); *Pudding chômeur* 1996 (d/sc).

Carrey, Jim

Actor; b. Newmarket, Ont., 1962. Years as a stand-up comic on the comedy club circuit landed Carrey a part in a short-lived sitcom, *The Duck Factory*, and small parts in several films. It wasn't until his rubbery face, manic energy, and general goofiness in the TV series *In Living Color* got him the lead in the low-budget comedy *Ace Ventura: Pet Detective* that Carrey became an overnight sensation. With the success of *The Mask, Dumb and Dumber, Ace Ventura: When Nature Calls,* and *The Truman Show,* Carrey has become one the highest-paid actors in Hollywood and the natural successor to Jerry Lewis's 'stupid' style of physical comedy. **Films and television include:** *All in Good Taste* 1981; *Introducing Janet* 1981 (TV); *Copper Mountain* 1982 (TV); *Finder Keepers* 1984; *The Duck Factory* 1984 (series); *Once Bitten* 1985; *Peggy Sue Got Married* 1986; *Earth Girls Are Easy* 1988; *The Dead Pool* 1988; *The Pink Cadillac* 1989; *In Living Color* 1990–4 (series); *High Strung* 1991; *Doing Time on Maple Drive* 1992; *Ace Ventura: Pet Detective* 1994; *Dumb and Dumber* 1994; *The Mask* 1994; *Batman Forever* 1995; *Ace Ventura: When Nature Calls* 1995; *The Cable Guy* 1996; *Liar Liar* 1997; *The Truman Show* 1998; *Simon Birch* 1998; *Man on the Moon* 1999; *Me, Myself and Irene* 2000; *Dr Seuss' How the Grinch Stole Christmas* 2000.

Carrière, Marcel

Director and sound engineer; b. Bouchette, Que., 1935. Carrière entered the world of film as a sound engineer for the NFB, where he worked for more than a decade before moving on to directing. As sound engineer, his love of experimenting led him to the forefront of the direct-cinema movement: in *Les Raquetteurs,** for example, he recorded direct sound before it could be synched with the camera. After co-directing *La Lutte,** Carrière made the transition to solo directing, which he first explored with *Villeneuve, peintre-barbier* and perfected with *Avec tambours et trompettes.** He has worked mainly in documentary, but has also contributed a few notable fiction films, the most memorable of which is perhaps the sociological satire *OK ... Laliberté.* **Films include:** *Les Raquetteurs* 1958 (sr); *La Lutte* 1961 (co-d/sr); *Québec–USA* 1962 (sr); *Seul ou avec d'atures* 1962 (sr); *Lonely Boy* 1962 (co-sr); *À Saint-Henri le cinq septembre* 1962 (sr); *Pour la suite du monde* 1963 (sr); *À tout prendre* 1963 (sr); *Le Temps perdu* 1964 (sr); *Le Chat dans le sac* 1964 (sr); *Jusqu'au cou* 1964 (sr); *Stravinsky* 1965 (sr); *La Fleur de l'âge: Geneviève* 1965 (sr); *Les Festin des morts* 1965 (sr); *Villeneuve, peintre-barbier* 1965 (d); *Ce soir-là Gilles Vigneault ...* 1966 (sr); *Avec tambours et trompettes* 1967 (d, CFA-SD); *OK ...*

Laliberté 1973 (d/co-sc); *Ping Pong* 1974
(d); *Jeux de la xxie Olympiade* 1977 (co-d).

Carry On, Sergeant!
1928 98m *prod* Canadian International
Films, *exp* William Clarke, Edward
Johnston, *p/d/sc* Bruce Bairnsfather, *ph*
Bert Cann, *ed* Bruce Bairnsfather, Bert
Cann, *assist. ed* Gordon Sparling, *mus*
Ernest Dainty; *with* Hugh Buckler,
Jimmie Savo, William Stewart, Nancy
Ann Hargreaves, Louis Cardi. This film,
made with an eye to the British market,
was shot at the Trenton studios in Ontario and was the most costly film
($500,000) in the history of Canadian
silent cinema. *Carry On, Sergeant!* is the
story of four friends who join the army
to fight in the First World War. After
years of trench warfare, one of the men
(Buckler) meets a French woman working the taverns. He sleeps with her, but
is overcome with guilt and is later killed
in battle. His wife (Hargreaves) back
home believes he died a hero and re-
members him with love. This sentimental story, which doesn't back away from
the unpleasant (the film was heavily
criticized for the affair between a Canadian soldier and a 'prostitute'), was released at the end of the silent era, and
after a brief theatrical run, it disappeared from view. A new print was
struck in the 1970s by the Ontario Film
Institute.

Carson, Jack
Actor; b. Carmen, Man., 1910; d. 1963.
Carson, a versatile character and supporting actor, appeared in eighty films
between 1935 and 1961. The tall, beefy,
rugged Manitoban, one of Warner Bros.
excellent stock company of character actors was usually cast as the wise guy
who wound up decking the likes of
James Cagney and James Mason. He is
best remembered for his malevolent per-

formances in *Mildred Pierce* opposite
Joan Crawford, as the studio press flak
in Judy Garland's musical version of *A
Star Is Born*, and as Paul Newman's
older brother in *Cat on a Hot Tin Roof*.
Films include: *Stage Door* 1937; *You Only
Live Once* 1937; *Bringing up Baby* 1938;
Carefree 1938; *Destry Rides Again* 1939;
Mr Smith Goes to Washington 1939; *Ty-
phoon* 1940; *The Bride Came C.O.D.* 1941;
Love Crazy 1941; *Mr and Mrs Smith* 1941;
The Strawberry Blonde 1941; *Gentleman
Jim* 1942; *The Male Animal* 1942; *The Hard
Way* 1943; *Arsenic and Old Lace* 1944; *Hol-
lywood Canteen* 1944; *Shine on Harvest
Moon* 1944; *Mildred Pierce* 1945; *Romance
on the High Seas* 1948; *It's a Great Feeling*
1949; *Dangerous When Wet* 1953; *A Star Is
Born* 1954; *Ain't Misbehavin'* 1955; *Cat on
a Hot Tin Roof* 1958; *Tarnished Angels*
1958; *Rally round the Flag, Boys!* 1958; *The
Bramble Bush* 1960; *King of the Roaring
20s: The Story of Arnold Rothstein* 1961.

Carter, Peter
Director and producer; b. U.K., 1933; d.
1982. Carter, a director and producer
who made a significant contribution to
English-Canadian cinema for nearly
twenty years, was best known for his
highly acclaimed 1971 film, *The Rowdyman,** starring Gordon Pinsent.* Trained
in Britain, Carter came to Canada in
1955, and joined Crawley Films as an
editor and assistant director. He later
directed and produced several CBC-TV
series during the 1960s and lent his production skills to Paul Almond's *Isabel**
and *The Act of Heart.** Before his death at
age forty-eight, Carter was based in Los
Angeles. **Films and television include:**
Isabel 1968 (ap); *The Act of the Heart* 1970
(ap); *A Fan's Notes* 1972 (ap); *The
Rowdyman* 1972 (d); *Highballin'* 1978 (d);
A Man Called Intrepid 1978 (d, TV); *Rituals* 1978 (d); *Jack London's Klondike Fever*
1980 (d); *Kavik the Wolf-Dog* 1980 (d); *The

Intruder Within 1981 (d, TV); *Highpoint* 1984 (d).

Cat Came Back, The
1988 7m37s *prod* NFB, *exp* Ches Yetman, *p* Richard Condie, Cordell Barker, *d/sc/an* Cordell Barker, *mus* John McCullock. This film, one of the most popular animated shorts produced by the NFB, tells the wacky and very funny tale of a man who wants nothing more than to get rid of his crazy cat. During one of his many attempts to do away with the freaky feline, the frustrated pet owner blows himself up. He believes he is finally free of his nemesis, but even in the afterlife the cat comes back. Cordell Barker's clever animation combines wonderfully with the well-known folk song. It's a classic that is entertaining for both children and adults, and it received an Academy Award nomination for Animated Short. (V)

Cattrall, Kim
Actor; b. Liverpool, U.K., 1956. Cattrall trained at American Academy of Dramatic Arts in New York, and appeared on the Canadian stage and in tax-sheltered films of the 1970s and early 1980s (few will forget her enthusiasm as the sexually voracious gym instructor in Bob Clark's* hugely popular adolescent farce, *Porky's*) before she found her niche as a sexy comedienne in Hollywood movies. Often poorly utilized, Cattrall played the object of desire in *Mannequin* and Tom Hanks's uptight wife in *The Bonfire of the Vanities*. She also commanded attention in the Oliver Stone television drama *Wild Palms* and landed a lead in the popular *Sex and the City* series. **Films and television include:** *Rosebud* 1975; *Deadly Harvest* 1977; *Crossbar* 1979 (TV); *Tribute* 1980; *Porky's* 1981; *Ticket to Heaven* 1981; *Police Academy* 1984; *Hold-Up* 1985; *Turk 182!* 1985;

City Limits 1985; *Big Trouble in Little China* 1986; *Mannequin* 1987; *Masquerade* 1988; *Midnight Crossing* 1988; *Palais Royale* 1988; *Brown Bread Sandwiches* 1989; *The Return of the Musketeers* 1989; *Honeymoon Academy* 1990; *Bonfire of the Vanities* 1990; *Star Trek VI: The Undiscovered Country* 1991; *Split Second* 1992; *Wild Palms* 1993 (TV); *Double Suspicion* 1994; *The Heidi Chronicles* 1995 (TV); *Unforgettable* 1996; *Where the Truth Lies* 1996; *Invasion* 1997 (TV); *Creature* 1998 (TV); *Sex and the City* 1998–present (series); *Baby Geniuses* 1999; *36 Hours to Die* 1999 (TV).

Chairy Tale, A
1957 10m *prod* NFB, *exp* Tom Daly, *p* Herbert Taylor, *d* Norman McLaren, Claude Jutra, *an* Evelyn Lambart, *mus* Ravi Shankar, Chatur Lal, Maurice Blackburn; *with* Claude Jutra. Norman McLaren* used pixilation (which he also used in *Neighbours*) to tell the amusing, surrealistic tale of a young man (Jutra*) who struggles to sit on a chair (animated by Lambart*) that refuses to cooperate. The humourous, hopeless struggle of the young man to impose his will on an otherwise inanimate object evolves into a moral lesson about compromise and cooperation. Academy Award nomination for Animated Short. (V)

Challenge for Change
1966–80 *prod* NFB. An innovative program that began in the late 1960s as a way of using film and video to promote social change and put the means of communication into the hands of the people. The program informally originated with Tanya Ballantyne's *The Things I Cannot Change** (1966) and gained credence with Colin Low's* remarkable series of twenty-seven films made on Fogo Island, Newfoundland, during the summer of 1967. In 1969, the program was established as a studio within the NFB

specifically mandated by the federal cabinet 'to prepare Canadians for social change.' Over 140 films were produced under the Challenge for Change banner before federal-government funding was withdrawn. By 1980 the program had quietly withered away.

Chambers, Jack

Filmmaker and artist; b. London, Ont., 1931; d. 1978. A celebrated visual artist, Jack Chambers was also a vastly influential figure in the evolution of experimental film in Canada. He pursued the poetics of perception in his work, and even wrote an aesthetic manifesto in 1969 entitled 'Perceptual Realism.' His deceptively simple films contain dizzying combinations of sound and silence, darkness and light, original and archival footage, and abstraction and representation. After almost three decades, Chambers's feature-length masterpiece, *The Hart of London,** continues to haunt and inspire, and it has influenced filmmakers from Bruce Elder* to Philip Hoffman.* **Films include:** *Mosaic* 1966; *Hybrid* 1967; *Little Red Riding Hood* 1967; *R34* 1967; *Circle* 1969; *The Hart of London* 1970.

Champagne Safari, The

1995 94m *prod* Field Seven Films, NFB, *exp* John Walker, *p/d* George Ungar, *sc* Steve Lucas, John Kramer, Harold Crooks, *ph* Floyd Crosby, Kirk Tougas, John Walker, Douglas Kiefer, Joan Hutton, Mathieu Roberts, *ed* John Kramer, *mus* Normand Roger, *narr* Colm Feore, David Hemblen, Jim Morris. In a strikingly original personal vision, director George Ungar unravels at least part of the little-known story of Charles Bedaux, the French-born venture capitalist, playboy, and crypto-fascist who was most famous for introducing the concept of time management to American industry. The wealthy entrepreneur was eccentric for sure, and much of the film focuses on his unsuccessful 1934 trek through the Canadian Rockies, transporting bulk quantities of luxury items (thus the film's title). Ungar manages to pack a great deal of information into the film while withholding judgment of Bedaux, opting instead for an ambiguous conclusion, effectively maintaining his subject's considerable mystique. (V) **Awards include:** GA: Feature Documentary.

Champions, Parts I and II, The

1978 113m *prod* NFB, *exp* Peter Katadotis, Paul Wright, *p* Donald Brittain, Janet Leissner, *d/sc/narr* Donald Brittain, *ph* Andreas Poulsson, *ed* Steven Kellar, Ted Remerowski, *mus* Art Phillips. René Lévesque and Pierre Trudeau – one a separatist the other a federalist – were life-long political foes. Their intertwined careers are the focus of these two NFB documentaries: Part I covers the earlier years up to 1967; Part II covers the years from 1967 to 1977. Using photos, newsreel footage, and interviews with friends and colleagues, these films provide a background to the titanic struggle of these two men for the hearts and minds of Canadians and Quebecers. Most of the footage had been seen elsewhere, but it was Brittain's* genius to fit the pieces together, and to make sense of it all. It's a great passion play, starring two compelling, opposite political figures who were nevertheless prisoners of each other. (V) **Awards include:** CFA: Feature Documentary.

Champions, Part III: The Final Battle, The

1986 87m *prod* NFB, CBC, *exp* Barrie Howells, *p* Adam Symansky, Donald Brittain, *d/sc/narr* Donald Brittain, *ph* Andreas Poulsson, *ed* Richard Bujold, *mus* Eldon Rathburn. The third (and best) of *The Champions* trilogy of films covers the years between 1977 and 1986. Using the same techniques of the previous two films, Brittain* reveals the turbulent, behind-the-scenes dramas during the first Quebec referendum on separation and Trudeau's repatriation of the Canadian Constitution. In so doing, Brittain also traces each man's fall from grace, and documents the moment when their historic battles slipped into the realm of popular myth. (V)

Changeling, The
1980 107m *prod* Tiberius Film Productions, *exp* Mario Kassar, Andrew Vajna, *p* Joel B. Michaels, Garth Drabinsky, *d* Peter Medak, *sc* William Gray, Diana Maddox, *ph* John Coquillon, *ed* Lilla Pedersen, Lou Lombardo, *mus* Rick Wilkins; *with* George C. Scott, Trish Van Devere, Melvyn Douglas, Jean Marsh, John Colicos, Barry Morse. Although it received mixed reviews, *The Changeling* went on to perform extremely well in the United States and remains one of the highest-grossing and most popular Canadian features ever made. Scott plays a music lecturer and composer who moves into a grandiose Seattle mansion to recover from a personal tragedy. Inevitably, the house turns out to be haunted, this time by the avenging spirit of a child whose murder was covered up by a changeling (Douglas), who grew up to inherit a fortune and become a powerful industrialist and senator. This middling haunted-house tale, well shot and nicely designed, has a few good moments but only under-par performances by the two veteran Hollywood leads. (V) **Awards include:** GA: Picture, Adapted Screenplay, Foreign Actor (Scott), Foreign Actress (Van Devere), Cinematography, Art Direction, Overall Sound; Golden Reel Award.

Chapman, Christopher
Producer, director, cinematographer, and editor; b. Toronto, 1927. Chapman is a gifted and naturally talented director and photographer of poetic films. His first short, *The Seasons* (shot in 1952), captured the Canadian Film Award for Film of the Year for its twenty-six-year-old director. In *A Place to Stand*, Ontario's official film made for Expo 67, Chapman pioneered multi-image techniques, displaying as many as fifteen images simultaneously on a 70mm screen with a twelve-track sound system. These techniques were later adopted by the Imax Corporation for its premiere film, *Tiger Child*, at Expo 70 in Japan. Chapman shot several of his films in the IMAX format, including *Toronto the Good* and *Volcano*. **Films include:** *The Seasons* 1953 (p/d/ph/ed, CFA-FY, CFA-NTS); *Saguenay* 1962 (d/ph); *Enduring Wilderness* 1964 (ph); *Expedition Bluenose* 1964 (ph); *The Persistant Seed* 1964 (d/ph/co-ed); *The Magic Molecule* 1964 (co-d/ph); *A Place to Stand* 1967 (co-p/d/ph/ed); *Ontario* 1970 (p/d); *Toronto the Good* 1973 (p/d/ed); *Volcano* 1974 (p/d/ed); *A Sense of Humus* 1976 (d/ph/ed); *Kelly* 1981 (d); *Pyramid of Roses* 1982 (co-p/d/ed); *The Wilderness* 1984 (d/ph/ed); U.S. pavillon film at Expo 86.

Chat dans le sac, Le
1964 74m *prod* NFB, *p* Jacques Bobet, *d/sc/ed* Gilles Groulx, *ph* Jean-Claude Labrecque, *mus* John Coltrane, Antonio Vivaldi; *with* Barbara Ulrich, Claude Godbout, Manon Blain, Véronique Vilbert. This essential film in the early development of Quebec cinema is as important to *le québécois* as its contemporary *Nobody Waved Good-Bye** was to English-Canadian filmmakers. *Le Chat dans le sac* uses documentary, direct-

cinema techniques and Godardian dis-
tancing devices to tell the story of a
young, Hamlet-like Quebec journalist
(Godbout), who struggles to come to
terms with the society around him. His
Anglo-Jewish girlfriend (Ulrich) is too
concerned about her career in the theatre to worry about social problems and
identity. Eventually, he leaves Montreal
for the countryside to meditate in isolation. As he says at one point: 'I am Québécois, so I must find my own way.' (V)

Chaykin, Maury

Actor; b. Brooklyn, N.Y., 1950. Chaykin
hs been lauded as 'Canada's top character actor of his generation.' He studied
acting at the State University of New
York in Buffalo and founded a theatre
group that toured Canada in the late
1960s. Since then, Chaykin has been
working non-stop, blazing a trail across
stage, screen, and television as a masterful portrayer of eccentric and melancholic loners. He has also shown considerable range in his performances
moving from the American labour boss
in Donald Brittain's *Canada's Sweetheart:
The Saga of Hal C. Banks** through the
spaced-out rock star in *Whale Music** to
the sex-obsessed games player in Atom
Egoyan's *The Adjuster** – perhaps his finest role. **Films and television include:**
Riel 1979 (TV); *Nothing Personal* 1980; *The
Kidnapping of the President* 1980; *Death
Hunt* 1981; *Soup for One* 1982; *Curtains*
1983; *Of Unknown Origin* 1983; *War
Games* 1983; *Highpoint* 1984; *Mrs Soffel*
1984; *Def-Con 4* 1985; *Turk 182!* 1985;
Overdrawn at the Memory Bank 1985 (TV);
The Suicide Murders 1985 (TV); *Canada's
Sweetheart: The Saga of Hal C. Banks* 1985
(TV); *Race for the Bomb* 1986 (TV); *Meat-
balls III* 1987; *Nowhere to Hide* 1987; *Iron
Eagle II* 1988; *Millennium* 1988; *Stars and
Bars* 1988; *Twins* 1988; *George's Island*
1989; *Cold Comfort* 1989; *Dances with
Wolves* 1990; *Mr Destiny* 1990; *Where the
Heart Is* 1990; *The Adjuster* 1991; *Con-
spiracy of Silence* 1991 (TV); *Montréal vu
par ...* 1991; *My Cousin Vinny* 1992; *Leav-
ing Normal* 1992; *The Pianist* 1992; *Hero*
1992; *Beethoven's 2nd* 1993; *Buried on Sunday* 1993; *Sommersby* 1993; *Camilla* 1994;
Money for Nothing 1994; *Whale Music* 1994
(GA-A); *Cutthroat Island* 1995; *Unstrung
Heroes* 1995; *Devil in a Blue Dress* 1995; *A
Life Less Ordinary* 1997; *Northern Lights*
1997; *The Sweet Hereafter* 1997; *The Mask
of Zorro* 1998; *Love and Death on Long Island* 1998; *Mouse Hunt* 1998; *Pale Saints*
1998; *Jerry and Tom* 1998; *Entrapment* 1999;
Joan of Arc 1999 (TV); *Mystery, Alaska*
1999; *Jacob Two-Two Meets the Hooded
Fang* 1999; *The Golden Spiders: A Nero
Wolfe Mystery* 2000 (TV, as Wolfe); *The
Art of War* 2000; *Nero Wolfe* 2001 (series).

Cherry, Evelyn and Lawrence

Evelyn: Director and producer; b.
Evelyn Spice, Yorkton, Sask., 1904; d.
1990. **Lawrence:** Director and producer;
b. Saskatchewan, ca 1900; d. 1966. As
pioneering social activists and documentary filmmakers, Evelyn and Lawrence Cherry made over 100 films in
fifty years. Evelyn, originally a journalist, went to England in the mid-1930s
where she worked for John Grierson* at
the General Post Office Film Unit. There
she meet and married Lawrence Cherry.
The couple returned to Canada and
joined the NFB, where they were given
responsibility for agricultural films.
Evelyn left the Board in 1950, but Lawrence continued directing and producing there until 1957. They established
Cherry Film Productions in Regina in
1961, and Evelyn continued producing
films after her husband's death in 1966.
Films include: *Prairie Winter* 1935; *By
Their Own Strength* 1940; *New Horizons*
1940; *Windbreaks for the Prairies* 1942;
That They May Live 1942; *Soil for Tomor-*

row 1945; *Land for Men* 1945; *Water for the Prairies* 1950.

Chetwynd, Lionel

Writer; b. London, U.K., 1940. Chetwynd, who immigrated to Canada in 1948, is most famous for his script (with Mordecai Richler*) for *The Apprenticeship of Duddy Kravitz,* which was nominated for an Academy Award for Best Adapted Screenplay in 1975. Chetwynd wrote two other Canadian features – *Goldenrod** and *Two Solitudes*, which he also directed – but since then has worked almost exclusively for American television. Recently he wrote a number of biblical reenactments for cable television and has become a conservative activist in the Los Angeles film community. **Films and television include:** *The Apprenticeship of Duddy Kravitz* 1974 (co-sc, AAN-SC); *Johnny We Hardly Knew Ya* 1975; *Goldenrod* 1976 (p/sc); *Quintet* 1977 (story); *It Happened One Christmas* 1977; *Two Solitudes* 1978 (d/sc); *A Whale for the Killing* 1980 (TV); *Escape from Iran: The Canadian Caper* 1980 (TV); *Miracle on Ice* 1981 (TV); *Sadat* 1982 (TV); *Children in the Crossfire* 1984 (TV); *The Hanoi Hilton* 1987; *The Heroes of Desert Storm* 1992 (TV); *Doomsday Gun* 1994 (TV); *Jacob: A TNT Bible Story* 1994 (TV); *Kissinger and Nixon* 1995 (TV); *Joseph* 1995 (TV); *Falling from the Sky: Flight 174* 1995 (TV); *Ruby Ridge: An American Tragedy* 1996 (TV); *The Man Who Captured Eichmann* 1996 (TV); *Moses* 1996 (TV); *P.T. Barnum* 1999 (TV); *Varian's War* 2001 (d/sc).

Chong, Rae Dawn

Actor; b. Vancouver, 1962; daughter of Tommy Chong. Rae Dawn Chong won a Genie for her performance in *Quest for Fire,** a part that required her to act in the nude and speak a special language devised by novelist Anthony Burgess. She has since appeared in *Choose Me, The*

Color Purple, and *Tales from the Darkside.* **Films and television include:** *Quest for Fire* 1982 (GA-A); *Cheech and Chong's The Corsican Brothers* 1984; *Beat Street* 1984; *Choose Me* 1984; *City Limits* 1984; *The Color Purple* 1985; *Commando* 1985; *American Flyers* 1985; *Soul Man* 1986; *The Squeeze* 1987; *The Principal* 1987; *Far Out Man* 1990; *Tales from the Darkside: The Movie* 1990; *Curiosity Kills* 1990; *The Borrower* 1991; *Chaindance* 1991; *Prison Stories: Women on the Inside* 1991 (TV); *Denial* 1991; *Amazon* 1992; *Dangerous Relations* 1993; *Boca* 1994; *Boulevard* 1994; *The Break* 1994; *Crying Freeman* 1995; *Hideaway* 1995; *Power of Attorney* 1995; *Starlight* 1996; *Highball* 1997; *Goodbye America* 1997; *The Alibi* 1997 (TV); *For Hope* 1997 (TV); *Small Time* 1998; *Valentine's Day* 1998 (TV); *Dangerous Attraction* 1999; *Mysterious Ways* 2000 – present (series); *The Visit* 2000.

Chong, Tommy

Actor, director, and writer; b. Edmonton, 1938; father of Rae Dawn Chong. Tommy Chong perfected his lunatic hippy persona with partner Cheech Marin, performing improvisational theatre in the late 1960s in Vancouver. Their successful real-life version of 'The Fabulous Furry Freak Brothers' led to several best-selling comedy albums. They moved smoothly into film, and *Cheech and Chong's Up in Smoke* became one of the box-office success stories of the late 1970s. Chong went on to write and direct four sequels before the duo broke up in 1985. **Films include:** *Cheech and Chong's Up in Smoke* 1978 (sc/a/mus); *Cheech and Chong's Next Movie* 1980 (d/sc/a); *Cheech and Chong's Nice Dreams* 1981 (d/sc/a/mus); *It Came from Hollywood* 1982 (a); *Things Are Tough All Over* 1982 (a); *Cheech and Chong's Still Smokin'* 1983 (d/sc/a); *Yellowbeard* 1983 (a); *Cheech and Chong's The Corsican Brothers* 1984 (d/sc/a); *After*

Hours 1985 (a); *Far Out Man* 1990 (d/a); *FernGully: The Last Rainforest* 1992 (voice); *McHale's Navy* 1997 (a).

Christie, Albert

Director, producer, and writer; b. London, Ont., 1886; d. 1951. Like his better-known countryman Mack Sennett,* Al Christie was in Hollywood almost from the beginning, first as a writer then as a producer and director of comic shorts. By 1916 he had set-up his own production company, a virtual laugh factory that turned out a great many inexpensive, simple-minded but popular two-reel comedies and a few full-length features. He ended his career in the late 1930s producing for Columbia and other studios.

Churchill, Berton

Actor; b. Toronto, 1876; d. 1940. Churchill, a Toronto-born character actor, began his career as a labour leader in New York City before taking bit parts in Broadway plays. He graduated into film in the early 1920s, appearing in over 150 films in less than ten years. He usually played the sourpuss businessman or the small-town mayor, and is probably best remembered for his role as Gatewood (the banker on the run with the stolen cash) in the John Ford classic, *Stagecoach*.
Films include: *Nothing but the Truth* 1929; *I Am a Fugitive from a Chain Gang* 1932; *Babbitt* 1934; *Steamboat 'round the Bend* 1935; *Dimples* 1936; *Stagecoach* 1939.

Churchill's Island

1941 22m *prod* NFB, *p/d/ed* Stuart Legg, *mus* Lucio Agostini, *narr* Lorne Greene. *Churchill's Island*, a classic example of the NFB wartime propaganda films made for the *Canada Carries On** series, is a compilation film describing the Battle of Britain and the steadfast resolve of the British people in the face of the German onslaught. It was the first NFB film

to win an Academy Award, giving credibility to the fledgling organization and the methods of its founder, John Grierson.* (V) **Awards include:** AA: Documentary.

Cinéma Vérité: Defining the Moment

2000 102m *prod* NFB, *exp* Sally Bochner, Doris Girard, *p* Eric Michel, Adam Symansky, *d* Peter Wintonick, *sc* Kirwan Cox, *ph* Françis Miquet, *ed* Marlo Miazga, Peter Wintonick. Once it was an avant-garde documentary movement, but today, the freewheeling, spontaneous methods of *cinéma-vérité* have been mainstreamed into everything from investment company commercials to *NYPD Blue*. Don't expect Peter Wintonick's feature documentary to run the movement through a fine-tooth analysis machine that gives the definitive word on the relationship of *cinéma-vérité* to reality. Instead, this picture is an affectionate homage to a 'small band of rebel filmmakers' – the aging men and the few women – who expanded moviemaking vocabulary with hand-held, wild-tracked films such as *Titticut Follies*, *Harlan County USA*, *Don't Look Back*, and *Lonely Boy*.* We meet them and enjoy many of the striking film moments they created. (V)

City of Gold

1957 21m40s *prod* NFB, *exp/co-ed* Tom Daly, *d/ph* Colin Low, Wolf Koenig, *sc/co-ed* Roman Kroitor, *mus* Eldon Rathburn, *narr* Pierre Berton. A classic example of the work done by the NFB's acclaimed Unit B. Wolf Koenig* and Colin Low* created an engaging look at Dawson City during the Klondike gold rush with the brilliant use of black-and-white still photographs and an insightful commentary by author Pierre Berton. One of the most popular and honoured films produced by the NFB under Tom Daly,* its innovative panning technique creates the impression that the still pictures are actually moving. (V) **Awards include:** CFA: Film of the Year; AAN: Short Documentary.

Clark, Bob
Director, producer, and writer; b. New Orleans, La., 1939. Clark turned down bids to play pro football to complete a drama major at the University of Miami. With the success of his low-budget horror classic *Children Shouldn't Play with Dead Things*, Clark moved to Montreal in 1973 and came to dominate Canadian commercial filmmaking for a decade. He followed *Children* with *Black Christmas*,* a box-office hit starring Margot Kidder,* and then, from 1978 to 1981, he directed *Murder by Decree*,* *Tribute*,* and *Porky's** – three of the most successful films produced in the tax-shelter era.* Sad to say, the sophomoric *Porky's* remains the Canadian box-office champ. Clark returned to the United States in 1984; his career, like his locale, has gone south since. **Films and television include:** *Dead of Night* 1972 (p/d); *Deathdream* 1972 (d); *Children Shouldn't Play with Dead Things* 1973 (d); *Black Christmas* 1974 (p/d); *Breaking Point* 1976 (p/d); *Murder by Decree* 1979 (p/d, GA-D); *Tribute* 1980 (d); *Porky's* 1981 (co-p/d/sc, GRA); *Porky's II: The Next Day* 1982 (p/d/sc); *A Christmas Story* 1983 (co-p/d/co-sc, GA-SC); *Rhinestone* 1984 (d); *Turk 182!* 1985 (d); *From the Hip* 1987 (p/d/sc); *Loose Cannons* 1989 (d/sc); *The American Clock* 1993 (d, TV); *Stolen Memories: Secrets from the Rose Garden* 1995 (d, TV); *Derby* 1995 (d, TV); *The Ransom of Little Chief* 1998 (d, TV); *Baby Geniuses* 1999 (d/co-sc); *I'll Remember April* 1999 (d).

Clark, Susan
Actor; b. Nora Golding, Sarnia, Ont., 1940. Clark was a leading lady of Holly-wood films of the late 1960s following a stage career that she began as a child. A graduate of London's Royal Academy of Dramatic Art, she made her screen debut in *Banning* with Robert Wagner in 1967 and went on to win an Emmy for her portrayal of the athlete 'Babe' Didrickson in the television movie *Babe*. She married her co-star of that production, Alex Karras; he later co-starred with her in the American television series, *Webster*. Returning to Canada, she appeared in Bob Clark's *Murder by Degree** and *Porky's.** More recently Clark has appeared in a number of TV movies, including *Butterbox Babies*, which she also produced. **Films and television include:** *Banning* 1967; *Madigan* 1968; *Coogan's Bluff* 1968; *Tell Them Willie Boy Is Here* 1969; *Skullduggery* 1969; *Wanda* 1970; *The Forbin Project* 1970; *Valdez Is Coming* 1971; *Skin Game* 1971; *Fat City* 1972; *Airport* 1974; *The Midnight Man* 1974; *The Apple Dumpling Gang* 1975; *Night Moves* 1975; *Babe* 1975 (TV); *Amelia Earhart* 1976 (TV, as Earhart); *Double Negative* 1978; *North Avenue Irregulars* 1978; *Murder by Decree* 1979; *Real Life* 1979; *City on Fire* 1979; *Porky's* 1981; *Nobody's Perfekt* 1981; *Maid in America* 1982 (p/a, TV); *Webster* 1983–7 (series); *Lana in Love* 1991; *Tonya and Nancy: The Inside Story* 1994 (TV); *Snowbound: The Jim and Jennifer Stolpa Story* 1994 (TV); *Butterbox Babies* 1995 (p/a, TV); *Emily of New Moon* 1997–9 (series).

Clarkson, Wayne
Administrator; b. Amherst, N.S., 1948. Clarkson, who began his career at the Canadian Film Institute, was chosen by Bill Marshall, the founder of Toronto's Festival of Festivals, to serve as director after the festival's second year of operation. During Clarkson's tenure, the festival grew to become one of the most important in North America. Clarkson also

helped launch Perspective Canada, a yearly showcase for Canadian film and filmmakers. In 1985, he was appointed the first chairman and CEO of the Ontario Film Development Corporation, the provincial film-funding agency that was responsible in large part for the explosion of filmmaking talent in Ontario during the late 1980s and early 1990s. Clarkson now heads Norman Jewison's* Canadian Film Centre, a virtual hothouse for the production of low-budget feature films.

Clearcut

1991 98m *prod* Cinexus, Famous Players Films, *exp* Stephen J. Roth, Stephen Alix, *p* Stephen J. Roth, Ian McDougall, *d* Richard Bugajski, *sc* Rob Forsyth, *novel* M.T. Kelly, *ph* François Protat, *ed* Michael Rea, *mus* Shane Harvey; *with* Ron Lea, Graham Greene, Michael Hogan, Rebecca Jenkins, Tom Jackson, Floyd Red Crow Westerman. Directed by Polish emigré Richard Bugajski, *Clearcut* attacks the smug liberal pieties of many movies about racial issues by daring to suggest that sometimes action, violent action, speaks far more eloquently than words. A Toronto lawyer (Lea) is hired to help a native community defend its land against a local logging company in Northern Ontario. He loses the case, and control of his life as well, when a mysterious Indian (Greene*) appears out of nowhere and proceeds to act out the lawyer's darkest anger against the mill owner (Hogan). This violent and disturbing film hammers home the point that liberal tolerance isn't necessarily the solution, but rather, as Bugajski sees it, part of the problem. (V)

Cleveland, George

Actor; b. Sydney, N.S., 1886; d. 1957. Cleveland, a veteran of the stage from 1903, played character parts in some 150 movies. He was typically cast as a crusty but kindly old man, and he played Gramps in the original *Lassie* television series. **Films and television include:** *Monte Carlo Nights* 1934; *Revolt of the Zombies* 1936; *Streets of New York* 1939; *The Haunted House* 1940; *All That Money Can Buy* 1941; *The Spoilers* 1942; *The Big Street* 1942; *Drums of Fu Manchu* 1943; *Dakota* 1945; *Courage of Lassie* 1946; *My Wild Irish Rose* 1947; *Carson City* 1952; *Walking My Baby Back Home* 1953; *Lassie* 1954–7 (series).

Cloutier, Suzanne

Actor; b. Ottawa, 1927. Cloutier is a Quebec actress who began her professional career as a New York model. She played in numerous international films during the 1940s and 1950s, notably as the doomed Desdemona in Orson Welles's version of Shakespeare's *Othello*. She later married (then divorced) Peter Ustinov. **Films include:** *Temptation* 1946; *Au royaume des cieux* 1949; *Juliette ou la clef des songes* 1950; *Derby Day* 1951; *Othello* 1952; *Doctor in the House* 1954; *Romanoff and Juliet* 1961; *Whiskers* 1997 (TV).

Coeur au poing, Le

1998 97m *prod* Cité-Amérique, *exp* Marie-France Lemay, *p* Lorraine Richard, *d* Charles Binamé, *sc* Charles Binamé, Monique Proulx, *ph* Pierre Gill, *ed* Claude Palardy, *mus* Richard Grégorie, Yves Desrosiers, Lhasa de Sela; *with* Pascale Montpetit, Anne-Marie Cadieux, Guy Nadon, Guylaine Tremblay. This is the second film in Charles Binamé's* improvised, *cinéma-vérité*-style trilogy about urban Montreal. (The other two films are *Eldorado*,* 1995, and *La Beauté de Pandore*, 2000.) Hand-held cameras whirl after Louise (Monpetit*), a lost soul who confronts despair by offering her obedient service to people she bumps into on the street – for exactly one hour. Louise's sometimes sexual life lessons build to a violent crisis. Then she tenderly reconciles with Paulette (Cadieux), the older sister she depends on. Recalling the wide-eyed and bewildered protagonists of *Juliet of the Spirits* and *Breaking the Waves*, Louise tries to connect with humanity by casting her fate to the wind. Montpetit's volatile performance echoes Binamé's jump-cutting, sky-tripping direction. (V) **Awards include:** PJ: Actress (Montpetit); Supporting Actress (Cadieux).

Cold Comfort
1989 90m *prod* Norstar Entertainment, *exp* Peter Simpson, Dan Johnson, *p* Ilana Frank, Ray Sager, *d/ph* Vic Sarin, *sc* Richard Beattie, L. Elliott Simms, *play* Jim Garrard, *ed* Nick Totundo, *mus* Jeff Danna, Mychael Danna; *with* Maury Chaykin, Paul Gross, Margaret Langrick. Cinematographer Vic Sarin* made his directorial debut with this adaptation of a play by Jim Garrard. Like *The Collector* and *Misery*, *Cold Comfort* puts a hapless kidnapping victim in the hands of maniacal people with complicated needs. Floyd (Chaykin*) brings home a travelling salesman (Gross*) for the pleasure of his captivating teenage daughter (Langrick). After several episodes of sadistic powerplay, the nymphet performs a striptease for both the salesman and her daddy. Unabashedly relishing the comic perversity of its characters, *Cold Comfort* imagines rural Canada neither as a paragon of austere stoicism, nor as a winter wonderland – it's a hotbed of thwarted lust. (V)

Colicos, John
Actor; b. Toronto, 1928; d. 2000. Colicos was a distinguished stage actor whose performance as Winston Churchill in *The Soldiers*, which played on Broadway

and London's West End, earned outstanding notices. He had guest roles in hundreds of television shows from the mid-1950s right up through the 1990s, including the legendary *Gunsmoke*, *Mission Impossible*, *Star Trek*, and *Star Trek: Deep Space Nine*, and he also played a recurring character on the short-lived series *Battlestar Galactica*. Colicos occasionally appeared in films, most notably a co-starring role in *Anne of the Thousand Days*, and as Jessica Lang's unloved (and ultimately murdered) husband in the 1981 remake of *The Postman Always Rings Twice* with Jack Nicholson. **Films and television include:** *Forbidden Journey* 1950; *Passport to Treason* 1955; *War Drums* 1957; *Wuthering Heights* 1958 (TV); *The Count of Monte Cristo* 1958 (TV); *Oliver Twist* 1959 (TV); *Treasure Island* 1960 (TV); *Dulcima* 1968 (TV); *Anne of the Thousand Days* 1969 (as Cromwell); *Raid on Rommel* 1971; *Doctors' Wives* 1971; *The Wrath of God* 1972; *Scorpio* 1973; *The National Dream* 1974 (TV, as Van Horne); *Breaking Point* 1976; *King Solomon's Treasure* 1977; *Battlestar Galactica* 1978–9 (series); *The Changeling* 1980; *Phobia* 1980; *The Postman Always Rings Twice* 1981; *Nowhere to Hide* 1987; *I'll Take Manhattan* 1987 (TV); *Shadow Dancing* 1988; *Love and Hate: The Story of Colin and Joann Thatcher* 1989 (TV); *X-Men* 1992 (voice, series); *The Last Don* 1997 (TV).

Comic Book Confidential
1988 85m *prod* Sphinx Productions, *exp* Don Haig, *p* Ron Mann, Martin Harbury, *d* Ron Mann, *sc* Ron Mann, *bp* Nichol, *ph* Robert Fresco, Joan Churchill, *ed* Robert Kennedy, Ron Mann, *mus* Shadowy Men on a Shadowy Planet, Dr. John, and others; *with* William M. Gaines, Jack Kirby, Stan Lee, Frank Miller, Will Eisner, Robert Crumb, Lynda Barry, Gilbert Shelton, and others. *Comic Book Confi-*

dential profiles twenty-two of the most significant artists and writers working in comic books, graphic novels, and strip-art in North America today. From Jack Kirby's *Captain America* and the superhero fervour of the war years, through Will Eisner's cinematic *The Spirit*, to the anti-comic book crusades of the 1950s and the irreverent *Mad* magazine, the film traces the origins and progress of the popular comic-book medium. Television aside, perhaps no other twentieth-century medium as been as widely maligned. Director Ron Mann* (in arguably his best film to date) makes a strong case for cultural redemption. (V, CD–ROM) **Awards include:** GA: Feature Documentary.

Coming Home
1973 84m *prod* NFB, *p* Tom Daly, Colin Low, *d* Bill Reid, *ph* Barry Perles, *ed* David Wilson. *Coming Home* is a completely unrehearsed record on film, edited to viewing length, of a few days' visit to the home of Bill Reid's parents. It represents a genuine but futile attempt to bridge the barrier (or 'generation gap' as it was called then) between Reid, his brother, and his mother and father. (V) **Awards include:** CFA: Theatrical Documentary.

Company of Strangers, The
1990 101m *prod* NFB, *exp* Colin Neale, Rina Fraticelli, Peter Katadotis, *p/ed* David Wilson, *d* Cynthia Scott, *sc* Gloria Demers, *ph* David de Volpi, *mus* Marie Bernard; *with* Alice Diabo, Constance Garneau, Winifred Holden, Cissy Meddings, Mary Meigs, Catherine Roche, Michelle Sweeney, Beth Webber. Eight women with an average age of seventy-three, find themselves stranded in the Quebec countryside when their tour bus breaks down. Using non-professional actors, director Cynthia Scott* elicits some lively and truly moving performances as the script draws on the women's real-life experiences while they wait in an abandoned farmhouse for help to come. *Company of Strangers* is a film about people who are old, rather than a traditional film about old people. There are no pat conclusions or romantic, fatal diseases. Instead there are just eight women who have seen the changes the century has brought, and the film allows the viewer to discover the value of each one. The result is a surprising and insightful drama. (V) **Awards include:** GA: Editing.

Condie, Richard
Animator; b. Vancouver, 1942. Although Richard Condie was born in Vancouver and worked at the NFB headquarters in Montreal for much of the 1990s, his roots are in Winnipeg's zany filmmaking community. During the 1970s and 1980s, Condie and fellow NFB animators Cordell Barker and Brad Caslor created cheeky, off-the-wall work, fully in keeping with the independent films made at the same time by Winnipeg filmmakers Guy Maddin* and John Paizs. The taciturn, painfully shy Condie let his imagination soar in his two masterpieces: *Getting Started*, a hymn to procrastination, and *The Big Snit*,* a wry fable about marital squabbling, Scrabble, and nuclear war. Both *The Big Snit* and his more recent computer-generated short, *La Salla*, received Academy Award nominations. **Films include:** *Oh Sure* 1977; *John Law and the Mississippi Bubble* 1978; *Getting Started* 1979; *The Big Snit* 1985 (AAN-AS); *The Cat Came Back* 1988 (p); *The Apprentice* 1991; *La Salla* 1997 (AAN-AS).

Confessionnal, Le
1995 100m *prod* Cinémaginaire, Enigma Film (U.K.), Cinéa (France), *p* Denise

Robert, David Puttnam, Philippe Carcassonne, Steve Norris, *d/sc* Robert Lepage, *ph* Alain Dostie, *ed* Emmanuelle Castro, *mus* Sacha Puttnam; *with* Lothaire Bluteau, Patrick Goyette, Jean-Louis Millette, Kristin Scott Thomas, Ron Burrage, Richard Frechette. Robert LePage's* powerful debut as a film director tells the story of a young man (Bluteau*), who returns from a three-year trip to China to attend his father's funeral. He searches to find a missing half-brother (Goyette) and uncovers some unpleasant family secrets. Flashbacks to the 1950s are framed around the shooting of Alfred Hitchcock's *I Confess* in Quebec City. *Le Confessionnal* engages viewers from start to finish, and Lepage's transitions from present to past and back are astonishing. The juxtapositions with the Hitchcock film shoot are cleverly done, and the film offers a startling reminder of how much has changed in Quebec since 1952. (V) **Awards include:** GA: Picture, Director, Art Direction, Claude Jutra Award.

Conquest

1999 92m *prod* Shaftesbury Films, Heartland Motion Pictures, Greenpoint Films (U.K.) *p* Christina Jennings, Stephen Onda, *d* Piers Haggarad, *sc* Rob Forsyth, *ph* Gerald Packer, *ed* Ralph Brunjes, *mus* Ron Sures; *with* Lothaire Bluteau, Tara FitzGerald, Monique Mercure, David Fox, Eugene Lipinski. This off-beat romantic comedy is set in the fading prairie town of Conquest, Saskatchewan. Daisy (FitzGerald), a pretty lady from the north of England, arrives one sunny day in a bright red Alfa Romeo that promptly breaks down, forcing her to stay for repairs. Pincer (Bluteau*), an idealistic banker who has moved back to the town of his birth to run the bank that the farmers depend upon, sets out to seduce Daisy with the town as he

imagines it. Her very presence begins to perk things up and, as if by magic, colours begin to return. This film is a rarity in Canadian cinema: a love story told straight up with a charming touch of magic realism. (V) **Awards include:** GA: Supporting Actress (Mercure).

Corral

1954 11m27s *prod* NFB, *p* Tom Daly, *d/sc* Colin Low, *ph* Wolf Koenig, *mus* Eldon Rathburn, Stan Wilson, Al Harris. This beautiful, deceptively simple documentary about a cowboy who ropes and saddles a horse, effectively breaking it in, was shot in southwestern Alberta. Although the film is less than twelve minutes long, it reaches poetic heights through its elegant cinematography, artful editing, and two-guitar score (played by Wilson and Harris). It is one of the NFB's and Colin Low's* crowning achievements. (V)

Cosmos

1997 100m *prod* Max Films, *exp/p* Roger Frappier, *d/sc* André Turpin, Arto Paragamian, Denis Villeneuve, Marie-Julie Dallaire, Jennifer Alleyn, Manon Briand, *ph* André Turpin, *ed* Richard Comeau, *mus* Michel A. Smith; *with* Igor Ovadis, David La Haye, Audrey Benoît, Marie-Hélène Montpetit, Pascale Contamine, Sébastien Joannette. *Cosmos* was the brainchild of veteran producer Roger Frappier.* For this compilation film, he enlisted the talents of six rising young Quebec filmmakers. Each was asked to write and direct a segment that somehow featured Cosmos, a scruffy-looking, good-natured cabbie with a clear-eyed philosophical bent. Frappier merged their diverse views into a single vision of modern urban life, punctuated by just the right amount of existentialism and absurdity. The film is ripe with simple joys and unknown terrors, genuine moments of connection and circumstances marked by sheer dumb luck. (V)

Coté, Guy L.

Archivist, producer, director, editor, and writer; b. Ottawa, 1925. As a Rhodes Scholar from Quebec in 1947, Coté became involved with the amateur film society at Oxford University. At the NFB, which he joined after graduation, he pursued a great many interests, one of which was building the largest film reference library in Canada. He was a founding member and the first president of the Canadian Federation of Film Societies, and he subsequently launched the Cinématheque québécoise, the National Film Archives, and the Montreal World Film Festival. As an editor, he worked on Roman Kroitor's and Wolf Koenig's *Lonely Boy*,* and as a producer he worked with Pierre Perrault* and Michel Brault* on a number of important films including *Le Règne du jour*,* *Un Pays sans bon sens!*,* and *L'Acadie, L'Acadie?!?*.* **Films include:** *Railroaders* 1958 (d/sc/ed); *Roughnecks: The Story of Oil Drillers* 1960 (d/sc/ed); *Lonely Boy* 1962 (ed with John Spotton); *Le Règne du jour* 1967 (co-p); *De mère en fille* 1968 (p); *Beluga Days* 1968 (co-p); *Les Voitures d'eau* 1969 (co-p); *Un Pays sans bon sens!* 1970 (co-p); *Où êtes vous donc?* 1979 (p); *L'Acadie, l'Acadie?!?* 1971 (co-p); *Tranquillement, pas vite* 1972 (d/ed); *Les Deux Côtes de la médaille* 1974 (d/ed); *Rose et Monsieur Charbonneau* 1976 (d/co-sc/ed); *Monsieur Journault* 1976 (d/co-sc/ed); *On est au coton* 1976 (co-p).

Crash

1996 98m *prod* Alliance Communications, *exp* Robert Lantos, Jeremy Thomas, *p/d/sc* David Cronenberg, *book* J.G. Ballard, *ph* Peter Suschitzky, *ed* Ronald Sanders, *mus* Howard Shore; *with* James Spader, Holly Hunter, Rosanna Arquette, Elias Koteas, Deborah Unger. Advertising executive James Ballard (Spader) and his wife Catherine (Unger) lead complex, if hollow, sexual lives. Following a near fatal car crash, they are drawn into the bizarre world of scientist and photographer Vaughan (Koteas*), a specialist in restaging famous car crashes, who teaches them new and disturbing ways to have sex. An intentionally controversial film, *Crash* is neither pornographic nor dull, as its many critics have claimed, but rather a brilliant, detached look at sexual obsession. The film maintains, with rigid assurance, its cool-as-highly-polished-steel concept that some people can be sexually aroused by car wrecks. Intensely erotic and surprisingly witty, *Crash* is a cerebral ride, an end-of-the-millennium meditation on sex, death, and alienation. (V) **Awards include:** GA: Director, Adapted Screenplay, Cinematography, Editing, Sound Editing; Golden Reel Award; Cannes: Special Jury Prize.

Crawley, Budge and Judith

Budge: Producer and director; b. Frank Ratford Crawley, Ottawa, 1911; d. 1987. **Judith:** Director, editor, and writer; b. Judith Sparks, Ottawa, 1914; d. 1986. The indefatigable Budge Crawley was Canada's original movie mogul. Under his stewardship, Crawley Films produced more than 4,000 shorts and industrials, Canada's first animated television series (*The Tales of the Wizard of Oz*), and several features, including *The Luck of Ginger Coffey*,* *The Rowdyman*,* and *Janis*.* His wife, Judith, started out as a script supervisor. As the company grew, she became director, editor, cinematographer, and even lab technician on many films. She wrote the narration for the Academy Award–winning documentary, *The Man Who Skied down Everest*.* **Budge Crawley's films and television include:**

Ile d'Orleans 1938 (p/d); *Canadian Power* 1940 (p/d); *Canadian Landscape* 1941 (d/ph); *The Loon's Necklace* 1948 (p/d, CFA-FY); *Newfoundland Scene* 1952 (p/d, CFA-FY, CFA-NTS); *The RCMP* 1959–60 (p, series); *The Tales of the Wizard of Oz* 1962 (p, series); *Amanita Pestilens* 1962 (exp); *The Luck of Ginger Coffey* 1964 (exp, CFA-FF); *The Rowdyman* 1972 (exp); *Janis* 1974 (exp); *The Man Who Skied down Everest* 1975 (exp, AA-FD); *Heartland Reggae* 1982 (exp). **Judith Crawley's films include:** *Ile d'Orléans* 1938 (sc/ed); *Canadian Power* 1940 (sc/ed); *Canadian Landscape* 1941 (ed); *West Wind: The Story of Tom Thomson* 1942 (ph/ed); *Alexis Tremblay: Habitant* 1943 (ph); *The Loon's Necklace* 1948 (sc/ed); *Legend of the Raven* 1957 (p/sc, CFA-AE); *The Man Who Skied down Everest* 1975 (sc).

Cree Hunters of Mistassini

1974 58m *prod* NFB, *exp* Len Chatwin, *p* Colin Low, *d* Boyce Richardson, Tony Ianzelo, *sc/narr* Boyce Richardson, *ph* Tony Ianzelo, *ed* Ginny Stikeman. This beautifully crafted and evocative portrait of the lifestyle and culture of the Cree Indians of Northern Quebec is one of the best films to come out of the NFB's Challenge for Change* program. The filmmakers meet with three Cree hunting families as they build their traditional winter camps and partake in hunting rituals that predate the arrival of Europeans in North America. Cree beliefs and ecological principals, which are under threat of being destroyed by the construction of huge hydro dams on the James Bay watershed, are sensitively examined. (V) **Awards include:** CFA: Documentary.

Cronenberg, David

Director, producer, and writer; b. Toronto, 1943. If David Cronenberg did not exist, would we invent him? Could we invent him? Perhaps no Canadian filmmaker has had such a singular career path, navigating his way from the university independent filmmaking scene of the 1960s to critically reviled commercial excrescences of the tax-shelter era,* and more recently, to the well-heeled approval of international art-house and festival circuits. Lauded as a late-twentieth-century taboo-bashing genius by some, and loathed as a puritanical body-fearing reactionary by others, Cronenberg's emergence is without parallel in this country. Moreover, his decidedly idiosyncratic oeuvre also represents a challenge to the critical paradigms and terms used to define Canadian film. Faced with phallic underarm growths spreading fatal diseases, exploding heads, videos slurped into human abdomens, men transformed into insects, and talking typewriters, the critical problem persists: just how do we talk about the work of David Cronenberg?

Cronenberg attended the University of Toronto, earning a BA in literature. An enthusiastic reader of science fiction, the budding filmmaker eschewed the documentary-realist tradition of his contemporaries, and introduced unprecedented levels of fantasy into Canadian film. After his late 1960s experimental, austere sci-fi shorts (*Stereo* and *Crimes of the Future*), Cronenberg plunged deep into a bloody biological Babylon in a series of 1970s horror films. Fusing the genre's ample and flexible narrative conventions with his own ideas about desire, repression, the body, and technology, Cronenberg developed a reputation, with *Shivers*,* *Rabid*,* and *The Brood*, as perhaps the most original, unflinching, no-holds-barred practitioner of the modern horror film. While he confounded 'tasteful' critical opinion in Canada, he also found himself to be a bankable genre auteur who could muster impressive budgets and still maintain a degree of artistic control.

Since 1980, Cronenberg's distinctive and influential vision (can we imagine Atom Egoyan* without David Cronenberg?) has explored, with increasing precision and restraint, several recurring themes: the paranormal (*Scanners** and *The Dead Zone*); the pervasiveness of visual media systems (*Videodrome**); the unsettling intersections of biology, technology, and identity (*The Fly* and *Dead Ringers**); and most recently and most Canadian of all, the tortured psychologies of delusion (*Dead Ringers*, *Naked Lunch*,* and *M. Butterfly*). In addition to his remarkable cinematic career, Cronenberg has directed for television, made several commercial spots for Ontario Hydro and Nike, and acted both in his own films and those of others.

These days, Cronenberg no longer draws outrage from the middle-brow arbiters of 'good taste.' His films are equally disturbing but seldom as viscerally off-putting as his earlier work – or perhaps we've all been jaded by the mediated, image-saturated culture his work presaged. At its increasingly chilling best, however, Cronenberg's more recent work still tests the limits of critical and audience response in contemporary Canadian film culture. His 1996 film, *Crash*,* based on a short story by J.G. Ballard, received a Special Jury Prize in official competition at Cannes in 1996. **Films include:** *Transfer* 1966 (p/d/sc/ph/ed); *From the Drain* 1967 (p/d/sc/ph/ed); *Stereo* 1969 (p/d/sc/ph/ed); *Crimes of the Future* 1970 (p/d/sc/ph/ed); *Shivers* 1975 (d/sc); *Rabid* 1977 (d/sc); *Fast Company* 1979 (d/co-sc); *The Brood* 1979 (d/sc); *Scanners* 1981 (d/sc); *Videodrome* 1983 (d/sc, GA-D); *The Dead Zone* 1983 (d); *Into the Night* 1985 (a); *The Fly* 1986 (d/co-sc/a); *Dead Ringers* 1988 (p/d/co-sc, GA-P, GA-D, GA-

ASC); *Nightbreed* 1990 (a); *Naked Lunch* 1992 (p/d/sc, GA-P, GA-D, GA-ASC); *Blue* 1992 (a); *M. Butterfly* 1993 (d); *To Die For* 1995 (a); *Blood and Donuts* 1995 (a); *Crash* 1996 (p/d/sc, GA-D, GA-ASC, GRA); *Last Night* 1998 (a); *eXistenZ* 1999 (co-p/d/sc); *Camera* from *Preludes* 2000 (d/sc).

Cronyn, Hume

Actor; b. Hume Blake Jr, London, Ont., 1911. Cronyn came from a family with strong Canadian heritage links to early settlers, politicians, and the founder of Labatt Breweries, but he turned away from his McGill University law studies to pursue a stage career. He hit the boards in New York in 1932 and was tempted by Alfred Hitchcock in 1943 to ply his talents in cinema with *Shadow of a Doubt*. Cronyn also adapted the screenplays for Hitchcock's *Rope* and *Under Capricorn*. Cronyn worked mainly on the stage, often with his celebrated wife, Jessica Tandy, but he made regular forays onto the screen to play flamboyant and idiosyncratic character roles: the sadistic guard who beats a prisoner to the music of a Wagnerian opera in *Brute Force*; the abrasive attorney in the original *The Postman Always Rings Twice*; and his Academy Award–nominated performance in Fred Zinnemann's *The Seventh Cross* opposite Spencer Tracy. Cronyn and Tandy (who died in 1994) were a remarkable couple whose creative and personal partnership was eulogized in Deepa Mehta's *Camilla*. **Films and television include:** *The Cross of Lorraine* 1943; *The Phantom of the Opera* 1943; *Shadow of a Doubt* 1943; *Lifeboat* 1944; *Blonde Fever* 1944; *Main Street after Dark* 1944; *The Seventh Cross* 1944 (AAN-SA); *The Sailor Takes a Wife* 1945; *The Beginning of the End* 1946; *The Green Years* 1946; *A Letter for Eve* 1946; *The Postman Always Rings Twice* 1946; *Ziegfeld Follies*

1946; *Brute Force* 1947; *Rope* 1948 (adaptation); *The Bride Goes Wild* 1948 *Under Capricorn* 1949 (adaptation); *Top o' the Morning* 1949; *People Will Talk* 1951; *Crowded Paradise* 1955; *Sunrise at Campobello* 1960; *Cleopatra* 1963; *Hamlet* 1964; *The Arrangement* 1969; *Gaily, Gaily* 1969; *There Was a Crooked Man* 1970; *Conrack* 1973; *The Parallax View* 1974; *Honky Tonk Freeway* 1981; *Rollover* 1981; *The World According to Garp* 1982; *Impulse* 1984; *Brewster's Millions* 1985; *Cocoon* 1985; *Batteries Not Included* 1987; *Cocoon: The Return* 1988; *Christmas on Division Street* 1991; *Broadway Bound* 1992; *The Pelican Brief* 1993; *Camilla* 1994; *Marvin's Room* 1996; *12 Angry Men* 1998 (TV); *Seasons of Love* 1999 (TV); *Sea People* 1999 (TV).

Cry of the Wild

1973 88m *prod* NFB, *p* William Brind, *d/sc/ed/narr* Bill Mason, *ph* Bill Mason, James Blake, *mus* Larry Crosley; *with* Bill Mason. This feature-length documentary, one of the most successful and popular films ever produced by the NFB, made over one million dollars in the first week of its release in the United States. Bill Mason* spent two years shooting *Death of a Legend*, a film about the many unfounded myths surrounding the northern timber wolf that have caused it to be hunted to the point of extinction. *Cry of the Wild*, a vivid account of that shoot, portrays not only an intimate (and loving) account of the life of wolves, but also the evolving relationship and understanding that Mason developed with them. (V)

Cube

1998 91m *prod* Cube Libre, Feature Film Project (Canadian Film Centre), *exp* Colin Brunton, *p* Mehra Meh, Betty Orr, *d* Vincenzo Natali, *sc* Andre Bijelic, Vincenzo Natali, Graeme Manson,

ph Derek Rogers, *ed* Jon Sanders, *mus* Mark Korven; *with* Maurice Dean Wint, Nicky Guadagni, David Hewlett, Nicole deBoer, Andrew Miller, Julian Richings. Brilliant set design and smart plotting are compromised by some atrocious acting in this enigmatic sci-fi thriller about six people trapped inside a deadly Rubik's cube. Each 'room' looks like the others but some contain deadly traps, as one unfortunate inmate (Richings) discovers in the opening sequence as he is sliced-and-diced in a spectacular manner. Unfortunately, this is the high point; this clever film disintegrates into repetitious squabbling as the survivors try to find their way out of the cube. The existential musing caused a sensation in Japan and France, where it broke all box-office records for a Canadian feature. (V)

Curzi, Pierre

Actor; b. Montreal, 1946. The National Theatre School-trained Curzi ranks among Quebec's most talented actors. His nuanced performance on screen as Napoléon Plouffe in Gilles Carle's *Les Plouffe** made him a instant star and propelled him into central roles in a series of films, including in *Les Fleurs sauvages* and *Les Yeux rouges ou les vérités accidentelles*. He resurrected Napoléon in *Le Crime d'Ovide Plouffe*, and after playing several more good-guy roles, went on to shine in the complexity of darker portrayals such as Pierre in *Le Déclin de l'empire américain** and Gildor in *Pouvoir intime,** a film that he co-wrote with Yves Simoneau.* **Films and television include:** *On est loin du soleil* 1971; *Bulldozer* 1974; *Tu brûles ... tu brûles* 1973; *L'Amour blessé* 1975; *Parlez-nous d'amour* 1976; *Avoir 16 ans* 1980; *Riel* 1979 (TV); *La Cuisine rouge* 1980; *Suzanne* 1980; *Fantastica* 1980; *Les Plouffe* 1981; *Les Fleurs sauvages* 1982; *Les Yeux rouges ou* *les vérités accidentelles* 1982; *Maria Chapdelaine* 1983; *Le Crime d'Ovide Plouffe* 1984; *Le Jour 'S' ...* 1983; *Caffè Italia Montréal* 1985; *Pourvoir intime* 1986 (co-sc/a); *Le Déclin de l'empire américain* 1986; *Dans le ventre du dragon* 1989; *Les Filles de Caleb* 1990–1 (series); *C'était le 12 du 12 et Chili avait les blues* 1992; *Le Cri de la nuit* 1996; *Matroni et moi* 1999.

Czerny, Henry

Actor; b. Toronto, 1959. Henry Czerny caught the world's attention with his mesmerizing performance as a sexual predator in the NFB co-production of John N. Smith's *The Boys of St Vincent*,* the realistic story of abuse at a boy's orphanage. His chilling portrayal of the pedophiliac brother won him accolades worldwide, and landed him coveted roles as the White House weasel opposite Harrison Ford in *Clear and Present Danger*, and as Tom Cruise's boss in *Mission Impossible*. **Films and television include:** *The Taming of the Shrew* 1988 (TV); *The Boys of St Vincent* 1993 (TV); *Cold Sweat* 1993; *Buried on Sunday* 1993; *I Love a Man in Uniform* 1993; *Anchor Zone* 1994; *Clear and Present Danger* 1994; *Jenipapo* 1995; *The Michelle Apartments* 1995; *When Night Is Falling* 1995; *Choices of the Heart: The Margaret Sanger Story* 1995 (TV); *Mission Impossible* 1996; *Promise the Moon* 1997 (TV); *The Ice Storm* 1997; *Kayla* 1997; *Glory and Honor* 1998 (TV); *My Father's Shadow: The Sam Sheppard Story* 1998 (TV); *P.T. Barnum* 1999 (TV); *External Affairs* 1999 (TV).

D

Daly, Tom

Producer and editor; b. Toronto, 1918. Daly, a major figure in the illustrious history of the NFB, joined the Board in 1940 as a production assistant and rose to become executive producer of Unit B in 1951. This catchall unit was home to filmmakers such as Wolf Koenig,* Colin Low,* Roman Kroitor,* Gerald Potterton,* Don Owen,* and Arthur Lipsett,* whose award-winning films of the 1950s and 1960s brought international recognition for their innovative approaches to documentary and animation. Daly, a sensitive and energetic producer, was also widely acknowledged as one of the NFB's best editors and an inspiration to his colleagues. He retired in 1984 with a legacy of more than 300 films produced during forty years of dedicated service. **Films and television include:** *Our Northern Neighbour* 1943 (d/ed); *Who Will Teach Your Child?* 1948 (CFA-TS); *Family Circles* 1949 (CFA-NTS); *Feelings of Depression* 1950 (CFA-NTS); *Family Tree* 1950 (CFA-SPA); *Royal Journey* 1951 (CFA-FF); *Age of the Beaver* 1952 (CFA-SPA); *The Romance of Transportation in Canada* 1953 (p/ed, AAN-AS); *Paul Tomkowicz: Street-Railway Switchman* 1954 (p/ed with Roman Kroitor); *Corral* 1954 (p/ed); *Riches of the Earth* 1954 (CFA-NTS); *The Jolifou Inn* 1955; *Gold* 1955 (CFA-TS); *It's a Crime* 1957; *City of Gold* 1957 (p/ed, AAN-SD); *A Chairy Tale* 1957 (AAN-AS); *Blood and Fire* 1958 (TV); *The Living Stone* 1958 (AAN-SD); *The Days before Christmas* 1958 (TV); *The Back-Breaking Leaf* 1959 (TV); *Glenn Gould – Off the Record* 1959 (TV); *Glenn Gould – On the Record* 1959 (TV); *Roughnecks: The Story of Oil Drillers* 1960; *Universe* 1960 (p/ed, CFA-FY, CFA-TS, AAN-AS); *Very Nice, Very Nice* 1961 (p with Colin Low, AAN-AS); *Lonely Boy* 1962 (CFA-FY); *My Financial Career* 1962 (p with Low, AAN-AS); *Christmas Cracker* 1963 (AAN-AS); *Free Fall* 1964 (p with Low); *The Hutterites* 1964 (p with Kroitor); *I Know an Old Lady Who Swallowed a Fly* 1964; *The Great Toy Robbery* 1964; *Toronto Jazz* 1964; *Nobody Waved Good-Bye* 1964; *Es-*

kimo Artist: Kenojuak 1964 (AAN-SD); Stravinsky 1965; Helicopter Canada 1966 (AAN-SD); Labyrinth 1967 (ed); Christopher's Movie Matinee 1969; Un Pays sans bon sens! 1970; Prologue 1970; Legend 1970 (CFA-AE); N-Zone 1970; Sad Song of Yellow Skin 1970; The Sea 1971 (CFA-TS); This Is a Photograph 1971 (CFA-TS); Cowboy and Indian 1972; Coming Home 1973 (CFA-TD); Action: The October Crisis of 1970 1973 (co-p); Reaction: A Portrait of a Society in Crisis 1973 (co-p); Waiting for Fidel 1974; One Man 1977; Co Hoedeman, Animator 1980; North China Commune 1980; Musical Magic: Gilbert and Sullivan in Stratford 1984 (TV).

Dance Me Outside

1995 87m prod Yorktown Productions, Shadow Shows, exp Norman Jewison, Sarah Hayward, p Brian Dennis, Bruce McDonald, d Bruce McDonald, sc Bruce McDonald, Don McKellar, John Frizzell, book W.P. Kinsella, ph Miroslav Baszak, ed Michael Pacek, mus Mychael Danna; with Ryan Black Adam Beach, Jennifer Podemski, Lisa Lacroix, Michael Greyeyes, Kevin Hicks, Hugh Dillon. This adaptation of a story by W.P. Kinsella focuses on young Indians living on a Northern Ontario reserve. Silas Crow (Black) and his buddy Frank Fencepost (Beach) are enjoying a late summer weekend when Crow's sister (Lacroix) arrives home with her white yuppie lawyer husband (Hicks). A Saturday night bar brawl leads to a young woman's death at the hands of a white troublemaker (Dillon), who is only given a light sentence and is soon out of jail. The young men vow revenge. Bruce McDonald's* film is fast-paced and entertaining, but it is not an auteur-driven work. The conventional (and disappointing) Hollywood storytelling techniques of executive producer Norman Jewison* are clearly evident. The film

led to a short-lived CBC-TV series, The Rez. (V) **Awards include:** GA: Editing, Sound Editing.

Dancing in the Dark

1986 98m prod Dancing in the Dark Productions, exp Don Haig, p Anthony Kramreither, d/sc Leon Marr, ph Vic Sarin, ed Tom Berner; with Martha Henry, Richard Monette, Rosemary Dunsmore, Neil Munro. This grim tale of domestic failure features a powerful performance by Martha Henry* as Edna Cormice, the devoted housewife who has spent twenty years establishing a safe and comfortable life with her husband, Harry (Monette). Despite her obsessive dedication to their home, their tranquil existence is undone with a single phone call. Following a harrowing act of revenge, Edna tirelessly examines her life from a hospital room, searching endlessly for the fatal flaw that she believes must have led to Harry's betrayal. **Awards include:** GA: Adapted Screenplay, Actress (Henry), Art Direction.

Dansereau, Fernand

Producer, director, and writer; b. Montreal, 1928; brother of Jean Dansereau. Fernand Dansereau, originally a labour reporter for Le Devoir, joined the NFB in 1955. He contributed to the founding of the French unit, and produced many films for Temps Présent, a television series that became the principal showcase for NFB filmmakers from Quebec during the early 1960s. He also produced Perrault's Pour la suite du monde,* undoubtedly the most influential film of the period. Fernand Dansereau left the NFB in 1968 to establish his own film and television production company, In-Media. In 1990 he adapted Les Filles de Caleb, the popular novel by Arlette Cousture, for the television series directed by Jean Beaudin.* **Films include:** Alfred ... 1956 (sc);

La Communauté juive de Montréal 1957
(d/sc); *Les Suspects* 1957 (sc); *La Maître
de Pérou* 1958 (d/sc, three films); *Les
Mains nettes* 1958 (sc); *Pays neuf* 1958 (d/
ed); *John Lyman, peintre* 1959 (d/sc/ed);
La Canne à pêche 1959 (d/ed, two films);
Pierre Leaulieu 1960 (d/sc); *Les Adminis-
trateurs* 1960 (co-d); *Golden Gloves* 1961
(co-p); *Bûcherons de la Manouane* 1962
(co-p); *Québec-U.S.A. ou l'invasion pacifique* 1962 (p); *Jour après jour* 1962 (co-p,
CFA-AE); *Congrès* 1962 (co-d); *Pour la
suite de monde* 1963 (p, CFA-FY); *À Saint-
Henri le cinq septembre* 1964 (p); *Champlain*
1964 (co-p); *Le Festin des morts* 1965 (d/
ed); *Ça n'est pas le temps des romans* 1966
(d/sc, CFA-S); *Confrontation* 1967 (d);
St-Jérôme 1967 (d); *Tout les temps, tout les
temps, tout les temps ...?* 1970 (d); *Québec
ski* 1970 (d/ed); *Faut aller parmi l'monde
pour le savoir* 1971 (d); *Vivre entre les mots*
1972 (d); *Contrat d'amour* 1973 (d/ed);
Simple Histoire d'amour 1976 (d); *Thetford
au milieu de notre vie* 1980 (d/co-sc/co-
ed); *Doux aveux* 1982 (d/co-sc); *L'Autre
Côte de la lune* 1994 (d).

Dansereau, Jean

Producer; b. Montreal, 1930; brother of
Fernand Dansereau. Jean Dansereau
worked at the NFB as a director and editor from 1957 until 1964 when he left to
join the private sector. As a producer, in
addition to his work for the Board, he
produced films for André Forcier* (*Bar
salon,* Kalamazoo*), Francis Mankiewicz*
(*Les Beaux Souvenirs*), Denys Arcand* (*Le
Confort et l'indifférence*), and Claude Jutra*
(*La Dame en couleurs*). **Films include:** *Le
Jeu de l'hiver* 1962 (co-d/co-ph/ed);
Congrès 1962 (co-d); *Gymastique* 1964 (d);
Confrontation 1967 (ed); *Le Viol d'une
jeune fille douce* 1968 (a); *St-Jerome* 1968
(ed); *Comment vit le Québécois* 1968 (co-
d); *À soir on fait peur au monde* 1969 (d);
Le Martien de Noël 1971 (p); *Le Grand

Sabordage 1973 (a); *Montreal Blues* 1974
(p); *Bar salon* 1975 (exp); *M'en revenant
par les épinettes* 1977 (p/co-sc/ed); *Un
Mois à Woukang* 1980 (p); *La Vie com-
mence en janvier* 1980 (p); *On est rendus
devant le monde!* 1980 (co-p); *Quelques
chinoises nous ont dit ...* 1981 (p); *La
Surditude* 1981 (p); *Les Beaux Souvenirs*
1981 (p); *Le Confort et l'indifférence* 1982
(co-p); *Au pays de Zom* 1983 (p); *Debout
sur leur terre* 1983 (p); *La Journée d'un curé
de campagne* 1983 (exp); *Le Dernier Glacier*
1984 (p); *La Dame en couleurs* 1985 (exp);
Kalamazoo 1988 (exp).

Dansereau, Mireille

Director and writer; b. Montreal, 1943.
Dansereau, who came to filmmaking after fifteen years in dance, is a pioneer in
the field and co-founder of Quebec's
L'Association coopérative de productions audio-visuelles (ACPAV). She is
still best known in English Canada for
*La Vie rêvée,** an episodic narrative about
two women whose obsession for an
older man finally leads them back to
each other and away from market-
driven images of female desire. After
making documentaries for the NFB,
Dansereau went on to successfully
adapt Marie-Claire Blais's dark, experimental novel, *Le Sourd dans la ville*.
Films include: *Moi, un jour* 1967 (p/d/
sc/ed); *Compromise* 1968 (p/d/sc/ed);
Forum 1969 (d); *Coccinelle* 1970 (d/ed);
La Vie rêvée 1972 (d/co-sc); *J'me marie,
j'me marie pas* 1973 (d); *Le Père ideal* 1973
(d); *Basement* 1974 (p); *Rappelle-toi* 1975
(co-d); *Famille et variations* 1977 (d);
L'Arrache-coeur 1979 (d/sc); *Les Baltes à la
recherche d'un pays* 1980 (d); *Les Nordiques
ou un peuple ans artifice* 1980 (d); *Le Frère
André* 1982 (d/co-sc); *Le Sourd dans la
ville* 1987 (d/sc); *Entre elle et moi* 1992
(d/sc); *Les Marchés de Londres* 1996 (d/
sc); *La Vie d'abord* 1999 (d/sc).

Darcus, Jack

Director, producer, writer, and editor;
b. Vancouver, 1941. Darcus, a leading
figure in the development of an independent film scene in British Columbia,
studied fine arts and philosophy at the
University of British Columbia, where
his directorial efforts began. His penetrating dramas – *Great Coups Of History*
and *Proxyhawks* – signalled a new cinematic energy from the West Coast in
the late 1960s. His films have dramatized Canada–United States relations
(*Deserters*) and explored the dangers and
disillusionments of middle age (*Kingsgate*). *Overnight*, a satire on the precari-
ous nature of the Canadian film industry, tells the story of an actor who ends
up working in porn films to survive and
is encouraged by a proud fellow performer with the immortal rallying cry:
'We may be small, we may be dirty, but
we're Canadian!' **Films include:** *Great
Coups of History* 1969 (p/d/sc/ed);
Proxyhawks 1970 (p/d/sc/ed/a); *Wolf-
pen Principle* 1974 (d/sc); *Deserters* 1983
(p/d/sc/ed); *Overnight* 1986 (p/d/sc);
Kingsgate 1989 (p/d/sc); *The Portrait*
1992 (d); *Silence* 1997 (p/d).

David, Pierre

Producer and distributor; b. Montreal,
1944. Born to a prominent Quebec family, the energetic and prolific David entered the business of making movies in
his early twenties. By age twenty-eight
he had established his own distribution
company, Mutual Films. In 1979, with
Denis Héroux* and Victor Solnicki, he
formed Filmplan International, the company that produced the early David
Cronenberg* hits *The Brood, Scanners,*
and *Videodrome** (along with many
dreadful films during the tax-shelter
era*). In 1982 David moved to Los Angeles where he continues to work, producing films at a furious pace, including

Oliver Stone's Oscar-winning *Platoon*,
the Richard Gere hit *Internal Affairs*, and
Wes Craven's Wishmaster. **Films include:**
Bingo 1974; *Les Aventures d'une jeune
veuve* 1974; *Parlez-nous d'amour* 1975;
Mustang 1975; *Je suis loin de toi mignonne*
1976; *Born for Hell* 1976; *Panique* 1976;
Eclair au chocolat 1979; *The Brood* 1979;
Hog Wild 1980; *Dirty Tricks* 1981; *Scan-
ners* 1981; *Gas* 1981; *Visiting Hours* 1982;
Funny Farm 1983; *Videodrome* 1983; *Going
Berserk* 1983; *Of Unkown Origin* 1983;
Covergirl 1984; *Breaking All the Rules*
1985; *The Vindicator* 1986; *Platoon* 1986
(AA-P); *Hot Pursuit* 1986; *The Great Land
of Small* 1987; *Pin* 1989; *Internal Affairs*
1990; *The Perfect Bride* 1991; *Scanners II:
The New Order* 1991; *Scanners III: The
Takeover* 1992; *Distant Cousins* 1993;
Scanner Cop 1993 (p/d); *Serial Killer* 1995
(p/d); *Scanner Cop II* 1995; *Never Too Late*
1996; *Wes Craven's Wishmaster* 1997; *Man
of Her Dreams* 1997; *Little Men* 1998; *The
Night Caller* 1998; *The Landlady* 1997;
Rites of Passage 1999; *A Clean Kill* 1999.

Davidovich, Lolita

Actor; b. Lolita David, Toronto, 1961.
Davidovich, the daughter of Yugosla-
vian parents who settled in Ontario,
made an auspicious debut in 1989 as the
stripper who enchanted Louisiana governor Earl Long (played by Paul Newman) in *Blaze*. The film was directed by
Ron Shelton, to whom Davidovich later
became engaged. Since then she has
starred in the biopic *Cobb* (opposite
Tommy Lee Jones), *Younger and Younger*
(with Donald Sutherland*), for which
she won the 1993 Best Actress Award at
the Tokyo International Film Festival,
and *Intersection* (with Richard Gere). In
addition, Davidovich joined Oliver
Stone's ensemble cast in *JFK*. For television, Davidovich earned a Golden Globe
nomination for the drama *Harvest of Fire*.
Films and television include: *Blindside*

1986; *Adventures in Babysitting* 1987; *Blaze* 1989; *The Object of Beauty* 1991; *JFK* 1991; *Prison Stories: Women on the Inside* 1991 (TV); *Leap of Faith* 1992; *Raising Cain* 1992; *Younger and Younger* 1993; *Cobb* 1994; *Intersection* 1994; *Trial at Fortitude Bay* 1994 (TV); *For Better or Worse* 1995; *Salt Water Moose* 1996; *Harvest of Fire* 1996 (TV); *Jungle2Jungle* 1997; *Touch* 1997; *Gods and Monsters* 1998; *Mystery, Alaska* 1999; *4 Days* 1999; *No Vacancy* 1999; *Play It to the Bone* 1999.

Davidson, William

Director, producer, and editor; b. Toronto, 1928. Davidson joined the NFB in 1948 and directed or edited a number of films for the *Canada Carries On** series. In 1955 he returned to Toronto, where he worked briefly for the CBC, then produced and directed two early English-Canadian features: *Now That April's Here*, which was based on four short stories by Morley Callaghan, and *The Ivy League Killers*, a melodrama about juvenile delinquency. Neither film received wide distribution, and Davidson rejoined the CBC as an executive producer for children and youth programs. He developed, wrote, and directed a number of series including *Razzle Dazzle*, *Adventures in Rainbow Country*, and *Starlost*. **Films include:** *Now That April's Here* 1958 (p/d/ed); *The Ivy League Killers* 1959 (p/d/ed); *Lions for Breakfast* 1975 (d); *Marie-Anne* 1978 (ap); *The Shape of Things to Come* 1979 (p).

Day, Richard

Art director; b. Victoria, B.C., 1896; d. 1972. Day, an illustrator and a captain in the Canadian army during the First World War, decided to try his luck in 1920s Hollywood. A chance meeting with Erich von Stroheim led him to work on *Foolish Wives* and *Greed*, films that set a new standard for realistic art direction. He was with MGM from 1923 to 1930, and from 1939 to 1943 he headed the art department at 20th Century-Fox. Day was nominated twenty times for an Academy Award, the most ever for an art director. **Films include:** *Foolish Wives* 1922; *Merry-Go-Round* 1923; *Greed* 1925; *The Merry Widow* 1925; *Queen Kelly* 1928; *The Wedding March* 1928; *Anna Christie* 1930; *Whoopee!* 1930 (AAN-AD); *Arrowsmith* 1931 (AAN-AD); *The Front Page* 1931; *Indiscreet* 1931; *Rain* 1932; *Hallelujah, I'm a Bum* 1933; *Roman Scandals* 1933; *The Affairs of Cellini* 1934 (AAN-AD); *Nana* 1934; *The Call of the Wild* 1935; *Clive of India* 1935; *Barbary Coast* 1935; *The Dark Angel* 1935 (AA-AD); *Les Miserables* 1935; *Dodsworth* 1936 (AA-AD); *Dead End* 1937 (AAN-AD); *Hurricane* 1937; *Stella Dallas* 1937; *The Goldwyn Follies* 1938 (AAN-AD); *Drums along the Mohawk* 1939; *The Hound of the Baskervilles* 1939; *Rose of Washington Square* 1939; *Young Mr. Lincoln* 1939; *Down Argentine Way* 1940 (AAN-AD); *The Grapes of Wrath* 1940; *Lillian Russell* 1940 (AAN-AD); *The Mark of Zorro* 1940; *Blood and Sand* 1941 (AAN-AD); *Charley's Aunt* 1941; *How Green Was My Valley* 1941 (AA-AD); *Man Hunt* 1941; *Tobacco Road* 1941; *Swamp Water* 1941; *Western Union* 1941; *The Black Swan* 1942; *My Gal Sal* 1942 (AA-AD); *This above All* 1942 (AA-AD); *The Ox-Bow Incident* 1943; *Coney Island* 1943; *The Razor's Edge* 1946 (AAN-AD); *Captain from Castile* 1947; *The Ghost and Mrs Muir* 1947; *Miracle on 34th Street* 1947; *Force of Evil* 1948; *Joan of Arc* 1948 (AAN-AD); *A Streetcar Named Desire* 1951 (AA-AD); *Hans Christian Andersen* 1952 (AAN-AD); *On the Waterfront* 1954 (AA-AD); *Exodus* 1960; *Cheyenne Autumn* 1964; *The Greatest Story Ever Told* 1965 (AAN-AD); *Valley of the Dolls* 1967; *The Boston Strangler* 1968; *Tora! Tora! Tora!* 1970 (AAN-AD).

Deadly Currents

1991 115m *prod* Associated Producers,

exp David Green, Jeff Sackman, Robert Topol, *p* Simcha Jacobovici, Elliott Halpern, Ric Esther Bienstock, *d* Simcha Jacobovici, *ph* Mark Mackay, *ed* Steve Weslak, *mus* Stephen Price. Shot during the height of the first Intifada, when Palestinian youths carried on an almost daily running battle with Israeli soldiers, *Deadly Currents* probes the dangerous and murky world of Arab-Israeli politics. Simcha Jacobovici (who was born in Israel) has obtained remarkably candid footage of all classes on both sides, but one individual stands out: a half-crazed street performer in Jerusalem who claims Arab and Israeli parentage, and douses himself in blood-red paint, screaming at the passersby, daring them to question the logic of his actions. He's an apt but troubling symbol of the region's violent impasse. (V) **Awards include:** GA: Feature Documentary.

Dead Ringers
1988 113m *prod* The Mantle Clinic II, *exp* Silvio Tabat, Carol Baum, *p* David Cronenberg, Marc Boyman, *d* David Cronenberg, *sc* David Cronenberg, Norman Snider, *book* Bari Woods, Jack Geasland, *ph* Peter Suschitzky, *ed* Ronald Sanders, *mus* Howard Shore; *with* Jeremy Irons, Geneviève Bujold, Shirley Douglas, Stephen Lack, Heidi Von Palleske. The basic premise of *Dead Ringers* is derived from a novel based on a true incident. Twin gynecologists, Elliot and Beverly Mantle, played exquisitely and to perfection by Irons, encounter a famous actress (Bujold*) and carry on an affair with her. Elliot, pretending to be Beverly, seduces her, and she ends up falling for Beverly. This situation leads to a rapid downhill spiral for the brothers into pills, eventual drug addiction, and death. Although fairly restrained for Cronenberg,* the film contains several brilliant set pieces. One particularly lurid touch is that inside the Mantle clinic operating theatre, the doctors and nurses wear blood-red surgical masks and gowns. Beverly designs and commissions a range of special gynecological instruments for treating 'mutant' women. Laid out on a trolley, they are truly the stuff of nightmares. (V) **Awards include:** GA: Picture, Director, Adapted Screenplay, Actor (Irons), Art Direction, Cinematography, Editing, Musical Score, Sound Editing.

De Carlo, Yvonne
Actor; b. Peggy Yvonne Middleton, Vancouver, 1922; d. 1996. The woman who portrayed Lily Munster in the ghoulish television show *The Munsters* was once titled 'the most beautiful girl in the world.' Although her mother wanted her little girl to be a famous ballerina, De Carlo wanted to act. By 1943 she was signed to Paramount Studios and, in her own words, 'usually cast as an exotic native.' She played the title role in *Salome*, followed by *The Song of Scheherazade* and *Slave Girl*, and became typecast as a temptress, representing Hollywood's idea of an Arabian Nights beauty. De Carlo showed a special knack for comedy in the British-made *The Captain's Paradise*. **Films and television include:** *This Gun for Hire* 1942; *Road to Morocco* 1942; *For Whom the Bell Tolls* 1943; *Kismet* 1944; *Salome* 1945; *The Song of Scheherazade* 1947; *Brute Force* 1947; *Slave Girl* 1947; *Criss Cross* 1949; *Hurricane Smith* 1952; *Fort Algiers* 1953; *The Captain's Paradise* 1953; *The Ten Commandments* 1956; *McLintock!* 1963; *The Munsters* 1964–6 (series); *Munster Go Home!* 1966; *It Seemed like a Good Idea at the Time* 1975; *The Man with Bogart's Face* 1980.

Déclin de l'empire américain, Le
1986 101m *prod* Corporation Image M and M, NFB, *exp* Pierre Gendron, *p* René Malo, Roger Frappier, *d/sc* Denys

Arcand, *ph* Guy Dufaux, *ed* Monique Fortier, *mus* François Dompierre; *with* Rémy Girard, Dorothée Berryman, Pierre Curzi, Louise Portal, Gabriel Arcand, Dominique Michel, Daniel Brière, Geneviève Rioux. A brillant black comedy of manners built around a series of satiric and witty conversations about sex, love, and life between several Montreal academics who are friends, or lovers, or both. The group includes a serial adulterer, an AIDS sufferer, and a divorcée in a sadomasochistic relationship. It's as if these aging professors are the former militants of Quebec's faded Quiet Revolution who are now locked into a sexual roundelay as their only outlet for action and iconoclasm. Just as *Le Chat dans le sac** in 1964 was the rallying cry for a militant generation, *Le Déclin de l'empire américain* is its epitaph. In post-(first) referendum Quebec, Denys Arcand* perfectly captures a society in transition, with a frantic desire for individual happiness, which may or may not be historically linked to the decline of the American empire. This Academy Award–nominated film was embraced by English-Canadian audiences like no other Québécois film since Claude Jutra's *Mon oncle Antoine.** (V) **Awards include:** GA: Picture, Director, Original Screenplay, Supporting Actor (Arcand), Supporting Actress (Portal), Editing, Overall Sound, Sound Editing; Golden Reel Award; AAN: Foreign-Language Film; Cannes: International Film Critics' Prize.

Demers, Rock

Producer; b. St-Cécile-de-Levrard, Que., 1933. Demers is the only Canadian producer whose public persona audiences can identify with his movies. In 1980, after a career as a distributor, exhibitor, and supporter of movie culture, Demers launched a series of children's films that he dubbed Tales for All. Shot in French or English, this remarkable series projects a humanist outlook, entertaining children around the world without resorting to mutant kickboxers tearing heads off aliens. Both *The Dog Who Stopped the War** and *The Tadpole and the Whale** were genuine box-office success stories in Canada. **Films and television Include:** *The Dog Who Stopped the War / La Guerre des tuques* 1984 (GRA); *The Peanut Butter Solution* 1985; *Bach and Broccoli* 1986; *Le Jeune Magicien* 1986; *The Great Land of Small* 1987; *Summer of the Colt* 1987; *Tommy Tricker and the Stamp Traveller* 1988; *The Tadpole and the Whale* 1988 (GRA); *Bye bye chaperon rouge* 1989; *Fierro ... l'été des secrets* 1989; *The Case of the Witch Who Wasn't* 1989; *Pas de répit pour Mélanie* 1990; *Vincent and Me* 1990; *La Championne* 1991; *Why Havel?* 1991; *The Clean Machine* 1992; *The Return of Tommy Tricker* 1994; *La Vie d'un héros* 1994; *V'là cinéma: la vie de Charles Pathé* 1994; *Le Silence des fusils* 1996; *Hathi* 1998; *Dancing on the Moon* 1998; *More Tales from the City* 1998 (TV); *P.T. Barnum* 1999 (TV).

De Mille, Katherine

Actor; b. Katherine Lester, Vancouver, 1911; d. 1995. Orphaned as a child, Lester was adopted by legendary Hollywood director Cecil B. de Mille at the age of nine. She played a variety of supporting roles and exotic leads during the 1930s and 1940s. She was also one of Anthony Quinn's five wives. **Films include:** *Madam Satan* 1930; *Viva Villa!* 1934; *Belle of the Nineties* 1934; *Call of the Wild* 1935; *Charlie Chan at the Olympics* 1937; *Blockade* 1938; *Ellery Queen Master Detective* 1946; *Aloma of the South Seas* 1941; *Black Gold* 1947; *Unconquered* 1947.

Dewhurst, Colleen

Actor; b. Montreal, 1926; d. 1991. Dewhurst, the daughter of a professional hockey player, made her Broadway debut in 1952. Often critically acclaimed for her performances on stage and television, she is best known to Canadian audiences as Marilla in the 1985 CBC-TV production of *Anne of Green Gables,* and as the alcoholic mother in Allan King's *Termini Station.* She was also memorable in two Academy Award–winning films: Woody Allen's *Annie Hall,* in which she played Diane Keaton's mother, and Fred Zinnemann's *The Nun's Story.* Her tempestuous relationship with American actor George C. Scott, whom she married twice, made for some intriguing performances when the two appeared together on stage and screen. **Films and television include:** *The Nun's Story* 1959; *Medea* 1959 (TV); *Man on a String* 1960; *A Fine Madness* 1966; *The Crucible* 1967 (TV); *The Cowboys* 1971; *The Last Run* 1971; *McQ* 1974; *A Moon for the Misbegotten* 1975 (TV); *Annie Hall* 1977; *Ice Castles* 1978; *When a Stranger Calls* 1979; *Final Assignment* 1980; *Guyana Tragedy: The Story of Jim Jones* 1980 (TV); *The Third Walker* 1980; *Tribute* 1980; *The Dead Zone* 1983; *Alice in Wonderland* 1983 (TV); *You Can't Take It with You* 1984 (TV); *Anne of Green Gables* 1985 (TV); *The Boy Who Could Fly* 1986; *Sword of Gideon* 1986 (TV); *Anne of Green Gables – The Sequel* 1987 (TV); *Obsessed* 1988 (GA-SA); *Termini Station* 1989; *Kaleidoscope* 1990 (TV); *Lantern Hill* 1990 (TV); *Dying Young* 1991; *Bed and Breakfast* 1992.

Dmytryk, Edward

Director and editor; b. Grand Forks, B.C., 1908; d. 1999. Dmytryk, the son of Ukrainian immigrants, was born in British Columbia, but after his mother died his father took him to San Francisco. By age fifteen he was working for Paramount as a messenger boy, and he moved up through the ranks to assistant editor. His first directing assignment

came in 1935 with *The Hawk,* and he was nominated for an Academy Award for *Crossfire* in 1947. As one of the original Hollywood Ten, he was found guilty of Communist affiliations (he had been a party member) and was blacklisted; however, in 1951 he gave testimony to the House of Un-American Activities ('naming names') and was once again allowed to direct in Hollywood where he continued to work until the mid-1970s. **Films include:** *The Royal Family of Broadway* 1930 (ed); *College Rhythm* 1934 (ed); *The Hawk* 1935; *Murder Goes to College* 1937 (ed); *Golden Gloves* 1940; *Confessions of Boston Blackie* 1941; *Seven Miles from Alcatraz* 1942; *Hitler's Children* 1943; *Murder, My Sweet* 1944; *Back to Bataan* 1945; *Cornered* 1945; *Crossfire* 1947 (AAN-D); *Give Us This Day* 1949; *The Sniper* 1952; *Broken Lance* 1954; *The Caine Mutiny* 1954; *The End of the Affaire* 1955; *The Left Hand of God* 1955; *Raintree County* 1957; *The Young Lions* 1958; *Walk on the Wild Side* 1962; *The Carpetbaggers* 1964; *Alvarez Kelly* 1966; *Shalako* 1968; *Bluebeard* 1972; *Hollywood on Trial* 1976 (a).

Dog Who Stopped the War, The

1984 91m prod Les Productions La Fête, *exp* Claude Bonin, *p* Rock Demers, Nicole Robert, *d* André Melançon, *sc* Danyèle Patenaude, Roger Cantin, André Melançon *ph* François Protat, *ed* André Corriveau, *mus* Germain Gauthier; *with* Cédric Jourde, Maripierre D'Amour, Julien Élie, Duc Minh Vu, Maryse Cartwright, Luc Boucher. This drama of camaraderie and rivalry, the first film in Rock Demers's* Tales for All series, is a modest and endearing children's tale of two gangs of school children who spend their winter break immersed in a war game in which the victors win an extraordinary ice fortress. Good-natured at first, the game gradually turns antagonistic and eventually reaches an abrupt and disturbing conclusion, teaching the youths a difficult but valuable lesson. (V) **Awards include:** GA: Editing; Golden Reel Award.

Donovan, Paul and Michael

Paul: Director and writer; b. Antigonish, N.S., 1954. **Michael:** Producer; b. Antigonish, 1953. The Donovan brothers first stumbled into filmmaking while attending Dalhousie University. There Michael studied law and Paul physics, but a course in film appreciation taken by Paul changed their lives. Paul went on to the London Film School. When he returned to Halifax, the brothers formed Salter Street Films in 1979. Their first films were less than stellar, but they persisted and in 1986 the company's focus changed to television with Codco, the Newfoundland sketch-comedy group. The success of *CODCO* on the CBC led to *This Hour Has 22 Minutes*, probably the best satirical show on television since *SCTV*. In 2001 Salter Street was bought out by Alliance Atlantis. **Films and television include:** *South Pacific 1942* 1981 (p/d/sc); *Siege* 1983 (p/d/sc); *Defcon-4* 1985 (p/d/sc); *CODCO* 1986–93 (exp, series); *The Squamish Five* 1988 (d, TV); *George's Island* 1989 (d/co-sc); *Buried on Sunday* 1993 (p/d/co-sc); *Life with Billy* 1993 (p/d, TV); *This Hour Has 22 Minutes* 1994–present (exp, series); *Paint Cans* 1994 (p/d/sc); *Lexx: The Dark Zone Stories* 1997–present (exp, series); *Emily of New Moon* 1997–9 (exp, series); *Made in Canada* 1998–present (exp, series); *Jacob Two-Two Meets the Hooded Fang* 1999 (exp); *Cod: The Fish That Changed the World* (exp, TV).

Doohan, James

Actor; b. Vancouver, 1932. Famous for his role as Montgomery 'Scotty' Scott in the successful television and film series *Star Trek*, James Doohan has had little luck doing much else. After time in the army, he started an acting career, studying in New York, and then returned to Canada to work in early Canadian television. After heading for Hollywood and Paramount Studios, Doohan got a job on *Star Trek* that lasted nearly thirty years. Stereotyped as his Scotty character, Doohan has accepted his fate and is a regular on the Trekkie convention circuit. **Films and television include:** *Flight into Danger* 1956 (TV); *Bus Riley's Back in Town* 1965; *Star Trek* 1966–9 (series); *Man in the Wilderness* 1971; *Pretty Maids All in a Row* 1971; *Star Trek: The Motion Picture* 1979; *Star Trek II: The Wrath of Khan* 1982; *Star Trek III: In Search of Spock* 1984; *Star Trek IV: The Voyage Home* 1986; *Star Trek V: The Final Frontier* 1989; *Star Trek VI: The Undiscovered Country* 1991; *National Lampoon's Loaded Weapon* 1993; *Star Trek: Generations* 1994.

D'Orsay, Fifi

Actor; b. Yvonne Lussier, Montreal, 1904; d. 1983. One of twelve children of a postal clerk, and educated in a convent, D'Orsay started out as a typist, moved on to vaudeville, and then starred in some of the first movie musicals, usually as a Parisian sexpot. Her first film, *They Had to See Paris*, was with the legendary Will Rogers in 1929. D'Orsay's star dimmed after 1935, but she kept active with occasional movies, television work, and lecturing on religion. **Films include:** *They Had to See Paris* 1929; *Hot for Paris* 1929; *Those Three French Girls* 1930; *Women of All Nations* 1931; *Girl from Calgary* 1932; *Going Hollywood* 1933; *Three Legionnaires* 1937; *What a Way to Go!* 1964; *Assignment to Kill* 1968.

Double Happiness

1995 110m *prod* First Generation Films, *p* Stephen Hegyes, Rose Lam Waddell, *d/sc* Mina Shum, *ph* Peter Wunstorf, *ed* Alison Grace, *mus* Shadowy Men on a Shadowy Planet; *with* Sandra Oh, Alannah Ong, Stephen Chang, Frances You, Johnny Mah, Callum Keith Rennie. This entertaining coming-of-age story explores the often troubled relationship between cultures and generations. Jade Li (Oh) is an irreverent twenty-two-year-old aspiring actress who lives at home with her strict Chinese family. She wants to move out and pursue her independence, but she is stopped by the memory of her brother, who was disowned for a similar act. Jade's parents desperately want her to marry a Chinese man, but her situation is complicated by her deepening relationship with Mark (Rennie*), a white university student. The film skilfully examines the struggles of the young woman as she attempts to balance her individuality and freedom with her culture and her family's rigid demands. (V) **Awards include:** GA: Actress (Oh).

Drabinsky, Garth

Producer and exhibitor; b. Toronto, 1948. Drabinsky, a lawyer by training and the boy wonder of Canadian cinema, produced his first feature, *The Disappearance*, in 1977 (released in 1981). In 1978 he joined forces with pioneering exhibitor Nat Taylor* and formed Pan Canadian Distribution. A year later, the pair built their first Cineplex cinema, an eighteen-screen complex in Toronto's Eaton Centre. Drabinsky went on to buy out the Odeon chain of theatres and between 1984 and 1989 (when he eventually lost control of his company to MCA) he built the second-largest theatre chain in North America. He left the world of Canadian cinema forever changed when, at age 41, he started a lucrative and controversial career producing megamusicals. **Films include:** *The Silent Partner*

1978 (CFA-FF); *The Changeling* 1980 (GA-P, GRA); *Tribute* 1980; *The Disappearance* 1981; *The Amateur* 1981; *Losin' It* 1983.

Dreamspeaker

1977 75m *prod* CBC, *p* Ralph L. Thomas, *d* Claude Jutra, *sc* Anne Cameron, *ph* John Seale, *ed* Toni Trow, *mus* Jean Cousineau; *with* Ian Tracey, George Clutesi, Jacques Hubert, Robert Howard. After setting a school on fire, Peter (Tracey), an emotionally disturbed eleven-year-old boy, is placed in a juvenile detention centre. He's hostile and prone to violent fits of self-strangulation. Peter manages to escape into the British Columbia wilderness where he meets up with a native shaman (or dreamspeaker) and his mute friend. Peter finds a solution to the troubling voices in his head through the shaman's spiritualism. But after authorities return him to the detention centre, Peter hangs himself. Director Claude Jutra* offers no happy endings but instead an insightful and emotionally charged look at native spiritualism and mental illness. Made for the CBC-TV anthology series *For the Record.**

Dressler, Marie

Actor; b. Leila Marie Koerber, Cobourg, Ont., 1869; d. 1934. Dressler was a light-opera singer and star on the vaudeville stage before moving into pictures. She made her film debut in Mack Sennett's* 1914 screen version of her popular stage hit, *Tillie's Punctured Romance*, co-starring with Charlie Chaplin. With the advent of sound, this large, ferociously genial actress became one of Hollywood's most popular stars, delivering several commanding performances in the early 1930s. She played with Greta Garbo in *Anna Christie*, and with Jean Harlow in *Dinner at Eight*. In 1930, she won the Best Actress Academy Award

for her role opposite Wallace Beery in
Min and Bill, but she is perhaps best remembered as the irrepressible main
character in *Tugboat Annie,* her last film.
Films include: *Tillie's Punctured Romance*
1914; *Tillie's Tomato Surprise* 1915; *Breakfast at Sunrise* 1927; *Bringing up Father*
1928; *The Hollywood Revue of 1929* 1929;
The Vagabond Lover 1929; *Anna Christie*
1930; *Min and Bill* 1930 (AA-A); *Emma*
1932 (AAN-A); *Dinner at Eight* 1933; *Tugboat Annie* 1933.

Driessen, Paul

Animator; b. Nimegue, Holland, 1940.
An ongoing fascination with the elements that make up an animated film
places Paul Driessen closer to the camp
of Michael Snow* than that of Disney.
His characters continually butt into and
out of the frame, often questioning the
meaning of the stories they are in. His
masterpiece, *The End of the World in Four
Seasons,* presents a storyboard gone
awry: in a world divided into four mini-
screens, his seasonal creations are buf-
feted by events taking place above, below, and beside them. This philosophical
Dutchman became acquainted with the
NFB while animating *Yellow Submarine*
(1968) in London for Canadian expatriate George Dunning.* After a five-year
stint at the Board in the early 1970s,
Driessen began to divide his time between Canada and Holland, a practice
he continues today. **Films include:** *Air*
1972; *Le Bleu perdu* 1972; *Cat's Cradle* 1974;
An Old Box 1975; *The Same Old Story* 1981;
Tip Top 1984; *The End of the World in Four
Seasons* 1995; *3 Misses* 1999 (AAN-AS);
The Boy Who Saw the Iceberg 2001.

Drug Addict

1948 33m *prod* NFB, *p/d/sc* Robert Ander-
son, *ph* Jean-Marie Couture, *ed* Victor
Jobin, *mus* Robert Fleming, *narr* Jack
Scott. *Drug Addict,* the first film to deal

sympathetically with drug addiction,
advocates treatment rather than jail. The
action follows the addictive poppy from
the fields to the streets, and uses real-life
addicts to demonstrate the torments of
drug abuse. Since Hollywood wouldn't
even allow mention of drugs in American films, *Drug Addict* was denied entry
into the United States, and the NFB
didn't actively promote the film.
Awards include: CFA: Documentary.

Drylanders

1963 69m *prod* NFB, *p* Peter Jones, *d*
Donald Haldane, *sc* M. Charles Cohen,
ph Reginald H. Morris, *ed* John Kemeny,
Kirk Jones, *mus* Eldon Rathburn; *with*
Frances Hyland, James Douglas, Lester
Nixon, Mary Savage, William Fruet,
Don Francks. The NFB's first English-
language feature is an epic story of the
hardships faced by settlers attempting to
farm the dry land of the Canadian prairies at the beginning of the twentieth
century. The film portrays the trials of
the Greer family over thirty years as
they struggle to survive bitterly cold
winters, scorching hot summers, unre-
lenting drought, and the Great Depression. The film is technically sound but
lacks emotional impact. (V)

Dufaux, Georges

Cinematographer and director; b. Lille,
France, 1927; brother of Guy Dufaux.
Georges Dufaux has been a mainstay of
Quebec cinema since the late 1950s. He
began with the NFB as a cameraman on
the *Candid Eye** series and in the 1970s
made many important social documentaries. He has directed in collaboration
with Clément Perron* and contributed
distinctive camera work on a number of
features, including Paul Almond's
Isabel, Léa Pool's *La Femme de l'hôtel,*
and André Forcier's *Une Historie
inventée.* **Films and television include:**

Les Brûles 1958 (TV); *The Days before Christmas* 1958 (co-ph, TV); *À Saint-Henri le cinq septembre* 1962 (co-ph); *Alexis Ldouceur, Métis* 1963 (co-ph); *La Fleur de l'âge* 1967; *YUL 871* 1966 (co-ph); *C'est pas la faute à Jacques Cartier* 1968 (d/sc/ed with Clément Perron, TV); *Isabel* 1968 (CFA-PH); *Stop* 1971; *Fortune and Men's Eyes* 1971; *Taureau* 1973; *À votre santé* 1974 (d/ph/ed, TV); *Partis pour la gloire* 1975; *Les Jardins d'hiver* 1976 (d/ph/co-ed); *Jeux de la xxie olympiade* 1977 (co-d/co-ph); *Going the Distance* 1979 (co-ph); *Les Beaux Souvenirs* 1981; *La Femme de l'hôtel* 1984; *Bayo* 1985; *Une Historie inventée* 1990; *Hotel Chonicles* 1990; *Le Vent de Wyoming* 1994; *De l'art et la manière chez Denys Arcand* 2000 (d/ph).

Dufaux, Guy

Cinematographer; b. Lille, France, 1943; brother of Georges Dufaux. Guy Dufaux, a fine arts student who emigrated to Canada in the mid-1960s, has established himself as one of the country's leading cinematographers. Over the years he has worked with many of Quebec's best directors, including Jean Pierre Lefebvre,* Yves Simoneau,* Micheline Lanctôt,* Jean-Claude Lauzon,* and Denys Arcand.* In the mid-1980s, Guy Dufaux's work signalled a shift in style from traditional documentary-influenced filming to a more stylized, formalistic cinematography. In films ranging from *Pouvoir intime** to *Un Zoo la nuit** and *Jésus de Montréal,** he has created some of the most striking images in Quebec cinema. **Films include:** *Les Smattes* 1972; *Les Dernières Fiançailles* 1973; *Le Vieux Pays où Rimbaud est mort* 1977; *Avoir 16 ans* 1980; *Les Fleurs sauvages* 1982; *St Lawrence: Stairway to the Sea* 1982; *Le Jour 'S ...'* 1984; *Sonatine* 1984; *Bach and Broccoli* 1986; *Le Déclin de l'empire américain* 1986; *Equinoxe* 1986; *Pouvoir intime* 1986; *Un Zoo la nuit* 1987

(GA-PH); *Pin* 1988; *Milk and Honey* 1988; *Jésus de Montréal* 1989 (GA-PH); *Moody Beach* 1990; *Montréal vu par ...* 1991 (co-ph); *Sam and Me* 1991; *Léolo* 1992; *Camilla* 1994; *Le Polygraphe* 1996; *Joyeux calvaire* 1996 (TV); *Stardom* 2000; *The Great Gatsby* 2001 (TV).

Duguay, Christian

Director; b. Montreal, 1957. Duguay, a graduate of Concordia University, began his professional career as a cameraman and jack of all trades, working in documentaries, commercials, and music videos. He became known as an expert with the steadicam and shot many movies of the week in the United States. As a director for hire, he helmed the *Scanner* sequels and *Screamers,** a sci-fi action vehicle based on a book by Philip K. Dick. He gained respectable attention with the CBC drama, *Million Dollar Babies*, based on the Dionne Quintuplets, then returned to the action genre with *The Assignment* and *The Art of War,** which quickly became the highest-grossing Canadian feature since the release of *Porky's** in 1980. **Films and television include:** *Scanners ii: The New Order* 1991; *Live Wire* 1992; *Scanners iii: The Takeover* 1992; *Adrift* 1993 (TV); *Model by Day* 1994 (TV); *Snowbound: The Jim and Jennifer Stolpa Story* 1994 (TV); *Million Dollar Babies* 1994 (TV); *Screamers* 1995; *The Assignment* 1997 (d/ph); *Joan of Arc* 1999 (TV); *The Art of War* 2000.

Duke, Daryl

Director and producer; b. Vancouver, 1930. Daryl Duke, a graduate of the University of British Columbia, began his career in the 1960s working as a producer and director on such CBC-TV shows as *Closeup* and *Telescope*. In 1973, he directed his acclaimed first feature *Payday* (with Rip Torn) and in 1978 he won the Best Director at the Canadian

Film Awards for *The Silent Partner*.*
Duke went on to launch and co-own an
independent Vancouver television sta-
tion. In the past two decades, he has
worked primarily on American televi-
sion productions, directing such mini-
series epics as *The Thorn Birds*, *Florence
Nightingale*, and *Tai-Pan*. **Films and tel-
evision include:** *Wojeck* 1966 (series);
The Children 1970 (TV); *The President's
Plane Is Missing* 1971 (TV); *Payday* 1973;
I Heard the Owl Call My Name 1974 (TV);
They Only Come out at Night 1975 (TV);
Griffin and Phoenix 1976; *Shadow of the
Hawk* 1976; *The Silent Partner* 1978
(CFA-D); *The Return of Charlie Chan* 1979
(TV); *The Thorn Birds* 1980 (TV); *Florence
Nightingale* 1985 (TV); *Tai-Pan* 1986 (TV);
Long Lance 1986 (TV); *When We Were
Young* 1989 (TV); *Columbo: Caution! Mur-
der Can Be Hazardous to Your Health* 1991
(TV); *Fatal Memories* 1992 (TV).

Dumbrille, Douglas

Actor; b. Hamilton, Ont., 1890; d. 1974.
An acting late-starter, Dumbrille sold his
southern Ontario onion farm in 1924
when he was thirty-four years old and
left for Hollywood. Versatile, and often
villainous, Dumbrille played lawyers,
politicians, judges, and evil potentates
in more than 250 films. As Mohammed
Khan in *Lives of a Bengal Lacer*, he told
Gary Cooper and Franchot Tone, 'We
have ways to make men talk.' **Films include:** *Broadway Bill* 1934; *Treasure Island*
1934; *Lives of a Bengal Lancer* 1935; *Cardinal Richelieu* 1935; *Crime and Punishment*
1935; *Mr. Deeds Goes to Town* 1936; *Coun-
terfeit Lady* 1936; *A Day at the Races* 1937;
The Buccaneer 1938; *The Three Musketeers*
1939; *The Big Store* 1941; *Road to Zanzibar*
1941; *Du Barry Was a Lady* 1943; *Lost in a
Harem* 1944; *Road to Utopia* 1946; *Abbott
and Costello in the Foreign Legion* 1950;
Son of Paleface 1952; *Julius Caesar* 1953;
The Ten Commandments 1956; *The Buccaneer* 1958; *Shock Treatment* 1964.

Dunning, George

Animator; b. Toronto, 1920; d. 1979. As a
young man, Dunning worked for Norman McLaren* at the NFB. In 1949, he
and fellow NFB-grad Jim McKay created
one of Toronto's first animation studios,
Graphic Associates. There he gave
Michael Snow* his first job in film. After
his move to England in the mid-1950s,
Dunning did a variety of commercial
work, and eventually made a cartoon
series based on the Beatles for BBC-TV.
This led to the film that Dunning will always be associated with: *Yellow Submarine*, the Peter Max-influenced pop-art-
meets-rock-'n'-roll feature that became
an instantly recognizable pop icon of the
1960s. **Films and television include:**
Grim Pastures 1944; *Three Blind Mice*
1945; *Cadet Rousselle* 1946 (with Colin
Low); *Family Tree* 1950 (with Eve
Lambart, CFA-SPA); *The Wardrobe* 1959;
The Flying Man 1962; *The Apple* 1962; *The
Beatles* 1966 (series); *Canada Is My Piano*
1967; *Yellow Submarine* 1968; *Moon Rock*
1970; *Along These Lines* 1974.

Dunning, John, and André Link

Producers and distributors. **Dunning:** b.
Montreal, 1927. **Link:** b. Budapest, Hungary, 1932. John Dunning and André
Link represent the longest lasting and
most successful producing partnership
in Canadian film history to date. The
pair came together in 1962 to form Cinépix distribution. By 1969 they were into
production with *Valerié** (the first of a
mini-boom dubbed 'maple-syrup porn'),
directed by Denis Héroux.* Later came a
lucrative partnership with fellow producer Ivan Reitman* resulting in the
first two Cronenberg* features – *Shivers**
and *Rabid** – and Reitman's own breakthrough film, *Meatballs*.* Cinépix merged
with Cinenexus and Famous Players to
form C/FP which later merged with the
Los Angeles-based Lions Gate Films. A
rarity in Canadian film production,

Dunning and Link have forged a pro-
duction/distribution empire based on
commercially successful, exploitative
films. **Films include:** *Valérie* 1969 (co-p/
co-sc); *L'Intiation* 1970; *Love in a Four Letter World* 1969; *Le Diable est parmi mous*
1972; *Across This Land with Stompin' Tom
Connors* 1973; *Shivers* 1975; *The Mystery
of the Million Dollar Hockey Puck* 1975;
Death Weekend 1976; *Rabid* 1977; *Ilsa the
Tigress of Siberia* 1977; *Blackout* 1978;
Meatballs 1979 (GRA); *Hot Dogs* 1980;
Happy Birthday to Me 1981; *My Bloody
Valentine* 1981; *Spacehunter: Adventures in
the Forbidden Zone* 1983; *The Vindicator*
1986; *Snake Eater* 1989; *Whispers* 1989;
Princes in Exile 1990; *Snake Eater II: The
Drug Buster* 1991; *Snake Eater III: His Law*
1992; *Bullet to Beijing* 1995; *Midnight in
St Petersburg* 1995; *Ski School II* 1995;
Vibrations 1995; *L'Homme idéal* 1996;
Bounty Hunters 1996; *Mask of Death* 1996;
La Conciergerie 1997; *Stag* 1997; *I'm Losing
You* 1998; *Jerry and Tom* 1998; *Johnny
Skidmarks* 1998.

Duparc, Marguerite
Producer and editor; b. France, 1933; d.
1982. After her arrival in Quebec from
France in 1955, Duparc worked in distribution, where she met her future husband, Jean Pierre Lefebvre.* She subsequently edited all of his films and
produced many of them through their
production company, Cinak. She also
edited and produced for other Québécois filmmakers, most notably Denys
Arcand* (*Réjeanne Padovani**). At the
time of her premature death due to
cancer, Duparc was finishing her film
Histoires pour Blaise with director Yves
Rivard. **Films include:** *Le Révolutionnaire*
1965 (ed); *Jusqu'au coeur* 1969 (ed); *Mon
oeil* 1971 (ed); *Les Maudits Sauvages* 1971
(ed); *La Maudite Galette* 1972 (p/ed); *Ultimatum* 1973 (p/ed); *Réjeanne Padovani*
1973 (p/co-ed with Denys Arcand); *Les
Dernières Fiançailles* 1973 (p/ed); *L'Amour*

blessé 1977 (p/ed); *Le Vieux Pays où Rimbaud est mort* 1977 (co-p/ed); *Avoir 16 ans*
1980 (p/ed); *Les Fleurs sauvages* 1982
(p/ed).

Dupuis, Roy
Actor; b. Amos, Que., 1964. Dupuis
studied at the National Theatre School,
and began work in films in the late
1980s after a successful career in theatre.
His star status in Quebec, however, was
assured by his steamy heart-throb performance in the enormously popular
SRC series, *Les Filles de Caleb*. Since then
he has starred in the film version of
*Being at Home with Claude** and the sci-fi
thriller *Screamers.** Dupuis played the
father of the Dionne quints in *Million
Dollar Babies*, and found regular employment in the television action series
Nikita. **Films and television include:**
Lance et compte 1986 (series); *Dans le
ventre du dragon* 1988; *Jésus de Montréal*
1989; *Les Filles de Caleb* 1990–1 (series);
Scoop 1991–5 (series); *Being at Home
with Claude* 1992; *Blanche* 1993 (series);
Cap Tourmente 1993; *C'était le 12 du 12
et Chili avait les blues* 1993; *Million
Dollar Babies* 1994 (TV); *Screamers*
1996; *L'Homme idéal* 1996; *Nikita* 1996–
2000 (series); *J'en suis* 1997; *Aire libre*
1997.

Durbin, Deanna
Actor and singer; b. Edna Mae Durbin,
Winnipeg, 1921. As a teenager, Deanna
Durbin became an instant singing star
of global proportions when her first
feature rescued Universal from the brink
of bankruptcy in 1937. With her first
four films – *Three Smart Girls, 100 Men
and a Girl* with Leopold Stokowski, *Mad
about Music*, and *That Certain Age* –
Durbin's stardom rivalled that of 20th
Century-Fox's Shirley Temple. In 1938
Durbin shared a Special Academy
Award with Mickey Rooney 'for bringing to the screen the spirit and personifi-

cation of youth.' After another decade in the limelight, she retired to the south of France in secluded goddess-like fashion. There are still Deanna Durbin fan clubs worldwide. **Films include:** *Three Smart Girls* 1936; *100 Men and a Girl* 1937; *Mad about Music* 1938; *That Certain Age* 1938; *Three Smart Girls Grow Up* 1939; *Spring Parade* 1940; *Christmas Holiday* 1944; *Can't Help Singing* 1944; *Because of Him* 1946; *For the Love of Mary* 1948.

Dwan, Allan

Director and producer; b. Joseph Aloysius Dwan in Toronto, 1885; d. 1981. Dwan left Toronto with his family at the age of eleven, studied engineering at Notre Dame, and landed a job at Essanay Films in 1909. He was sent to Hollywood in 1911, where he stayed and learned directing skills from the actors. Between 1911 and 1913 he turned out more than 250 one-reelers, mostly westerns. His engineering background was useful for solving early technical problems and he is credited with inventing the dolly shot (using a car) in 1915. Dwan's career peaked in the 1920s with a series of highly successful Douglas Fairbanks (*Robin Hood, The Iron Mask*) and Gloria Swanson (*Manhandled, Wages of Virtue*) vehicles. He continued directing well into the 1950s, and shot his last film at the age of seventy-six. **Films include:** *David Harum* 1915; *A Girl of Yesterday* 1915; *Robin Hood* 1922; *Zaza* 1923 (p/d); *Manhandled* 1924 (p/d); *Her Love Story* 1924 (p/d); *Wages of Virtue* 1924 (p/d); *Stage Struck* 1925 (p/d); *The Iron Mask* 1929; *While Paris Sleeps* 1932; *Heidi* 1937; *Rebecca of Sunnybrook Farm* 1938; *Suez* 1938; *The Three Musketeers* 1939; *Frontier Marshall* 1939; *Up in Mabel's Room* 1944; *Brewster's Millions* 1945; *Getting Gertie's Garter* 1945 (d/co-sc); *Rendezvous with Annie* 1946 (d/ap); *Sands of Iwo Jima* 1949; *Silver Lode* 1954; *Tennes-*

see's Partner 1955 (d/co-sc); *Hold Back the Night* 1956; *The River's Edge* 1957; *The Restless Breed* 1957.

E

Edwards, Harry J.

Director; b. London, Ont., 1888; d. 1952. Edwards entered films in 1912 as a prop boy and gradually worked his way up to director of comedy shorts under fellow expat Mack Sennett.* He developed into one of the best comedy directors of the silent period, working with Harry Langdon, Ben Turpin, Carole Lombard, and many others. He is perhaps best remembered as the director of *Tramp, Tramp, Tramp* (1926), one of Langdon's finest comedies.

Egoyan, Atom

Director, producer, and writer; b. Cairo, Egypt, 1960. Born into an Armenian family and raised in Victoria, British Columbia, Atom Egoyan has emerged as not only the most commercially successful member of the Toronto new wave* but also as a cultural voice that speaks to a hip, more inclusive vision of Canadian society. His preoccupations with family tragedies, sexual obsessions, and the intense difficulty that people have in communicating with each other, clearly strike a chord with both critics and a growing portion of the film-going public.

A trio of edgy, darkly comic and psychologically resonant tales, beginning with *Family Viewing** and continuing through *Speaking Parts** and *The Adjuster,** established Egoyan's highly influential sensibility. In these films, the collision of utterly disparate types – an aging patriarch with a phone sex operator; a death-obsessed scriptwriter with a shallow wannabe actor; a kinky role-playing couple with a maladjusted family – is charted with philosophical brio and a bemused equanimity. While busily plotting increasingly baroque scenarios, Egoyan pursued a formal, experimental course, positioning video as a major device in his films – particularly in *Speaking Parts*, in which a sequence involving mutual masturbation via a visual phone hook-up created a controversy.

It was with *Calendar** that Egoyan discovered a way to enter an audience's heart as well as its mind. In his only starring role, he played a Canadian photographer of Armenian descent who loses his wife (played by his partner Arsinée Khanjian*) to a travel guide while shooting calendar shots of churches in Armenia. Though Egoyan used devices typical of his earlier work (such as video and erotic phone scenes) *Calendar* achieved a finer intimacy and rapport with its viewers.

Returning to higher budgets, professional actors, and increased production values, Egoyan attained commercial success with *Exotica.** The scenario, set mostly in a decadent nightclub that looks as if it was designed by Cocteau after an opium dream, is propelled by the repressed desires of an accountant who has lost his family, and with them, his reason to live. Elaborately constructed with myriad plot developments and a memorable cast of characters, the film moves beyond textural concerns in the scenes between Bruce Greenwood* (the alienated accountant) and Mia Kirshner (the conflicted nightclub stripper). Their relationship is poignant and terrifying in ways that previous films never achieved.

Egoyan's next film garnered awards at Cannes and Academy Award nominations. *The Sweet Hereafter** recounts the difficult tale of a small town's recovery from a school bus disaster that claimed the lives of the majority of the children. While Egoyan's shifting perspective reveals the grief experienced by key figures in the drama, he gradually focuses on the conflicting paths of redemption offered by two people: a lawyer (Ian Holm), who wants to attach blame to an institution for the tragedy; and a crippled survivor (Sarah Polley*), whose desire is to allow the town's inhabitants to accept their loss and move on. These two characters form the emotional and moral core of the film.

Atom Egoyan is that rarest of breeds, a true auteur. As a brilliant visual stylist and an accomplished screenwriter, he has already created an impressive body of work. His success has helped to establish Canadian cinema in the international film scene. **Films include:** *Howard in Particular* 1979 (p/d/sc); *After Grad with Dad* 1980 (p/d/sc); *Peep Show* 1981 (p/d/sc); *Open House* 1982 (p/d/sc); *Next of Kin* 1984 (p/d/sc); *Family Viewing* 1987 (p/d/sc/co-ed); *La Boîte à soleil* 1988 (a); *Speaking Parts* 1989 (p/d/sc/co-ed); *The Adjuster* 1991 (co-p/d/sc); *Montréal vu par ...* 1991 (co-d/co-sc); *Gross Misconduct* 1992 (d, TV); *Calendar* 1993 (co-p/d/sc/ed/a); *Exotica* 1994 (co-p/d/sc, GA-P, GA-D); *Curtis's Charm* 1995 (exp); *Sarabande* from *Yo-Yo Ma Inspired by Bach* 1997 (d/sc, TV); *The Sweet Hereafter* 1997 (co-p/d/sc, GA-D, GA-P, AAN-D, AAN-ASC); *Babyface* 1998 (exp); *Felicia's Journey* 1999 (d/sc, GAA-SC); *Krapp's Last Tape* 2000 (d/ed); *The Line* from *Preludes* 2000 (d/sc).

Elder, Bruce

Filmmaker; b. Hawkesbury, Ont., 1947. Sprawling, stirring, dense, solipsistic, indulgent, interminable, brilliant: all these characterizations have been used to describe the films of Bruce Elder. All are true. Elder was one of the key figures to emerge from the Toronto experimental scene of the 1970s, and his rigorous films range from short works to marathon-length meditations such as *Lamentations: A Monument for the Dead World*. In addition to his gargantuan filmography, Elder is also a perceptive commentator on Canadian cinema. His critical writing (especially his book *Image and Identity*) has opened new and deepened old debates about film in Canada. **Films include:** *Breath / Light / Birth* 1975; *She Is Away* 1975; *Permutations and Combinations* 1976; *Barbara Is a Vision of Loveliness* 1976 (CFA-AE); *Unremitting Tenderness* 1977; *Look! We Have Come Through!* 1978; *The Art of Worldly Wisdom* 1979; *Trace* 1980; *Sweet Love Remembered* 1980; *1857 (Fool's Gold)* 1981; *Illuminated Texts* 1982; *Lamentations: A Monument for the Dead World* 1985; *Azure Serene: Mountains, Rivers, Sea and Sky* 1992.

Eldorado

1995 *prod* Cité-Amérique, *exp* Monique Messier, Michel Gauthier, Lorraine Richard, *p* Lorraine Richard *d* Charles Binamé, *sc* Charles Binamé, Lorraine Richard, *ph* Pierre Gill, *ed* Michel Arcand, *mus* Claude Lamothe, Francis Dhomont; *with* Pascale Bussières, Pascale Montpetit, Robert Brouilette, Isabel Richer, James Hyndman, Macha Limonchik. Set in Montreal during the summer of 1994, *Eldorado* tells the distressing tale of six alienated and aimless youths struggling to make sense of their lives. These members of the lost generation search for meaning on the streets of Montreal while engaging in risky sex, fighting, raving, and Rollerblading. The extensive use of hand-held cameras, natural lighting, and improvised dialogue gives the film a raw look and feel that effectively matches the subject matter. (V)

Emporte-moi

1999 94m *prod* Cité-Amérique, Cinéma Télévision Inc., Catpics (Switzerland), Haut et Court (France), *exp* Louis Laver-dière, *p* Lorraine Richard, Alfi Sinniger, Carole Scotta, *d/sc* Léa Pool, *ph* Jeanne Lapoirie, *ed* Michel Arcand, *mus* ECM; *with* Karine Vanasse, Pascale Bussières, Miki Manojlovic, Nancy Huston, Anne-Marie Cadieux, Monique Mercure. In this highly regarded film, which is based on her own adolescence during the early 1960s, director Léa Pool* explores the dilemmas of a teenage girl, Hannah (Vanasse) and her relationship with her suicidal mother (Bussières*) and Jewish father (Manojlovic), who is traumatized by the Holocaust. In danger of being smothered, Hannah gropes for a sense of identity by bonding with the seductive and defiant screen image of Anna Karina in Jean-Luc Godard's *Vivre sa vie*. *Emporte-moi*'s yearning lyricism is exemplified by a sequence in which Hanna and another girl drift toward each other at a high school party and end up kissing tenderly in an alley. (V) **Awards include:** PJ: Actress (Vanasse), Supporting Actress (Bussières), Art Direction.

Entre la mer et l'eau douce

1968 85m *prod* Coopératio Inc, *p* Pierre Patry, *d* Michel Brault, *sc* Denys Arcand, Michel Brault, Marcel Dubé, Gérald Godin, Claude Jutra, *ph* Bernard Gosselin, Michel Brault, Jean-Claude Labrecque, *ed* Michel Brault, Werner Nold, *mus* Claude Gauthier; *with* Claude Gauthier, Geneviève Bujold, Paul Gauthier, Robert Charlebois, Louise Latraverse. Brault's* most poetic and richly complex fiction feature, a seminal film in Quebec cinema, concerns Claude Tremblay (Claude Gauthier), who leaves his small town for Montreal, where he falls in love with an actress, Geneviève (Bujold*). Tremblay enters a singing contest that launches his career, but as he becomes more famous, he drifts apart from his lover. When he tries to go home, he understands that things have changed forever. Contrasting Tremblay's Quiet Revolution–inspired restlessness with the eternal flow of the St Lawrence River, Brault's evocative, episodic, often improvised first fiction feature is a startling work. *Entre la mer et l'eau douce* is an engaging combination of Heraclitus and Thomas Wolfe: the river is never the same and you really can't go home again.

Ernie Game, The

1968 88m *prod* NFB, CBC, *exp* Robert Allen, *p* Gordon Burwash, *d/sc* Don Owen, *ph* Jean-Claude Labrecque, *ed* Roy Ayton, *mus* Kensington Market, Leonard Cohen; *with* Alexis Kanner, Judith Gault, Jackie Burroughs, Derek May, Anna Cameron, Leonard Cohen. Don Owen* risked his career when he surreptitiously turned an educational half-hour into one of the few English-Canadian dramatic features made during the 1960s. Just as the young hero of Owen's *Nobody Waved Good-Bye** thumbs his nose at his stifling parents, the filmmaker resisted the Griersonian dictum that Canadian moviemakers were ordained to record life and not imagine it. In his follow-up picture, Owen went further. The eponymous protagonist of *The Ernie Game* is not merely a suburban kid who craves a little freedom; he's a 'schizie' lost boy with a maddening indifference to real life. The carrot-topped Ernie flirts and floats through Montreal, driving himself into a terminal state of confusion. **Awards include:** CFA: Feature Film, Director.

Erreur boréale, L'

1999 68m *prod* ACPAV, NFB, *p* Bernadette Payeur, *d* Richard Desjardins, Robert Monderie, *sc* Richard Desjardins, *ph* Jacques Leduc, *ed* Alain Belhumeur, *mus* Jean-François Groulx, Benoit Groulx. Due to an unholy alliance of big business and lax government regulations, the great boreal forests of Quebec are being systematically plundered. Filmmaker and musician Richard Desjardins' passionate documentary makes it clear that clearcutting (which is euphemistically called 'selective harvesting') what was once the largest forested area the world has lead to an ecological disaster. He travels the province, interviewing not only ministry flaks and business 'suits' but also those who make a living of the forests – the outfitters and the Cree – and his conclusions are unsettling. When the original European settlers came to Quebec they found a land of unimaginable natural wealth and beauty. Now large parts of the province are clearcut wasteland. (V) **Awards include:** PJ: Feature Documentary.

Evangeline

1914 5 reels *prod* Canadian Bioscope Co., *exp* H.H.B. Holland, G.J.B. Metzler, *d* E.P. Sullivan, William Cavanaugh, *sc* Marguerite Marquis, *poem* Henry Wadsworth Longfellow, *ph* H. Thomas Oliver, William Thompson; *with* Laura Lyman, John F. Carleton, E.P. Sullivan, William Cavanaugh. This film is based on Longfellow's famous poem describing the expulsion of the Acadians in 1755 and the undying love of Evangeline (Lyman) and Gabriel (Carleton), and was shot entirely on location in Nova Scotia. *Evangeline* is considered the first dramatic feature produced in Canada, although both Cavanaugh and Sullivan were American stage actors.

Every Child

1980 6m13s *prod* NFB, *p* Derek Lamb, *d/an* Eugene Fedorenko, *sc* Derek Lamb, Patrice Arbour, Bernard Carez, *ph* Robert Humble, Richard Moras. This animated short, made in conjunction with the United Nations' Declaration of

Children's Rights, was one section of an hour-long film that consisted of ten six-minute shorts, each illustrating one of the ten principles of the Declaration. NFB animator Eugene Fedorenko's contribution, *Every Child*, is the story of a baby who appears mysteriously on the doorstep of a busy businessman who passes it on a block; no one wants to take care of a child that has no name or nationality. (V) **Awards include:** AA: Animated Short.

Evolution

1971 10m21s *prod* NFB, *exp* Robert Verrall, *d/p/sc/an* Michael Mills, *ph* Kjeld Nielsen, *mus* Doug Randle. This amusing take on how life came into being on this planet begins with the single-cell amoebae that romped about the ocean depths, and continues with the first amphibious creatures that crawled onto land and the progenitors of modern man. It received an Academy Award nomination for Animated Short. (V)

eXistenZ

1999 97m *prod* Alliance Atlantis Communications, Serendipity Point Films, *p* Robert Lantos, Andras Hamori, David Cronenberg, *d/sc* David Cronenberg, *ph* Peter Suschitzky, *ed* Ronald Sanders, *mus* Howard Shore; *with* Jennifer Jason Leigh, Jude Law, Ian Holm, Willem Dafoe, Christopher Eccleston, Don McKellar, Sarah Polley. *eXistenZ*, David Cronenberg's* follow-up to the austere, provocative *Crash*,* is like a 1940s screwball comedy crossed with a hilariously icky fever dream. The principals in Cronenberg's slap-happiest movie are the brilliant virtual-reality game designer Allegra Geller (Jason Leigh) and the security agent Ted Pikul (Law). After an assassination attempt on Geller with a gun that fires human teeth, the couple hits the road. Despite his typically screwball male inhibitions, Ted gets sucked into Allegra's game, a virtual-reality adventure undulating with erotic subtext and peculiar life forms. In a woodland Chinese restaurant, the 'special' is a slithering mess the waiter recommends because 'mutant reptiles and amphibians produce previously unknown taste sensations.' (V) **Awards include:** GA: Editing.

Exotica

1994 102m *prod* Ego Film Arts, *p* Atom Egoyan, Camelia Frieberg, *d/sc* Atom Egoyan, *ph* Paul Sarossy, *ed* Susan Shipton, *mus* Mychael Danna; *with* Bruce Greenwood, Mia Kirshner, Don McKellar, Arsinée Khanjian, Elias Koteas, Sarah Polley. The most complex of the many interconnected relationships in this film is between a thirty-something tax auditor (Greenwood*), who is a regular patron of Exotica, and the table dancer whom he always requests. Kirshner, a very convincing Lolita who is in fact not too many years past her own minority, invariably starts out her routine dressed as a schoolgirl. Their relationship is intensely ritualized and it is only with the film's gradual unravelling that we fully understand its hidden meaning. Atom Egoyan's* box-office breakthrough, *Exotica* is a film that displays a faith in cinema as a vehicle for provocation and intellectual complexity. He creates a dreamy atmosphere that reflects the partial, fragmented way the characters' pasts are uncovered, bit by eloquent bit. (V) **Awards include:** GA: Picture, Director, Original Screenplay, Supporting Actor (McKellar), Art Direction, Costumes, Cinematography, Musical Score; Cannes: International Film Critics' Prize.

Experimental Film

It seems paradoxical and strangely typi-

cal that Canada's internationally renowned avant-garde cinema can trace
its origins to, of all places, the Canadian
government. As with most things cinematic in Canada, experimental film began at the NFB, where it was unwit-
tingly nurtured by the very man whose
approach to filmmaking would later fuel
the experimentalists' rebellion – John
Grierson.* When Grierson hired Norman McLaren,* he had no idea that this
quiet animator would help to inspire a
movement that radically opposed the
empirical principles of the documentary.
Working with the cinematic medium in
entirely new ways, playfully and profoundly foregrounding the artifices of
his own image-making, McLaren deto-
nated the perceptual frameworks of the
institution that employed him, and in
the process, he expanded the possibilities of Canadian cinematic expression.
This pursuit of possibilities remains the
chief characteristic of that other essential
Canadian filmmaking tradition – the experimental film.

Rooted in early European avant-garde
movements and influenced by the
American avant-garde cinema of the
1940s and 1950s, experimental filmmaking in Canada began to emerge fully
in the 1960s. Although some experimental work continued to be produced inside the NFB by McLaren, Arthur Lipsett,* and others, the most significant
avant-garde filmmaking took place beyond the NFB. Concentrated primarily,
but not exclusively in Toronto and Vancouver, experimental filmmaking flourished within the independent film
scenes, on university campuses, and in
the burgeoning visual arts community.
During the 1960s, Canadian experimental film rose to international prominence
and critical acclaim with the groundbreaking works of Michael Snow*
(*Wavelength,** 1967), Joyce Wieland*

(*Rat Life and Diet in North America,**
1968), and Jack Chambers* (*The Hart of
London,** 1970).

The tradition gathered formal and
philosophical momentum in the 1970s
and 1980s with the films of Bruce Elder,*
David Rimmer,* Ellie Epp, Al Razutis,*
Chris Gallagher, Vincent Grenier, Peter
Mettler,* Barbara Sternberg,* and others.
In addition to the continuing work of
these directors, Sheridan College in
Oakville, Ontario, gave rise to the 'Niagara Escarpment school.' Rick Hancox,*
Richard Kerr,* Philip Hoffman,* Mike
Hoolboom,* Gary Popovich, and Steve
Sanguedolce produced highly personal,
autobiographical work while maintaining the structuralist, experimental
tradition. In the 1990s experimental
filmmaking, always restless and incor-
porating new image-making media into
its open-ended forms, continued to offer
startling, influential work. Just as the
documentary tradition once dominated
the structures of fiction in Canadian cinema, now formal and philosophical investigations, once the exclusive preserve
of the experimental film, are increasingly evident in recent Canadian narrative feature filmmaking.

In under four decades, the elusive,
protean experimental film tradition has
yielded a vast, complex, vital body of
work essential to our understanding of
Canadian cinema. Then and now, experimental film contests the assump-
tions of narrative cinema, the empirical
claims of the documentary, and the va-
lidity of its own complex processes of
image-making. The experimental accu-
sation, boldly and often breathtakingly
rendered, contends that audiences must
challenge their very ways of seeing.
Evolving in a creative dialectic with the
documentary (in spite of Grierson, or
because of him), the rich and vibrant
Canadian experimental film tradition

continues to both construct and detonate images in order to investigate what is present and, perhaps, illuminate what is absent.

F

Falardeau, Pierre

Director and writer; b. Montreal, 1946. Falardeau is one of Quebec's most politically involved filmmakers. Along with actor Julien Poulin, he created a series of political videos in the 1970s on the general theme of anti-oppression. In 1981, the team made the jump to fiction with the short *Elvis Gratton*, starring Poulin as a most unflattering parody of the culturally oppressed Quebecker. They made two more shorts, and then compiled the three into a feature-length video. The success of the video put the duo in the limelight and encouraged them to make a follow-up feature, *Elvis Gratton: Miracle à Memphis*, in 1999. Falardeau has also made two politically charged features, *Le Party* and *Octobre.** **Films and video include:** *Les Canadiens sont là* 1973; *À force de courage* 1976; *Pea Soup* 1978; *Speak White* 1980; *Elvis Gratton* 1981 (GA-LAS, short version); *Les Vacances d'Elvis Gratton* 1983; *Pas encore Elvis Gratton!* 1985; *Elvis Gratton* 1985 (long version); *Le Party* 1989; *Le Temps des bouffons* 1993; *Octobre* 1994; *Elvis Gratton: Miracle à Memphis* 1999.

Falls, The

1991 90m *prod* Primitive Features, *exp* George Flak, Clare Odgers, *p* Michael McMahon, Brian Dennis, *d/sc* Kevin McMahon, *ph* Douglas Koch, *ed* Michael McMahon, *mus* Kurt Swinghammer. This ambitious and brilliantly realized documentary sets out to capture the terrible beauty of Niagara Falls, the crass industries that have risen up around the Falls, and the odd obsessions of people drawn to them. A man matter-of-factly recalls the fools he has seen tumble over the Falls to their deaths, and a Love Canal mother speaks with cold rage about the birth defects visited upon the children born near that chemical cesspool. The film also recreates the feelings of wonder and dread that must have filled the first Europeans who looked upon the Falls. McMahon keeps the film funny when it should be and absurd when it must be. (V)

Family Viewing

1987 86m *prod* Ego Film Arts, *p/d/sc* Atom Egoyan, *ph* Robert MacDonald, *ed* Atom Egoyan, Bruce McDonald, *mus* Mychael Danna; *with* David Hemblen, Aidan Tierney, Gabrielle Rose, Arsinée Khanjian, Selma Keklikian, Jeanne Sabourin. Atom Egoyan's* second feature centres around a malcontented youth (Tierney) who lives with his father (Hemblen) in a high-tech, sterile apartment. The young man is drawn to his dying grandmother (Keklikian) who lies unhappily in a hospital bed. There he finds friendship with the daughter (Khanjian*) of his grandmother's roommate, who works in a phone-sex establishment and occasionally as a prostitute. The two scheme to get the grandmother out of the hospital and into their care. This complex and allusive film uses video images (TVs, monitors, home video) as an ironic counterpoint to a family that can't connect in real life. It established Egoyan as a major director but it is curiously lifeless and let down by performances that are never fully realized. (V)

Famine Within, The

1990 90m *prod* Direct Cinema Limited, *p/d/sc/narr* Katherine Gilday, *ph* Joan Hutton, *ed* Petra Valier. A meticulous, well-researched documentary that analyses the contemporary problem of North American women's self-image. Mostly composed of talking heads, *The Famine Within* nevertheless manages to hold together remarkably well. The film presents the case that the modern image of the tall, rail-thin supermodel runs counter to nature and biology, and that women are tyrannized by cultural ideals of beauty imposed upon them by patriarchy and the diet industry, to the point where one painfully thin young women (who speaks for many) says, 'I'd rather be dead than fat.' An important, insightful film. **Awards include:** GA: Feature Documentary.

Far Shore, The

1976 105m *prod* Far Shore Inc., *exp* Pierre Lamy, *p* Judy Steed, Joyce Wieland, *d* Joyce Wieland, *sc* Bryan Barney, *ph* Richard Leiterman, *ed* George Appleby, Brian French, *mus* Douglas Pringle; *with* Céline Lomez, Frank Moore, Lawrence Benedict, Sean McCann, Susan Petrie. A critical and box-office failure, *The Far Shore* is nevertheless an important compendium of Joyce Wieland's* major thematic concerns: Wieland was an early feminist, and she was also an ardent nationalist and environmentalist. Eulalie (Lomez), a young French-Canadian woman, marries a wealthy industrialist who turns out to be a brute in more ways than one. She seeks solace with a more sensitive soul, a painter named Tom (Moore), and runs away with him to the backwoods of the Canadian north. Visually, the film is a treat, thanks to Richard Leiterman's* luscious imagery and Wieland's nod to the work of the Group of Seven. Although she was unable to escape the trappings of strained melodrama, she nevertheless manages to construct a moving portrait of courage and conviction. **Awards include:**

CFA: Supporting Actor (Moore), Cinematography, Art Direction.

Felicia's Journey

1999 116 *prod* Alliance Atlantis Pictures, Icon Productions (U.K.), *exp* Paul Tucker, Ralph Kamp, *p* Bruce Davey, *d/sc* Atom Egoyan, *novel* William Trevor, *ph* Paul Sarossy, *ed* Susan Shipton, *mus* Mychael Danna; *with* Bob Hoskins, Elaine Cassidy, Arsinée Khanjian, Peter McDonald, Claire Benedict. Egoyan's* adaptation of William Trevor's novel is one of the filmmaker's most accessible works to date. A pregnant Irish teenager, Felicia (Cassidy) travels to England in search of her boyfriend. By chance, she meets an executive chef named Hilditch (chillingly played by Hoskins) and the story of how she became pregnant soon emerges. Hilditch offers her shelter in the childhood home he shared with his mother Gala (Khanjian,* seen in poignant flashbacks). Felicia has no idea that this 'nice little man' is actually filled with demons that have taken their toll on other young women he has 'helped.' Egoyan departs from his usual emotionally overwrought, ensemble films for a more suspenseful, personable drama. With a touch of Hitchcock, he offers an intimate look at two desperate people while leaving the viewer on edge throughout the proceedings. (V) **Awards include:** GA: Adapted Screenplay, Actor (Hoskins), Cinematography, Musical Score.

Femme de l'hôtel, La

1984 89m *prod* ACPAV, *p* Bernadette Payeur, *d* Léa Pool, *sc* Léa Pool, Michel Langlois, Robert Gurik, *ph* Georges Dufaux, *ed* Michel Arcand, *mus* Yves Laferrière; *with* Louise Marleau, Paule Baillargeon, Marthe Turgeon, Serge Dupire. Swiss-born director Léa Pool's* debut feature, set in a Montreal hotel during the making of a film, is an authoritative investigation of identity, solitude, and the role of fiction in understanding experience. Andrea (Baillargeon*), a film director who is struggling against writer's block, becomes obsessed with Estelle (Marleau), a woman she meets at the hotel. Increasingly, Estelle's own troubled life informs Andrea's fictional character and the actor who is to portray her. Despite occasional lapses into the ossified excesses of European art-house cinema, Pool carefully controls her memorable modernist tale of female alienation and spiritual desolation. In the film Montreal is identified as 'an island that doesn't feel like an island.' As Pool once described it, *La Femme de l'hotel* is a fascinating drama about 'rootlessness, not belonging, and internal exile.' **Awards include:** GA: Actress (Marleau), Song.

Feore, Colm

Actor; b. Boston, Mass., 1959. Feore attended the National Theatre School in Montreal and began working at Stratford Festival in 1983; he appeared in over forty productions, along with a stint as director. In 1993, during the run of *Romeo and Juliet*, he was approached to play the lead role in François Girard's* critically acclaimed *Thirty-Two Short Films about Glenn Gould.** Feore now divides his time between Canadian and American film productions such as *Face/Off*, *The Red Violin,** *City of Angels*, and *The Insider*. Most recently, he played Marcus in Julie Taymor's film adaptation of *Titus Andronicus*, opposite Anthony Hopkins' Titus. **Films and television include:** *The Boys from Syracuse* 1986 (TV); *A Nest of Singing Birds* 1987 (TV); *The Taming of the Shrew* 1988 (TV); *Iron Eagle* ii 1988; *Bethune: The Making of a Hero* 1990; *Beautiful Dreamers* 1990; *Romeo and Juliet* 1993 (TV); *Thirty-Two Short Films about Glenn Gould* 1994

(as Gould); *The Champagne Safari* 1995 (narr); *Truman* 1995 (TV); *The Boor* 1996; *Liberty! The American Revolution* 1997 (TV); *The Escape* 1997 (TV); *Face/Off* 1997; *The Herd* 1998; *The Red Violin* 1998; *The Lesser Evil* 1998; *Airborne* 1998; *The Wrong Guy* 1998; *Creature* 1998 (TV); *City of Angels* 1998; *Titus* 1999; *The Insider* 1999; *Forget Me Never* 1999 (TV); *Striking Poses* 1999; *Storm of the Century* 1999 (TV); *Nuremberg* 2000 (TV); *The Virginian* 2000 (TV); *The Caveman's Valentine* 2001.

Ferguson, Graeme

Cinematographer, director, and producer; b. Toronto, 1929. Ferguson, the co-founder and former president of Imax Corporation, found his calling doing summer jobs at the NFB while he was a political science student at the University of Toronto. In the late 1950s, he moved to New York to work on such films as the Academy Award–nominated *Rooftops of New York*. Returning to Canada for Expo 67, Ferguson designed and directed *Polar Life*, a multi-screen installation that was one of the fair's biggest hits. The success of that film led to Ferguson's creation of the IMAX system of projection in 1968 with Roman Kroitor* and Robert Kerr. His *North of Superior** defined the IMAX style: breathtaking scenes of nature captured in a swooping, epic manner. **Films include:** *Rooftops of New York* 1960 (ph); *The Legend of Rudolph Valentino* 1963 (p/d/co-sc); *The Love Goddesses* 1965 (co-p/d/co-sc); *Polar Life* 1967 (co-p/d/ph); *North of Superior* 1971 (co-p/d/ph/ed); *Snow Job* 1974 (p/d); *Man Belongs to Earth* 1974 (co-p/d); *Ocean* 1977 (p/d); *Hail Columbia!* 1982 (co-p/d/ph); *The Dream Is Alive* 1985 (p/d); *Blue Planet* 1991 (p); *Destiny in Space* 1994 (p); *Into the Deep* 1994 (p).

Fight: Science against Cancer, The

1951 21m *prod* NFB, *p* Guy Glover, *d* Morten Parker, *ph* Grant McLean, ed Douglas Tunstell, *an* Evelyn Lambart, Colin Low, *mus* Louis Applebaum. This important documentary from the NFB received wide distribution in both Canada and the United States. It traces, by means of greatly magnified sequences brilliantly animated by Colin Low* and Evelyn Lambart,* the growth and multiplication of a single fertilized cell into an adult man, and asks why, after the body has reached maturity, some outlaw cells begin a persistent and subversive growth of their own. The animation techniques developed by Low and Lambart were later used in *Universe.* * (V) **Awards include:** CFA: Special Award; AAN: Short Documentary.

Filiatrault, Denise

Actor, director, and writer; b. Montreal, 1931. Filiatrault was made famous by her role in one of Quebec television's funniest series ever, *Moi et l'autre*, but her creative talents show considerable virtuosity. From her comic beginnings, she moved into drama, fashioning an explosive screen presence in numerous films, including *La Mort d'un bûcheron*, *Les Beaux dimanches*, *Les Plouffe** (as Cécile Plouffe, a spinster tortured by an impossible love, for which she won a Genie), and *Le Crime d'Ovide Plouffe*. As a director, Filiatrault made her debut with *C't'à ton tour Laura Cadieux*, a popular screen adaptation of Michel Tremblay's novel, which she followed in 1999 with *Laura Cadieux ... la suite*. **Films and television include:** *Moi et l'autre* 1966 (series); *Le P'tit vient vite* 1972 (TV); *La Mort d'un bûcheron* 1973; *Il était une fois dans l'est* 1973; *Les Beaux Dimanches* 1974; *Par le sang des autres* 1974; *Le Plumard en folie* 1974; *Gina* 1975; *Mado* 1976; *Le Soleil se lève en retard* 1976; *Chez Denise* 1977 (series); *Au revoir ... à lundi* 1979; *Fantastica* 1980; *Les Plouffe* 1981 (GA-SA); *Le Crime d'Ovide Plouffe* 1984; *L'Adolescente sucre d'amour* 1985; *Blue la magnifique*

1989 (TV); *Imogène: les légumes maudits* 1991 (TV); *Nelligan* 1991; *Alisée* 1991; *Denise ... aujourd'hui* 1991 (series); *Au nom du père et du fils* 1993 (series); *Moi et l'autre* 1995 (series); *C't'à ton tour Laura Cadieux* 1998 (d/sc); *Laura Cadieux ... la suite* 1999 (d/sc).

Final Offer: Bob White and the Canadian Auto Workers Fight for Independence

1985 79m *prod* NFB, CBC, *exp* John Spotton, *p* John Kramer, Sturla Gunnarsson, Robert Collison, *d* Sturla Gunnarsson, Robert Collison, *sc* Robert Collison, *ph* Len Gilday, *ed* Jeff Warren, *mus* Jack Lenz, *narr* Henry Ramer. With unfettered access, the filmmakers provide a fly-on-wall observational view of the dramatic 1984 contract negotiations between the United Auto Workers and General Motors. As a result of tensions that developed between the Canadian and American sections of the union, Bob White, the charismatic head of the Canadian sector, pulled his members out of the international union and formed his own. The film is a primer for anyone interested in the complexities of Canada / U.S. relations, and it provides a remarkable portrait of revolutionary events. (V) **Awards include:** GA: Feature Documentary.

First Winter

1981 27m *prod* NFB, *exp* Roman Kroitor, *p* John N. Smith, Sam Grana, *d* John N. Smith, *sc* Gloria Demers, *ph* David de Volpi, *ed* Richard Todd, *mus* Tadhg de Brun. A historical drama about the first winter spent in Canada by a family of Irish settlers in 1830. After the father leaves for the logging camps, the mother falls ill and dies, leaving the children to cope by themselves. This moving film about the struggle to survive enormous hardships and a deadly climate received an Academy Award nomination for Live-Action Short. (V)

Five Senses, The
1999 106n *prod* Five Senses Productions, *exp* Charlotte Mickie, Ted East, David Ginsburg, *p* Camelia Frieberg, Jeremy Podeswa, *d/sc* Jeremy Podeswa, *ph* Gregory Middleton, *ed* Wiebke Von Carolsfeld, *mus* Alexina Louie, Alex Pauk; *with* Mary-Louise Parker, Pascale Bussières, Brendan Fletcher, Marco Leonardi, Nadia Litz, Daniel MacIvor, Molly Parker, Gabrielle Rose, Philippe Volter. *The Five Senses* follows the interconnected lives of five characters – each of whom has a particular relation to one of the human senses – and is structured around the search for a lost child. The film develops into five-part harmony as the collective stories evoke the age-old quest for love and the barriers that prevent its realization. Eschewing the traditional happy ending guaranteed by Hollywood romances, director Jeremy Podeswa* creates a rich and ultimately moving chronicle of our universal longing for a connection with someone, anyone. However, the film's art-house pretentions only served to restrict its box-office appeal. (V) **Awards include:** GA: Director.

Flamenco at 5:15
1984 29m *prod* NFB, *exp* Adam Symansky, Kathleen Shannon, *p* Cynthia Scott, Adam Symansky, *d* Cynthia Scott, *ph* Paul Cowan, *ed* Paul Demers, Cynthia Scott, *mus* Antonio Robledo. This documentary from the NFB's Studio D presents a record of senior students at the National Ballet School of Canada as they are taught the ancient art of flamenco by two great Spanish teachers: Susana and Antonio Robledo. The film captures beautiful young dancers as they learn the passion and mythic power of the dance, inspired by the extraordinary energy of Susana. (V) **Awards include:** AA: Short Documentary.

Florida, La
1993 111m *prod* Pierre Sarrazin Productions, Les Films Vision 4, *exp* Claude Bonin, Jacques Bonin, Pierre Sarrazin, Suzette Couture, *p* Pierre Sarrazin, Claude Bonin, *d* George Mihalka, *sc* Pierre Sarrazin, Suzette Couture, *ph* René Ohashi, *ed* François Guill, Yves Chaput, *mus* Milan Kymlicka; *with* Rémy Girard, Pauline Lapointe, Marie-Josée Croze, Guillaume Lemay-Thivièrge, Raymond Bouchard, Micheal Sarrazin, Margot Kidder. *La Florida* is a satirical comedy that blends the American dream – financial independence – with the Québécois dream – a life of sunny luxury in Florida. Léo (Girard*), a retired bus driver, moves his family to Hollywood Beach, where he has purchased a ramshackle motel with his life savings. At first things seem to go well, but soon Léo is being hustled by local land speculators while his wife (Papointe) develops a romantic attachment to a has-been lounge singer (Sarrazin*). However, after several bad turns, things eventually work out for *la famille*. This film was very popular in Quebec, and the opening sequence, with the family packing up to leave during a Montreal blizzard, is one of the most resonant in Canadian cinema. **Awards include:** Golden Reel Award.

Flowers on a One-Way Street
1967 57m *prod* NFB, *p* Joseph Koenig, *d/sc* Robin Spry, *ph* Douglas Keifer, *ed* Christopher Cordeau, *mus* Ravi Shankar. Robin Spry's* first major film is one of the best documentaries from the 1960s to cover that brief moment in time when the hippy revolution was in full flower and hopes ran high. The hippies wanted to close down Yorkville Avenue in Toronto to car traffic, while the powers that be – police and politicans – wanted them off the street. The resulting conflict

was played out on the street and in the council chambers of Toronto's City Hall. The film shoot became the centre of controversy when police accused the filmmakers of encouraging street demonstrations, and the NFB brass in Montreal got very nervous. (V)

Forbidden Love: The Unashamed Stories of Lesbian Lives

1993 85m *prod* NFB, *exp* Rena Fraticelli, *p* Margaret Pettigrew, Ginny Stikeman, *d/sc* Aerlyn Weissman, Lynne Fernie, *ph* Zoe Dirse, *ed* Cathy Gulkin, Denise Beaudoin, *mus* Kathryn Moses; *with* Stephanie Morganstern, Lynne Adams, Marie-Jo Therio, George Thomas. A rich and rewarding look at the lesbian subculture of the 1950s and 1960s as expressed through the lurid and often amusing pulp novels of the period. Books such as *Women of Evil, Man Hater,* and *Lesbians in Black Lace* are seen as key to the development of lesbian consciousness in the 1950s, historical markers of the undocumented history of lesbian lives. A variety of women aged forty to seventy are interviewed and talk candidly about coming out, while actors (Morganstern and Adams) act out fictional scenes of lesbian desire. (V) **Awards include:** GA: Feature Documentary.

Forcier, André

Director and writer; b. Montreal, 1947. The vitality of the Quebec film scene depends on regular booster shots from a certifiable *enfant terrible*. Forcier, the *eminence grise* of iconoclasts, has been making loopy, disrespectful human comedies for nearly thirty years. A typical Forcier picture is a topsy-turvy mix of harsh realism and goofy fantasy, a poverty-stricken, intoxicating world of bars, rooming houses and boxing gyms. His portraits of people on the fringes include *Bar salon,** *Au clair de la lune** (in which a dreamy albino bum takes a walk in the sky), and *Une Histoire inventée* (in which a lusty actress is followed through the streets by forty adoring lovers). In *Le Vent du Wyoming,* Forcier celebrates cabaret acts, somnambulism, and boxing; like all his work, it is poetic and absurd. **Films include:** *Le Retour de l'Immaculée Conception* 1971 (d); *Night Cap* 1974 (d/sc); *Bar salon* 1975 (d/co-sc); *L'Eau chaude, l'eau frette* 1976 (d/co-sc); *Au clair de la lune* 1983 (d/co-sc); *Kalamazoo* 1988 (d/co-sc); *Une Histoire inventée* 1990 (d/co-sc); *Le Vent du Wyoming* 1994 (d/co-sc); *La Comtesse de Baton Rouge* 1997 (d/sc).

Ford, Glenn

Actor; b. Gwyllyn Samuel Newton, Quebec City, 1916. This unprepossessing figure with a crew cut and a shy grin was a Hollywood leading man for forty years, starring in more than eighty films. His credits range from Fritz Lang's classic film noir thriller *The Big Heat* to the relaxed comedy of Daniel Mann's *The Teahouse of the August Moon* opposite Marlon Brando. Ford specialized in well-meaning, ordinary men, who were tough when the chips were down. He made his name in *Gilda*, opposite Rita Hayworth, and is best remembered for his charming / tough roles in Richard Brooks's *The Blackboard Jungle*, Frank Capra's *A Pocketful of Miracles*, and Vincent Minnelli's *The Courtship of Eddie's Father*. **Films include:** *Adventures of Martin Eden* 1942; *Gilda* 1946; *The Loves of Carmen* 1948; *Lust for Gold* 1949; *Convicted* 1950; *Affair in Trinidad* 1952; *The Big Heat* 1953; *Human Desire* 1954; *Blackboard Jungle* 1955; *The Fastest Gun Alive* 1956; *The Teahouse of the August Moon* 1956; *3:10 to Yuma* 1957; *Cowboy* 1958; *The Gazebo* 1960; *A Pocketful of Miracles* 1961; *The Four Horsemen of the Apocalypse*

1962; *The Courtship of Eddie's Father* 1963; *Fate Is the Hunter* 1964; *Is Paris Burning?* 1966; *Smith* 1969; *Battle of Midway* 1976; *Superman* 1978; *Happy Birthday to Me* 1980.

Forteresse, La

See *Whispering City / La Forteresse*

For the Record

1976–84 series *prod* CBC. The series *For the Record* presented the most consistently high-quality journalistic dramas ever produced by CBC-TV. These films stand collectively as a remarkable body of work created by a number of Canada's best filmmakers. Directors were drawn from the private sector and individual shows were intensely controversial; for example, Peter Pearson's *Tar Sands*, starring Kenneth Welsh,* resulted in a public feud and a lawsuit launched by the premier of Alberta. **Films:** *The Insurance Man from Ingersoll* 1976 (d Peter Pearson); *Nest of Shadows* 1976 (d Peter Pearson); *A Thousand Moons* 1976 (d Gilles Carle); *Kathy Karbuks Is a Grizzly Bear* 1976 (d Peter Pearson); *What We Have Here Is a People Problem* 1976 (d Francis Mankewicz); *Maria* 1977 (d Allan King); *Someday Soon* 1977 (d Don Haldane); *Dreamspeaker* 1977 (d Claude Jutra); *Hank* 1977 (d Don Haldane); *Ada* 1977 (d Claude Jutra); *The Tar Sands* 1977 (d Peter Pearson); *A Matter of Choice* 1978 (d Francis Mankewicz); *Scoop* 1978 (d Anthony Perris); *Dying Hard* 1978 (d Don Haldane); *Seer Was Here* 1978 (d Claude Jutra); *Cementhead* 1979 (d Ralph L. Thomas); *Don't Forget 'Je me souviens'* 1979 (d Robin Spry); *Homecoming* 1979 (d Gilles Carle); *Certain Practices* 1979 (d Martin Lavut); *Every Person Is Guilty* 1979 (d Paul Almond); *One of Our Own* 1979 (d William Fruet); *The Winnings of Frankie Walls* 1980 (Martin Lavut); *Harvest* 1980 (d Giles Walker); *Maintain the Right* 1980 (d Les Rose); *A Question of the Sixth* 1980 (d Graham Parker); *Lyon's Den* 1980 (d Graham Parker); *A Far Cry from Home* 1981 (d Gordon Pinsent); *Snowbirds* 1981 (d Peter Pearson); *Running Man* 1981 (d Donald Brittain); *Cop* 1981 (d Al Waxman); *The Final Edition* 1981 (d Peter Rowe); *An Honourable Member* 1982 (d Donald Brittain); *By Reason of Insanity* 1982 (d Donald Shebib); *High Card* 1982 (d Bill Gough); *Becoming Laura* 1982 (d Martin Lavut); *Blind Faith* 1982 (d John Trent); *Ready for Slaughter* 1983 (d Allan King); *Out of Sight, Out of Mind* 1983 (d Zale Dalen); *Reasonable Force* 1983 (d Peter Rowe); *Moving Targets* 1983 (d John Trent); *Kate Morris, Vice-President* 1984 (d Danièle Suissa); *I Love a Man in Uniform* 1984 (d Don McBrearty); *Slim Obsession* 1984 (d Donald Shebib); *Hide and Seek* 1984 (d René Bonnière); *Rough Justice* 1984 (d Peter Yalken-Thomson); *Change of Heart* 1984 (Anne Wheeler).

Fortune and Men's Eyes

1971 102m *prod* Cinemex, *p* Lester Persky, Lewis Allen, *d* Harvey Hart, *sc/play* John Herbert, *ph* Georges Dufaux, *ed* Douglas Robertson, *mus* Galt Mac-Dermot; *with* Wendell Burton, Michael Greer, Zooey Hall, Danny Freedman. Based on the play by John Herbert, who also wrote the script. *Fortune and Men's Eyes* is the story of Smitty (Burton), a naive young boy, who is placed in prison with hardened criminals for a minor crime. He is brutalized and raped nightly by a fellow cell mate Rocky (Hall). When Smitty finally stands up to Rocky and beats him in a fist fight, he becomes emboldened and in turn brutalizes a new cell mate (Freedman). The play is a denunciation of a harsh system that victimized young offenders, but the film sensationalizes the material and leaves an unpleasant taste. **Awards include:**

CFA: Supporting Actor (Freedman), Editing.

Fournier, Claude
Director, writer, cinematographer, and editor; b. Waterloo, Que., 1931. Fournier began his career in journalism, then moved to Radio-Canada as a news cameraman. He joined the NFB in 1956 as a writer and director, and worked on early direct-cinema films such as *La Lutte** with Michel Brault* and Claude Jutra.* He left the Board to work in the United States with famed documentary filmmakers Richard Leacock and D.A. Pennebaker, then returned to Montreal in 1963 to set up his own company. In 1970, he directed *Deux femmes en or* – one of a group of films known as 'maple-syrup porn,' and one of the most successful Québécois films of its time. Fournier has continued his career in Quebec in both film and television, and he is one of the most durable filmmakers of his generation. **Films and television include:** *La Lutte* 1961 (co-d/co-ph/co-ed); *À Saint-Henri le cinq septembre* 1962 (co-ph); *Le Dossier Nelligan* 1969 (d/sc/co-ph/ed); *Deux Femmes en or* 1970 (d/co-sc/ph/ed); *Les Chats bottés* 1971 (d/co-sc/ph/ed); *La Pomme, la queue ... et les pépins!* 1974 (d/co-sc/ph/ed); *Alien Thunder* 1974 (d/ph); *Je suis loin de toi mignonne* 1976 (d/co-sc/ph/ed); *La Notte dell'alta marea* 1977 (co-sc); *The Newcomers* 1977 (co-d, series); *A Special Day* 1977 (co-sc); *Hot Dogs* 1980 (d/co-sc/ph/co-ed); *Jack London's Tales of the Klondike* 1981 (co-d, series); *Bonheur d'occasion* 1983 (d/co-sc); *The Tin Flute* 1983 (d/co-sc/ph); *Les Tisserands du pouvoir* 1988 (d); *Les Tisserands du pouvoir II: La Révolte* 1988 (d); *Golden Fiddles* 1990 (d, series); *J'en suis!* 1997 (d/sc).

Fox, Michael J.
Actor; b. Edmonton, 1961. After appearing in Disney's first PG-rated film, *Midnight Madness*, Fox was cast as the irrepressible yuppie-in-training in the highly successful television sitcom *Family Ties*, for which he won three consecutive Emmys. He transferred easily to film when he was asked to replace Eric Stoltz in Robert Zemeckis's *Back to the Future* and its two sequels. Fox's attempts at serious drama, such as *Casualties of War* and *Bright Lights, Big City*, didn't meet with equal success, and he wisely chose to stay with the light comedy of *The Hard Way* and *The American President*. In 2000, Parkinson's disease forced him to leave his top-rated television series *Spin City*. **Films and television include:** *Midnight Madness* 1980; *Family Ties* 1982–9 (series); *Back to the Future* 1985; *Teen Wolf* 1985; *Light of Day* 1987; *Bright Lights, Big City* 1988; *Back to the Future II* 1989; *Casualties of War* 1989; *Back to the Future III* 1990; *The Hard Way* 1991; *Doc Hollywood* 1991; *For Love or Money* 1993; *Homeward Bound: The Incredible Journey* 1993 (voice); *Blue in the Face* 1995; *The American President* 1995; *The Frighteners* 1996; *Mars Attacks!* 1996; *Spin City* 1996–2000 (series); *Stuart Little* 1999 (voice of Stuart).

Frappier, Roger
Producer and director; b. St-Joseph-de-Sorel, Que., 1945. Frappier worked in all areas of the film business from critic to television commercial director until he found his true vocation as a hands-on producer. While at the NFB in the early 1980s, he assembled a group of writer-directors who collaborated on developing edgy, urban dramas. The script for Denys Arcand's *Le Déclin de l'empire américain** emerged from the process that Frappier had set in motion. With that film's phenomenal success, Frappier rose to the ranks of the top producers of feature films in Quebec. His

many other films include Yves Simoneau's *Pouvoir intime*,* Arcand's *Jésus de Montréal*,* and Jean-Claude Lauzon's *Un Zoo la nuit*.* In 1999, he was awarded the Albert-Tessier Award for exceptional achievement in the Quebec film industry. **Films include:** *Le Grand Film ordinaire* 1970 (p/d); *Gaston Mir* 1971 (d/ ed); *Faut aller parmi l'monde pour le savoir* 1971 (ed); *Réjeanne Padovani* 1973 (a); *On a raison de se révolter* 1974 (co-p); *L'Infonie inachevée ...* 1974 (d/ed); *Le Ventre de la nuit* 1977 (co-d); *Kouchibouguac* 1977 (p); *Primera pregunta sobre la felicidad* 1978 (co-p); *La Loi de la ville* 1979 (p); *La Fiction nucléaire* 1979 (p); *De la rourbe et du restant* 1980 (p); *Cordélia* 1980 (co-p); *Le Confort et l'indifférence* 1982 (co-p); *Le Dernier Glacier* 1984 (d with Jacques Leduc); *Le Déclin de l'empire américain* 1986 (p with René Malo, GA-P, GRA, AAN-FLF); *Pouvoir intime* 1986 (co-p); *Anne Trister* 1986 (co-p); *Un Zoo la nuit* 1987 (co-p, GA-P); *Jésus de Montréal* 1989 (co-p, GA-P, GRA, AAN-FLF); *Ding et Dong, le film* 1990 (p, GRA); *The Dark Side of the Heart* 1992 (co-p); *La Vie fantôme* 1992 (p); *Love and Human Remains* 1994 (co-p); *L'Enfant d'eau* 1995 (co-p); *Sous-sol* 1996 (p); *Cosmos* 1997 (p); *La Comtesse de Baton Rouge* 1997 (p); *Un 32 août sur terre* 1998 (p); *2 secondes* 1998 (p); *Le Onzième* 1998 (co-p); *Matroni et moi* 1999 (p); *La Vie après l'amour* 2000 (co-p); *Maelström* 2000 (co-p, GA-P).

Frenchkiss: La Génération du rêve Trudeau
See *Just Watch Me: Trudeau and the '70s Generation*

Frieberg, Camelia
Producer; b. Toronto, 1959. Frieberg attended school in Vermont and began her career as a freelance journalist. Her infatuation with film came when she covered the Toronto International Film Festival and then left for a stint in Los

Angeles. After several false starts on low-budget projects, she found her footing with emerging members of the Toronto new wave.* She became a key producing partner with Atom Egoyan,* and won two Best Picture Genies. **Films include:** *The Adjuster* 1991 (p with Atom Egoyan); *Masala* 1992 (co-p); *Eclipse* 1994 (p with Jeremy Podeswa); *Exotica* 1994 (p with Egoyan, GA-P); *The Sweet Hereafter* 1997 (p with Egoyan, GA-P); *The Fishing Trip* 1998 (exp); *The Five Senses* 1999 (p with Podeswa).

Fruet, William
Director and writer; b. Lethbridge, Alta., 1933. Fruet attended the National Theatre School of Canada and acted in *Drylanders*,* the first NFB dramatic feature. He was prominent player on the English-Canadian film scene in the 1970s, writing films such as *Goin' down the Road*,* *Rip-Off*,* and *Slipstream*.* His directorial debut, *Wedding in White*,* won a Canadian Film Award for Best Picture in 1972 and is still considered a classic of the period. In a disappointing career move, Fruet went on to make several slice-an-dice films during the tax-shelter era,* including *Search and Destroy* and *Spasms*. Since the mid-1980s he has directed exclusively for television. **Films and television include:** *Drylanders* 1963 (a); *Goin' down the Road* 1970 (sc); *Rip-Off* 1971 (sc); *Wedding in White* 1972 (d/sc, CFA-FF); *Slipstream* 1973 (sc); *125 Rooms of Comfort* 1974 (co-sc); *Death Weekend* 1976 (d/sc); *One of Our Own* 1979 (d, TV); *Search and Destroy* 1979 (d); *Cries in the Night* 1980 (d); *Baker County, U.S.A.* 1982 (d); *Trapped* 1982 (d); *Spasms* 1983 (d/sc); *Bedroom Eyes* 1984 (d) *Brothers by Choice* 1986 (d, TV); *Killer Party* 1986 (d); *Chasing Rainbows* 1988 (d, series).

Furey, Lewis
Composer, director, and actor; b. Lewis Greenblatt, Montreal, 1949. Furey was a

classical violinist before he turned to the Euro-pop, art-cabaret music that led him first to film composing, and then to acting and directing. As a composer, his slippery rhythms and witty harmonies spiced up pictures by Gilles Carle* and other moviemakers. In 1985, after acting opposite Carole Laure* in Carle's *L'Ange et la femme*, and falling in love with her, Furey directed *Night Magic*, a musical fantasy he scripted with Leonard Cohen. The picture, which starred Laure, didn't win over many fans, but this didn't stop Furey from pursuing a career as a feature film and straight-to-video director. **Films include:** *La Tête de Normande St-Onge* 1975 (mus, CFA-M); *L'Ange et la femme* 1977 (a/mus); *Rubber Gun* 1978 (mus); *Jacob Two-Two Meets the Hooded Fang* 1978 (mus); *Agency* 1979 (mus); *Au revoir ... à lundi* 1980 (mus); *Fantastica* 1980 (a/mus); *Maria Chapdelaine* 1983 (mus, GA-M); *Night Magic* 1985 (d/sc/a/mus, GA-S); *The Peanut Butter Solution* 1985 (mus); *Shades of Love* 1987–8 (mus, series); *Shadow Dancing* 1990 (d); *Rats and Rabbits* 2000 (co-p/d/co-sc).

Furie, Sidney J.
Director; b. Toronto, 1933. Furie, who was once described by British film critic Leslie Halliwell as the 'Canadian director with a restless camera,' began his career as a writer for CBC-TV. He directed two stylish, prescient teenage rebellion films at the end of the 1950s: *A Dangerous Age* and *A Cool Sound from Hell*. Since there was no infrastructure in place to make feature films in English Canada, Furie sought cinematic employment in England, where he directed *The Young Ones* and *The Ipcress File* with Michael Caine. Later, perhaps inevitably, he moved to Hollywood, where he made a number of stylish and insubstantial films including *The Lady Sings the Blues*, *Gable and Lombard*, and *Iron Eagle*. **Films include:** *A Dangerous Age* 1958; *A Cool*

Sound from Hell 1959; *The Young Ones* 1961; *The Boys* 1962; *The Leather Boys* 1964; *The Ipcress File* 1965; *The Appaloosa* 1966; *Lady Sings the Blues* 1972; *Little Fauss and Big Halsy* 1973; *Gable and Lombard* 1976; *The Boys in Company C* 1978; *The Entity* 1983; *Iron Eagle* 1986; *Superman IV: The Quest for Peace* 1987; *Iron Eagle II* 1988; *Ladybugs* 1992; *Iron Eagle IV* 1995.

G

Garber, Victor
Actor and singer; b. London, Ont., 1949. Garber, an accomplished stage actor and singer is a two-time Tony nominee for his Broadway roles in *Damn Yankees* and *Sweeney Todd*. He was also nominated by the Screen Actors Guild for his part as the ship's designer in James Cameron's* megalithic film, *Titanic*. In 1999, he played Daddy Warbucks in the television version of *Annie*. His other film appearances include *The First Wives Club, Sleepless in Seattle*, and Atom Egoyan's *Exotica*.* **Films and television include:** *Godspell* 1973 (as Jesus); *Tartuffe* 1978 (TV); *The Days and Nights of Molly Dodd* 1987–8 (series); *Liberace: Behind the Music* 1988 (TV); *Grand Larceny* 1991 (TV); *The First Circle* 1991 (TV); *I'll Never Get to Heaven* 1992; *E.N.G.* 1992–4 (series); *Life with Mikey* 1993; *Dieppe* 1993 (TV); *Woman on the Run: The Lawrencia Bembenek Story* 1993 (TV); *Sleepless in Seattle* 1993; *Exotica* 1994; *Kleptomania* 1995; *Jeffrey* 1995; *The First Wives Club* 1996; *Titanic* 1997; *Rodgers and Hammerstein's Cinderella* 1997 (TV); *How Stella Got Her Groove Back* 1998; *Annie* 1999 (TV); *Love and Murder* 2000 (TV); *Deadly Appearances* 2000 (TV); *The Wandering Soul Murders* 2001 (TV); *A Cold Kind of Death* 2001 (TV); *Torso* 2001 (TV).

Gate, The
1987 92m *prod* Alliance Entertainment, *p* John Kemeny, Andras Hamori, *d* Tibor

Takacs, *sc* Michael Nankin, *ph* Thomas Vamos, *ed* Rit Wallis, *mus* Michael Hoenig, J. Peter Robinson; *with* Stephen Dorff, Louis Tripp, Christa Denton, Kelly Rowan, Jennifer Irwin. A storm brings down an ancient tree in the backyard of a Spielbergian suburban family home, and as soon as the parents leave for a long weekend, demons from Hell are unleashed on the unsuspecting teens (Dorff, Tripp and Denton). *The Gate*, a horror flick in the vein of *Poltergeist*, concentrates on the traditional fears of children – strange noises in the night, moving shadows, the death of a family pet, a monster in the closet – and although the happy ending is predictable, there are some truly frightening moments. The pint-size, flesh-eating demons (created by special effects wizard Randall William Cook, who also worked on *Ghostbusters* and *The Thing*) are particularly spooky and unpleasant. (V) **Awards include:** Golden Reel Award.

Gélinas, Gratien

Actor, director, and writer; b. St-Tite-de-Champlain, Que., 1909; d. 1999. Gélinas, a star of the Quebec stage from 1936, was considered by many to be the godfather of the province's theatre. In 1948, Gélinas wrote *Tit-coq** (*The Cocky One*) and performed it hundreds of times in both French and English. *Tit-coq* was eventually made into a film that became the most successful feature shot in Quebec during the mini-boom of the 1940s and early 1950s and it won Film of the Year at the 1953 Canadian Film Awards. As a playwright, an actor, a theatre manager, and the chairman of the Canadian Film Development Corporation (Telefilm Canada) from 1969 to 1978, Gélinas represents one of the early links between the English- and French-speaking Quebec culture. **Films include:** *Tit-coq* 1953 (p/co-d/sc/a, CFA-FY, CFA-FF); .

Red 1969 (a, CFA-SA); *Cordélia* 1978 (a); *Agnes of God* 1985 (a); *Les Tisserands du pouvoir* 1988 (a); *Les Tisserands du pouvoir II: La Révolte* 1988 (a).

George, Chief Dan

Actor; b. Burrard Indian Reserve, North Vancouver, 1899; d. 1981. After working for twenty-eight years as a longshoreman, an injury on the job inadvertently led to a career in acting for the then forty-seven-year-old George. He got his first role in 1960 on CBC-TV's *Caribou County*. Then Disney came knocking with the feature *Smith*, touting George as 'the real thing.' His most famous role was in Arthur Penn's *Little Big Man* as Old Lodge Skins (a part that had originally been offered to Laurence Olivier). He received an Academy Award nomination for his poignant performance opposite Dustin Hoffman. **Films include:** *Smith* 1969; *Little Big Man* 1970 (AAN-SA); *Cancel My Reservation* 1972; *Harry and Tonto* 1974; *The Bears and I* 1974; *Alien Thunder* 1974; *Man Belongs to the Earth* 1974; *Cold Journey* 1975; *Shadow of the Hawk* 1976; *The Outlaw Josey Wales* 1976; *Centennial* 1978 (series); *Spirit of the Wind* 1979; *Americathon* 1979; *Nothing Personal* 1980.

George and Rosemary

1987 8m48s *prod* NFB, *exp* Douglas MacDonald, *p* Eunice Macaulay, *d/sc/an* Alison Snowden, David Fine, *ph* Pierre Landry, Jacques Avoine, Robin Bain, *ed* Paul Demers, *mus* Patrick Godfrey, *narr* Cec Linder. A delightful piece of animation from the couple (Alison Snowden and David Fine) who would go on to make the Academy Award–winning *Bob's Birthday** and the animated series *Bob and Margaret*. This short hits just the right whimsical note, showing, in a wry, subtle, and charming manner, that even though the facade may crumble, golden-agers can still rekindle passions and find love. (V) **Awards include:** GA: Live-Action Short; AAN: Animated Short

Gina

1975 94m *prod* Les Productions Carle-Lamy, *exp* Luc Lamy, *p* Pierre Lamy, *d/sc/ed* Denys Arcand, *ph* Alain Dostie, *mus* Michel Pagliaro, Benny Barbara; *with* Céline Lomez, Claude Blanchard, Frédérique Collin, Serge Thériault, Gabriel Arcand, Paule Baillargeon. Parallel story lines draw an exploited hotel stripper (Lomez) who is sent to work a small Quebec town, a drunken gang of hell-raising snowmobilers, and a film crew attempting to shoot a political documentary about exploited textile workers (echoing Denys Arcand's* own NFB-banned documentary *On est au coton*) together into a potent mixture of action and observations on workers, violence against women, and film as a political tool.

Girard, François

Director and writer; b. Saguenay-Lac-St-Jean, Que., 1963. This technically innovative filmmaker stunned English Canada with his brilliant feature *Thirty-Two Short Films about Glenn Gould,** which garnered Genies for Girard as Best Director and Rhombus Media for Best Picture. Structured in thirty-two parts, the film utilized drama, documentary, animation, and performance art to offer insights into the life of an enigmatic Canadian genius. Those who had seen *Le Dortoir*, Girard's award-winning collaboration with the dance troupe Carbone 14, were probably less surprised that Girard could score a triumph with difficult material. His *The Red Violin** won eight Genies (including Best Picture and Best Director) in 1998 and went on to become the most successful Canadian arthouse feature to date. **Films and video**

include: *Das Brunch* 1983; *Human Scope* 1984; *Le Train* 1985; *Tango, Tango* 1986; *Montréal Danse* 1988; *Cargo* 1990; *Le Dortoir* 1991; *Le Jardin des ombres* 1993; *Thirty-Two Short Films about Glenn Gould* 1994 (d/co-sc, GA-D); *Remembering Othello: Interview with Suzanne Cloutier* 1995 (d, TV); *The Sound of Carceri* from *Yo-Yo Ma Inspired by Bach* 1997 (d/sc, TV); *The Red Violin* 1998 (d/co-sc, GA-D, GA-SC).

Girard, Rémy

Actor; b. Jonquière, Que., 1950. Girard, a one-time law student turned theatre actor, made his film debut during the 1980s. Now he is one of the busiest performers on Quebec's bustling entertainment scene, visible in everything from television commercials to high drama. An unlikely leading man, chubby and open-faced, Girard slips easily into the role of the modern Everyman. But he also has a puckish quality that gives his characters an ironic amusement with the condition of their lives. Winner of three acting Genies, Girard is most remembered for the jovial lecher in Denys Arcand's *Le Déclin de l'empire américain.** **Films and television include:** *Les Yeux rouges ou les vérités accidentelles* 1982; *Le Crime d'Ovide Plouffe* 1984; *Trouble* 1985; *Le Lys cassé* 1986; *Le Déclin de l'empire américain* 1986; *Les Portes tournantes* 1988 (GA-SA); *Kalamazoo* 1988; *Le Chemin de Damas* 1988; *Les Tisserands du pouvoir* 1988; *Les Tisserands du pouvoir II: La Révolte* 1988; *Jésus de Montréal* 1989 (GA-SA); *Dans le ventre du dragon* 1989; *Rafales* 1990; *Les Archives* 1991; *Amoureux fou* 1991 (GA-A); *Montréal vu par ...* 1991; *L'Empire des lumières* 1991; *Scoop* 1991–5 (series); *La Florida* 1993; *Blanche* 1993 (series); *Le Secret de Jérôme* 1994; *Neige au soleil* 1995; *L'Homme idéal* 1996; *Lilies* 1996; *Fish Tale Soup* 1996; *Le Siège de l'âme* 1997; *Les Boys* 1997; *Les Boys II* 1998; *The Red Violin* 1998; *Free Money* 1998.

Glenn Gould – Off the Record

1959 30m *prod* NFB, *exp* Tom Daly, *p/d/ed* Wolf Koenig, Roman Kroitor, *ph* Wolf Koenig, *narr* Stanley Jackson. This informal portrait – part of the NFB's *Candid Eye** series – of Canada's certifiable musical genius in splendid isolation, retreating from the world to the family cottage on Lake Simcoe, playing an old Chickering piano for an audience that consists solely of his pet collie and the film crew, walking in the woods, and conversing with associates. (V)

Glenn Gould – On the Record

1959 30m *prod* NFB, *exp* Tom Daly *p/d/ed* Wolf Koenig, Roman Kroitor *ph* Wolf Koenig *narr* Stanley Jackson. This documentary portrait of the piano virtuoso as a young man shows Gould in New York during a recording session at Columbia Records. The camera follows Gould as he takes a cab to the studio, banters with the studio engineers, and then, alone at the piano, fastidiously records Bach's *Italian Concerto*. (V)

Glover, Guy

Producer and administrator; b. London, U.K., 1908; d. 1988. Glover's career as a senior producer at the NFB spanned more than thirty-five years and covered more than 200 films. He arrived from England in 1913 and studied at the University of British Columbia. He joined the Board in 1941, and three years later he was put in charge of the French unit. From 1954 to 1963, he oversaw television production, and from 1969 to 1974 he was director of the English program. Four of his films received Academy Award nominations. **Films include:** *Listen to the Prairies* 1945; *Challenge: Science against Cancer* 1950; *The Fight: Science against Cancer* 1951 (CFA-SPA, AAN-SD); *Opera School* 1952 (CFA-TS); *Herring Hunt* 1953 (AAN-SD); *Farewell Oak Street* 1953 (CFA-TS); *The Stratford Adventure* 1954 (CFA-FY, CFA-FF, AAN-SD); *Window on Canada* series 1954–6; *The Colour of Life* 1955; *Les Matins nettes* 1958; *Les Brûlés* 1958; *River with a Problem* 1961; *Morning on the Lièvre* 1961 (CFA-TS); *The Promised Land* 1962; *Lewis Mumford on the City* 1963 (six films); *Bethune* 1964; *23 Skidoo* 1964; *Angel* 1966 (CFA-AE); *Never a Backward Step* 1966 (CFA-FD); *Fluxes* 1967; *The Street* 1976 (CFA-AS, AAN-AS); *Poets on Film* 1977 (three films).

Godbout, Jacques

Writer and director; b. Montreal, 1933. When Godbout joined the NFB in 1958 as a dialogue writer, he was already a published poet and an aspiring novelist, and he had worked in Ethiopia teaching literature. He quickly rose to directorial status, collaborating notably with French documentarian Jean Rouch and rising to head of French production. In 1966, *YUL 871* established his reputation as a stylish filmmaker and this highly acclaimed film, together with the 1971 musical comedy *IXE-13*, allowed Godbout to bring his unique literary flair to cinema. A provocative critic and commentator on Québécois, English-Canadian, and global culture, Godbout's output has been as prolific in literature as in film. He has written over a dozen books and directed more than twenty films, including the poetic *Alias Will James** in 1988. **Films include:** *Les Dieux* 1961 (d with Georges Dufaux); *Pour quelques arpents de neige* 1962 (d with Dufaux); *À Saint-Henri le cinq septembre* 1964 (ed/narr); *Rose et Landry* 1963 (d); *Paul-Émile Borduas* 1963 (d/sc/ed); *Le Monde va nous prendre pour des sauvages* 1964 (d); *Fabienne sans son Jules* 1964 (d/sc); *Huit témoins* 1965 (d); *YUL 871* 1966 (d); *Vivre sa ville* 1967 (d); *Kid Sentiment* 1968 (d/co-sc/ed); *Les Vrais Cousins* 1970 (d); *IXE-13* 1972 (d/sc); *La Gammick* 1974 (d/co-sc); *Les Troubles de Johnny* 1974 (d);

L'Invasion 1975 (d); *Aimez-vous les chiens?* 1976 (d); *Arsenal* 1976 (d); *Derrière image* 1978 (d); *Deux episodes dans la vie d'Hubert Aquin* 1979 (d/co-sc); *Distortions* 1981 (d); *Un Monologue nord-sud* 1982 (d); *Comme en californie* 1983 (d); *Alias Will James* 1988 (d/sc); *Le Mouton noir* 1992 (d); *Le Sort de l'amérique* 1996 (d/co-sc).

Goin' down the Road
1970 87m *prod* Evdon Films, *p/d/ed* Donald Shebib, *sc* William Fruet, *ph* Richard Leiterman, *mus* Bruce Cockburn; *with* Doug McGrath, Paul Bradley, Jayne Eastwood, Cayle Chernin, Nicole Morin. Pete (McGrath) and his pal Joey (Bradley) are two wistful roustabouts from the Maritimes with thirty bucks and an abused Chevrolet labelled 'My Nova Scotia Home.' They pack up and head for Toronto where they find temporary work in a soft-drink factory, drown their troubles in beer, and make various futile attempts to improve themselves. Joey marries a girl (Eastwood) he has made pregnant, then loses his job. After robbing a food store, Pete and Joey, still believing there is a better life somewhere, take to the road once more. Don Shebib's* first feature was the most influential English-Canadian film of its generation with absolutely perfect performances by McGrath and Bradley, and is still an impressive piece of realist cinema. Its intelligent blend of fiction and documentary realism gives the film a clarity and insight into the lives of marginal people sharing a universal burden of existence, unable to cope even with their own aspirations but never losing their dignity. **Awards include:** CFA: Feature Film, Actor (McGrath and Bradley).

Going the Distance
1979 89m *prod* NFB, *exp* Robert Verrall, Jacques Bobet, *d/sc* Paul Cowan, *ph* Georges Dufaux, Pierre Letarte, Tony Westman, Paul Cowan, *ed* Paul Cowan, Steven Kellar, Jeepy Macadam, Rosemaire Shapley, *narr* Michael Kane. *Going the Distance* is the official film of the eleventh Commonwealth Games held in Edmonton in August, 1978. Eight athletes from four continents, selected to illustrate the nature of individual effort, were filmed in their home countries and in competition in Edmonton. The film received an Academy Award nomination for Feature Documentary. (V)

Goldenrod
1976 98m *prod* Film Funding Productions, Talent Associates (U.S.), *exp* David Susskind, *p* Gerry Arbeid, Lionel Chetwynd, *d* Harvey Hart, *sc* Lionel Chetwynd, *novel* Herbert Harker, *ph* Harry Makin, *ed* Ralph Brunjes, Peter Shatalow, Ron Wisman, *mus* Franklin Boyd; *with* Tony LoBianco, Donald Pleasence, Gloria Carlin, Donnelly Rhodes, Will Darrow McMillan, Ian McMillan. Made for American television with a limited theatrical release in Canada, *Goldenrod* stars Tony LoBianco as Jesse, a broncobuster from Alberta. Jesse is put out of action by a broken pelvis, deserted by his wife (Carlin), and left to care for his two sons (Will and Ian McMillan). After descending to the point of a suicide attempt, Jesse is slowly restored by the loyalty of his sons and a comeback on the rodeo circuit. His wife returns and the family unit is restored in a tearful reunion. Sentimental and badly acted, the film plays fast and loose with both accents and location. LoBianco brings Arkansas to Alberta, and when Jesse and his buddies want to go drinking, they head for Estevan, which is in the southeast corner of Saskatchewan. **Awards include:** CFA: Director.

Gosselin, Bernard
Cinematographer and director; b. Drummondville, Que., 1934. Gosselin joined the title department of the NFB in 1956,

and served as assistant cameraman, location manager, and assistant editor before shooting his first film, *Golden Gloves*, in 1961. His hand-held camera work for Denys Arcand,* Pierre Perrault,* Michel Brault,* and Claude Jutra* represents a significant contribution to early direct cinema in Quebec. **Films include:** *Golden Gloves* 1961 (co-ph); *Alexis Ladouceur, Métis* 1962 (co-ph); *Seul ou avec d'autres* 1962 (ph/co-ed); *Le Jeu de l'hiver* 1962 (d/co-ph); *Bûcherons de la Manouane* 1962 (co-ph); *Pour la suite du monde* 1963 (co-ph); *À tout prendre* 1964 (co-ph); *60 Cycles* 1965 (co-ph, CFA-PH); *Avec tambours et trompette* 1967 (co-ph); *Le Règne du jour* 1967 (co-ph); *La Visite du général de Gaulle au Québéc* 1967 (ph); *Entre la mer et l'eau douce* 1968 (co-ph); *Le Beau Plaisir* 1968 (d with Michel Brault and Pierre Perrault); *Les Voitures d'eau* 1969 (ph); *Capture* 1969 (d/co-ph); *L'Odyssée de Manhattan* 1970 (d/ph/ed); *Passage au nord-ouest* 1970 (d/ph); *Le Martien de Noel* 1971 (d); *Un Pays sans bon sens!* 1971 (co-ph); *César et don canot d'écorce* 1971 (d/ph); *Réjeanne Padovani* 1972 (a); *Les Raquettes des Atchikameg* 1973 (d/ph); *Jean Carignan, violoneux* 1975 (d/ph); *Un Royaume vous attend* 1976 (ph); *La Veillée des veillées* 1976 (d/co-ph); *Le Goût de la farine* 1977 (ph); *Le Retour à la terre* 1977 (ph); *Le Pays de la terre sans arbre ou le Mouchouânipi* 1980 (ph); *Gens d'Abitibi* 1980 (ph); *L'Arche de verre* 1994 (d/ed).

Grana, Sam

Producer and actor; b. Saverio Grana, Foggia, Italy, 1948. Grana emigrated to Canada at the age of six with his family and landed in Montreal. He joined the NFB in 1967, and worked primarily as a producer and director in Montreal and Halifax. In 1982, he was persuaded to take on his first acting role as Alex, the philandering husband, in John N. Smith's *Masculine Mystique*.* The film was a surprise hit. Grana reprised his role of Alex to less success in two sequels, *90 Days* and *The Last Straw*. He also produced *Train of Dreams, Welcome to Canada,** and *The Boys of St Vincent.** Grana served as the first head of Film New Brunswick. **Films and television include:** *Une Simple Histoire d'amour* 1973 (p); *SDL-1 Shakedown* 1977 (d); *Driving below Daylight* 1978 (d); *First Winter* 1981 (p, AAN-LAS); *The Way It Is* 1982 (p); *Running Scared* 1985 (co-p); *The Masculine Mystique* 1985 (a); *90 Days* 1985 (a); *Train of Dreams* 1987 (p); *The Last Straw* 1987 (a); *The Boulevard of Broken Dreams* 1988 (co-p); *Welcome to Canada* 1989 (p/co-sc/co-ed); *Toivo: Child of Hope* 1990 (p); *Nuit et silence* 1990 (p); *Oliver Jones in Africa* 1990 (p); *The Boys of St Vincent* 1992 (p/co-sc/a, TV); *Chronicle of a Genocide Foretold* 1996 (p, TV); *Never Too Late* 1996 (co-p); *Barbed War and Mandolins* 1997 (co-p/co-sc); *Victor-Martin, Diane and John* 1997 (p).

Grass

2000 80m *prod* Sphinx Productions, *exp* Keith Clarkson, *p/d* Ron Mann, *sc* Solomon Vesta, *ed* Robert Kennedy, *ad* Paul Mavrides, *mus* Guido Luciani, *narr* Woody Harrelson. Years in the making, this feature documentary from Ron Mann,* Canada's foremost film archivist, is a funny and sardonic exposé on the evolution of marijuana use in North America. Narrated by Woody Harrelson, a pro-grass activist, and designed by comic artist Paul Mavides, *Grass* ranges across a variety of misconceptions and fallacies that have helped cloak the pervasive weed in a shroud of paranoiac mystery. Mann focuses on Ted Anslinger, an American scientist and first 'drug czar,' who convinced the U.S. government that marijuana was a dangerous drug that lead users to violence and heroin addiction. The film forcefully demonstrates that despite a multi-billion dollar 'war on drugs,' the weed is as popular as ever. (V) **Awards include:** GA: Feature Documentary.

Greenberg, Harold

Producer; b. Toronto, 1930; d. 1996. The mourners at Harold Greenberg's funeral filled two chapels and spilled out the door of the building. Many were film industry people who came to pay their last respects to a man they thought of as simply 'Harold' – an unpretentious guy who began with a single photo shop and expanded a retail photography business into Astral Communications, one of the most powerful companies in Canadian media. Aided by members of his family, Greenberg did it all, from producing hit movies to launching pay-TV and specialty channels. Along the way, this genial entrepreneur and philanthropist contributed both time and money to the promotion of Canada's film culture. After his death, the Foundation to Underwrite New Drama, a fund he created in 1986 to foster the work of Canadian screenwriters, was renamed the Harold Greenberg Fund. **Films and television include:** *The Neptune Factor* 1972; *The Merry Wives of Tobias Rouke* 1972; *Slipstream* 1973; *Seizure* 1974; *Breaking Point* 1976; *The Little Girl Who Lives down the Lane* 1977; *The Uncanny* 1977; *In Praise of Older Women* 1978; *Rituals* 1978; *City on Fire* 1979; *A Man Called Intrepid* 1979 (TV); *Death Ship* 1979; *Mary and Joseph: A Story of Faith* 1979 (TV); *Terror Train* 1980; *Crunch* 1981; *Porky's* 1981 (GRA); *Being Different* 1981; *Tulips* 1981; *Porky's II: The Next Day* 1982; *Hard Feelings* 1982; *Hot Touch* 1982; *Maria Chapdelaine* 1983; *Tell Me That You Love Me* 1983; *Draw!* 1984.

Greene, Graham

Actor; b. Six Nations Reserve, Ont., 1952. Greene, a member of the Oneida nation, is best known for his Academy Award-nominated performance in *Dances with Wolves* opposite Kevin Costner. He worked as an audio technician for rock bands before becoming involved in theatre in Britain and Toronto, and scored supporting roles in *Running Brave, Revolution,* and *Pow-Wow Highway.* An actor of uncommon intensity, Greene gave an astonishing performance in Richard Bugajski's seldom seen *Clearcut.** He also appeared to good effect as the sole survivor of a pre–First World War Indian tribe in the cable TV movie *The Last of His Tribe* opposite Jon Voight. **Films and television include:** *Running Brave* 1983; *Revolution* 1985; *Pow-Wow Highway* 1988; *Dances with Wolves* 1990 (AAN-SA); *Clearcut* 1991; *Thunderheart* 1992; *The Last of His Tribe* 1992 (TV); *North* 1994; *Maverick* 1994; *Camilla* 1994; *Far from Home: The Adventures of Yellow Dog* 1995; *Die Hard with a Vengence* 1995; *The Education of Little Tree* 1998; *Shadow Lake* 1999 (TV); *Grey Owl* 1999.

Greene, Lorne

Actor; b. Ottawa, 1915; d. 1987. Before his ascent to American television's pantheon of pioneer patriarchs as *Bonanza's* Pa Cartwright (television's second-longest running western series, on air from 1959 to 1973), Greene was Canada's 'voice of doom.' After graduating from Queen's University, Greene began in radio. His rich basso profundo soon became the voice of choice in countless Second World War newsreels and documentaries for the NFB's *World in Action** series. After his move to the United States in the 1950s, Greene appeared on television, on Broadway, and on screen in mostly forgettable Hollywood fare. Late in his career, as if to rise to the heavens again, Greene starred as Commander Adama in the moderately successful sci-fi television series, *Battlestar*

Galactica. **Films and television include:**
The World in Action 1942–5 (narr); *The Money Makers* 1952 (TV); *Farewell Oak Street* 1953 (narr); *The Silver Chalice* 1954; *Tight Spot* 1955; *Autumn Leaves* 1956; *Peyton Place* 1957; *The Buccaneer* 1958; *Bonanza* 1959–73 (series); *A Matter of Fat* 1969 (narr); *Earthquake* 1974; *Tidal Wave* 1975; *Roots* 1977 (TV); *Jack London's Klondike Fever* 1979; *Battlestar Galactica* 1978–80 (series); *Lorne Greene's New Wilderness* 1982–7 (host, series); *The Canadian Conspiracy* 1986 (TV).

Greenwood, Bruce

Actor; b. Noranda, Que., 1956. It took twenty years of hard work before Bruce Greenwood became an overnight star in Roger Donaldson's political thriller, *Thirteen Days*. Greenwood studied acting at the University of British Columbia, but he considered a career as a professional skier before showing up for a part as an extra in *First Blood*, Sylvester Stallone's first Rambo film, which was shot in British Columbia. From there Greenwood built an impressive resume of credits, including Genie nominations for his intense performances in Atom Egoyan's *Exotica** and *The Sweet Hereafter.** His performance in the latter film attracted the attention of Hollywood studios, and led to his plum role as John F. Kennedy saving the world from nuclear disaster. **Films and television include**: *First Blood* 1982; *Peyton Place: The Next Generation* 1985 (TV); *The Malibu Bikini Shop* 1985; *Striker's Mountain* 1985 (TV); *St. Elsewhere* 1986–8 (series); *The Climb* 1986; *Jake and the Fatman* 1987 (TV); *Twist of Fate* 1989 (TV); *Wild Orchid* 1990; *Summer Dreams: The Story of the Beach Boys* 1990 (TV as Dennis Wilson); *The Little Kidnappers* 1990 (TV); *Knots Landing* 1991–2 (series); *The Great Pretender* 1991 (TV); *Passenger 57* 1992;

Adrift 1993 (TV); *Woman on the Run: The Lawrencia Bembenek Story* 1993 (TV); *Paint Cans* 1994; *Heart of a Child* 1994 (TV); *Exotica* 1994; *Naomi and Wynonna: Love Can Build a Bridge* 1995 (TV); *The Absolute Truth* 1997 (TV); *Fathers' Day* 1997; *The Sweet Hereafter* 1997; *Disturbing Behaviour* 1998; *Double Jeopardy* 1999; *Thick as Thieves* 1999; *Rules of Engagement* 2000; *Thirteen Days* 2000.

Grey Fox, The

1983 91m *prod* Mercury Pictures, *exp* David Brady, *p* Peter O'Brian, *d* Phillip Borsos, *sc* John Hunter, *ph* Frank Tidy, *ed* Frank Irvine, *mus* Michael Conway Baker, The Chieftains; *with* Richard Farnsworth, Jackie Burroughs, Kenneth Pogue, Wayne Robson, Timothy Webber, Gary Reineke. Bill Minor (Farnsworth), an infamous American stage robber, is released 'into the twentieth century' after thirty-three years in San Quentin Prison. Following a botched train heist, Minor flees northward to British Columbia. Under the name of Bill Edwards, Minor passes as a prospector, does some horse rustling, befriends the local RCMP officer, and takes a lover – a fiery feminist photographer played by Jackie Burroughs.* Eventually his past catches up with him and he returns to jail. This revisionist western in the tradition of *Butch Cassidy and the Sundance Kid* is set in a mythic, nostalgic Canada where manners receive respect, where order is preferable to law, and fair play is more important than self-promotion. Farnsworth gives a terrific performance as the gentlemanly bandit and shines in his scenes with Burroughs. *The Grey Fox* signalled the arrival of a major directorial talent in Phillip Borsos* and is probably the single most successful feature-film debut in the history of Canadian cinema. (V) **Awards include:** GA: Picture,

Director, Original Screenplay, Supporting Actress (Burroughs), Art Direction, Musical Score.

Greyson, John

Director and writer; b. London, Ont., 1960. A product of the radical video movement that characterized the downtown art scene of 1980s Toronto, Greyson has remained true to his roots while creating critically acclaimed feature films. His unique combination of wit and didacticism makes him a force for the mainstream to reckon with, particularly as he creates tales that are unabashedly gay in style and content. *Urinal*, a Berlin film festival winner, combined video and film aesthetics, as did his astonishing *Zero Patience*,* a musical that featured the ghosts of Sir Richard Burton and a nearly mythical carrier of the AIDS virus. *Lilies*,* a prison drama that deals with guilt, homosexuality, priests, and young love, won the Genie for Best Picture in 1996. **Films include:** *Moscow Does Not Believe in Queers* 1986 (d/sc); *Urinal* 1988 (d/sc/co-ed); *The Making of 'Monsters'* 1991 (d/sc); *Zero Patience* 1994 (d/sc); *Lilies* 1996 (d); *Uncut* 1998 (d/sc); *The Law of Enclosures* 2000 (d/sc).

Grierson

1973 58m *prod* NFB, *exp* David Bairstow, *p/d* Roger Blais, *sc/narr* Donald Brittain, *ph* Eugene Boyko, Lewis McLeod, Michel Thomas-d'Hoste, Magi Torruella, Jacques Fogel, *ed* Les Halman, John Kramer, Annick de Bellefeuille. This film is an impressive tribute to John Grierson,* the Scottish-born documentary pioneer who, in 1939, was put in charge of the fledgling NFB. Over the years, he propagated his faith in the drama of everyday life, and his ideas about the 'creative interpretation of reality' influenced generations of Canadian

documentary filmmakers. (V) **Awards include:** CFA: Documentary.

Grierson, John

Producer and administrator; b. Deanston, Scotland, 1898; d. 1972. While not a Canadian by birth or citizenship, John Grierson is the single most important figure in the development of a Canadian film culture. As a public servant, broadcaster, critic, producer, and teacher, Grierson personified the term 'charismatic.' This tough, witty Scotsman had the idealism needed to imagine the form of non-fiction film and the practical skills required to turn his vision into a movement that would spread around the world.

Grierson was the first to apply the word 'documentary' to film; in a 1927 review of Flaherty's *Moana*, he defined a documentary as 'the creative interpretation of reality.' In 1929, turning from theorist to director, he made *Drifters*, a film about the North Sea herring fishers. His direction of this film, using striking camera and editing techniques that had been developed by Eisenstein in *Potemkin*, was so assured that it turned a potentially dull subject into a first-rate work of cinema.

After the success of *Drifters*, Grierson was able to persuade the British government to form a documentary unit, first at the Empire Marketing Board (1931–3) and then at the General Post Office (1933–7). As head of production, Grierson unleashed such talents as Len Lye, Paul Rotha, Cavalcanti, Basil Wright, and Norman McLaren* on a receptive film public. During that time, Grierson produced such classics as Lye's abstract animated *Rainbow Dance*, Cavalcanti's marvellous *Pett and Pott*, and Basil Wright's acclaimed *Night Mail*.

Having established the documentary

principle in Britain, Grierson arrived in Canada in 1939 to set up the NFB at the behest of Prime Minister Mackenzie King. He assembled a new group of fine filmmakers including Raymond Spottiswoode, Stuart Legg,* and the newly arrived McLaren. In 1941, the NFB won its first of many Academy Awards for *Churchill's Island*.* Grierson arranged for NFB films to be screened as shorts before commercial features, allowing Canadians the opportunity to see their own images on the screen, week after week. He also consciously nurtured the talent of young Canadians, employing such future film producers and directors as James Beveridge, Sydney Newman,* Guy Glover,* and Tom Daly.*

In 1945, Grierson left the NFB to form a film production unit for the United Nations and UNESCO. Soon afterward he found himself 'greylisted' for his past associations with radicals (one of his secretaries had known the famous Russian spy and defector Igor Gouzenko). Grierson returned to England where he tried his hand as the executive producer for Group Three. Eventually, he returned to his native Scotland, where he hosted *This Wonderful World* for television. At the close of his career, Grierson made his way back to Canada, and spent his final years teaching at McGill University. He always remained true to his credo that 'the ordinary affairs of people's lives are more dramatic and vital than all the false excitement you [fiction filmmakers] can muster.' **Films include:** *Drifters* 1929 (p/d/ph/ed); *Upstream* 1931 (p); *Industrial Britain* 1933 (p); *The Fishing Banks of Skye* 1934 (p/d); *So This Is London* 1934 (p); *The Song of Ceylon* 1935 (p); *Night Mail* 1936 (p); *The Brave Don't Cry* 1952 (exp).

Grocer's Wife, The

1992 104m *prod* Medusa Film Produc-

tions, *exp* Gregory E. Lavier, *d/sc* John Pozer, *ph* Peter Wunstorf, *ed* Reginald Dean Harkema, John Pozer, *mus* Mark Korven; *with* Simon Webb, Susinn McFarlen, Nicola Cavendish, Jay Brazeau, Andrea Rankin, Leroy Schultz. Set in the industrial hell of Trail, British Columbia, *The Grocer's Wife* is a decidedly bent comic drama about a man (Webb) who spends his days checking the emissions from the town's giant smoke stack. After his domineering mother (Rankin) dies from the pollution, his life takes a bizarre turn when an itinerant American stripper (McFarlen) moves into her bedroom. To make matters worse, the local grocer's wife (Cavandish) lusts after the young man. This unsettling fairy tale – director John Pozer's completely original 'no-budget' feature debut – is shot in dense black and white and features an epic soundtrack. **Awards include:** GA: Claude Jutra Award.

Gross, Paul

Actor, writer, and producer; b. Calgary, Alta., 1959. Gross is the current golden boy of Canadian television. By the age of fourteen, he was doing commercials to finance his drama studies at the University of Alberta. He worked the circuit of regional theatres while developing his writing abilities. After a stint as playwright-in-residence at the Stratford Festival, Gross moved to the Grand Theatre in London, Ontario, to work with artistic director Robin Phillips. Shifting to television, he wrote *Gross Misconduct*, which was directed by Atom Egoyan.* However, it was the series *Due South* (in which Gross embodied the wholesome character of RCMP Constable Benton Fraser) that brought him to the public's attention. His film credits include *Whale Music*,* *Married to It* and the black comedy *Paint Cans*.*

Films and television include: *In This Corner* 1985 (sc, TV); *Chasing Rainbows* 1988 (a, TV); *Divided Loyalties* 1989 (a, TV); *Cold Comfort* 1989 (a); *Getting Married in Buffalo Jump* 1990 (a, TV); *Married to It* 1991 (a); *Buried on Sunday* 1992 (a); *Gross Misconduct* 1993 (sc, TV); *Tales of the City* 1993 (a, TV); *Aspen Extreme* 1993 (a); *Whale Music* 1994 (a); *Paint Cans* 1994 (a); *Due South* 1994–9 (p/a, series); *20,000 Leagues under the Sea* 1997 (a, TV); *Murder Most Likely* 1999 (p/a, TV).

Groulx, Gilles

Director, writer, and editor; b. Montreal, 1931. Died 1994. Groulx never settled into the relative mainstream of filmmaking that was pursued by some of his colleagues. Instead, with his splintering, questioning approach, he became known for his socially committed documentaries. *Les Raquetteurs,** shot in 1958 with Michel Brault,* pioneered direct cinema and had a profound influence on modern Quebec film. His 1964 landmark feature *Le Chat dans le sac** explored Quebec's emerging identity and the relationship between the Québécois and *les autres* through the hero's affair with a young Jewish woman. An auto crash in 1981 left Groulx with severe brain damage and he lived out the rest of his life painting – active, but forgotten. **Films include:** *Les Raquetteurs* 1958 (ed/co-d with Michel Brault); *Normétal* 1959 (d/sc); *Les Brûlés* 1959 (co-ed); *La France sur un caillou* 1960 (ed/co-d with Claude Fournier); *Golden Gloves* 1961 (d/ed); *Seul ou avec d' autres* 1962 (co-ed); *Voir Miami* 1962 (d/ed); *Un Jeu si simple* 1964 (d/ed/narr); *Le Chat dans le sac* 1964 (d/sc/ed); *Entre tu et vous* 1969 (d/sc); *Où êtes vous donc?* 1970 (d/sc/ed); *Place de l'équation* 1973 (d); *24 heures ou plus ...* 1977 (d/sc/ed); *Primera pregunta sobre la felicidad / Première question sur le bonheur* 1977 (d); *Au pays de Zom* 1983 (d/sc/ed).

Gruben, Patricia

Filmmaker; b. Chicago, Ill., 1948. Gruben, one of Canada's most respected avant-garde filmmakers, emigrated to Canada from Texas in 1972 and has taught film at Simon Fraser University since 1984. Her 1981 film, *Sifted Evidence*, stands as a landmark exploration of feminist and colonial issues, using language against itself to complicate the story of one woman's trip to Mexico in search of matriarchal history. After a poorly received foray into commercial features, Gruben refocused her attention to produce *Ley Lines*, a tour-de-force return to experimental methods that pursues the idea of family across the ages, according to an associative logic all its own. **Films include:** *Shifted Evidence* 1982; *Low Visibility* 1984; *Deep Sleep* 1990; *Ley Lines* 1993; *Before It Blows* 1997.

Guerre des tuques, La

See *Dog Who Stopped the War, The*

Guy Maddin: Waiting for Twilight

1997 60m *prod* Marble Island Pictures, *exp* Richard Findlay, *p* Laura Michalchyshyn, *d/sc* Noam Gonick, *ph* Noam Gonick, Christle Leonard, Evan Tristan, Caelum Vatnsdal, Greg Mefferd, *ed* Bruce Little, *mus* Aradia Baroque Ensemble, Jeff Gillman, *narr* Tom Waits; *with* Guy Maddin. No one makes motion pictures quite like Guy Maddin.* In films such as *Archangel** and *Careful,** the born-and-bred Winnipeger achieves a synthesis of madcap parody, retro-aesthetics, and dreamy poeticism that the late Jean Cocteau would have applauded. Noam Gonick's portrait of the filmmaker neatly escapes the deadening hagiography of many Canadian arts documentaries. We see Maddin lolling around in bed, getting a haircut, and shooting his extravagant reverie, *Twi-*

light of the Ice Nymphs. As a bonus,
Gonick includes excerpts from an an-
cient cable television show on which
Maddin and some pals hilariously im-
personate crazed white supremacists.
Tom Waits' raspy narration hits the spot.

Gypsies of Svinia, The

1999 95m *prod* NFB, *exp* Graydon
McCrea, *p* Joe MacDonald, *d/ph* John
Paskievich, *ed* K. George Godwin, John
Paskievich. This documentary, which
focuses on gypsies living in Svinia
(a village in Slovakia), is a devastating
look at a defeated people living in abject
poverty. The film manages to illuminate
the problems faced by the Roma, who
live in filthy conditions – with no toilets
or furniture – and are overwhelmingly
reviled by their Slovak neighbours. Efforts of some Canadian activists to find
solutions to the daunting situation of the
Roma are defeated both by the passivity
of the people and by the ingrained ha-
tred on the part of some Slovaks who
lament that Hitler failed to finish them
off in his death camps. A harrowing, disturbing film about medieval conditions
in the heart of modern Europe. (V)

H

Haig, Don

Producer and editor; b. Winnipeg, 1933.
Don Haig moved to Toronto in 1956 and
joined CBC-TV as an editor. He shortly
left the corporation and in 1963 set-up
his own company, Film Arts, with director Beryl Fox and Vancouver producer
and director Allan King.* He edited the
legendary CBC public affairs program
This Hour Has Seven Days and several of
the early direct-cinema documentaries
shot by Richard Leiterman.* In 1974,
Haig produced his first feature, Patrick
Loubert's *125 Rooms of Comfort*, and in

1984 he acted as associate producer on
Brigette Berman's* Academy Award–
winning documentary, *Artie Shaw: Time
Is All You've Got*.* With genial guidance
and generosity, he nurtured the growth
of a Toronto film culture for two decades
before moving on to produce for the
NFB in 1994. **Films and television include:** *One More River* 1963 (ed, TV); *This
Hour Has Seven Days* 1964–6 (ed, series);
The Mills of the Gods: Viet Nam 1965 (ed,
TV); *The National Dream* 1974 (ed, TV);
125 Rooms of Comfort 1974 (p); *Summer's
Children* 1981 (p); *Alligator Shoes* 1981
(exp); *Alex Colville, the Splendour of Order*
1984 (exp, TV); *Unfinished Business* 1984
(exp, TV); *Samuel Lount* 1985 (exp, TV);
Artie Shaw: Time Is All You've Got 1985
(ap, AA-FD); *Dancing in the Dark* 1986
(exp); *I've Heard the Mermaids Singing*
1987 (exp); *Comic Book Confidential* 1988
(exp, GA-FD); *Growing up in America*
1988 (co-p); *Termini Station* 1989 (exp);
Elizabeth Smart: On the Side of Angels
1991 (exp, TV); *Secret Nation* 1992 (exp);
Twist 1993 (exp); *Who's Counting?
Marilyn Waring on Sex, Lies and Global
Economics* 1995 (exp); *Kid Nerd* 1997
(exp); *Moving Pictures* 2000 (exp).

Hancox, Rick

Filmmaker; b. Toronto, 1946. Rick
Hancox is an important figure in the
development of experimental film in
Canada as much for his filmmaking as
his for influence. From 1973 to 1985 he
taught at Sheridan College, where he
was instrumental in shaping the sensibilities of a new generation of filmmakers. Hancox's students included docu-
mentarians Janis Cole and Holly Dale,
and experimental filmmakers Mike
Hoolboom,* Philip Hoffman,* and Richard Kerr.* Inspired by his own mentor,
American independent filmmaker
George Semsel, Hancox instilled in his
students an interest in converging ques-

tions around memory, landscape, and documentary convention. The subsequent trend in Canadian experimental cinema in the 1980s toward personal cinema and experimental documentary can be largely attributed to Hancox. **Films include:** *I, a Dog* 1970; *House Movie* 1972; *Wild Sync* 1973; *Home for Christmas* 1978; *Zum Ditter* 1979; *Waterworx (A Clear Day and No Memories)* 1982; *Beach Events* 1984; *Moose Jaw (There's a Future in Our Past)* 1992.

Hanging Garden, The
1997 91m *prod* Triptych Media, Galafilm, Emotion Pictures, *p* Louise Garfield, Arnie Gelbart, Thom Fitzgerald, *d/sc* Thom Fitzgerald, *ph* Daniel Jobin, *ed* Susan Shanks, *mus* John Roby, Ashley MacIssac, Heather Rankin, Mary Jane Lamond; *with* Chris Leavins, Kerry Fox, Seana McKenna, Peter MacNeill, Troy Veinotte, Sarah Polley. Director Thom Fitzgerald's masterful feature debut is both revelatory and mysterious. A young gay man (Leavins) returns to his Nova Scotia home, some ten years after apparently taking his own life. The film concerns a reconciliation between his repressed past and family life and his bolder, openly gay adult personality. Fitzgerald's penchant for surreal family situations is in full display. The film features an accomplished ensemble cast with a noteworthy cameo by fiddler savant Ashley MacIsaac. One of the most auspicious debuts by a Canadian filmmaker since Jean-Claude Lauzon's *Un Zoo la nuit.** (V) **Awards include:** GA: Original Screenplay, Supporting Actor (MacNeill), Supporting Actress (McKenna), Claude Jutra Award.

Hangman's Bride, The
1997 20m *prod* Word of Mouth Productions, *p/d/sc* Naomi McCormack, *ph* Jonathan Freeman, *ed* Josephine

Massarella. Based on the true story of Françoise Laurent and Jean Corolère, this clever tale of an imprisoned servant girl who escapes her tragic fate won a Genie. It's a classic tale of unexpected love in an unlikely place, developed with considerable panache. McCormack's attention to detail and careful recreation of eighteenth-century Montreal make this historical episode come alive, an important reminder that our history is not as dull as we might believe. **Awards include:** GA: Live-Action Short.

Hard Core Logo
1996 96m *prod* Terminal City Pictures, Shadow Shows, *p* Christine Haebler, Brian Dennis *d* Bruce McDonald, *sc* Noel S. Baker, *book* Michael Turner, *ph* Danny Nowak, *ed* Reginald Harkema, *mus* Swamp Baby, Shaun Tozer; *with* Hugh Dillon, Callum Keith Rennie, John Pyper-Ferguson, Bernie Coulson, Bruce McDonald. When an early 1980s punk group reunites for a final farewell tour across the Canadian west, group leaders Joe Dick (perfectly depicted by real-life rocker Dillon) and Billy Talent (Rennie*) bring their ongoing personal feud along for the ride. Director Bruce McDonald* (who appears in the film as himself) is in his element with this satiric effort and pumps up the volume throughout the zany proceedings. Along with documentary-style footage, he combines clever effects shots with a driving, hardcore soundtrack. Baker's screenplay retains key elements from the Brad Turner book and makes it all work on screen. It's McDonald's strongest cinematic work to date. (V)

Hard Part Begins, The
1974 86m *prod* Odyssey Films, Auric Films, *exp* Ratch Wallace, *p* John Hunter, Derrett Lee, *d* Paul Lynch, *sc* John

Hunter, *ph* Robert Saad, *ed* William Gray, *mus* Ian Guenther; *with* Donnelly Rhodes, Nancy Belle Fuller, Paul Bradley, Linda Sorensen, Doug McGrath. *The Hard Part Begins*, one of the finest features from the early 1970s, is about a country singer Jim King (Rhodes) who travels the small-town circuit in Southern Ontario with his band but dreams of Nashville. In one disastrous week, King watches an old friend die, his Toronto recording contract disappears, his girlfriend (Fuller) leaves him, and he is beaten up in a brawl. As one of English-Canadian cinema's quintessential losers – or dreamers – King resolves to go on playing. Rhodes gives a stellar performance, Paul Lynch's direction is solid, and John Hunter's script is particularly evocative of small towns and the dreariness of life on the road with a second-rate bar band.

Hart, Harvey

Director; b. Toronto, 1928; d. 1989. Hart, a University of Toronto graduate, got his start during the 1950s working as a producer and director for the CBC. After directing a variety of American television series from *Mannix* to *Alfred Hitchcock Presents* in the 1960s, Hart returned to Canada in 1970. Known for his 'international style,' he made several features, including *Fortune and Men's Eyes** (which proved intensely controversial), *Goldenrod** (which won him a Canadian Film Award for Best Director), *The Pyx*, and *Utilities*. In his later years, Hart devoted most of his time to American television projects such as the mini-series *East of Eden*. **Films and television include:** *Bus Riley's Back in Town* 1965; *The Young Lawyers* 1970–1 (series); *Fortune and Men's Eyes* 1971; *The Pyx* 1973; *Shoot* 1976; *Mahoney's Last Stand* 1976; *Goldenrod* 1976 (CFA-D); *Captains Courageous* 1977 (TV); *The Prince of Central Park* 1977 (TV); *Utilities* 1981; *The High Country*

1981; *East of Eden* 1981 (TV); *Getting Even* 1983; *Spenser: For Hire* 1985–8 (series); *Beverly Hills Madam* 1986 (TV); *Passion and Paradise* 1989 (TV); *Dick Francis: Blood Sport* 1989 (TV).

Hartman, Phil

Actor; b. Brantford, Ont., 1949; d. 1998. This Canadian-born comedian, like his contemporaries, John Candy* and Dan Aykroyd,* found fame and success south of the border. In the mid-1980s, Hartman linked up with Paul Reubens and co-wrote the Tim Burton hit, *Pee-Wee's Big Adventure*. Later he joined the cast of *Saturday Night Live* and provided a variety of voices for the animated series *The Simpsons*. His career in film was about to take off when, in a shocking twist of fate, his third wife killed him and then herself in a fit of jealous rage in 1998. **Films and television include:** *Cheech and Chong's Next Movie* 1980; *Pee-Wee's Big Adventure* 1985 (co-sc); *Saturday Night Live* 1986–94 (TV); *The Simpsons* 1988–98 (voices, series); *So I Married an Axe Murderer* 1993; *NewsRadio* 1995–8 (series); *Sgt Bilko* 1996; *Jingle All the Way* 1996; *Small Soldiers* 1998.

Hart of London, The

1970 79m *prod* Chambers Productions, *p/d/ph/ed* Jack Chambers. *The Hart of London*, Jack Chambers'* final master work in his short but brilliant career, is a film of epic scope, a powerful statement about the thorny bond between life and death. The core of the film revolves around newsreel footage of a hart that wandered into London in 1954. This rather quaint episode quickly turns ugly as we watch the animal's capture and eventual slaughter in graphic detail. Chambers' insistent pairing of oppositional elements, creates an experience rich in ambiguity, that reminds us of the dangers inherent in even the most wondrous of moments.

Heartaches

1981 92m *prod* Rising Star Films, *exp* Joseph Beaubien, Nicole Boisvert, Claude Giroux, Michael Bennahum, *p* Pieter Kroonenburg, David Patterson, Jerry Raibourn, *d* Donald Shebib, *sc* Terence Heffernan, *ph* Vic Sarin, *ed* Gerry Hambling, Peter Boita, Barbara Brown-McKay, *mus* Michael Martin; *with* Margot Kidder, Annie Potts, Robert Carradine, Winston Rekert, George Touliatos. In this variation on Shebib's* own *Goin' down the Road,** two women head for Toronto – Bonnie (Potts) to escape her past and Rita (Kidder*) in search of a future. Strangers when they meet on a bus, the two lodge together and find work in a mattress factory. Rita begins an affair with the nephew of the factory owner (Rekert), which ends in betrayal, while Bonnie reunites with her boyfriend (Carradine), whom she had been fleeing. It is an accomplished, well-directed film, but nonetheless is sentimental in tone and has none of the real pain of Shebib's earlier works. Kidder is terrific as the foul-mouthed, man-hungry Rita. **Awards include:** GA: Original Screenplay, Actress (Kidder), Foreign Actress (Potts).

Heavy Metal

1981 90m *prod* Heavy Metal Animation Co., *exp* Leonard Mogel, *p* Ivan Reitman, *supervising d* Gerald Potterton, *sc* Dan Goldberg, Len Blum, *source Heavy Metal* comics with original art and stories by Richard Corben, Angus McKie, Dan O'Bannon, Thomas Warkentin, and Berni Wrightson, *ed* Janice Brown, *mus* Elmer Bernstein, Black Sabbath, Blue Oyster Cult, Cheap Trick, Devo, Donald Fagen, and others; *voices* Jackie Burroughs, John Candy, Joe Flaherty, Don Francks, Eugene Levy. Canada's most successful animated feature is actually six short films animated by hundreds of artists overseen by NFB veteran Gerald Pot-terton* and based on selected stories from the French-American fantasy magazine of the same name. Sexually graphic, very violent, with a mixture of grisly horror and low humour, *Heavy Metal* has the distinction of being the last R-rated animated feature to be released by a major Hollywood studio. Its original box-office performance was not overwhelming but the film remained a staple of midnight screenings throughout the 1980s. The theatrical release of a digitally remastered version in 1996 is a testament to the film's popularity among connoisseurs (mostly young men) of the genre. (V) **Awards include:** GA: Overall Sound, Sound Editing; Golden Reel Award.

Hébert, Anne

Writer; b. St-Catherine-de-Fossambault, Que., 1916; d. 2000. Hébert, the author of *Kamouraska*, *Héloise*, *Les Enfants du sabbat*, and many other novels, worked as a scriptwriter with the NFB in Montreal from 1953 to 1954. Her co-scripting effort with Claude Jutra* led to a somewhat marred film version of *Kamouraska** which may have gone too far to preserve the novel's aleatory approach to memory. Hébert denounced Yves Simoneau's* version of her novel *Les Fous de bassan*, but some see it as a better film than Jutra's. Her short story 'La Canne à peche' was made into a memorable film by Fernand Dansereau* in 1959. Hébert moved to Paris in the mid-1950s, but returned to Quebec shortly before her death. **Films include:** *The Charwoman* 1954 (sc); *La Canne à peche* 1959 (sc); *Kamouraska* 1973 (co-sc).

Helicopter Canada

1966 50m *prod* NFB, *p* Peter Jones, Tom Daly, *d/ph* Eugene Boyko, *ed* Rex Tasker, *narr* Stanley Jackson. This popular NFB film, which was made for the Centennial Commission, was shot entirely from a helicopter in Panavision, and portrays a breathtaking panoramic view of Canada from coast to coast. (V) **Awards include:** CFA: Special Award; AAN: Short Documentary.

Hemingway: A Portrait

1999 18m *prod* Productions Pascal Blais, Imagica Corp. (Japan), Denstu Tec (Japan), HNK Enerprises 21 (Japan), Panorama Animation Studio of Yaroslavl (Russia), *exp* Jean-Yves Martel, Shizuo Ohashi, *p* Bernard Lajoie, Tatsuo Shimamura, *d* Erik Canuel, *ph* Bernard Lajoie, *ed* Denis Papillon, *mus* Michel Corriveau. This lavish but fairly ordinary docudrama romanticizing the life of the American writer Ernest Hemingway was shot in conjunction with the Academy Award–winning animated IMAX short *The Old Man and the Sea** on the occasion of the centenary of Hemingway's birth. **Awards include:** GA: Short Documentary.

Henry, Martha

Actor; b. Greenville, Mich., 1938. Martha Henry, one of Canada's foremost stage actors, came to Canada in 1959 to act at the Crest Theatre in Toronto, and subsequently attended the newly founded National Theatre School of Canada. Her expansive career as an actor includes nineteen seasons at Stratford, the Broadway musical *Pal Joey* in 1986, and Genie Award–winning performances in *The Wars,* Dancing in the Dark,* Mustard Bath,* and *Long Day's Journey into Night.** She made her directorial stage debut with *Brief Lives* in 1980 and won accolades as the artistic director of the Grand Theatre in London, Ontario, in the late 1980s. Henry is a Companion of the Order of Canada. **Films include:** *Empire Inc.* 1982 (TV); *The Wars* 1983 (GA-A); *Dancing in the Dark* 1986 (GA-A); *White Light* 1991; *Mustard Bath* 1994 (GA-SA); *Long Day's Journey into Night* 1996 (GA-A).

Héroux, Claude

Producer; b. Montreal, 1942; brother of Denis Héroux. Claude Héroux produced *In Praise of Older Women** and a whole slew of tax-shelter era* bombs, as well as David Cronenberg's breakthrough films, *Scanners** and *Videodrome.** Since the mid-1980s he has produced exclusively for Quebec television. **Films and television include:** *Pas de vacances pour les idoles* 1965; *7 fois ... (par jour)* 1971; *Un Enfant comme les autres ...* 1972; *Quelques arpents de neige* 1972; *J'ai mon voyage!* 1973; *Y a toujours moyen de moyenner!* 1973; *Par les sang des autres* 1974; *Y a pas d'mal à se faire du bien* 1974; *Je t'aime* 1974; *Pousse mais pousse égal* 1975; *Breaking Point* 1975; *Jacques Brel Is Alive and Well and Living in Paris* 1975; *The Uncanny* 1977; *In Praise of Older Women* 1978; *Angela* 1978; *City on Fire* 1979; *The Brood* 1979; *Hog Wild* 1980; *Scanners* 1981; *Dirty Tricks* 1981; *Visiting Hours* 1982; *Videodrome* 1983; *Of Unknow Origin* 1983; *Au nom de tous les miens* 1983; *Funny Farm* 1983; *Going Berserk* 1983; *Covergirl* 1984; *For Those I Loved* 1986 (TV); *Lance et compte* 1987 (series); *Formule un* 1988 (TV); *René Lévesque* 1993 (TV); *Le Sorcier* 1994 (TV); *Les Bâtisseurs d'eau* 1996 (TV).

Héroux, Denis

Producer and director; b. Montreal, 1940; brother of Claude Héroux. While studying history at the University of Montreal, Denis Héroux collaborated with fellow students Denys Arcand* and Stéphane Venne on a bemused film about student life called *Seul ou avec d'autres.* By the late 1960s, this urbane Montrealer had become one of Quebec's first successful private industry moviemakers with the erotic hit, *Valérie.** Héroux went on to pioneer international co-productions with such films as *Atlantic City** and *Quest for Fire** and was a co-founder of Alliance Entertainment, a company he left toward the end of the 1980s. **Films**

include: *Seul ou avec d'autres* 1962 (co-d);
Jusqu'au cou 1964 (d); *Pas de vacances pour
les idoles* 1965 (d); *Valérie* 1969 (d/co-sc);
L'Amour humain 1970 (d); *L'Initiation*
1970 (d); *7 fois ... (par jour)* 1971 (d); *Un
enfant comme les autres ...* 1972 (d); *Quelques
arpents de neige* 1972 (d); *J'ai mon voyage!*
1973 (d); *Y a toujours moyen de moyenner!*
1973 (p/d); *Y a pas d'mal à se faire du bien*
1974 (p); *Pousse mais pousse égal* 1975 (d);
*Jacques Brel Is Alive and Well and Living in
Paris* 1975 (d); *Born for Hell* 1976 (d/sc);
The Uncanny 1977 (d); *The Little Girl Who
Lives down the Lane* 1977 (co-p); *Tomorrow
Never Comes* 1978 (ap); *Blood Relatives*
1978 (co-p); *Violette Nozière* 1978 (co-p);
L'Homme en colère 1979 (co-p); *À nous
deux* 1979 (co-p); *Atlantic City* 1980 (co-p,
AAN-P); *Les Plouffe* 1981 (exp); *Quest for
Fire* 1982 (exp); *Louisiana* 1984 (co-p); *Le
Crime d'Ovide Plouffe* 1984 (exp); *The
Blood of Others* 1984 (co-p); *This Park Is
Mine* 1984 (co-p); *The Bay Boy* 1984 (co-p,
GA-P); *Mario* 1984 (co-p); *Le Matou* 1985
(exp); *Eddy and the Cruisers* II: *Eddy Lives*
1989 (exp); *Black Robe* 1991 (exp, GA-P).

High Grass Circus
1976 57m *prod* NFB, *exp* Colin Low, *p*
William Brand, *d* Torben Schioler, Tony
Ianzelo, *ph* Tony Ianzelo, *ed* Torben Schioler. The film follows the Royal Brothers' Circus, the only surviving Canadian
tent circus, during its 1976 summer season and documents a twenty-four-hour
day in the life of the performers, observ-
ing not only the people but also the me-
chanics behind a circus in transit. It received an Academy Award nomination
for Short Documentary. (V)

Highway 61
1992 110m *prod* Shadow Shows, *p* Colin
Brunton, Bruce McDonald, *d* Bruce
McDonald, *sc* Don McKellar, *ph* Miro-
slaw Baszak, *ed* Michael Pacek, *mus*
Nash the Slash; *with* Valerie Buhagiar,
Don McKellar, Earl Pastko, Art Berg-

mann, Tracy Wright, Jello Biafra. It has
been said that Canadians are really
Americans, 'but they don't know it yet.'
The statement might be crude hyper-
bole, but certainly the relationship between 'us' and 'them' is more intricate
than our cultural traditionalists would
like us to believe. Bruce McDonald's*
follow-up to his debut feature *Roadkill**
was one of the first Canadian movies to
get real about how most Great White
Northerners feel about the land that lies
due south. In *Highway 61*, a Pickerel
Falls barber (McKellar*) rides down to
mythical New Orleans with a world-
weary rock 'n' roller (Buhagiar). Although they find tacky trailer parks and
mindless violence, their lives are heightened by the experience. (V)

Hill, Arthur
Actor, b. Melfort, Sask., 1922. Hill, a stage
actor, graduated from the University of
British Columbia and moved to England
in 1948. He appeared on Broadway in
the late 1950s and starred in the original
production of *Who's Afraid of Virginia
Woolf?* for which he won a Tony Award.
Later he went to Hollywood where he
played a variety of supporting roles and
the occasional lead. **Films and televi-
sion include:** *The Young Doctors* 1961;
The Ugly American 1963; *Harper* 1966;
Petulia 1968; *Don't Let the Angels Fall*
1969; *Rabbit Run* 1970; *Owen Marshall,
Counselor at Law* 1971–4 (series, as
Marshall); *The Andromeda Strain* 1971;
The Killer Elite 1975; *Futureworld* 1976; *A
Bridge Too Far* 1977; *Riel* 1979 (TV); *The
Champ* 1979; *Dirty Tricks* 1981; *The Ama-
teur* 1982; *Something Wicked This Way
Comes* 1983 (narr); *One Magic Christmas*
1985.

Hiller, Arthur
Director; b. Edmonton, 1923. Like his
contemporary, Norman Jewison,* Hiller
graduated from CBC-TV in the early

1950s in Toronto to mainstream American feature filmmaking. After a series of forgettable films, such as *Popi* and *The Tiger Makes Out*, Hiller scored a huge hit with *Love Story*, the Ryan O'Neal and Ali MacGraw weepie that became one of the top-grossing films of the 1970s and earned him an Academy Award nomination for Best Director. In a long and efficient career, Hiller has shown talent with light comedy – *The In-Laws* and *Outrageous Fortune* – but he is most memorable as the director of Paddy Chayefsky's sardonic *Hospital*. **Films include:** *The Wheeler Dealers* 1963; *The Americanization of Emily* 1964; *Tobruk* 1967; *The Tiger Makes Out* 1967; *Love Story* 1970 (AAN-D); *The Out-of-Towners* 1970; *The Hospital* 1971; *Plaza Suite* 1971; *Man of La Mancha* 1972; *The Man in the Glass Booth* 1974; *W.C. Fields and Me* 1976; *Silver Streak* 1976; *The In-Laws* 1979 (co-p/d); *Making Love* 1982; *Author! Author!* 1982; *The Lonely Guy* 1984 (p/d); *Outrageous Fortune* 1987; *See No Evil, Hear No Evil* 1989; *Taking Care of Business* 1990; *The Babe* 1992; *Married to It* 1993; *Beverly Hills Cop III* 1994.

Hirsch, Michael
See Nelvana Studios.

Hoedeman, Co
Animator; b. Amsterdam, Holland, 1940. Hoedeman's mature work neatly divides into two parts. Hoedeman the fantasist has turned Russian dolls, trains, and sand sculptures into the stuff of dreams in, respectively, *Matrioska*, *Tchou-tchou*, and the Academy Award–winning *The Sand Castle*.* Hoedeman the mentor uses puppets to transform native fables and social concerns into well-meaning but pedestrian films such as *Lummaq* and *The Sniffing Bear*. One sings; the other doesn't. Hoedeman left the Netherlands for the NFB in 1965. After a

try-out as an assistant on educational films, he found a permanent home in French production as a full-time animator in 1968. **Films include:** *Continental Drift* 1968; *Oddball* 1969; *Matrioska* 1970; *Tchou-tchou* 1972; *Monsieur Pointu* 1975 (ph); *The Sand Castle* 1978 (AA-AS); *The Treasure of the Grotoceans* 1980; *Masquerade* 1984; *Charles and François* 1987; *The Box* 1989; *The Sniffing Bear* 1992; *The Garden of Ecos* 1996; *Ludovic: The Snow Gift* 1998; *Ludovic: A Crocodile in My Garden* 2000.

Hoffman, Philip
Filmmaker; b. Kitchener, Ont., 1955. Philip Hoffman is a leading figure in the experimental cinema movement known as diarist or personal cinema. One of his earliest and most successful films *?O, Zoo! (The Making of a Fiction Film)** is considered by many as a classic of this form. Hoffman, a graduate of Sheridan College's Media Arts program during Rick Hancox's* tenure, inherited an interest in memory, landscape, and documentary convention. Mixing home-movie footage with his own luscious cinematography, Hoffman deftly merges documentary practice with personal reflections and fictional codes in ways that elaborate larger themes such as the intersection between the personal and historical. **Films include:** *On the Pond* 1978; *River* 1979–83; *The Road Ended at the Beach* 1983; *Somewhere between Jalostotitlan and Encarnacion* 1984; *?O, Zoo! (The Making of a Fiction Film)* 1986; *passing through/torn formations* 1988; *Technilogic Ordering* 1992–3; *CHIMERA* 1995; *Destroying Angel* (d with Wayne Salazar) 1998; *Kokoro Is for Heart* 1999.

Holland, Andrew and George
Exhibitors. **Andrew:** b. Ottawa, 1844; d. 1929. **George:** b. Nepean, Ont., 1846; death date unknown. On 21 July 1896

the *Ottawa Daily Citizen*, announcing the first-ever Canadian public film screening outside Quebec, reported that 'The Holland Bros. have the Canadian control of this wonderful invention.' That invention was the Vitascope, an early Edison projection system marketed by the two brothers from Ottawa. Unlike Edison himself, these two entrepreneurs immediately recognized the potential of moving-image technology. In 1894, as 'agents for the Smith Premier Typewriter, Edison Phonograph, and the Sorley Storage Battery,' they had opened the world's first kinetoscope parlour in New York City; their expansion to Ottawa marked the beginning of Canada's fascination with cinematographic devices.

Homme à tout faire, L'

1980 99m *prod* Corp. Image M and M, *exp* Jean-Claude Lord, *p* René Malo, *d/sc* Micheline Lanctôt, *ph* André Gagnon, *ed* Annick de Bellefeuille, *mus* François Lanctôt; *with* Jocelyn Bérubé, Andrée Pelletier, Gilles Renaud, Paul Dion, Danielle Schneider, Marcel Sabourin. This film tells the sensitive, eloquent tale of a romantic dreamer (Bérubé) who leaves his Gaspé home after his wife of ten months leaves him for another man. First he arrives in Quebec City where he has a fling with a young girl, then he moves to Montreal where he is hired as a handyman to renovate the basement of a bored suburban housewife (Pelletier). They begin an affair which is cut short by the jealous husband, and he has to move on again. This gentle comedy of manners marked an auspicious directorial debut by former actress Micheline Lanctôt.*

Hoolboom, Mike

Filmmaker; b. Toronto, 1959. Prolific and protean, Mike Hoolboom has produced over a large body of work, ranging from experimental shorts to daring feature-length dramas. Hoolboom's often cinematically breathtaking films are as visually inventive as Derek Jarman's, and as politically courageous as Pier Paolo Pasolini's in their exploration of the troubling intersections of desire, the body, and the nation-state in the chaotic, late twentieth century. A major talent whose work has been acclaimed both here and abroad, Hoolboom twice captured the Best Short Film Award at the Toronto International Film Festival for his films about living with HIV: *Frank's Cock* and *Letters from Home*. **Films include:** *White Museum* 1986; *Svetlana* 1988; *From Home* 1988; *Mexico* 1992 (d with Steve Sanguedolce); *Kanada* 1993; *Valentine's Day* 1994; *Frank's Cock* 1994; *House of Pain* 1995; *Letters from Home* 1996; *Panic Bodies* 1998.

Houde, Germain

Actor; b. Petit-Saguenay, Que., 1952. Germain Houde is predisposed by his physique to playing tough-guy parts; his screen characters have ranged from cruel criminals to corrupt policemen. His first cinematic role, a courageous one indeed, was in Anne Claire Poirier's* acclaimed *Mourir à tue-tête*,* where he played the vicious rapist. He won Genies for best supporting actor for his performances as a rural simpleton in *Les Bons Débarras** and as a brutal cop in *Un Zoo la nuit*.* He played the central role in the films *Love-moi* and *L'Assassin jouait du trombone*, and has been featured in numerous Quebec television series, including *Les Filles de Caleb*, *Scoop* and *Omertà*. **Films and television include:** *Mourir à tue-tête* 1979; *Les Bons Débarras* 1980 (GA-SA); *Lucien Brouillard* 1983; *Un Zoo la nuit* 1987 (GA-SA); *La Nuit avec Hortense* 1988; *Terminal City Riochet* 1989; *Love-moi* 1990; *Les Filles de Caleb* 1990–1 (series); *L'Assassin jouait du trombone*

1991; *Léolo* 1992; *Scoop* 1991–5 (series); *Le Secret de Jérôme* 1994; *La Vengeance de la femme en noir* 1997; *Omertà II: La Loi du silence* 1997 (TV); *Omertà III: Le Dernier des hommes d'honneur* 1999 (TV).

Hounds of Notre Dame, The
1980 95m *prod* Fraser Film Associates, *p* Fil Fraser, *d* Zale Dalen, *sc* Ken Mitchell, *ph* Ron Orieux, *ed* Barry Freeman, *mus* Maurice Marshall; *with* Thomas Peacocke, Frances Hyland, Barry Morse, David Ferry. *The Hounds of Notre Dame* portrays thirty-six hours in the life of Père Athol Murray (Peacocke), a hard-drinking, chain-smoking Catholic priest, teacher, political activist, and coach of the school hockey team, the Hounds. Peacocke gives a powerful performance as Murray who defies his superior (Morse*) and gives anti-CCF speeches in 1940s Saskatchewan. The film received outstanding reviews, and Peacocke won a Genie for Best Actor, but it only received limited distribution and came to symbolize the problems inherent in producing quality Canadian features. When he received his award, Peacocke spoke out forcefully about the frustrations of acting in a film that 'no one gets a chance to see.' **Awards include:** GA: Actor (Peacocke).

Howard, Kathleen
Actor and singer; b. Clifton (Niagara Falls), 1880; d. 1956. Trained in opera, Howard sang at major houses in Europe, and spent twelve seasons at the Metropolitan Opera (1916–28). She also wrote about fashion and in 1928 became the editor of *Harper's Bazaar*. In another career move, she went to Hollywood in the 1930s and starred as W.C. Field's wife in *It's a Gift* and *The Man on the Flying Trapeze*. She continued with character roles until her retirement in 1950. **Films include:** *Death Takes a Holiday* 1934; *It's a Gift* 1934; *The Man on the Flying Trapeze* 1935; *Ball of Fire* 1942; *Laura* 1944; *Shady Lady* 1945; *The Bride Goes Wild* 1948; *The Pary Girl* 1950; *Born to Be Bad* 1950.

Hunger
1973 11m22s *prod* NFB, *p* René Jodoin, *d/an* Peter Foldès, *ph* Alan Ward, Richard Michaud, *ed* Pierre Lemelin, *mus* Pierre Brault. This biting satire of conspicuous consumption was the first animated short made with the aid of a computer. A man eats, at first sparingly. His appetite then grows to alarming proportions, yet he is haunted by images of starving people. A powerful wordless film about gluttony. (V) **Awards include:** Cannes: Special Jury Prize for animation; AAN: Animated Short.

Huston, Walter
Actor; b. Walter Houghston, Toronto, 1884; d. 1950. Distinguished character actor of stage and screen, has been described as 'possibly the best American actor ever.' Ironically, Huston was brought up in Toronto. His busy film career began in 1928 when he was already a seasoned veteran of the stage. He quickly rose through the ranks to play leads in D.W. Griffith's *Abraham Lincoln*, William Wyler's *Dodsworth*, William Dieterle's *The Devil and Daniel Webster* and René Clair's *And Then There Were None*. Although Houston was not noted as a singer, Kurt Weill and Maxwell Anderson composed 'September Song' for him to perform on Broadway in *Knickerbocker Holiday*. He received four Academy Award nominations and finally won for his performance as the grizzled prospector in *The Treasure of the Sierra Madre*, directed by his son, John Houston. **Films include:** *The Virginian* 1929; *Abraham Lincoln* 1930; *The Criminal Code* 1930; *Rain* 1932; *Dodsworth* 1936

(AAN-A); *The Light That Failed* 1939; *The Devil and Daniel Webster* 1941 (AAN-A); *The Maltese Falcon* 1941; *The Shanghai Gesture* 1941; *Swamp Water* 1941; *Why We Fight* 1942 (voice); *Yankee Doodle Dandy* 1942 (AAN-SA); *The Outlaw* 1943; *Dragon Seed* 1944; *And Then There Were None* 1945; *Dragonwyck* 1946; *Duel in the Sun* 1947; *The Treasure of the Sierra Madre* 1948 (AA-SA); *Summer Holiday* 1948; *The Furies* 1950.

Hutt, William

Actor; b. Toronto, 1920. William Hutt is one of the best-known and respected figures in Canadian theatre. He began his career at the University of Toronto and joined the Stratford Festival for its first season in 1953. He has since appeared in over seventy Stratford productions, playing all the great roles, including Hamlet, Lear, Macbeth, and Falstaff. He has occasional forayed into film and television, winning the ACTRA Award in 1974 for his role as Sir John A. Macdonald in CBC's *The National Dream*, and the Best Actor Genie for *Long Day's Journey into Night** in 1996. **Films and television include:** *Oedipus Rex* 1957; *There Was a Crooked Man* 1960; *Henry V* 1966 (TV); *The Fixer* 1968; *The National Dream* 1974 (TV); *The Shape of Things to Come* 1979 (voice); *The Wars* 1983; *The Kid Who Couldn't Miss* 1983 (narr); *Covergirl* 1984; *Much Ado about Nothing* 1987 (TV); *Long Day's Journey into Night* 1995 (GA-A).

Hutterites, The

1964 28m *prod* NFB, *p* Tom Daly, Roman Kroitor, *d* Colin Low, *ph/ed* John Spotton, *narr* Stanley Jackson. The Hutterites are an Anabaptist religious group who live communally in colonies. Persecuted for hundreds of years in Europe (where their leader Jacob Hutter was burned at the stake in 1536), they settled in the United States in the mid-1800s then mi-grated to the Canadian prairies in 1918. This NFB film, shot in black and white by the award-winning John Spotton,* was made at one of the Hutterite colonies in Alberta and shows all aspects of their daily life. (V) **Awards include:** CFA: Cinematography.

I

Ianzelo, Tony

Cinematographer and director; b. Tony Ianuzielo, Toronto, 1935. Ianzelo, the son of Italian immigrants, studied at Ryerson in Toronto and joined the NFB as a camera assistant. In 1966, he directed his first film, *Antonio*, a moving portrait of his father. He proved to be a talented cinematographer, and in partnership with Boyce Richardson* directed and shot some of the most important NFB films about the Cree of Northern Quebec and life in communist China. Two of his films, *Blackwood** and *High Grass Circus,** were nominated for Academy Awards. *Transitions*, which he directed with Colin Low, was the first film to be shot in IMAX 3-D. **Films include:** *Antonio* 1966 (d/ph/co-ed); *The Best Damn Fiddler from Calabogie to Kaladar* 1968 (ph, TV, CFA-PH); *Don't Knock the Ox* 1970 (d/ph, CFA-TS); *Goodbye Sousa* 1973 (d/co-ph, CFA-TS); *Cree Hunters of Mistassini* 1974 (ph/co-d with Boyce Richardson, CFA-SD); *Our Land Is Our Life* 1974 (ph/co-d with Richardson); *Blackwood* 1976 (co-d/ph, AAN-SD); *High Grass Circus* 1976 (co-d/ph, AAN-SD); *Cree Way* 1977 (d/co-ph); *North China Commune* 1979 (ph/co-d with Richardson); *North China Factory* 1980 (ph/co-d with Richardson); *China: A Land Transformed* 1980 (ph/co-d with Richardson); *From Ashes to Forest* 1984 (d/ph); *Transitions* 1986 (d with Colin Low); *Emergency/Urgence* 1988 (d with

Low); *The First Emperor of China* 1989
(co-d); *Momentum* 1992 (d with Low).

If You Love This Planet
1983 26m *prod* NFB, *exp* Kathleen Shannon, *p* Edward Le Lorrain, *d/ed* Terre
Nash, *ph* André-Luc Dupont, Susan
Trow, Don Virgo, *mus* Karl Duplessis.
Terre Nash's* directorial debut became
an international sensation when it was
labelled 'propaganda' by U.S. President
Ronald Reagan's conservative administration and banned from showing in the
United States. The film is devastating in
its simplicity. Renowned peace activist
Dr Helen Caldicott delivers a lecture
about precisely what a nuclear war
would mean in terms of human casualties. Nash then cuts from shots of the
eloquent Caldicott to horrifying black-
and-white footage of the atomic bomb-
ings of Hiroshima and Nagasaki. *If You
Love This Planet* is one of the definitive
films of the peace movement. During
her Oscar-acceptance speech Nash
thanked the Reagan administration for
the added publicity it had brought to
the film. (V) **Awards include:** AA: Short
Documentary.

I'll Find a Way
1978 26m *prod* NFB, *exp* Kathleen Shannon, *p* Yuki Yoshida, *d* Beverly Shaffer,
ph Hideaki Kobayashi, *ed* Ginny Stikeman, *mus* Larry Crosley. Upon its release, *I'll Find a Way* proved another
coup – and provided an Academy
Award – for the now-defunct NFB wom-
en's Studio D. This deceptively simple
film about a young girl facing spina
bifada with inspiring courage, follows
nine-year-old Nadia DeFranco through
an average week, from meeting with her
schoolmates, to her family life, to gener-
ally coping with her disability. The title
comes from the final line of the film,
when Nadia describes how she'll man-

age in life despite pervasive negative at-
titudes about the disabled. Director
Beverly Shaffer* returned to Nadia's life
in 1999 to capture her decision to marry
in *Just a Wedding*. (V) **Awards include:**
AA: Live-Action Short.

I Love a Man in Uniform
1993 98m *prod* Miracle Pictures, *exp*
Alexandra Raffé, *p* Paul Brown, *d/sc*
David Wellington, *ph* David Franco,
ed Susan Shipton, *mus* Ron Sures, The
Tragically Hip; *with* Tom McCamus,
Brigitte Bako, Kevin Tighe, David
Hemblen. Henry Adler (McCamus) is a
bank clerk and aspiring actor who becomes increasingly angered with the
surrounding urban violence. When he
lands a role of a 'cop-on-the-edge' in a
television crime series, he develops an
unhealthy identification with the character and he eventually loses his grip on
reality as his identity is overwhelmed by
his alter-ego. McCamus's skillful performance makes watching Henry's de-
generation into a power-hungry, corrupt
cop creepy fun. (V) **Awards include:**
GA: Actor (McCamus), Supporting Actor (Tighe).

Images of a Dictatorship
1999 50m *prod* Macumba International,
p Patricio Henriquez, Raymonde Pro-
vencher, Robert Cornellier, *d* Patricio
Henriquez, *ph* Raúl Cuevas, *ed* Jean-
Marie Drot, *mus* Robert M. Lepage. Chil-
ean cameraman Raúl Cuevas spent seventeen years documenting life in Chile
under the ruthless military dictatorship
of Augusto Pinochet. The film, arranged
in a series of tableaux by Montreal director Patricio Henriquez, provides a close-
up look at Pinochet's brutal regime and
those who opposed him. Behind-the-
scenes glimpses of guerrilla activity are
mixed with footage of street demonstrations and police violence. Pinochet ap-

pears in several unguarded moments, talking and laughing with his supporters, unaware that his actions were being recorded for posterity. **Awards include:** PJ: Documentary.

In Praise of Older Women

1978 110m *prod* RSL Productions, Astral Bellevue Pathé, *exp* Stephen J. Roth, Harold Greenberg, *p* Robert Lantos, Claude Héroux, *d* George Kaczender, *sc* Paul Gottlieb, *novel* Stephen Vizinczey, *ph* Miklos Lente, *ed* George Kaczender, Peter Wintonick, *mus* Tibor Polgar; *with* Karen Black, Tom Berenger, Susan Strasberg, Helen Shaver, Marilyn Lightstone. This film, which is based on Stephen Vizenczey's slight but popular coming-of-age novel about a Hungarian Lothario, created quite a stir when it was first released. The world premiere at the Toronto Festival of Festivals in 1978 caused a near riot as the tickets were oversold and the crowd became unruly. All this gave the film an edge of controversy that in retrospect seems undeserved. It is a mildly titillating tale of an immature young man (Berenger) and his various conquests, rather than a groundbreaking sexual revelation such as *Last Tango in Paris*. (V) **Awards include:** CFA: Actress (Shaver), Supporting Actress (Lightstone), Cinematography, Art Direction.

In the Gutter and Other Good Places

1993 56m *prod* Ladder to the Moon Productions, *p/d/sc/narr* Cristine Richey, *ph* Douglas Munro, Philip Letourneau, *ed* Jack Morbin, *mus* Adrian Belew; *with* Colin Sinclaire, Ron Beards, Jean Leduc. In a poignant, humorous, and gut-wrenching look at urban street life, director Cristine Richey focuses on three 'dumpster divers' as they collect bottles and other recyclables from garbage cans to earn money. One, Ron, is a former en-

gineer who lost his family and privileged position to alcoholism. Another, Colin, who was considered a genius as a child, offers a thoughtful rant on society's wasteful ways; his suicide is a slap in the face for viewers. *In the Gutter* is an eye-opener and the cinematography makes the big city look lonely and unforgiving – a disturbing sign of the times. **Awards include:** GA: Feature Documentary.

Ireland, John

Actor; b. Victoria, B.C., 1914; d. 1992. Although Ireland's run at accumulating more than 100 on-screen credits landed him in some shabby pictures during the 1970s and 1980s, his career featured many high spots. He was discovered by Margaret Webster while he was studying under Alfred Lunt and Lynn Fontanne. Webster cast him as the lead in her 1941 Broadway production of *Macbeth*. His work on the big screen includes John Ford's *My Darling Clementine*, Howard Hawks's *Red River*, and Stanley Kubrick's *Spartacus*. He was nominated for an Academy Award for his role in *All the King's Men*. In his later years, Ireland returned to Canada to write his memoirs and star in tax-shelter era* bombs such as *Incubus* and *Tomorrow Never Comes*. **Films include:** *A Walk in the Sun* 1946; *My Darling Clementine* 1946; *Joan of Arc* 1948; *Red River 1948*; *All the King's Men* 1949 (AAN-SA); *I Shot Jesse James* 1949; *The Return of Jesse James* 1950; *Queen Bee* 1955; *Gunfight at the O.K. Corral* 1957; *Party Girl* 1958; *Spartacus* 1960; *55 Days at Peking* 1963; *The Ceremony* 1963; *The Fall of the Roman Empire* 1964; *Farewell, My Lovely* 1975; *Tomorrow Never Comes* 1977; *The Shape of Things to Come* 1979; *Incubus* 1982.

Irwin, Mark

Cinematographer; b. Toronto, 1950. This

boy wonder of Canadian cinematographers, who studied film at York University, had shot scores of feature films and documentaries by the time he reached his mid-twenties. In 1976 Irwin shot the CBC-TV series *The Newcomers* and his first feature, *Starship Invasion*. He was once dubbed the 'prince of darkness,' both for his distinctive low-light shooting style and for his body of work, which includes Paul Lynch's *Blood and Guts* and six David Cronenberg* films. Since the mid-1980s, Irwin has primarily shot big-budget Hollywood films such as *Vampire in Brooklyn* and *Something about Mary*. **Films and television include:** *Point of No Return* 1976; *Starship Invasion* 1977; *Blood and Guts* 1978; *Jimmy Playing with Time* 1979 (TV); *The Brood* 1979; *Fast Company* 1979; *Tanya's Island* 1980; *Cries in the Night* 1980; *Scanners* 1980; *Bix: Ain't None of Them Play like Him Yet* 1981; *Baker County, U.S.A.* 1982; *Videodrome* 1983; *Dead Zone* 1983; *Artie Shaw: Time Is All You've Got* 1985; *A Child's Christmas in Wales* 1986 (TV); *The Fly* 1986; *Youngblood* 1986; *The Hanoi Hilton* 1987; *The Blob* 1988; *Bat 21* 1988; *Fright Night Part II* 1989; *Robocop 2* 1990; *Showdown in Little Tokyo* 1991; *Passenger 57* 1992; *Man's Best Friend* 1993; *D2: The Mighty Ducks* 1994; *Wes Craven's New Nightmare* 1994; *Dumb and Dumber* 1994; *Vampire in Brooklyn* 1995; *Kingpin* 1996; *Scream* 1996; *Something about Mary* 1998; *10 Things I Hate about You* 2000; *Road Trip* 2000.

Irwin, May

Actor; b. May Campbell, Whitby, Ont., 1862; d. 1938. May Irwin was a popular, lively stage performer during the 1890s, and she appeared in *The Kiss* with John Rice in 1896, the first Edison film to be shown in Canada. Although it amounted to nothing more than a close-up of two people kissing on the cheek, the film caused a sensation and was the first to be condemned as immoral.

Isabel

1968 108m *prod* Quest Film Productions, *p/d/sc* Paul Almond *ph* Georges Dufaux, *ed* George Appleby, *mus* Harry Freedman; *with* Geneviève Bujold, Marc Strange, Gerard Parkes, Al Waxman. *Isabel*, the first of Paul Almond's* trilogy of films made with Geneviève Bujold* (see also *The Act of the Heart* and *Journey*) was one of the first Canadian features to be picked up for distribution by a Hollywood major (Paramount). A young woman (Bujold) returns to her parent's home in Gaspé and must deal with her mother's death. Days after the funeral she is left in a dark, lifeless home with her ailing uncle (Parkes) and images of the family's history, which includes domestic violence and incest. Her relationship with a local (Strange) helps her to escape her dark past. The film's cinematography perfectly mirrors the young woman's feelings with its dark, foggy landscapes. The film presents one of Bujold's early English-speaking roles, along with fine supporting performances by Waxman,* Parkes, and Strange. **Awards include:** CFA: Actor (Parkes), Actress (Bujold), Cinematography, Editing.

I've Heard the Mermaids Singing

1987 84m *prod* Vos Productions, *exp* Don Haig, *p* Patricia Rozema, Alexandra Raffé, *d/sc/ed* Patricia Rozema, *ph* Douglas Koch, *mus* Mark Korven; *with* Sheila McCarthy, Paule Baillargeon, Ann-Marie MacDonald, John Evans, Brenda Kamino, Richard Monette. Patricia Rozema's* debut feature is a gentle comedy about Polly (McCarthy*), an 'organizationally impaired person Friday,' who works for a chic downtown art dealer (Baillargeon*). Polly's story is told in the form of a self-confession, taped on video. As she talks and mimics in front of the camera, her relationship with the dealer is told in flashbacks. The strange dependency that develops between the two women is shattered by the arrival of the dealer's lesbian lover. At times whimsical to a fault, the film is wholly dependent on McCarthy's extraordinary performance as Polly. Her sweet innocence is completely credible and never mawkish. (V) **Awards include:** GA: Actress (McCarthy), Supporting Actress (Baillargeon); Cannes: Prix de la Jeunesse.

J

Jacobi, Lou
Actor; b. Toronto, 1913. Jacobi appeared on stage from an early age, and entered films in the late 1950s as the father in *The Diary of Anne Frank*. He played character parts in a number of good films – *Irma la douce* with Shirley MacLaine, Woody Allen's *Everything You Always Wanted to Know about Sex*, and *My Favourite Year* with Peter O'Toole – usually as a comic, bumbling type. **Films and television include:** *The Diary of Anne Frank* 1959; *Song without End* 1960; *Irma la douce* 1963; *Cotton Comes to Harlem* 1970; *Little Murders* 1971; *The Dean Martin Show* 1971–3 (TV); *Everything You Always Wanted to Know about Sex* 1972; *Next Stop, Greenwich Village* 1976; *Roseland* 1977; *The Magician of Lublin* 1979; *The Lucky Star* 1980; *Arthur* 1981; *My Favorite Year* 1982; *Off Your Rocker* 1982; *Isaac Littlefeathers* 1984; *Avalon* 1990; *I.Q.* 1994.

J.A. Martin photographe
1977 101m *prod* NFB, *p* Jean-Marc Garand, *d* Jean Beaudin, *sc* Jean Beaudin, Marcel Sabourin, *ph* Pierre Mignot, *ed* Jean Beaudin, Hélène Girard, *mus* Maurice Blackburn; *with* Marcel Sabourin, Monique Mercure, Marthe Thiéry, Catherine Tremblay, Mariette Duval. A wife (Mercure*) takes a coura-geous decision to leave her five children at home and accompany her husband (Sabourin*) on his yearly summer tour as an itinerant photographer. They travel through the backwoods of late-nineteenth-century Quebec shooting weddings and baptisms and, more importantly, rediscovering each other. This marvelously observed, slow-paced film, one of the best ever produced by the NFB, has little plot but many rewarding interludes and extraordinary performances from the two leads, especially Mercure who won the Best Actress Award at the Cannes Film Festival. (V) **Awards include:** CFA: Feature Film, Director, Actress (Mercure), Cinematography, Editing, Art Direction, Sound Re-recording; Cannes: Best Actress (Mercure).

Janis
1974 97m *prod* Crawley Films, *exp* Budge Crawley, *d/ed* Howard Alk, Seaton Findlay, *mus* Janis Joplin. This is undoubtedly the most complete film ever made about Janis Joplin, who was one of great rock and blues singers from the 1960s. The idea for the film began when Budge Crawley* saw footage shot during the Festival Express concert tour that crossed Canada just months before Joplin died of a drug overdose in 1970. Crawley spent the next four years tracking down all available film footage on Joplin (including performances at Montrey Pop and Woodstock) and secured permission from her parents to release it as a feature in 1974. The film combines compelling concert performances with rehearsals and frank backstage interviews. **Awards include:** CFA: Theatrical Documentary.

Jésus de Montréal
1989 118m *prod* Max Films, Gérard Mital Productions, NFB, *exp* Monique Létourneau, *p* Roger Frappier, Pierre Gendron,

d/sc Denys Arcand, *ph* Guy Dufaux *ed* Isabelle Dedieu, *mus* Yves Laferrière; *with* Lothaire Bluteau, Rémy Girard, Monique Miller, Johanne Marie Tremblay, Catherine Wilkening, Robert Lepage. The plot follows a group of actors who have been asked by the Catholic church to revitalize the Passion play on Montreal's Mount Royal. The results are electrifying. The troupe, led by unemployed actor Daniel Coulombe (Bluteau*), creates a breathtaking reinterpretation that incorporates ancient texts, historical and theological debates about Christ, and even Hamlet's famous soliloquy. As the production becomes a hit, the lines between fiction and reality become blurred, particularly for Daniel. The play also becomes a media sensation, much to the alarm of church authorities. When the church intervenes to stop the production, the replication of the tale of Christ's persecution and death grows to eerie proportions. This Borgesian weaving of the real and the fictional, the perceived and the invisible – Denys Arcand's* most rewarding fiction feature to date – is an analysis of power, institutional authority, rampant materialism, and the spiritual vacuum in modern Quebec society. (V) **Awards include:** GA: Picture, Director, Original Screenplay, Actor (Bluteau), Supporting Actor (Girard), Art Direction, Costumes, Cinematography, Editing, Musical Score, Overall Sound, Sound Editing; Golden Reel Award; AAN: Foreign-Language Film; Cannes: Jury Prize.

Jewison, Norman

Director and producer; b. Toronto, 1926. Jewison received his early training at CBC-TV. In 1960, he left Canada for the world of Hollywood, where he made a remarkable series of successful features and became one of America's hottest directors of the 1960s. *The Russians Are Coming, the Russians Are Coming, In the Heat of the Night, The Thomas Crown Affair*, and *Fiddler on the Roof* generated a total of fifteen Academy Award nominations, including two for Best Picture and Best Director. Jewison's career slipped badly in the 1970s, but he regained his footing with *Moonstruck*, a film that again generated Academy Award nominations for Best Picture and Best Director. Jewison returned to Toronto in 1987 to establish the Canadian Film Centre and has since been active in the Canadian film scene, producing Bruce McDonald's *Dance Me Outside** in 1994. In 1999, he received the Irving G. Thalberg Award for lifetime achievement at the Academy Awards. **Films include:** *40 Pounds of Trouble* 1963 (d); *The Cincinnati Kid* 1965 (d); *The Russians Are Coming, the Russians Are Coming* 1966 (p/d, AAN-P); *In the Heat of the Night* 1967 (d, AAN-D); *The Thomas Crown Affair* 1968 (p/d); *Gaily, Gaily* 1969 (p/d); *Fiddler on the Roof* 1971 (p/d, AAN-D, AAN-P); *Billy Two Hats* 1973 (p); *Jesus Christ Superstar* 1973 (p/d/sc); *Rollerball* 1975 (p/d); *... And Justice for All* 1979 (p/d); *A Soldier's Story* 1984 (p/d, AAN-P); *Agnes of God* 1985 (p/d); *Moonstruck* 1987 (p/d, AAN-D, AAN-P); *In Country* 1989 (p/d); *Other People's Money* 1991 (p/d); *Dance Me Outside* 1994 (exp); *Bogus* 1996 (p/d); *The Hurricane* 1999 (co-p/d).

John and the Missus

1986 95m *prod* Peter O'Brian Productions, Independent Pictures, Big Island Motion Pictures, CBC, *exp* Peter O'Brian, Howard Rosen, *p* Peter, O'Brian, John Hunter, *d/sc/novel* Gordon Pinsent, *ph* Frank Tidy, *ed* Bruce Nyznik, *mus* Michael Conway Baker; *with* Gordon Pinsent, Jackie Burroughs, Randy Follett, Jessica Steen, Timothy Webber. *John and the Missus*, written by, directed by, and starring Gordon Pinsent, is also based on Pinsent's novel. The film is a sentimental look back to a time when small Newfoundland communities were a way of life to be treasured. John is a miner, but there is nothing left to mine. When the government comes to close down the pit – and by extension the town – John resists. When resistance proves futile, he literally uproots his house and sails away. **Awards include:** GA: Actor (Pinsent), Musical Score.

Johnny Mnemonic

1995 98m *prod* Alliance Productions, *exp* Staffan Ahrenberg, Victoria Hamburg, Robert Lantos, B.J. Rack, *p* Don Carmody, *d* Robert Longo, *sc/short story* William Gibson, *ph* François Protat, *ed* Ronald Sanders, *mus* Brad Fiedel; *with* Keanu Reeves, Dina Meyer, Ice-T, Takeshi, Dolph Lundgren, Henry Rollins. William Gibson, the pioneer of cyberpunk, based the script on his own short story. On paper *Johnny Mnemonic* reads like an amusing intellectual adventure set in *Blade Runner* terrain. A twenty-first century courier (Reeves*), who can download computer information directly into his brain, is on the run from a variety of nasties intent on pulling his plug. However the film, New York artist Robert Longo's first, is a terrible bore – shot in a flat manner, with Reeves at his wooden worst. The script would likely have worked better as an animated feature. (V) **Awards include:** Golden Reel Award.

Jones, Mike, Andy, and Cathy

Mike: Director, actor, writer, and cinematographer; b. St John's, Nfld., 1944; **Andy:** Director, writer, and actor; b. St John's, Nfld., 1948; **Cathy:** Actor and writer; b. St John's, Nfld., 1955. The multi-talented Jones family is Newfoundland's comic gift to the rest of Canada. Founders of the Codco comedy

troupe (along with Mary Walsh* and Robert Joy*), Mike, Andy, and Cathy have been skewing the establishment, politicians, and sacred cows for more than twenty-five years. Mike Jones was a founding member of the Newfoundland Independent Filmmaker's Co-op in 1975, and in 1976 he began production of his ambitious, decidedly quirky satire of Newfoundland politics, *The Adventure of Faustus Bidgood,** starring Andy in the title role. The film was finally released ten years later. Both Andy and Cathy appeared the television series *CODCO* during the 1980s, but Andy left the show when the CBC brass tried to censor his biting satires of the Catholic Church. Cathy, along with Mary Walsh, eventually moved on to create the very popular *This Hour Has 22 Minutes*. **Mike Jones's films include:** *Morning* 1972 (d); *Grand Larceny* 1974 (d); *Codpieces: A Codco Sampler* 1976 (d); *Dolly Cake* 1977 (d); *Aerial View* 1979 (a); *Sisters of the Silver Scalpel* 1982 (d); *Swashbucklers of '82* 1982 (d); *Stations* 1983 (co-sc/a); *Outport Lesbians* 1985 (a); *The Adventure of Faustus Bidgood* 1986 (co-p/co-d/co-sc/ph/ed); *Secret Nation* 1992 (d/co-ph); *Congratulations* from *Preludes* 2000 (d/sc/a). **Andy Jones's films and television include:** *Outport Lesbians* 1985 (a); *The Adventure of Faustus Bidgood* 1986 (co-p/co-d/co-sc/a); *CODCO* 1986–9 (a/co-sc, series); *Coleslaw Warehouse* 1992 (a); *Secret Nation* 1992 (a); *Buried on Sunday* 1993 (a); *Life with Billy* 1993 (a,TV); *Paint Cans* 1994 (a); *Kids in the Hall: Brain Candy* 1996 (a); *Extraordinary Visitor* 1998 (a); *Rain, Drizzle, and Fog* 1998 (a); *When Ponds Freeze Over* 1998 (a); *Dooley Gardens* 1999–2000 (a, series); *Preludes* 2000 (a). **Cathy Jones's films and television include:** *Outport Lesbians* 1985 (d/a); *The Adventure of Faustus Bidgood* 1986 (a); *CODCO* 1986–93 (a/co-sc, series); *Secret Nation* 1992 (a); *This Hour Has 22 Minutes*

1994–present (a/co-sc, series); *Preludes 2000* (a).

Jory, Victor

Actor; b. Dawson City, Yukon, 1902; d. 1982. Jory was educated at the University of California, and entered films from the stage at the beginning of the sound era. He played occasional leads and then numerous character roles in a variety of films, mostly B pictures, usually as the evil-eyed heavy: he was Injun Joe in *The Adventures of Tom Sawyer*, he gave Shirley Temple a hard time in *Susannah of the Mounties*, and he was particularly memorable as the racist husband in *The Fugitive Kind* opposite Marlon Brando and Joanne Woodward. **Films include:** *Pride of the Legion* 1932; *State Fair* 1933; *The Devil's in Love* 1933; *Madame Du Barry* 1934; *A Midsummer Night's Dream* 1935; *Escape from Devil's Island* 1935; *Bulldog Drummond at Bay* 1937; *The Adventures of Tom Sawyer* 1938; *Each Dawn I Die* 1939; *Man of Conquest* 1939; *Susannah of the Mounties* 1939; *Gone with the Wind* 1939; *The Shadow* 1940; *Charlie Chan in Rio* 1941; *The Loves of Carmen* 1948; *Canadian Pacific* 1949; *The Man from Alamo* 1953; *Cat-Women of the Moon* 1953; *The Fugitive Kind* 1960; *The Miracle Worker* 1962; *Cheyenne Autumn* 1964; *Jigsaw* 1968; *Mackenna's Gold* 1969 (narr); *A Time for Dying* 1971; *Papillon* 1973; *The Boy Who Talks to Whales* 1975; *The Mountain Men* 1980.

Joshua Then and Now

1985 118m (127m TV version) *prod* RSL Productions, *p* Robert Lantos, Stephen J. Roth, *d* Ted Kotcheff, *sc/novel* Mordecai Richler, *ph* François Protat, *ed* Ron Wisman, *mus* Philippe Sarde; *with* James Woods, Gabrielle Lazure, Alan Scarfe, Michael Sarrazin, Alan Arkin, Linda Sorensen. This collaboration of director Kotcheff* and writer Richler* was highly anticipated (due mainly to the success of their earlier project, *The Apprenticeship of Duddy Kravitz**), but it died at the box office. *Joshua Then and Now* is one of those artificially constructed 1980s miniseries/feature hybrids. It evokes similar feelings to *Duddy*, and owes much to Richler's freestyle, semi-autobiographical tone. The fine ensemble cast is led by James Woods, whose life is complicated by a mixed marriage (his wife is a rich Wasp, he's a poor Jew). The film has stood the test of time as a serio-comic soaper full of colourful characters (Alan Arkin is a standout as Woods's father), but critics rightly noted the choppy editing. (V) **Awards include:** GA: Supporting Actor (Arkin), Supporting Actress (Sorensen), Cinematography, Art Direction, Costumes.

Jour après jour

1962 28m *prod* NFB, *p* Fernand Dansereau, Victor Jobin, Hubert Aquin, *d/sc* Clémont Perron, *ph* Guy Borremans, *ed* Anne Claire Poirier, *mus* Maurice Blackburn. This direct-cinema documentary portrays life in a small Quebec paper mill town, where most the inhabitants derive their living from the mill. The filmmakers, however, chose to shoot in a highly contrived style that emphasized the editing structure and the combination of sync and non-sync sound. (V) **Awards include:** CFA: Arts and Experimental, Cinematography.

Journey

1972 88m *prod* Quest Film Productions, *p/d/sc* Paul Almond, *ph* Jean Boffety, *ed* Honor Griffith, James Mitchell, *mus* Luke Gibson, Nexus; *with* Geneviève Bujold, John Vernon, Beata Hartig, Meg Hogarth. This is the last film in Paul Almond's* trilogy with Geneviève Bujold* (see also *Isabel* and *The Act of the Heart*). It tells an allegorical story of a young woman (Bujold) who is found floating down a river on a log. She is rescued by a man (Vernon*) who carries her to Undersky, his commune in the Quebec wilderness. Haunted by memories from her past, the woman remains uncommunicative until she begins to respond to her natural surroundings. Finally, she travels back up the river to confront her nightmares. Pretentious and obscure, it is the weakest film in the trilogy, and it ended Almond's attempts to create a commercial art-house cinema in Quebec.

Joy, Robert

Actor; b. St John's, Nfld., 1951. Robert Joy, a Rhodes Scholar, was a founding member of Newfoundland's famed Codco comedy troupe, with whom he worked as an actor, musician, writer, and composer for three years. He moved to New York to work in off-Broadway productions and became part of the New York Shakespeare Festival and a regular on Broadway. Joy has appeared in numerous Canadian films (including *Ticket to Heaven** and *Atlantic City**) as well as Milos Forman's *Ragtime* and the cult hit *Desperately Seeking Susan* with Madonna. **Films and television include:** *Atlantic City* 1980; *Ragtime* 1981; *Ticket to Heaven* 1981; *Desperately Seeking Susan* 1985; *The Adventure of Faustus Bidgood* 1986; *Radio Days* 1987; *Millennium* 1988; *Shadows and Fog* 1991; *Grand Larceny* 1991 (TV): *The Dark Half* 1993; *Henry and Verlin* 1994; *Waterworld* 1995; *Harriet the Spy* 1996; *The Divine Ryans* 1999; *The Bookfair Murders* 2000 (TV); *Nuremberg* 2000 (TV); *Haven* 2001 (TV).

Just Watch Me: Trudeau and the '70s Generation

1999 75m *prod* NFB, *exp* Louise Lore, *p* Gerry Flahive, Yves Bilsaillon, *d* Catherine Annau, *ph* Ronald Plante, *ed* Craig Webster. This lively, crowd-pleasing documentary is about Pierre Trudeau's extraordinary impact on the generation that came of age during the 1970s. The men and women who appear in *Just Watch Me* (or *Frenchkiss: La Génération du rêve Trudeau*, the more appropriate and sexier French title), who are now in their mid-thirties, once bought into Trudeau's visions and goals, especially his determined attempt to make Canada bilingual. On another level, director Annau and her eight subjects were electrified by Trudeau's erotic charge – his almost magical ability to sexualize English and French Canadians and the relationship between them. The dream to which the French title refers was not just about linguistic harmony. It was also about a Canada where French and English speakers found the exotic 'other' breathtakingly alluring. (V) **Awards include:** GA: Feature Documentary.

Jutra, Claude

Director, writer, and actor; b. Montreal, 1930; d. 1986. Trained as a doctor, Jutra emerged as a prominent filmmaker during the early stages of the 1960s counterculture movement. In Montreal, this meant a network of hangouts ranging from poets' coffee houses to nightclubs where black R & B bands jived for wannabe hipsters and their soulful chicks. This milieu is the world of Jutra's autobiographical debut feature *À tout prendre.** In it, he plays himself as a discontented rambler, who during the process of terminating an interracial affair with Johanne, a lanky Haitian model, reveals that he's gay. This film, shot in an improvised style reminiscent of the French New Wave, displayed Jutra's fascination with free-spirited, poetry-over-narrative moviemaking.

At the height of his career, Jutra's work became more traditional in both form and content. *Mon oncle Antoine,** which is still regarded by many critics as the best Canadian film ever made, is an archetypal, serio-comic initiation story set in a small town during the 1940s. His next feature, *Kamouraska,** based on a novel by Anne Hébert,* is a lavish period piece constructed around the classic nineteenth-century heroine's memories of a tempestuous love affair. *Kamouraska* was radically cut for its initial release after a difficult shoot, and was then lambasted as a disappointing follow-up to *Mon oncle Antoine.*

Following another debacle, *Pour le meilleur et pour le pire,* Jutra fell out of favour in Quebec and accepted television and theatrical film assignments in English-speaking Canada. Like many of his Quebec pictures, Jutra's English-language films are concerned with turbulent emotion and even mental breakdown, especially in the young. In *Ada* and *Dreamspeaker** he successfully conveys his mistrust of healing institutions.

Moving back to a bigger budget production, Jutra and producer Beryl Fox attempted to film the probably unfilmable Margaret Atwood novel *Surfacing.* The failure of this production hurt both of their careers. Jutra returned to form with *By Design,* a screwball comedy about a lesbian couple who are determined to become parents. This film won over many fans, including *New Yorker* critic Pauline Kael, who called it a 'Lubitsch sex comedy stripped of the glamor but not the fun.'

During the early 1980s, Jutra discovered he had Alzheimer's disease, and as a former doctor, he was acutely aware of its effects. He directed *La Dame en couleur* – his last film, which has been both admired and dismissed for its nightmarish story line – while contending with symptoms of the disease. Jutra drowned himself in the St Lawrence in

1986, a suicide anticipated in the final shot of *À tout prendre,* where he steps off a pier into the glistening river.

Since Jutra's death, no one has questioned his successes, and his failures have been reconsidered. A restored director's cut of *Kamouraska* in 1995 has led some critics to compare it to pictures such as *Dr Zhivago* and *Gone with the Wind.* Since 1993, the Academy of Canadian Cinema and Television has presented the Claude Jutra Award at the Genies to the best director of a first feature, and in 1999 Quebec producer Roger Frappier* launched the Prix Jutra awards for Quebec film.

Claude Jutra lives on as a benevolent and influential guiding spirit of quality in Canadian feature filmmaking. Whether or not *Mon oncle Antoine* is the best Canadian movie ever made, Jutra worked with absolute sincerity and a passion for cinema. **Films and television include:** *Le Dément du lac Jean-Jeunes* 1948 (d); *Mouvement perpétuel* 1949 (d); *Jeunesses musicales* 1956 (d); *A Chairy Tale* 1957 (a/co-d with Norman McLaren, AAN-AS); *Les Mains nettes* 1958 (d); *Anna la bonnes* 1959 (d/sc); *Félex Leclerc, troubadour* 1959 (d); *Fred Barry, comédien* 1959 (d/sc); *Le Niger, jeune république* 1961 (d/co-ed); *Golden Gloves* 1961 (co-ph); *La Lutte* 1961 (co-d/co-ph/co-ed); *Québec–USA, ou l'invasion pacifique* 1962 (d with Michel Brault); *Petit discours de la méthode* (co-d/ed); *À tout prendre* 1964 (d/sc/ed/a, CFA-FF); *Comment savoir* 1966 (d/ed); *Rouliroulant* 1966 (d); *Entre la mer et l'eau douce* 1968 (co-sc); *Le Viol d'une jeune fill douce* 1968 (a); *Wow!* 1970 (d/sc/co-ed); *Mon oncle Antoine* 1971 (d/a/co-ed, CFA-D, CFA-FF); *Kamouraska* 1973 (d/co-sc/co-ed, CFA-SPA); *Pour le meilleur et pour le pire* 1975 (d/sc); *Québec fête juin 75* 1976 (co-d/ed); *Ada* 1977 (d/sc, TV); *Arts Cuba* 1977 (d); *Dreamspeaker* 1977 (d, TV); *Two Solitudes*

1978 (a); *Seer Was Here* 1978 (d/co-sc, TV); *The Wordsmith* 1979 (d, TV); *Surfacing* 1981 (d); *By Design* 1982 (d); *La Dame en couleurs* 1985 (d/sc); *My Father, My Rival* 1985 (d).

K

Kaczender, George
Director and editor; b. Budapest, Hungary, 1933. Kaczender worked as an assistant director in Hungary before emigrating to Canada where he joined the NFB as an editor in 1957. He began directing shorts for the Board in 1963, but in the early 1970s he left to establish his own production company. He directed the controversial *In Praise of Older Women** which was a box-office hit, but since then he has mostly made routine melodramas. Despite several attempts, he has been unable to break through the Hollywood barrier. **Films and television include:** *Nahanni* 1962 (ed); *Ballerina* 1963 (d/sc/ed); *Phoebe* 1964 (d/sc); *You're No Good* 1965 (d/sc); *Don't Let the Angels Fall* 1969 (d); *U-Turn* 1973 (d/co-sc/ed); *In Praise of Older Women* 1978 (d/co-ed); *Agency* 1980 (d/co-ed); *Your Ticket Is No Longer Valid* 1981 (d); *Prettykill* 1987 (d); *Christmas on Division Street* 1991 (d, TV); *Betrayal of Trust* 1994 (d, TV); *Indiscretion of an American Wife* 1998 (d, TV).

Kamouraska
1973 124m (restored director's cut 173m) *prod* Les Productions Carle-Lamy, Parc Film (France), *p* Pierre Lamy, Mag Bodard, *d* Claude Jutra, *sc* Anne Hébert, Claude Jutra, *novel* Anne Hébert, *ph* Michel Brault, *ed* Renée Lichtig, *mus* Maurice Le Roux; *with* Geneviève Bujold, Richard Jordan, Philippe Léotard, Marcel Cuvelier, Suzie Baillargeon, Camille Bernard. Claude Jutra's* adaptation of Anne Hébert's* famous novel is a slow-moving, stunningly beautiful film – thanks in large part to the work of ace cinematographer Michel Brault* – set in nineteenth-century Quebec. As the film opens, Elisabeth (Bujold*) is at the deathbed of her second husband (Cuvelier). She relives her past through a series of flashbacks, telling the story of how her love affair with an American doctor (Jordan) led to the murder of her first husband (Léotard), the brutish seigneur of Kamouraska. This lush period piece with a touch of David Lean had a big budget (at one million dollars it was the most expensive Canadian film of its time) but received only lukewarm praise by the critics and died at the box office. Bujold, in one of her most demanding roles, convincingly plays a naive young woman in some scenes and a woman decades older in others. (V) **Awards include:** CFA: Actress (Bujold), Supporting Actress (Bernard), Art Direction, Special Award.

Kanehsatake: 270 Years of Resistance
1993 119m *prod* NFB, *exp* Colin Neale, *p* Alanis Obomsawin, Wolf Koenig, *d/sc* Alanis Obomsawin, *ph* Roger Rochat, Jean-Claude Labrecque, Phillippe Amiguet, Susan Trow, François Brault, Barry Perles, Zoe Dirse, Jocelyn Simard, André-Luc Dupont, Savas Kalogeras, *ed* Turji Luhovy. A passionate point-of-view documentary about the Oka Crisis of 1990. When the crisis broke with the killing of a Quebec provincial police officer, NFB director Alanis Obomsawin* was the only filmmaker to stay behind the barricades for the full length of the resulting siege. Although the film is historically inaccurate and ignores the fact that the so-called Mohawk 'warriors' were, in part, protecting their turf for profitable cigarette and gun smuggling,

it is nevertheless a powerful reminder of the years of systematic abuse and neglect of First Nations people by both federal and provincial governments. (V)

Karmina

1996 109m *prod* Lux Films, *p* Nicole Robert, *d* Gabriel Pelletier, *sc* Ann Burke, Andrée Pelletier, Gabriel Pelletier, *ph* Eric Cayla, *ed* Gaétan Huot, *mus* Patrick Bourgeois; *with* Isabelle Cyr, Robert Brouillette, Raymond Cloutier, Sylvie Potvin, France Castel. 'Young' vampire Karmina (Cyr) flees Transylvania on her wedding day to live with an eccentric aunt, Esmeralda (Potvin), in Quebec. Esmeralda gives Karmina a potion to restore her to human life. Karmina falls in love with Phillipe (Brouillette), a rock musician she meets through a video dating service. Then Vlad (Cloutier), her ex-fiancé vampire, shows up in Montreal to reclaim his bride. The wacky premise offers an interesting, sardonic update of the vampire genre, and the scene featuring a vampire's coffin on an airport baggage carousel is priceless. (V) **Awards include:** GA: Art Direction, Costumes.

Keating, Lulu

Producer, director, and writer; b. Antigonish, N.S., 1952. Keating, an East Coast producer and director, made her first film in 1980. *Lulu's Back in Town*, which consists of stills shot on an animation camera, was part of a national tour and played at the Smithsonian Institution in Washington. In 1985, she directed the award-winning documentary *Rita MacNeil in Japan*. *The Midday Sun*, a feature she shot in Zimbabwe, was the first Canadian drama filmed entirely in Africa. Keating also wrote and directed *Madam Ada: More Class than Flash*, a documentary about the legendary madam, and *The Moddy Brood*, an animated documentary. **Films and televi-**sion included: *Lulu's Back in Town* 1980 (d/an); *Rita MacNeil in Japan* 1985 (d, TV); *Enterprising Women* 1987 (co-d/sc, TV); *The Midday Sun* 1989 (d/sc); *In Service* 1990 (d, TV); *Ann and Maddy* 1992 (co-p/d); *Romancing the Odds* 1997 (d/sc); *Madame Ada: More Class than Flash* 1998 (d/sc, TV); *The Moody Beach* 1999 (d/sc/narr).

Kemeny, John

Producer; b. Budapest, Hungary, 1925. When Kemeny moved to Canada in 1957 he began one of the longest and most successful careers in Canadian filmmaking. At the NFB, he served for twelve years and produced more than eighty films, including Donald Brittain's *Memorandum,** Tanya Ballantyne's *The Things I Cannot Change,** and Colin Low's* series of twenty-seven films made on Fogo Island. Kemeny eventually left the NFB, and in 1973 he produced *The Apprenticeship of Duddy Kravitz.** In 1979, with Denis Héroux,* he founded the International Cinema Corporation (ICC). Their first collaboration, *Atlantic City,** starring Burt Lancaster, was nominated for five Academy Awards, including Best Picture, the only Canadian drama to receive that honour to date. Later ICC merged with Robert Lantos's* RSL Productions to form Alliance Entertainment, and soon afterward Kemeny left the company to pursue solo television projects. **Films and television include:** *Drylanders* 1963 (co-ed); *Bethune* 1964 (d/sc/(sc/co-p with Donald Brittain); *Three Fishermen* 1964 (co-d); *Three Country Boys* 1964 (co-d); *The Visit* 1964 (d/ed); *Memorandum* 1965; *Ladies and Gentlemen ... Mr Leonard Cohen* 1965; *No Reason to Stay* 1966; *The Things I Cannot Change* 1966; *Newfoundland Project* 1967 (twenty-seven films); *Encounter with Saul Alinsky* 1967 (two films); *Pow-Wow at Duck Lake* 1967; *The Best Damn Fiddler from*

Calabogie to Kaladar 1968 (TV, CFA-FY);
Saul Alinsky Went to War 1968; *Don't Let
the Angels Fall* 1969; *7 Fois ... (par jour)*
1971; *The Apprenticeship of Duddy Kravitz*
1974 (CFA-FY); *White Line Fever* 1975;
Shadow of the Hawk 1976; *Atlantic City*
1980 (AAN-P); *Les Plouffe* 1981; *Quest for
Fire* 1982 ; *Louisiana* 1984; *Mario* 1984; *Le
Crime d'Ovide Plouffe* 1984; *The Bay Boy*
1984 (GA-P); *The Blood of Others* 1984; *Le
Matou* 1985; *The Park Is Mine* 1986 (TV);
The Gate 1987 (GRA); *Murderers among
Us: The Simon Wiesenthal Story* 1989 (TV);
The Josephine Baker Story 1991 (TV).

Kent, Larry

Director, writer, and producer; b. Johan-
nesburg, South Africa, 1937. Of all the
filmmakers from the 1960s, Larry Kent
is the most consistently and unjustly
underrated. His films suffer from a puz-
zling neglect by canon builders and critics alike. Kent came to Vancouver at the
age of nineteen. His low-budget, mid-
1960s feature films *The Bitter Ash** and
*Sweet Substitute** were stylistically brash
and sexually frank dramas of post-ado-
lescent angst. After moving to Montreal
in the late 1960s, his work – often skep-
tical assessments of 1960s idealism and
groundbreaking examinations of feminist themes – led him further into the
margins. Sadly, his impressive feature
Mothers and Daughters went unnoticed
and unreleased. **Films include:** *The Bitter Ash* 1963 (p/d/sc); *Sweet Substitute*
1964 (p/d/sc, CFA-SPA); *High* 1968
(p/d/sc); *Facade* 1969 (co-p/d/sc); *The
Apprentice* 1970 (d); *High Stakes* 1987 (d);
Mothers and Daughters 1992 (d/sc).

Kerr, Richard

Filmmaker; b. St Catharines, Ont., 1952.
Richard Kerr is one of a group of experimental filmmakers – including Philip
Hoffman,* Rick Hancox* – who use
landscape and documentary convention

to explore interior states. Kerr's work is
distinguished by its overt formalism, always referring to the medium and its attendant properties. Eschewing the more
personal focus of his contemporaries,
Kerr instead evokes social and political
realities. His films that indulge his love-
hate relationship with American culture,
as in *The Last Days of Contrition* and
Cruel Rhythm, are particularly effective.
After a rather frustrating attempt at feature filmmaking (*the willing voyeur ...*),
Kerr branched out to explore a wide
range of media, from videos, to installa-
tions, to light boxes adorned with film
strips. **Films include:** *Hawkesville to
Wallenstein* 1977; *Vesta Lunch (Cookin' at
the Vesta)* 1978; *On Land over Water* 1984;
The Last Days of Contrition 1988; *Machine
in the Garden* 1991; *Cruel Rhythm* 1991;
McLuhan 1993; *the willing voyeur ...* 1996;
never confuse movement with action 1998;
human tragedy on a grand scale 1999.

Khanjian, Arsinée

Actor; b. Beruit, Lebanon, 1958. Arsinée
Khanjian came to Canada at age seventeen. She studied drama in Montreal
and completed a Masters degree in political science at l'Université de Montréal. She moved to Toronto in 1984
where she appeared in her first film,
Atom Egoyan's *Next of Kin*. She married
Egoyan* and has served as his creative
muse, starring in all of his features.
More recently, she stretched her acting
talent and won a Gemini for her role as
a desperate mother in Ken Finkleman's
CBC drama series, *Foolish Hearts*. **Films
and television include:** *Next of Kin* 1984;
Family Viewing 1987; *La Boite à soleil* 1988;
Speaking Parts 1989; *The Adjuster* 1991;
Montréal vu par ... 1991; *Calendar* 1993
(co-p/a); *Exotica* 1994; *Yo-Yo Ma Inspired
by Bach* 1997 (TV); *The Sweet Hereafter*
1997; *Foolish Hearts* 1999 (TV); *Felicia's
Journey* 1999.

Kidder, Margot

Actor; b. Yellowknife, N.W.T., 1948. Kidder, one of the most interesting leading ladies of the 1970s, toiled on the television assembly line before making audiences sit up and take notice with her eerie interpretation of separated Siamese twins in Brian De Palma's *Sisters*. In 1975, Kidder directed a medium-length film, *And Again*, which did not gain commercial success; fifteen years later she studied directing at the Canadian Film Centre. She is best known as Lois Lane in Christopher Reeve's four Superman films (1978–87). In 1981, she won a Genie for her standout performance in Don Shebib's *Heartaches*,* but her career since the Superman films has been plagued with uneven performances, and a near-fatal car accident in 1990 left her with a permanent back injury. **Films and television include:** *The Best Damn Fiddler from Calabogie to Kaladar 1968* (TV); *Gaily, Gaily 1969; Quackser Fortune Has a Cousin in the Bronx 1970; Sisters 1973; A Quiet Day in Belfast 1974* (CFA-A); *Black Christmas 1974* (CFA-A); *92 in the Shade 1975* (TV); *The Great Waldo Pepper 1975; And Again 1975* (d/sc); *Superman 1978; The Amityville Horror 1979; Superman II 1980; Willie and Phil 1980; Heartaches 1982* (GA-A); *Superman III 1983; Louisiana 1984; Superman IV: The Quest for Peace 1987; Mob Story 1989; White Room 1990; La Florida 1993; Henry and Verlin 1994; The Planet of Junior Brown 1997* (TV).

King, Allan

Director and producer; b. Vancouver, 1930. King is a director of both documentary and fiction who has blurred the distinction between the two. He was educated at the University of British Columbia and pursued his interest in cinema at the Vancouver Film Society. He joined the Vancouver film unit of the CBC in 1954, and then left for a six-year stint working in England. On his return to Canada in 1967 he settled in Toronto, where he directed three genre busting, ethically unsettling, fly-on-the-wall observational films he called 'actuality dramas': *Warrendale,* *A Married Couple,** and *Come on Children*. Since the mid-1970s, King has worked largely in the fictional mode and in television. He directed and produced the popular *Who Has Seen the Wind,* *Silence of the North*, and *Termini Station*. **Films and television include:** *Skid Row 1956* (d, TV); *Rickshaw 1960* (d); *Running Away Backwards 1964* (d); *Warrendale 1967* (p/d, CFA-D, CFA-FY, CFA-FF); *A Married Couple 1969* (p/d); *Come on Children 1973* (p/d); *A Bird in the House 1973* (d, TV); *Baptizing 1975* (d, TV); *Red Emma 1976* (d, TV); *Maria 1977* (d, TV); *Who Has Seen the Wind 1977* (p/d, GRA); *One Night Stand 1978* (p/d, TV); *The Silence of the North 1981* (d); *Who's in Charge? 1983* (p/d, TV); *Ready for Slaughter 1983* (d, TV); *Termini Station 1989* (p/d); *All the King's Men 1991* (d, TV); *Leonardo Da Vinci 1996* (d, TV); *The Dragon's Egg: Making Peace on the Wreckage of the Twentieth Century 1999* (p/d, TV).

Kissed

1997 78m *prod* Boneyard Film, *exp* John Pozer, *p* Dean English, Lynne Stopkewich, *d* Lynne Stopkewich, *sc* Angus Faser, Lynne Stopkewich, *short story* Barbara Gowdy, *ph* Gregory Middleton, *ed* John Pozer, Peter Roeck, Lynne Stopkewich; *with* Molly Parker, Peter Outbridge, Jay Brazeau, Natasha Morley, Jessie Winter Mudie. Lynne Stopkewich's debut feature plays a nervy game. Although viewers are curious about Sandra (Parker*) and her erotic attraction to dead young men, they are also fearful of spending an evening with their heads stuck in a barf bag. The relief is palpable when audiences realize that Stopkewich has transformed the tormented protagonist of Barbara Gowdy's story into a warm-hearted spiritual quester who delights in the 'energy given off when a thing turns into its opposite.' Briskly paced, dryly funny, and at times ridiculous, *Kissed* is graced by Molly Parker's career-making performance as the Happy Necrophile. **Awards include:** GA: Actress (Parker).

Klein, Bonnie Sherr
Director and producer; b. Philadelphia, Pa., 1941. Klein is best known for *Not a Love Story: A Film about Pornography,** her controversial 1981 investigation into the sex trade. The film ignited a wide-ranging debate about pornography and was banned in Ontario and Saskatchewan, but went on to become one of the most popular films the NFB has ever made. After moving to Canada in 1967 to protest the Vietnam War, Klein joined the NFB's Challenge for Change* program, and made a series of films about the American social activist Saul Alinsky. She moved back to the United States in 1970 to establish a community channel in Rochester and direct for PBS, then returned to Canada in 1975. Her 1989 film with Terre Nash,* *Russian Diary*, provided a memorable last glimpse of the Soviet Union before its transition by glasnost. **Films include:** *Pow-Wow at Duck Lake* 1967 (d); *Encounter with Saul Alinsky* 1967 (d); *Organizing for Power: The Alinsky Approach* 1968 (d, five films); *VTR St-Jacques* 1969 (d); *Patricia's Moving Picture* 1978 (d); *Not a Love Story: A Film about Pornography* 1981 (d); *Speaking Our Peace* 1985 (p/d); *Dark Lullabies* 1985 (p); *Russian Diary* 1989 (p/d with Terre Nash).

Klymkiw, Greg
Producer; b. Winnipeg, 1959. Klymkiw studied English and theatre at the University of Manitoba. As a freelance journalist, he contributed to the CBC, the *Winnipeg Sun*, and *Cinema Canada*. From 1979 to 1982, he was the manager and programmer at the Festival Cinema in Winnipeg, and from 1988 to 1992 he was director of marketing and distribution for the Winnipeg Film Group. During this time, Prairie surrealist cinema flourished and Klymkiw became known as its tireless and inventive promoter. He was also Guy Maddin's* producer on *Tales from the Gimli Hospital,** *Archangel,** and *Careful.** In 1997, he joined the Canadian Film Centre as a producer mentor on the Feature Film Project. **Films include:** *Tales from the Gimli Hospital* 1988 (exp/a); *Archangel* 1990 (p/a); *Smoked Lizard Lips* 1991 (p/a); *Careful* 1992 (p); *Jack of Hearts* 1993 (exp); *The Last Supper* 1995 (p/co-sc); *Symposium* 1996 (p); *City of Dark* 1997 (p); *Zabava* 1999 (d/sc/a); *Vinyl* 2000 (co-p); *Preludes* 2000 (a).

Knox, Alexander
Actor; b. Strathroy, Ont., 1907; d. 1995. Knox was educated at the University of Western Ontario, and first appeared on the London stage before going to Hollywood at the outbreak of the Second World War. He worked steadily as a distinguished character actor and was nominated for an Academy Award for his lead as President Wilson in *Wilson*. However, his left-wing political views caused him to clash with the McCarthyites. He returned to England in the early 1950s, where he continued to work in film (notably *Accident* and *You Only Live Twice*) and as a playwright and novelist. His only Canadian film, *Joshua Then and Now,** came in 1985 at the end of his career. **Films and television include:** *The Sea Wolf* 1941; *This above All* 1942; *Commandos Strike at Dawn* 1943; *Wilson* 1944 (AAN-A); *Two of a Kind* 1951; *Europa '51/The Greatest Love* 1951; *Intent to Kill* 1958; *The Vikings* 1958; *The Wreck of the Mary Deare* 1959; *Crack in the*

Mirror 1960; *The Longest Day* 1962; *The Damned* 1963; *Woman of Straw* 1964; *Modesty Blaise* 1966; *Khartoum* 1966; *Accident* 1967; *You Only Live Twice* 1967; *How I Won the War* 1967; *Villa Rides* 1968; *Nicholas and Alexandra* 1971; *Churchill and the Generals* 1979 (TV); *Tinker, Tailor, Soldier, Spy* 1980 (TV); *Gorky Park* 1983; *Joshua Then and Now* 1985.

Koenig, Wolf

Director, producer, cinematographer, and animator; b. Dresden, Germany, 1927. Koenig is the type of 'complete' filmmaker that the NFB traditionally relied on to create key projects. In the early 1950s, Koenig filmed Norman McLaren's* Academy Award–winning *Neighbours,** animated Colin Low's *The Romance of Transportation in Canada,** and was the cinematographer on Low's *Corral.** Koenig was one of the principals associated with direct cinema at the NFB Unit B, co-directing such non-fiction gems as *City of Gold** with Low* and *Glenn Gould – Off the Record,** *Glenn Gould – On the Record,** and *Lonely Boy** with Roman Kroitor.* He was also the executive producer of the NFB animation department during some of its finest years. A canny veteran, Koenig retired from the NFB in 1995 and remains active in the independent sector. **Films include:** *Neighbours* 1952 (ph); *The Romance of Transportation in Canada* 1953 (co-an, AAN-AS); *Corral* 1954 (ph); *Gold* 1955 (sc/ph/ed); *City of Gold* 1957 (d/ph with Colin Low, CFA-FY, AAN-SD); *It's a Crime* 1957 (d); *The Days before Christmas* 1958 (co-p/co-d/co-ed); *Blood and Fire* 1958 (co-p/ed); *Glenn Gould – Off the Record* 1959 (p/d with Roman Kroitor, also ph); *Glenn Gould – On the Record* 1959 (p/d with Kroitor, also ph); *The Back-Breaking Leaf* 1959 (co-p); *Lonely Boy* 1962 (ph/co-d with Kroitor, CFA-FY); *The Great Toy Robbery* 1964 (co-p); *The Drag* 1965 (co-p, AAN-AS); *Stravinsky* 1965 (ph/ed/co-d with Kroitor); *What on Earth!* 1966 (co-p, AAN-AS); *The House That Jack Built* 1967 (co-p, AAN-AS); *N-Zone* 1970 (co-ph); *Psychocratie* 1970 (co-p, CFA-FY); *Hot Stuff* 1971 (co-p); *The Family That Dwelt Apart* (p, CFA-AS, AAN-AS); *The Street* 1976 (exp, AAN-AS); *The Hottest Show on Earth* 1977 (co-p/co-d/co-sc, CFA-SD); *Spinnolio* 1977 (p, CFA-AS); *Eve Lambart* 1978 (exp/ph); *Why Men Rape* 1979 (co-p/co-ed); *Ted Baryluk's Grocery* 1982 (co-p, GA-SD); *John Cat* 1984 (d/sc); *Connection* 1986 (d/ed); *Kanehsatake: 270 Years of Resistance* 1993 (co-p).

Kotcheff, Ted

Director and producer; b. Toronto, 1931. Ted Kotcheff is best known in Canada for his solid screen adaptations of two novels by his close friend Mordecai Richler*: *The Apprenticeship of Duddy Kravitz** and *Joshua Then and Now.** Kotcheff started as a stagehand at CBC-TV in Toronto. In 1959 he moved to England to work on television dramas with producer and future NFB commissioner Sydney Newman.* While there he directed *Life at the Top*, written by Richler and starring Laurence Harvey. He also directed *Outback* with Donald Pleasence in Australia before arriving in Hollywood in the 1970s, where he directed Sylvester Stallone in *First Blood*, the first of the Rambo series. Now based in Los Angeles, Kotcheff directs and produces mostly for American television. **Films and television include:** *Life at the Top* 1965; *Outback* 1971; *Billy Two Hats* 1973; *The Apprenticeship of Duddy Kravitz* 1974; *Fun with Dick and Jane* 1976; *Someone's Killing the Great Chiefs of Europe* 1978; *North Dallas Forty* 1979 (d/sc); *First Blood* 1982; *Uncommon Valour* 1983 (exp/d); *Joshua Then and Now* 1985; *Weekend at Bernie's* 1989; *Folks!* 1992; *Family of Cops* 1995 (TV); *The Shooter* 1995; *A Strange Affair* 1996 (TV); *Borrowed Hearts* 1997 (TV);

Crime in Connecticut: The Story of Alex Kelly 1999 (TV); *Law and Order: Special Victims Unit* 1999–present (p/d, series).

Koteas, Elias

Actor; b. Monteal, 1961. Elias Koteas came from a Greek background. He studied at Vanier College in Montreal then left for the United States to pursue an acting career. His breakout film was *Malarek* in 1989, for which he received a Genie nomination. Following that success he appeared in two *Teenage Mutant Ninja Turtle* mall movies and earned recognition for his work in Egoyan's *Exotica,** receiving a second Genie nomination. Subsequently, David Cronenberg* cast him as the collision-obsessed Vaughn in the highly vaunted (but simultaneously much maligned) *Crash.** This, combined with a compelling screen *gravitas* akin to that of Robert DeNiro, established Koteas in the industry, garnering him a variety of roles in *Gattaca, Apt Pupil, Fallen,* and *The Thin Red Line.* **Films and television include:** *One Magic Christmas* 1985; *Private Sessions* 1985 (TV); *Some Kind of Wonderful* 1987; *Onassis: The Richest Man in the World* 1988 (TV); *Full Moon in Blue Water* 1988; *Tucker: The Man and His Dream* 1988; *Friends, Lovers and Lunatics* 1989; *Malarek* 1989; *Desperate Hours* 1990; *Teenage Mutant Ninja Turtles* 1990; *Almost an Angel* 1990; *Look Who's Talking Too* 1990; *The Adjuster* 1991; *The Habitation of Dragons* 1992 (TV); *Teenage Mutant Ninja Turtles III* 1993; *Exotica* 1994; *Camilla* 1994; *Sugartime* 1995 (TV); *The Prophecy* 1995; *Power of Attorney* 1995; *Hit Me* 1996; *Crash* 1996; *Gattaca* 1997; *Apt Pupil* 1998; *Living Out Loud* 1998; *Fallen* 1998; *The Thin Red Line* 1999.

Kroitor, Roman

Director and producer; b. Yorkton, Sask., 1926. Kroitor, a technical innovator, has pioneered new cinematographic ap-

proaches for decades. In the 1950s, he was one of the first filmmakers to use the new lightweight cameras, and his *Labyrinth** project with Colin Low* was one of the most brilliant multi-screen efforts at Expo 67. As an NFB veteran and one of the leading members of the direct-cinema movement, Kroitor contributed to the *Candid Eye** series and directed *Lonely Boy** with Wolf Koenig.* He also co-founded the Imax Corporation with Graeme Ferguson* and Robert Kerr, and he produced and wrote *Tiger Child,* the first film partially shot in the revolutionary format, directed by Donald Brittain.* **Films include:** *Age of the Beaver* 1952 (ed); *Paul Tomkowicz: Street-Railway Switchman* 1954 (d/co-sc); *City of Gold* 1957 (sc/co-ed); *Blood and Fire* 1958 (co-p); *The Days before Christmas* 1958 (co-p/co-d/co-ed); *Glenn Gould – Off the Record* 1959 (p/d with Wolf Koenig); *Glenn Gould – On the Record* 1959 (p/d with Koenig); *The Back-Breaking Leaf* 1959 (co-p); *Cars in Your Life* 1960 (co-p); *Universe* 1960 (sc/co-d with Colin Low); *The Days of Whiskey Gap* 1961 (co-p); *Festival in Puerto Rico* 1961 (p/co-d/co-ed with Koenig); *Lonely Boy* 1962 (p/co-d with Koenig, CFA-FY); *The Living Machine* 1962 (co-p/d); *Toronto Jazz* 1964 (p); *Nobody Waved Good-Bye* 1964 (p with Don Owen); *Legault's Place* 1964 (p with Tom Daly); *Above the Horizon* 1964 (co-p/co-d); *The Hutterites* 1964 (p with Daly); *The Baymen* 1965 (p); *Stravinsky* 1965 (p/co-d with Koenig); *Little White Lies* 1966 (co-p); *Labyrinth* 1967 (d with Low); *Tiger Child* 1971 (p/sc); *Propaganda Message* 1974 (p with Koenig); *Circus World* 1974 (p/d); *Man Belongs to the Earth* 1974 (co-p); *Bargain Basement* 1976 (p); *For Gentlemen Only* 1976 (exp); *Listen Listen Listen* 1976 (exp); *Striker* 1976 (exp); *Henry Ford's America* 1977 (co-p); *One Man* 1977 (p); *Back Alley Blue* 1977 (exp); *Bekevar Jubilee* 1977 (exp); *Breakdown* 1977 (exp); *Flora: Scenes from a*

Leadership Convention 1977 (exp); *Happiness Is Your Loving Teacher* 1977 (exp); *Hold the Ketchup* 1977 (exp); *I Wasn't Scared* 1977 (exp); *Sail Away* 1977 (exp); *Margaret Laurence: First Lady of Manawaka* 1978 (co-p); *The Red Dress* 1978 (exp); *So Long to Run* 1978 (exp); *Voice of the Fugitive* 1978 (exp); *Why Men Rape* 1979 (exp); *In the Labyrinth* 1979 (d with Low); *Bravery in the Field* 1979 (exp, AAN-S); *Northern Composition* 1979 (exp); *Revolution's Orphans* 1979 (co-p); *Twice upon a Time* 1979 (co-p); *Challenger: An Industrial Romance* 1980 (exp); *Acting Class* 1980 (exp); *Coming Back Alive* 1980 (p with Koenig); *First Winter* 1981 (exp, AAN-LAS); *Hail Columbia!* 1982 (co-p); *We Are Born of Stars* 1985 (p/sc); *Heartland* 1987 (p); *The Last Buffalo* 1990 (co-p); *Echoes of the Sun* 1990 (co-p/co-d); *Rolling Stones at the Max* 1991 (co-d).

L

Labrecque, Jean-Claude

Cinematographer and director; b. Quebec City, 1938. Labrecque, who trained at the NFB, is one of most talented of the first wave of Quebec filmmakers of the 1960s. He shot many of the key films of the period, including *À tout prendre** and *Le Chat dans le sac,** before he turned to directing in 1965. In 1967 he left the Board to set up his own production company. Throughout his career, his interests have focused on matters of concern to the Québécois people, whether it be sports, culture, or politics. His best-known films include the documentary *La Visite du général De Gaulle au Québec* and his second fiction film, *Les Vautours,* an eloquent and charming personal meditation on the birth of a generation. **Films and television include:** *À tout prendre* 1963 (co-ph); *Jusqu'au cou* 1964

(co-ph); *Le Chat dans le sac* 1964 (ph); *60 Cycles* 1965 (d/co-ph, CFA-PH); *La Vie heureuse de Léopold Z.* 1965 (ph); *De mère en fille* 1966 (co-ph, TV); *Notes for a Film about Donna and Gail* 1966 (ph); *La Visite du général De Gaulle au Québec* 1967 (d); *Le Règne du jour* 1967 (co-ph); *Ce soir-là, Gilles Vigneault ...* 1968 (co-ph); *Entre la mer et l'eau douce* 1968 (co-ph); *The Ernie Game* 1968 (ph, TV); *Essai à la mille* 1970 (d, CFA-AE); *Les Maudits Sauvages* 1971 (ph); *Les Smattes* 1972 (d/co-sc); *Les Corps célestes* 1973 (ph); *Les Beaux Dimanches* 1974 (ph); *Les Vautours* 1975 (d/ed); *Jeux de la XXIe olympiade* 1977 (co-d); *L'Affaire Coffin* 1980 (d); *Les Années de rêves* 1984 (d/co-sc); *67 bis, boulevard Lannes* 1990 (d); *André Mathieu, musicien* 1993 (d); *Kanehsatake: 270 Years of Resistance* 1993 (co-ph); *De l'autre côté de la lune* 1993 (ph); *L'Aventure des compagnons de Saint-Laurent* 1995 (d); *Anticosti au temps des Menier* 1999 (d).

Labyrinth

1967 45m *prod* NFB, *p* Roman Kroitor, Colin Low, Hugh O'Connor, *d* Roman Kroitor, Colin Low, *ph* Walter Lassally, and others, *ed* Tom Daly, *mus* Eldon Rathburn. This multi-chamber installation by the NFB was the undisputed hit of Expo 67. Conceived and designed by Roman Kroitor* and Colin Low,* with the participation of many others, *Labyrinth* consisted of three chambers based on the Greek myth about Theseus' descent into the labyrinth to kill the Minotaur. The first chamber had screens on the floor and on the walls. The second chamber was a transitional passageway formed by mirrored prisms that, when the lights went out, blinked like a million stars. The third chamber was an auditorium containing five screens where the symbolic struggle was played out. The separate films were later compiled into a single flat-screen film, which was released as *In the Labyrinth* in 1979. The installation provided inspiration in the development of the IMAX process.

Lamb, Derek

Producer and animator; b. London, U.K., 1936. Lamb developed his animation skills at the NFB in the late 1950s and scored a major success with *I Know an Old Lady Who Swallowed a Fly* in 1964. From 1966 through 1971, he taught animation at Harvard, and in 1976 he returned to the NFB as head of the English animation department. During his five years there, he produced two Academy Award winners, *Special Delivery* and *Every Child*,* as well as such lauded shorts as *The Sweater** and *Afterlife*.* Lamb's exceptional talents as a script editor and a teacher inspired animators such as John Weldon,* Sheldon Cohen, Ishu Patel,* and Eugene Fedorenko to produce mature, often challenging work while maintaining a focused narrative line. **Films include:** *I Know an Old Lady Who Swallowed a Fly* 1964 (d); *Mr Frog Went a-Courting* 1974 (m); *Bead Game* 1977 (p, AAN-AS); *The Hottest Show on Earth* 1977 (co-p/co-d/co-sc, CFA-SD); *Spinnolio* (exp, CFA-AS); *Why Me* 1978 (co-p/co-d, AAN-AS); *Afterlife* 1978 (p); *Special Delivery* 1979 (p, AA-AS); *Every Child* 1980 (p/co-sc, AA-AS); *The Sweater* 1980 (exp); *Kate and Anna McGarrigle* 1981 (exp); *The Tender Tale of Cinderella Penguin* 1981 (exp, AAN-AS); *Narcissus* 1983 (exp); *Real Inside* 1984 (exp); *Karate Kids* 1995 (p/d).

Lambart, Evelyn

Animator; b. Ottawa, 1914; d. 1999. Eve Lambart, the first woman animator at the NFB, was overshadowed by her partner on many films, the legendary Norman McLaren.* Lambart made significant contributions to *Begone Dull Care*,* *Around Is Around*,* and *Now Is the Time*,* and her work on *A Chairy Tale** (where she made a chair come to life to the comic frustration of Claude Jutra*) won her an Academy Award nomination. She began by specializing in graphics and maps, which were used extensively in *The World in Action** series. Later she developed her own technique, using paper cut-outs of animal characters in morality tales for children (*Mr Frog Went a-Courting*, *The Town Mouse and the Country Mouse*). **Films include:** *Maps in Action* 1945 (an); *Begone Dull Care* 1949 (d/an/ed with Norman McLaren, CFA-SPA); *Family Tree* 1950 (d/an with George Dunning, CFA-SPA); *Challenge: Science against Cancer* 1950 (an with Colin Low); *Around Is Around* 1951 (an with McLaren, CFA-SPA); *Now Is the Time* 1951 (an with McLaren, CFA-SPA); *The Fight: Science against Cancer* 1951 (an with Low, CFA-SPA, AAN-SD); *O Canada* 1952 (d/an); *Rhythmetic* 1956 (p/d/an with McLaren); *A Chairy Tale* 1957 (an with McLaren, AAN-AS); *Lines – Horizontal* 1961 (d/an with McLaren, CFA-AE); *Lines – Vertical* 1962 (d/an with McLaren); *Mosiac* 1965 (d/an with McLaren); *Paradise Lost* 1970 (d); *The Story of Christmas* 1973 (d/an); *Mr Frog Went a-Courting* 1974 (d/an); *The Lion and the Mouse* 1976 (d/an); *The Town Mouse and the Country Mouse* 1980 (d/an).

Lamothe, Arthur

Director, producer, writer, and editor; b. Saint-Mont, France, 1928. Canada's greatest ethnographic filmmaker was born in the Pyrenees region of France and came to Canada in 1953. After turning his hand to a variety of jobs, including work in the lumberjack camps in Northern Quebec, Lamothe eventually joined the NFB. His first film, *Bûcherons de la Manouane*,* recounted his experiences in the camps. This film, which is considered by critics to be one of the most influential documentaries in Québécois cinema, was the beginning of a career spanning thirty years and sixty films, detailing hidden social issues with a keen analytical mind and a sensitivity toward the subject matter. Perhaps his most ambitious work was a twelve-part chronicle of the First Nations of Northern Quebec (*Carcajou et le péril blanc* and *La Terre de l'homme*) produced for Quebec television. **Films and television include:** *Bûcherons de la Manouane* 1962 (d/co-ed); *De Montréal à Manicouagan* 1963 (d/sc); *La Neige a foundu sur la Manicouagan* 1965 (d/sc/ed): *Le Train du Labrador* 1967 (d); *Poussière sur la ville* 1968 (d/ed); *Ce soir-là, Gilles Vigneault ...* 1968 (d/co-ed); *Les Mépris n'aura qu'un temps* 1970 (p/d); *La Route du fer* 1972 (d); *La Mort d'un bûcheron* 1973 (sc with Gilles Carle); *Les Corps célestes* 1973 (sc with Carle); *Carcajou et le péril blanc* 1977 (p/d, series); *La Terre de l'homme* 1980 (p/d, series); *Equinoxe* 1986 (d/co-sc); *Ernest Livernois, photographe* 1989 (d); *La Conquête de l'amérique* 1992 (d, two films); *L'Echo des songes* 1992 (d); *Le Silence des fusils* 1996 (d).

Lamy, André

Administrator and producer; b. Montreal, 1932; brother of Pierre Lamy. André Lamy was the head of the NFB and the film commissioner from 1975 to 1979, and in 1980 he was appointed head of the CFDC (Telefilm Canada). **Credits include:** *Le Viol d'une jeune fille douce* 1968; *The Valour and the Horror* 1991 (three films, TV).

Lamy, Pierre

Producer; b. Montreal, 1926; d. 1998; brother of André Lamy. Pierre Lamy was one of Quebec's most prolific and successful movie producers. He started as a Radio-Canada producer in the 1950s and in 1971 joined forces with director Gilles Carle* (Productions Carle-Lamy)

to produce many of the early films of Denys Arcand* and Claude Jutra* as well as all of Carle's films. After splitting with Carle in 1975, Lamy went on to produce films for Joyce Wieland,* Allan King,* Francis Mankiewicz,* and Arthur Lamothe.* **Films and television include:** *Pas de vacances pour les idoles* 1965; *Le Viol d'une jeune fille douce* 1968; *Red* 1970; *Deux femmes en or* 1970; *Les Mâles* 1971; *Les Smattes* 1972; *La Maudite Galette* 1972; *La Vraie Nature de Bernadette* 1972; *La Mort d'un bûcheron* 1973; *La Conquête* 1973; *Kamouraska* 1973; *Les Corps célestes* 1973; *Il était une fois dans l'est* 1974; *Gina* 1975; *Pour le meilleur et pour le pire* 1975; *Tout feu tout femme* 1975; *La Tête de Normande St-Onge* 1975; *Chanson pour Julie* 1976; *The Far Shore* 1976; *Le Soleil se lève en retard* 1977; *Who Has Seen the Wind* 1977 (GRA); *La Terre de l'homme* 1980 (series); *Les Beaux Souvenirs* 1981; *Contrecoeur* 1983; *La Dame en couleurs* 1985; *Ernest Livernois, photographe* 1989.

Lanctôt, Micheline

Actor and director; b. Montreal, 1947. Lanctôt made an indelible impression as the restless, questing heroine of Gilles Carle's* masterpiece, *La Vraie Nature de Bernadette*. Soon after, she created another memorable character, Richard Dreyfuss's beguiling, long-suffering girlfriend in *The Apprenticeship of Duddy Kravitz*.* Following an unhappy sojourn in Los Angeles with director Ted Kotcheff,* Lanctôt returned to Quebec and built her present career as a moviemaker with a reputation for unsentimental, unconventional, probing films. Her directorial debut, *L'Homme à tout faire*,* was a critical success as was her 1993 release, *Deux actrices*. *Sonatine*,* which probes a suicidal bond between two alienated teenage girls, was the first Canadian feature to win the Golden Lion Award at the Venice Film Festival, and it also won Lanctôt a Genie for Best Director. **Films and television include:** *La Vraie Nature de Bernadette* 1972 (a, CFA-A); *Noel et Juliete* 1973 (a); *Voyage en grande Tartarie* 1973 (a); *Les Corps célestes* 1973 (a); *Child under a Leaf* 1974 (a); *The Apprenticeship of Duddy Kravitz* 1974 (a); *Ti-cul tougas* 1975 (a); *A Token Gesture* 1975 (d); *Blood Relatives* 1978 (a); *Blood and Guts* 1978 (a); *Mourir à tue-tête* 1979 (a); *L'Homme à tout faire* 1980 (d/sc); *Sonatine* 1984 (d/sc, GA-D); *La Ligne de chaleur* 1988 (co-sc); *Le Chemin de Damas* 1988 (a, TV); *Onzième spéciale* 1988 (d, TV); *L'Affaire Coffin* 1990 (a); *Deux actrices* 1993 (p/d/sc/ed); *La Vie d'un héros* 1994 (d/sc); *J'en suis* 1997 (a); *Le Coeur au poing* 1998 (a); *Aujourd'hui ou jamais* 1998 (a); *Quand je serai parti ... vous vivez encore* 1999 (a).

Lantos, Robert

Producer and distributor; b. Budapest, Hungary, 1949. Lantos became involved in film at McGill University in Montreal, and formed his first company, Vivafilm, in 1972. He quickly moved into production during the tax-shelter era* with Gilles Carle's *L'Ange et la femme*, George Kaczender's *In Praise of Older Women,* and Ted Kotcheff's *Joshua Then and Now.** In 1985, he formed Alliance Entertainment with Stephen Roth, Denis Héroux,* and John Kemeny.* Since then Alliance has become Canada's largest production and distribution company with a succession of hit television shows such as *Night Heat, E.N.G., Due South,* and features including Bruce Beresford's *Black Robe,** David Cronenberg's *Crash,** and Atom Egoyan's *The Sweet Hereafter.** In 1998, after the merger of the company with Atlantis Communications, Lantos stepped aside as the head of Alliance. He continues to produce features in Canada and abroad. **Films include:** *L'Ange et la femme* 1977; *In Praise of Older Women* 1978; *Agency* 1979; *Suzanne* 1980; *Joshua Then and Now* 1985; *Night Magic* 1985; *Black Robe* 1991 (GA-P, GRA); *Whale Music* 1994; *Johnny Mnemonic* 1995 (GRA); *Crash* 1996 (GRA); *The Sweet Hereafter* 1997 (GA-P); *Strike!* 1998; *eXistenZ* 1999; *Sunshine* 1999 (GA-P).

Larkin, Ryan

Animator; b. Montreal, 1943. Larkin, a gifted animator with a unique style, was once described as the 'Frank Zappa of animation films.' He trained at Montreal's École du Musée des beaux-arts to be a painter then switched to film through an animation workshop conduced by Norman McLaren,* who oversaw his first films, *Syrinx* and *Cityscape.* Larkin's *Walking** was nominated for an Academy Award, but unfortunately drugs over took his talent and he left the NFB in the early 1970s. He has not worked since and most recently was found homeless on the streets of Montreal – a sad end to a career with such great promise. **Films include:** *Syrinx* 1965 (d/an, CFA-TS); *Cityscape* 1966 (p/d/an); *Burning Fox* 1966 (an); *ABC of First Aid* 1966 (an); *Walking* 1968 (p/d/an, AAN-AS); *Street Musique* 1972 (p/d/an).

Last Night

1998 94m *prod* Rhombus Media, *exp* Caroline Benjo, Carole Scotta, *p* Niv Fichman, Daniel Iron, *d/sc* Don McKellar, *ph* Doug Koch, *ed* Reginald Harkema, *mus* Alex Pauk, Alexina Louie; *with* Don McKellar, Sandra Oh, Callum Keith Rennie, Sarah Polley, Geneviève Bujold, David Cronenberg. With wit and poignancy, director-writer Don McKellar* depicts the final hours in the lives of a group of Torontonians as they await the end of the world. In scenarios that are alternately hilarious, tragic, and absurd, they struggle to find some semblance of meaning in what's left of their lives.

Intriguingly, McKellar offers no reason for the impending doom; he simply indicates that the people know it's coming. This film also sets a precedent: for a country that isn't supposed to have its own star system, *Last Night* arguably features Canada's first ever all-star cast, with standout performances by McKellar, Callum Keith Rennie,* Sandra Oh, David Cronenberg,* and Geneviève Bujold.* (V) **Awards include:** GA: Actress (Oh), Supporting Actor (Rennie), Claude Jutra Award; Cannes: Prix de la Jeunesse.

Laure, Carole

Actor; b. Shawinigan, Que., 1950. Following a troubled childhood, Laure embarked on a career in music. Her charismatic beauty attracted director Gilles Carle,* who cast her in *La Mort d'un bûcheron*, *La Tête de Normand St-Onge*, and the sensuous and controversial, *L'Ange et la femme*. During the filming of *L'Ange*, the sultry actress became romantically involved with musician and filmmaker Lewis Furey,* who eventually directed her in *Night Magic*, a fantasy film written by Leonard Cohen. In pictures such as Bernard Blier's 1978 Academy Award–winning *Get Out Your Handkerchiefs*, as well as in her singing career, Laure seems to be permanently eroticized – a dark, sulky, lubricious post-Bardot actress who has reinvented the screen goddess. **Films include:** *The Apprentice* 1971; *Mon enfance à Montréal* 1971; *Fleur bleue* 1971; *IXE-13* 1972; *La Mort d'un bûcheron* 1973; *Les Corps célestes* 1973; *Sweet Movie* 1974; *La Tête de Normande St-Onge* 1975; *Born for Hell* 1976; *Spécial Magnum* 1976; *La Menace* 1977; *La Jument-vapeur* 1977; *L'Eau chaude l'eau frette* 1977; *L'Ange et la femme* 1977; *Get Out Your Handkerchiefs* 1977; *Au revoir ... à lundi* 1979; *Inside Out* 1979 (TV); *Fantastica* 1980; *Un Assassin qui passe* 1981; *Croque la vie* 1981; *Maria Chapdelaine* 1983; *À mort l'arbitre* 1984; *The Surrogate* 1984; *Night Magic* 1985; *Sauve-toi, Lola* 1986; *La Nuit avec Hortense* 1988; *Thank You Satan* 1988; *Flight from Justice* 1993; *Elles ne pensent qu'à ça* 1994; *Bluffer's Hand* 1999; *Rats and Rabbits* 2000 (co-p/a).

Lauzon, Jean-Claude

Director and writer; b. Montreal, 1953; d. 1997. Amazingly, Lauzon's reputation is based on only three films: a short, *Piwi*; his debut feature, *Un Zoo la nuit*;* and the surreal *Léolo*,* which was screened in competition at Cannes in 1992. Lauzon's legend is that of a troubled dropout who transformed himself into a wiry, intense artist who was able to express semi-autobiographical, down and dirty themes with elegant craftsmanship. Despite his success, Lauzon frequently expressed doubts about his profession, claiming that he preferred to shoot commercials and that hunting and flying bush planes were more satisfying than moviemaking. Tragically, his passion for flying took his life. He was killed in an accident in Northern Quebec in 1997. **Films:** *Piwi* 1982; *Un Zoo la nuit* 1987 (d/sc, GA-D, GA-SC); *Léolo* 1992 (d/sc, GA-SC).

Lawrence, Florence

Actor; b. Hamilton, Ont., 1886; d. 1938. Lawrence, the most popular actress at the Biograph studios, starred in many of D.W. Griffith's early films. Since it was the company's policy not to promote actors lest they demand more money, she was simply called 'The Biograph Girl.' In 1910, producer Carl Laemmle offered her a lucrative contract to work for his Independent Motion Picture Company of America; there she became known as 'The IMP Girl.' Thanks to one of Laemmle's outrageous publicity stunts (he claimed she was killed in a traffic accident), Lawrence became the first star whose real name became known to the public. Lawrence's career was effectively over by the mid-1920s, and she committed suicide on Christmas Day, 1938.

Leaf, Caroline

Animator; b. Seattle, Wash., 1946. Using simple means – sand, silhouettes, and drawings etched directly onto film – Caroline Leaf has created films that possess the disturbing power of dreams. She imparts true narrative depth to her work by concentrating on carefully delineated shifts in her characters' circumstances. In the Academy Award–nominated *The Street,** a boy in the Montreal Jewish ghetto achieves his goal of getting a bedroom through his grandmother's death. The Kafkaesque *The Metamorphosis of Mr. Samsa* evokes the nightmare of an ordinary man being turned into a cockroach. In her prize-winning comeback film, *Two Sisters*, the ugliness of sibling rivalry reaches Gothic proportions. **Films include:** *The Owl Who Married a Goose* 1974 (CFA-AS); *The Street* 1976 (AAN-AS); *The Metamorphosis of Mr. Samsa* 1977; *Interview* 1979 (d with Veronika Soul); *Kate and Anna McGarrigle* 1981; *Two Sisters* 1993.

Leduc, Jacques

Director, cinematographer, and writer; b. Montreal, 1941. Throughout his career, Leduc has been fascinated by the lives and fates of ordinary Québécois. As a cameraman and latterly a director, Leduc was involved with the NFB's direct-cinema movement. After his controversial non-fiction film *Cap d'espoir* was banned, Leduc slowly moved away from documentaries to dramas. His fiction features, from the celebrated *Tendresse ordinaire* through to *La Vie fantôme*, have continued to emphasize how work and the daily grind of events can affect an individual's emotional and romantic

life. **Films and television include:** *Il ne faut pas mourir pour ça* 1967 (ph); *Chantel en vrac* 1967 (d); *Ce soir-là, Gilles Vigneault ...* 1968 (co-ph); *Nominingue ... depuis qu'il existe* 1968 (d, TV); *Cap d'espoir* 1969 (d); *Mon amie Pierrette* 1969 (ph); *Là ou ailleurs* 1969 (d); *Mon oeil* 1971 (co-ph); *On est loin du soleil* 1971 (d); *Tendresse ordinaire* 1973 (d); *Ultimatum* 1975 (ph); *Le Ventre de la nuit* 1978 (co-d); *Du grand large aux grands lacs* 1982 (co-ph, TV); *Debout sur leur terre* 1983 (co-ph); *Torngat* 1984 (ph); *Le Dernier Glacier* 1984 (co-d/co-sc/ph); *La Femme de l'hôtel* 1984 (a); *Trois pommes à côté du sommeil* 1989 (d/co-sc); *Au chic resto pop* 1990 (ph); *Montréal vu par ...* 1991 (co-d/co-sc); *La Vie fantôme* 1992 (d/co-sc); *Tu as crié Let Me Go* 1997 (ph); *L'Age de braise* 1998 (d); *L'Erreur boréale* 1999 (ph).

Lefebvre, Jean Pierre

Director and writer; b. Montreal, 1941. While other filmmakers of his generation attempted to access the mainstream, Lefebvre, once a movie critic, has never turned away from ultra-low-budget personal cinema. Film historian Peter Morris has called him 'the best and brightest of Canadian cinema.' Between 1964 and 1998 Lefebvre directed twenty-three features. *Les Dernières Fiançailles, L'Amour blessé, Le Vieux Pays ou Rimbaud est mort,** *Les Fleurs sauvages* (which won the International Critics' Prize at Cannes in 1982), and many other films approach human frailty and incertitude with an eccentric, self-referential mix of wit, surreal contrast, and reverie. Respected for his integrity, Lefebvre is also a skillful teacher of screenwriting, directing, and the use of democratizing technology such as Hi-8 video. In 1995, he won Quebec's prestigious Prix Albert-Tessier, a yearly homage made to artists and intellectuals. **Films include:** *L'Hommonan* 1964 (p/d/sc/ph); *Le Révolutionnaire*

1965 (p/d/sc); *Patricia et Jean-Baptiste* 1968 (p/d/sc/a); *Il ne faut pas mourir pour ça* 1968 (d/co-sc); *Mon amie Pierrette* 1969 (d/sc); *Jusqu'au coeur* 1969 (d/sc); *La Chambre blanche* 1969 (d/sc); *Entre tu et vous* 1970 (p); *Un Succès commercial ou Q-bec My Love* 1970 (d/sc); *Ainsi soient-ils* 1971 (p); *Jean-Françoise-Xavier de ...* 1971 (p); *Mon oeil* 1971 (d/sc); *Les Maudits Sauvages* 1971 (d/sc); *Réjeanne Padovani* 1973 (a); *Les Dernières Fiançailles* 1973 (d/sc); *On n'engraisse pas les cochons à l'eau claire* 1975 (d/sc); *Ultimatum* 1975 (d/sc); *I'Ile jaune* 1975 (a); *L'Amour blessé* 1977 (d/sc); *Le Vieux Pays où Rimbaud est mort* 1977 (d/co-sc); *Le Gars des vues* 1978 (d); *Avoir 16 ans* 1980 (d/co-sc); *Les Fleurs sauvages* 1982 (d/sc); *Au rythme du mon coeur* 1983 (d/ph/ed/narr); *Le Jour 'S ...'* 1984 (d/co-sc/mus); *Alfred Laliberté, sculpteur* 1987 (d/sc); *La Boite à soleil* 1988 (d/sc/mus); *Le Fabuleux Voyage de l'ange* 1991 (d/sc); *Aujourd'hui ou jamais* 1998 (d); *See You in Toronto* from *Preludes* 2000 (d/sc).

Leiterman, Douglas

Producer; b. South Porcupine, Ont., 1927; brother of Richard Leiterman. Douglas Leiterman co-created (with Patrick Watson) CBC-TV's seminal public affairs program, *This Hour Has Seven Days*. Leiterman also produced some of CBC's most insightful documentaries during the turbulent 1960s. **Films and television include:** *One More River* 1963 (p/co-d, TV); *Summer in Mississippi* 1964 (exp, TV); *The Mills of the Gods: Viet Nam* 1965 (exp, TV, CFA-FY); *This Hour Has Seven Days* 1964–6 (co-p, series); *By Design* 1982 (exp); *Millennium* 1988 (p); *Termini Station* 1989 (exp).

Leiterman, Richard

Cinematographer; b. South Porcupine, Ont., 1935; brother of Douglas Leiterman. Richard Leiterman is one of the best and most famous Canadian cinematographers. His early work at the CBC and on low-budget features such as *Goin' down the Road,* *Rip-Off,* *Wedding in White,* and *Between Friends* virtually defined the look of early English-Canadian cinema – hand-held direct cinema shot with style and grace. In the 1990s he mostly shot movies of the week for American television, and he now teaches cinematography at Sheridan College. **Films and television include:** *One More River* 1963 (TV); *Summer in Mississippi* 1964 (TV); *This Hour Has Seven Days* 1964–6 (series); *A Married Couple* 1969; *High School* 1969 (TV); *Goin' down the Road* 1970; *Rip-Off* 1971; *Wedding in White* 1972; *Between Friends* 1973; *Come on Children* 1973 (ap); *Recommendation for Mercy* 1975; *The Far Shore* 1976 (CFA-PH); *Who Has Seen the Wind* 1977; *Surfacing* 1980; *Wild Horse Hank* 1980 (TV); *The Silence of the North* 1981 (GA-PH); *Ticket to Heaven* 1981; *Hail Columbia!* 1982; *Maria Chapdelaine* 1983 (co-ph); *My American Cousin* 1985; *Striker's Mountain* 1985 (TV); *And Then You Die* 1987; *Watchers* 1988; *Stephen King's It* 1990 (TV); *To Grandmother's House We Go* 1992 (TV); *Without a Kiss Goodbye* 1993 (TV); *Don't Talk to Strangers* 1994 (TV); *Pocahontas: The Legend* 1995; *Far from Home: The Adventures of Yellow Dog* 1995; *Murder on the Iditarod Trail* 1995 (TV); *Into the Arms of Danger* 1997 (TV); *Country Justice* 1997 (TV); *The Spree* 1998 (TV).

Legg, Stuart

Director; b. London, U.K., 1910; d. 1988. Stuart Legg was a talented British documentary filmmaker who was recruited by John Grierson* and played a major role in the early days of the NFB. Legg oversaw the production of the *Canada Carries On* series and also produced and directed most of the films for *The World in Action* series. His *Churchill's Island* (1942) was the first NFB film to win an Academy Award, and his hard-hitting, propagandistic films set the style and tone of the Board during the war years. In 1945 he left the Board and returned to England.

Léolo

1992 107m *prod* Les Productions du Verseau, Flach Film, NFB, *exp* Aimée Danis, Claudette Viau, *p* Lyse Lafontaine, Isabelle Fauvel, Jean-François Lepetit, *d/sc* Jean-Claude Lauzon, *ph* Guy Dufaux, *ed* Michel Arcand, *mus* Richard Grégoire; *with* Maxime Collin, Ginette Reno, Pierre Bourgault, Julien Guiomar, Germain Houde. This captivating and sometimes disturbing tale concerns an imaginative young boy (Collin) and his eccentric family living in working-class Montreal. With unimpeded candour, the youngster records his observations about life in his notebook, exposing his memories, dreams, and nightmares. The boy's name is really Leo, but he insists on being called Léolo because he believes his conception involved a sperm-laden tomato imported from Sicily. The film beautifully – and at times brutally – tells the story of the rich fantasy life Léolo creates in order to cope with the squalor of his tenement existence and bizarre family life. (V) **Awards include:** GA: Original Screenplay, Editing.

Lepage, Robert

Director, writer, and actor; b. Quebec City, 1958. In 1995, visionary theatre director Robert Lepage soared to the top of the Canadian film scene with his first picture, *Le Confessionnal.** This visually arresting exploration of familial secrets and lies garnered ecstatic reviews and took four Genies, including Best Director. But a year later, Lepage's follow-up, an adaptation of one of his own plays, *Le Polygraphe*, met with lukewarm reviews, audience indifference, and a Genie

shut-out. He rebounded in 1998 with the award-winning *Nô,** a witty dissection of Quebec's separatist impulses and the October Crisis. **Films include:** *Jésus de Montréal* 1989 (a); *Montréal vu par ...* 1991 (a); *Tectonic Plates* 1992 (sc/a); *Le Confessionnal* 1995 (d/sc, GA-D, CJA); *Le Polygraphe* 1996 (d/sc); *Nô* 1998 (d/co-sc); *Stardom* 2000 (a); *Possible Worlds* 2000 (d).

Levy, Eugene

Actor and writer; b. Hamilton, Ont., 1946. Originally interested in singing, Levy attended McMaster University in Hamilton, Ontario, where he met director and producer Ivan Reitman.* This led to a role in Reitman's first feature, *Cannibal Girls*. Levy gained attention as a writer and comedian in the popular *SCTV* series. While the careers of other *SCTV* alumni flourished in Los Angeles, Levy kept his base in Toronto, appearing in a variety of film and television productions, including *Waiting for Guffman* (for which he won an Independent Spirit Award for Best Screenplay) and the teenage sex romp *American Pie*. Levy has said, 'The thing that works best for me is riding a very fine reality line, and having people wonder: Is it supposed to be funny or not?' **Films and television include:** *Cannibal Girls* 1973; *SCTV* 1977–84 (co-sc/a, series); *Running* 1979; *Nothing Personal* 1980; *Heavy Metal* 1981 (voice); *Double Negative* 1982; *Going Berserk* 1983; *National Lampoon's Vacation* 1983; *Splash* 1984; *The Last Polka* 1985 (sc/a, TV); *Armed and Dangerous* 1986; *Club Paradise* 1986; *Bride of Boogedy* 1987 (TV); *Speed Zone!* 1989; *Father of the Bride* 1991; *Stay Tuned* 1992; *Sodbusters* 1994 (d/sc, TV); *I Love Trouble* 1994; *Father of the Bride Part II* 1995; *Multiplicity* 1996; *Dogmatic* 1996; *Waiting for Guffman* 1996 (sc/a); *Holy Man* 1998; *Almost Heroes* 1998; *Richie Rich's Christmas Wish* 1998 (TV); *American Pie* 1999; *Unglued* 1999;

D.O.A. 1999 (sc/a, TV); *Best in Show* 2000 (co-sc/a); *American Pie 2* 2001.

Lies My Father Told Me
1975 102m *prod* Pentacle VIII Productions, Pentimento Productions, *exp* Michael Harrison, Arnold Issenman, Arnold Shniffer, *p* Anthony Bedrich, Harry Gulkin, *d* Ján Kadár, *sc/short story* Ted Allan, *ph* Paul van der Linden, *ed* Edward Beyer, Richard Marks, *mus* Sol Kaplan; *with* Yossi Yadin, Len Birman, Marilyn Lightstone, Jeffrey Lynas, Ted Allan. This delightful and often funny adaptation of Ted Allan's* original story offers viewers a look at Montreal's vibrant Jewish immigrant community in the 1920s. It revolves around the magical relationship between a six-year-old boy (Lynas) and his Orthodox grandfather (Yadin), who travels through the neighbourhood on a horse-drawn cart selling rags, bottles, and other odds and ends. The boy is devastated by his grandfather's death. Fine performances by the entire cast along with an accurate recreation of old Montreal make this film an excellent time capsule of a time and era long gone. This film was the final feature made by Czech director Ján Kadár. **Awards include:** CFA: Film of the Year, Adapted Screenplay, Actress (Lightstone), Sound Recording, Sound Re-recording; AAN: Original Screenplay.

Life Classes
1987 117m *prod* Picture Plant, *exp/d/sc/ed* William D. MacGillivray, *p* Stephen Reynolds, *mus* Alexander Tilley, William D. MacGillivray; *with* Jacinta Cormier, Leon Dubinsky, Evelyn Garbary, Mary Izzard. In Bill MacGillivray's* second feature, a young woman (Cormier) gets pregnant and leaves her limiting Cape Breton home for the big city. In Halifax, Mary lives out a life-changing experience that is not at all like the misadventures we might expect from such a melodramatic premise. She goes to work as a nude model for art classes, discovers her own creativity, and reconnects with her roots. Few movies portray a naked woman's body the way MacGillivray does here: it is sensual, but it is also a repository of power and spiritual growth. (V)

Lilies
1996 95m *prod* Triptych Media, Galafilm, *p* Anna Stratton, Robin Cass, Arnie Gelbart, *d* John Greyson, *sc* Michel-Marc Bouchard, Linda Gaboriau, *ph* Daniel Jobin, *ed* André Corriveau, *mus* Mychael Danna; *with* Brent Carver, Marcel Sabourin, Aubert Pallascio, Jason Cadieux, Danny Gilmore, Matthew Ferguson, Rémy Girard. The effortless shifts between the two settings in *Lilies* – a prison in 1952 and a small Quebec town in 1912 – produce a magical, dreamlike atmosphere, one that inspires us to believe that anything can happen. The story centres on an aging bishop (Sabourin*) who visits a prison to hear a confession. The bishop is confined himself, made to watch a play put on by the prisoners, and thereby forced to come to terms with his own past sins and desires. To his credit, director John Greyson* exhibits enormous control over the material (and the play-within-a-play structure), in effect normalizing the unconventional casting (all major parts, regardless of gender, are played by men) and tempering the sensational melodrama of this unusual tale of revenge. (V) **Awards include:** GA: Picture, Art Direction, Costumes, Overall Sound.

Lillie, Beatrice
Actor; b. Toronto, 1894; d. 1989. Bea Lillie, a popular stage comedienne in England and America, was the daughter of an actress and a British Army Officer who became a Canadian government of-

ficial. At age fifteen, Lillie, her sister, and her mother toured southern Ontario as the Lillie Trio, and Lillie made her London, England, debut in 1914. She became known for her quick-witted, inventive, comic style ('the toast of two continents') and was extremely popular both on stage and on radio, but the few films she made were mainly vehicles that failed to capture her at her best. She counted Noel Coward, Charlie Chaplin, and Winston Churchill as friends and in 1920 she became the wife of Sir Robert Peel. **Films include:** *Exit Smiling* 1926; *The Show of Shows* 1929; *Are You There?* 1930; *Dr. Rhythm* 1938; *On Approval* 1944; *Around the World in Eighty Days* 1956; *Thoroughly Modern Millie* 1967.

Linder, Cec

Actor; b. Poland, 1921; d. 1992. Linder, who was raised in Timmins, Ontario, appeared in films in England the United States. He also appeared in a number of Canadian films during the tax-shelter era.* He is perhaps best known as the CIA agent Felix Leiter in *Goldfinger*, the third (and best) Bond film. **Films and television include:** *Crack in the Mirror* 1960; *Lolita* 1962; *Goldfinger* 1964; *Do Not Fold, Staple, Spindle or Mutilate* 1967; *Explosion* 1969; *Foxy Lady* 1971; *A Touch of Class* 1973; *Sunday in the Country* 1974; *Why Rock the Boat?* 1974; *The Clown Murders* 1976; *Vengeance Is Mine* 1976; *Point of No Return* 1976; *Ragtime Summer* 1977; *Deadly Harvest* 1977; *High-Ballin'* 1978; *I Miss You, Hugs and Kisses* 1978; *Something's Rotten* 1979; *City on Fire* 1979; *An American Christmas Carol* 1979 (TV); *The Courage of Kavir the Wolf Dog* 1980; *F.D.R.: The Last Year* 1980 (TV); *Atlantic City* 1980; *Heavenly Bodies* 1984; *Perry Mason Returns* 1985 (TV); *Perry Mason: The Case of the Shooting Star* 1986 (TV); *George and Rosemary* 1987 (narr); *Skate!* 1988 (TV).

Link, André

See Dunning, John, and André Link.

Lipsett, Arthur

Director, editor, and writer; b. Montreal, 1936; d. 1986. Arthur Lipsett, the ghost of experimental film in the NFB documentary machine, was one of Canadian cinema's most original artists and a key figure in the development of experimental cinema. Lipsett was hired as an editor at the NFB animation department in 1958, and he worked on several masterpieces by Norman McLaren.* He soon began reworking stock footage into stunning collage films that were harshly critical of contemporary culture (including *Very Nice, Very Nice** and *Free Fall*). His later films are increasingly metaphysical and filled with elusive, even opaque cinematic poetry, and demonstrate a transcendental quality rare in Canadian cinema. After leaving the NFB in the early 1970s, Lipsett's output came to a virtual standstill. He took his own life in 1986. **Films include:** *Hors-d'oeuvre* 1960 (co-d); *Very Nice, Very Nice* 1961 (d/ed, AAN-AS); *Experimental Film* 1963 (d/ed); *Free Fall* 1964 (d/ed); *21–87* 1964 (d/sc); *A Trip down Memory Lane* 1965 (d/co-p/ed); *N-Zone* 1970 (d/co-sc).

Lockhart, Gene

Actor; b. London, Ont., 1891; d. 1957. A veteran of vaudeville and the stage, Lockhart played solid character parts in over 100 films, both as the nice guy (Bob Cratchit in *A Christmas Carol*) and as the villian (Molotov in *Mission to Moscow*). He was also the father of actress June Lockhart. **Films include:** *Crime and Punishment* 1935; *Algiers* 1938; *A Christmas Carol* 1938; *His Girl Friday* 1940; *Geronimo* 1940; *Meet John Doe* 1941; *Billy the Kid* 1941; *The Sea Wolf* 1941; *All That Money Can Buy* 1941; *They Died with Their Boots On* 1942; *Mission to Moscow* 1943; *Going*

My Way 1944; *Miracle on 34th Street* 1947; *Joan of Arc* 1948; *Down to the Sea in Ships* 1949; *Madame Bovary* 1949; *The Inspector General* 1949; *A Girl in Every Port* 1952; *Carousel* 1956; *The Man in the Gray Flannel Suit* 1956.

Lonely Boy

1962 27m *prod* NFB, *exp* Tom Daly, *p* Roman Kroitor, *d* Wolf Koenig, Roman Kroitor, *ph* Wolf Koenig, *ed* John Spotton, Guy L. Coté. *Lonely Boy* captures the minutia of the life of Ottawa teen heartthrob Paul Anka during the glory days of his early career from his screaming adolescent fans to his rather sleazy management team. The film, undoubtedly one of the greatest in the NFB oeuvre, has become a classic of the *cinéma-vérité* documentary movement. With an astounding eye for detail, directors Wolf Koenig* and Roman Kroitor* have caught Anka's interactions with his handlers, and a still photographer who can't quite get his flashbulb to work. This fascinating and trailblazing examination of the absurdity of celebrity status, captures Anka's smooth performance style, especially when he sings his signature number that inspired the film's title. (V) **Awards include:** CFA: Film of the Year.

Long Day's Journey into Night

1996 173m *prod* Rhombus Media, *p* Daniel Iron, Niv Fichman *d* David Wellington, *play* Eugene O'Neil, *ph* David Franco, *ed* Susan Shipton, *mus* Ron Sures; *with* William Hutt, Martha Henry, Tom McCamus, Peter Donaldson, Martha Bruns. This straightforward, powerful rendition of the Stratford Festival production of one of the great plays of the twentieth century was shot for television by Toronto's Rhombus Media. The film, which enjoyed a modest theatrical release and swept the acting Genie Awards in 1996, is arguably more faithful to O'Neil's original than the 1962 version starring Katharine Hepburn and Ralph Richardson. (V) **Awards include:** GA: Actor (Hutt), Actress (Henry), Supporting Actor (Donaldson), Supporting Actress (Burns).

Longfellow, Brenda

Producer, director, and writer; b. Copper Cliff, Ont., 1954. Longfellow is well-known in Canadian film studies for her theoretical work on feminist and international cinema. She teaches and directs between articles (or writes between films). Her politically engaged film practice has taken her from *Our Marilyn*, an impressionistic comparison of two icons, Marilyn Monroe and Marilyn Bell, to *Gerda*, a feminist analysis of the Gerda Munsinger sex scandal, and *A Balkan Journey: Fragments from the Other Side of War*, an investivation of the role of female activists in the former Yugoslavia. *Shadow Maker: Gwendolyn MacEwen, Poet*, her film about the troubled Toronto poet, won a Genie, while *Our Marilyn*, which is still her most emotionally affecting work, shared the grand prize at Oberhausen and won the Prix du Publique in Montreal. **Films include:** *Our Marilyn* 1987; *Gerda* 1992; *A Balkan Journey: Fragments from the Other Side of War* 1996; *Shadow Maker: Gwendolyn MacEwen, Poet* 1998 (GA-SD).

Loon's Necklace, The

1948 11m6s *prod* Crawley Films, *p/d* Budge Crawley, *sc* Douglas Leechman, *ph* Grant Crabtree, *ed* Judith Crawley. This short uses masks created by First Nations tribes in British Columbia to tell the tale of how the loon received its distinctive neckband. The film, made by the legendary Crawley Films and sponsored by Imperial Oil, was probably the most successful sponsored film of the period, and helped to establish Budge

Crawley's* reputation as Canada's leading independent filmmaker. It became a staple of 1950s classrooms and also won Film of the Year at the first Canadian Film Awards in 1948. **Awards include:** CFA: Film of the Year.

Lord, Jean-Claude
Director, writer, and editor; b. Montreal, 1943. Lord, the creator of Quebec's beloved television series *Lance et compte* (*He Shoots, He Scores*), has always been interested in dealing with political themes in a commercial, Hollywood style. *Bingo* explores the October Crisis through the story of a college student named François. *Parlez-nous d'amour* deals with the shady side of art. *Panique* is a thriller that deals with issues of pollution and ecology. Lord also directed one commercially successful English-language film, *Visiting Hours*, and has developed a number of successful Quebec televison series. He has written or co-written most of his own films. **Films and television include:** *Trouble-fête* 1964 (co-sc); *Les Colombes* 1972 (p/d/sc/ed); *Bingo* 1974 (d/co-sc/ed); *Parlez-nous d'amour* 1976 (d/co-sc/co-ed); *Panique* 1977 (d/co-sc/ed); *Éclair au chocolat* 1979 (d/co-sc/ed); *L'Homme à tout faire* 1980 (exp); *Visiting Hours* 1982 (d/co-ed); *Covergirl* 1984 (d); *Toby McTeague* 1986 (d); *Lance et compte* 1986 (d, series); *The Tadpole and the Whale* 1988 (d); *Eddy and the Cruisers II: Eddy Lives* 1989 (d); *Mindfield* 1989 (d); *Landslide* 1992 (d).

Lotus Eaters, The
1993 100m *prod* Mortimer and Ogilvy Productions, *exp* Alexandra Raffé, *p* Sharon McGowan, *d* Paul Shapiro, *sc* Peggy Thompson, *ph* Thomas Burstyn, *ed* Susan Shipton, *mus* John Sereda; *with* Sheila McCarthy, R.H. Thomson, Michelle Barbara Pelletier, Francis Hyland, Paul Soles. A hip Montreal

teacher, Miss Andrew (Pelletier) moves to Galiano Island in British Columbia, around 1964. Her unorthodox ways irk the school's principal, the staid and conservative Mr Kingswood (Thomson*). His young daughter, Zoe, takes a shine to the teacher's beatnik style, while her older sister, Cleo, is more concerned with The Beatles, and mom (McCarthy*) is focused on being a homemaker. Meanwhile, Kingswood's and Andrew's heated exchanges lead to a heat of another kind. In television director Paul Shapiro's hands, this slight, entertaining little picture from writer Peggy Thompson seems more like a movie of the week. R.H. Thomson has been better, and McCarthy is given little to work with. (V) **Awards include:** GA: Actor (McCarthy), Original Screenplay, Sound Editing.

Loubert, Patrick
See Nelvana Studios.

Louis 19, le roi des ondes
1994 93m *prod* Les Films Stock International, Eiffel Productions, *p* Richard Sadler, Jacques Dorfmann, *d* Michel Poulette, *sc* Emile Gaudreault, Sylvie Bouchard, Michel Michaud, *ph* Daniel Jobin, *ed* Denis Papillon, *mus* Jean-Marie Benoît; *with* Martin Drainville, Agathe de la Fontaine, Dominique Michel, Patricia Tulasne, Gilbert Lachance, Jean L'Italien. Louis (Drainville), a television addict, wins a competition launched by Channel 19 in Montreal to find a viewer whose life will be broadcast live, twenty-four hours a day, for three months. His very ordinariness makes him the perfect choice, appealing to all sectors of the viewing public. Before long Louis is a celebrity. When he meets a girl (de la Fontaine) and falls in love, the ratings soar, but he wants out of a life that has become an intrusive nightmare. His

scheme to make love on air is a hilarious conclusion to a very smart satire on television and its craven attempts to grab ratings at any cost. The American remake, *Ed TV* directed by Ron Howard, was not as funny. (V) **Awards include:** GA: Claude Jutra Award; Golden Reel Award.

Louisiana
1984 128m (186m TV version) *prod* International Cinema Corp., Films A2 (France), Filmax (France), RAI TV2 (Italy), *p* John Kemeny, Denis Héroux, *d* Philippe de Broca, *sc* Etienne Périer, Dominique Fabre, Charles Isreal, *books* Maurice Denuzière, *ph* Michel Brault, *ed* Henri Lanoe, *mus* Claude Bolling; *with* Margot Kidder, Ian Charleson, Victor Lanoux, Andréa Ferreol, Len Cariou, Lloyd Bochner. This sweeping saga of the Old South dates back to the heyday of a production strategy that *Cinema Canada* once dubbed 'minee-feechies.' These hybrids functioned both as television mini-series and (in an abbreviated form) theatrical features. *Louisiana*, directed by Philippe de Broca, the breeziest of 1960s French New Wavers, and shot by Canadian ace cinematographer Michel Brault,* was the most lavish of the hybrids. This kitsch-filled tale concerns a feisty southern belle (Kidder*) whose dilemmas include her family's lost plantation and her tragically emasculated lover (Charleson) – *Gone with the Wind* meets *The Sun also Rises*, with Kidder doing a sub-par Vivien Leigh. The feature film version was cut so frenetically that it plays like the mini-series on speed. (V)

Love and Death on Long Island
1998 93m *prod* Imagex, Skyline Films (U.K.), British Broadcasting Corp. (U.K.), Mikado Films (Italy), *p* Steve Clark-Hill, Christopher Zimmer, *d/sc* Richard

Kwietniowski, *novel* Gilbert Adair, *ph* Oliver Curtis, *ed* Susan Shipton, *mus* The Insects, Richard Grassby-Lewis; *with* John Hurt, Jason Priestly, Fiona Loewi, Sheila Hancock, Maury Chaykin. John Hurt, an actor seemingly destined to play doomed sufferers, and Jason Priestly,* best known for his eight-year gig on *Beverly Hills 90210*, are unlikely co-stars, but the duo play off each other beautifully in this story about a repressed British writer who is infatuated with a handsome star of teen flicks. The subdued chemistry between Hurt and Priestly accounts for the film's sincerity. This male menopause melodrama recalls *Death in Venice*, but is also very different in that Hurt's Giles De'Ath and Priestly's Ronnie Bostock do actually make contact. The picture is perhaps a little too genial and relaxed for its own good; however, it's funny and touching, and never stoops to caricature. (V)

Love and Human Remains
1994 100m *prod* Max Films, Atlantis Films, *exp* Roger Frappier, Pierre Latour, *p* Roger Frappier, Peter Sussman, *d* Denys Arcand, *sc/play* Brad Fraser, *ed* Alain Baril, *mus* John McCarthy; *with* Thomas Gibson, Ruth Marshall, Cameron Bancroft, Mia Kirshner, Joanne Vannicola, Matthew Ferguson. This film is a well-meaning but ultimately disappointing effort to bring Brad Fraser's wildly successful stage play, *Unidentified Human Remains and the True Nature of Love*, to the big screen. The talent certainly seemed to be in place, with two-time Academy Award–nominee Denys Arcand* at the helm and Fraser penning his own adaptation, but the spooky sensuality that worked in so many stage productions didn't translate onto the screen. The plot, about a group of cynical urbanites who cope with a serial killer among them, remains intact,

but Arcand's first English-language foray ultimately seems lifeless. (V)
Awards include: GA: Adapted Screenplay.

Love Come Down

2001 101m *prod* Conquering Lion Pictures, The Film Works, *exp* Larenz Tate, *p* Eric Jordan, Damon D'Oliveira, Clement Virgo, *d/sc* Clement Virgo, *ph* Dylan Macleod, *ed* Susan Maggi, *mus* Aaron Davis, John Lang; *with* Larenz Tate, Deborah Cox, Martin Cummins, Rainbow Sun Francks, Sarah Polley, Barbara Williams. Clement Virgo's* second feature is the tale of two brothers – one black (Tate), the other white (Cummins) – who share the same mother but have different fathers. Their mother (Williams) is in jail for murdering her abusive second husband, an event both boys witnessed. The black brother strives to be a stand-up comedian and falls for the adopted daughter (Cox) of wealthy Jewish parents. The white brother is a club boxer who tries to keep his sibling away from drugs and on the straight and narrow. With a confusing flashback structure and weak ending, the film is not entirely successful, but Virgo displays a natural gift for directing actors even when his writing skills let him down.
Awards include: GA: Supporting Actor (Cummins), Overall Sound, Sound Editing.

Low, Colin

Director, producer, animator, and administrator; b. Cardston, Alta., 1926; father of Stephen Low. Like his mentor, Norman McLaren,* Colin Low has worked in animation and documentary with his eyes clearly fixed on the experimental in form and the socially relevant in content. He directed *The Romance of Transportation in Canada,** a key advance for the NFB in character-driven animation, and *Corral,** a lyrical celebration of the Canadian cowboy. He co-directed the multi-award-winning *City of Gold,** a film that bought historical photographs of the Klondike gold rush to life. For Expo 67, he created the extravagant *Labyrinth** project, and in 1967 he lived on the remote Fogo Island to document a community in economic and social crisis. In 1976 Low returned to the NFB to become head of regional production. He received Quebec's prestigious Prix Albert Tessier in 1997. **Films include:** *Cadet Rousselle* 1947 (co-an with George Dunning); *Time and Terrain* 1947 (d/an/ed); *Challenge: Science against Cancer* 1950 (an with Evelyn Lambart); *The Fight: Science against Cancer* 1951 (an with Lambart, CFA-SPA, AAN-SD); *Age of the Beaver* 1952 (d, CFA-SPA); *The Romance of Transportation in Canada* 1953 (d, AAN-AS); *Corral* 1954 (d/sc); *Riches of the Earth* 1954 (d, CFA-NTS); *The Joulifou Inn* 1955 (p/d/ed); *Gold* 1955 (d, CFA-TS); *City of Gold* 1957 (d/ph with Wolf Koenig, CFA-FY, AAN-SD); *Universe* 1960 (d with Roman Kroitor, CFA-FY, CFA-TS, AAN-AS); *Hors-d'oeuvre* 1960 (co-p); *Very Nice, Very Nice* 1961 (co-p, AAN-AS); *Circle of the Sun* 1961 (d/sc); *The Peep Show* 1962 (p); *My Financial Career* 1962 (co-p, AAN-AS); *The Ride* 1963 (p); *21–87* 1964 (co-p); *I Know an Old Lady Who Swallowed a Fly* 1964 (p); *Free Fall* 1964 (co-p); *The Hutterites* 1964 (d); *Labyrinth* 1967 (d with Kroitor); *Newfoundland Project* 1967 (d, twenty-seven films); *The Sea* 1971 (co-p, CFA-TS); *Memo from Fogo* 1972 (p); *Here Is Canada* 1972 (co-p); *Coming Home* 1973 (co-p, CFA-TD); *In Search of the Bowhead Whale* 1974 (exp); *Cree Hunters of Mistassini* 1974 (p, CFA-FD); *Waiting for Fidel* 1974 (exp); *High Grass Circus* 1976 (exp, AAN-SD); *Blackwood* 1976 (exp, AAN-SD); *Path of the Paddle* 1977 (four films, p with Bill Mason); *Running Time* 1978 (exp);

Starlife 1983 (p); *We Are Born of Stars* 1985 (co-an); *Transitions* 1986 (co-d/sc); *Beavers* 1988 (co-sc); *Emergency / Urgence* 1988 (co-d); *Momentum* 1992 (co-d); *Moving Pictures* 2000 (d/co-sc/narr).

Low, Stephen

Director; b. Montreal, 1950; son of Colin Low. Stephen Low has become a specialist in giant-screen moviemaking, taking the IMAX camera into the depths of the ocean (*Titanica**), the habitat of a family of beavers (*Beavers*), into the sky with a flock of Canadian geese (*Skyward*), and in an Indy car doing 250 mph (*Super Speedway*). In 1995, he produced and directed *Across the Sea of Time*, a time-travelling drama that married archival stereo images with IMAX 3-D, the cutting edge of motion-picture technology. **Films include:** *Challenger: An Industrial Romance* 1980; *Skyward* 1985; *Beavers* 1988; *Titanica* 1992; *The Last Buffalo* 1992; *Across the Sea of Time* 1995; *Super Speedway* 1997.

Loyalties

1986 99m *prod* Lauron International, Dumbarton Films (U.K.), *p* William Johnston, Ronald Lillie, *d* Anne Wheeler, *sc* Sharon Riis, *ph* Vic Sarin, *ed* Judy Krupanzsky; *with* Susan Wooldridge, Kenneth Welsh, Tantoo Cardinal, Tom Jackson, Vera Martin. Still her best work, Anne Wheeler's* debut feature is a gem of resonating subtext. When an upscale British couple (Wooldridge and Welsh*) relocate in the Albertan outback, you're not quite sure what they're doing in such an alien environment. However, finely tuned writing, directing, and acting let us know that their relationship has been corroded by an event that is not named until the end of the picture. *Loyalties* is further distinguished by Vic Sarin's* spacious, elegant cinematography and Tantoo Cardinal's* performance as a Métis woman whose luminous humanity contrasts with the twisted soul of Ken Welsh's character. (V) **Awards include:** GA: Costumes.

Luck of Ginger Coffey, The

1964 100m *prod* Crawley Films, Roth-Kershner Productions (U.S.), *exp* Budge Crawley, *p* Leon Roth, *d* Irvin Kershner, *sc/novel* Brian Moore, *ph* Manny Wynn, *ed* Antony Gibbs, *mus* Bernardo Segáll; *with* Robert Shaw, Mary Ure, Liam Redmond, Tom Harvey, Libby McClintock, Leo Leyden. An unemployed dreamer (Shaw) moves his family from Ireland to Montreal in search of a better life. His wife (Ure) and daughter (McClintock) hate their new surroundings, but Ginger struggles and manages to find work as a copy editor on a Montreal paper. The film, which is based on Brian Moore's* autobiographical novel of the same name, is well-crafted, with a great deal of care paid to the Montreal locations, and the cast is uniformly excellent. However, because it was directed by an American (Kershner, who would later direct *The Empire Strikes Back*) and had a British lead, it wasn't considered 'Canadian' by critics when it was first released. It won Best Feature Film at the Canadian Film Awards, and a viewing print has recently been restored for television. **Awards include:** CFA: Feature Film.

Lutte, La

1961 28m *prod* NFB, *exp* Jacques Bobet, *d* Michel Brault, Claude Jutra, Marcel Carrière, Claude Fournier, *ph/ed* Michel Brault, Claude Fournier, Claude Jutra, *mus* J.S. Bach, Antonio Vivaldi. This important, early direct-cinema documentary on professional wrestlers and the crowds at the Montreal Forum was made collectively by some of Quebec's best filmmaking talent. Nothing escapes the probing, hand-held camera that records the spectacle with humour. (V)

M

Macartney-Filgate, Terence

Director, producer, and cinematographer; b. Scotland, 1924. Macartney-Filgate, an influential figure in the development of new forms of documentary in Canada, joined the fabled Unit B of the NFB in 1956. He worked extensively as a producer and cinematographer on the groundbreaking *Candid Eye** series of film portraits of Canadian life, and helped refine the free-form, unscripted, observational approach of the direct-cinema movement. He left the NFB in 1960 to work independently, but rejoined Board briefly in the late 1960s during the Challenge for Change* program, and he went on to produce several major docudramas. Macartney-Filgate's most memorable films are *The Back-Breaking Leaf,* Up against the System*, and *Dieppe 1942*. **Films and television include:** *The Days before Christmas* 1958 (co-d, TV); *Blood and Fire* 1958 (d, TV); *Police* 1958 (d/co-ph, TV); *The Back-Breaking Leaf* 1959 (d/co-ph, TV); *End of the Line* 1959 (d/co-ph, TV); *Cars in Your Life* 1960 (d/ph, TV); *Primary* 1960 (ph); *Pinter People* 1960 (ph); *Robert Frost: A Lover's Quarrel* 1962 (d/co-ph); *Composers USA: Avant Garde* 1966 (d/ph); *Marshall McLuhan* 1967 (d); *Christopher Plummer* 1967 (d); *Up against the System* 1969 (d/ph); *A.Y. Jackson: A Portrait* 1970 (d); *Henry David Thoreau: The Beat of a Different Drummer* 1972 (p/d); *The Time Machine* 1972 (p/d); *Lucy Maude Montgomery: The Road to Green Gables* 1975 (p/d/ph); *Grenfell of Labrador: The Great Adventure* 1977 (p/d/ph, TV); *The Hottest Show on Earth* 1977 (co-d, CFA-SD); *Fields of Endless Days* 1978 (co-p/d); *Dieppe 1942* 1979 (p/d, TV); *Magical Eye* 1989 (co-p/d/ph); *Timothy Findley: Anatomy of a Writer* 1991 (p/d, TV).

MacDonald, Wallace

Actor and producer; b. Sydney, N.S., 1891; d. 1978. MacDonald, who is virtually unknown today, was a mainstay in Hollywood for about forty-five years. He began his career in 1914 as one of Mack Sennett's* Keystone Kops (including seven shorts with Charlie Chaplin) and continued working as an actor into the sound era. In the late 1930s he moved behind the camera, and produced more than 100 B-movies before his retirement in 1959.

MacGillivray, William D.

Director, writer, and producer; b. St John's, Nfld., 1946. MacGillivray, a founder of the Atlantic Filmmakers Cooperative in Halifax in 1974, has made lasting contributions to the development of film culture in Atlantic Canada. Out of his fiercely independent production company, Picture Plant, MacGillivray wrote and directed several critically acclaimed films, including *Stations** and *Life Classes.** MacGillivray's intelligent, introspective, and formally complex films are concerned with the pressures of mass culture and commercialization on the individual imagination and identity. 'Tell your own stories, get to know who you are,' exhorts his protagonist in *Understanding Bliss*. It is MacGillivray's own credo. **Films and television include:** *Aerial View* 1979 (d); *Stations* 1983 (p/d/co-sc/co-ed); *Life Classes* 1987 (p/d/sc/ed); *I Will Make No More Boring Art* 1988 (p/d/sc/ed/mus); *Vacant Lot* 1989 (d/sc); *Understanding Bliss* 1990 (exp/d/co-sc/co-ed); *Gullage's* 1996–8 (p/d/sc, series).

Maddin, Guy

Director and writer; b. Winnipeg, 1957. Maddin began his career as a student of economics at the University of Manitoba. With two short films and four gloriously idiosyncratic features, he has single-handedly invented an imaginary Canadian cinematic history, moving from 1920s prairie expressionist and surrealist movements through that creaky era between silent and sound cinema to the arrival of our own colour talkies. His prodigious imagination offers up murky sagas of diseased male rivalry (*Tales from the Gimli Hospital**), love and amnesia in the First World War (*Archangel**), and lust and incest in a repressed alpine village (*Careful**). All are rendered in luminous Canadian pastiches of Buñuel, Vigo, Cocteau, von Sternberg, Lang, and Murnau. **Films include:** *The Dead Father* 1986; *Tales from the Gimli Hospital* 1988; *Archangel* 1990; *Careful* 1992; *Odilon Redon* 1996; *Twilight of the Ice Nymphs* 1997; *The Heart of the World* from *Preludes* 2000 (d/sc).

Maelström

2000 88m *prod* Max Films, *p* Roger Frappier, Luc Vandel, *d/sc* Denis Villeneuve, *ph* André Turpin, *ed* Richard Comeau, *mus* Pierre Desrochers; *with* Marie-Josée Croze, Jean-Nicolas Verreault, Stéphanie Morgenstern, Pierre Lebeau. Denis Villeneuve's* follow-up to his auspicious feature debut, *Un 32 août sur terre,** again focuses on a young woman (Croze) who is dissatisfied with her pampered lifestyle and is pushed to the brink of suicide by a car accident. Here, she leaves a bar one night and drunkenly hits an old fish-monger who later dies. But, as in *Un 32 août*, life has a few twists and turns in store for this hapless heroine. She meets the son of her victim (Verrault), a Norwegian deep sea diver, and falls in love. This oddly humorous tale is told by a monstrous fish who provides ironic commentary throughout the film, much like a Greek chorus. (V) **Awards include**: GA: Picture, Director, Original Screenplay, Actress (Croze), Cinematography.

Making of 'Monsters,' The

1991 35m *prod* Canadian Centre for Advanced Film Studies, *p* Laurie Lynd, *d/sc* John Greyson, *ph* Almerinda Tarvassos, *ed* Miume Jan, *mus* Glenn Schellenberg; *with* Stewart Arnott, Claire Coulter, David Gardner, Taborah Johnson. On a summer night in 1985, five teenage boys attacked and killed a gay man in Toronto's High Park. They were out of jail in less than three years. *The Making of 'Monsters'* is a fictional documentary that chronicles a movie-of-the-week version of the event. The movie-within-the-movie is produced by Hungarian Marxist Georg Lukacs and directed by Bertolt Brecht who, inexplicably, appears as a catfish in a bowl. The film brilliantly satirizes Brechtian theatre while simultaneously exploring the issue of anti-gay violence.

Malo, René

Producer and distributor; b. Joliette, Que., 1942. Malo, who worked as a variety show and record producer before entering the film industry, is a major industry player. He built Malofilm into one of Canada's most successful distributors of Canadian features. As a producer, Malo has been behind some of the best films made in Quebec, including Micheline Lanctôt's *Sonatine,** Denys Arcand's *Le Déclin de l'empire américain,** and Francis Mankiewicz's *Les Portes tournantes*. Malo once said that producers should react to scripts 'like a normal person on the street.' **Films include:** *Panique* 1977; *L'Homme à tout faire* 1980; *Le Ruffian* 1983; *Sonatine* 1984; *Lune et miel* 1985; *Le Déclin de l'empire américain* 1986 (p with Roger Frappier, GA-P, GRA, AAN-FLF); *Tinamer* 1987; *Les Portes tournantes* 1988; *Trois pommes à côte du sommeil* 1988; *Pin* 1989; *Blind Fear* 1989; *Internal Affairs* 1990; *Scanners II: The New Order* 1991; *Scanners III: The Takeover* 1991; *Scanner Cop* 1994; *Ladies Room* 1999.

Mankiewicz, Francis

Director; b. Shanghai, China, 1944; d. 1993. Francis Mankiewicz, who belonged to the same clan as writer-director Joe (*All about Eve*) and writer Herman (*Citizen Kane*), directed one of the most moving of all Canadian films. *Les Bons Débarras** concerns the loving but destructive relationship between a manipulative young girl and her tempestuous mother. This picture, which won eight Genies, was followed by more Québécois features and provocative English-language dramas such as *Love and Hate*, the first Canadian television drama to be shown on U.S. prime-time television. Mankiewicz had a gift for exploring intricate and even dysfunctional relationships with compassion, finesse, and minimal sentimentality. **Films and television include:** *Les Temps d'une chasse* 1972 (d/sc); *What We Have Here Is a People Problem* 1976 (d, TV); *A Matter of Choice* 1978 (d, TV); *Une Amie d'enfance* 1978; *Les Bons Débarras* 1980 (GA-D); *Les Beaux Souvenirs* 1981; *And Then You Die* 1987; *Les Portes tournantes* 1988 (d/co-sc); *Love and Hate: The Story of Colin and Joann Thatcher* 1989 (TV); *Conspiracy of Silence* 1991 (TV).

Mann, Ron

Director and producer; b. Toronto, 1958. A *wunderkind*, Mann directed his first documentary feature, *Imagine the Sound*, at the age of twenty-one. This idiosyncratic look at avant-garde jazz won an award at the Chicago Film Festival, as did his follow-up, *Poetry in Motion.** Mann is also a pioneer in digitalizing film – *Poetry in Motion* was one of the first to be released in a digital format. Through investigations of comics, popular dance, or marijuana, Mann has made it his project to make marginal cultures accessible to larger audiences. **Films include:** *Imagine the Sound* 1981 (p/d); *Poetry in Motion* 1982 (p/d); *The New Cinema* 1983 (exp); *Listen to the City* 1984 (p/d); *Comic Book Confidential* 1988 (p/d, GA-FD); *Special of the Day* 1989 (exp); *Twist* 1992 (p/d); *Brakhage* 1998 (exp); *Grass* 2000 (p/d, GA-FD).

Manners, David

Actor and writer; b. Rauff de Ryther Duan Acklom in Halifax, 1901; d. 1998. Manners was a prolific writer as well as a stage and movie actor who claimed lineage that dated back to William the Conqueror. He played the second lead of many of Universal's horror classics of the 1930s, including the naive Jonathan Harker in Tod Browning's *Dracula* and one of the explorers who discover Boris Karloff in *The Mummy*. He starred with Bela Lugosi and Karloff in Edgar G. Ulmer's classic *The Black Cat*, and he also played opposite Katharine Hepburn in *A Bill of Divorcement* and *A Woman Rebels*. In the 1940s Manners left Hollywood for the New York stage and a career as a novelist. **Films include:** *Kismet* 1930; *Dracula* 1931; *The Miracle Woman* 1931; *A Bill of Divorcement* 1932; *The Greeks Had a Word for Them* 1932; *The Mummy* 1932; *Roman Scandals* 1933; *The Black Cat* 1934; *Jalna* 1935; *The Mystery of Edwin Drood* 1935; *A Woman Rebels* 1936.

Manufacturing Consent: Noam Chomsky and the Media

1992 167m *prod* Necessary Illusions Productions, NFB, *exp* Dennis Murphy, Colin Neale, *p* Mark Achbar, Peter Wintonick, Adam Symansky, *d/sc* Mark Achbar, Peter Wintonick, *ph* Francis Miquet, Mark Achbar, Barry Perles, Norbert Bunge, Ken Reeves, Kip Tougas, Antonin Lhotsky, Peter Wintonick, *ed* Peter Wintonick, *mus* Carl Schultz; *with* Noam Chomsky. This clever documentary profiles the ideas of Chomsky, one of the most prominent intellectuals of the twentieth century. The linguist and media analyst is only interviewed in one sequence; elsewhere, the film-makers opt to rely primarily on pouring through mediated images of Chomsky. *Manufacturing Consent* is at once an intelligent analysis of Chomsky's ideas and a careful deconstruction of the documentary form itself. Chomsky has argued in countless articles and books that the media, while not conspiratorial, definitely operates by unwritten rules about what to report and what not to report. His theories have evoked extremely divided responses, from those (on the left) who consider him a genius, to those (on the right) who think he's a crackpot. (V)

Man Who Skied down Everest, The

1975 84m *prod* Crawley Films, Ishihara International Productions (Japan), *p/d* Budge Crawley, *sc* Judith Crawley, *diary* Yuichiro Miura, *ph* Mitsuji Kanau, Shigeru Kawamoto, Kikumatsu Soda, Takeshi Kimura, Masaru Ohtaki, Ryo Yano, Kenji Fukuhara, *ed* Bob Cooper, Millie Moore, *mus* Larry Crosley, *narr* Douglas Rain. Yuichiro Miura was a daredevil Japanese skier who set world speed records. This film covers his 1970 trek through the Himalayas to ski down Mount Everest. Budge Crawley* purchased the filmed record of the event, and Judith Crawley* fashioned a script from Miura's diary to accompany the footage. The resulting movie was extremely popular and was the first feature-length Canadian film to win an Academy Award. **Awards include:** AA: Feature Documentary

Margaret's Museum

1996 118m *prod* Ranfilm, Les Productions Télé-Action, Imagex, Glace Bay

Pictures, Skyline (U.K.), *exp* Marilyn Belec, *p* Mort Ransen, Christopher Zimmer, Claudio Luca, Steve Clark-Hall, *d* Mort Ransen, *sc* Gerald Wexler, Mort Ransen, *short story* Sheldon Currie, *ph* Vic Sarin, *ed* Rita Roy, *mus* Milan Kymlicka, The Rankin Family; *with* Helena Bonham Carter, Clive Russell, Kate Nelligan, Kenneth Welsh, Craig Olejnik. Margaret (Bonham Carter) is an eccentric, strong-willed woman living in a Cape Breton coal-mining town, who is determined not to marry a miner. She falls for a charming rogue (Russell), who also doesn't want the life of a miner. They marry, but the need for money leads him down the mine, and Margaret is faced with the inevitable tragedy. Vic Sarin's* stunning cinematography is just one of the highlights of this entertaining movie, and director Mort Ransen* achieves stellar performances from Bonham Carter and an excellent supporting cast. The hard life of the coal miners is intertwined with some touching and often humorous moments of family, love, and death. (V) **Awards include:** GA: Actress (Bonham Carter), Supporting Actor (Welsh), Supporting Actress (Nelligan), Costumes, Musical Score.

Maria Chapdelaine

1983 107m (220m TV version) *prod* Astral Bellevue Pathé, Radio-Canada, T.F.1 Films (France), *exp* Harold Greenberg, *p* Murray Shostak, Robert Baylis, *d* Gilles Carle, *sc* Gilles Carle, Guy Fournier, *novel* Louis Hémon, *ph* Pierre Mignot, Richard Leiterman, *ed* Avdé Chiriaeff, *mus* Lewis Furey; *with* Carole Laure, Nick Mancuso, Claude Rich, Amulette Garneau, Yoland Guérard, Pierre Curzi. *Maria Chapdelaine* is based on Louis Hémon's bestselling novel, set in the Lac Saint-Jean region of Quebec in the early years of the twentieth century. The beautiful Maria (Laure*), who dreams of an easier life than the one she must endure in the wilderness, gives her heart to a handsome lumberjack (Mancuso) and waits for his return. The film was designed as a feature/mini-series hybrid and directed by veteran Gilles Carle.* Unfortunately, it never really rises above the glorious rustic setting. The lovers are too beautiful and well-coiffed to be believable, and they rarely appear on the screen together. An expensive, boring failure. (V) **Awards include:** GA: Cinematography, Art Direction, Costumes.

Married Couple, A

1969 96m *prod* Allan King Assoc., *p/d* Allan King, *ph* Richard Leiterman, *ed* Arla Saare, *mus* Zalman Yanovsky, Douglas Bush; *with* Antoinette, Billy and Bogart Edwards. Shot over ten weeks, this direct-cinema portrait of a troubled young couple in their seventh year of marriage straddles the line between documentary and fiction. The film crew records the couple's lives as they fight about everything – from money, to who will take the car, to how to use a vacuum cleaner properly. Although the film is not scripted and there are no professional actors, the couple seem to 'act out' their lives for the cameras in this frightening depiction of domestic life.

Masala

1992 105m *prod* Divani Films, *p* Camelia Frieberg, Srinivas Krishna, *d/sc* Srinivas Krishna, *ph* Paul Sarossy, *ed* Michael Munn, Srinivas Krishna, *mus* Leslie Winston, The West Indian Company, Asha Bosle; *with* Madhuri Bhatia, Srinivas Krishna, Saeed Jaffrey, Sakina Jaffrey. This film, an uneven, comedic look at the lives of Indian immigrants in Toronto, focuses on two families, and in particular on Krishna (Srinivas Krishna),

who returns to his relatives five years after he refused to join his immediate family on a doomed flight to India. While reluctant to form attachments, Krishna encounters his cousin Rita (Sakina Jaffrey), who tries to draw him out of his emotional isolation. In a fantastical story of exceptionally good fortune and terribly bad karma, a Hindu God (Saeed Jaffrey) appears on grandma's television screen and characters spontaneously break into song. (V)

Masculine Mystique, The

1985 87m *prod* NFB, *exp* Robert Verrall, Andy Thomson, *p/d* John N. Smith, Giles Walker, *sc* John N. Smith, Giles Walker, David Wilson, *ph* Andrew Kitzanuk, *ed* David Wilson, *mus* Richard Gresko; *with* Stefan Wodoslawsky, Char Davies, Sam Grana, Eleanor MacKinnon, Mort Ransen, Felice Grana. *The Masculine Mystique*, one of the NFB's attempts to produce 'alternative dramas,' casts an amused eye on how four rather unliberated men – all NFB employees – cope with feminism and modern day women. Essentially a docudrama, the film alternates between scenes of personal lives and encounter sessions where the men bare their souls, question each other's motives, and try to confront their feelings about the women with whom they are involved. It's an honest, often amusing, and touching account of a contemporary problem. (V)

Mason, Bill

Director, editor, and cinematographer; b. Winnipeg, 1929; d. 1989. Mason was one of the world's best directors and photographers of nature films. From 1962 to 1984 he worked at the NFB where he directed, shot, and edited some of the Board's most popular shorts, including the enduring *Paddle to the Sea.* * His one and only feature documentary, *Cry of the*

Wild,* grossed one million dollars in the
first week of release in 1973 and went on
to become the most successful feature
ever produced by the Board. Mason, a
devoted naturalist and expert canoeist,
was also the author of *The Path of the
Paddle* (1980). **Films include:** *Paddle to
the Sea* 1966 (d/ph/ed, AAN-S); *The Rise
and Fall of the Great Lakes* 1968 (d/sc/ph/
ed/an); *Blake* 1969 (d/ph/ed, AAN-S);
Death of a Legend 1971 (d/ph/ed); *Cry of
the Wild* 1973 (d/sc/ed/co-ph/narr); *In
Search of the Bowhead Whale* 1974 (d/ed/
co-ph/narr); *Wolf Pack* 1974 (d/ph/ed);
Path of the Paddle 1977 (d/ed/narr, four
films); *Song of the Paddle* 1978 (d/ed); *The
Land That Devours Ships* 1984 (d/ph/ed/
an); *Waterwalker* 1984 (p/d/ed/narr).

Massey, Raymond

Actor; b. Toronto, 1896; d. 1983. Raymond, brother of Vincent Massey, the
first Canadian-born Governor General
of Canada, was being groomed for an
illustrious career in the family farm-
implement business when, during the
First World War, an impromptu minstrel
show led him into a post-war acting career on the British stage. Because of his
lanky taciturnity he was typecast early
on as the embodiment of authority, and
when he arrived in Hollywood in 1931,
Massey was instantly cast as Sherlock
Holmes. He played a number of similar
characters, turning in a succession of
strong performances. He won an Academy Award nomination for his portrayal
of Abraham Lincoln in *Abe Lincoln in Illinois* and was also exceptional as James
Dean's father in *East of Eden*. In the
1960s, he created the memorable Dr
Gillespie in the *Dr Kildare* television series. **Films and television include:** *The
Speckled Band* 1931; *The Scarlet Pimpernel*
1935; *Things to Come* 1936; *The Prisoner of
Zenda* 1937; *Drums* 1938; *Abe Lincoln in
Illinois* 1940 (AAN-A); *The Santa Fe Trail*

1940; *49th Parallel* 1941; *Reap the Wild
Wind* 1942; *Desperate Journey* 1942; *Arsenic and Old Lace* 1944; *The Woman in the
Window* 1944; *Stairway to Heaven* 1946;
Mourning Becomes Electra 1947; *The Foun-
tainhead* 1949; *Carson City* 1952; *Battle
Cry* 1955; *East of Eden* 1955; *The Naked
and the Dead* 1958; *The Great Imposter*
1960; *Dr Kildare* 1961–6 (series); *How the
West Was Won* 1962; *Mackenna's Gold*
1969.

Maxwell, Lois

Actor; b. Lois Ruth Hooker, Kitchener,
Ont., 1927. Maxwell had spells in Hollywood and Italy, but spent the majority
of her film career in England. Here her
pleasant personality was always welcome, if somewhat wasted, in playing
the unflappable Miss Moneypenny in
fourteen James Bond films over a
period of twenty-four years. From *Dr No*
to *A View to a Kill*, Maxwell added a touch
of humour and class to the longest-
running joke in the history of cinema –
Moneypenny's 'unrequited love' for
Bond. **Films include:** *Aida* 1953; *Lolita*
1962; *Dr No* 1962; *Come Fly with Me* 1963;
The Haunting 1963; *From Russia with Love*
1963; *Goldfinger* 1964; *Thunderball* 1965;
You Only Live Twice 1967; *On Her Majes-
ty's Secret Service* 1969; *Diamonds Are Forever* 1971; *Live and Let Die* 1973; *The Man
with the Golden Gun* 1974; *The Spy Who
Loved Me* 1977; *Ragtime Summer* 1977;
Moonraker 1979; *For Your Eyes Only* 1981;
Octopussy 1983; *A View to a Kill* 1985;
Martha, Ruth and Edie 1987.

May, Derek

Director and writer; b. London, U.K.,
1932; d. 1992. Poet Leonard Cohen once
described his friend Derek May as a
man with an acute sense of 'upset' – an
uncanny ability to turn seemingly ordinary ideas on their heads and make
them fascinating. May was trained in

visual arts (painting, sculpting), and his remarkable films offer evidence of Cohen's theory. May joined the NFB in 1965 as an assistant editor, and went on to direct films, such as *Angel* and *Pandora*, that merged documentary, experimental, and personal styles. His final film, *Projections* – a beguiling and insightful portrait of another artist of 'upset,' Krzyztof Wodicko – was an impressive swan song for a filmmaking life too soon cut short. **Films include:** *Angel* 1966 (CFA-AE); *The Ernie Game* 1968 (ad); *A Film for Max* 1970; *Pandora* 1971; *Sananguagat: Inuit Masterworks* 1974; *Mother Tongue* 1979; *Boulevard of Broken Dreams* 1987; *Projections* 1992.

McCarthy, Sheila

Actor; b. 1956. Sheila McCarthy made her first notable impression on the Canadian movie scene as the airborne, quirky Polly in Patricia Rozema's *I've Heard the Mermaids Singing** in 1987. She also won her first Genie for that performance. When Rozema* and McCarthy worked together again, on *White Room*, the response was less than favourable. However, little harm was done to McCarthy's career, which has hummed along at a steady pace with varied roles in conventional Hollywood pictures (*Die Hard 2*, *Paradise*), local fare such as *The Lotus Eaters** (which brought her a second Genie) and *George's Island*, and stage roles at the Stratford and Shaw festivals and the Grand Theatre in London, Ontario. **Films and television include:** *Waiting for the Parade* 1984 (TV); *Love and Larceny* 1985 (TV); *Passion: A Letter in 16mm* 1985; *A Nest of Singing Birds* 1987 (TV); *I've Heard the Mermaids Singing* 1987 (GA-A); *Friends, Lovers and Lunatics* 1989; *Beethoven Lives Upstairs* 1989 (TV); *George's Island* 1989; *Beautiful Dreamers* 1990; *Back to the Beanstalk* 1990 (TV); *Die Hard 2* 1990; *White Room* 1990; *Pacific Heights* 1990; *Montréal vu par ...* 1991; *Stepping Out* 1991; *Paradise* 1991; *The Lotus Eaters* 1993 (GA-A); *The Possession of Michael D.* 1995 (TV); *The Marriage Bed* 1996 (TV); *House Arrest* 1996; *Emily of New Moon* 1997–9 (series); *More Tales of the City* 1998 (TV); *Virtual Mom* 2000 (TV).

McDonald, Bruce

Director and editor; b. Toronto, 1954. McDonald, the self-styled rock 'n' roll director of Toronto's new wave,* has constructed an identity – scruffy, hip, funny – that is cannily in sync with his movies. He is a graduate of Ryerson Polytechnic University's film department and the Toronto independent production scene of the 1980s. *Roadkill*,* his funky low-budget feature debut, launched his career in 1990. That film and its follow-up, *Highway 61*,* are contemporary road films featuring quirky characters, dollops of debauchery, and hot music strung together by an ironic comic tone. McDonald co-scripted, with Don McKellar* and John Frizzell, an adaptation of W.P. Kinsella's *Dance Me Outside** in 1994, and he released his best film, the mock-documentary *Hard Core Logo*,* in 1996. **Films and television include:** *Knock! Knock!* 1985 (p/d/sc/ed); *Family Viewing* 1987 (co-ed); *Comic Book Confidential* 1988 (co-ed); *The Mysterious Moon Men of Canada* 1988 (co-p/ed, GA-LAS); *Speaking Parts* 1989 (co-ed); *Roadkill* 1990 (co-p/d/co-sc/a); *Highway 61* 1992 (co-p/d); *Dance Me Outside* 1994 (d/co-sc); *Hard Core Logo* 1996 (d/a); *Platinum* 1997 (d, TV); *Elimination Dance* 1998 (d/co-sc); *Scandalous Me: The Jacqueline Susann Story* 1998 (d, TV); *Twitch City* 1998, 2000 (d, series).

McKellar, Don

Actor, writer, and director; b. Toronto, 1962. To connoisseurs of Canadian cin-

ema, McKellar is best known for his collaborations with Bruce McDonald.* He wrote *Roadkill** and *Highway 61,** co-wrote *Dance Me Outside,** and appeared in *Roadkill* and *Highway 61*. McKellar also co-wrote (with François Girard*) the Genie-winning *Thirty-Two Short Films about Glenn Gould** and *The Red Violin.** Sometimes called a 'renaissance man' for his diversity and originality, McKellar is also a prodigious writer for the stage (*The Drowsy Chaperone, 86: An Autopsy*) and television (*Twitch City*).
His role as an idiosyncratic pet shop owner in Egoyan's *Exotica** won him a Best Supporting Actor Genie and his feature directorial debut, *Last Night,** earned him the Prix de la Jeunesse at Cannes. **Films and television include:** *Roadkill* 1990 (co-sc/a); *The Adjuster* 1991 (a); *Highway 61* 1992 (sc/a); *Blue* 1992 (d/sc); *Thirty-Two Short Films about Glenn Gould* 1994 (co-sc); *Exotica* 1994 (a, GA-SA); *Dance Me Outside* 1994 (co-sc); *Joe's So Mean to Josephine* 1997 (a); *When Night Is Falling* 1995 (a); *The Red Violin* 1998 (co-sc/a, GA-SC, PJ-SC); *Last Night* 1998 (d/sc/a, CJA); *Twitch City* 1998, 2000 (sc/a, series); *The Herd* 1999 (a); *eXistenZ* 1999 (a); *Waydowntown* 2000 (a); *A Word from the Management* from *Preludes* 2000 (d/sc).

McLaren, Norman
Animator; b. Stirling, Scotland, 1914; d. 1987. When John Grierson* offered the young Scottish animator 'forty dollars a week and a chance to make films,' McLaren accepted and wound up staying at the NFB for the rest of his working life. He established the department of animation in 1942 and spent most of his career creating innovative animated and documentary films. His pixilated anti-war allegory, *Neighbours,** won an Academy Award for Best Short Documentary in 1953, and *A Chairy Tale,**

made with Evelyn Lambart* and Claude Jutra,* was nominated in 1958. Most of McLaren's animated work, like the jazzy *Begone Dull Care,** was drawn directly onto film, but he also used cut outs of shapes, traditional cartoon elements, and in the lyrical *Pas de deux*, stroboscopic effects. **Films include:** *V for Victory* 1941 (p/d/an); *Hen Hop* 1942 (p/d/an); *C'est l'aviron* 1944 (p/d); *Alouette* 1944 (d/an with René Jodoin); *Fiddle-de-dee* 1947 (p/d/an); *Dots* 1948 (p/d/an, CFA-SPA); *Loops* 1948 (p/d/an, CFA-SPA); *Begone Dull Care* 1949 (p/d/an/ed with Eve Lambart, CFA-SPA); *Around Is Around* 1951 (p/d/an with Lambart, CFA-SPA); *Now Is the Time* 1951 (d/an with Lambart, CFA-SPA); *A Phantasy* 1952 (p/d/an, CFA-SPA); *Neighbours* 1952 (p/d/an/mus, CFA-SPA, AA-SD); *Blinkity Blank* 1955 (p/d/an); *Rhythmetic* 1956 (p/d/an with Lambart); *A Chairy Tale* 1957 (d with Claude Jutra, AAN-AS); *Lines – Horizontal* 1961 (d/an with Lambart, CFA-AE); *Lines – Vertical* 1962 (d/an with Lambart); *Christmas Cracker* 1963 (co-d, AAN-AS); *Canon* 1964 (d with Grant Munro, CFA-AE); *Mosaic* 1965 (p/d/an with Lambart); *Pas de deux* 1968 (p/d, AAN-AS); *Spheres* 1969 (p/d/an with Jodoin); *Ballet Adagio* 1971 (p/d/an); *Narcissus* 1983 (d).

Meatballs
1979 94m *prod* Haliburton Films, *exp* André Link, John Dunning, *p* Dan Goldberg, *d* Ivan Reitman, *sc* Dan Goldberg, Janis Allen, Len Blum, Harold Ramis, *ph* Don Wilder, *ed* Debra Karen, *mus* Elmer Bernstein; *with* Bill Murray, Harvey Atkin, Kate Lynch, Russ Banham. Ivan Reitman's* follow-up to the hugely successful *National Lampoon's Animal House* (which he co-produced) is less frantic and more sentimental but definitely in the same mould. Relying on juvenile, bawdy humour and the hip,

anti-establishment attitude of *Animal House*, *Meatballs* is set in a summer camp for misfits overseen by head counsellor Murray in his first starring role. His motivational rallying cry to his team of losers as they take on an opposing team from a rich kid's camp is: 'It just doesn't matter!' Despite its critical drubbing, *Meatballs* remains one of the most popular Canadian films of all time and spawned two dreadful sequels. (V) **Awards include:** GA: Screenplay, Actress (Lynch); Golden Reel Award.

Mehta, Deepa
Director and writer; b. Bombay, India, 1949. Although Mehta's father was a film distributor and she grew up watching popular Bombay musicals, her university studies led to a degree in philosophy, not film. In 1973, she immigrated to Canada and married Paul Saltzman. Together they established Sunrise Films. Mehta proved to be an industrious and talented writer, editor, and director of short films and documentaries. Her features include *Sam and Me*, which won an Honorable Mention at Cannes in 1991, *Camilla* (with Jessica Tandy and Bridget Fonda), and *Fire*, the first of a trilogy set in India. Her reputation in the Canadian film industry is of a woman not to be trifled with. **Films include:** *At 99: A Portrait of Louise Tandy Murch* 1974 (d, CFA-SD); *Martha, Ruth and Edie* 1987 (co-d); *Sam and Me* 1991 (d); *Camilla* 1994 (d); *Fire* 1997 (d/sc); *Earth* 1999 (d/sc).

Melançon, André
Director, actor, and writer; b. Rouyn-Noranda, Que., 1942. Melançon set out to become a youth guidance counsellor before he veered into film, but filmmaking soon became his primary activity. After making several films for adults, he produced a trio of shorts for

kids that confirmed the direction of his career. Thereafter he became one of Quebec's most acclaimed children's filmmakers, directing such award-winning cultural icons as *The Dog Who Stopped the War** and *Bach and Broccoli*, both part of the Tales for All series. His insight into young minds has been lauded, as has his taste for experimenting. He has also pursued a career as an actor, mostly in supporting roles. **Films include:** *Charles Gagnon* 1970 (p/d); *L'Enfant et les mathématiques* 1971 (d); *Le Professeur et les mathématiques* 1971 (d); *Des armes et les hommes* 1973 (d); *Taureau* 1973 (a); *Réjeanne Padovani* 1973 (a); *Partis pour la glorie* 1975 (a, CFA-A); *Comme les six doigts de la main* 1978 (d/sc); *Les Vrais Perdants* 1979 (d); *L'Espace d'un été* 1980 (d); *Odyssey of the Pacific* 1982 (a); *The Dog Who Stopped the War / La Guerre des tuques* 1984 (d/sc); *Les Lys cassé* 1986 (d); *Equinoxe* 1986 (a); *Bach and Broccoli* 1986 (d/co-sc); *Pouvoir intime* 1986 (a); *The Great Land of Small* 1987 (a); *The Tadpole and the Whale* 1988 (co-sc); *Les Matins infidèles* 1989 (a); *Rafales* 1990 (d).

Memoradum
1965 58m *prod* NFB, *p* John Kemeny, *d* Donald Brittain, John Spotton, *sc* Donald Brittain, *ph/ed* John Spotton. In this documentary – one of his best – Donald Brittain* uses a blend of *cinéma-vérité* and stock footage to tell the story of a Canadian Holocaust survivor who returns to Bergen-Belsen with his son on the twentieth anniversary of his liberation from the death camp. It is a conceptually complex work that combines the present with the past to offer a powerful and deeply moving testament to 'murder by memorandum,' Hitler's final solution to the 'Jewish problem.' (V)

Mental Mechanisms
1947–50 prod NFB. This series of four

dramatized films about mental health was made in the late 1940s by the NFB for the Department of National Health and Welfare. The four films are: *The Feeling of Hostility, The Feeling of Rejection, Over Dependency,* and *Feelings of Depression.* The aim of the series was to depict the causes of mental illness, remove its stigma, and suggest possible cures. The films were widely viewed and much admired by psychiatrists and mental health professionals.

Mercure, Monique
Actor; b. Montreal, 1930. As an actor, Mercure exudes dignity, strength, and an alluring enigmatic quality. She began her film career in numerous bit parts and secondary roles, but in 1970, this former music student with the no-nonsense gaze broke through to a wider audience in Denis Héroux's* raunchy sex comedy, *Deux femmes en or.* The next year she played an aging village temptress in *Mon oncle Antoine.** Mercure's period role in *J.A. Martin photographe** won her Best Actress at Cannes and the Canadian Film Awards. The Mercurian persona reached its apotheosis when she played a sinister dominatrix with extraordinary powers in Cronenberg's *Naked Lunch.** **Films include:** *Félix Leclerc* 1959; *À tout prendre* 1963; *Ce n'est pas le temps des romans* 1964; *Le Festin des morts* 1965; *Ca n'est pas les temps des romans* 1966; *Waiting for Caroline* 1967 (TV); *Don't Let the Angels Fall* 1969; *Love in a 4 Letter World* 1970; *Deux femmes en or* 1970; *Finalement ...* 1971; *Mon oncle Antoine* 1971; *Françoise Durocher, Waitress* 1971; *Le Temps d'une chasse* 1972; *Il était une fois dans l'est* 1974; *Pour le meilleur et pour le pire* 1975; *Les Vautours* 1975; *L'Amour blessé* 1975; *L'Absence* 1976; *Parlez-nous d'amour* 1976; *J.A. Martin photographe* 1977 (CFA-A); *La Chanson de Roland* 1978; *Quintet* 1979; *Stone Cold*

Dead 1980; *La Cuisine rouge* 1980; *The Third Walker* 1980; *Odyssey of the Pacific* 1982; *Une Journée en taxi* 1982; *La Quarantaine* 1982; *Contrecoeur* 1983; *Les Années de rêves* 1984; *The Blood of Others* 1984; *La Dame en couleurs* 1985; *Les Bottes* 1986; *Qui a tiré sur nos histoires?* 1986; *Dans le ventre du dragon* 1988; *Montréal vu par ...* 1991; *Naked Lunch* 1992 (GA-SA); *The Red Violin* 1998; *Conquest* 1999 (GA-SA); *Emporte-moi* 1999.

Mettler, Peter
Director, producer, cinematographer, and editor; b. Toronto, 1958. Peter Mettler is one of the most important figures to emerge out of Toronto's new wave* of the early 1980s. He studied filmmaking at Ryerson Polytechnic University, and worked as cinematographer for Atom Egoyan,* Bruce McDonald,* Patricia Rozema,* and others. Mettler's own films are astonishing dramas of technology and perception that examine cinema's mysteries of sound and vision while enacting them on screen. He blurs the borders between experimental and narrative cinema, and always displays a stunning visual and aural design. **Films include:** *Reverie* 1976 (p/d/sc/ph/ed); *Poison Ivy* 1978 (p/d/sc/co-ph/ed); *Home Movie* 1979 (p/d/sc/ph/ed); *Lancalot Freely* 1980 (p/d/sc/ph/ed); *Gregory* 1981 (p/d/sc/co-ph/ed); *Scissere* 1982 (co-p/d/sc/ph/ed); *Open House* 1982 (ph); *David Roche Talks to You about Love* 1982 (ph); *Next of Kin* 1984 (ph); *Kabaret de la Vita* 1984 (ph); *Trip around Lake Ontario* 1984 (ph); *Eastern Avenue* 1985 (p/d/ph/ed); *Passion: A Letter in 16mm* 1985 (ph); *Knock! Knock!* 1985 (ph); *Walking after Midnight* 1986 (co-ph); *Artist on Fire: The Work of Joyce Wieland* 1987 (ph); *Family Viewing* 1987 (ph); *Top of His Head* 1989 (d/sc/co-ph/co-ed); *Tectonic Plates* 1992 (d/co-ph, adapted from a play by Robert Lepage);

Picture of Light 1996 (co-p/d/ph/ed/ narr); *Balifilm* 1997 (p/d/ph/ed); *Leda and the Swan* 1998 (co-ph); *Krapp's Last Tape* 2000 (ph).

Michaels, Lorne

Producer and writer; b. Lorne Lipowitz, Toronto, 1945. Michaels was in his early twenties and was already writing and producing comedy specials for CBC-TV when he broke into U.S. television as a writer for the groundbreaking *Rowan and Martin's Laugh-In*. He was the original producer of *Saturday Night Live*, he won a parcel of Emmys, and he launched the film careers of John Belushi, Dan Aykroyd,* Gilda Radner, Chevy Chase, and many others. In 1980, he wrote and produced *Gilda Live*, a film version of Radner's Broadway show directed by Mike Nichols. In the 1990s, he scored major box-office hits with another *SNL* graduate, Mike Myers,* in *Wayne's World* and its sequel. Michaels also produced *Brain Candy*, starring the Kids in the Hall, another of his discoveries.
Films and television include: *Saturday Night Live* 1975–80, 1985–present (series); *The Rutles* 1978 (TV); *Gilda Live* 1980; *Three Amigos!* 1986; *The Kids in the Hall* 1989–95 (series); *Wayne's World* 1992; *Wayne's World 2* 1993; *Coneheads* 1993; *Tommy Boy* 1995; *Black Sheep* 1996; *The Kids in the Hall Brain Candy* 1996; *Night at the Roxbury* 1998; *Superstar* 1999.

Mills of the Gods: Viet Nam, The

1965 56m *prod* CBC, *exp* Douglas Leiterman, *p/d* Beryl Fox, *ph* Erik Durschmied, *ed* Don Haig. This documentary, which was made for the CBC-TV *Document* series, was one of first films to deal in a serious way with the impact of the war in Vietnam on the people who fought it (the Americans) and those who were being 'saved' from communism (the South Vietnamese). **Awards include:** CFA: Film of the Year.

Mon oncle Antoine

1971 104m *prod* NFB, *p* Marc Beaudet, *d* Claude Jutra, *sc* Clémont Perron, *ph* Michel Brault, *ed* Claude Jutra, Claire Boyer, *mus* Jean Cousineau; *with* Jean Duceppe, Jacques Gagnon, Lyne Champagne, Olivette Thibault, Claude Jutra, Monique Mercure. In a mining town in the late 1940s in Quebec, Benoît (Gagnon), a fifteen-year-old orphan goes to live with his uncle Antoine (Duceppe), the town's undertaker. Young Benoît quietly observes the hypocrisy, joy, despair, carnality, class tension, and strange melancholy of the adults who surround him. On Christmas night, he is taken by his uncle to a farm to collect the body of a young boy who has died. Consistantly rated by critics as the best Canadian feature ever made, the film also has been accused of presenting a backward-looking postcard of an earlier Quebec society. It is. It is also, more importantly, a perceptive, subtle, and emotionally devastating portrait of pre–Quiet Revolution Quebec. Tracing the vast personal and political fissures about to tear open the rural Catholic Quebec heartland, Jutra's* episodic narrative structure and inspired use of landscape render unforgettable this portrait of a sad, wintry town and the end of innocence. (V) **Awards include:** CFA: Feature Film, Director, Original Screenplay, Cinematography, Actor (Duceppe), Supporting Actress (Thibault), Musical Score, Overall Sound.

Monpetit, Pascale

Actor; b. Montréal-Nord, Que., 1960. Monpetit, who trained at the Conservatoire de Théâtre de Montréal, is renowned for her heart-wrenching emotional abandon and frequent tears. Never one to shy away from intense roles, her screen debut came in *H*, where she played a heroin addict undergoing withdrawal, a role that earned her a

Genie. Her transition to leading roles followed rapidly, starting with the 1994 television drama *Soho*. Monpetit found an artistic soulmate in director Charles Binamé* in the mid-1990s and has been featured in his films since, including *Eldorado*,* as a heart-broken and therapy-addicted woman, *Le Coeur au poing*,* and *La Beauté de Pandore*. **Films and television include:** *H* 1991 (GA-A); *Blanche* 1993 (TV); *Eclipse* 1994; *Soho* 1994 (TV); *Eldorado* 1995; *L'Incompris* 1996 (TV); *Le Coeur au poing* 1998 (PJ-A); *La Beauté de Pandore* 2000.

Montréal vu par ...

1991 127m *prod* Cinémaginaire, Atlantis Films, *exp* Michel Houle, Peter Sussman, *p* Denise Robert, *d* Patricia Rozema, Jacques Leduc, Michel Brault, Atom Egoyan, Léa Pool, Denys Arcand, *sc* Patricia Rozema, Marie-Carole de Beaumont, Jacuqes Leduc, Hélène Le Beau, Michel Brault, Atom Egoyan, Léa Pool, Paule Baillargeon, *ph* Guy Dufaux, Pierre Letarte, Jean Pépine, Eric Cayla, Pierre Mignot, Paul Sarossy, *ed* Susan Shipton, Pierre Vernier, Jacques Gagné, Dominque Fortin, Alain Baril, *with* Sheila McCarthy, Charlotte Laurier, Monique Mercure, Maury Chaykin, Arsinée Khanjian, Rémy Girard. This cinematic tribute to the city of Montreal on the occasion of the 350th anniversary of the first European settlement on the island consists of six short films directed by Patricia Rozema,* Jacques Leduc,* Michel Brault,* Atom Egoyan,* Léa Pool,* and Denys Arcand.*

Moore, Brian

Writer; b. Belfast, Northern Ireland, 1921; d. 1999. Moore, an internationally acclaimed novelist, was also known for writing screenplays between books. Two of his novels became Canadian-made feature films based on his own screen treatments. The first, *The Luck of Ginger Coffey*,* was inspired by Moore's four-year stint as a proofreader and reporter at the Montreal *Gazette*. The second, *Black Robe*,* was brought to the screen in 1991 and won several Genies. Moore became a Canadian citizen in the 1950s, but he moved to California, where he died. **Films include:** *The Luck of Ginger Coffey* 1964; *Torn Curtain* 1966; *The Blood of Others* 1984; *Black Robe* 1991 (GA-ASC).

Moranis, Rick

Actor; b. Toronto, 1954. Moranis started in show business as a radio deejay and stand-up comic, and this eventually led him to Toronto's famed Second City comedy troupe. With the launch of the *SCTV* series, he teamed up with Dave Thomas to create the endearing, toque-wearing, beer-swilling McKenzie brothers in 'The Great White North'; their antics spawned the box-office hit *Strange Brew*.* Moranis successfully transposed his comic nerd character from *SCTV* to the big time in 1984 in Ivan Reitman's* smash hit *Ghostbusters*. Since then he has starred in Disney's *Honey, I Shrunk the Kids*, in *Parenthood* and *L.A. Story* opposite Steve Martin, and as Barney Rubble in *The Flintstones*. **Films and television include:** *SCTV* 1977–84 (co-sc/a, series); *Strange Brew* 1983 (a/d/sc with Dave Thomas); *Ghostbusters* 1984; *Streets of Fire* 1984; *Brewster's Millions* 1985; *Little Shop of Horrors* 1986; *Spaceballs* 1987; *Ghostbusters* II 1989; *Honey, I Shrunk the Kids* 1989; *Parenthood* 1989; *L.A. Story* 1991; *The Flintstones* 1994.

Morse, Barry

Actor; b. London, U.K., 1918. As Lt. Philip Gerard in the very popular American television series *The Fugitive*, Barry Morse played one of the most doggedly determined cops in television history. His pursuit of Richard Kimble (David Janssen) week after week kept viewers glued to the screen until the final capture, the single most highly rated show of its time. Morse was never less good in countless made-for-television productions and Canadian features, but never in a part that mattered so much. *Space: 1999*, his second series appearance, proved to be an expensive failure. **Films and television include:** *The Fallen Idol* 1959 (TV); *Treasure Island* 1960 (TV); *The Fugitive* 1963–7 (series); *Justine* 1969; *Puzzle of a Downfall Child* 1970; *Space: 1999* 1975–6 (series); *Love at First Sight* 1977; *One Man* 1977; *Power Play* 1978; *The Shape of Things to Come* 1979; *Riel* 1979 (TV); *Jack London's Klondike Fever* 1980; *The Martian Chronicles* 1980 (TV); *The Changeling* 1980; *Cries in the Night* 1980; *Hounds of Notre Dame* 1980; *A Tale of Two Cities* 1980 (TV); *The Winds of War* 1983 (TV); *Sadat* 1983 (TV); *Race for the Bomb* 1986 (TV); *Hoover vs the Kennedys: The Second Civil War* 1987 (TV); *War and Remembrance* 1989 (TV); *Glory! Glory!* 1989 (TV); *JFK: Reckless Youth* 1993 (TV).

Mourir à tue-tête

1979 96m *prod* NFB, *p* Jacques Gagné, Anne Claire Poirier, *d* Anne Claire Poirier, *sc* Anne Claire Poirier, Marthe Blackburn, *ph* Michel Brault, *ed* André Corriveau, *mus* Maurice Blackburn; *with* Julie Vincent, Germain Houde, Paul Savoie, Monique Miller, Micheline Lanctôt. This brutal, compelling, and angry film tackles the subject of rape in its most heinous form. One night Suzanne (Vincent) is brutally attacked. The experience traumatizes her, effects her relationship with her lover (Savoie), and eventually leads to her suicide. The narrative provides the basis for a wider social, cultural, and political discussion about violence against women. A filmmaker and editor (Miller and Lanctôt*)

are making a documentary about Suzanne. Their discussions about how their film will deal with the rape raise larger questions about rape as a social issue. (V)

Moyle, Allan

Director, writer, and actor; b. Arvida, Que., 1947. Moyle is the Diogenes of Canadian cinema, wandering about the planet looking for an honest project. He helped found the Players' Club at McGill University. A year later, he moved to San Francisco to absorb the best of the youth-quake culture. Then he crossed the continent to New York, where he studied acting with legendary director Nicholas Ray. Moyle had a small part in the hippie-era classic, *Joe*, and in 1974 marked his screenwriting debut with *Montreal Main*.* With *The Rubber Gun* in 1978, he became a director. Since that time Moyle has distinguished himself in the teen-film genre with *Times Square*, *Pump up the Volume*, *Empire Records*, and *New Waterford Girl*.* **Films include:** *Joe* 1970 (a); *Montreal Main* 1974 (co-p/co-sc/a); *East End Hustle* 1976 (co-sc/a); *The Morning Suite* 1976 (a); *The Rubber Gun* 1978 (co-p/d/co-sc/a); *Rabid* 1977 (a); *Outrageous!* 1977 (a); *Times Square* 1980 (d); *Pump up the Volume* 1990 (d/sc); *The Gun in Betty Lou's Handbag* 1992 (d); *Empire Records* 1995 (d); *New Waterford Girl* 2000 (d); *X Change* 2001 (d, TV).

Murder by Decree

1979 124m *prod* Ambassador Films, Sands Films (U.K.), *exp* Len Herberman, Robert Goldstone, *p* René Dupont, Bob Clark, *d* Bob Clark, *sc* John Hopkins, *novel* Elwyn Jones and John Lloyd, *ph* Reginald H. Morris, *ed* Stan Cole, *mus* Carl Zittrer, Paul Zaza; *with* Christopher Plummer, James Mason, David Hemmings, Susan Clark, Anthony Quayle, John Gielgud, Frank Finlay, Donald

Sutherland, Geneviève Bujold. *Murder by Decree* features Sherlock Holmes vs Jack the Ripper in the most elaborate and expensive Canada / U.K. co-production ever mounted. It's a splendid, detailed period reconstruction of Victorian London complete with swirling fog and rattling hansom cabs. The dense story is based on the unfounded notion that Jack the Ripper was a member of the royal household. Plummer* is particularly effective (if temperamentally wrong) as Holmes, and Mason gives what is perhaps the best screen portrayal of Dr Watson. The film tries very hard to please, with strong supporting performances from Sutherland,* Bujold,* and Clark,* but it is overly long and has an unsatisfactory, pat ending. (V)

My American Cousin

1985 89m *prod* Okanagan Motion Picture Co., Borderline Productions, Independent Pictures, *p* Peter O'Brian, *d/sc* Sandy Wilson, *ph* Richard Leiterman, *ed* Haida Paul; *with* Margaret Langrick, John Wildman, Richard Donat, Jane Mortifee, T.J. Scott, Camille Henderson. Sandy Wilson's* debut feature film has emerged as something of an English-Canadian classic, operating simultaneously as a deeply personal film and as a metaphor for the inferiority complex of our national psyche. Margaret Langrick is endearing as the teenage girl living in rural British Columbia who becomes infatuated with her handsome American cousin (Wildman), who has come to visit for the summer. Despite its specific Canadian subject matter, Wilson's sweet storyline and the charm of her characters gave the film a universal appeal that ultimately led to its international success. It was followed by a much less successful sequel, *American Boyfriends*. (V) **Awards include:** GA: Picture, Director, Screen-

play, Actor (Wildman), Actress (Langrick), Editing.

Myers, Mike

Actor, writer, and producer; b. Toronto, 1964. Myers, a graduate of Toronto's comedy club circuit and the *Second City Revue*, was picked by fellow Canadian, producer Lorne Michaels,* to write skits for the long-running *Saturday Night Live*. Myers soon became a regular on-camera player and extended his popular skit about two suburban dudes with their own local cable show into the hugely successful *Wayne's World* and its sequel. In 1997, Myers created the character of Austin Powers, the randy, buck-toothed spy in *Austin Powers: International Man of Mystery*, a spoof on James Bond and all things British from the 'swinging sixties.' Its sequel, *The Spy Who Shagged Me*, was a box-office champ of 1999, second only to *Star Wars Episode I*. **Films and television include:** *Saturday Night Live* 1989–94 (series); *Wayne's World* 1992 (co-sc/a); *So I Married an Axe Murderer* 1993 (a); *Wayne's World 2* 1993 (co-sc/a); *Austin Powers: International Man of Mystery* 1997 (co-p/sc/a); *54* 1998 (a); *Austin Powers: The Spy Who Shagged Me* 1999 (co-p/co-sc/a).

My Financial Career

1963 6m38s *prod* NFB, *p* Tom Daly, Colin Low, *d/an* Gerald Potterton, Grant Munro, *short story* Stephen Leacock, *mus* Eldon Rathburn, *narr* Stanley Jackson. This animated cartoon portrays Stephen Leacock's witty and duly famous account of a young man's first attempt to open a bank account. When he goes in to make a deposit he is so overwhelmed by the institution that nothing he says comes out right and he finally flees in confusion. The film received an Academy Award nomination for Animated Short. (V)

N

Naked Lunch

1992 115m *prod* Recorded Picture Co., Naked Lunch Productions, *p* Jeremy Thomas, Gabriella Martinelli, *d/sc* David Cronenberg, *novel* William S. Burroughs, *ph* Peter Suschitzky, *ed* Ronald Sanders, *mus* Howard Shore; *with* Peter Weller, Judy Davis, Ian Holm, Julian Sands, Monique Mercure, Roy Scheider. David Cronenberg's* attempt to bring dramatic life to William Burroughs's most famous novel is inspired but limited in its appeal. Cronenberg creates a drug-induced fantasy based on Burroughs's life while he was writing the book, rather than a page-by-page adaptation of the novel. The author is represented by Will Lee (portrayed effectively by Weller), a part-time exterminator who accidentally shoots his wife, Joan (Davis). Viewers follow Lee through an underworld that includes opium-filled nightclubs and typewriters that are transformed into talking insects. This surreal work filled with hallucinogenic images is a visual treat but it becomes a bit tedious after a while. The film certainly works better for those who are familiar with Burroughs's writings. (V) **Awards include:** GA: Picture, Director, Adapted Screenplay, Supporting Actress (Mercure), Cinematography, Art Direction, Overall Sound, Sound Editing.

Narizzano, Silvio

Director; b. Montreal, 1927. Narizzano came from an Italian-American background and trained at the CBC before moving on to the BBC in the early 1960s. He directed the aging star Tallulah Bankhead in the Hammer horror film *Die! Die! My Darling* then gained international fame as the director of *Georgy Girl*, a film that virtually defined the 'swinging London' scene of the 1960s. The film did huge box-office business and made Lynn Redgrave a star. His subsequent films were much less successful but he did secure a footnote in the Canadian film canon with *Why Shoot the Teacher?*,* starring Bud Cort and Samantha Eggar, which won the Golden Reel Award in 1978. **Films and television incude:** *Die! Die! My Darling!* 1965; *Georgy Girl* 1966; *Blue* 1968; *Loot* 1970; *Redneck* 1972 (p/d); *The Sky Is Falling* 1976; *Why Shoot the Teacher?* 1977; *Come Back, Little Sheba* 1977 (TV); *The Class of Miss MacMichael* 1978; *The Body in the Library* 1984 (TV).

Nash, Terre

Director, writer, and editor; b. Nanaimo, B.C., 1949. Nash gained international attention in 1983 when her anti-nuclear film, *If You Love This Planet*,* was denounced by the U.S. Justice Department as propaganda and went on to win an Academy Award. Working freelance with the NFB women's unit, Nash made a specialty of profiling smart, politically engaged women in films ranging from *Speaking Our Peace*, to *A Love Affair with Politics: A Portrait of Marion Dewar*, and *Who's Counting? Marilyn Waring on Sex, Lies and Global Economics*.* Compelling and beautiful to watch, *Who's Counting?* presents ingenious visual analogies to illustrate the alternative economic analyses developed by Waring, a former New Zealand MP. **Films include:** *If You Love This Planet* 1983 (d/ed, AA-SD); *Speaking Our Peace* 1985 (d/sc with Bonnie Sherr Klein); *A Love Affair with Politics: A Portrait of Marion Dewar* 1987 (d/ed); *Russian Diary* 1989 (p/d with Klein); *Who's Counting? Marilyn Waring on Sex, Lies and Global Economics* 1995 (d/ed); *My Left Breast* 2000 (ed).

National Film Board of Canada, The

The creation of the National Film Board of Canada is the central event in the history of Canadian cinema. According to the National Film Act of 1939, the purpose of the NFB was 'to make and distribute films designated to help Canadians in all parts of Canada to understand the ways of living and the problems of Canadians in other parts.' The Board was set up by Mackenzie King's Liberal government in the last months before the start of the Second World War, and almost immediately it became an important tool in mobilizing the nation for the war effort. Canada's first film commissioner, John Grierson,* a self-styled propagandist who had spearheaded the documentary movement in Britain, directed his filmmaking team to show Canada to Canadians while stirring them into action to support British efforts to end the Nazi threat in Europe. Grierson established partnerships with Famous Players theatres in Canada and *Time* magazine's popular newsreel *The March of Time* in the United States to distribute NFB films, a strategy that paid immediate dividends when the Board won an Academy Award for Stuart Legg's *Churchill's Island** in 1941, its first of ten (and counting) Academy Awards.

The post-war period proved to be a time of grave uncertainty. Grierson left the Board to set up a film unit for the United Nations and was subsequently implicated in the Gouzenko spy scandal. Although the charges were unfounded, the scandal left the Board with a 'pink' hue during the cold war epoch, and when the time came to establish Canada's first television network in 1952, the task was given to CBC Radio and not the NFB. In 1956, in a move designed to distance itself from the political heat of Ottawa, the NFB opened a new headquarters in suburban Montreal with the largest sound studios and most complete production facilities outside of Hollywood.

The NFB hit its stride during the late 1950s and 1960s, producing important and stylistically revolutionary documentaries, shorts, animation, and feature films. Animator Norman McLaren* led the way with the Academy Award–winning *Neighbours** (1952). His protégés Colin Low,* Wolf Koenig,* Roman Kroitor,* and others, combined to produce innovative and award-winning documentaries such as *Corral** (1954), *City of Gold** (1957), and *Universe** (1960) for Tom Daly's* Unit B. The new headquarters also provided a focal point for a new generation of talented Québécois filmmakers – Pierre Perrault,* Michel Brault,* Gilles Groulx,* Bernard Gosselin,* Claude Jutra,* Denys Arcand* – who created many of their early works in the *cinema-vérité* style. Jutra's *Mon oncle Antoine,** produced by the Board in 1971, is still considered the finest feature ever shot in this country.

Expo 67 provided an opportunity for the NFB to become involved in multi-screen productions and the projection of ultra-wide films, which led directly to the creation of the IMAX format by Roman Kroitor and Graeme Ferguson.* The 1970s saw the flowering of two remarkable producers: Kathleen Shannon,* who was chosen to head Studio D, the Board's first unit for women filmmakers, and Derek Lamb,* who was brought in to head the English animation department. These units excelled and brought more glory to the Board with such Academy Award winners as Beverly Shaffer's *I'll Find a Way** (1978), John Weldon's and Eunice Macaulay's *Special Delivery* (1979), Eugene Fedorenko's *Every Child** (1980) and Terre Nash's *If You Love This Planet** (1983).

Many of the most successful NFB

films of the past few years have been co-productions with the private sector or in conjunction with CBC-TV: *The Boys of St Vincent** (1992), *The Valour and the Horror* (1991), *Manufacturing Consent: Noam Chomsky and the Media** (1992). Recent cuts in staff and the closing of the Montreal lab have put the NFB on notice that it cannot continue to rely on the level of public support it has enjoyed in the past. Despite its central role in the creation of a film culture in Canada, the NFB must now rely increasingly on the creation of challenging and distinctly Canadian work for the global television market in the digital universe.

Neighbours
1952 8m10s *prod* NFB, *p/d/an/m* Norman McLaren, *ph* Wolf Koenig; *with* Jean-Paul Ladouceur, Grant Munro. Norman McLaren's* most famous and perhaps most personal and powerful film uses pixillation techniques to tell the story of two neighbours who come to blows and eventually kill each other (and their families) over the possession of a flower. (V) **Awards include:** CFA: Special Award; AA: Short Documentary; AAN: One Reel / Short Subject.

Nelligan, Kate
Actor; b. Patricia Colleen Nelligan, London, Ont., 1951. This charismatic performer began her varied and justly celebrated international career on the London stage in the 1970s with the National Theatre of Great Britain and the Royal Shakespeare Company. She won the London Critics Best Actress Award in 1979. Since then, she has appeared on Broadway and in Hollywood in films by such diverse directors as Garry Marshall, Barbra Streisand, and Woody Allen – most memorably in the title role of *Eleni* in 1985. A performer of passion and intelligence, Kate Nelligan captured the Best Supporting Actress Award at the Genies for her role in *Margaret's Museum*.* **Films and television include:** *The Romantic Englishwoman* 1975; *Dracula* 1979; *Eye of the Needle* 1981; *Without a Trace* 1983; *Eleni* 1985; *Love and Hate: The Story of Colin and Joann Thatcher* 1989 (TV); *White Room* 1990; *Prince of Tides* 1991 (AAN-SA); *Frankie and Johnny* 1991; *Shadows and Fog* 1991; *Wolf* 1994; *Million Dollar Babies* 1994 (TV); *How to Make an American Quilt* 1995; *Margaret's Museum* 1996 (GA-SA); *Up Close and Personal* 1996; *U.S. Marshals* 1998; *Boy Meets Girl* 1999; *Into the Deep* 1999 (narr); *The Cider House Rules* 1999; *Blessed Stranger: After Flight 111* 2000 (TV).

Nelvana Studios
Nelvana Studios was formed in 1971 by three producers and animators who were also good friends: **Michael Hirsch** (b. Brussells, 1946), **Patrick Loubert** (b. Ontario, 1947), and **Clive Smith** (b. London, U.K., 1944). The company has evolved from a live-action and animation house that made local educational and broadcast fare to one of the most important producers of children's television programs in the world. After the box-office failure of their ambitious early 1980s animation feature *Rock and Rule* nearly ruined the company, the Nelvana triumvirate recovered its equilibrium with the much safer *The Care Bears Movie*,* which was a Golden Reel Award winner and a huge hit in the United States. Following a decision to concentrate on the half-hour children's broadcast market, Nelvana has since gone on to create such popular high-quality series as *Babar*, *Tintin*, and *Little Bear*. **Films include:** *Rock and Rule* 1983 (d, Smith; p, Hirsh and Loubert); *The Care Bears Movie* 1985 (p, GRA); *The Care Bears Movie II* 1986 (p); *Babar: The Movie* 1989 (p); *Pippi Longstocking* 1997

(d, Smith; p, Hirsh and Loubert); *Babar: The King of the Elephants* 1999 (p).

Never a Backward Step

1966 57m *prod* NFB, *p* Guy Glover, *d* Donald Brittain, Arthur Hammond, John Spotton. This film provides an intimate profile of Roy Herbert Thomson (Baron Thomson of Fleet), a small-town businessman from Northern Ontario who ended up owning hundreds of newspapers in the United States, Canada, Britain, and the Commonwealth. The filmmakers obtained permission to follow him around for a few days to capture the many sides of this very ordinary Canadian who, by the dint of hard work and luck, became one of the most powerful men in the world. (V) **Awards include:** CFA: Feature Documentary.

Neville, John

Actor; b. London, U.K., 1925. Neville is an accomplished stage and screen actor with a career spanning two continents and four decades. He was hand picked by director Terry Gilliam for the lead role in *The Adventures of Baron Munchausen*, and most recently has been seen as the Well-Manicured Man on the *X-Files* television series and film. The British-born Neville has considered himself to be an Albertan since he fell in love with Edmonton and founded the Citadel Theatre, where he was artistic director from 1973 to 1978. **Films and television include:** *The Life of Henry v* 1957 (TV); *Oscar Wilde* 1959; *Hamlet* 1959 (TV, as Hamlet); *Mr Topaze* 1961; *Billy Budd* 1962; *A Study in Terror* 1965; *Riel* 1979 (TV); *The Adventures of Baron Munchausen* 1988 (as the Baron); *Grand* 1990 (series); *Dieppe* 1993 (TV); *Journey to the Center of the Earth* 1993 (TV); *The Road to Wellville* 1994; *Little Women* 1994; *Baby's Day Out* 1994; *The X-Files* 1995–9 (series); *Dangerous Minds* 1995; *The Song Spinner* 1995 (TV); *Swann* 1996; *Sabotage* 1996; *High School High* 1996; *The Fifth Element* 1997; *Regeneration* 1998; *Urban Legend* 1998; *X-Files: The Movie* 1998; *Sunshine* 1999; *Dinner at Fred's* 1999; *Water Damage* 2000.

Newman, Sydney

Producer and administrator; b. Toronto, 1917; d. 1997. Newman first joined the NFB in 1941 as a film editor. In 1945, he became a producer on the *Canada Carries On** series, and in 1947 he was appointed executive producer of Unit C. In 1952, he joined CBC-TV where he was the supervisor of dramatic production. Later, he moved to England where he eventually became head of the drama group at BBC-TV. On his return to Canada, he was appointed film commissioner and head of the NFB during its most turbulent period (1970–5). He censored or banned several films (most famously Denys Arcand's *On est au coton**), and moderated the Board's role as social activist, but he also established regional production centres and stimulated feature production. From 1975 to 1977, he was a special adviser on film to the Secretary of State.

New Waterford Girl

2000 97m *prod* Sienna Films, Imagex Production, *exp* Christopher Zimmer, Ted East, Victor Lowery, *p* Jennifer Kawaja, Julia Sereny, *d* Allan Moyle, *sc* Tricia Fish, *ph* Derk Rogers, *ed* Susan Maggi, *mus* Geoff Bennett, Longo Hai, Ben Johannesen; *with* Liane Balaban, Tara Spencer-Nairn, Nicholas Campbell, Mary Walsh, Andrew McCarthy, Mark McKinney. This delightful comedy concerns a teenage girl (Balaban) who wants to leave her home in New Waterford, Cape Breton, to study art in New York. Her parents (Walsh* and Campbell) think she'd be better off becoming a nurse. The town is full of loser boys and the only way out is to get 'knocked up,' so she and a friend (Spencer-Nairn), a newcomer to town with a wicked right hook, come up with a scheme to fake her pregnancy. Tricia Fish's sensitive script has a strong sense of place, and under Allan Moyle's* excellent direction, the film becomes a fresh take on an old-fashioned coming-of-age story with strong performances by the two young leads. (V)

Nielsen, Leslie

Actor; b. Regina, 1926. Nielsen, the son of a Royal Canadian Mountie and the brother of a deputy prime minister, grew up in the Northwest Territories where, according to him, 'there was lots of Viking discipline.' After studying voice and acting with Lorne Greene,* Nielsen launched his film career in the mid-1950s. For more than two decades he played stolid leading men, including the captains in *Forbidden Planet* and *The Poseidon Adventure*. A self-confessed 'closet comedian,' he reinvigorated his image by sending up those former roles in *Airplane!* and the *Naked Gun* films. His Inspector Drebin character became a pop icon of the 1990s. **Films include:** *Forbidden Planet* 1956; *Tammy and the Bachelor* 1957; *Harlow* 1965; *The Plainsman* 1966; *The Poseidon Adventure* 1972; *Amsterdam Kill* 1977; *City on Fire* 1979; *Airplane!* 1979; *Prom Night* 1980; *The Naked Gun: From the Files of Police Squad* 1988; *Naked Gun 2½: The Smell of Fear* 1991; *Naked Gun 33⅓ : The Final Insult* 1994; *Dracula: Dead and Loving It* 1995; *Spy Hard* 1996; *Mr Magoo* 1997; *Wrongfully Accused* 1998; *Santa Who?* 2000 (TV).

Nô

1998 83m *prod* In Extremis Images, *p* Bruno Jobin, *d* Robert Lepage, *sc* Robert Lepage, André Morency, *ph* Pierre

Mignot, *ed* Aube Foglia, *mus* Michel Cote; *with* Marie Brassard, Anne-Marie Cadieux, Richard Fréchette, Alexis Martin. In a bid for greater accessibility, Robert Lepage* made this jaunty follow up to his dourly Kafkaesque *Le Polygraph*. A pregnant Québécoise actress (Cadieux) appears in a tacky performance of a French farce in the Canadian pavilion at the 1970 Osaka world fair. This staging collides ironically with events back in Montreal, where Sophie's separatist lover (Martin) and his pals are planning to blow up something. The inept conspirators act more like the Three Stooges than the tragic freedom-fighters of FLQ lore. Theatre and real life are interwoven throughout the film, but life isn't always a bad farce. The solemn choreography of masked Japanese Nô actors suggest the higher planes that humans can achieve in a fully ripened culture. (V)

Nobody Waved Good-Bye

1964 80m *prod* NFB, *exp* Tom Daly, *p* Roman Kroitor, Don Owen, *d/sc* Don Owen, *ph* John Spotton, *ed* Donald Ginsberg, John Spotton, *mus* Eldon Rathburn; *with* Peter Kastner, Julie Biggs, Claude Rae, Toby Tarnow, Charmion King, John Vernon, John Sullivan. Peter (Kastner), an eighteen-year-old who lives with his parents and sister in a middle-class Toronto suburban wasteland in the early 1960s, is a rebel without a cause or a clue. He argues with his parents, skips school, makes his girlfriend pregnant (she leaves him), and is exploited by a hostile adult world when he leaves home. He finally runs away with stolen money and a stolen car. The film's mundane storyline is overcome by beautiful performances and the purity of its intentions. Originally slated as a half-hour docudrama on juvenile delinquency for Unit B of the NFB, *Nobody*

Waved Good-Bye went on to win critical acclaim in New York, and subsequently in Canada, and remains a seminal – if flawed – film in the development of early English-Canadian cinema. It was also the first film to give Toronto a cinematic identity.

North of Superior

1971 18m *prod* Multiscreen Corp., *p/d/sc/ ph* Graeme Ferguson, *ed* Toni Trow, *mus* Bill Houston. This premiere IMAX film, commissioned for the world's first IMAX screen at Ontario Place in Toronto, offers viewers a towering, breathtaking, wide-screen look at the almost untouched world of Northern Ontario, circa 1970. Aerial shots provide an inflight effect that was much imitated in future IMAX films. *North of Superior* is still the best trip.

Not a Love Story: A Film about Pornography

1981 96m *prod* NFB, *exp* Kathleen Shannon, *p* Dorothy Todd Hénaut, *d* Bonnie Sherr Klein, *ph* Pierre Letarte, *ed* Anne Henderson, *mus* Ginette Bellavance. Definitely the NFB's most controversial film to date, *Not a Love Story* reflects the high-tide mark of the anti-pornography feminist sentiment. Director Bonnie Klein* interviewed porn actors and sex workers about the horrors of the trade, and enlisted anti-porn pundits to discuss their sentiments about the industry and its effects on society at large. Ironically, while fuelling the ongoing debate – allowing the intelligentsia to battle it out – the film also became popular among porn enthusiasts who flocked to see its graphic imagery. Another irony occurred when the film was banned in Ontario for its pornographic content – the very pornography the filmmakers were arguing so passionately against. (V)

Now Is the Time

1951 3m *prod* NFB, British Film Institute, *p/d* Norman McLaren, *an* Norman McLaren, Evelyn Lambart. This early experimentation in 3-D by Norman McLaren* and Evelyn Lambart* was commissioned by the British Film Institute for the Festival of Britain in 1951 (see also *Around Is Around*). **Awards include:** CFA: Special Award.

O

Obomsawin, Alanis

Director, producer and writer; b. New Hampshire, U.S.A., 1932. Obomsawin, who was brought up on the Abenaki reservation near Montreal, built a career as a singer and storyteller, performing both her own haunting tales and chants and traditional First Nations material. In the 1970s, she began making documentaries celebrating First Nations life and exposing the repercussions of white injustice. NFB films such as *Incident at Restigouche* and *No Address* deal with the realities of being victimized, poor, and self-destructive. *Kanehsatake: 270 Years of Resistance,** a retelling of the 1990 Oka standoff between Mohawks and the Canadian army, won her international acclaim. Obomsawin has become a leading voice for First Nations people in Canada, and she was named a Member of the Order of Canada in 1983. **Films include:** *Christmas at Moose Factory* 1971 (d/sc); *Eliza's Horoscope* 1976 (a); *Amisk* 1977 (p/d); *Mother of Many Children* 1977 (p/d/sc/narr); *Incident at Restigouche* 1984 (co-p/d/sc/narr); *Richard Cardinal: Cry from a Diary of a Métis Child* 1986 (co-p/d/sc); *Poundmaker's Lodge: A Healing Place* 1987 (co-p/d/sc); *No Address* 1988 (co-p/d/sc); *Walker* 1992 (d); *Kanehsatake: 270 Years of Resistance* 1993 (co-p/d/sc/narr); *My Name Is Kahentiiosta*

1996 (p/d/sc); *Spudwrench* 1997 (p/d/sc); *Rocks at Whiskey Trench* 2000 (p/d/sc/narr).

O'Brian, Peter
Producer; b. Toronto, 1947. Peter O'Brian has built a reputation as a fiercely independent producer willing to take risks with first-time feature directors. His Independent Pictures has produced two Genie winners: Phillip Borsos's* splendid *The Grey Fox** and Sandy Wilson's *My American Cousin.** O'Brian took a sabbatical to run Jewison's Canadian Film Centre in the early 1990s, and then returned to filmmaking to produce what turned out to be Borsos's last film, *Far from Home*. He has described his career as a mission 'to contribute to and be responsible for quality Canadian films that are unabashedly from this country.' **Films include:** *Love at First Sight* 1977; *Outrageous!* 1977 (ap); *Blood and Guts* 1978; *Fast Company* 1979; *The Grey Fox* 1983 (GA-P); *My American Cousin* 1985 (GA-P); *One Magic Christmas* 1985; *John and the Missus* 1986; *Milk and Honey* 1988; *Far from Home: The Adventures of Yellow Dog* 1995.

Octobre
1994 97m *prod* ACPAV, NFB, *exp* André Dupuy, *p* Bernadette Payeur, Marc Daigle, *d/sc* Pierre Falardeau, *ph* Alain Dostie, *ed* Michel Arcand, *mus* Richard Grégoire; *with* Hugo Dubé, Luc Picard, Pierre Rivard, Denis Trudel, Serge Houde, Julie Castonguay. This film presents an account of the October Crisis of 1970 from the point of view of the terrorists. Pierre Falardeau,* one of the most political of Québécois directors and a committed separatist, attempted to humanize the FLQ kidnappers. The narrative unfolds inside their house as they deal with the pressures and conflicts of the situation. The film caused a stir when federal funding agencies initially refused to back the project. Upon release it was essentially ignored in English Canada, but it found an audience in Quebec, where it was heralded as a bold attempt to come to terms with one of the most volatile moments in recent Canadian history. (V)

Oedipus Rex
1957 87m *prod* Oedipus Rex Productions, *p* Leonid Kipnis, *d* Tyrone Guthrie, *play* Sophocles (based on a version by W.B. Yates), *ph* Roger Barlow, *ed* Irving Lerner, Richard Meyer, *mus* Louis Applebaum, Cedric Thorpe Davie; *with* Douglas Campbell, Eleanor Stuart, Robert Goodier, William Hutt, Douglas Rain. This straightforward film record of the Stratford Festival production of the Greek classic was directed by the noted British actor Tyrone Guthrie, co-founder of the Festival. It received a modest theatrical release in the United States and Canada and is one of only a handful of English-Canadian features produced during the 1950s.

O'Hara, Catherine
Actor; b. Toronto, 1954. O'Hara came from the Toronto suburbs and Burnhamthorpe Collegiate to land a job as the hat-check girl for Toronto's *Second City Revue* in 1974. A few days later she joined the touring company, and when Gilda Radner bolted for *Saturday Night Live* in New York, O'Hara joined the legendary troupe. She was in all fifty-two episodes of *SCTV* (1977–84), and along with *SCTV* alumni John Candy,* Rick Moranis,* and Martin Short,* she landed in big-budget Hollywood films. O'Hara launched her film career in Martin Scorsese's *After Hours*. She was in Tim Burton's *Beetlejuice*, and played the harried mother in Chris Columbus's megahit *Home Alone* and its sequel. **Films and**

television include: *SCTV* 1977–84 (series); *Nothing Personal* 1980; *After Hours* 1985; *Heartburn* 1986; *Beetlejuice* 1988; *Home Alone* 1990; *Home Alone 2: Lost in New York* 1992; *The Nightmare before Christmas* 1993 (voice); *The Paper* 1994; *Waiting for Guffman* 1997; *Home Fries* 1998; *The Life before This* 1999 (GA-SA); *Best in Show* 2000.

Olcott, Sidney

Director; b. John Sidney Alcott, Toronto, 1873; d. 1949. This energetic, profilic director of shorts in the silent era was first an actor, then manager of the Biograph studios in New Jersey. Olcott co-directed the first version of *Ben Hur* in 1907. He was the first director to shoot regularly on location and is still recognized as a pioneering director of westerns. In 1915, he joined Aldof Zukor's Famous Players and directed several Mary Pickford* shorts.

Old Man and the Sea, The

1999 22m *prod* Les Productions Pascal Blais, Imagica Corporation (Japan), Dentsu Tec (Japan), NHK Enterprises 21 (Japan), Panorama Studio of Yaroslavl (Russa), *exp* Jean-Yves Martel, Shizuo Ohashi, *p* Bernard Lajoie, Tatsuo Shimanura, *d/sc* Alexandre Petrov, *an* Alexandre Petrov, Dimitri Petrov, *ph* Serguei Rechetnikoff, *ed* Denis Paillon, *mus* Normand Roger; *voices* Gordon Pinsent, Kevin Dehaney. This film version of Hemingway's classic tale of a Cuban fisherman's struggle to land a giant marlin in the Gulf Stream was the first animated IMAX short. Russian animator Alexandre Petrov painstakingly painted 29,000 individual oil-on-glass frames in order to create the beautiful effect of a painting that is constantly moving. The film was screened in conjunction with Erik Canuel's documentary, *Hemingway: A Portrait*,* which was also co-produced by Montreal's Les Productions Pascal Blais. **Awards include:** PJ: Animation; AA: Animated Short.

One Magic Christmas

1985 89m *prod* The North Pole Picture Co., Walt Disney Pictures (U.S.), *exp/d* Phillip Borsos, *p* Peter O'Brian, *sc* Thomas Meehan, *ph* Frank Tidy, *ed* Sidney Wolinsky, *mus* Michael Conway Baker; *with* Mary Steenburgen, Harry Dean Stanton, Elizabeth Harnois, Gary Basaraba, Arthur Hill, Wayne Robson. This decidedly downbeat Christmas fantasy was made in the Capra mould. Mary Steenburgen plays a dispirited mother (her unemployed husband is shot in a bank robbery and her children are kidnapped and nearly drowned) whose renewed belief in Christmas is helped along by the appearance of a slightly menacing but kindly angel (Stanton). After she mails a letter to Santa asking for help, her husband returns, and the whole town unites to sing Christmas carols. A well-crafted, old-fashioned film that has become a staple of seasonal television. (V) **Awards include:** GA: Overall Sound, Sound Editing.

On est au coton

1976 158m *prod* NFB, *p* Guy L. Coté, Pierre Maheu, Marc Beaudet, *d* Denys Arcand, *ph* Alain Dostie, *ed* Pierre Bernier. The left-leaning thesis of this film – the exploitation of Quebec textile workers by their American bosses – made the NFB management nervous, which in turn, made the film famous. It was shot in 1970, the same year as the October Crisis, and the NFB felt that any film this provocative could only cause more trouble. Consequently, film commissioner Sidney Newman* held back the release of *On est au coton* for six years. However, Denys Arcand's* gritty *cinéma-vérité* documentary was clandestinely transferred onto video and widely distributed throughout Quebec, making Arcand's name synonymous with radical politics. The making of this film also forms one of storylines in *Gina*,* a dramatic feature made by Arcand five years later. (V)

Only Thing You Know, The
1972 82m *prod* Clarke Mackey Films, *p/d/sc* Clarke Mackey, *ph* Paul Lang, *ed* Clarke Mackey, Iain Ewing, Becky Shechter, *mus* Paul Craven, Iain Ewing; *with* Anne Knox, John Denos, Allan Royal, Linda Huffman, Iain Ewing. Ann (Knox) is an eighteen-year-old of strict middle-class upbringing who is exasperated with her parents and her tedious life. After meeting Scott (Royal) in a bar, she moves in with him, but when he appears incapable of committing himself to the relationship she becomes disillusioned and takes up with Paul (Denos), Scott's vagrant Californian buddy. Later Ann returns home. A coming-of-age story in the tradition of *Nobody Waved Good-Bye*,* Clarke Mackey's first feature sensitively etches the pain, wonder, and awkwardness of becoming an adult. **Awards include:** CFA: Actress (Knox).

Ontkean, Michael
Actor; b. Vancouver, 1946. The son of actors, Ontkean joined his father's repertory company at four and was later a child actor at the Stratford Festival. However, he was also a talented hockey player. Ontkean was offered a contract by the New York Rangers, but turned it down, preferring instead to play hockey on television (*The Rookies*) and the big screen (*Slap Shot*). He is perhaps best known for the role of Sheriff Harry S. Truman in David Lynch's television cult favourite, *Twin Peaks*. **Films and television include:** *The Peace Killers* 1971; *Pickup on 101* 1972; *Necromancy* 1972; *The Rookies* 1972–4 (series); *Slap Shot* 1977; *Willie and Phil* 1980; *Making Love* 1982; *The Blood of Others* 1984; *Maid to Order* 1987; *The Allnighter* 1987; *Clara's Heart* 1988; *Street Justice* 1989; *Cold Front* 1989; *Bye Bye Blues* 1989; *Postcards from the Edge* 1990; *Twin Peaks* 1990–1 (series); *Whose Child Is This? The War for Baby Jessica* 1993; (TV); *Family Album* 1994 (TV); *The Stepford Husbands* 1996 (TV); *Swann* 1996; *Summer of the Monkeys* 1998.

Ordres, Les
1974 107m *prod* Les Productions Prisma, Les Ordres Inc., *exp* Bernard Lalonde, *d/sc* Michel Brault, *ph* François Protat, *ed* Yves Dion, *mus* Philippe Gagnon; *with* Hélène Loiselle, Jean Lapointe, Guy Provost, Claude Gauthier, Louise Forestier. Consistently rated by critics as one of the best Canadian features ever made, this subtle blend of fiction and documentary realism is a chilling portrayal of what can happen in a liberal democracy when the state imposes its power. When FLQ terrorists kidnapped a British diplomat and murdered a Quebec cabinet minister, Prime Minister Pierre Trudeau ordered the Canadian army onto the streets of Montreal. Five hundred ordinary citizens, with no connection to the terrorists, were summarily arrested and held without charge. *Les Ordres* focuses on five of those 500 and details, in a realistic manner, their experiences in prison. Eventually all are released with no explanation or apology. The film is Michel Brault's* finest fictional feature, and it won top awards at Cannes and the Canadian Film Awards. **Awards include:** CFA: Film of the Year, Feature Film, Director, Original Screenplay; Cannes: Best Director Award.

Ouimet, Léo-Ernest
Exhibitor and distributor; b. St-Martin, Que., 1877; d. 1972. Ouimet, a trained

electrician who started with $50 and used Lumière equipment, began showing films in Montreal on a regular basis in 1905. He began Canada's first film exchange in 1906 and opened his first 'Ouimetoscope' the same year. By 1907, he had built the largest (1,200 seats) luxury theatre in North America. The next year he experimented with sound equipment. Although the Ouimetoscope was well ahead of its time, cheaper nickelodeons eventually cornered the market. Ouimet continued in the business as both a distributor (he had the Canadian rights to Pathé films) and a producer of newsreels. In 1951, Ouimet received a presentation at the third Canadian Film Awards in recognition of his pioneering work in distribution, exhibition, and production.

Outrageous!

1977 96m *prod* Film Consortium of Canada, *p* William Marshall, Henk Van der Kolk, *d/sc* Richard Benner, *short story* Margaret Gibson Gilboord, *ph* James B. Kelly, *ed* George Appleby, *mus* Paul Hoffert; *with* Craig Russell, Hollis McLaren, Richert Easley, Allan Moyle, David McIlwraith, Helen Shaver. This low-budget gem from the tax-shelter era* was a major breakthrough for English-Canadian cinema. It received critical raves and wide theatrical release. It's an unassuming, insightful film in which two marginal characters – Russell,* a gay hairdresser trying to make it as a drag artist, and McLarlen, a former mental patient still haunted by demons – come together to build a fragile web of mutual dependency. Witty and well-written, the film's success was in large part due to Russell's remarkable gifts as a female impersonator (his Mae West is dead-on), but it wasn't much of a stretch; he had been a star on drag circuit before his movie breakthrough. Russell's attempts to revive the role ten years later in *Too Outrageous!* proved disastrous. **Awards include:** CFA: Musical Score.

Owen, Don

Director and writer; b. Toronto, 1935. In 1964, while he was an employee at the NFB, Owen, a former University of Toronto anthropology student and poet, was assigned to direct a half-hour documentary project about a probation officer and a juvenile delinquent. Owen disobeyed orders, and instead delivered an edgy, urgent, now legendary feature called *Nobody Waved Good-Bye.** It was the first feature film to give Toronto a cinematic identity. Owen followed up with two more features: the intriguing *Notes for a Film about Donna and Gail*, and a perceptive drama of late 1960s Canuck zeitgeist, *The Ernie Game.** After leaving the NFB in 1969, Owen directed several unsatisfactory productions for television, including *Unfinished Business*, the 1984 sequel to *Nobody Waved Good-Bye*. **Films and television include:** *Runner* 1962 (d); *Toronto Jazz* 1964 (d); *Nobody Waved Good-Bye* 1964 (co-p/d/sc); *You Don't Back Down* 1965 (d); *High Steel* 1965 (d/sc/ed, CFA-E); *Ladies and Gentlemen ... Mr. Leonard Cohen* 1965 (d with Donald Brittain); *Monique Leyrac in Concert* 1965 (d); *Notes for a Film about Donna and Gail* 1966 (d/co-sc); *A Further Glimpse of Joey* 1967 (d); *Gallery, a View of Time* 1967 (d/sc/ed); *The Ernie Game* 1968 (d/sc, TV, CFA-D); *Subway or Spain* 1970 (d, TV); *Snow in Venice* 1971 (d, TV); *Richler of St Urbain* 1971 (d, TV); *Graham Coughtry in Ibiza* 1971 (d, TV); *Changes* 1971 (d, TV); *Cowboy and Indian* 1972 (d/ed); *Far from Home* 1971 (p/d/ph/ed, TV); *The St Lawrence* 1971 (d, TV); *Partners* 1976 (co-p/d/co-sc); *Holstein* 1978 (d/ph, TV); *Spread Your Wings: Tanya's Puppet* 1981 (d, TV); *Unfinished Business* 1984 (co-p/d, TV).

?O, Zoo! (The Making of a Fiction Film)

1986 23m *p/d/sc/ph/ed* Philip Hoffman, *mus* Tucker Zimmerman. The success of *?O, Zoo!*, the film that brought Philip Hoffman* to international attention, marked the shift in Canadian experimental film in the 1980s away from structuralism toward a more personal cinema. Begun as a documentary on the making of Peter Greenaway's *A Zed and Two Naughts*, Hoffman's treatise on reality as a construct turns conventional documentary film practice on its head. Familiar codes give way to family memories that, in turn, merge with personal reflections until the whole notion of an objective truth collapses. The result, in which facts are suspect and fiction seems to be the only thing we can count on, is a brilliant statement on the fictions spun throughout our lives.

P

P4W: Prison for Women

1981 90m *prod* Spectrum Films, *p/d/ed* Janis Cole, Holly Dale, *ph* Nesya Shapiro, *mus* Susie, Kas. Directors Janis Cole and Holly Dale fought with authorities for four years to gain access to the inmates of the Prison for Women, Canada's only federal jail for women convicted of murder (now closed). Once the pair got behind the walls, however, they found the women eager to talk – so much so that the filmmakers were able to fashion a candid portrait from an unlikely subject. The unobtrusive style of the film is perfectly suited to the brutal honesty of the inmates' stories. Mixing *cinéma-vérité* with interviews, the filmmakers created a poignant picture of a group of women struggling to maintain their individuality, their sanity, and their closest relationships. **Awards include:** GA: Feature Documentary.

Paddle to the Sea

1966 28m *prod* NFB, *p* Julian Biggs, *d/ph/ed* Bill Mason, *mus* Louis Applebaum, *narr* Stanley Jackson. This film, based on a story by Holling C. Holling, lovingly tells the tale of a little hand-carved Indian in a canoe, launched in the spring towards the sea. As the canoe passes through the system of rivers and lakes into the Gulf of St Lawrence, viewers gain vivid impressions of Canada's vast landscape and life along the waterways. Perhaps Bill Mason's* most famous film, it was immensely popular (especially in classroom screenings) and earned an Academy Award nomination for Best Short. (V)

Paint Cans

1994 100m *prod* Salter Street Films, *exp* Michael Donovan, Paul Donovan, *p/d/sc/book* Paul Donovan, *ph* Les Krizan, *ed* David Ostry, *mus* Marty Simon, Christopher L. Stone; *with* Chas Lawther, Robyn Stevan, Bruce Greenwood, Andy Jones, Paul Gross, Anne-Marie MacDonald, Neve Campbell, Don Francks. Wick Burns (Lawther), a self-serving, nasty bureaucrat, is second-in-command at the Toronto office of a government film-financing agency. Burns is obsessed with his work and spends most of his time dealing with meglomaniac producers and directors. A trip to a major European film festival leads to a failed romance and a murder, but due to an odd set of circumstances, Burns becomes the head of the agency. Lawther is exquisitely slimy as the bureaucrat, and the film features an excellent supporting cast with Paul Gross,* Bruce Greenwood,* Neve Campbell,* and Andy Jones.* Regretfully, the film never found an audience, and director Paul Donovan* was left in the doghouse with government film-funding agencies. *Paint Cans* is a Canadian version of Robert Altman's *The Player*. (V)

Painted Door, The

1984 24m *prod* NFB, Atlantis Films, *exp* Robert Verrall, Michael MacMillian, *p* Michael MacMillian, Janice Platt, *d* Bruce Pittman, *sc* Joe Wiesenfeld, *short story* Sinclair Ross, *ph* Savas Kalogeras, *ed* Margaret Van Eerdewijk, *mus* Bruce Levy; *with* Linda Goranson, Eric Peterson, August Schellenberg. This dark and downbeat film, set during a cold, stormy, Canadian prairie winter, is based on a short story by Sinclair Ross. During a blizzard, Anne (Goranson) stays alone in the farmhouse while husband John (Schellenberg) leaves to help his ailing father. Neighbour Stephen (Peterson) comes over to help with the chores. By late evening, when John hasn't returned, Anne sleeps with Stephen. She awakes the next day to the horrible realization of what she has done. The strong cast offers a touching and realistic portrayal of an unrequited love that, once set free, quickly comes crashing down. The film received an Academy Award nomination for Live-Action Short. (V)

Paperback Hero

1973 93m *prod* Agincourt Productions, *p* John Bassett, James Margellos, *d* Peter Pearson, *sc* Les Rose, Barry Pearson, *ph* Don Wilder, *ed* Kirk Jones, *mus* Ron Collier; *with* Keir Dullea, Elizabeth Ashley, John Beck, Dayle Haddon, Franz Russell. Rick Dillon (Dullea), a small-town, prairie hockey player, considers himself a modern-day gunslinger on and off the ice, and he spends his off-ice time womanizing or getting into bar-room brawls. His irresponsible, idyllic life is shaken up when the hockey team disbands, an event that tragically leads to a 'high noon' with the local police. The film has been dubbed '*The Rowdyman** Goes West,' but Dullea is no Gordon Pinsent,* and his character seems imported from a second-rate American western. While *Paperback Hero* is undoubtedly one of the finest films ever made about prairie life, the story lacks cohesion. It's a collection of memorably funny scenes and interesting episodes punctuated with Gordon Lightfoot's catchy hit tune, 'If You Could Read My Mind.' **Awards include:** CFA: Cinematography, Editing, Sound Re-recording.

Paperland: The Bureaucrat Observed

1979 58m *prod* NFB, CBC, *exp* Barrie Howells, Paul Wright, *p* Marrin Canell, Donald Brittain, *d* Donald Brittain, *sc* Donald Brittain, Ronald Blumer, John Random, *ph* Douglas Kiefer, Barry Perles, *ed* Richard Todd. This documentary exposes the absurdities of bureaucratic behaviour with humour and irreverence. In scenes from Ottawa, communist Hungary, the Vatican (home to the world's oldest bureaucracy), and the tiny Virgin Islands (where a lone bureaucratic literally changes hats to carry out his various functions), the film brings insight to the essential irrationality of a system that can cause intelligent individuals to commit collective absurdities. (V) **Awards include:** GA: Feature Documentary.

Paradise

1985 15m20s *prod* NFB, *exp* Douglas MacDonald, *p/d* Ishu Patel, *an* Ishu Patel, George Ungar, *ph* Pierre Landry, *mus* Gheorghe Zamfir. This stunningly beautiful piece of animation from Ishul Patel* uses innovative mixed-media techniques – cut outs, multiple exposures, and backlit perforated backgrounds – to tell a fable with a simple but strong moral message. Within an emperor's crystal palace lives a beautiful bird of spectacular plumage. Outside, a blackbird watches enviously, and strives to obtain what it covets, only to discover that a golden cage is no substitute for the freedom of the open skies. The film received an Academy Award nomination for Animated Short. (V)

Parasite Murders, The
See *Shivers*.

Parker, Cecilia
Actor; b. Fort William, Ont., 1905; d. 1993. Parker, the daughter of a British Army Officer, was trained as an opera singer in Toronto, but she ended up in Hollywood in the 1930s. There she appeared mostly in western and action pictures before gaining popularity in the Andy Hardy series of films in which she played Andy's older sister, Marion. **Films include:** *Mystery Ranch* 1932; *Naughty Marietta* 1935; *Ah, Wilderness!* 1935; *A Family Affair* 1937; *Judge Hardy's Children* 1938; *Love Finds Andy Hardy* 1938; *Out West with the Hardy's* 1938; *Andy Hardy Gets Spring Fever* 1939; *Andy Hardy Meets a Debutante* 1940; *The Courtship of Andy Hardy* 1942; *Andy Hardy Comes Home* 1958.

Parker, Gudrun
Director, producer, and writer; b. Gudrun Bjerring, Winnipeg, 1920; wife of Morten Parker. Gudrun Bjerring, a pioneering woman director and one of the first in Canada, joined the NFB in the early 1940s and became head of the educational unit. Her films were often lyrical documentaries that reflected her interest in music, culture, and young children. She retired from filmmaking to raise a family, and returned in 1963 as president of Parker Film Associates, a company she ran with her husband. **Films include:** *Listen to the Prairies* 1945 (p/d/sc); *Who Will Teach Your Child?* 1948 (co-p/co-ed, CFA-TS); *Children's Concert* 1949 (p/d); *Family Circles* 1949 (co-sc); *Royal Journey* 1951 (co-d, CFA-FF); *Opera School* 1952 (d, CFA-TS);

A Musician in the Family 1953 (d); *The Stratford Adventure* 1954 (sc).

Parker, Molly
Actor; b. Vancouver, 1972. This west coast beauty was raised on a 'hippie' farm in Pitt Meadows, British Columbia, and began ballet lessons at the age of three. Parker studied dance at the Royal Winnipeg Ballet school and acting at Vancouver's Gastown Actors' Studio. She performed in many American television shows, but her most outstanding role was Glenn Close's daughter in the Emmy Award–winning *Serving in Silence*. In Canada, her performance as Hope in Bruce McDonald's* bathrobe-television mini-series, *Twitch City* (which followed closely on the heels of her Genie-winning role in *Kissed**) moved her into the fast lane, with roles in István Szabó's *Sunshine** and Jeremy Podeswa's *The Five Senses*.* **Films and television include:** *The Ranger, the Cook and a Hole in the Sky* 1995 (TV); *Little Criminals* 1995; *Falling from the Sky: Flight 174* 1995 (TV); *Serving in Silence: The Margarethe Cammermeyer Story* 1995 (TV); *Ebbie* 1995 (TV); *Titanic* 1996 (TV); *Bliss* 1997; *Kissed* 1997 (GA-A); *Intensity* 1997 (TV); *Twitch City* 1998, 2000 (series); *The Five Senses* 1999; *Sunshine* 1999; *Sweethearts of the World* 1999; *The Intruder* 1999; *Waking the Dead* 1999; *Wonderland* 1999; *Ladies Room* 2000; *The Centre of the World* 2001..

Parker, Morten
Director and producer; b. Winnipeg, 1919; husband of Gudrun Parker. Morten Parker joined the NFB in 1943 and was responsible for the Board's labour films. He also directed some of its most prestigious documentaries, including *The Fight: Science against Cancer** and *The Stratford Adventure,** both of which were nominated for Academy Awards. **Films include:** *Family Circles* 1949 (co-p/

d/co-sc, CFA-NTS); *Challenge: Science against Cancer* 1950 (d); *The Fight: Science against Cancer* 1951 (d, AAN-SD); *Labour in Canada* series 1953-5 (d, five films); *The Stratford Adventure* 1954 (d, AAN-SD).

Patel, Ishu
Animator; b. Jalsan, India, 1942. A visionary philosophy combined with innovative technical prowess has allowed this gifted animator to produce a unique body of work. Trained in Switzerland, Patel found a congenial working environment at the NFB in the 1970s. There he created abstract worlds for a series of films, using beads, intricately designed backgrounds, and back-lit plasticine figures. From *How Death Came to Earth*, through *Afterlife*,* to *Divine Fate*, Patel has pursued his project of animating religious and mythical concepts and tales with great art and style. His masterpiece remains *Paradise*,* a parable about envy that is as luminous as the castle in which the tale is played out. **Films include:** *How Death Came to Earth* 1971; *Bead Game* 1977 (AAN-AS); *Afterlife* 1978 (CFA-AS); *Paradise* 1985 (AAN-AS); *Divine Fate* 1993.

Pays sans bon sens!, Un (Wake Up, Mes bons amis!)
1970 118m *prod* NFB, *p* Tom Daly, Guy L. Coté, Paul Larose, *d* Pierre Perrault, *ph* Michel Brault, Bernard Gosselin, *ed* Yves Leduc; *with* Didier Dufour, Maurice Chaillot. Less a celebration of a culture than an investigation into a problem, *Un Pays sans bon sens!* was Perrault's* wake-up call to Quebecers that their only future is in a free country called Quebec. Interviewers (Dufour and Chaillot) roam about Canada and even go to France in an attempt to gather data about Québécois culture. While specifically examining what images are essential for the 'Quebec Family Album' (as

Dufour keeps explaining), the film implies that, both geographically and culturally, Canada is, indeed, 'a ridiculous kind of country' – the literal translation of the French title. (V)

Pearl's Diner
1993 14m30s *p/d/sc/an* Lynn Smith, *ed* Abbey Neidik, Lynn Smith, *mus* Zander Ary. *Pearl's Diner* is a painstakingly crafted, quiet film in the best sense of the word – short on plot but heavy on insight. Using a cut-out animation technique, Smith skilfully mixes bits and pieces from magazines and adds some paints and sketches of her own to create an astonishingly detailed portrait of a group of lonely diner regulars and their devoted waitress. Narrative trajectory becomes unnecessary in her hands: Smith's collage style, subtly nuanced and highly evocative, says it all. **Awards include:** GA: Animated Short.

Pearson, Peter
Director and writer; b. Toronto, 1938. Pearson won scores of awards for his early features, including his stunning debut film, *The Best Damn Fiddler from Calabogie to Kaladar*,* and *Paperback Hero*,* the best film made about the Canadian prairies. He is also well-known as a screenwriter and is co-author (with Robin Spry*) of the award-winning *One Man*. Pearson made several documentaries for CBC-TV and the NFB and directed several of the innovative dramas for the CBC series *For the Record*.* In the 1980s, he headed Telefilm Canada's Broadcast Fund, and he was CEO of the federal-funding agency from 1985 to 1987. **Films and television include:** *The Best Damn Fiddler from Calabogie to Kaladar* 1968 (d, TV, CFA-D); *Encounter with Saul Alinsky* 1967 (d, two films); *Saul Alinsky Went to War* 1968 (d with Donald Brittain); *The Dowry* 1969 (d/sc); *Paper-*

back Hero 1973 (d); *Only God Knows* 1974 (d, TV); *The Insurance Man from Ingersoll* 1976 (d, TV); *Kathy Karbuks Is a Grizzly Bear*, 1976 (d, TV); *Nest of Shadows* 1976 (d, TV); *The Tar Sands* 1977 (d/co-sc, TV); *One Man* 1977 (d/co-sc); *Snowbirds* 1981 (d, TV).

Perfectly Normal

1990 104m *prod* Bialystock and Bloom, *exp* Rafe Engle, *p* Michael Burns, *d* Yves Simoneau, *sc* Eugene Lipinski, Paul Quarrington, *ph* Alain Dostie, *ed* Ronald Sanders, *mus* Richard Gregoire; *with* Robbie Coltrane, Michael Riley, Deborah Duchene, Eugene Lipinski, Kenneth Welsh, Patricia Gage. *Perfectly Normal* combines two staples of Canadiana – beer and hockey – with opera. Lorenzo (Riley) spends his time working in a brewery, playing hockey, and driving cab by night. His life changes when one of his passengers, a gregarious American chef (Coltrane) who loves opera, ends up living in his home. Eventually, the chef convinces Lorenzo to think big and open an opera-themed Italian restaurant. A classy opening night of opera and linguine turns into a hilarious hockey brawl. This entertaining comedy features stand out performances by Riley, Coltrane, and Kenneth Welsh* as an over-the-top, Don Cherryesque coach. The slow-motion game sequences work perfectly with the classical soundtrack, and director Simoneau* injects a Québécois sensibility into this Anglo-Canadian tale. (V) **Awards include:** GA: Original Screenplay.

Perrault, Pierre

Director; b. Montreal, 1927; d. 1999. The rugged Perrault, the most traditionally nationalistic Quebec filmmaker, was the Gilles Vigneault of Quebec cinema. After working in documentary radio, Perrault became known for *Pour la suite*

*de monde,** a film shot with Michel Brault* that presented the textures of life in rural Quebec by allowing the subjects to speak for themselves. Films such as *La Bête lumineuse** explored the way *le québécois* communicate while dealing with such topics as nationalist sensibilities and relationships between men and nature or men and men. Perrault, who was also a poet, made films that favoured traditional occupations such as hunting and fishing while lamenting the encroachment of the modern world on deeply rooted ways of life. **Films include:** *Whalehead* 1959 (sc); *Pour la suite du monde* 1963 (d with Michel Brault, CFA-FY, CFA-SPA); *Le Règne du jour* 1967; *Belgua Days* 1968 (co-d); *Les Voitures d'eau* 1969; *Le Beau Plaisir* 1969 (d with Brault and Bernard Gosselin); *Un Pays sans bon sens!* 1970; *L'Acadie, l'Acadie ?!?* 1971 (d with Brault); *Tickets s.v.p.* 1973; *Un Royaume vous attend* 1976; *Le Retour à la terre* 1976; *Le Goût de la farine* 1977; *C'était un Québécois en Bretagne, Madame!* 1977; *Gens d'Abitibi* 1980; *Le Pays de la terre sans arbre ou le Mouchouânipi* 1980; *La Bête lumineuse* 1982; *Les Voiles bas et en travers* 1983; *La Grand Allure* 1984; *La Toundra* 1992; *L'Oumigmag ou l'objectif documentaire* 1993; *Cornouailles* 1994.

Perron, Clémont

Director, producer, and writer; b. East Brompton, Que., 1929; d. 1999. Perron received a classical education from the Jesuits before obtaining a degree in philosophy and literature from Université Laval. He began working as a screenwriter at the NFB, where he wrote *Mon oncle Antoine** for Claude Jutra*, *Stop* for Jean Beaudin,* and *Les Smattes* for Jean-Claude Labrecque.* Beginning in 1960, he explored directing with projects such as *Georges-P. Vanier, soldat, diplomate, gouverneur général* and the better-known

*Jour après jour,** a direct-cinema documentary on the working conditions in pulp and paper mills. He left the NFB in 1986 and continued screenwriting in the private sector. **Films and television include:** *Georges-P. Vanier, soldat, diplomate, gouverneur général* 1960 (d/sc); *Jour après jour* 1962 (d/sc, CFA-AE); *Caroline* 1964 (d/sc/ed with Georges Dufaux); *Salut Toronto!* 1965 (d); *C'est pas la faute à Jacques Cartier* 1966 (d/sc/ed with Dufaux, TV); *Les Acadiens de la dispersion* 1968 (p, TV); *Kid Sentiment* 1968 (p); *Mon amie Pierrette* 1969 (p); *We Are All ... Picasso!* 1969 (p); *Mon oncle Antoine* 1971 (sc, CFA-SC); *Stop* 1971 (sc); *Les Smattes* 1972 (sc); *Taureau* 1973 (d/sc); *Jusqu'au coeur* 1974 (p); *Partis pour la glorie* 1975 (d/sc); *Vieillard et l'enfant* 1985 (sc); *Le Marchand de jouets* 1989 (sc).

Perry, Matthew

Actor; b. Williamstown, Mass., 1969. Raised in Ottawa, Perry is the only child of Suzanne and actor John Perry. When Matthew was ten (and had become an accomplished tennis player), his mother married CTV news anchorman Keith Morrison. Perry began acting when he was about twelve, and at age fifteen, he moved to Los Angeles to test his tennis and acting skills. Tennis didn't go so well, but in 1994 he won the coveted role of Chandler Bing on the megahit *Friends*. He enhanced his television career with a string of light comedies including *Three to Tango* and *The Whole Nine Yards*. **Films and television include:** *Second Chance* 1987–8 (series); *A Night in the Life of Jimmy Reardon* 1988; *She's Out of Control* 1989; *Sydney* 1990 (series); *Call Me Anna* 1990 (TV); *Home Free* 1993 (series); *Deadly Relations* 1993 (TV); *Parallel Lives* 1994 (TV); *Friends* 1994–present (series); *Fools Rush In* 1997; *Almost Heroes* 1998; *Three to Tango* 1999; *The Whole Nine Yards* 2000.

Petrie, Daniel

Director; b. Glace Bay, N.S., 1920. After studying communications at St Francis-Xavier University in Antigonish, Nova Scotia, Petrie went to the United States to attend Columbia and Northwestern universities. Working for most of his career in the United States, Petrie achieved critical acclaim for his 1961 screen adaptation of Lorraine Hansberry's play *A Raisin in the Sun*, which starred Sidney Poitier. He has since directed many productions for both cinema and television. In 1984, Petrie captured the Best Picture Genie for *The Bay Boy,** which starred a young Kiefer Sutherland* and Liv Ullmann in a semi-autobiographical story about growing up in Cape Breton. One of his sons, Daniel Petrie Jr, wrote *Beverly Hills Cop* (1984), and his other son Donald Petrie directed *Mystic Pizza* (1988). **Films and television include:** *The Bramble Bush* 1960; *A Raisin in the Sun* 1961; *Stolen Hours* 1963; *The Idol* 1966; *The Spy with the Cold Nose* 1966; *The Neptune Factor* 1973; *Buster and Billie* 1974; *Lifeguard* 1976; *The Betsy* 1977; *Resurrection* 1980; *Fort Apache, the Bronx* 1981; *The Bay Boy* 1984 (d/sc, GA-P); *The Dollmaker* 1984 (TV); *Cocoon: The Return* 1988; *Lassie* 1994; *The Assistant* 1997; *Seasons of Love* 1999 (TV).

Pickford, Jack

Actor and director; b. Jack Smith, Toronto, 1896; d. 1933; brother of Lottie and Mary Pickford. Jack Pickford followed his more famous sister Mary's footsteps, first on stage and then into film, starting with Biograph in 1910. In Hollywood, he became a star in his own right, and later a director and producer. Heavy drinking and fast living caught up with him, and he died at the age of thirty-seven. **Films include:** *White Roses* 1910; *For Her Brother's Sake* 1911; *Musketeers of Pig Alley* 1913; *A Girl of Yesterday* 1915;

Tom Sawyer 1917; *Great Expectations* 1917; *Tom and Huck* 1918; *Through the Back Door* 1921 (co-d); *Little Lord Fauntleroy* 1921 (co-d); *The Hill Billy* 1924 (p/a); *Gang War* 1928.

Pickford, Lottie

Actor; b. Lottie Smith, Toronto, 1900; d. 1936; sister of Jack and Mary Pickford. Lottie, the youngest of the Pickfords, followed her brother and sister on the New York stage and then in Hollywood. Like Mary, she had curly hair, but she didn't have her sister's star power. Lottie played minor roles (sometimes with her siblings), but died of a heart attack at age thirty-six.

Pickford, Mary

Actor and producer; b. Gladys Smith, Toronto, 1893; d. 1979; sister of Jack and Lottie Pickford. Mary Pickford appeared on the Toronto stage at age four, and was a star on Broadway before appearing in her first film for D.W. Griffith in 1909. Known as Little Mary, 'America's Sweetheart,' she became the first Hollywood star and the most popular and financially successful woman in silent cinema. In films such as *Rebecca of Sunnybrook Farm*, *Pollyanna*, and *Little Lord Fauntleroy*, Pickford played the heroine with idealism, spunk, and a subtle suggestion of the nymphet. She formed United Artists with Griffith, Charlie Chaplin, and Douglas Fairbanks in 1919, and married Fairbanks in 1920. Pickford made over 200 films in twenty-five years and dominated American cinema until the coming of sound, when her Little Mary character went out of favour with audiences. She won the Academy Award for Best Actress for *Coquette* and was given an Honorary Academy Award in 1976.
Films include: Over 140 shorts from 1909 to 1912; *In the Bishop's Carriage* 1913; *Tess of the Storm Country* 1914; *Cinderella*

1914; *Rags* 1915; *A Girl of Yesterday* 1915 (sc/a); *Madame Butterfly* 1915; *The Foundling* 1916; *The Poor Little Rich Girl* 1917; *A Romance of the Redwoods* 1917; *A Little Princess* 1917; *Rebecca of Sunnybrook Farm* 1917; *Daddy-Long-Legs* 1919; *Captain Kidd, Jr* 1919; *Pollyanna* 1920; *Studs* 1920; *The Love Light* 1921 (p/a); *Little Lord Fauntleroy* 1921 (p/a); *Through the Back Door* 1921 (p/a); *Tess of the Storm Country* 1922 (p/a); *Rosita* 1923 (p/a); *Little Annie Rooney* 1925 (p/a); *My Best Girl* 1927 (p/a); *Coquette* 1929 (p/a, AA-A); *The Taming of the Shrew* 1929.

Picture of Light

1996 83m *prod* Grimthorpe Films, *exp* Andreas Züst, *p* Peter Mettler, Alexandra Gill, *d/sc/ph* Peter Mettler, *ed* Peter Mettler, Mike Nunn, Alexandra Gill, *mus* Jim O'Rourke. On the surface, this hallucinatory and lyrical picture is a document of a journey to the Canadian Arctic Circle in an effort to capture the northern lights on film. Deeper consideration reveals much more. The film, which combines glimpses of the eccentric characters that inhabit this remote portion of the planet with spectacular shots of the aurora borealis, contemplates the relationship between nature and technology and examines the gap separating reality from our perception of reality as seen through the filters of the mass media. (V)

Pidgeon, Walter

Actor; b. Saint John, N.B., 1897; d. 1984. Like most talented Canadians of his generation, Pidgeon flew south. Although he worked in silent films, he only emerged as a leading man in the sound era, appearing in eighty-five films between 1928 and 1978. Durable, and frequently cast as a man of principle or a doting husband, Pidgeon reached his peak in the 1940s as the co-star in

John Ford's *How Green Was My Valley*, William Wyler's *Mrs Miniver* and Mervin LeRoy's *Madame Curie*, and he garnered Academy Award nominations for his performances opposite Greer Garson in the two latter films. From the mid-1940s on, he was assigned mostly character roles. His dignified screen presence opposite another expatriate Canuck, Leslie Nielsen,* lent credibility to the sci-fi cult classic *Forbidden Planet*. **Films include:** *Rockabye* 1932; *Big Brown Eyes* 1936; *Saratoga* 1937; *The Girl of the Golden West* 1938; *Nick Carter, Master Detective* 1939; *Dark Command* 1940; *Man Hunt* 1941; *How Green Was My Valley* 1941; *Mrs Miniver* 1942 (AAN-A); *Madame Curie* 1943 (AAN-A); *Mrs Parkington* 1944; *Weekend at the Waldorf* 1945; *That Forsyth Woman* 1949; *The Miniver Story* 1950; *Calling Bulldog Drummond* 1951; *Soldiers Three* 1951; *The Bad and the Beautiful* 1952; *Executive Suite* 1954; *The Last Time I Saw Paris* 1954; *Forbidden Planet* 1956; *Voyage to the Bottom of the Sea* 1961; *Advise and Consent* 1962; *Funny Girl* 1968; *The Neptune Factor* 1973; *Won Ton Ton, the Dog Who Saved Hollywood* 1976.

Pilon, Daniel

Actor; b. Montreal, 1940; brother of Donald Pilon. Daniel Pilon was cast with his brother Donald in Gilles Carle's *Le Viol d'une jeune fille douce* and *Red*. Since then, in addition to pursuing a film career in Europe and Quebec, he has appeared in thousands of episodes of various television soaps, such as *Dallas, Ryan's Hope*, and *The Guiding Light*. **Films and television include:** *Le Viol d'une jeune fille douce* 1968; *Red* 1970; *Après-ski* 1971; *Les Smattes* 1972; *Le Diable est parmi nous* 1972; *La Mort d'un bûcheron* 1973; *Brannigan* 1975; *Starship Invasions* 1977; *Plague* 1979; *Dallas* 1984–5 (series); *Ryan's Hope* 1984–7 (series); *The Guiding Light* 1988–9 (series); *Malarek* 1989; *Scanners III: The Takeover* 1992; *Sirens* 1993 (series); *Danielle Steel's*

No Greater Love 1996 (TV); *Suspicious Minds* 1997; *Obsessed* 1988; *The Collectors* 1999; *Bonanno: A Godfather's Story* 1999 (TV); *36 Hours to Die* 1999 (TV).

Pilon, Donald

Actor; b. Montreal, 1938; brother of Daniel Pilon. Donald Pilon virtually became the alter ego of director Gilles Carle* who cast him in eight films. Between 1968 and 1974, his name appeared in the credits of more than two dozen feature films, mostly in central roles; he won a Canadian Film Award for *La Vraie Nature de Bernadette*. Pilon has also dabbled in English cinema and in television, notably in the Quebec television series *Duplessis*. **Films and television include:** *Le Viol d'une jeune fille douce* 1968; *Red* 1970; *Deux femmes en or* 1970; *Les Mâles* 1971; *Bulldozer* 1974; *Les Smattes* 1972; *La Vraie Nature de Bernadette* 1972 (CFA-SA); *The Pyx* 1973; *Les Corps célestes* 1973; *Child under a Leaf* 1974; *Gina* 1975; *Duplessis* 1977 (series); *I Miss You, Hugs and Kisses* 1978; *A Man Called Intrepid* 1979 (TV); *Fantastica* 1980; *Les Plouffe* 1981; *Cook and Peary: The Race to the Pole* 1983 (TV); *Le Crime d'Ovide Plouffe* 1984; *Keeping Track* 1986; *Une Histoirie inventée* 1990; *Le Vent du Wyoming* 1994; *C't'à ton tour Laura Cadieux* 1998; *Laura Cadieux ... la suite* 1999.

Pindal, Kaj

Animator; b. Copenhagen, Denmark, 1927. A naturally gifted cartoonist, Pindal worked as an animator in Sweden and at Denmark's legendary Nordisk Film before emigrating to Canada and the NFB in 1957. His love of machinery and outrageous character designs qualified the puckish Pindal for a prime spot in the Board's burgeoning animation department during the 1960s and 1970s. There he won kudos for his sprightly animation of Derek Lamb's *I Know an Old Lady Who Swallowed a Fly* and *What on Earth!,** his own satirical peek at car culture. Pindal has remained an important influence in Canadian animation through teaching stints at Sheridan College, ongoing work on the barnyard *Peep* creatures, and the animation, with Lamb, of the Third World heroes, *The Karate Kids*. **Films include:** *Horsd'oeuvre* 1960; (co-d/an); *The Peep Show* 1962 (d/sc/an); *I Know an Old Lady Who Swallowed a Fly* 1964 (an); *What on Earth!* 1966 (d/an with Les Drew, AAN-AS); *The Hottest Show on Earth* 1977 (co-an); *Peep and the Big Wide World* 1988 (d/sc/an); *The Karate Kids* 1989 (co-an).

Pinsent, Gordon

Actor, writer, and director; b. Grand Falls, Nfld., 1930. Pinsent, a versatile character actor and one of the most enduring Canadian screen talents, has also seen two of his novels – *The Rowdyman** and *John and the Missus** – brought to the screen. He starred in both productions and directed the latter. Pinsent began his career at the Manitoba Theatre Centre, and from there moved to the Stratford Festival, across Canada's theatrical circuit, and to the United States. His film credits include *Who Has Seen the Wind** and *Jack London's Klondike Fever*; his small-screen work includes *A Gift to Last*, *Due South*, and *Power Play*. He has been awarded the Order of Canada, two Genies, two ACTRA awards, and the 1997 Earle Grey Award for lifetime achievement. **Films and television include:** *The Forest Rangers* 1964 (series); *Lydia* 1964 (TV); *Quentin Durgens, M.P.* 1966 (series); *The Thomas Crown Affair* 1968; *The Rowdyman* 1972 (sc/a, CFA-A); *Blacula* 1972; *Only God Knows* 1974; *Newman's Law* 1974; *The Heatwave Lasted Four Days* 1975 (TV); *A Gift to Last* 1976–80 (sc/a, series); *Who Has Seen the Wind* 1977; *Jack London's Klondike Fever* 1980 (GA-SA); *Escape from Iran: The Canadian Caper* 1980 (TV); *A Far Cry from Home*

1981 (d, TV); *Silence of the North* 1981; *The Devil at Your Heels* 1981 (narr); *The Life and Times of Edwin Alonzo Boyd* 1982 (TV); *Ready for Slaughter* 1983 (TV); *A Case of Libel* 1984 (TV); *John and the Missus* 1986 (d/sc/a, GA-A); *Two Men* 1988 (d, TV); *Termini Station* 1989; *Babar: The Movie* 1989 (voice); *Blood Clan* 1991; *In the Eyes of a Stranger* 1992 (TV); *Due South* 1994–9 (series); *A Vow to Kill* 1995 (TV); *A Holiday for Love* 1996 (TV); *Pale Saints* 1997; *Pippi Longstocking* 1997 (voice); *Power Play* 1998–2000 (series); *Win, Again!* 1999 (sc/a, TV); *The Old Man and the Sea* 1999 (voice).

Place Called Chiapas, A

1999 93m *prod* Canada Wild Productions, *p* Nettie Wild, Kirk Tougas, Betsy Carson, *d* Nettie Wild, *sc* Nettie Wild, Manfred Becker, *ph* Kirk Tougas, Nettie Wild, *ed* Manfred Becker, *mus* Joseph Pepe Sanza, Salvador Ferreras, Celso Machado, Laurence Mallerup. This documentary portrays the true story of how a group of white, middle-class, politically correct filmmakers, posing as journalists, travelled to southern Mexico to cover the Zapatista uprising. Eager to please, director Nettie Wild demonizes the Mexican authorities and dutifully waits around until subcomandante Marcos shows up to tell his side of the story from behind a mask and heavily armed bodyguards. While undoubtedly the living conditions in the state of Chiapas are deplorable by Canadian standards and local human rights are regularly trampled on by a distant government, this point-of-view documentary is so fawning as to give the genre a bad name. (V) **Awards include:** GA: Feature Documentary.

Plouffe, Les

1981 169m (227m TV version) *prod* International Cinema Corporation, *exp* Denis Héroux, John Kemeny, *p* Justine Héroux,

d Gilles Carle, *sc* Roger Lemelin, Gilles Carle, *novel* Roger Lemelin, *ph* François Protat, *ed* Yves Langlois, *mus* Stéphane Venne, Claude Denjean; *with* Emile Genest, Juliette Huot, Denise Filiatrault, Gabriel Arcand, Pierre Curzi, Serge Dupire, Anne Létourneau, Gérard Poirier, Donald Pilon, Stéphane Audran. Roger Lemelin's famous novel had already been serialized for Radio-Canada and CBC Radio and made into a hugely successful téléroman for Quebec television during the 1950s. This big-budget version was shot both for a television mini-series and (in a shorter version) for theatrical release. In the movie version, the relationship between the sensitive, repressed son Ovide (Arcand*) and Rita (Létourneau), a tease pursued by all the young men, is the central focus. The film nostagically captures the past years of the Great Depression and the events leading up to the Second World War, a time when traditional Quebec society was undergoing radical changes. (V)
Awards include: GA: Director, Adapted Screenplay, Supporting Actress (Filiatrault), Art Direction, Costumes, Musical Score, Song.

Plummer, Christopher

Actor; b. Montreal, 1927. Plummer, an actor in the classical mould, has taken on innumerable larger-than-life roles. Working in the theatre, film, and television in the United States, England, and Canada, Plummer has played Hamlet, Rudyard Kipling, and, of course, Baron von Trapp opposite Julie Andrews in *The Sound of Music*, one of the most popular films of all time. The most memorable of his many Canadian film roles are the psychopathic thief who terrorizes Elliott Gould in *The Silent Partner** and Sherlock Holmes to James Mason's Dr Watson in Bob Clark's *Murder by Decree.** He also played Brad Pitt's dubious Big Daddy in *12 Monkeys* and *60 Minutes'* Mike Wallace in *The Insider.* Plummer won a Tony for his portrayal of the legendary actor John Barrymore in a one-man play on Broadway in 1997. He is the father of actress Amanda Plummer (*The Fisher King, Pulp Fiction*).
Films and television include: *Wind across the Everglades* 1958; *The Fall of the Roman Empire* 1964; *The Sound of Music* 1965; *Inside Daisy Clover* 1966; *The Night of the Generals* 1967; *Oedipus the King* 1968; *The Royal Hunt of the Sun* 1969; *Waterloo* 1970; *The Pyx* 1973; *The Return of the Pink Panther* 1975; *The Man Who Would Be King* 1975; *Conduct Unbecoming* 1975; *International Velvet* 1978; *The Silent Partner* 1978; *Murder by Decree* 1979 (GA-A); *The Disappearance* 1981; *The Amateur* 1981; *Little Gloria: Happy at Last* 1982 (TV); *Dragnet* 1987; *The Man Who Planted Trees* 1987 (narr); *Kingsgate* 1989; *The First Emperor of China* 1989 (narr); *Where the Heart Is* 1990; *Star Trek VI: The Undiscovered Country* 1991; *Wolf* 1994; *Dolores Claiborne* 1995; *12 Monkeys* 1995; *The Insider* 1999; *Nuremberg* 2000 (TV); *American Tragedy* 2000 (TV).

Podeswa, Jeremy

Director, writer, and producer; b. Toronto, 1962. After just two feature films, Jeremy Podeswa has already established himself as a major talent. In 1999, he won the Best Director Genie for *The Five Senses,** and shortly after its release *Variety* included him in the international survey of 'Tomorrow's Hot Exports.' His filmography, though brief (two shorts, two features to date), is a thematically rich and comprehensive body of work devoted to mining the depths of the age-old quest for love. To his credit, he avoids cheap sentiment and saccharine solutions, choosing instead to present his favourite theme in all its glorious messy complexity. **Films include:** *David*

Roche Talks to You about Love 1983; *Nion (in the Kabaret de la Vita)* 1986; *Eclipse* 1994; *The Five Senses* 1999 (GA-D); *24fps* from *Preludes* 2000 (d/sc).

Poetry in Motion

1982 90m *prod* Sphinx Productions, *exp* Murray Sweigman, *p/d* Ron Mann, *ph* Robert Fresco, *ed* Peter Wintonick; *with* Allen Ginsberg, Charles Bukowski, Tom Waits, Michael Ondaatje, and others. This film portrays twenty-five major poets in performance, emphasizing poetry as an oral art. With only momentary cuts to interviews, *Poetry in Motion* simply reveals one great poet after another, building waves of themes or techniques through the arrangement of the readings. Some of the poets were filmed in a studio setting, some in live performance before an audience, and some in their homes. All read from their own work and occasionally offer reflections on their art. (V)

Poirier, Anne Claire

Director, producer, writer, and editor; b. St-Hyacinthe, Que., 1932. Poirier prefigured the feminist movement with such films as *De mère en fille* and became the dominant force behind women's production at the NFB. For rhetorical force, nothing in her oeuvre matches the 1979 docudrama *Mourir à tue-tête,** which combines footage of ritual clitoridectomy with an episodic narrative to convey the emotional disintegration and eventual suicide of a nurse victimized by rape. More recently Poirier won a Genie Award for *Tu es crié Let Me Go*, a painful documentary about the murder of her daughter. **Films include:** *Jour après jour* 1962 (ed); *Stampede* 1962 (co-d); *30 Minutes, Mr Plummer* 1963 (d/sc/ed); *La Fin des étés* 1964 (d/ed); *Les Ludions* 1965 (d/ed); *De mère en fille* 1968 (d/sc); *La Savoir-faire s'impose* 1971 (d/ed); *J'me*

marie, j'me marie pas 1973 (p); *Les Filles, c'est pas pareil* 1974 (p); *Les Filles du roy* 1974 (p/d/co-sc); *Le Temps de l'avant* 1975 (p/d/co-sc); *Ti-dré* 1976 (p); *Skakti* 1976 (p); *Surtout l'hiver* 1976 (p); *Raison d'être* 1977 (p); *Familles et variations* 1977 (p); *Les Héritiers de la voilence* 1977 (p); *La P'tite Violence* 1977 (p); *Québec à vendre* 1977 (p); *Mourir à tue-tête* 1979 (co-p/d/co-sc); *La Quarantaine* 1982 (d/co-sc); *Tu as crié Let Me Go* 1997 (d/sc, GA-FD).

Polley, Sarah

Actor; b. Toronto, 1979. Polley, who has been acting since the age of four and starred in a big-budget Hollywood movie at eight, has become one of the hottest young actors in Canada, a remarkable achievement for a high school dropout. Torn between left-wing activism (she has worked for the NDP and the Ontario Coalition against Poverty) and the life of a movie star, Polley brings a refreshing youthful honesty to her performances. She excelled in Egoyan's* ensemble drama, *The Sweet Hereafter.** **Films and television include:** *One Magic Christmas* 1985; *Ramona* 1987 (series); *The Adventures of Baron Munchausen* 1988; *Babar: The Movie* 1989 (voice); *Road to Avonlea* 1989–95 (series); *Exotica* 1994; *Joe's So Mean to Josephine* 1997; *The Sweet Hereafter* 1997; *The Hanging Garden* 1997; *The Planet of Junior Brown* 1997 (TV); *White Lies* 1998 (TV); *Last Night* 1998; *eXistenZ* 1999; *Go* 1999; *Guinevere* 1999; *The Life before This* 1999; *Preludes* 2000.

Pool, Léa

Director and writer; b. Soglio, Switzerland, 1950. Montreal-based Pool has won many festival prizes for such coolly stylized pictures as *La Femme de l'hôtel,** *Anne Trister,** and *La Demoiselle sauvage*, all of which explore themes of isolation, artistic crisis, identity confusion and ambiguous sexuality from a feminist perspective. The style and texture of Pool's films are so European auteur that in *Mouvements de désir,* a film set on a train speeding across Canada, the characters might as well be travelling to Geneva. One of her best films, the short *Urgence* (her part of the *Montréal vu par ...** compilation film) evokes the swirling memories of a woman being rushed to the hospital in the aftermath of an accident. **Films include:** *Strass Café* 1979; *La Femme de l'hôtel* 1984; *Anne Trister* 1986; *À corps perdu* 1988; *Hôtel chronicles* 1990; *La Demoiselle sauvage* 1991; *Montréal vu par ...* 1991 (co-d/co-sc); *Mouvements du désir* 1994; *Gabrielle Roy* 1999 (TV); *Emporte-moi* 1999 (d/sc); *Lost and Delirious* 2001.

Porky's
1981 98m *prod* Astral Bellevue Pathé (Canada), Melvin Simon Productions (U.S.), *exp* Harold Greenberg, Melvin Simon, *p* Don Carmody, Bob Clark, *d/sc* Bob Clark, *ph* Reginald H. Morris, *ed* Stan Cole, *mus* Carl Zittrer, Paul Zaza; *with* Dan Monahan, Mark Herrier, Wyatt Knight, Roger Wilson, Kaki Hunter, Kim Cattrall. This raunchy teen comedy, a rehash of *American Graffiti* via *Animal House,* is about a group of frat boys in 1950s Florida trying to get laid. *Porky's* made a ton of money (Greenberg* built the Astral Communications empire on the profits), spawned two sequels, and it has enshrined itself as the most reviled film in the Canadian canon. The reviews were so harsh (*Variety* called it 'astonishingly vulgar ... has to be seen to be believed') and the worldwide box office so huge (exceeding $100 million) that no other Canadian film even comes close. *Porky's* has been dismissed as an aberration, a bad joke, but given the comic extremes of *Dumb and Dumber* and *American Pie,* the film's juvenile, foul-mouthed humour seems more like a harbinger of

things to come. (V) **Awards include:** Golden Reel Award.

Portal, Louise
Actor; b. Chicoutimi, Que., 1950. Fresh out of the Conservatoire d'art dramatique de Montréal, Portal began with two screen roles: a small part in *La Vie rêvée,** and the spunky adolescent in *Taureau,* a performance that won her general acclaim and inspired great expectations. Her career has since diversified into television, theatre, music, and literature, but she made a noted return to film in 1979 with the central character in Jean Beaudin's *Cordelia,* followed by a role in Arcand's *Le Déclin de l'empire américain,** for which she won a Genie. That film established Portal as a mature actor with an eloquent ability to render the vulnerability of her characters. Other touching performances include those in *Sous-sol** and *Full Blast.* **Films include:** *La Vie rêvee* 1972; *Taureau* 1973; *Les Beaux Dimanches* 1974; *Les Deux Pieds dans la même bottine* 1974; *Vie d'ange* 1979; *Mourir à tue-tête* 1979; *Cordélia* 1980; *Larose, Pierrot et la Luce* 1982; *Le Déclin de l'empire américain* 1986 (GA-SA); *Exit* 1986; *Tinamer* 1987; *Histoire infâme* 1987; *Mes meilleurs copains* 1988; *Les Amoureuses* 1992; *Sous-sol* 1996; *Le Grand Serpant du monde* 1998; *Souvenirs intimes* 1999; *Quand je serai parti ... vous vivrez encore* 1999; *Full Blast* 1999.

Possible Worlds
2000 93m *prod* The East Side Film Company, In Extremis Images, *exp* Victor Loewy, Charlotte Mickie, Ted East, *p* Sandra Cunningham, Bruno John, *d* Robert Legage, *sc/play* John Mighton, *ph* Jonathan Freeman, *ed* Susan Shipton, *mus* Ron Proulx; *with* Tom McCamus, Tilda Swinton, Sean McCann, Rick Miller, Gabriel Gascon. *Possible Worlds,* Robert Lepage's* first English-language

film – and the first not based on his own material – is a difficult film to describe properly. George Barber (McCamus), a seemingly ordinary man, has an extraordinary ability to exist in an infinite number of possible worlds. As he searches for the love of his life (Swinton), he meets her again and again, each time in a different world. The film, part love story, part thriller (it starts with George's death and the removal of his brain), is wholly intriguing. Haunting and beautifully shot, *Possible Worlds* is a dreamlike exploration of parallel universes. **Awards include:** GA: Editing, Art Direction.

Post Mortem

1999 92m *prod* Coop Vidéo de Montreal, *p/ed* Lorraine Dufour, *d/sc* Louis Bélanger, *ph* Jean-Pierre St-Louis, *mus* Guy Bélanger, Steve Hill; *with* Gabriel Arcand, Sylvie Moreau, Hélène Loiselle, Sarah Lecompte-Bergeron. This urban fable about karma, ironic twists of fate, and the quivering line between life and death is Quebec's most striking feature-film debut since Yves Simoneau's *Pouvoir intime** (1986). Linda – vividly played by Sylvie Moreau – is both a loving single mom and a ruthless thief; she lures men into hotel rooms, knocks them out, and grabs their wallets. Yet, despite her crimes, we like her because she lives to dance the twist with her daughter. The second character, a lonely morgue attendant struggling to hold onto his dignity, is brought to life by Gabriel Arcand* in a finely tuned, near-silent performance. Director Louis Bélanger skilfully makes us think we're one step ahead of the narrative when we're actually lagging behind. (V) **Awards include:** GA: Actress (Moreau), Original Screenplay, Claude Jutra Award; PJ: Picture, Director, Screenplay, Actor (Arcand), Editing.

Potterton, Gerald

Director and animator; b. London, U.K., 1931. Few Canadian careers have been as colourful as that of Gerald Potterton. He collaborated with Harold Pinter (*Pinter People*), Buster Keaton (*The Railrodder*), and Donald Pleasance (*The Rainbow Boys*), ran his own studio, and directed the animated feature *Heavy Metal** for Ivan Reitman.* Arriving in Canada in the mid-1950s, Potterton was in the forefront of the animation wave that shook the NFB. By the early 1960s, he found himself twice nominated for Academy Awards (for *My Financial Career** and *Christmas Cracker*). His comic sense proved equally adept in both live-action and animated films, allowing him to direct features, theatrical shorts, and television programs in either format. **Films include:** *Huff and Puff* 1955 (an with Grant Munro); *It's a Crime* 1957 (an); *Hors-d'oeuvre* 1960 (co-d/co-an); *My Financial Career* 1963 (d/an with Munro, AAN-AS); *The Ride* 1963 (d); *Christmas Cracker* 1963 (co-d, AAN-AS); *The Railrodder* 1965 (d/sc/co-ed); *Pinter People* 1968 (p/d); *The Charge of the Snow Brigade* 1970 (p/d/sc); *Tiki-Tiki* 1971 (p/d); *A Child under Leaf* 1973 (p); *The Rainbow Boys* 1973 (d/sc); *The Remarkable Rocket* 1975 (d); *Raggedy Ann and Andy* 1977 (an); *Heavy Metal* 1981 (supervising d); *The Awful Fate of Melpomenus Jones* 1983 (d/an).

Pour la suite du monde

1963 105m *prod* NFB, *exp* Fernand Dansereau, *p* Jacques Bobet, *d* Pierre Perrault, Michel Brault, *ph* Michel Brault, Bernard Gosselin, *ed* Werner Nold, *mus* Jean Cousineau, Jean Meunier. For centuries the inhabitants of Île-aux-Coudres, a small island in the St Lawrence River, trapped beluga whales by sinking a weir of saplings into the offshore mud at low tide. After 1920, the practice was abandoned. In 1962, a team of NFB filmmakers led by Pierre Perrault* and Michel Brault* arrived on the island to make a direct-cinema documentary about the people and their isolated life, and they encouraged the islanders to revive the practice of beluga fishing. The resulting film was hugely popular in Quebec and became a classic of Canadian cinema. It has been consistently ranked by critics as one of the best ever made, and it represents a major development in the direct-cinema movement, moving away from simple observation to a more immediate participation and a greater emphasis on the words of the people portrayed. (V) **Awards include:** CFA: Film of the Year, Special Award.

Pouvoir intime
1986 84m *prod* Les Films Vision 4, NFB, *exp* Francine Forest, *p* Claude Bonin, *d* Yves Simoneau, *sc* Yves Simoneau, Pierre Curzi, *ph* Guy Dufaux, *ed* André Corriveau, *mus* Richard Grégoire; *with* Marie Tifo, Pierre Curzi, Jacques Godin, Robert Gravel. This fast-moving heist flick adroitly demonstrated that a Canadian could make an offbeat, stylish genre film. Yves Simoneau* fools around with sex, death, existential irony, and witty camera moves. The plot involves a band of thieves who hijack an armoured truck only to be stymied by a guard (Gravel) who is going through a relationship crisis. This poor jumpy guy locks himself into the rear of the vehicle with the loot, refusing to hand it over. As in Tarantino's *Reservoir Dogs*, Simoneau's criminals undermine cool professionalism with human frailties. (V)

Pratley, Gerald
Archivist and journalist; b. London, U.K., 1923. Pratley, who came to Canada in 1946, first worked as a scriptwriter for CBC Radio. In 1948, he hosted 'This Week in the Movies,' the first show of its kind in Canada to deal seriously with film appreciation. In 1968 he founded and became director of the Ontario Film Institute, and he held that position until 1990 when the Institute merged with the Toronto International Film Festival to become Cinematheque Ontario and The Film Reference Library. Pratley had built up an impressive archives and an extensive book collection. He was chairman of the Canadian Film Awards from 1969 to 1976, and he ran the Stratford Film Festival from 1970 to 1976.

Preludes
2000 50m *prod* Rhombus Media, *exp* Niv Fichman. *Preludes* consists of ten five-minute films made to celebrate the twenty-fifth anniversary of the Toronto International Film Festival. The project was commissioned by festival director Piers Handling and overseen by producer Niv Fichman. One film was screened prior to a festival gala, and all ten have since been packaged as a single film by TMN–The Movie Network. **The films:** *Camera p* Jody Shapiro, *d/sc* David Cronenberg, *ph* André Pienaar, *ed* Ronald Sanders, *mus* Howard Shore; *with* Les Carlson. *The Line p* Jody Shapiro, *d/sc* Atom Egoyan, *ph* Paul Sarossy, *ed* David Wharnsby, *mus* Mychael Danna. *Congratulations p* Paul Pope, Jody Shapiro, *d/sc* Mike Jones, *ph* Robert J. Petrie, *ed* Derek Norman, *mus* Paul Steffler; *with* Mike Jones, Andy Jones, Cathy Jones. *See You in Toronto p* Edouard Faribault, Jody Shapiro, *d/sc* Jean Pierre Lefebvre, *ph* Robert Vanherveghen; *with* Marcel Sabourin. *The Heart of the World p* Jody Shapiro, *d/sc/ph* Guy Maddin, *ed* Guy Maddin, deco dawson; *with* Leslie Bais, Caelum Vatnsdal, Shaun Balbar, Greg Klymkiw. *A Word from the Management*

p Jody Shapiro, *d/sc* Don McKellar, *ph* Douglas Koch, *ed* Christopher Donaldson. **24fps** *p* Jody Shapiro, *d/sc* Jeremy Podeswa, *ph* Greg Middleton, *ed* David Wharnsby, *mus* Alex Pauk, Alexina Louie. *This Might Be Good p* Jody Shapiro, *d/sc* Patricia Rozema, *ph* André Pienaar, *ed* Michelle Czukar, *mus* Lesley Barber; *with* Sarah Polley, Don McKellar, Mark McKinney, Fides Krucker. *Prelude p* Jody Shapiro, *d/sc* Michael Snow, *ph* Luc Montpellier, *ed* David Wharnsby, *mus* CCMC, Michael Snow; *with* Ester Jun, Diane Sidik, Bill Chan, Tuan Tran, Leanne Poon, Robert Lee. *Legs Apart p* Peter Lhotka, Jody Shapiro, *d/sc* Anne Wheeler, *ph* David Frazee, *ed* Lara Mazur, *mus* Tim McCauley; *with* Patricia Harras, Hrothgar Mathews, Alec Willows, Tom Butler, Gabrielle Rose.

Prevost, Marie

Actor; b. Marie Bickford Dunn, Sarnia, Ont., 1898; d. 1937. Prevost was educated in a convent school in Montreal and later at a Los Angeles high school. By age eighteen she had become one of Mack Sennett's* bathing beauties. She stayed with Sennett until 1921, then went to Universal, where she was promoted to leading-lady status, and starred in three films by Ernst Lubitsch – *The Marriage Circle, Three Women,* and *Kiss Me Again.* Her career peaked in the mid-1920s, but by the mid-1930s she had developed a serious weight problem. Attempts at a crash diet proved fatal; she was found dead at her home of extreme malnutrition in 1937. **Films include:** *Secrets of a Beauty Parlor* 1917; *Yankee Doodle in Berlin* 1919; *Down on the Farm* 1920; *A Parisian Scandal* 1921; *Her Night of Nights* 1922; *The Marriage Circle* 1924; *Three Women* 1924; *Kiss Me Again* 1925; *Other Women's Husbands* 1926; *Man Bait* 1926; *Up in Mabel's Room* 1926; *Getting Gertie's Garter* 1927; *A Blonde for a Night* 1928; *The Godless Girl* 1929; *Party Girl* 1930; *Sweethearts on Parade* 1930; *Reckless Living* 1931; *Three Wise Girls* 1932; *Parole Girl* 1933.

Priestly, Jason

Actor; b. Vancouver, 1969. Priestly's grandfather was a circus acrobat, and his mother, a ballerina. Priestly himself began working in television commercials as a child, but he focused on school sports until his graduation, when he landed guest appearances on the sitcom *21 Jump Street.* He was reportedly spotted by Tori Spelling, who encouraged her father, Aaron, to cast him as nice guy Brandon Walsh on *Beverly Hills 90210.* In film, Priestly made his mark in 1997 in *Love and Death on Long Island** with John Hurt. On the directorial front, Priestly started behind the camera with episodes of *90210* and moved to directing music videos for the Canadian band Barenaked Ladies – a warmup for the documentary, *Barenaked in America.* **Films and television include:** *The Boy Who Could Fly* 1986; *Nowhere to Run* 1989; *Sister Kate* 1989–90 (series); *Beverly Hills 90210* 1990–8 (series); *Calendar Girl* 1993; *Tombstone* 1993; *Love and Death on Long Island* 1997; *Eye of the Beholder* 1999; *Barenaked in America* 1999 (p/d/a); *Kiss Tomorrow Goodbye* 1999 (exp/d/a); *The Highwayman* 2000 (exp/a); *Homicide: The Movie* 2000 (TV).

Profession of Arms, The

1983 57m *prod* NFB, *exp* Barrie Howells, *p* Michael Bryans, Tina Viljoen, William Brind, John Kramer, *d* Michael Bryans, Tina Viljoen, *sc/narr* Gwynne Dyer, *ph* Douglas Kiefer, Paul Cowan, Susan Trow, Kent Nason, Andy Kitzanuk, Sava Kalogeras, *ed* Tina Viljoen, *mus* Larry Crosley. *The Possession of Arms,* part three of a seven-part NFB series entitled *War,* hosted by Gwynne Dyer, examines the nature, evolution, and consequences of modern warfare. With extraordinary frankness, officers from six countries recount combat experiences and explain how sophisticated technology is changing the nature of their profession. The film received an Academy Award nomination for Short Documentary. (V)

Prom Night

1980 92m *prod* Simcom, *exp* Deanne Judson, *p* Peter Simpson, *d* Paul Lynch, *sc* William Gray, *ph* Robert New, *ed* Brian Ravok, *mus* Paul Zaza, Carl Zitter; *with* Jamie Lee Curtis, Leslie Nielsen, Casey Stevens, Eddie Benton, Antoinette Bower. Fresh from the success of *Halloween*, Jamie Lee Curtis cemented her early reputation as the 'scream queen' with this slasher tale of revenge. Four witnesses to a young girl's accidental death years ago are targets of a stalking killer on the night of the high school prom. While definitely inferior to *Halloween* and *Carrie*, the two films that provide the framework for this low-budget knock-off, *Prom Night* survives as a cult favourite in the genre and is the subject of a trivia question in Wes Craven's *Scream*. The film also provided a franchise of sorts for producer Peter Simpson, since three terrible sequels of diminishing returns were made over the next twelve years. (V)

Q

Qualen, John

Actor; b. Vancouver, 1899; d. 1987. Of Norwegian parents, Qualen was born in Vancouver and brought up in Illinois. He got his start in vaudeville and appeared in more than 100 films, portraying a variety of character roles, often as a well-meaning patsy. He played the father of the Dionne Quints in *Five of a*

Kind and is perhaps best remembered as the crazed 'Muley' Graves in the 1940 John Ford classic, *The Grapes of Wrath*. **Films include:** *Street Scene* 1931; *Arrowsmith* 1931; *The Farmer Takes a Wife* 1935; *The Three Musketeers* 1935; *Seventh Heaven* 1937; *Nothing Sacred* 1937; *Five of a Kind* 1938; *His Girl Friday* 1940; *The Grapes of Wrath* 1940; *Long Voyage Home* 1940; *All That Money Can Buy* 1941; *Jungle Book* 1942; *The Arabian Nights* 1942; *Casablanca* 1943; *Song of Scheherazade* 1947; *Hans Christian Andersen* 1952; *The Searchers* 1956; *Anatomy of a Murder* 1959; *North to Alaska* 1960; *Two Rode Together* 1961; *The Man Who Shot Liberty Valance* 1962; *Cheyenne Autumn* 1964.

Quest for Fire

1982 110m *prod* International Cinema Corporation, Belstar Production (France), Stephan Films (France), *exp* Michael Gruskoff, *p* Denis Héroux, John Kemeny, *d* Jean-Jacques Annaud, *sc* Gérard Brach, *novel* J.-H. Rosny Sr, *language* Anthony Burgess, *adviser* Desmond Morris, *ph* Claude Agostini, *ed* Yves Langlois, *mus* Philippe Sarde; *with* Rae Dawn Chong, Everett McGill, Ron Pearlman, Nameer El-Kadi. *Quest for Fire* is difficult to take too seriously at any level and it compares poorly with Kubrick's *2001: A Space Odyssey*, a film dealing with similar themes of primitive growth leading to spiritual understanding. However, *Quest* succeeds by not taking itself seriously and is at times funny, tense, and touching, as three hapless humans (McGill, Pearlman, and El-Kadi) travel across a prehistoric landscape (shot in Kenya, Scotland, Iceland, and Northern Ontario) in search of live-preserving fire. Their language was created by Anthony Burgess and their body movements by Desmond Morris, author of *Naked Ape*. Rae Dawn Chong* stands out as a tribal nymphet who teaches the

trio how to make fire – and love. (V)
Awards include: GA: Actress (Chong),
Editing, Overall Sound, Sound Editing;
AA: Make-up.

Quiet Day in Belfast, A

1974 88m *prod* Vision IV Productions,
exp Milad Bassada, Stan Feldman, *p/d*
Milad Bassada, *sc* Jack Gray, *play*
Andrew Angus Dalrymple, *ph* Harry
Makin, *ed* Simon Christopher Dew, *mus*
Greg Adams, Eric Robertson; *with* Barry
Foster, Margot Kidder, Sean McCann,
Leo Leyden. *A Quiet Day in Belfast*, the
first Canadian dramatic feature to be
shot on location, suffers from an uncertain script and lacklustre direction. Although it tries to take an even-handed
approach to 'the troubles' of Northern
Ireland, the characters are cardboard
cut outs and first-time director Milad
Bassada can't seem to get a handle on
the material. The result is a flat, stilted
film that offers only a few interesting
patches. **Awards include:** CFA: Actress
(Kidder).

R

Rabid

1977 91m *prod* DAL Productions, *exp*
André Link, Ivan Reitman, *p* John Dunning, *d/sc* David Cronenberg, *ph* René
Verzier, *ed* Jean Lafleur, *mus* Ivan
Reitman; *with* Marilyn Chambers, Frank
Moore, Joe Silver, Patricia Gage. *Rabid*
combines some of director David Cronenberg's* most unpleasant obsessions
while he was working with cheaper
budgets (when many fans argue he was
at his best). The film features porn star-
let Marilyn Chambers as a woman
whose plastic surgery operation leads to
her being stung by a wicked bloodlust
(much like a vampire), and she infects
her victims with a form of rabies. Typically, *Rabid* has dark humour, some
rather campy gore, and Chambers bares
it all for the camera. Not for all tastes,
undoubtedly, but essential viewing for
students and enthusiasts of Cronenberg.
(V)

Raffé, Alexandra

Producer; b. Singapore, 1955. Raffé, who
came to Canada in 1978, spent ten years
with Xerox before finding her calling as
a hands-on producer of Patricia Rozema's* wildly successful *I've Heard the
Mermaids Singing.* Coming just one year
after the creation of the Ontario Film
Development Corporation (OFDC), the
success of *Mermaids* launched Toronto's
new wave* and led the way to the smart
film festival and commercial marketing
of a series of low-budget films by Atom
Egoyan,* Bruce McDonald,* Peter
Mettler,* and others. Raffé's next film,
Rozema's *White Room*, didn't fare so
well, but she regained her footing with
three films in 1993: *I Love a Man in Uniform,* The Lotus Eaters,* and John Greyson's* groundbreaking gay musical *Zero
Patience.* Raffé served as head of the
OFDC from 1995 to 1998. **Films include:**
Passion: A Letter in 16mm 1985; *I've Heard
the Mermaids Singing* 1987; *White Room*
1990; *Battle of the Bulge* 1991; *The Lotus
Eaters* 1993; *I Love a Man in Uniform* 1993;
Zero Patience 1994.

Rain, Douglas

Actor; b. Winnipeg, 1928. A classically
trained actor who studied his craft at the
Old Vic Theatre School in London, Rain
has pursued a successful career on the
stage. However, when director Stanley
Kubrick went looking for a 'smoothing'
voice for HAL 9000, the computer who
takes control of the flight to Jupiter in
2001: A Space Odyssey, he found it in
Rain. Rain repeated the role in the sequel, *2010*, and Woody Allen used him

to great effect for the voice of the evil computer in *Sleeper*. **Films and television include:** *Oedipus Rex* 1957; *1+1: Exploring the Kinsey Reports* 1961; *Henry v* 1966 (TV); *2001: A Space Odyssey* 1968 (voice); *Sleeper* 1973 (voice); *The Man Who Skied down Everest* 1975 (narr); *2010* 1984 (voice); *Love and Larceny* 1985 (TV); *Donald Brittain: Filmmaker* 1992 (narr).

Ransen, Mort
Director, producer, and writer; b. Montreal, 1933. Like many of his contemporaries, Mort Ransen began his filmmaking career at the NFB and later moved into private-sector production. While at the Board, he made a number of short documentary portraits of his restless generation culminating, in 1968, in his direction of one of the most peculiar, engaging, and telling examinations of the 1960s ever filmed, *Christopher's Movie Matinee*. After producing several notable shorts in the 1970s, Ransen left the NFB in 1984 to work independently, turning his attention to feature dramas such as *Bayo* and *Falling over Backwards*. His 1996 film, *Margaret's Museum,** won rave reviews both internationally and in Canada, and captured a multitude of Genie Awards. **Films include:** *Jacky Visits the Zoo* 1962 (d/sc); *John Hirsch: A Portrait of a Man and a Theatre* 1965 (d); *No Reason to Stay* 1966 (d/co-sc); *The Circle* 1967 (d/sc); *Christopher's Movie Matinee* 1969 (d/ed); *You Are on Indian Land* 1969 (d); *Untouched and Pure* 1970 (co-d); *The Street* 1976 (voice); *Running Time* 1978 (d/sc/ed/mus); *The Masculine Mystique* 1985 (a); *Bayo* 1985 (d/co-sc); *Falling over Backwards* 1990 (co-p/d/sc); *Margaret's Museum* 1996 (p/d/co-sc).

Raoul Wallenberg: Buried Alive
1983 78m *prod* Rubicon Film Productions, *exp/ph* David Yorke, *p* Wayne Arron, David Harel, *d* David Harel, *sc* Peter David Lauterman, David Harel, *ed* Roushell Goldstein, *mus* Tony Kosinee, Jack Lenz, *narr* Pierre Berton. This detailed and well-researched documentary tells the story of Raoul Wallenberg, the extraordinary Swedish diplomat who personally managed to save thousands of Hungarian Jews during the Holocaust only to be arrested by the Russians after the war, accused of being an American spy. The key strength of the film is the numerous interviews with survivors who personally owe their lives to Wallenberg's intervention. He created legal-looking Swedish visas to fool the Nazis (fully understanding the German obsession for bureaucratic formality) and literally snatched people from the jaws of death. The last part of the film focuses on the persistent rumours of Wallenberg's life in the Soviet Gulags. **Awards include:** GA: Feature Documentary.

Raquetteurs, Les
1958 15m *prod* NFB, *p* Louis Portugais, *d* Gilles Groulx, Michel Brault, *ph* Michel Brault, *ed* Gilles Groulx. This early direct-cinema documentary about a convention of snowshoers held in Sherbrooke in 1958 provdes a revealing and sympathetic portrait of ritual and communal life in rural Quebec. It is an important film that marked the beginnings of the French unit at the NFB and established cinematographer and director Michel Brault* as a major force in the documentary movement in Canada and abroad.

Rasky, Harry
Director, writer, and producer; b. Toronto, 1928. This internationally acclaimed Canadian filmmaker is best known for his biographies of famous people including *The Song of Leonard Cohen*, *Homage to Chagall: The Colours of Love*, and *Stratasphere*. Rasky's unique,

innovative documentary films have often been dubbed 'Raskymentaries' for their combination of documentary and fiction-film elements. Rasky began his career as a newspaper and radio journalist and then wrote and directed CBC news programs in the early 1950s. From 1957 through the 1960s, he made freelance documentaries for every major English-language network, and is considered a 'chronicler of greatness and historical atrocities.' **Films include:** *An Invitation to a Royal Wedding* 1972; *Tennessee Williams' South* 1973; *Next Year in Jerusalem* 1974; *Homage to Chagall: The Colours of Love* 1977; *The Peking Man Mystery* 1977; *Arthur Miller on Home Ground* 1981; *The Song of Leonard Cohen* 1981; *Being Different* 1981; *Stratasphere* 1984; *Karsh: The Searching Eye* 1986; *The War against the Indians* 1992; *Prophecy* 1995.

Rat Life and Diet in North America
1968 14m *p/d/ph/ed* Joyce Wieland. Wieland's* funniest and most political film, a narrative of sorts, follows the adventures of a pair of rodents who escape their feline captors to journey to Canada in search of freedom. Remaining true to her structuralist roots, Wieland plays with narrative convention, disrupting the flow of the story with everything from title cards to messy splices. Thematically, the film marked the beginning of a particularly nationalistic time in Wieland's life and art, as she reached beyond pure formalism to make a political statement. *Rat Life* is not just a parable of oppression and rebellion, but also an incisive comment about the dangers of U.S. imperialism, cultural or otherwise.

Raymont, Peter
Director and producer; b. Ottawa, 1950. Raymont, a graduate of Queen's University, worked as a producer, director, and editor at the NFB from 1972 to 1978. In

1978, he formed his own company, Investigative Productions, and has since produced and directed documentaries, mostly for CBC and for PBS in the United States. Raymont is a socially and politically engaged filmmaker, and his films have covered a wide range of topics from a Conservative leadership convention to the plight of Jews in Africa and American manipulation of news from Central America. He was a founding member of the Canadian Independent Film Caucus. **Films and television include:** *River, Planet Earth* 1974 (d); *The Working Class on Film* 1975 (co-d); *Flora: Scenes from a Leadership Convention* 1977 (d/sc/ed); *The Art of the Possible* 1978 (d/sc/ed); *Magic in the Sky* 1981 (p/d/sc); *Falasha: Exile of the Black Jews* 1982 (d, TV); *Prisoners of Debt: Inside the Global Banking Crisis* 1982 (d, TV); *On the Polar Sea: A Yukon Adventure* 1983 (co-p/d/co-sc, TV); *The Brokers* 1984 (p/d); *With Our Own Two Hands* 1985 (p/d, TV); *Haiti: The Politics of Aid* 1987 (p/sc, TV); *The World Is Watching* 1988 (p/d/co-sc, GA-SD); *As Long as the Rivers Flow* 1991 (p, series); *Voices from the Shadows* 1992 (p/d, TV); *Hearts of Hate* 1994 (p/d/co-sc, TV); *The Sceptic's Journey* 1995 (d/sc/narr, TV); *Invisible Nation: Policing the Underground* 1996 (p, TV); *A Scattering of Seeds: The Creation of Canada* 1998 (p, series); *The New Ice Age: A Year in the Life of the NHL* 1998 (p/d, series); *Toronto: City of Dreams* 2000 (p, TV).

Razutis, Al
Filmmaker; b. Bamberg, Germany, 1946. This Vancouver-based teacher, critic, and filmmaker produced two major cycles of thematically linked short experimental films: *Amerika*, an epic, phantasmagoric, and decidedly dystopian descent into the gloom of western industrialized society; and *Visual Essays: Origins of Film*, described by Razutis as a

'structural investigation of the primitive silent cinema.' In these larger works and in more recent films, Razutis's frequently ferocious interrogations of contemporary culture utilize a variety of optical and sonic techniques (collage, layering, etc.) to penetrate and illuminate the contours of the cacophony of modernity. **Films include:** *Amerika* 1972–83 (Reel 1: *The Cities of Eden, Software / Head Title, Vortex, Atomic Gardening, Motel Row Part I, Refrain, 98.3 KHz: Bridge at Electrical Storm, Motel Row Part II*. Reel 2: *The Wasteland and Other Stories ..., Refrain, Motel Row Part III, 98.3 KHz: Bridge at Electrical Storm Part II, The Wildwest Show, A Message from Our Sponsor, Photo Spot/ Terminal Cityscapes*. Reel 3: *Refrain, Exiles, The Lonesome Death of Leroy Brown, [Fin; O Kanada], Closing Credits*); *Visual Essays: Origins of Film* 1973–84 (*Lumière's Train [Arriving at the Station], Méliès Catalogue, Sequels in Transfigured Time, Ghost: Image, For Artaud, Storming the Winter Palace*).

Reaction: A Portrait of Society in Crisis

1974 58m *prod* NFB, *p* Tom Daly, Normand Cloutier, Robin Spry, *d* Robin Spry, *ph* Douglas Keifer, *ed* Shelagh Mackenzie. *Reaction* was shot during the October Crisis of 1970 when a British diplomat was kidnapped and a Quebec cabinet minister killed, and is a companion film to *Action: The October Crisis of 1970*.* It provides a portrait of a minority community under pressure, as anglophones candidly express their feelings about what is happening around them. (V)

Reason over Passion

1969 82m *prod* Corrective Films, *p/d/ph/ ed/m* Joyce Wieland. Experimental film doyenne Joyce Wieland* once described her feature film as being 'about the pain

and joy of living in a very large space.' Structured in three parts with a prelude, the film contains the national anthem, a dissection of Pierre Trudeau's affirmation that reason over passion is the theme of his intellectual and political project, and fleeting images of Canada's vast territories. Wieland's film, a sprawling, heterogenous, contentious, experimental road movie, not only dissents from Trudeau's rationalist certainty, but also offers one of the most haunting journeys you'll ever take across the gargantuan land we call, however tenuously, home.

Red Violin, The

1998 138m *prod* Rhombus Media, Mikado Films (Italy), New Line Cinema (U.S.), Channel Four (U.K.), *p* Niv Fichman, *d* François Girard, *sc* Don McKellar, François Girard, *ph* Alain Dostie, *ed* Gaetan Huot, *mus* John Corigliano; *with* Samuel L. Jackson, Greta Scacchi, Jason Flemyng, Sylvia Chang, Colm Feore, Don McKellar, Carlo Cecchi, Christoph Koncz. The story of an ill-fated 'red' violin is told through its various owners. From its creator, a seventeenth-century master violinmaker (Cecchi), the instrument passes through the ages to a child prodigy (Koncz), an English virtuoso (Flemyng), a Chinese Communist official (Chang), and finally to a Montreal auction room where it is coveted by many, but stolen at the last moment by a musicologist (Jackson) hired to prove its authenticity. The film is epic in scope, intelligently realized by screenwriters McKellar* and Girard,* and well directed by Girard. It is perhaps overly long and falters on occasion, but it is visually magnificent, with meticulous period recreations and an Academy Award–winning classical score. The film was a box-office hit and is the most successful art-house Canadian feature made to date. (V) **Awards include:** GA: Picture, Director, Original Screenplay, Cinematography, Art Direction, Costumes, Musical Score, Overall Sound; PJ: Picture, Director, Screenplay, Supporting Actor (Feore), Cinematography, Editing, Art Direction, Sound; AA: Musical Score.

Reeves, Keanu
Actor; b. Beirut, Lebanon, 1965. Toronto-trained Reeves moved quickly from the troubled teens in *River's Edge* and *The Prince of Pennsylvania* to the goofy but goodhearted dude in *Bill and Ted's Excellent Adventure* and its sequel to classical roles in *Dangerous Liaisons* and *Much Ado about Nothing*. His straightforward approach and good looks made him a major star in *Speed*. With the phenomenal success of *The Matrix*, Reeves has become one of the highest-paid actors in Hollywood. **Films include:** *Youngblood* 1986; *River's Edge* 1987; *The Prince of Pennsylvania* 1988; *Dangerous Liaisons* 1988; *Bill and Ted's Excellent Adventure* 1989; *I Love You to Death* 1990; *Bill and Ted's Bogus Journey* 1991; *My Own Private Idaho* 1991; *Bram Stoker's Dracula* 1992; *Much Ado about Nothing* 1993; *Little Buddha* 1993; *Speed* 1994; *Johnny Mnemonic* 1995; *A Walk in the Clouds* 1995; *Chain Reaction* 1996; *Devil's Advocate* 1997; *The Matrix* 1999; *The Replacements* 2000; *The Watcher* 2000; *The Gift* 2000; *Sweet November* 2001.

Regeneration
1998 113m *prod* Rafford Films, Norstar Entertainment, BBC Films (U.K.), The Scottish Arts Council (U.K.), *exp* Saskia Sutton, Mark Shivas, *p* Allan Scott, Peter Simpson, *d* Gilles MacKinnon, *sc* Allan Scott, *novel* Pat Barker, *ph* Glen MacPherson, *ed* Pia Di Ciaula, *mus* Mychael Danna; *with* Jonathan Pryce, James Wilby, Jonny Lee Miller, Stuart Bunce, Tanya Allen. *Regeneration* is a fictionalized account of a historical encounter in 1917, between noted psychologist William Rivers (Pryce) and British war poets Siegfried Sassoon (Wilby) and Wilfred Owen (Bunce) in a Scottish mental hospital. The film, based on Pat Barker's Booker Prize–winning novel, is beautifully shot, and features an especially fine performance by Pryce as the conflicted doctor who understands that if he is successful in curing his shell-shocked patients they will be sent back to the front to die. Unfortunately, this intense exploration of ideas – the nature of courage, art, suffering, emotional ravages of war and healing – lacks dramatic focus. (V)

Région centrale, La
1971 180m *p/d* Michael Snow, *ph* Pierre Abbeloos. In a brilliant convergence of form and content, camera movement becomes the *raison d'être*. Rarely, if ever, has a film so clearly delineated the role of this machine in our reception and perception of the object filmed. To make the film, Michael Snow* worked with a technician to design a mechanized camera that was able to move without human intervention in every direction imaginable. To further erase the influence of humans, Snow filmed in the remote reaches of Northern Quebec, where his camera roamed the landscape, in a manner both systematic and arbitrary. *La Région centrale* is not just a dry technological experiment, it is both an exhilarating celebration of cinema's unique qualities and a clever joke on the landscape tradition in Canadian art.

Règne du jour, Le
1967 118m *prod* NFB, *p* Jacques Bobet, Guy L. Coté, *d* Pierre Perrault, *ph* Bernard Gosselin, Jean-Claude Labrecque, *ed* Yves Leduc, Jean Lepage. This film, the second in a trilogy (see also *Pour la*

suite du monde* and Les Voitures d'eau*)
follows the extended Tremblay family as
they travel to western France to discover
their roots. Director Pierre Perrault*
records their reactions to contradictions
between the real France and the imaginary homeland they had envisioned.
Back home on Île-aux-Coudres, the
Tremblays discuss their impressions and
feelings of cultural isolation. Perrault, a
committed separatist who initiated the
trip, produced the film as a profound
expression of Québécois reality. **Awards
include:** CFA: Cinematography (B+W),
Overall Sound.

Reid, Kate
Actor; b. Daphne Kate Reid, London,
U.K., 1930; d. 1993. Kate Reid, one of
Canada's most respected and talented
dramatic actresses, was at home on the
stage, radio, television, and film. She
grew up in Oakville, Ontario, and studied at the Royal Conservatory of Music
in Toronto. In 1952, she appeared with
Lorne Greene* in Ted Allan's The Money
Makers, the first Canadian stage play to
be transferred to television. She played a
variety of major roles on Broadway, including Martha in the original stage
version of Who's Afraid of Virginia Woolf.
Her Canadian films were mostly tax-
shelter-era* bombs, but she distinguished herself as Burt Lancaster's nagging
girlfriend in Atlantic City,* for which she
won a Genie for Best Supporting Actress. **Films and television include:** A
Dangerous Age 1958; 1 + 1 (Exploring the
Kinsey Reports) 1961; The Invincible Mr
Disraeli 1963 (TV); This Property Is Condemned 1966; The Andromeda Strain 1971;
The Best Damn Fiddler from Calagbogie to
Kaladar 1968 (TV); The White Oaks of Jalna
1972 (series); The Rainbow Boys 1973; A
Delicate Balance 1973 (TV); Shoot 1976;
Equus 1977; Plague 1979; Crossbar 1979

(TV); Circle of Two 1981; Death Ship 1980;
Atlantic City 1980 (GA-SA); Double Nega-
tive 1982; Dallas 1982–3 (series, as Aunt
Lil Trotter); The Blood of Others 1984;
Highpoint 1984; No Sad Songs 1985 (narr);
Death of a Salesman 1985 (TV); Christmas
Eve 1986 (TV); Sweet Hearts Dance 1988;
Signs of Life 1989; Bye Bye Blues 1989;
Raw Nerve 1990; The Last Best Year 1990
(TV); Deceived 1991; Teamster Boss: The
Jackie Presser Story 1992 (TV); Murder in
the Heartland 1993 (TV).

Reitman, Ivan
Director and producer; b. Czechoslovakia, 1950. Reitman has been directing
and producing films since his student
days at McMaster University, and has
been associated with some of the biggest
box-office successes in Canadian cinema. He produced Cronenberg's* first
two features, Shivers* and Rabid,* and
the animated Heavy Metal,* and he directed Meatballs.* In the United States
since the late 1970s, he produced National Lampoon's Animal House, John
Belushi's first film, and went on to build
an impressive career as one of the most
reliable and successful director-produc-
ers in Hollywood with a string of hits
such as Stripes, Ghostbusters (one of the
most successful comedies of all time and
a big part of 1980s pop culture), Twins,
Ghostbusters ii, Kindergarten Cop, Dave,
and Father's Day. **Films include:** The
Columbus of Sex 1969 (p/ph); Foxy Lady
1971 (p/d/ed/mus); Cannibal Girls 1973
(exp/d); Shivers 1975 (p/mus); Death
Weekend 1976 (p/mus); Rabid 1977 (exp/
mus); Ilsa the Tigress of Siberia 1977 (exp);
Blackout 1978 (exp); National Lampoon's
Animal House 1978 (co-p); Meatballs 1979
(d); Heavy Metal 1981 (p, GRA); Stripes
1981 (p/d); Spacehunter: Adventures in the
Forbidden Zone 1983 (exp); Ghostbusters
1984 (p/d); Twins 1988 (p/d); Ghost-

busters ɪɪ 1989 (p/d); *Kindergarten Cop* 1990 (p/d); *Beethoven* 1992 (p); *Dave* 1993 (p/d); *Junior* 1994 (p/d); *Space Jam* 1996 (p); *Father's Day* 1997 (p/d); *Six Days, Seven Nights* 1998 (p/d); *Road Trip* 2000 (exp).

Réjeanne Padovani

1973 94m *prod* Cinak Compagnie Cinématographique, *p* Marguerite Duparc, *d* Denys Arcand, *sc* Denys Arcand, Jacques Benoit, *ph* Alain Dostie, *ed* Marguerite Duparc, Denys Arcand, *mus* Christoph Willibald Glück, Walter Boudreau; *with* Luce Guilbeault, Jean Lajeunesse, Roger Lebel, Margot McKinnon, René Caron, Pierre Thériault, Frédérique Collin, Céline Lomez. *Réjeanne Padovani* is about a corrupt Montreal-area contractor (Lajeunesse), his political entourage, hired thugs, and divorced wife (Guilbeault), who only wants to see her children. The occasion is a party to celebrate the opening of a new highway. While the rich and powerful dine and drink upstairs, the strong-arm types hang out with cops and hookers in the basement. When the wife shows up unannounced, she sets in motion a series of events that ultimately leads to her death and burial beneath the highway. This biting social satire helped establish Denys Arcand's* reputation as one of Quebec's top directors and as one not afraid to tackle political matters in feature films. **Awards include:** CFA: Original Screenplay.

Rennie, Callum Keith

Actor; b. Sunderland, U.K., 1960. Raised in Edmonton, Rennie did not begin acting until the age of twenty-five, when he appeared on stage at the Edmonton Fringe Festival. Mina Shum's *Double Happiness** marked the point where film audiences sat up and took note of his performance abilities, and he followed up with a lead in *Curtis's Charm*. Rennie

locked in the cult crowd with Bruce McDonald's* mock-documentary, *Hard Core Logo,** at which point he landed in the popular television series *Due South* opposite Paul Gross.* He has also done a rash of edgy film and television projects, including Don McKellar's *Last Night,** the television series *Twitch City*, and David Cronenberg's *eXistenZ.** **Films and television include:** *Frank's Cock* 1994; *Timecop* 1994; *Valentine's Day* 1994; *Double Happiness* 1995; *Falling from the Sky: Flight 174* 1995 (TV); *Little Criminals* 1995; *Curtis's Charm* 1996; *Hard Core Logo* 1996; *Letters from Home* 1996; *Unforgettable* 1996; *My Life as a Dog* 1996 (series); *For Those Who Hunt the Wounded Down* 1996 (TV); *Due South* 1997–9 (series); *Men with Guns* 1997; *Excess Baggage* 1997; *Masterminds* 1997; *Last Night* 1998 (GA-SA); *Twitch City* 1998, 2000 (series); *The Life before This* 1999; *eXistenZ* 1999; *The Highwayman* 2000; *Torso* 2001 (TV); *Momento* 2001.

Rennie, James

Actor; b. Toronto, 1889; d. 1965. Rennie, a minor, handsome leading man during the silent period, was more famous for his marriage to Dorothy Gish (the younger sister of Lillian) in 1920 than he was for his acting roles. His marriage didn't survive, but his career continued well into the 1940s.

Rhapsody in Two Languages

1934 11m *prod* Associated Screen News, *d/sc/ed* Gordon Sparling, *ph* Alfred Jacquemin, *mus* Howard Fogg. This short, the most famous of the *Canadian Cameo* series by Gordon Sparling,* depicts Montreal from sunrise to sunset with the use of music and special optical effects.

Richardson, Boyce

Director and writer; b. New Zealand,

1928. Richardson worked as a journalist and editor with the *Montreal Star* from 1957 to 1971, and then joined the NFB's Challenge for Change* program in 1971. He wrote and directed a number of films on the Northern Cree with director and cinematographer Tony Ianzelo.* In the late 1970s, he travelled to China with Ianzelo for a series of films on the people living in the Chinese communist state. **Films include:** *Chissibi – la mort d'un fleuve* 1973 (co-d); *Cree Hunters of Mistassini* 1974 (sc/narr/co-d with Tony Ianzelo, CFA-FD); *Our Land Is Our Life* 1974 (sc/co-d with Ianzelo); *North China Commune* 1979 (d with Ianzelo); *North China Factory* 1980 (d with Ianzelo); *China: A Land Transformed* 1980 (d with Ianzelo); *Moving Pictures* 2000 (co-sc).

Richler, Mordecai
Writer; b. Montreal, 1931; d. 2001. Richler, who grew up in the Jewish immigrant section of Montreal, was an acerbic satirist with one recurring theme. In his various screenplays, including adaptations of his novels *The Apprenticeship of Duddy Kravitz* * (a credit he shared with Lionel Chetwynd*) and *Joshua Then and Now,* * both of which were directed by close friend Ted Kotcheff,* Richler focused on the sense of failure that can accompany material success. In the 1975 Academy Award–nominated *Duddy*, the twitching hustler (played by Richard Dreyfuss), is revealed to be missing something at his core. In a 1965 British picture, *Life at the Top* (also directed by Kotcheff), man-on-the-make Joe Lampton (Laurence Harvey) suffers from a double dose of dissatisfaction as he deals with the perils of upward mobility and an unhappy marriage. **Films include:** *The Wild and Willing* 1962 (co-sc); *Life at the Top* 1965 (sc); *The Apprenticeship of Duddy Kravitz* 1974 (co-sc, AAN-ASC); *Fun with Dick and Jane* 1976 (co-sc); *Joshua Then and Now* 1985 (sc).

Rimmer, David
Filmmaker; b. Vancouver, 1942. Vancouver-based David Rimmer, one of Canadian experimental cinema's most internationally acclaimed filmmakers, has assembled a remarkable body of meditative, subtle films that expose and investigate the material properties of the very images of which they are constituted. His most celebrated early films include *Surfacing on the Thames* * and *Canadian Pacific.* * Rimmer's more recent films (*Black Cat, White Cat* and *Lizard Music*) have merged his philosophical and aesthetic preoccupations in a striking stylistic hybrid of documentary and diary, infused with the insistent interrogations of image and epistemology that is evident in his earlier work. **Films include:** *Treefall* 1970; *Variations on a Cellophane Wrapper* 1970; *Surfacing on the Thames* 1970; *Real Italian Pizza* 1971; *Watching for the Queen* 1973; *Canadian Pacific* 1974; *Canadian Pacific* II 1975; *Shades of Red* 1982; *As Seen on TV* 1986; *Along the Road to Altamira* 1986; *Black Cat, White Cat. It's a Good Cat If It Catches the Mouse* 1989; *Local Knowledge* 1992; *Jack Wise: Language of the Body* 1998.

Rip-Off
1971 88m *prod* Phoenix Film Productions, *p* Bennet Fode, *d* Don Shebib, *sc* William Fruet, *ph* Richard Leiterman, *ed* Don Shebib, Tony Lower, *mus* Murray McLauchlan, Gene Martynec; *with* Don Scardino, Ralph Endersby, Mike Kukulewich, Peter Gross, Susan Petrie. Director Don Shebib's* second feature (sandwiched between the far superior *Goin' down the Road* * and *Between Friends**) is a light-hearted, coming-of-age story about four high school friends desperately trying to be hip and gain acceptance among their peers. A disastrous weekend in the country, where the four try to establish a commune, leads them to discover the realities of life.

Roadkill

1990 80m *prod* Mr. Shack Motion Pictures, *exp* Keith Bates, *p* Colin Brunton, Bruce McDonald, *d* Bruce McDonald, *sc* Don McKellar, *ph* Miroslaw Baszak, *ed* Mike Munn, *mus* Nash the Slash, The Cowboy Junkies, The Ramones; *with* Valerie Buhagiar, Don McKellar, Larry Hudson, Gerry Quigley, Earl Pasko, Bruce McDonald. *Roadkill*, one of the most original films to emerge from the Toronto new wave,* is director Bruce McDonald's* debut feature. Described as a rock 'n' roll road movie, it concerns the adventures of Ramona (Buhagiar), a naive assistant to a maniacal rock promoter (Quigley), who is sent to track down a band called the Children of Paradise who have gone missing in Northern Ontario. She comes across a pot-addled cabbie (Hudson), a rock-video crew led by a director (McDonald) with visions of widescreen grandeur, and an aspiring serial killer (McKellar*). Ramona eventually does find the band, but it ultimately matters less than what she discovers about herself. (V)

Roberge, Guy

Administrator; b. St-Ferdinand-d'Halifax, Que., 1915. Roberge, who was film commissioner and head of the NFB from 1957 to 1965, was the first French Canadian to hold that position. He initiated many changes at the Board, including scrapping the long-running theatrical series *Canada Carries On** and initiating French-language film and television production. Roberge lobbied persistently for the creation of a feature-film fund that would stand apart from the NFB and the CBC. He took the matter to cabinet but was transferred to Paris as the *agent général* for Quebec before the legislation to create the Canadian Film Development Corporation (now Telefilm Canada) was enacted by Parliament in 1967.

Robertson, John

Director; b. London, Ont., 1878; d. 1964. This likeable, lightweight director of the silent era began as an actor for Vitagraph in 1915, but soon switched to directing. Probably his best-known silent film was the John Barrymore version of *Dr. Jekyll and Mr. Hyde* (1920). He also directed such stars as Greta Garbo and fellow expat Mary Pickford* in her 1922 remake of *Tess of the Storm Country*.

Robson, Mark

Director and editor; b. Montreal, 1913; d. 1978. Robson, who was educated at the University of California at Los Angeles, was a respected Hollywood craftsman. He began as a prop boy for Fox and became Robert Wise's assistant, editing *Citizen Kane* (uncredited) and *The Magnificent Ambersons* (credited). He directed Boris Karloff in *Isle of the Dead* and *Bedlam*, and Humphrey Bogart in *The Harder They Fall*, and he received back-to-back Academy Award–nominations for the trashy, but influential *Peyton Place* and the Ingrid Bergman hit, *Inn of the Sixth Happiness*. His most commercial success came at the end of his career in 1974 with *Earthquake*. **Films include:** *The Magnificent Ambersons* 1942 (co-ed); *Cat People* 1942 (ed); *Journey into Fear* 1943 (ed); *I Walked with a Zombie* 1949 (ed); *Isle of the Dead* 1945 (d); *Bedlam* 1946 (d/co-sc); *Home of the Brave* 1949 (d); *Champion* 1949 (d); *Phffft* 1954 (d); *The Bridges at Toko-Ri* 1955 (d); *The Harder They Fall* 1956 (d); *Peyton Place* 1957 (d, AAN-D); *Inn of the Sixth Happiness* 1958 (d, AAN-D); *From the Terrace* 1960 (p/d); *Nine Hours to Rama* 1963 (p/d); *The Prize* 1963 (d); *Von Ryan's Express* 1965 (exp/d); *Lost Command* 1966 (p/d); *Valley of the Dolls* 1967 (exp/d); *Happy Birthday Wanda June* 1971 (d); *Earthquake* 1974 (p/d); *Avalanche Express* 1979 (d).

Roffman, Julian

Producer and director; b. Montreal, 1919; d. 2000. A cross-border director who made most of his films in the United States, Roffman was responsible for two notable low-budget horror films: *The Bloody Brood*, and *The Mask*, the only 3-D feature to be made in Canada. He studied film in New York and in 1940 joined the NFB where he became responsible for the Armed Service Production Program. In the late 1950s, he joined forces with distributor Nat Taylor* to form Taylor-Roffman Productions and produce the two features. *The Mask* was the first Canadian feature to be extensively marketed in the United States. **Films include:** *The Bloody Brood* 1959 (p/d); *The Mask* 1961 (p/d); *Explosion* 1969 (p); *The Pyx* 1973 (p); *The Glove* 1978 (d/sc).

Rolling Stones at the Max

1991 85m *prod* The BCL Group, Imax Corp., Promotour U.S. (U.S.), *exp* Michael Cohl, André Picard, *d* Julien Temple, Roman Kroitor, David Douglas, Noel Archambault, *ph* David Douglas, Andrew Kitzanuk, Haskell Wexler, *ed* Daniel Blevins; *mus/with* The Rolling Stones. This IMAX production, shot during the Rolling Stones 1990 Steel Wheels tour, was not only the first concert film but also the first feature-length film to be made in the IMAX format. It is, without a doubt, the best concert film of the legendary 'greatest rock 'n' roll band in the world.'

Romance of Transportation in Canada, The

1953 11m *prod* NFB, *p/ed* Tom Daly, *d* Colin Low, *sc* Guy Glover, *an* Wolf Koenig, Robert Verrall, *ph* Lyle Enright, *mus* Eldon Rathburn, *narr* Max Ferguson. Colin Low's* whimsical look at the development of transportation since the arrival of the Europeans, part of the *Canada Carries On** series, was a major breakthrough in character animation at the NFB. It was influenced not by the abstract style of animation of pioneered by Norman McLaren,* but instead by the popular United Productions of America style. The film uses incident and a plot line to tell the story – with wit and tongue-in-cheek seriousness – of how Canada's vast distances and great obstacles have been overcome. **Awards include:** AAN: Animated Short; Cannes: Palme d'or for animation.

Rowdyman, The

1972 94m *prod* Canart Films, *exp* Budge Crawley, *p* Lawrence Dane, *d* Peter Carter, *sc* Gordon Pinsent, *ph* Edmund Long, *ed* Michael C. Manne, *mus* Ben McPeek; *with* Gordon Pinsent, Frank Converse, Will Geer, Linda Goranson. Will Cole (Pinsent*), a rebellious, irresponsible Newfoundlander, takes a carefree attitude to his life, but reality catches up to him when the old man who was his mentor (played effectively by Geer) lies on his deathbed. Cole must take responsibility for a friend's (Converse) death in an industrial accident and deal with the departure of his girlfriend (Goranson) for Toronto. *The Rowdyman* is based on Pinsent's screenplay, and director Carter* provided him with a generous cinematic background for his comedic and dramatic talents. The film, which became Pinsent's calling card, was popular at the time of its release and still stands up as one of the best films ever made about life on the Rock. **Awards include:** CFA: Actor (Pinsent).

Royal Journey

1951 54m *prod* NFB, *p* Tom Daly, *d* David Bairstow, Gudrun Parker, *sc* Leslie McFarlene, *ph* Osmond Borradaile,

Grant McLean, *ed* Ronald Dick, Victor Jobin, *mus* Louis Applebaum, *narr* Elwood Glover. This documentary account of the five-week visit of young Princess Elizabeth to Canada and the United States in the fall of 1951 was the first major film to use the single emulsion Eastmancolor stock. With its theatrical release in Canada, it quickly became the most popular film made by the NFB up to that time. **Awards include:** CFA: Feature Film.

Rozema, Patricia

Director, producer, and writer; b. Kingston, Ont., 1958. Patricia Rozema, one of Canada's most accomplished and internationally recognized filmmakers, was raised in Sarnia, Ontario, by Dutch Calvinist parents. Throughout her narrative feature film work she has maintained an elegant feminist consciousness while drawing male characters with compassion. Most notably, Rozema has established herself as an exceptional and distinctly sensual visual stylist. Her films are characterized by self-referential narration, idiosyncratic protagonists (who are often struggling artists), formal adventurousness, and the use of fairy tales, mythology, and poetry as structuring notions. Rozema's debut feature is one of Canada's most celebrated and circulated success stories. *I've Heard the Mermaids Singing,** a serious comedy about a socially inept Girl Friday (a standout performance by Sheila McCarthy*) was made for a mere $350,000, and was remarkably successful not only critically, but also commercially. The film went on to win the coveted Prix de la Jeunesse at Cannes in 1987 and was recently voted one of the Top Ten Canadian films of the century. Rozema followed up this success with *White Room*, an ambitious and dark contemporary tale of fame. In her third feature, the semi-autobiographical

*When Night Is Falling,** Rozema crafts a lyrical lesbian love story involving a Christian professor and a circus performer. Her subsequent project, the richly textured *Six Gestures* (part of the *Yo-Yo Ma Inspired by Bach* series), was awarded a Prime Time Emmy. Rozema's next two films, however, marked an exit from Canadian production. *Mansfield Park* (U.K.) is a sophisticated revisionist adaptation of Jane Austen's novel, and *Happy Days*, an Irish production, is a film version of Samuel Beckett's absurdly despairing play in which a woman lives partially buried in a mound. **Films include:** *Passion: A Letter in 16mm* 1985 (d); *I've Heard the Mermaids Singing* 1987 (co-p/d/sc/ed); *White Room* 1990 (exp/d/sc/ed); *Montréal vu par ...* 1991 (co-d/co-sc); *When Night Is Falling* 1995 (d/sc); *Curtis's Charm* 1996 (exp); *Six Gestures* from *Yo-Yo Ma Inspired by Bach* 1997 (d/sc, TV); *Mansfield Park* 1999 (d/sc); *Happy Days* 2000 (d); *This Might Be Good* from *Preludes* 2000 (d/sc).

Rubbo, Michael

Director, producer, writer, and editor; b. Melbourne, Australia, 1938. Rubbo was both a student in anthropology and an experienced traveller. His MA thesis on film at Stanford University, *The True Source of Knowledge*, landed him a job at the NFB, where he worked until 1984. He made a series of films dealing with humanitarian issues, including *Sad Song of Yellow Skin* in Vietnam and *Waiting for Fidel* in Cuba, often featuring himself as a deliberately intrusive on-screen presence. His departure from the Board coincided with a move into children's fiction. He directed four of Rock Demers's* Tales for All: *The Peanut Butter Solution*, *Tommy Tricker and the Stamp Traveller*, *Vincent and Me*, and *The Return of Tommy Tricker*. Later he returned to Australia where he continues to work in the private sector. **Films include:** *The True Source of Knowledge* 1964 (p/d/ph/ed); *Mrs Ryan's Drama Class* 1969 (d); *Sad Song of Yellow Skin* 1970 (d/sc/narr); *Wet Earth and Warm People* 1971 (d/sc/ed); *Cold Pizza* 1972 (p); *Jalan, Jalan: A Journey in Sundanese Java* 1973 (d/sc/ed); *The Man Who Can't Stop* 1973 (d/sc); *Waiting for Fidel* 1974 (co-p/d/ed); *I Am an Old Tree* 1975 (co-p/d/sc/ed); *Solzhenitsyn's Children ... Are Making a Lot of Noise in Paris* 1978 (d/sc/ed); *Daisy: The Story of a Facelift* 1982 (co-p/d/ed); *Margaret Atwood: Once in August* 1984 (co-p/d/ co-sc/ed); *Atwood and Family* 1985 (co-p/d/co-sc/ed); *The Peanut Butter Solution* 1985 (d/co-sc); *Tommy Tricker and the Stamp Traveller* 1988 (d/sc); *Vincent and Me* 1990 (d/sc); *The Return of Tommy Tricker* 1994 (d/sc).

Rubes, Jan

Actor and singer; b. St Volyne, Czechoslovakia, 1920. Rubes graduated from the Prague Conservatory of Music in 1945, and immigrated to Canada in 1948 to pursue music. He was an original member of the Opera Festival Company of Toronto (later the Canadian Opera Company). Acting, his second love, drew him to the stage at the Stratford Festival and eventually to film and television where he developed into a distinguished character actor. He is perhaps best remembered at Kelly McGillis's Amish grandfather in Peter Weir's *Witness*. He is married to actress and theatre producer Susan Rubes. **Films and television include:** *Forbidden Journey* 1950; *The Incredible Journey* 1963; *Lions for Breakfast* 1975; *Mr. Patman* 1981; *Your Ticket Is No Longer Valid* 1981; *The Amateur* 1981; *Charlie Grant's War* 1984 (TV); *One Magic Christmas* 1985; *Witness* 1985; *Kane and Abel* 1985 (TV); *Dead of Winter* 1987; *Blood Relations* 1988; *The Kiss* 1988; *The Outside Chance of Maximilian Glick* 1988;

Something about Love 1988; *Blind Fear* 1989; *Courage Mountain* 1989; *Divided Loyalties* 1989 (TV); *The Amityville Curse* 1990; *Class Action* 1991; *Deceived* 1991; *D2: The Mighty Ducks* 1994; *The Birds II: Land's End* 1994 (TV); *Mesmer* 1994; *Serving in Silence: The Margarethe Cammermeyer Story* 1995 (TV); *The Marriage Bed* 1996 (TV); *Never Too Late* 1997; *The White Raven* 1998; *Boozecan* 1999; *Snow Falling on Cedars* 1999; *What Katy Did* 1999 (TV).

Rubinek, Saul

Actor; b. Wolfrathausen, Germany, 1948. Saul Rubinek was born in a German refugee camp, and grew up in Toronto where he co-founded Toronto Free Theatre and established himself on stage in both Canada and the United States. He had his film debut in *Agency* and won a Genie Award in 1982 for his performance in *Ticket to Heaven*.* Although he has appeared mostly in supporting roles in U.S. movies (opposite Alan Alda in *Sweet Liberty* and Clint Eastwood and Gene Hackman in *Unforgiven*), he did receive particular acclaim for his starring performance as an Orthodox Jewish rabbi in the provocative 1992 Canadian film, *The Quarrel*. He played a recurring character in the popular television series *Frasier*, and directed his first feature, *Jerry and Tom*, in 1998. **Films and television include:** *Agency* 1979; *Death Ship* 1980; *Ticket to Heaven* 1981 (GA-SA); *Soup for One* 1982; *By Design* 1982; *Young Doctors in Love* 1982; *The Terry Fox Story* 1983; *Sweet Liberty* 1985; *The Suicide Murders* 1986 (TV); *Wall Street* 1987; *The Outside Chance of Maximilian Glick* 1988; *Obsessed* 1988; *The Quarrel* 1990; *Falling over Backwards* 1990; *Man Trouble* 1991; *The Bonfire of the Vanities* 1990; *Unforgiven* 1992; *Driving Miss Daisy* 1992; *And the Band Played On* 1993; *True Romance* 1993; *Undercover Blues* 1993; *Death Wish V: The Face of Death* 1994; *I Love Trouble* 1994;

Getting Even with Dad 1994; *Hiroshima* 1995 (TV); *Nixon* 1995; *Ink* 1996 (series); *Open Season* 1996; *Memory Run* 1996; *Color of Justice* 1997 (TV); *Hostile Intent* 1997; *Fraiser* 1998–2000 (series); *Pale Saints* 1998; *Jerry and Tom* 1998 (p/d/a); *Past Perfect* 1998; *Bad Manners* 1998; *Dick* 1999; *36 Hours to Die* 1999 (TV); *The Golden Spiders: A Nero Wolfe Mystery* 2000 (TV); *The Bookfair Murders* 2000 (TV).

Rude

1995 87m *prod* Conquering Lion Productions, Feature Film Project, *exp* Colin Brunton, *p* Damon D'Oliveira, Karen King, *d/sc* Clement Virgo, *ph* Barry Stone, *ed* Susan Maggi, *mus* Aaron Davis, John Lang; *with* Maurice Dean Wint, Rachael Crawford, Clark Johnson, Richard Chevolleau, Sharon M. Lewis, Melanie Nicholls-King. The themes of sin and redemption are not coincidental in this triptych of stories set over an Easter weekend. Young black Torontonians living in a housing project move in the sphere of Rude (a honey-voiced DJ on a local pirate radio station), who offers a meta-narration on the flux of life and her own brand of benediction. Director Clement Virgo's* debut feature is ambitious: he tries to juggle the three stories simultaneously to create a coherent whole. However, the only story that really works is about an ex-con (Dean Wint) trying to go straight while his brother (Johnson) continues to deal drugs; the other two stories are unnecessarily elliptical and poorly acted. (V)

Russell, Craig

Actor; b. Russell Craig Eadie, Toronto, 1948; d. 1990. There was no competition when Russell laid claim to the title of 'Canada's best-known female impersonator.' At sixteen, he founded the Mae West Fan Club with a phony list of twenty-five names; four years later, he

was West's secretary for nine months. West became the inspiration for his best impersonation. His lead role as a gay hairdresser in the surprise 1977 hit film *Outrageous!** was bewitching. A decade later, because he agreed to cut out booze and drugs during production, Russell added some shine to the otherwise lacklustre sequel, *Too Outrageous!*. Unfortunately, his addictions took his life in 1990. **Films include:** *Outrageous!* 1977; *Nothing Personal* 1980; *Too Outrageous!* 1987.

S

Sabourin, Marcel

Actor and writer; b. Montreal, 1935. Sabourin worked primarily in the theatre before giving himself up to cinema in 1967 with *Il ne faut pas mourir pour ça*, for which he both wrote the screenplay, with Jean Pierre Lefebvre,* and took the starring role. The film marked the beginning of a fruitful relationship with Lefebvre, who cast him in nine films. The various characters Sabourin played for Lefebvre established his talent for playing weak, cowardly men, but did not restrict his possibilities. One of his most impressive roles was the photographer in *J.A. Martin photographe,** a film he wrote with Jean Beaudin.* Sabourin has maintained a penchant for adventure throughout his career; his name also appears in the credits of a number of shorts and low-budget features. **Films include:** *Il ne faut pas mourir pour ça* 1968 (co-sc/a); *Deux femmes en or* 1970; *On es loin du soleil* 1971; *Les Maudits Sauvages* 1971; *La Maudite Galette* 1972; *Les Smattes* 1972; *Le Temps d'une chasse* 1972; *La Mort d'un bûcheron* 1973; *Taureau* 1973; *Les Dernières Fiançailles* 1973; *Bingo* 1974; *Gina* 1975; *Mustang* 1975; *Eliza's Horoscope* 1976; *J.A. Martin photographe* 1977 (co-sc/a); *Le Vieux Pays ou Rimbaud est mort* 1977; *Riel* 1979 (a, TV); *Cordélia* 1980; *L'Homme à tout faire* 1980; *Mario* 1984; *Le Jour 'S ...'* 1984; *Equinoxe* 1986; *Les Portes tournates* 1988; *Le Fabuleux Voyage de l'ange* 1991; *Wind from Wyoming* 1994; *Lilies* 1996; *Aujourd'hui ou jamais* 1998; *L'Age de braise* 1998; *Souvenirs intimes* 1999; *Preludes* 2000.

Sarin, Vic
Cinematographer and director; b. Srinagar, Kashmir, India, 1941. Sarin, one of Canada's best cameramen, has worked with a number of top directors on such features as Mort Ransen's *Margaret's Museum*,* Anne Wheeler's *Bye Bye Blues** and Don Shebib's *Heartaches.** In 1989, Sarin made a strong feature-film directing debut with *Cold Comfort.** He has numerous credits on many CBC-TV productions, and he also directed the documentary *The Other Kingdom* and the television movie *Family Reunion*. Known for his stunning shots of Canada's winter landscape, Sarin once said he came to the 'Great White North' because of the snow. **Films and television include:** *The Insurance Man from Ingersoll* 1975 (TV); *Riel* 1979 (TV); *Bix: Ain't None of Them Play like Him Yet* 1981; *Heartaches* 1981; *Rumours of Glory* 1983; *The Other Kingdom* 1984; *The Suicide Murders* 1986 (TV); *Loyalties* 1986; *Dancing in the Dark* 1986; *Family Reunion* 1987 (d/ph, TV); *Bye Bye Blues* 1989; *Love and Hate: The Story of Colin and Joann Thatcher* 1989 (TV); *Cold Comfort* 1989 (d/ph); *Whale Music* 1994; *Margaret's Museum* 1996; *In His Father's Shoes* 1997 (d, TV); *Sea People* 1999 (d, TV).

Sarrasine, La
1992 109m *prod* ACPAV, NFB, *exp* Lise Abastado, Léon G. Arcand, *p* Marc Daigle, *d* Paul Tana, *sc* Bruno Ramirez, Paul Tana, *ph* Michel Caron, *ed* Louise Surprenant, *mus* Pierre Desrochers; *with* Tony Nardi, Enrica Maria Modugno, Jean Lapointe, Gilbert Sicotte. Based on true events from turn-of-the-century Montreal, *La Sarrasine* is a beautifully shot, sensitively told story of a young Italian couple making their way in Québécois society. Giuseppe (superbly played by Nardi) is a humble tailor with big ambitions. His wife (Modugno) is lovingly devoted to him, helping when she can while running a boarding house for single Italian men. Through an unfortunate set of circumstances, Giuseppe is implicated in the murder of a local bully. He is saved from the gallows by the efforts of his wife but is condemned to life in prison. Melancholic and poignant, the film is a measured study of intolerance and of cultures in conflict, rendered with beauty and precision. **Awards include:** GA: Actor (Nardi).

Sarrazin, Michael
Actor; b. Jacques Michel André Sarrazin, Quebec City, 1940. Michael Sarrazin prepared for the stage at New York's Actors Studio. He made his screen debut in NFB documentaries, and came to feature films via American television, often cast as a younger man undergoing initiation at the hands of older men. He connected with youthful audiences in the 1968 surfing saga *The Sweet Ride*, which co-starred Jacqueline Bisset, and played opposite Jane Fonda in the harrowing melodrama *They Shoot Horses, Don't They?*, but he never got beyond the brink of stardom. In recent years he's taken many unsympathetic roles, including white-collar criminals. His brother Pierre Sarrazin, produced the 1993 Golden Reel Award-winner, *La Florida*. **Films and television include:** *Romeo and Jeannette* 1965 (TV); *The Doomsday Flight* 1966 (TV); *Gunfight in Abilene* 1967; *The Flim-Flam Man* 1967;

The Sweet Ride 1968; *They Shoot Horses Don't They?* 1969; *Sometimes a Great Notion* 1971; *The Groundstar Conspiracy* 1972; *The Life and Times of Judge Roy Bean* 1972; *Harry in Your Pocket* 1973; *For Pete's Sake* 1974; *The Reincarnation of Peter Proud* 1975; *The Loves and Times of Scaramouche* 1975; *The Gumball Rally* 1976; *Caravans* 1978; *Double Negative* 1980; *The Seduction* 1982; *Keeping Track* 1985; *Joshua Then and Now* 1985; *Sword of Gideon* 1986 (TV); *Captive Hearts* 1987; *Passion and Paradise* 1989 (TV); *Malarek* 1989; *La Florida* 1993; *Bullet to Beijing* 1995; *Midnight in St Petersburg* 1995; *The Peacekeeper* 1996; *Thunder Point* 1996 (TV); *The City* 1998–2000 (series); *The Second Arrival* 1998.

Scanners

1981 103m *prod* Filmplan International, *exp* Pierre David, Victor Solnicki, *p* Claude Héroux, *d/sc* David Cronenberg, *ph* Mark Irwin, *ed* Ronald Sanders, *mus* Howard Shore; *with* Jennifer O'Neill, Stephen Lack, Patrick McGoohan, Lawrence Dane, Michael Ironside, Robert Silverman. When David Cronenberg* made *Scanners*, he pulled off a tricky balancing act that he learned in his early years as a commercial moviemaker, operating as both schlockmeister and auteur of dark, existential fables. *Scanners* is a pleasantly cheesy, derivative sci-fi horror picture with echoes of *A Clockwork Orange*, *Carrie*, and Chris Marker's *La Jetée*. The premise sets up a confused, but powerfully telepathic young man (Lack) who's tracking down a fellow 'scanner,' a megalomaniacal creep (Ironside) who gets off on using his mental prowess to blow up people's heads. Naturally, the movie exhibits Cronenbergian motifs ranging from penetration anxieties to the mutation of human beings into something disturbingly different. The picture spawned several

sequels aimed at the teenage horror market. (V)

Scissere

1982 87m *prod* Collaborative Effort Productions, *p* Ron Repke, Peter Mettler, Alfred Mettler, *d/sc/ph/ed* Peter Mettler; *with* Greg Krantz, Natalie Olanick, Sandy MacFadyen, Anthony Downes. Peter Mettler's* first feature, a student film produced at Ryerson, is a daring experiment with narrative form. In an exercise that was to influence much of his future work (particularly *Top of His Head*) Mettler sustains a single subjective point of view throughout the film. Recently released from a heroin rehabilitation clinic, Scissere (Krantz), attempts to rediscover the outside world, only to experience a disturbing series of fragmented perceptions, mirrored in the film's dramatic trajectory. Employing a variety of cinematic techniques and materials, Mettler's formal strategy invites viewers to participate in this construction of reality. It is this process that raises the film from pure experiment to profound statement.

Scott, Cynthia

Director and actor; b. Winnipeg, 1939. Known as a talented documentarian who made solid, social-purpose, slice-of-life films, Scott won an Academy Award in 1984 for *Flamenco at 5:15*.* She gained international attention with her endearing docudrama, *The Company of Strangers*,* about seven elderly women stranded at a deserted farmhouse. The film, which features non-professional actors and spontaneous dialogue, is both heartwarming and radical, and it raked in over a dozen major awards. In her other incarnation as an actress, Scott played a corporal in *Aliens* and a waitress in *Rush*. **Films include:** *For the Love of Dance* 1981 (co-d); *Gala* 1982 (co-d);

Flamenco at 5:15 1984 (d/co-p/co-ed, AA-SD); *Aliens* 1986 (a); *The Company of Strangers* 1990 (d); *Rush* 1992 (a).

Screamers
1996 105m *prod* Allegro Films, *exp* Charles Fries, Josée Bernard, Masao Takiyama, *p* Tom Berry, Franco Battista, *d* Christian Duguay, *sc* Dan O'Bannon, Miguel Tejada-Flores, *short story* Philip K. Dick, *ph* Rodney Gibbons, *ed* Yves Langlois, *mus* Normand Corbeil; *with* Peter Weller, Roy Dupuis, Jennifer Rubin, Andy Lauer. This dystopian futuristic action flick has impeccable credentials. Dan O'Bannon (who wrote Ridley Scott's *Alien*) based the script on a short story by sci-fi visionary Phillip K. Dick. Screamers are 'Autonomous Mobile Swords,' feisty little robots that slice and dice human flesh on a mining planet called Sirius 6B. Exploited human miners, trapped in this nasty world, are fighting a vicious war with an energy company that recklessly endangers their health. The stoical hero (Weller) believes that peace looms on the horizon and risks being cuisinarted to achieve it. While the movie displays some smarts, its visual chops that pass for style are strictly *déja vu*, as are the recycled motifs from David Cronenberg* pictures and *The Thing*.

Scream from Silence, A
See *Mourir à tue-tête*.

Sennett, Mack
Producer, director, and actor; b. Mikall Sinnott, Danville, Que., 1880; d. 1960. Mack Sennett, the founder of the Keystone Studios and creator of the Keystone Kops, was a self-styled 'King of Comedy.' He worked the vaudeville circuit until a chance encounter with fellow Canadian Marie Dressler* in New York landed him in film. He directed and acted in comedies for D.W. Griffith, and in 1912, set up his own studios in Los Angeles. Sennett launched the careers of such comic geniuses as Charlie Chaplin, Mabel Normand, Frank Capra, Harold Lloyd, and Fatty Arbuckle. Failing to change his formalistic style of slapstick comedy, he eventually lost favour with audiences. He directed and produced his last film in 1935. **Credits include:** Actor with D.W. Griffith's stock company 1908–11; *p/d/sc* over 1,000 short comedies 1911–35.

Shaffer, Beverly
Director; b. Montreal, 1945. Shaffer, a skilled documentarist with a great eye for detail, joined the NFB in the mid-1970s and is best known for her work on the *Children of Canada* series (1975–8), including *I'll Find a Way*,* for which she won an Academy Award in 1978. More recently, Shaffer directed seven instalments for the Board's *Children of Jerusalem*, a series that explored questions of identity and cultural conflict through profiles of Arab and Jewish youths. Shaffer's 1987 film, *To a Safer Place*, won awards for its uplifting story of an incest survivor in her thirties who succeeded in building a full life after years of abuse. **Films and television include:** *I'll Find a Way* 1978 (AA-LAS); *The Way It Is* 1982; *I Want to be an Engineer* 1983; *To a Safer Place* 1987; *Children of Jerusalem* 1991–4 (seven films, TV); *Just a Wedding* 1999.

Shannon, Kathleen
Producer and director; b. Vancouver, 1935; d. 1998. Kathleen Shannon joined the NFB in 1956 as a music editor, worked her way into picture editing, and produced and directed her first film in 1971. However, her greatest contribution to documentary filmmaking was the founding of the NFB's Studio D. Her strong feminist views and her belief that

films are meant to affect change in the world were behind the forthright mandate of Studio D 'to make films by, for, and about women.' Under her tutelage Studio D produced films such as *Not a Love Story** and the Academy Award winner *If You Love This Planet.** Shannon ran Studio D from 1975 to 1986, and oversaw the production of more than 100 films. She was named an officer of the Order of Canada. **Films include:** *Mothers Are People* 1974 (p/d); *Some American Feminists* 1977; *How They Saw Us: Women at War* 1977; *How They Saw Us: Women at Work* 1977; *I'll Find a Way* 1978 (exp, AA-LAS); *Eve Lambart* 1978; *Not a Love Story: A Film about Pornography* 1981; *The Way It Is* 1982; *Dream of a Free Country: A Message from Nicaraguan Women* 1983 (p/d); *If You Love This Planet* 1983 (exp, AA-SD); *Flamenco at 5:15* 1983 (exp, AA-SD); *Abortion: Stories from North and South* 1984; *On Our Own* 1984; *Behind the Veil: Nuns* 1984; *Speaking Our Peace* 1985; *A Writer in the Nuclear Age: A Conversation with Margaret Laurence* 1985; *To a Safer Place* 1987; *Goddess Remembered* 1989; *Russian Diary* 1989.

Shatner, William

Actor, director, and producer; b. Montreal, 1931. Although his family hoped to enlist him in their *schmatte* business, Shatner turned to acting and eventually transformed a short television gig (the original *Star Trek* series ran from 1966–9) into an internationally recognized icon. James T. Kirk, captain of the Starship Enterprise, operates as a pop-culture hero who upholds the value of the human race in the cold darkness of zero gravity. While he is not exactly an emotional volcano, he champions empathy and compassion over pure logic. Shatner's long-running portrayal of this earnest, somewhat absurd figure, through seven films in fifteen years, often dis-

plays humour and refreshing self-parody. **Films and television include:** *The Brothers Karamazov* 1958; *Judgment at Nuremberg* 1961; *The Intruder* 1962; *The Outrage* 1974; *Incubus* 1965; *Star Trek* 1966–9 (series); *Star Trek: The Motion Picture* 1979; *Riel* 1979 (TV); *The Kidnapping of the President* 1980; *Airplane II: The Sequel* 1982; *Star Trek II: The Wrath of Khan* 1982; *Star Trek III: In Search of Spock* 1984; *Star Trek IV: The Voyage Home* 1986; *Star Trek V: The Final Frontier* 1989 (d/a/story); *Star Trek VI: The Undiscovered Country* 1991; *Star Trek: Generations* 1994; *Tekwar* 1994–5 (exp, series); *Free Enterprise* 1999 (as himself); *Miss Congeniality* 2000.

Shaver, Helen

Actor; b. St Thomas, Ont., 1951. Shaver began her acting career at age sixteen when she won a scholarship to the Banff School of Fine Arts. She played character roles in several Canadian features during the 1970s (*Outrageous!*,* *In Praise of Older Women*,* *Who Has Seen the Wind**) before she gained attention in 1985 as the repressed teacher who makes a wary, but liberating foray into lesbianism in Donna Deitch's moving *Desert Hearts*. Shaver is perhaps best known as Paul Newman's long-suffering wife in *The Color of Money*. She also starred opposite Donald Sutherland* in Phillip Borsos's* ill-fated *Bethune: The Making of a Hero.** **Films and television include:** *Wolfen Principle* 1973; *Shoot* 1976; *Starship Invasions* 1977; *Outrageous!* 1977; *Who Has Seen the Wind* 1977; *In Praise of Older Women* 1978 (CFA-A); *The Amityville Horror* 1979; *Off Your Rocker* 1982; *Harry Tracy, Desperado* 1982; *The Osterman Weekend* 1983; *Best Defense* 1984; *Desert Hearts* 1985; *The Park Is Mine* 1986 (TV); *The Color of Money* 1986; *The Believers* 1987; *Walking after Midnight* 1988; *Land before Time* 1988 (voice); *Bethune: The Making of a Hero* 1990; *Zebrahead* 1992;

Morning Glory 1993 (TV); *Ride with the Wind* 1994 (TV); *The Forget-Me-Not Murders* 1994 (TV); *Without Consent* 1994 (TV); *Tremors 2: Aftershocks* 1995; *Open Season* 1995; *The Craft* 1996; *Poltergeist: The Legacy* 1997–present (series); *The Sweetest Gift* 1998 (TV); *Summer's End* 1999 (d, TV); *The Wishing Tree* 1999; *Common Ground* 2000 (TV); *We All Fall Down* 2000 (exp/a, GA-SA).

Shearer, Douglas

Sound recording engineer; b. Montreal, 1899; d. 1971; brother of Norma Shearer. Douglas Shearer founded the MGM sound department and was responsible for developing a revolutionary recording head at the dawn of the sound era. In addition to his seven Academy Awards for Sound Recording, he also received six awards from the Academy for technical achievement over the course of his long career. **Films include:** *The Broadway Melody* 1929; *Hallelujah* 1929; *Anna Christie* 1930; *The Big House* 1930 (AA-SR); *Min and Bill* 1930; *The Thin Man* 1934; *Naughty Marietta* 1935 (AA-SR); *A Night at the Opera* 1935; *San Francisco* 1936 (AA-SR); *Romeo and Juliet* 1936; *Ninotchka* 1939; *The Wizard of Oz* 1939; *Strike up the Band* 1940 (AA-SR); *The Philadelphia Story* 1940; *Thirty Seconds over Tokyo* 1944 (AA-SR); *Green Dolphin Street* 1947 (AA-SR); *The Asphalt Jungle* 1950; *The Great Caruso* 1951 (AA-SR); *Singin' in the Rain* 1952.

Shearer, Norma

Actor; b. Montreal, 1900; d. 1983; sister of Douglas Shearer. Norma landed her debut role at MGM in 1920 after a successful modelling career. A fortuitous marriage to legendary producer Irving Thalberg helped her to become one of the studio's leading ladies. She won an Academy Award in 1930 for *The Divorcee*, and led MGM through the first five years of the talkies with a string of hits including *Private Lives* and *The Barretts of Wimpole Street*. Thalberg died unexpectedly in 1936 and left Shearer a major shareholder in MGM. She delivered a witty performance in *The Women* before retiring in 1942. **Films include:** *Blue Water* 1924; *He Who Gets Slapped* 1924; *The Tower of Lies* 1925; *The Student Prince* 1927; *The Last of Mrs Cheyney* 1929; *Their Own Desire* 1929 (AAN-A); *The Divorcee* 1930 (AA-A); *A Free Soul* 1931 (AAN-A); *Private Lives* 1931; *Strange Interlude* 1932; *The Barretts of Wimpole Street* 1934 (AAN-A); *Romeo and Juliet* 1936 (AAN-A); *Marie Antoinette* 1938 (AAN-A); *Idiot's Delight* 1939; *The Women* 1939; *Her Cardboard Lover* 1942.

Shebib, Donald

Director and editor; b. Toronto, 1938. Shebib, a central figure in the development of English-Canadian cinema and an eloquent, compassionate chronicler of individual alienation and collective Canadian angst, made several award-winning, lucid documentaries for the NFB and CBC-TV prior to his feature work. After a remarkable cluster of features in the early 1970s – the seminal *Goin' down the Road,** *Rip-Off,** and his masterpiece, *Between Friends** – Shebib became frustrated by the process of bureaucratic film funding, chronic distribution problems, and subsequent box-office disappointments. He returned to form with Margot Kidder*and Annie Potts in *Heartaches,** but since then has worked primarily as a director for television, with only occasional forays into feature filmmaking. **Films and television include:** *Surfin'* 1964 (d/ph); *Satan's Choice* 1965 (d/ph); *San Francisco Summer 1967* 1967 (d/ph, TV); *Good Times Bad Times* 1969 (d/ph/ed, CFA-FD); *Goin' down the Road* 1970 (p/d/ed, CFA-FF); *Rip-Off* 1971 (d/co-ed); *Between*

Friends 1973 (d/ed); *Second Wind* 1976 (d/ed, CFA-E); *Once upon a Time in Genarro* 1974 (d, TV); *The Canary* 1975 (d, TV); *The Fighting Men* 1977 (d, TV); *Fish Hawk* 1979 (d); *Heartaches* 1981 (d); *By Reason of Insanity* 1982 (d, TV); *Slim Obsession* 1984 (d, TV); *The Climb* 1986 (d); *Little Kidnappers* 1990 (d, TV); *Change of Heart* 1992 (d); *The Ascent* 1994 (d); *The Pathfinder* 1996 (d, TV).

Sheehan, Nik

Director, producer, and writer; b. London, U.K., 1960. Sheehan's family immigrated to Canada in 1967 and settled in Ottawa. Sheehan moved to Toronto to become a writer and activist in the city's gay community. In 1985, in assocation with the NFB and the AIDS Committe of Toronto, he wrote, produced, and directed *No Sad Songs*, the first documentary to tackle HIV and AIDS in a serious manner. In 1997, he tracked down the elusive Toronto bad-boy writer Scott Symons in Morocco for the documentary *God's Fool*. **Films and television include:** *Tricoolair* 1977 (p/d); *Jeremy Lelion* 1978 (p/d); *The Brick* 1981 (p/d); *No Sad Songs* 1985 (p/d/sc); *Symposium* 1996 (p/d/sc); *God's Fool* 1998 (p/d/sc/ed, TV).

Shimkus, Joanna

Actor; b. Halifax, 1943. Shimkus started her career as a fashion model and traveled to Paris at the age of nineteen to pose for *Elle* magazine. There she had a modest but brief career in international films, including the dreadful *Boom!* with Elizabeth Taylor and Richard Burton. She retired shortly after her marriage to the American actor Sidney Poiter in 1976. **Films include:** *Paris vu par ...* 1965; *The Last Adventure* 1968; *Boom!* 1968; *The Lost Man* 1969; *The Virgin and the Gypsy* 1970; *The Marriage of a Young Stockbroker* 1971.

Shipman, Nell and Ernest

Nell: Actor, writer, and director; b. Helen Barham, Victoria, B.C., 1892; d. 1970. **Ernest:** Producer; b. Ottawa, 1871; d. 1931. The Shipmans married in 1911, and went to Hollywood in 1912, where Ernest promoted films written by and starring Nell. In 1915, Vitagraph produced Nell's script for *God's Country and the Woman*, a film in which she took the starring role. The couple returned to Canada, where Ernest produced *Back to God's Country*,* again written by and starring Nell, who appeared in the first nude scene in Canadian cinema. The film became the biggest box-office success of any Canadian feature during the silent era. The Shipmans separated shortly thereafter. Nell returned to the United States where she established her own production company. Ernest went on to produce six more silent features in Canada. **Nell Shipman's films include:** *God's Country and the Woman* 1915 (sc/a); *Back to God's Country* 1919 (sc/a); *Something New* 1920 (co-d/sc/a); *A Bear, a Boy and a Dog* 1920 (d/sc); *The Grub-Stake* 1922 (co-d/sc/a); *Trail of the Northwind* 1923 (d/sc/a); *The Light on Lookout* 1923 (d/sc/a). **Ernest Shipman's films include:** *Back to God's Country* 1919; *God's Crucible* 1921; *Cameron of the Royal Mounted* 1921; *The Man from Glengarry* 1922; *The Rapids* 1922; *Glengarry School Days* 1923; *Blue Water* 1924.

Shivers (The Parasite Murders)

1975 87m *prod* DAL Productions, *exp* Alfred Pariser, John Dunning, André Link, *p/mus* Ivan Reitman, *d/sc* David Cronenberg, *ph* Robert Saad, *ed* Patrick Dodd; *with* Paul Hampton, Joe Silver, Lynn Lowry, Allan Migicovsky. This early Cronenberg* feature has a low-rent B-movie look and feel, but he does a lot with very little. When residents of a singles life-style apartment building become riddled with a man-made parasite that acts as a powerful aphrodisiac and causes a deforming venereal disease, they become violent and sexually aggressive. Many elements of Cronenberg's later features can be seen in this early effort. The film, one of Ivan Reitman's* early successes as a producer, established Cronenberg's reputation for gross-out horror, and became a cult favourite. (V)

Short, Martin

Actor; b. Hamilton, Ont., 1950. Martin Short, the son of an Irish-born steel executive and his concert-violinist wife, began performing at McMaster University in Hamilton, Ontario, where he majored in social work. After graduation he moved to Toronto where he began his professional career in 1972 in the legendary production of *Godspell*. He joined the Second City improvisational group in 1977, and eventually became a cast member of *SCTV*. Short has had a spotty career on both television and film ever since. He made some dreadful comedies, but he did his annoying best as 'Franck,' the wedding coordinator from Hell, in the remake of *Father of the Bride*, and he won the prestigious Tony Award for his central role in the revival of *Little Me* on Broadway in 1999. **Films and television include:** *Lost and Found* 1979; *SCTV* 1981–3 (series); *Saturday Night Live* 1984–5 (series); *Three Amigos!* 1986; *Cross My Heart* 1987; *Innerspace* 1987; *Three Fugitives* 1989; *Andrea Martin ... Together Again* 1989 (TV); *Pure Luck* 1991; *Father of the Bride* 1991; *Captain Ron* 1992; *Clifford* 1994; *Father of the Bride Part II* 1995; *The Pebble and the Penguin* 1995 (voice); *Mars Attacks!* 1996; *Jungle2Jungle* 1997; *A Simple Wish* 1997; *Merlin* 1998 (TV); *The Prince of Egypt* 1998 (voice); *Alice in Wonderland* 1999 (TV, as the Mad Hatter); *Mumford* 1999; *The Martin Short Show* 1999 (series); *Get Over It* 2000.

Shum, Mina

Director and writer; b. Hong Kong, 1966. One of the freshest new voices in Canadian cinema, Vancouver-based Shum has so far made a specialty out of light-but-filling comedies exploring what it's like to be Chinese, Canadian, and female. Of her six short films, *Me, Mom and Mona* stands out for its stylishly loopy depiction of the main women in her life. Shum developed her semi-autobiographical first feature, *Double Happiness*,* while a resident at the Canadian Film Centre and it won awards both at home and in Germany and Italy. **Films include:** *Me, Mom and Mona* 1993; *Double Happiness* 1995; *Drive, She Said* 1998.

Silent Partner, The

1978 105m *prod* Tiberius Film Production, *exp* Garth Drabinsky, *p* Stephen Young, Joel B. Michaels, *d* Daryl Duke, *sc* Curtis Lee Hanson, *novel* Anders Bodelsen, *ph* Billy Williams, *ed* George Appleby, *mus* Oscar Peterson; *with* Elliott Gould, Christopher Plummer, Susannah York, Céline Lomez, John Candy. *The Silent Partner* is one of the few critical and commercial successes made during the tax-shelter era.* The script by Curtis Hanson (who later won Hollywood fame and a stack of Academy Awards for *L.A. Confidential*) is an unnerving blend of comedy and sudden violence. A robber (Plummer*) holds up a bank, but later discovers that the teller (Gould) managed to put aside $50,000 that the police assume was stolen. Plummer's attempts to recover the cash from Gould provide the suspense, while Gould's attempts to bed a fellow employee (York) provide the subplot. The script is uneven at times, and Gould's character annoyingly fatuous, but Plummer gives one of his best performances as the psychopathic thief, and the brutal murder of his girlfriend (Lomez) remains one of the most violently graphic scenes in Canadian film. **Awards include:** CFA: Feature Film, Director, Editing, Musical Score, Sound Editing, Sound Recording.

Silverheels, Jay

Actor; b. Harold J. Smith, Six Nations Reserve, Ont., 1919; d. 1980. Jay Silverheels (his father changed his son's name because of his speed on the track) was an all-star lacrosse player on the Canadian national team before he broke into movies playing bit parts in B westerns. When the popular *Lone Ranger* radio serial was brought to television in 1949, Silverheels was chosen to play Tonto, the Ranger's faithful sidekick, a role that made him the most recognizable First Nations actor on television or film. The series ended in 1961, but Silverheels continued in films until the early 1970s. He also became active in First Nations affairs; he founded the Indian Actors' Workshop in 1966, and was inducted into the First Americans Arts' Hall of Honor in 1998. **Films and television include:** *The Lone Ranger* 1949–61 (series); *Broken Arrow* 1950; *The Battle at Apache Pass* 1952; *Saskatchewan* 1954; *The Lone Ranger* 1956; *The Lone Ranger and the Lost City of Gold* 1958; *Alias Jesse James* 1959; *Smith* 1969; *The Man Who Loved Cat Dancing* 1973.

Simoneau, Yves

Director and writer; b. Quebec City, 1955. After directing several critically acclaimed Québécois pictures (including *Les Yeux rouges, Pouvoir intime,** *Les Fous de bassan,* and *Dans le ventre du dragon*) Simoneau directed *Perfectly Normal,** the most successful English-Canadian comedy ever made, and then took off for a career in Hollywood. Fond of genre plots and eye-popping style, Simoneau defined his approach in *Pouvoir intime,* a taut crime drama that spills over into existential anxiety and features bravura

camera moves and *trompe l'oeil* effects. In the United States, he has made films both for television and for theatrical release, including the 1994 thriller *Mother's Boys,* starring Jamie Lee Curtis. **Films and television include:** *Les Célébrations* 1979 (d/sc/ed); *Les Yeux rouges ou les vérités accidentelles* 1982 (d/sc); *Pour-quoi l'étrange Monsieur Zolock s'intéressait-il tant à la bande dessinée?* 1983 (GA-FD); *Trouble* 1985; *Pouvoir intime* 1986 (d/co-sc); *Les Fous de bassan* 1987 (d/co-sc); *Dans le ventre du dragon* 1988 (d/co-sc); *Perfectly Normal* 1990; *Memphis* 1991 (TV); *Till Death Us Do Part* 1992 (TV); *Cruel Doubt* 1992 (TV); *Amelia Earhart: The Final Flight* 1994 (TV); *Mother's Boys* 1994; *Free Money* 1998; *36 Hours to Die* 1999 (TV); *Nuremberg* 2000 (TV).

Slipstream

1973 93m *prod* Pacific Rim Films, *exp* Harold Greenberg, *p* James Margellos, *d* David Acomba, *sc* William Fruet, *ph* Marc Champion, *ed* Tony Lower, *mus* Brian Ahern; *with* Luke Askew, Patti Oatman, Eli Rill, Scott Hylands, Danny Freedman. *Slipstream* is perhaps the most inept film ever to win a major Canadian Film Award; it was in competition with *Kamouraska,** *Réjeanne Padovani,** *Between Friends,** and *Paperback Hero,** and its victory did a great deal of damage to the credibility of the international jury system of the Canadian Film Awards. The story concerns Mike (Askew), an Albertan disc jockey who runs a pirate station from a remote farmhouse. Mike becomes involved with Kathy (Oatman), a 'hippie chick,' but when pressures to play more mainstream music lead to a quarrel and Kathy leaves, Mike burns down the station and lands in a mental hospital, where Kathy returns to him. This boring and banal film is relieved only by some beautiful shots of the Prairies. **Awards include:** CFA: Feature Film, Director, Sound Editing.

195

Smith, Alexis

Actor; b. Gladys Smith, Penticton, B.C., 1921; d. 1993. A youthful, alluring leading lady of the 1940s and 1950s, Alexis Smith got her start first in Canadian summer stock and then at the Los Angeles City College, where she went to study. She was spotted by a Warner's talent scout and given a long-term contract. She retired at the end of the 1950s, but made a comeback in 1975 after a successful run on Broadway as a star of the musical *Follies*. **Films include:** *The Lady with Red Hair* 1940; *Gentleman Jim* 1942; *The Constant Nymph* 1943; *The Adventures of Mark Twain* 1944; *Rhapsody in Blue* 1945; *Of Human Bondage* 1946; *Night and Day* 1946; *Any Number Can Play* 1949; *Undercover Girl* 1950; *Here Comes the Groom* 1951; *The Eternal Sea* 1955; *Beau James* 1957; *The Young Philadelphians* 1959; *Once Is Not Enough* 1975; *The Little Girl Who Lives down the Lane* 1977; *Tough Guys* 1986.

Smith, Clive

See Nelvana Studios.

Smith, John N.

Director, producer, and writer; b. Montreal, 1943. When Smith switched from documentary to drama at the NFB, he turned out a string of movies in the 1980s that earnestly probed issues such as male sexuality (*The Masculine Mystique**), racism (*Train of Dreams*), and immigration (*Welcome to Canada**). With collaborators including Giles Walker,* Smith made economic use of non-professional actors and documentary techniques. In 1993, he filmed *The Boys of St Vincent*,* a powerful and controversial two-part television drama depicting the sexual violation of children in a Catholic orphanage. Excellent reviews and ratings in the United States led to a Hollywood assignment directing Michelle

Pfeiffer in *Dangerous Minds*, which became one of the top-grossing films of 1995. **Films and television include:** *Breathing Together: Revolution of the Electric Family* 1971 (ed); *The Heatwave Lasted Four Days* 1973 (exp, TV); *A Star Is Lost* 1974 (exp); *First Winter* 1981 (p/d, AAN-LAS); *For the Love of Dance* 1981 (co-p/co-d/co-ed); *Gala* 1982 (co-p/co-d/co-ed); *The Masculine Mystique* 1985 (p/d/sc with Giles Walker); *Sitting in Limbo* 1985 (p/d); *First Stop, China* 1985 (p/d); *Train of Dreams* 1987 (d/co-sc/ed); *Welcome to Canada* 1989 (d/co-sc/co-ed); *The Boys of St Vincent* 1993 (d, TV); *Dieppe* 1994 (d, TV); *Sugartime* 1995 (d, TV); *Dangerous Minds* 1995 (d); *A Cool, Dry Place* 1998 (d); *Revenge of the Land* 2000 (d, TV).

Snow, Michael

Filmmaker; b. Toronto, 1929. Snow began his remarkable career in Toronto in the early 1950s as a designer, animator, painter, and jazz musician. By 1963 he had moved to New York and was working with a community of American experimental filmmakers who were expanding the definitions of cinema through forays into graphic and structuralist films. Snow's provocative works from this era – *New York Eye and Ear Control*, *Wavelength*,* and *Back and Forth* – offer unique viewing experiences that delve into the relationship between the spectator and the image, qualifying Snow as the undisputed dean of structuralist cinema. His more recent films – *So Is This* and *Seated Figures* – are equally intelligent and compelling explorations of the nature of communication and signification. **Films include:** *A-Z* 1956; *New York Eye and Ear Control* 1964; *Wavelength* 1967; *Standard Time* 1967; *Back and Forth* 1969; *Dripping Water* 1969 (with Joyce Wieland); *La Région centrale* 1971; *Rameau's Nephew by Diderot (Thanx to*

Dennis Young) by Wilma Schoen 1974; *Presents* 1981; *So Is This* 1983; *Seated Figures* 1988; *Prelude* from *Preludes* 2000; *The Living Room* 2000.

Sonatine

1984 91m *prod* Corp. Image M and M, *exp* René Malo, *p* Pierre Gendron, *d/sc* Micheline Lanctôt, *ph* Guy Dufaux, *ed* Louise Surprenant, *mus* François Lanctôt; *with* Pascale Bussières, Marcia Pilote, Pierre Fauteux, Kliment Denchev, Pierre Girard. *Sonatine*, the second feature from actress-turned-director Micheline Lanctôt,* is a delicate exploration of female adolescent suicide. Lanctôt probes the bonds between two upper-middle-class girls (Pilote and Bussières,* in her first film) who allow their sense of social detachment to swell into a purple romantic impulse. Caught between childhood impressions and adult knowledge, the girls struggle in vain to bring life, art, and poetry into the stagnant, complacent world of adults. Shot with Bressonian austerity, the film is divided into three movements, each demonstrating a distinct cinematic style. **Awards include:** GA: Director; Venice Film Festival: Silver Lion.

Sous-sol

1996 90m *prod* Max Films, *p* Roger Frappier, *d/sc* Pierre Gang, *ph* Pierre Mignot, *ed* Florence Moureaux, Yves Chaput, *mus* Anne Bourne, Ken Myhr; *with* Louise Portal, Isabelle Pasco, Patrice Godin, Daniel Gadouas. In an era when so many films result from attitude than rather talent, director Pierre Gang's psychodrama affirms the values of delicate craftsmanship and acute psychological insight. There are few films, apart from *East of Eden*, that explore a son's fear of his mother's sexuality. In *Sous-sol*, eleven-year-old René (Moffat) accidentally sees his mother (Portal*) and father

(Gadouas) engage in a slightly kinky bedroom encounter. When dad is found dead the next morning, the boy assumes that Reine, a woman who delights in her sexual power, is responsible. Over the movie's long time span (1967–76), René struggles with the demons of his immobilizing sexual terror, without aging visibly until the final scene. Gang draws extraordinarily authentic performances from Moffat and Portal. (V) **Awards include:** GA: Original Screenplay.

Sparks, Ned

Actor; b. Edward Sparkman, Guelph, Ont., 1883; d. 1957. Sparks, a comic character actor with a dour countenance and raspy voice, was featured in numerous Hollywood silents and talkies after a long career on the vaudeville stage. He played the caterpillar in the 1933 version of *Alice in Wonderland*. **Films include:** *The Big Noise* 1928; *Nothing but the Truth* 1929; *Conspiracy* 1930; *The Miracle Man* 1932; *42nd Street* 1933; *Gold Diggers of 1933* 1933; *Lady for a Day* 1933; *Alice in Wonderland* 1933; *Imitation of Life* 1934; *One in a Million* 1937; *The Star Maker* 1939; *Stage Door Canteen* 1943; *Magic Town* 1947.

Sparling, Gordon

Director, producer, and editor; b. Toronto, 1900; d. 1994. Sparling's start with the Ontario Motion Picture Bureau in 1924 led to a forty-year career with the Canadian Government Motion Picture Bureau and Associated Screen News (ASN). During the 1930s, he was virtually the only creative filmmaker in the Canadian commercial film industry. He launched the *Canadian Cameo* series of theatrical shorts at ASN in 1932 and continued to direct and produce the series until 1955. During the Second World War, he was the head of the

Canadian Army Film and Photo Unit, producing and directing propaganda films. He returned to ASN and remained with the studio until the production department was closed down in 1957. **Films include:** *Carry on, Sergeant!* 1928 (assist. ed); *Canadian Cameo* series 1932–55, including *Rhapsody in Two Languages* 1934 (d/sc/ed); *Royal River* 1959 (co-d).

Speaking Parts

1989 92m *prod* Ego Film Arts, *exp* Atom Egoyan, Don Ranvaud, *p/d/sc* Atom Egoyan, *ph* Paul Sarossy, *ed* Bruce Mc-Donald, Atom Egoyan, *mus* Mychael Danna; *with* Patricia Collins, Robert Dodds, David Hemblen, Arsinée Khanjian, Gabrielle Rose, Michael McManus. 'People want things recorded,' says a character in Atom Egoyan's* third feature, 'parties, weddings, the usual.' *Speaking Parts* reflects on the 1980s fixation with video as a mausoleum of the past. The movie seems a bit quaint, compared to the eternal 'now' of the Internet but it features impeccable composition and smoothly somnolent rhythms as Egoyan's characters audition for the life roles they want to play: a lovestruck chambermaid (Khanjian*) pursues the object of her desire; a film writer (Rose) seeks an emotional replacement for her beloved dead brother; a young actor (McManus) hopes the film writer will get him a part he craves. The minimalist action revolves around a tasteful hotel where the male employees make themselves sexually available to the upscale guests. (V)

Special Day, A (Uno Gironata speciale)

1977 105m *prod* Canafox Films, Compagnia Cinematografica Champion (Italy), *p* Richard Hellman, Carlo Ponti, *d* Ettore Scola, *sc* Ruggero Maccari, Ettore Scola, Claude Fournier, Maurizio

Constanzo, *ph* Pasqualino De Santis, *ed* Raimondo Crocian, *mus* Armando Trovajoli; *with* Sophia Loren, Marcello Mastroianni, John Vernon, Françoise Berd. *A Special Day* portrays the simple, affecting story of a fleeting interlude in the lives of two people (Loren, playing against type as a lonely housewife married to a fascist bully, and Mastroianni, a homosexual facing deportation to the camps) who look out at each other across the courtyard. They are the only two that stay home when all others turn out for a monster rally held in Rome on 8 May 1938 to celebrate Hitler's historic visit. The two leads play off each other with practised ease, and veteran Italian director Ettore Scola artfully contrasts their brief encounter with the trumpeting of history. This small gem of a movie received an Academy Award nomination for Best Foreign-Language Film. (V)

Spencer, Michael

Producer and administrator; b. London, U.K., 1919. Spencer, a former producer and director of planning at the NFB, played a major role in the creation of the CFDC. In 1969, he was named executive director of the fledgling corporation. When he left in 1978, opinions differed on his contribution, but there is no doubt that during his tenure the film industry in Canada was transformed. Although chronically underfunded, the CFDC contributed funds to *Goin' down the Road,** *The Rowdyman,** *Paperback Hero,** *The Apprenticeship of Duddy Kravitz,** and many other seminal Canadian films, without which Canada wouldn't have a feature-film culture. **Credits include:** More than 60 NFB shorts 1941–54 (p).

Spotton, John

Director, producer, cinematographer, and editor; b. Toronto, 1927; d. 1991. The still of Buster Keaton on John Spotton's office wall at the NFB was an ironic recognition that *Buster Keaton Rides Again* was Spotton's big achievement in his long career as a supposedly pragmatic filmmaker. For over four decades, Spotton functioned as a jack of all trades – producing, directing, shooting, and editing films – mainly at the NFB. Although loyal to his bureaucratic masters, he was not averse to subversive activity, most notably in the case of *Nobody Waved Good-Bye*.* As Don Owen's cinematographer and editor, Spotton was complicit in the secretive expansion of a half-hour documentary on delinquents into a groundbreaking feature drama. Spotton also shot many of Tom Daly's* memorable direct-cinema efforts for Unit B, and co-directed the moving Holocaust film *Memorandum** with Donald Brittain.* **Films include:** *The Back-Breaking Leaf* 1959 (ed); *Circle of the Sun* 1961 (co-ph); *Runner* 1962 (ph); *Lonely Boy* 1962 (co-ed); *Nobody Waved Good-Bye* 1963 (ph/ ed); *The Hutterites* 1964 (ph/ed, CFA-PH); *High Steel* 1965 (ph); *Buster Keaton Rides Again* 1965 (d/ph/ed); *Memorandum* 1965 (ph/ed/co-d with Donald Brittain); *Never a Backward Step* 1966 (d with Brittain CFA-FD); *The People's Railway* 1973 (ph/ed/co-d with Brittain); *Circus World* 1974 (ph); *Have I Ever Lied to You Before?* 1976 (d); *Prisoners of Debt: Inside the Global Banking Crisis* 1983 (exp); *Final Offer: Bob White and the Canadian Auto Workers Fight for Independence* 1985 (exp, GA-FD); *Peep and the Big Wide World* 1988 (exp).

Spry, Robin

Director, producer, and writer; b. Toronto, 1939. Spry, a pioneer of the emerging English-Canadian film scene of the late 1960s, first became interested in film while attending university in Britain. When he returned to Canada in 1965, he joined the NFB as an assistant director and later made several docudramas focusing on social issues, including *Flowers on a One-Way Street*.* His first feature, *Prologue*, won a British Academy Award. Other works include the television film *Drying up the Streets* and the features *One Man*, *Suzanne*, and *Obsessed*. In recent years, he has produced films such as *Une Histoire inventée* and *Malarek* through his Montreal-based firm, Télé-scene. **Films and television include:** *Flowers on a One-Way Street* 1967 (d/sc); *Prologue* 1970 (co-p/d); *Québec: Duplessis et après ...* 1972 (a); *Action: The October Crisis of 1970* 1974 (co-p/d); *Reaction: A Portrait of a Society in Crisis* 1974 (co-p/ d); *Don't Forget 'Je me souviens'* 1979 (d, TV); *One Man* 1977 (d/co-sc); *Drying up the Streets* 1979 (d, TV); *Suzanne* 1980 (d/co-sc); *Keeping Track* 1985 (p/d); *À corps perdu* 1988 (co-p); *You've Come a Long Way, Ladies* 1988 (p, TV); *Obsessed* 1988 (co-p/d); *Malarek* 1989 (co-p); *Une Histoire inventée* 1990 (co-p); *A Cry in the Night* 1992 (d/sc, TV); *Myth of the Male Orgasm* 1993 (p); *On Dangerous Ground* 1995 (exp, TV); *Windsor Protocol* 1996 (exp, TV); *Thunder Point* 1996 (exp, TV); *Hiroshima* 1996 (exp, TV); *The Hunger* 1997–8 (exp, series); *Escape from Wildcat Canyon* 1998 (exp); *Arthur Conan Doyle's The Lost World* 2000–present (exp, series).

Stardom

2000 102m *prod* Alliance Atlantis, Serendipity Point Films, Cinémaginaire, Ciné b, *p* Robert Lantos, Denise Roberts, *d* Denys Arcand, *sc* Denys Arcand, J. Jacob Potashnik, *ph* Guy Dufaux, *ed* Isabelle Dedieu, *mus* François Dompierre; *with* Jessicca Paré, Dan Aykroyd, Robert Lepage, Charles Berling, Frank Langella, Camilla Rutherford, Thomas Gibson. *Stardom* is Arcand-lite. Canada's best-known satirist (*Le Déclin de l'empire* *américain** and *Jésus de Montréal**) turns his withering glance on the media attention given to the fashion industry. However, it's like using a shotgun to blast a gnat. Tina Menzel (Paré), a teenaged hockey player from Cornwell, Ontario, is spotted on a local cable-television program and launched on a high-flying modelling career that takes her to the runways of the world. Arcand* traces her rise and eventual return to Cornwell through mediated images such as television, talk shows, and an ever-present documentary filmmaker played by Lepage.* Unfortunately, the director appears to be slumming, and his take on celebrity and voyeurism is slight and dated. **Awards include:** GA: Costumes.

Stations

1983 86m *prod* Picture Plant, *d* William D. MacGillivray, *sc* William D. MacGillivray, Michael Jones, Lionel Simmons, *ph* Lionel Simmons, *ed* William D. MacGillivray, Lionel Simmons; *with* Michael Jones, Richard Boland, Libby Davies, Patricia Kipping. When Vancouver television journalist Tom Murphy (Jones*) learns of a friend's suicide back home in St John's, Newfoundland, he travels to the funeral by train. His station asks him to produce a documentary record of his pan-Canadian odyssey. As he travels, Murphy not only interviews his fellow passengers, but also begins to take stock of his own life. William D. MacGillivray's* first feature is a quiet, meditative 'rail movie' that penetrates the odd combination of displacement and roots that constitutes, for many Canadians, a kind of identity. Reminiscent of early Wim Wenders films, *Stations* is an absorbing examination of distinctly Canadian angst and the modes by which our culture expresses it.

Sternberg, Barbara

Filmmaker; b. Toronto, 1945. Sternberg, a tireless champion of experimental film since the mid-1970s, was one of the few women in Canada working in the genre at that time. Her films are both a product of and a challenge to the prevalent structuralist bent of her male counterparts. Sternberg's formally rigorous early films slowly gave way to no less demanding films of association with editing strategies that generate a sense of the fleeting and the ephemeral. Influenced by and quoting liberally from the writings of Gertrude Stein, Sternberg is driven by the same interest in repetition and the everyday. **Films include:** *Opus 40* 1979; *Transitions* 1982; *A Trilogy* 1985; *Tending towards the Horizontal* 1988; *At Present* 1990; *Through and Through* 19992; *Beating* 1995; *midst* 1997; *Like a Dream That Vanishes* 1999.

Stewart, Alexandra

Actor; b. Montreal, 1939. Alexandra Stewart studied art in Paris and became a fashion model before she was discovered by French director Louis Malle (whom she later married then divorced). Malle launched her career with *Le Feu follet*, considered by some critics to be his most accomplished film. Stewart also played secondary roles in Truffaut's *The Bride Wore Black* and *Day for Night*, and she starred opposite Warren Beatty in Arthur Penn's *Mickey One*. She made a string of Canadian films during the tax-shelter era,* including the controversial *In Praise of Older Women.* **Films and television include:** *Les Liaisons dangereuses* 1959; *Exodus* 1960; *Le Feu follet* 1963; *Mickey One* 1965; *Waiting for Caroline* 1967 (TV); *The Bride Wore Black* 1968; *Only When I Larf* 1968; *Zeppelin* 1971; *Day for Night* 1973; *Bingo* 1974; *Black Moon* 1975; *The Heat Wave Lasted Four Days* 1975 (TV); *In Praise of Older Women* 1978; *Final Assignment* 1980; *Agency* 1980; *The Last Chase* 1981; *Your Ticket Is No Longer Valid* 1981; *The Blood* *of Others* 1984; *Under the Cherry Moon* 1986.

Stratford Adventure, The
1954 40m *prod* NFB, *p* Guy Glover, *d* Morten Parker, *sc* Gudrun Parker, *ph* Donald Wilder, *ed* Douglas Tunstell, *mus* Louis Applebaum, *narr* John Drainie. This NFB documentary tells the story of the founding of what was to become North America's premiere Shakespearean festival, on the banks of the Avon River in the small Ontario town of Stratford. **Awards include:** CFA: Film of the Year, Feature Film; AAN: Short Documentary.

Strand: Under the Dark Cloth
1990 81m *prod* John Walker Productions, *p/d/ph* John Walker, *ed* Cathy Gulkin, John Kramer, Geoff Bowie, *mus* Jean Derome, René Lussier, *with* Georgia O'Keefe, Milton Brown, Fred Zimmerman, Cesare Zavattini. This poetic, beautifully shot, and deeply personal documentary brings into focus the life and career of Paul Strand, an important but little-known American twentieth-century pioneering photographer. Director and cinematographer John Walker* travelled to New York, Mexico, and France to investigate this complex and difficult imagemaker who influenced such diverse artists as the American painter Georgia O'Keefe and the Italian new-realist cinematographer Cesare Zevattini. For Walker, who began his own career as a still photographer, this film, which took years to shoot, was a labour of love. (V) **Awards include:** GA: Feature Documentary.

Strange Brew
1983 90m *prod* Strange Brew Film Productions, *exp* Jack Grossberg, *p* Louis M. Silverstein, *d* Rick Moranis, Dave Thomas, *sc* Rick Moranis, Dave Thomas, Steven De Jarnatt, *ph* Steven Poster, *ed* Patrick McMahon, *mus* Charles Fox; *with*

Dave Thomas, Rick Moranis, Max von Sydow, Paul Dooley, Lynne Griffin. *Strange Brew* is based on *SCTV*'s most endearing characters, the toque-wearing, beer-swilling Canucks from the Great White North, Bob and Doug McKenzie. The brothers translate fairly well onto the big screen with a silly script, penned by stars Rick Moranis* and Dave Thomas. The film is very loosely based on *Hamlet* and involves a nefarious plot launched by an evil villain played, hilariously, by Max von Sydow. *Strange Brew* was wildly successful in Canada, where it won the Golden Reel Award, but didn't do as well in the United States; MGM pulled it after small returns on a limited run. However, the film has proven to be a minor cult classic on television; despite sporadic attempts, a sequel has not yet materialized. (V) **Awards include:** Golden Reel Award.

Stratten, Dorothy
Actor and model; b. Vancouver, 1960; d. in 1980. While not a beauty as a child, Stratten came into her own in high school and attracted the attention of Paul Snider, a promoter and wannabe star. He convinced her to pose for *Playboy*, and in 1979 she was chosen to be a Playmate. In 1980, it was revealed that Stratten would be Playmate of the Year, but when the jealous Snider found out she was having an affair with director Peter Bogdonavich, he killed her and then himself. Since her death, Stratten has become something of a cult figure. Bob Fosse's biopix, *Star 80*, traced her short, tragic life. **Films include:** *Americathon* 1979; *Skatetown, U.S.A.* 1979; *Galaxina* 1980; *They All Laughed* 1981.

Street, The
1976 10m12s *prod* NFB, *exp* Wolf Koenig, *p* Guy Glover, *d/an* Caroline Leaf, *story* Mordecai Richler. *The Street* (based on a short story by Mordecai Richler*) is a

marvellously visual, stream-of-consciousness story, told from the point of view of a nine-year-old boy about the summer his grandmother died. The film is set in the St Urbain district of Richler's youth, and the character's are familiar from the *Duddy Kravitz* novel. However, the text of this beautiful award-winning film is completely upstaged by the fluid work of animator Caroline Leaf,* who uses soft, transformational watercolour wash and ink drawings on glass plates to create images with a striking three-dimensional quality that give the feeling of a painting constantly in motion. (V) **Awards include:** CFA: Animated Short; AAN: Animated Short.

Such a Long Journey
1999 113m *prod* The Film Works, Amy International Artists, *exp* Victor Solnicki, *p* Paul Stephens, Simon MacCorkindale, *d* Sturla Gunnarsson, *sc* Sooni Taraporevala, *novel* Rohinton Mistry, *ph* Jan Kiesser, *ed* Jeff Warren, *mus* Jonathan Goldsmith; *with* Roshan Seth, Soni Razdan, Om Puri, Ranjit Chowdhry, Kurush Deboo. Based on Rohinton Mistry's Govenor General Award–winning novel set in the teaming heart of Bombay, India, *Such a Long Journey* tells the tale of the Noble family. Gustad (Seth) is a dedicated bank clerk who finds his modest but peaceful life unravelling when he is asked to do a favour for an old friend working for the Bengali resistance: his rebellious son refuses to go to the school of his choice and leaves home; his daughter becomes sick with malaria; and his wife (Razdan) concocts spells to restore some semblance of order to the chaos. The film works well as a vehicle for some fine performances, and is well directed and emotionally effective, but fans of the novel found the pared-down script failed to capture the complexity and beauty of Mistry's story of a family – and India – in crisis. (V) **Awards include:** GA: Actor (Seth), Editing, Sound Editing.

Sunshine
1999 180m *prod* Alliance Atlantis Pictures, Kinowelt (Germany), ISL Film (Hungary), Dor Film (Hungary), *exp* Rainer Kolmel, Jonathan Debin, *p* Robert Lantos, Andras Hamori, *d* István Szabó, *sc* István Szabó, Israel Horovitz, *ph* Lajos Koltai, *ed* Dominique Fortin, Michael Arcand, *mus* Maurice Jarre; *with* Ralph Fiennes, Rosemary Harris, Rachel Weisz, Jennifer Ehle, Deborah Kara Ungar, Molly Parker, William Hurt. *Sunshine*, a chronicle of a Hungarian-Jewish family, the Sonnenschein's, over three generations, aims at epic status. Evoking some of the worst traumas of the twentieth century during its three-hour running time, the movie portrays victimized European Jews as courageous, but flawed and far from saintly. The focal point of each generational chapter is a male Sonnenschein whose drive to reach the apex of Hungarian society blinds him to the tragic reality that he will always remain an outsider. Fiennes plays all three – father, son, and grandson – with careful attention to detail. Although *Sunshine* is old-fashioned and faltering at times, it is an engrossing, thematically rich film that packs an emotional punch. **Awards include:** GA: Picture, Overall Sound, Sound Editing.

Surfacing on the Thames
1970 6m *p/d/ph/ed* David Rimmer. This early found-footage film is a remarkable transformation of original material. Rimmer* based his film on five feet of Second World War footage showing two ships passing on the Thames River. He systematically re-filmed and froze the frames until he achieved an abstracted

look, something akin to an impressionistic painting. The materiality of the film image is highlighted as every imperfection, watermark, and scratch, is brought to the fore. Legend has it that one critic actually believed he was looking at a work by the nineteenth-century English painter J.M.W. Turner. In his manipulation of the rather pedestrian footage, Rimmer has created both a lyrical gesture and an incisive meditation on the material basis of cinema.

Sutherland, Donald

Actor; b. Saint John, N.B., 1934; father of Kiefer Sutherland. Donald Sutherland is indisputably one of the world's most versatile actors. His career spans a vast and open cinematic terrain: from bit parts to leading roles, from American potboilers to European art-house cinema, from *Klute* to *M*A*S*H*, to *Fellini's Casanova*, to *Ordinary People*, to *Bethune: The Making of a Hero*.* He began his career as a stage actor, first in Canada, then in Britain before making his screen debut in 1964. Sutherland's unique screen presence has made him much in demand, and he has produced a body of work that is as beguilingly diverse as it is lengthy. **Films include:** *Castle of the Living Dead* 1964; *Dr. Terror's House of Horrors* 1964; *Die! Die! My Darling* 1965; *The Bedford Incident* 1965; *Promise Her Anything* 1966; *The Dirty Dozen* 1967; *Oedipus the King* 1968; *The Split* 1968; *The Act of the Heart* 1970; *Alex in Wonderland* 1970; *Start the Revolution without Me* 1970; *Kelly's Heroes* 1970; *M*A*S*H* 1970; *Johnny Got His Gun* 1971; *Klute* 1971; *Little Murders* 1971; *FTA* 1972 (p/sc/a); *Don't Look Now* 1973; *Steelyard Blues* 1973 (exp/a); *The Day of the Locust* 1975; *Fellini's Casanova* 1976; *The Eagle Has Landed* 1976; *1900* 1976; *The Kentucky Fried Movie* 1977; *Blood Relatives* 1978; *Invasion of the Body Snatchers* 1978; *National Lampoon's*

Animal House 1978; *Murder by Decree* 1979; *Bear Island* 1979; *A Man, a Woman and a Bank* 1979; *Ordinary People* 1980; *Nothing Personal* 1980; *The Disappearance* 1981; *Eye of the Needle* 1981; *Threshold* 1982 (GA-A); *Max Dugan Returns* 1982; *Revolution* 1985; *The Trouble with Spies* 1987; *A Dry White Season* 1989; *Lock Up* 1989; *Bethune: The Making of a Hero* 1990; *JFK* 1991; *Buffy the Vampire Slayer* 1992; *Six Degrees of Separation* 1993; *Younger and Younger* 1993; *Outbreak* 1995; *A Time to Kill* 1996; *The Assignment* 1997; *Fallen* 1998; *Without Limits* 1998; *Virus* 1999; *Instinct* 1999; *Space Cowboys* 2000; *The Art of War* 2000; *The Big Heist* 2001 (TV).

Sutherland, Kiefer

Actor and director; b. London, U.K., 1967; son of Donald Sutherland. Kiefer Sutherland appears to have taken much the same approach as his father. Following an impressive screen debut opposite Liv Ullmann in Daniel Petrie's* coming-of-age story *The Bay Boy*,* he took on an eclectic range of films and has become one of his generation's most consistent performers. **Films include:** *The Bay Boy* 1984; *Crazy Moon* 1986; *Stand by Me* 1986; *The Killing Time* 1987; *The Lost Boys* 1987; *Bright Lights, Big City* 1988; *1969* 1988; *Young Guns* 1988; *Flatliners* 1990; *Chicago Joe and the Showgirl* 1990 (d/a); *Flashback* 1990; *Young Guns II* 1990; *A Few Good Men* 1992; *The Three Musketeers* 1993; *A Time to Kill* 1996; *Truth or Consequences, N.M.* 1997 (d); *Dark City* 1998; *Woman Wanted* 2000 (d/a).

Sweater, The

1980 10m21s *prod* NFB, *exp* Derek Lamb, *p* David Verrall, Marrin Canell, *d/an* Sheldon Cohen, *sc/story/narr* Roch Carrier, *ed* David Verrall, *mus* Normand Roger. In the rural Quebec of Roch Carrier's boyhood, Maurice 'Rocket' Richard was king of the ice and Les Canadiens No. 9 was the only hockey sweater to wear, and the conflict between the two solitudes was played out on the hockey rink. This animated film is based on Carrier's funny and heartwarming short story about a boy whose mother orders him a hockey sweater from the Eaton's catalogue. A mistake is made and the boy receives a Toronto Maple Leaf jersey instead! (V)

Sweet Hereafter, The

1997 110m *prod* Ego Film Arts, *exp* Robert Lantos, Andras Hamori, *p* Atom Egoyan, Camelia Frieberg, *d/sc* Atom Egoyan, *novel* Russell Banks, *ph* Paul Sarossy, *ed* Susan Shipton, *mus* Mychael Danna, Toronto Consort; *with* Ian Holm, Tom McCamus, Sarah Polley, Bruce Greenwood, Gabrielle Rose, Alberta Watson, Arsinée Khanjian. Based on the novel by Russell Banks, *The Sweet Hereafter* recounts the events leading up to and following a school bus accident that kills fourteen children. The story follows the families whose lives irrevocably change, and a big-city lawyer (Holm) who shows up in the community hoping to sign people up for a class-action lawsuit. In the ensuing atmosphere of suspicion, guilt, and doubt, a surviving teenager (Polley*) manages to regain her strength and dignity, and by telling a lie, reunites the community and drives the lawyer from the town. Egoyan's* excellent adaptation of Banks's complex tale of guilt and redemption is told in a *Rashomon*-like fashion. The cast is seamlessly perfect, and Holm's central performance as the deeply flawed lawyer with a smouldering intelligence holds the screen with a magnetic core. (V) **Awards include:** GA: Picture, Director, Actor (Holm), Cinematography, Editing, Musical Score, Overall Sound, Sound Editing; AAN: Director and Adapted Screenplay; Cannes: Grand Jury Prize and International Film Critics' Prize.

Sweet Substitute

1964 85m *prod* Larry Kent Productions, *p/d/sc* Larry Kent, *ph* Richard Bellamy, *ed* Shelah Reljic, *m* Jack Dale; *with* Robert Howay, Angela Gann, Carol Pastinsky, Lanning Beckman. This quintessential independent feature from the early 1960s is the second feature from Vancouver director Larry Kent.* Like his earlier *The Bitter Ash,* *Sweet Substitute* is improvisational but is based on a structured outline. The film tells the tale of a randy college-bound student (Howay) who just wants to have sex. His girlfriend Kathy (Gann) wants marriage first, so he searches for women who are more willing. When one (Pastinsky) becomes pregnant, he makes a cowardly return to Kathy and the safer confines of middle-class respectability. The film was much admired by critics at the time of its release but since then has disappeared from view. **Awards include:** CFA: Special Award.

T

Tadpole and the Whale, The

1988 92m *prod* Les Productions La Fête, *p* Rock Demers, *d* Jean-Claude Lord, *sc* Jacques Bobet, André Melançon, *ph* Tom Burstyn, *ed* Hélène Giraud; *with* Fanny Lauzier, Denis Forest, Marina Orsini, Félix-Antoine Leroux, Jean Lajeunesse, Lise Thouin. *The Tadpole and the Whale*, the sixth film in Rock Demers's* Tales for All series, is a simple and affecting story of Daphne (the Tadpole of the title, played with winning charm by twelve-year-old Lauzier), a girl who has the ability to understand the language of dolphins and whales. She lives in idyllic splendour on the St Lawrence North

Shore, but her world is put in jeopardy when the estranged brothers who own the inn her parents operate want to sell it. Her efforts to bring the warring siblings together and save her beloved life with dolphins provides the dramatic focus to a predictable plot that could well be made for *The World of Disney*. (V) **Awards include:** Golden Reel Award.

Tales from the Gimli Hospital
1988 72m *prod* Extra Large Productions, Winnipeg Film Group, *exp* Greg Klymkiw, *p* Steve Snyder, *d/sc/ph/ed* Guy Maddin; *with* Michael Gottli, Angela Heck, Margaret-Anne MacLeod, Kyle McCulloch. This strange little film somehow manages to combine synchronized swimming, necrophilia, and buttock wrestling with an Icelandic legend and a unique expressionistic look. The story, set during a smallpox outbreak in turn-of-the-century Gimli, Manitoba, revolves around two men who share a hospital room. In an attempt to impress the nubile nurses, the men engage in a competitive exchange of bizarre tales from their individual pasts. As the men descend into madness, the stories eventually reveal their intertwined fates. (V)

Tana, Paul
Director and writer; b. Ancone, Italy, 1947. Tana has been a resident of Quebec since 1958, but his Italian origins make a noticeable appearance in his films, starting with *Les Grands Enfants*. His meeting with historian Bruno Ramirez, a specialist in Quebec immigration, proved decisive. They collaborated on the writing of *Caffè Italia Montréal*, a docu-fiction for which Tana won fame, which tells the story of three generations of Italian immigrants making their way in a culturally insular Montreal. Further collaborations include two fictional features, the masterful *La Sarrasine*,*

for which star Tony Nardi won the Best Actor Genie, and the less successful *La Déroute*, again starring Nardi. **Films include:** *Les Grands Enfants* 1980 (d); *Caffè Italia Montréal* 1985 (d/co-sc); *La Sarrasine* 1992 (d/co-sc); *La Déroute* 1998 (d/co-sc).

Tax-Shelter Era
The term used to identify those films made between 1974 and 1982, explicitly to take advantage of the provisions of the 100 per cent capital cost allowance introduced by the federal government in 1974 for feature films. The allowance created a tax shelter that enabled wealthy investors to deduct 100 per cent of their investment in certifiable Canadian films. The resulting boom in production of films made for tax purposes only occurred in the latter part of the 1970s and early 1980s. The federal regulations and restrictions were so complex that the scheme attracted professional investment brokers, accountants, and lawyers who took advantage of 'up front' fees and cared little about distribution. The films, which invariably featured second-rate Hollywood talent and were designed for international sales, for the large part, were dreadful. By 1982, when the tax rules were changed to reflect a 50 per cent write-off, the scheme had run its course. The increased production activity, however, created a large number of service jobs and a few of the films – *Who Has Seen the Wind** (1977), *The Silent Partner** (1978), *Murder by Decree** (1979), *Atlantic City** (1980), *The Grey Fox** (1983) – do have merit.

Taylor, Nat
Exhibitor, distributor, producer, and journalist; b. Toronto, 1906. An enigmatic, yet important figure in the development of a film culture in Canada, Taylor owned and operated the Twenti-

eth Century theatre circuit, the largest of the independents, and he opened the world's first 'twin' theatre in Ottawa in 1948. In 1942, with publisher Hye Bosin, he launched the *Canadian Film Weekly*, and used the paper as a platform to lobby for greater federal government involvement in feature-film production. He produced Julian Roffman's *The Mask*, which was the first Canadian feature marketed extensively in the United States; however, his lasting achievement was the introduction of multiplex cinemas, a concept that he developed for thirty years before launching the Cineplex chain with producer Garth Drabinsky* in 1979. **Films include:** *The Mask* 1961 (exp); *The Reincarnate* 1971 (exp).

Temps d'une chasse, Les
1972 98m *prod*, NFB, *p* Pierre Gauvreau, *d/sc* Francis Mankiewicz, *ph* Michel Brault, *ed* Werner Nold, *mus* Pierre Brault; *with* Guy L'Ecuyer, Marcel Sabourin, Pierre Dufresne, Olivier L'Ecuyer. This first feature from Francis Mankiewicz* (who would later make the masterful *Les Bons Débarras**) is a critical but not entirely unsympathetic examination of the rituals of male bonding. Three friends (Guy L'Ecuyer, Sabourin,* and Dufresne) and the son of one of the men (Olivier L'Ecuyer) spend a weekend hunting together in the Quebec bush. They pass the first night in a motel bar where they get drunk and harass the waitresses. Not much else happens in this character drama, but Mankiewicz's insight into their empty, desperate lives, and Michel Brault's* outstanding camera work make this one of the best films to come out of Quebec in the early 1970s. (V) **Awards include:** CFA: Cinematography, Overall Sound.

Tender Tale of Cinderella Penguin, The
1981 10m *prod* NFB, *exp* Derek Lamb, *p/d/an* Janet Perman, *ph* Pierre Landry,

Raymond Dumas, Jacques Avoine. In this fresh take on a centuries-old fairy tale, Cinderella is a penguin who loses her magic flipper as she runs to meet her midnight deadline. All ends well when Prince Charming finds the right webbed foot. The film received an Academy Award nomination for Animated Short. (V)

Terry Fox Story, The
1983 97m *prod* Robert Cooper Films, *exp* Gurston Rosenfeld, Michael Levine, *p* Robert Cooper, *d* Ralph Thomas, *sc* Edward Hume, *ph* Richard Ciupka, *ed* Ron Wiseman, *mus* Bill Conti; *with* Robert Duvall, Eric Fryer, Chris Makepeace, Rosalind Chao, Michael Zelniker. *The Terry Fox Story* is a fairly straightforward rendering of a story that has by now become overly familiar. Fryer's performance as the doomed runner is admirable and he is not afraid to shy away from the unpleasant bits. Fox was an emotional volcano, struggling to express what he felt about his leg, his disease, and the tremendous rush of emotion that was directed towards him as his run entered Ontario. Director Ralph Thomas wisely surrounded the newcomer (Fryer, like Fox, had lost his leg to cancer and this was his first role) with pros such as Robert Duvall and was able to capture the heroics of the story with striking images such as Fryer pounding down stretches of mind-numbingly lonely, empty highway. (V) **Awards include:** GA: Picture, Actor (Fryer), Supporting Actor (Zelniker), Editing, Overall Sound, Sound Editing.

Things I Cannot Change, The
1966 58m *prod* NFB, *p* John Kemeny, *d* Tanya Ballantyne, *ph* Paul Leach, *ed* William Brind. This striking documentary, which focuses on one Montreal family's struggle with poverty, is a remarkable film, full of poetic images,

heart-wrenching moments, and editing that was far ahead of its time. The fact that the patriarch of the Bailey family is clearly alcoholic, makes the situation faced by his wife and their numerous offspring even more dire. The film became notorious as a textbook case for ethical dilemmas in documentary filmmaking: the family complained that, after the film was aired nationally on CBC-TV, the notoriety they gained led to serious detrimental effects in their employment and housing – an ironic outcome for a film that was supposed to help the poor. (V)

Thirty-Two Short Films about Glenn Gould

1994 93m *prod* Rhombus Media, *p* Niv Fichman, *d* François Girard, *sc* François Girard, Don McKellar, *ph* Alain Dostie, *ed* Gaétan Huot, *mus* Glenn Gould; *with* Colm Feore. In essence, Glenn Gould was a translator. His legendary status is rooted in his reshaping of established musical texts, principally Bach and Beethoven, with a remarkable, idiosyncratic combination of technical mastery and artistic imagination. Gould also reinvented classical music culture with his provocative philosophical challenges to performance codes, new technologies, and the role of the artist. No conventional bio-pic, *Thirty-Two Short Films* is a striking cinematic orchestration of thirty-two separate visual and sonic fragments (dramatic re-enactment, documentary, animation, etc.) about Gould's life and work. Girard's* direction of Don McKellar's* script manages to both illuminate and mystify its elusive subject. (V)
Awards include: GA: Picture, Director, Cinematography, Editing.

Thomson, R.H.

Actor; b. Toronto, 1947. At university Thomson majored in math and physics, but he left the lab for the stage. This re-markably talented actor has over forty screen credits to his name, but despite the more lucrative fees for acting in Hollywood films, Thomson has resolutely remained in Canada. He has won every major acting award in theatre, film, and television and has shown considerable range – from the waterfront thug in *Canada's Sweetheart: The Saga of Hal C. Banks** to a survivor of the Holocaust in *The Quarrel*. Currently, he hosts CBC-TV's long-running *Man Alive* series, a role, he has said, that suits his opinionated disposition. **Films and television include:** *L'Homme en colère* 1979; *An American Christmas Carol* 1979 (TV); *Escape from Iran: The Canadian Caper* 1981 (TV); *Surfacing* 1981; *Les Beaux Souvenirs* 1981; *Ticket to Heaven* 1981; *If You Could See What I Hear* 1982 (GA-SA); *The Terry Fox Story* 1983; *Charlie Grant's War* 1983 (TV); *Canada's Sweetheart: The Saga of Hal C. Banks* 1985 (TV); *Samuel Lount* 1985; *Heaven on Earth* 1987; *Glory Enough for All* 1987 (TV); *And Then You Die* 1987; *Ford: The Man and the Machine* 1987 (TV); *Love and Hate: The Story of Colin and Joann Thatcher* 1989 (TV); *The Quarrel* 1990; *Mark Twain and Me* 1991 (TV); *The Lotus Eaters* 1993; *Max* 1994; *The Babymaker: The Dr Cecil Jacobson Story* 1994 (TV); *The Marriage Bed* 1996 (TV); *Net Worth* 1996 (TV); *Man Alive* 1996–present (host, series); *Twilight of the Ice Nymphs* 1997; *Hollywoodism: Jews, Movies, and the American Dream* 1998 (narr); *Crime in Connecticut: The Story of Alex Kelly* 1999 (TV); *P.T. Barnum* 1999 (TV).

Ticket to Heaven

1981 108m *prod* Ronald Cohen Productions, *exp* Ronald Cohen, *p* Vivienne Leebosh, *d* Ralph L. Thomas, *sc* Anne Cameron, Ralph L. Thomas, *book* Josh Freed, *ph* Richard Leiterman, *ed* Ron Wisman, *mus* Micky Erbe, Maribeth Solomon; *with* Nick Mancuso, Saul Rubinek, Meg Foster, Kim Cattrall,

R.H. Thomson, Jennifer Dale. David (Mancuso), a Torontonian, visits a friend in California and joins a commune. The constant singsongs and chanting sessions soon make it apparent that he has become involved with a cult. Meanwhile, his friend Larry (Rubinek*) becomes concerned and rallies friends and family to rescue David. Director Thomas brought talents honed on CBC-TV's *For the Record** to this much-praised film, which features strong performances by Mancuso, R.H. Thomson* (as a professional deprogrammer), and Rubinek. Yet, while the early brainwashing scenes are engaging and believable, the film meanders and the deprogramming section toward the end is all too brief. *Ticket to Heaven* ends up as a comfortable, non-threatening movie of the week. **Awards include:** GA: Picture, Actor (Mancuso), Supporting Actor (Rubinek), Editing.

Titanica

1992 90m *prod* Low Films International, Imax Corporation, *exp* André Picard, Joe MacInnis, *p* Stephen Low, Pietro Serapiglia, *d* Stephen Low, *ph* Ralph White, *ed* James Lahti, *narr* Leonard Nimoy. One of the most popular and highest-grossing Canadian films ever made, *Titanica* is a narrative-driven feature-length documentary about a crew who descended to the depths of the North Atlantic in 1991 to film the Titanic's remains. Though some of the shots of the ruins are a bit too long, the international crew is eccentric enough that our interest becomes focused on them and the state-of-the-art technology they used in the expedition rather than on the ill-fated ship. Extensive underwater shots on the IMAX screen leave viewers feeling damp by the final frames.

Tit-coq

1953 101m *prod* Les Productions Gratien Gélinas, *exp* Paul L'Anglais, *p/sc/play* Gratien Gélinas, *d* René Delacroix, Gratien Gélinas, *ph* Akos Farkas, *ed* Anton Van de Water, Roger Garand, *mus* Maurice Blackburn, Morris Davis; *with* Gratien Gélinas, Clément Latour, Monique Miller, Denise Pelletier. Gratien Gélinas's* immensely popular play started life as a film script, but when he had difficulty raising the financing, he began performing it on stage. By 1952 he was able to raise the money. The script, filmed essentially as it appeared on stage, tells the story of Tit-coq (Gélinas), a shy, awkward French-Canadian soldier with an irreverent sense of humour who falls for the sister (Miller) of a friend (Latour). She promises to wait for him when he is sent overseas but she doesn't. When Tit-coq returns he is once again alone in the world. The play made Gélinas a star in Quebec, and the film was a box-office hit in both languages. **Awards include:** CFA: Film of the Year, Feature Film.

Toronto New Wave

Toronto new wave is a catchy phrase for a spirited generation of English-Canadian filmmakers who came to cinematic maturity during the mid- to late-1980s, rather than an expression of a particular group aesthetic. Peter Mettler,* Bruce McDonald,* Atom Egoyan,* Patricia Rozema,* John Greyson,* Don McKellar,* and Ron Mann,* along with producers Camelia Frieberg,* Alexandra Raffé,* Colin Brunton, Janis Lundman, and others, came bursting on to the Canadian movie scene with fresh, original films that equally rejected Hollywood's conventional dramas and the earlier English-Canadian *cinéastes* (such as Don Shebib* and Don Owen*) who had made downbeat films about heartbreak and loss.

Most of Toronto's new wave, graduates of University of Toronto, Sheridan College, or Ryerson Polytechnic University's film department, gravitated to LIFT (Liaison of Independent Filmmakers of Toronto), a funky film co-op, the spiritual successor to the original Toronto Filmmakers Co-op, located in a downtown warehouse. Leading the way into features were Mettler (with *Scissere* in 1982) and Mann (with two exceptional documentaries – *Imagine the Sound* in 1981 on jazz, and *Poetry in Motion* in 1982). Egoyan followed in 1984 with *Next of Kin*, a fictional comic feature about identity. Many of the young filmmakers (all under 30) worked on each other's films. Mettler shot *Next of Kin*, Rozema's *Passion* (1985), and McDonald's *Knock! Knock!* (1985), while McDonald edited *Scissere*, Egoyan's *Family Viewing* (1987), and Mann's *Comic Book Confidential* (1988). McDonald also guest-edited the 1988 'Outlaw Edition' of *Cinema Canada*, which publicized the existence of this new breed of filmmakers. Despite the lack of a defining manifesto, these Toronto-based filmmakers existed through a close-knit sense of cooperation of a kind rarely seen in Canada since the growth of Quebec cinema in the early 1960s.

Two major events of the 1980s gave credence and cash to these young Toronto filmmakers. In 1984 Toronto's Festival of Festivals held the largest retrospective of Canadian films ever programed in Canada. This event launched Perspective Canada, an ongoing festival series that has become the most prestigious venue for launching English-Canadian features. In 1986, the doors to the Ontario Film Development Corporation (OFDC) opened, providing a much needed alternative to the narrow, experimental restrictions of the Ontario Arts Council and the bureaucratic red tape of Telefilm Canada in Montreal. From the

start, the OFDC was unofficially mandated to create an Ontario film culture. Under the guidance of its first CEO, Wayne Clarkson* (who, as the former head of the Toronto festival, had been partially responsible for launching Perspective Canada), it proceeded to do so.

The breakthrough came in 1987 when Rozema's first low-budget feature, *I've Heard the Mermaids Singing*,* won the Prix de la Jeunesse at Cannes. The film, and Rozema herself, received a tremendous amount of international press attention and *Mermaids* did something almost unheard of for an English-Canadian film – it actually made money at the box office. A number of key new-wave films followed in the wake of Rozema's stunning success: Egoyan's *Speaking Parts** (1989), *The Adjuster** (1991), and *Exotica** (which won the International Critics' Prize at Cannes in 1994); Bruce McDonald's *Roadkill** (1990), and *Highway 61** (1992), both written by Don McKellar; John Greyson's *Zero Patience** (1994); and Peter Mettler's *Top of His Head* (1989) and *Tectonic Plates* (1992).

What is remarkable about this group of filmmakers is that they, unlike previous generations, avoided the easy lure of big money and bigger films in Hollywood. Instead, like their cinematic mentor David Cronenberg,* they chose to stay in Canada and actually make a living while practising their chosen profession.

Trent, John

Producer, director, and writer; b. London, U.K., 1935; d. 1983. Trent came to Canada in 1960, starting out as a magazine writer then quickly moving into directing. He directed or produced more than 700 shows for Canadian and American television, including such popular Canadian series as *Wojeck*,

Quentin Durgens M.P., and *For the Record*.*
His film work consists mostly of dread-
ful early tax-shelter era* bombs such as
It Seemed like a Good Idea at the Time with
Anthony Newly, but later in his career
he directed the prestige CBC dramas
Riel and *Crossbar*. Trent was a founding
member of the Directors Guild of Cana-
da, and he formed his own production
company, Quadrant Films, with David
Perlmutter, in 1971. **Films and television include:** *Wojeck* 1966–8 (d, series);
The Bushbaby 1968 (p/d); *Homer* 1970 (d);
The Heart Farm 1970; *The White Oaks of
Jalna* 1972 (d, series); *Dead of Night* 1974
(exp); *Blue Blood* 1974 (p); *Sunday in the
Country* 1974 (d/sc); *It Seemed like a Good
Idea at the Time* 1975 (d/sc); *Find the Lady*
1976 (p/d/sc); *Love at First Sight* 1977
(exp); *The Fighting Men* 1977 (p); *Riel*
1979 (p, TV); *Crossbar* 1979 (d, TV);
Middle Age Crazy 1980 (d); *Best Revenge*
1984 (d).

32 août sur terre, Un
1998 88m *prod* Max Films, *p* Roger Frap-
pier, *d/sc* Denis Villeneuve, *ph* André
Turpin, *ed* Sophie Leblond, *mus* Nathalie
Boileau, Pierre Desrochers, Robert
Charlebois, Jean Leloup; *with* Pascale
Bussières, Alexis Martin, Sérge Thériault,
Richard Hamilton, Paule Baillargeon.
Denis Villeneuve's* debut feature is
predicated on a life-changing car crash.
In the aftermath of a highway mishap,
photo model Simone (Bussières*) goes
full-tilt existential and decides that con-
ceiving a baby with old flame Philippe
(Martin) is the only way to give her vacant life some meaning. Philippe reluc-
tantly agrees with the proviso that they
conceive in a desert. Villeneuve is a director who can hold your attention with
a wordless sequence and assemble
seamless montages. However, once the
odd couple hits the salt flats of Utah, his

Generation-X angst comedy loses its
bearings, and we wish Simone and
Philippe would cut the word play and
get on with it. They never do and things
end badly. (V) **Awards include:** PJ:
Actor (Martin).

Tribute
1980 124m *prod* Tiberius Film Corp.,
exp Lawrence Turman, David Foster,
Richard Bright, *p* Garth Drabinsky, Joel
Michaels, *d* Bob Clark, *sc/play* Bernard
Slade, *ph* Reginald Morris, *ed* Richard
Halsey, Stan Cole, Ian McBride, *mus* Ken
Wannberg; *with* Jack Lemmon, Robby
Benson, Lee Remick, John Marley, Kim
Cattrall, Gale Garnett, Colleen Dewhurst. Bernard Slade wrote the script for
his film version of his successful play.
Lemmon plays a bon vivant press agent
who learns he is dying of cancer and
wants only to reconcile himself with his
estranged son (Benson). Director Bob
Clark* seems helpless to rein in Lemmon, who mugs and clowns his way
through what is essentially an old-
fashioned Hollywood weepie. The film's
final scene, a tribute to Lemmon with
Benson and Remick (who gives the
film's best performance as Lemmon's
divorced wife) in attendance is effective,
but taken as a whole, the film is a less-
than-satisfactory star vehicle. (V)
Awards include: GA: Foreign Actor
(Lemmon).

U

Universe
1960 26m *prod* NFB, *p/ed* Tom Daly,
d Roman Koitor, Colin Low, *sc* Roman
Kroitor, *ph* Denis Gillson, Wolf Koenig,
design Sydney Goldsmith, Colin Low,
special effects Wally Gentleman, Herbet
Taylor, James Wilson, *mus* Eldon Rath-

burn, *narr* Stanley Jackson. Perhaps the NFB's most honoured film – with twenty-three major awards including an Academy Award nomination and a special award at Cannes – *Universe* is a marvel of animation made with such mathematical precision that it became required viewing by NASA technicians as they plotted to send a manned space craft to the moon. It also attracted the attention of Stanley Kubrick, who used techniques developed by the NFB team (led by Kroitor,* Low,* Goldsmith, and Gentleman) for the special effects in his groundbreaking epic *2001: A Space Odyssey*. Realistic animation takes the viewer on a trip through the universe from ground zero, Earth, to the farthest reaches of space. (V) **Awards include:** CFA: Film of the Year, Theatrical Short; AAN: Animated Short; Cannes: Jury Prize for animation.

V

Valérie
1969 95m *prod* Cinépix, *p* John Dunning, André Link, *d* Denis Héroux, *sc* Louis Gauthier, Denis Héroux, John Dunning, André Link, *ph* René Verzier, *ed* Jean Lafleur, *mus* Joe Cracy, Michel Paje; *with* Danielle Ouimet, Guy Godin, Yvan Ducharme, Claude Préfontaine. *Valérie* is the story of a comely young woman (Ouimet) who, upon leaving a convent with the leader of a motorcycle gang, discovers the hippy culture of Montreal and turns to prostitution. This improbable storyline, made famous by the frank display of nudity and sexuality, came from a culture that was still labouring under a strong sense of Catholic guilt. It was the first of a group of films now known as 'maple-syrup porn,' and it turned an unprecedented gross of over a million, making it the top domestic box-office film of its time. *Valérie* also launched the careers of John Dunning,* André Link,* and Denis Héroux.*

Vernon, John
Actor; b. Adolphus Vernon Agoposwicz, Montreal, 1932. In addition to his many films, both U.S. and Canadian (remember his growling dispensation of worldly wisdom to Peter in *Nobody Waved Good-Bye**?), Vernon starred in the legendary Canadian television series *Wojeck*. This distinguished stage and screen performer was often cast as the self-assured heavy or crafty villain. An underrated character actor, Vernon is undoubtedly the only human in history to have appeared in both an episode of *The Forest Rangers* and a film by Alfred Hitchcock (*Topaz*). He is perhaps best remembered as the mayor opposite Clint Eastwood in Don Siegel's *Dirty Harry*, and the thief who is viciously betrayed by Angie Dickenson in John Boorman's *Point Blank*. **Films and television include:** *1984* 1956 (voice of Big Brother); *Nobody Waved Good-Bye* 1964; *Wojeck* 1966–8 (series); *Point Blank* 1967; *Topaz* 1969; *Tell Them Willie Boy Is Here* 1969; *Justine* 1969; *Face-Off* 1971; *Dirty Harry* 1971; *Journey* 1972; *Fear Is the Key* 1972; *Charley Varrick* 1973; *The Black Windmill* 1975; *Sweet Movie* 1975; *Brannigan* 1975; *The Swiss Family Robinson* 1975 (TV); *The Outlaw Josey Wales* 1976; *The Uncanny* 1977; *A Special Day* 1977; *Angela* 1978; *National Lampoon's Animal House* 1978; *It Rained All Night the Day I Left* 1979; *Herbie Goes Bananas* 1980; *Fantastica* 1980; *Heavy Metal* 1981 (voice); *The Blue and the Gray* 1982 (TV); *Airplane* II: *The Sequel* 1982; *Chained Heat* 1983; *Curtains* 1983; *The Blood of Others* 1984; *Hail to the Chief* 1985 (TV); *Ernest Goes to Camp* 1987; *Killer Klowns from Outer Space* 1988; *I'm Gonna Git You Sucka* 1988; *Mob Story* 1989; *Wojeck* 1992 (TV); *The Naked Truth*

1992; *Hostage for a Day* 1994 (TV); *Sod-busters* 1994 (TV); *Family of Cops* 1995 (TV).

Verrall, David

Producer; b. Ottawa, 1948; son of Robert Verrall. David Verrall followed in his father's footsteps, joining the NFB in 1977 and rising to become head of the English animation department. His credits include *Bob's Birthday*,* which won an Academy Award, *When the Day Breaks*,* which was nominated for one, and the films of John Weldon.* **Films include:** *Laugh Lines: A Profile of Kaj Pindal* 1979 (p with Derek Lamb); *The Sweater* 1980 (co-p); *The Awful Fate of Melpomenus Jones* 1983 (p); *Real Inside* 1984 (p/d with John Weldon); *Narcissus* 1983 (p); *Elephantrio* 1985 (co-p); *Of Dice and Men* 1988 (p); *The Magical Eye* 1989 (p with Terence Macarthney-Filgate); *To Be* 1990 (p); *The Lump* 1991 (p); *Bob's Birthday* 1994 (co-p, AA-AS); *When the Day Breaks* 1999 (co-p, AAN-AS); *Village of Idiots* 2000 (co-p, GA-AS).

Verrall, Robert

Producer and animator; b. Toronto, 1928; father of David Verrall. Robert Verrall is a veteran NFB producer who joined the Board as an animator in 1945 under Norman McLaren* and contributed to such NFB classics as *The Romance of Transportation in Canada*,* *The Great Toy Robbery*, and *What on Earth!** He became director of English animation in 1967 and director of English production in 1972. In the 1980s he acted as executive producer on a number of NFB co-productions including Robin Philips's *The Wars*,* Claude Fournier's *The Tin Flute*, and Bruce Pitman's Academy Award–nominated *The Painted Door*.* **Films include:** *Three Blind Mice* 1945 (an with George Dunning); *Age of the Beaver* 1952 (an); *The Romance of Transportation in*

Canada 1953 (co-an, AAN-AS); *The Colour of Life* 1955 (co-an); *A Is for Architecture* 1959 (co-d); *Hors-d'oeuvre* 1960 (d/an with Gerald Potterton); *The Great Train Robbery* 1964 (co-p); *The Drag* 1965 (co-p, AAN-AS); *What on Earth!* 1966 (co-p, AAN-AS); *Cosmic Zoom* 1968 (co-p); *Psychocratie* 1970 (co-p, CFA-FY, CFA-AS); *Evolution* 1971 (exp, AAN-AS); *Christmas at Moose Factory* 1971 (exp); *Hot Stuff* 1971 (co-p); *Going the Distance* 1979 (exp, AAN-FD); *The Wars* 1983 (exp); *The Tin Flute* 1983 (exp); *Democracy on Trial: The Morgentaler Affair* 1984 (exp); *Incident at Restigouche* 1984 (exp); *The Painted Door* 1984 (exp, AAN-LAS); *The Masculine Mystique* 1985 (exp); *Bayo* 1985 (exp); *Richard Cardinal: Cry from a Diary of a Métis Child* 1986 (co-p).

Very Nice, Very Nice

1961 7m *prod* NFB, *p* Colin Low, Tom Daly, *d/ed* Arthur Lipsett. Arthur Lipsett's* brilliant first film was a revelation – a bold social critique presented in a rapid-fire montage style unique to Canadian cinema at the time. After working for two years in the animation department, a sound experiment conducted for fun prompted the twenty-five-year-old Lipsett to add images. The result was *Very Nice, Very Nice*, a rigorously composed film in which each image is richly suggestive and perfectly suited to his bleak vision. The film is not without moments of humour, but it ends on a bittersweet note. *Very Nice, Very Nice* received an Academy Award nomination for Animated Short. (V)

Videodrome

1983 87m *prod* Filmplan International ii, Universal Pictures (U.S.), *exp* Pierre David, Victor Solnicki, *p* Claude Héroux, *d/sc* David Cronenberg, *ph* Mark Irwin, *ed* Ronald Sanders, *mus* Howard Shore; *with* James Woods, Sonja Smits, Deborah

Harry, Peter Dvorsky, Les Carlson. David Cronenberg,* the visionary *schlockmeister*, has created a parallel universe that could be a nightmarish flip side of the Canadian Dream. *Videodrome*'s hero (an especially feral James Woods), a hustling cable-television operator who suggests Duddy Kravitz in the twenty-first century, seeks out the ultimate pornography to boost the ratings of his failing channel. Some claim that Cronenberg's debut feature, *Shivers*,* anticipated AIDS; certainly, *Videodrome* points toward today's quest for psycho-sexual fulfilment on the Web. Near the end of the movie, Woods is ravished by a monitor. (V) **Awards include:** GA: Director.

Vie heureuse de Léopold Z, La
1965 69m *prod* NFB, *exp* Jacques Bobet, *d/sc* Gilles Carle, *ph* Jean-Claude Labrecque, *ed* Werner Nold, *mus* Paul de Margerie; *with* Guy L'Écuyer, Paul Hébert, Suzanne Valéry, Monique Joy. On Christmas Eve in Montreal, snowplow driver Léopold Z. Tremblay (L'Écuyer) is busy clearing the streets of a heavy snowfall. But there's more in store today for this simple, amiable man. He must also find time to take out a loan, buy his wife a fur coat, take his son to choir practice, meet his cousin at the station, and watch her rehearse her nightclub act, all while evading detection by his boss. In this whimsical tale, the viewer follows Léopold on his adventurous day as everything falls neatly into place with warmth and good-natured humour. (V)

Vie rêvée, La
1972 85m *prod* ACPAV, *d* Mireille Dansereau, *sc* Mireille Dansereau, Patrick Auzépy, *ph* François Gill, Richard Rodrigue, Louis de Ernsted, *ed* Danielle Gagné, *mus* Emmanuel Charpentier; *with* Liliane Lemaître-Auger, Véronique

Le Flaguais, Jean-François Guité, Guy Foucault. *La Vie rêvée*, the first Quebec fiction feature to be directed by a woman (Mireille Dansersau*), offers a refreshing perspective on the politics of liberation. Two women – Isabelle (Lemaître-Auger) and Virginie (Le Flaguais) – who work in an advertising firm dream, sexually and otherwise, of finding the ideal man. As they become increasingly aware of their oppression and marginalization within popular media and within Quebec history and society, both women recognize that battles must be fought for respect and recognition. Consistently intelligent, the film is by turns lyrical, polemical, playful, sensual, amusing, and ferocious. While its Godardian influences are numerous, this film is an original detonation of Quebec machismo and a convincing call to arms for a generation of women left out of the cinematic articulation of their own experience of Quebec's emergent cultural nationalism. **Awards include:** CFA: Editing.

Vieux Pays où Rimbaud est mort, Le
1977 113m *prod* Cinak Compaigne Cinématographique, Filmoblic (France), Institut National de l'Audiovisuel (France), *p* Marguerite Duparc, Hubert Niogret, *d* Jean Pierre Lefebvre, *sc* Jean Pierre Lefebvre, Mireille Amiel, *ph* Guy Dufaux, *ed* Marguerite Duparc, *mus* Claude Fondrède; *with* Marcel Sabourin, Anouk Ferjac, Myriam Boyer, Roger Blin. The second film of Lefebvre's* 'Abel' trilogy follows Abel (Sabourin*) on a journey to France to visit the land of his ancestors. He discovers that his distance from the old country is more than geographical. Abel's three separate excursions within France provide a visually stunning exploration of identity, melancholy, and solitude. Through Abel's searching and personal encoun-

ters, Lefebvre reveals the paradoxes of living in a former colony. The film, made as the Parti Québécois came to power, is unfashionably critical of Quebec's colonial relationship to France, and remains a poetic commentary on how Canadians are perhaps still fighting the old colonial battles with European powers who could care less about former distant holdings of empire.

Villeneuve, Denis
Director and writer, b. Gentilly, Que., 1967. Villeneuve's intimate style was apparent from his beginnings on *Course destination monde*, the television show for which he produced highly subjective clips of his travels across the globe. In his first docu-fiction work, *REW FFWD*, he developed this style and added a more blatant taste for formal experimental filmmaking. After taking time out to produce music videos, he created a frantic and poignant sketch for the collaborative work *Cosmos*,* starring a strange and disarming David La Haye. Villeneuve's first feature film, *Un 32 août sur terre*,* with Pascale Bussières* and Alex Martin, furthered his oddball style, both formally and thematically, by offering a harshly edited psychological portrait reflecting the angst of a generation. **Films include:** *REW FFWD* 1994; *Cosmos* 1996 (co-d/co-sc); *Un 32 août sur terre* 1999 (d/sc); *Maelström* 2000 (d/sc, GA-D, GA-SC, PJ-D, PJ-SC).

Vinyl
2000 110m *prod* Vinyl Produicitons, *p* Alan Zweig, Greg Klymkiw, *d/ph* Alan Zweig, *ed* Christopher Donaldson, *mus* Drysdale. *Vinyl* is a penetrating, almost disturbing film about the compulsions of an antisocial cadre of quirky hobbyists who collect vinyl records. Director Alan Zweig's journey into a personal,

comic exploration of guilt and obsessive behaviour is wrapped around clever semantics and philosophical musings. He talks to fellow collectors such as Atom Egoyan* and Don McKellar,* to a guy who wants to collect every record ever made, and to a fellow whose apartment is so full of records that he has to move them to get into bed at night. Years in the making, this film portrays a naked, personal attempt by one lonely man to discover whether anyone shares his obsessions, and what the psychic costs are of his pursuit.

Virgo, Clement
Director and writer; b. Montego Bay, Jamaica, 1966. Virgo came to Canada at the age of eleven and grew up in Toronto's Regent Park housing project. A love of movies led him to a year at the Canadian Film Centre where he completed the script for *Rude*,* a film set in the Regent Park drug culture. It was the first feature created entirely by black Canadian filmmakers. It was invited to Cannes, where critics praised the inventive parallel story lines, but the film failed to find an audience. Virgo's next project, the television movie *The Planet of Junior Brown*, fared better, and also secured an Emmy nomination. His second feature, *Love Come Down*,* about two brothers, one black and the other white, who struggle with a family tragedy, firmly established Virgo's credentials as a bankable emerging talent. **Films include**: *A Small Dick Fleshy Ass Thang* 1991 (co-d/sc); *Split Second Pullout Technique* 1992 (d/sc); *Save My Lost Nigga' Soul* 1993 (d/sc); *Rude* 1995 (co-p/d/sc); *The Planet of Junior Brown* 1998 (d/co-sc, TV); *Love Come Down* 2001 (co-p/d/sc).

Voitures d'eau, Les
1969 110m *prod* NFB, *p* Jacques Bobet,

Guy L. Coté, *d* Pierre Perrault, *ph* Bernard Gosselin, *ed* Monique Fortier. This film is the final chapter in Pierre Perrault's* epic documentary project about the island community of Île-aux-Coudres (see also *Pour la suite du monde* and *Le Règne du jour*) and the extended Tremblay family. Once again Perrault used a direct-cinema style of filmmaking to capture particular events such as the building of a river schooner (which revived a long-dead tradition), a labour strike, and the family's departure from the island. By the time the film was made, the Tremblay family had become part of Québécois folklore tradition. Alexis, the head of the family, died just weeks after the shoot was finished, as if waiting for Perrault to complete his story. (V)

Volcano: An Inquiry into the Life and Death of Malcolm Lowry

1976 99m *prod* NFB, *exp* James de B. Domville, *p* Donald Brittain, Robert Duncan, *d/sc* Donald Brittain, John Kramer, *ph* Douglas Kiefer, *ed* John Kramer, *mus* Alain Clavier, *narr* Donald Brittain, *readings* Richard Burton. Considered to be Donald Brittain's* best work, *Volcano* is concerned with the life and times of British novelist Malcolm Lowry, and the creation of his novel, *Under the Volcano*, written in an alcoholic haze while Lowry was living in Mexico. The film tells its story in two ways: from the inside, through Lowry's own tortured words, read by Richard Burton; and from the outside, through interviews with friends and family who helplessly watched Lowry's self-destruction. Near the beginning of the film we see Brittain emptying a bottle of beer on Lowry's grave, a startling salute from one legendary hard-drinker to another. (V)
Awards include: CFA: Feature Documentary; AAN: Feature Documentary.

W

Wake Up, Mes bons amis!
See *Pays son bons sens!, Un.*

Walker, Giles
Director, producer, and writer; b. Dundee, Scotland, 1946. During the 1970s, Walker's name appeared on the credits of one film each year, as director, producer or screenwriter. *The Masculine Mystique** (co-directed with John N. Smith*), the first of a trio of NFB films dealing with issues of gender relations, shows Walker's experimental side, working with non-professional actors and the technique of improvisation. The two other films in the series, however, moved closer to an easy, palatable Hollywood style – successfully in *90 Days*, but less so in *The Last Straw*. Perhaps Walker's most successful fictional work is *Princes in Exile*, a film about a summer camp for children with cancer, notable for a delicate treatment of the subject and a moving lack of sentimentality.
Films include: *Freshwater World* 1974 (d/ed); *Descent* 1975 (co-d); *I Wasn't Scared* 1977 (d); *Bravery in the Field* 1979 (d/co-sc, AAN-LAS); *Twice upon a Time* 1979 (d); *Harvest* 1980 (d, TV); *The Masculine Mystique* 1984 (p/d/sc with John N. Smith); *90 Days* 1985 (co-p/d); *The Last Straw* 1987 (co-p/d/co-sc); *Princes in Exile* 1990 (d); *Ordinary Magic* 1993 (d); *Never Too Late* 1996 (d).

Walker, John
Cinematographer and director; b. Montreal, 1952. Walker got his start in photography and turned to documentary filmmaking as a cinematographer for Crawley Films in the 1970s. He directed his first film, *Chambers: Tracks and Gestures* (about Canadian artist Jack Chambers) for Atlantis Films in 1982. His passionate commitment to the documentary

form has led him to work around the world and to co-found the Canadian Independent Film Caucus, a lobby group for point-of-view documentaries. Walker represents the best in a new generation of Canadian documentary filmmakers, and is a natural successor to the lyrical tradition created by Colin Low.* **Films and television include:** *Chambers: Tracks and Gestures* 1982 (d/ph, TV); *Making Overtures* 1984 (ph, TV); *Blue Snake* 1985 (ph, TV); *A Winter Tan* 1988 (co-p/co-d/ph); *Calling the Shots* 1988 (ph); *Strand: Under the Dark Cloth* 1990 (p/d/ph, GA-FD); *The Hand of Stalin* 1990 (d/ph, two films, TV); *Distress Signals* 1991 (co-p/d/ph, TV); *Orphans of Manchuria* 1993 (d/co-ph, TV); *The Champagne Safari* 1995 (exp, GA-FD); *Tough Assignment* 1996 (co-p/d/ph, TV); *Utshimassits: Place of the Boss* 1997 (d/ph, TV); *The Fairy Faith* 2000 (p/d/sc/co-ph).

Walking

1968 5m6s *prod* NFB, *p/d/an* Ryan Larkin, *ph* Raymond Dumas, *mus* David Fraser, Pat Patterson, Christopher Nutter. This brief portrayal of talented NFB animator Ryan Larkin's* impressions of the way people walk received an Academy Award nomination for Animated Short. Larkin employed a variety of techniques (including line drawing and colour wash) to reproduce dream-like motions of people afoot with wit, humour, and individuality. (V)

Walsh, Mary

Actor and writer; b. St John's, Nfld., 1952. Walsh, Newfoundland's great comic gift to the rest of Canada, got her start with the legendary Codco troupe in the 1970s, along with co-founders Andy,* Mike,* and Cathy Jones* and Robert Joy.* She appeared in all and wrote many of the weekly skits on CBC-TV from 1986 to 1993. When the show

went off the air, she and Cathy Jones moved on to become regulars on *This Hour Has 22 Minutes*, the funniest show about television since *SCTV*. Walsh has built a reputation for fearless political satire combined with dramatic roles in a number of East Coast features, including legendary *The Adventure of Faustus Bidgood*.* **Films and television include:** *The Adventure of Faustus Bidgood* 1986; *CODCO* 1986–93 (a/co-sc, series); *Secret Nation* 1992; *Buried on Sunday* 1992; *The Boys of St Vincent* 1993 (TV); *This Hour Has 22 Minutes* 1994–present (a/co-sc, series); *Major Crime* 1998 (TV); *Rain, Drizzle, and Fog* 1998; *Extraordinary Visitor* 1998; *Dooley Gardens* 1999–2000 (series); *The Divine Ryans* 1999; *New Waterford Girl* 2000; *Cod: The Fish That Changed the World* 2000 (host, TV).

Warrendale

1967 110m *prod* Allan King Assoc., *exp* Patrick Watson, *p/d* Allan King, *ph* William Brayne, *ed* Peter Moseley. One of the most powerful films to come out of the 1960s, *Warrendale*, a direct-cinema documentary set in a treatment centre for emotionally disturbed children, focuses on the children's response when they are told of the death of the house cook, who was loved by all. The film was shot for CBC-TV, but the network backed out when the brass saw the footage. *Warrendale* was released theatrically, and received wide praise by critics in Canada and Europe. It won both the Film of the Year and Best Feature Film at the Canadian Film Awards and established Allan King* as one of Canada's leading documentary filmmakers. It was finally shown on Canadian television in 1999. **Awards include:** CFA: Film of the Year, Feature Film, Direction.

Wars, The

1983 120m *prod* Nielsen-Ferns International, NFB, Polyphon Film-und-Fernseh GmbH (Germany), *exp* Robert Verrall, *p* Richard Nielsen, *d* Robin Phillips, *sc/novel* Timothy Findley, *ph* John Coquillon, *ed* Tony Lower, *mus* Glenn Gould; *with* Brent Carver, Martha Henry, William Hutt, Ann-Marie MacDonald, Jackie Burroughs, Jean Leclerc, Domini Blythe. Hailed as a 'classic' on its release, Timothy Findley's adaptation of his own novel, directed by noted theatre director Robin Phillips, died at the box office and is rarely seen now, even on television. Phillips had no feel for cinematic flow, the cinematography was pedestrian, and the editing was inconsistent. The story centres on Robert Ross (Carver), an affluent young man from a repressed Toronto family ruled by a domineering mother (Henry*). When his retarded sister (MacDonald) dies, he enlists, and travels to France to fight in the First World War. The theatrical roots of the cast are evident – overall, the performances are strong but the end result is disappointing. **Awards include:** GA: Actress (Henry), Supporting Actress (Burroughs).

Watson, Lucile

Actor; b. Quebec City, 1879; d. 1962. Watson, a leading Hollywood character actor who trained at the American Academy of Dramatic Arts, came to the movies in 1934 after a successful career on Broadway. Typically she played well-bred, haughty matrons. She appeared with Carole Lombard and James Stewart in *Made for Each Other*, she was a member of the stellar ensemble cast of George Cukor's *The Women* (with fellow Canadian expat Norma Shearer*), and she was nominated for an Academy Award for her role as Bette Davis's mother in *Watch on the Rhine*. **Films include:** *What Every Women Knows* 1934; *Three Smart Girls* 1936; *Made for Each Other* 1939;

The Women 1939; *Waterloo Bridge* 1940; *Mr and Mrs Smith* 1941; *Watch on the Rhine* 1943 (AAN-SA); *The Thin Man Goes Home* 1945; *The Razor's Edge* 1946; *Song of the South* 1946; *The Emperor Waltz* 1948; *Little Women* 1949.

Wavelength

1967 45m *p/d/ph/ed* Michael Snow; *with* Hollis Frampton, Joyce Wieland. Canada's most famous experimental film, *Wavelength* is a modernist masterpiece and a monumental work in the history of cinema. Michael Snow's* meditation on cinematic practice takes the form of a seemingly continuous, forty-five-minute zoom progressing down the length of his New York loft. Snow systematically disrupts the flow of this movement with typical structuralist tropes such as jumpy splices and flashes of light, and cleverly breaks in with four human episodes – concise melodramas that recall what normally happens in a conventional cinematic space. It's exactly this precision and schematic austerity that so cogently expresses the most fundamental tenet of modernist art: in *Wavelength*, form does not shape content; form is content.

Waxman, Al

Actor and director; b. Albert Samuel Waxman, Toronto, 1935; d. 2001. Waxman, a versatile character actor, studied with Lee Strasberg at the Actor's Studio in New York. He worked mostly in television and gained national celebrity as Larry King in *The King of Kensington*, the CBC's popular situation comedy from the 1970s. He further cemented his reputation as one of Canada's most recognizable actors as Lt Samuels in the long-running ABC-TV series *Cagney and Lacey*. Waxman made a significant contribution to a number of features (most notably *Atlantic City**) and worked as an actor and a director on the stage. **Films and televi-**

sion include: *The Last Gunfighter* 1961; *Isabel* 1968; *The Crowd Inside* 1971 (p/d/sc/a); *Child under a Leaf* 1974; *Sunday in the Country* 1974; *The Heatwave Lasted Four Days* 1975 (TV); *My Pleasure Is My Business* 1975 (d); *A Star Is Lost!* 1974; *King of Kensington* 1975–9 (series); *The Clown Murders* 1976; *Vengeance Is Mine* 1976; *Wild Horse Hank* 1980 (TV); *Atlantic City* 1980; *Cop* 1981 (d, TV); *Heavy Metal* 1981 (voice); *Tulips* 1981 (d/a); *Double Negative* 1982; *Cagney and Lacey* 1982–8 (series); *Class of 1984* 1982; *Spasms* 1983; *Meatballs* III 1987; *Switching Channels* 1988; *The Return of Ben Casey* 1988 (TV); *Malarek* 1988; *Millennium* 1989; *Mob Story* 1989; *The Hitman* 1991; *White Light* 1991 (d); *I Still Dream of Jeannie* 1991 (TV); *The Diamond Fleece* 1992 (d, TV); *Live Wire* 1992; *Teamster Boss: The Jackie Presser Story* 1992 (TV); *Cagney and Lacey: The Return* 1994 (TV); *Net Worth* 1995 (TV); *Iron Eagle* IV 1995; *Gotti* 1996 (TV); *Bogus* 1996; *The Assignment* 1997; *At the End of the Day: The Sue Rodriguez Story* 1998 (TV); *Power Play* 1998 (series); *The Hurricane* 1999; *The Ride* 2000 (TV).

waydowntown

2000 83m *prod* Burns Films, *exp* Bryan Gliserman, Marguerite Rigott, *p* Shirley Vercuysse, Gary Burns, *d* Gary Burns, *sc* Gary Burns, James Martin, *ph* Patrick McLaughlin, *ed* Mark Lemmon, *mus* John Abram; *with* Fabrizio Filippo, Don McKellar, Marya Delver, Gordon Currie, Jennifer Clement. A group of twenty-something corporate drones bet a month's salary on who can last the longest without going outside the enclosed, soulless office and shopping mall complex where they work. Shot on digital video and transferred to film, *waydowntown* captures a sense of heightened realism in a suffocating world of offices, parking garages, and constantly humming air ventilators. The script is original and the performances uniformly engaging, including Don McKellar* as a masochistic employee who attempts to escape by smashing a pop bottle full of marbles against a pane of unbreakable glass. With moments of hallucinatory bizarreness (one of the characters is seen floating through the mall doing the breaststroke), Calgary director Gary Burns* has created an oddly funny movie about barely controlled insanity.

Wedding in White

1972 103m *prod* Dermet Productions, *p* John Vidette, *d/sc* William Fruet, *ph* Richard Leiterman, *ed* Tony Lower, *mus* Milan Kymlicka; *with* Donald Pleasence, Carol Kane, Doris Petrie, Leo Phillips, Paul Bradley, Doug McGrath. *Wedding in White* is set in a small prairie town in wartime Canada. Jeannie (Kane), a pretty, timid teenager, is raped by her brother's (Bradley) army buddy (McGrath). When her father (Pleasence), a drunk and overbearing bully, finds out he beats her and is at first ready to throw her out. Then he changes his mind and marries his daughter off to an old friend, a man in his fifties. Director William Fruet's* bleak vision of male oppression and brutality is at times painful to watch, but the film features some exceptional performances – especially by Pleasence, and by Petrie as the long-suffering mother. It remains a gem of early English-Canadian cinema. **Awards include:** CFA: Feature Film, Supporting Actress (Petrie), Art Direction.

Welcome to Canada

1989 86m *prod* NFB, *exp* Colin Neale, *p* Sam Grana, *d* John N. Smith, *sc* Sam Grana, John N. Smith, *ph* David de Volpi, Roger Martin, K. Shanmuganathan, Martin Duckworth, *ed* John N. Smith, Martial Ethier, Sam Grana; *with*

Noreen Power, Brendan Foley, Madonna Hawkins, Anandprasad Pathanjali, Charlene Bruff. Loosely based on true stories of impoverished refugees left to fend for themselves off Canada's east coast, *Welcome to Canada* explores the inevitable cultural clashes as eight Tamils from Sri Lanka are rescued in a howling gale and wait for the immigration officials to arrive in a remote Newfoundland community. Much of the film (shot with non-professional actors in documentary style) is taken up by tentative, frequently funny exchanges between the Tamils (who think they've been dropped off near Montreal) and their hosts (for whom Ceylon is the name of a tea). While avoiding both the politics of Canadian immigration policy and the racist backlash in the issue of illegal immigrants, the film nevertheless touches upon the questionable integrity of Canada's multicultural dream. (V)

Weldon, John
Animator; b. Belleville, Ont., 1945. In the comic world of John Weldon, average Canadians are confronted by absurd circumstances that tear away the fragile underpinnings of their lives. His Academy Award–winning *Special Delivery*, co-directed by Eunice Maccaulay, follows a postman, his wife, and her lover as they work their way through a darkly humorous scenerio of love, death, misunderstanding, and exile. Questions of identity are played out in several of Weldon's films. *To Be*, an animated sequel to *The Fly*, raises the ante on Hamlet's soliloquy by duplicating a scientist through a teleport machine. In his stylish *Real Inside* (made before *Who Framed Roger Rabbit*), a 'toon' (cartoon creation) applies for a job because he wants to be human. **Films include:** *Spinnolio* 1977 (CFA-AS); *Special Delivery* 1979 (AA-AS); *Real Inside* 1984; *Elephan-*

trio 1985; *Of Dice and Men* 1988; *To Be* 1990; *The Lump* 1991; *Scant Sanity* 1997; *Frank the Wabbit* 1998.

Welsh, Kenneth
Actor; b. Edmonton, 1942. With lead roles in *Perfectly Normal,** *Margaret's Museum,** *Whale Music,** and the CBC-TV movies *Dieppe* and *Love and Hate*, Welsh is a familiar face on Canadian screens, both big and small. He is equally well known south of the border with roles in such films as *The January Man*, *The Freshman*, and Clint Eastwood's *Absolute Power*. From 1976 to 1989 Welsh worked on and off Broadway, where his biggest hit was starring opposite Kathy Bates in Terrence McNally's *Frankie and Johnny*. Welsh also received good notices for the play he conceived, *Standup Shakespeare*, which the *New Yorker* called '77 minutes of enchantment.' **Films and television include:** *The Tar Sands* 1976 (TV); *Riel* 1978 (TV); *Empire Inc.* 1982 (series); *Loyalties* 1986; *And Then You Die* 1987; *The January Man* 1989; *Love and Hate: The Story of Colin and Joann Thatcher* 1989 (TV); *Perfectly Normal* 1990; *Grand Larceny* 1991 (TV); *Adrift* 1993; *Dieppe* 1994 (TV); *Legends of the Fall* 1994; *Whale Music* 1994; *Margaret's Museum* 1996 (GA-SA); *Hiroshima* 1996 (TV); *Absolute Power* 1997; *The Taking of Pelham One Two Three* 1998 (TV); *Scandalous Me: The Jacqueline Susann Story* 1998 (TV); *Love and Murder* 2000 (TV); *Who Killed Atlanta's Children?* 2000 (TV); *The Hound of the Baskervilles* 2000 (TV); *Revenge of the Land* 2000 (TV).

Whale Music
1994 101m *prod* Alliance Communications, Cape Scott Motion Pictures, *exp* Robert Lantos, David Hauka, *p* Raymond Massey, Steven DeNure, *d* Richard Lewis, *sc* Paul Quarrington, Richard Lewis, *novel* Paul Quarrington, *ph* Vic Sarin, *ed* Richard Martin, *mus* George

Blondheim, The Rheostatics; *with* Maury Chaykin, Cyndy Preston, Jennifer Dale, Paul Gross, Kenneth Welsh. Maury Chaykin* plays a washed-up rock star, haunted by ghosts, who lives in a ramshackle mansion by the ocean and is composing his magnum opus, a symphony for whales. Into his life comes a comely young groupie (Preston) who tries to revive the reclusive genius. The film, based on the Paul Quarrington novel, never finds its focus and is, quite frankly, a mess. Chaykin dominates and deservedly won a Genie for his performance, but Preston isn't in the same league, and the other characters come and go without making an impact. The mawkish ending – after running away, the girl returns and the whales appear – is embarrassing. (V) **Awards include:** GA: Actor (Chaykin).

What on Earth!
1966 9m35s *prod* NFB, *p* Robert Verrall, Wolf Koenig, *d/an* Les Drew, Kaj Pindal, *sc* Kaj Pindal, *ph* Kjeld Nielsen, *mus* Donald Douglas, *narr* Donald Brittain. This clever and funny satire on humanity's obsession with automobiles comes from the animation talents of Les Drew* and Kaj Pindal.* Invaders from Mars arrive and conclude that cars are the true inhabitants of Earth and that humans are parasites infesting the autos. The film received an Academy Award nomination for Animated Short. (V)

Wheeler, Anne
Director and producer; b. Edmonton, 1946. Following an eclectic early career in computer programming and music education, Wheeler has emerged as one of Canada's finest storytellers, blending the social conscience of an NFB documentary with a firm grip on story structure in such films as *Loyalties,** *Bye Bye Blues,** and *The War between Us*. Friend-

ships between women, the Second World War, and prairie history have been major concerns throughout her career, which began at Filmwest with *Great Grand Mothers*, a short film about pioneer women. Since then Wheeler has worked on some twenty-six film and television projects, including adaptations of two Margaret Laurence works – *To Set Our House in Order* and *The Diviners*. **Films and television include:** *Great Grand Mothers* 1975 (d); *Priory, the Only Home I've Got* 1978 (co-p, GA-SD); *A War Story* 1981 (p/d/sc); *Change of Heart* 1984 (d, TV); *To Set Our House in Order* 1985 (d); *Loyalites* 1986 (d); *Cowboys Don't Cry* 1988 (d); *Bye Bye Blues* 1989 (co-p/d/sc); *Angel Square* 1990 (d); *The Diviners* 1993 (d, TV); *The War between Us* 1995 (d, TV); *The Sleep Room* 1998 (d, TV); *Better than Chocolate* 1999 (d); *Legs Apart* from *Preludes* 2000 (d/sc); *Marine Life* 2001 (d).

When Night Is Falling
1995 93m *prod* Crucial Pictures, *p* Barbara Tranter, *d/sc* Patricia Rozema, *ph* Douglas Koch, *ed* Susan Shipton, *mus* Lesley Barber; *with* Pascale Bussières, Rachael Crawford, Henry Czerny, David Fox, Don McKellar, Tracey Wright. Patricia Rozema's* third feature is a modern fable about a young Calvinist theology student (Bussières*) who finds herself falling in love with another woman, a flamboyant circus performer (Crawford), a situation that makes her question her faith and her relationship with her boyfriend. Henry Czerny* rounds out the fine cast as Bussières' puzzled amour who is left behind by her new tryst. While the film won a certain lesbian following, it is essentially a fairly rudimentary coming-out story. It undoubtedly features some of the most erotic love scenes ever captured on Canadian celluloid and its overall serious mood is lightened by a touch of magic realism. (V)

When Ponds Freeze Over

1998 23m *prod* From Here Productions, *d/sc/an* Mary Lewis. One night in St John's, Newfoundland, a mother (Lewis) tells her daughter the story of how she fell through the ice while skating and saw her life flash before her eyes. Out of this terrifying accident and the panic of her escape from the cold water, Lewis mixes various styles of animation, dramatic reconstruction, and visual puns. The film won the award for best short at the Atlantic, the Toronto, and the Vancouver film festivals as well as the Genie for Live-Action Short: Lewis is the only filmmaker to date to achieve this quadruple distinction. **Awards include:** GA: Live-Action Short.

When the Day Breaks

1999 10m *prod* NFB, *p* David Verrall, Barrie Angus McLean, *d/an* Wendy Tilby, Amanda Forbis, *mus* Judith Gruber-Stitzwer. This animation short portrays urban life as lonely anonymity until a momentary encounter between the two main characters – a pig and a chicken – leads to an accidental death. The irony of the story is matched by the precisely rendered animal heads on the protagonists' hyper-realistic human bodies. The transcendent moment occurs when documents, photographs, and other debris of Chickenman's life flash by in a virtuoso montage. This popular film, one of the best examples of recent NFB animation, was a triple winner – at Cannes, at Annecy, and at the Genies – in addition to receiving an Academy Award nomination. (V) **Awards include:** GA: Animated Short; Cannes: Palme d'or for animation; AAN: Animated Short.

Whispering City / La Fortresse

1947 English version 91m, French version 99m *prod* Quebec Productions, *exp* Paul L'Anglais, *p* George Marton, *d* Fédor Ozep, *sc* Rain James, Leonard Lee, *ph* Guy Roe, *ed* Leonard Anderson, Douglas Bagier, Richard J. Jarvis, *mus* Morris C. Davis; *English version with* Helmut Dantine, Mary Anderson, Paul Lukas, John Pratt; *French version with* Paul Dupuis, Nicole Germain, Jacques Auger, Henri Letondal. This substandard Hollywood-style potboiler, which was shot simultaneously in French and English, was one of the first attempts to crack the American market with a Canadian-produced feature. Mary Roberts (Anderson / Germain), an American journalist in Quebec City, is investigating a mysterious death, and her intrepid search leads her to the upper echelons of Quebec's aristocratic elite. The French version did well in Quebec, but the English version fared poorly. Subsequent Quebec Productions films were shot in French only and achived considerable popular success for a period of nearly ten years.

Whistling Smith

1975 27m *prod* NFB, *exp* Ian McLaren, *p* Barrie Howells, Michael Scott, *d/ed* Michael Scott, Marrin Canell, *sc* Donald Brittain, *ph* Henry Fiks, *mus* Larry Crosley; *with* Bernie Smith. This short, shot on the mean streets of Vancouver's east side, explores the underbelly of big-city life with one tough cop who cares. Bernie 'Whistling' Smith's methods of policing are unorthodox. To the petty criminals, drug users, and prostitutes he encounters on his beat, he is not only the heavy hand of law, but also a friend and counsellor. The film received an Academy Award nomination for Short Documentary. (V)

White Museum

1986 32m *p/d/sc/ph/ed* Mike Hoolboom. An audacious and often hilarious early effort by master provocateur Mike Hoolboom,* *White Museum* is the cinematic equivalent of flipping the bird. Viewers must wait about thirty minutes to see the one and only image in the film. In the meantime, Hoolboom* expounds on everything from old girlfriends to making movies to living in the big city. With unabashed irony, he argues for a cinema without images, while simultaneously describing images he would show if he had the cash. For a film that appears on the surface to be literally about nothing, *White Museum* becomes a veritable cornucopia of semiotic jokes and meanings, and a rich statement on the nature of cinema itself.

Who Has Seen the Wind

1977 103m *prod* Allan King Assoc., *exp* Pierre Lamy, *p/d* Allan King, *sc* Patricia Watson, *novel* W.O. Mitchell, *ph* Richard Leiterman, *ed* Arla Saare, *mus* Eldon Rathburn; *with* Brian Painchaud, Douglas Junor, Patricia Hamilton, Gordon Pinsent, Chapelle Jaffe. The lush look of Allan King's* adaptation of W.O. Mitchell's classic Canadian tale is thanks to veteran cinematographer Richard Leiterman.* The story revolves around Brian (Painchaud), a young boy who lives a magical life on the Canadian prairies catching prairie dogs and playing with friends. The magic ends when his father (Pinsent*) falls ill, and he witnesses the harsh realities of adult life. This coming-of-age story provides a poignant look at life on the prairies during the Great Depression. The strong cast and director King created a film of quality – a rare exception during the dark days of the tax-shelter era.* **Awards include:** Golden Reel Award.

Who's Counting? Marilyn Waring on Sex, Lies and Global Economics

1995 94m *prod* NFB, *exp* Don Haig, Colin Neale, *p* Kent Martin, *d/ed* Terre Nash, *ph* Susan Trow, *mus* Penny Lang, Brian Eno, Daniel Lanois; *with* Marilyn Waring. Waring, the youngest woman to be elected to the New Zealand parliament, left politics to begin an exhaustive study of the role of women in economics. The result was a stinging and important book, *If Women Counted*. Like Nash's* previous film (*If You Love This Planet**), this compelling and important documentary is essentially a reportage of Waring's public lectures. An engaging performer with a flare of a stand-up comic, Waring is passionate in delivering her dual thesis: that the unacknowledged value of woman's work hides an exploitation of women and children worldwide, and that because the ecosystem is not factored into economic growth, environmental degradation accelerates. She points out that the international arms trade is the biggest growth industry, yet the amount of money spent on armaments in just two weeks could provide safe water for the entire world. (V)

Why Rock the Boat?

1974 112m *prod* NFB, *exp* James de Domville, *p/sc/book* William Weintraub, *d/mus* John Howe, *ph* Savas Kalogeras, *ed* Marie-Hélène Cuillemin; *with* Stuart Gillard, Tiiu Leek, Ken James, Henry Beckman, Patricia Gage, Budd Knapp. This film is based on William Weintraub's satiric novel about the Montreal newspaper world of the 1940s. Harry Barnes (Gillard) is an innocent, bashful, yet ambitious young reporter with the *The Daily Witness*. The managing editor (Beckman) is a hard-nosed reactionary who is out to please his advertisers and not rock the boat. On an assignment, Barnes falls for the beautiful union organizer and reporter (Leek) for a rival newspaper. His comic attempts to court her lead to a drunken, passionate pro-union speech at his own paper. It's a slight, humorous coming-of-age story with several engaging performances. **Awards include:** CFA: Adapted Screenplay, Actor (Gillard), Supporting Actor (Beckman).

Why Shoot the Teacher?
1977 99m *prod* Fraser Films, Lancer Teleproductions, *exp* Fil Fraser, *p* Lawrence Herzog, *d* Silvio Narizzano, *sc* James Defilce, *novel* Max Braithwaite, *ph* Marc Champion, *ed* Stan Cole, Max Benedict, *mus* Ricky Hyslop; *with* Bud Cort, Samantha Eggar, Chris Wiggins, Gary Reineke. American actor Bud Cort stars as Max Brown, a young, shy school teacher assigned to a one-room schoolhouse during a Canàdian prairie winter in the Great Depression. He finds the going tough because of the harsh elements and the even harsher hardscrabble kids he teaches. Over time, the earnest Max finds ways of surviving in this alien land and adjusts to the realities of life. However, the film too often lapses into farce and mawkish sentimentality and Silvio Nariazzano's* direction is only competent. *Why Shoot the Teacher?* was released at the same time as *Who Has Seen the Wind*,* a superior film dealing with life on the prairies during the dirty thirties. **Awards include:** GA: Adapted Screenplay; Golden Reel Award.

Wieland, Joyce
Filmmaker; b. Toronto, 1931; d. 1998. Wieland, who is considered the mother of Canadian experimental cinema, explored her woman-centred artist's territory through nineteen avant-garde films, one dramatic feature (*The Far Shore**), paintings, and political quilts. Her 1965 film, *Water Stark*, has been held up as a key instance of feminine *écriture*, drama-tizing the discovery of a filmic language based on the female body. *Reason over Passion** sums up an impassioned but critical approach to Canadian nationalism. Grounded in a sense of the female body/bawdy, Wieland's work consistently exploded categories of high and low art, the political and the personal, and the artistic and the domestic. **Films:** *Tea in the Garden* 1958 (with Warren Collins); *A Salt in the Park* 1959 (with Michael Snow); *Larry's Recent Behaviour* 1963; *Patriotism i* 1964; *Patriotism ii* 1964; *Water Stark* 1965; *Barbra's Blindness* 1965 (with Betty Ferguson); *Peggy's Blue Skylight* 1966; *Handtinting* 1968; *1933* 1968; *Sailboat* 1968; *Catfood* 1968; *Rat Life and Diet in North America* 1968; *Dripping Water* 1968 (with Snow); *Reason over Passion* 1969; *Pierre Vallières* 1972; *Solidarity* 1973; *The Far Shore* 1976 (co–p/d); *A and B in Ontario* 1984; *Birds at Sunrise* 1986.

Williams, Richard
Animator; b. Toronto, 1933. Williams, the animator who created the popular Pink Panther cartoon character and designed the introductory credits to the hugely popular films starring Peter Sellers, left school in Toronto at fifteen to make a failed bid to join the Disney studios. Eventually he arrived, with George Dunning,* in the swinging London of the early 1960s. Williams worked as a graphic artist, winning countless prizes for his animated television commercials. He also designed the clever title sequences for *What's New Pussycat?* (1965) and *A Funny Thing Happened on the Way to the Forum* (1966). In 1973, he earned an Academy Award for his animated version of Dickens's *A Christmas Carol*, and in 1988 he was responsible for the groundbreaking combination of live action and animation in Robert Zemeckis's *Who Framed Roger Rabbit*. **Films include:** *The Little Island* 1958; *A Lecture on Man:*

Love Me Love Me Love Me 1962; *Diary of a Madman* 1965; *A Christmas Carol* 1971 (AA-AS); *Raggedy Ann and Andy* 1977; *Who Framed Roger Rabbit* 1988; *Arabian Knight* 1995.

Williams, Steve

Animator and producer; b. Toronto, 1962. Steve Williams, one of the best and brightest of the new wave of computer animators, and a graduate of Sheridan College's famed animation school, first went to work for Toronto-based software innovators Alias Research, but quickly moved on to George Lucas's Industrial Light and Magic. There he was responsible for creating the liquid aliens in *The Abyss* and the shape-shifting villain in *Terminator 2: Judgment Day*. His realistic dinosaurs convinced Steven Spielberg to use computer animation rather than traditional puppets to create the t-rex and the raptors in *Jurassic Park*. Williams was nominated for an Academy Award for his work in transforming Jim Carrey* into a cartoon superhero in *The Mask*. **Films include:** *The Abyss* 1989; *Terminator 2: Judgment Day* 1991; *Jurassic Park* 1993; *The Mask* 1995 (AAN-SE); *Spawn* 1997 (co-p/an).

Wilson, Sandy

Director and writer; b. Penticton, B.C., 1947. Wilson began her film career in 1970 with *Pentiction Profile* and the promising experimental short *Growing Up in Paradise*, structured around her father's home movies. Talented but unfortunately cursed with a taste for pure Okanagan tree sap, she made a splash with her 1986 debut feature, *My American Cousin** (about a prepubescent girl's first big crush), but then floundered with the sequel, *American Boyfriends*. *Harmony Cats* was an even greater disappointment, pitting an arrogant city musician against country folk with predictable re-

sults. **Films include:** *Pentiction Profile* 1970; *The Bridal Shower* 1972; *Growing Up in Paradise* 1977; *My American Cousin* 1985 (co-p/d/sc, GA-D, GA-SC); *Mama's Going to Buy You a Mockingbird* 1988 (TV); *American Boyfriends* 1989 (d/sc); *Harmony Cats* 1993.

Winter Kept Us Warm

1965 81m *prod* Varsity Films, *exp* Ronald Thomson, *p/d* David Secter, *sc* John Porter, John Clute, David Secter, *ph* Robert Fresco, Ernest Meershoek, *ed* Michael Foytényi, *mus* Paul Hoffert; *with* John Labow, Henry Tarvainen, Janet Amos. This first English-Canadian gay feature (contemporary with Claude Jutra's* better-known *À tout prendre**) is more than just a historical curiosity. The film is loaded with the spirit and ingenuity of an independent filmmaker fighting the odds. David Secter, a twenty-two-year-old student, produced and directed it with only a small amount of cash from the Student Administrative Council of the University of Toronto. The story is as closeted as the lifestyle it depicts – subtly suggestive yet ultimately ambiguous. Doug (Tarvainen) is a dashing and popular senior who inexplicably takes a shy freshman, Peter (Labow), under his wing. As their friendship develops, it becomes clear that Doug's feelings go deeper than mere camaraderie. The film was invited to the Cannes Film Festival, but Secter's later work did not cash in on this early promise.

Winter Tan, A

1988 91m *p/d* Jackie Burroughs, Louise Clark, John Frizzle, John Walker, Aerlyn Weissman, *sc* Jackie Burroughs, *novel* Marsye Holder, *ph* John Walker, *ed* Alan Lee, *mus* John Lang, Ahmed Hassan; *with* Jackie Burroughs, Erando Gonzales, Javier Torres. Based on the writings of

Maryse Holder, posthumously published as *Give Sorrow Words*, this articulate and passionate film is a first-person account of Maryse (Burroughs*), a self-destructive woman who looks for romance and freedom in Mexico but finds mostly just sex. As she accumulates an astonishing list of conquests, she chronicles each experience and emotion in a series of explicit letters to her best friend Edith. Emotions run deeper when Maryse meets Miguel, but she withdraws from both his affections and her own sanity. Produced and directed collectively, this picture about one woman living on the edge smashes through the rules of conventional filmmaking to characterize a tragic figure (slut and saint simultaneously) with a sense of humour aciduous enough to eat through steel. (V) **Awards include:** GA: Actress (Burroughs).

Wiseman, Joseph
Actor; b. Montreal, 1918. Unforgettable as the arch fiend Dr No bent on destroying the world in the first James Bond film, Wiseman often played villains of a cerebral nature. Gaunt and sharp-eyed, he began his career on the American stage in 1935 and appeared in numerous television series from *The Untouchables* in the 1950s to *Law and Order* in the 1990s. He spent most of the 1960s with the Lincoln Centre Repertory Theatre in New York, and returned to Canada in 1974 to play the wealthy Uncle Benjy in Ted Kotcheff's *The Apprenticeship of Duddy Kravitz.** **Films and television include:** *With These Hands* 1950; *Detective Story* 1951; *Les Miserables* 1952; *Viva Zapata!* 1952; *The Silver Chalice* 1954; *The Prodigal* 1955; *The Garment Jungle* 1957; *The Unforgiven* 1960; *Dr No* 1962; *Bye Bye Braverman* 1968; *The Night They Raided Minsky's* 1968; *Stiletto* 1969; *Lawman* 1971; *The Valachi Papers* 1972 *The Appren-*

ticeship of Duddy Kravitz 1974; *QB VII* 1974 (TV); *Journey into Fear* 1975; *Homage to Chagall: The Colours of Love* 1977 (narr); *The Betsy* 1978; *Buck Rogers in the 25th Century* 1978; *Masada* 1981 (TV); *The Ghost Writer* 1984 (TV); *Seize the Day* 1986; *Crime Story* 1986–8 (series).

Woods, Donald
Actor; b. Ralph L. Zink, Brandon. Man., 1904; d. 1998. Woods, a regular in B movies during the 1930s and 1940s, played mainly nice guys and solid citizens, with the occasional second lead in major productions such as *A Tale of Two Cities, The Story of Louis Pasteur*, and *Watch on the Rhine*. He worked in the theatre and television during the 1950s and appeared in his last film, *True Grit* with John Wayne, in 1969. **Films include:** *She Was a Lady* 1934; *A Tale of Two Cities* 1935; *The Story of Louis Pasteur* 1936; *Anthony Adverse* 1936; *Charlie Chan on Broadway* 1937; *Mexican Spitfire* 1940; *I Was a Prisoner of Devil's Island* 1941; *Watch on the Rhine* 1943; *The Bridge at San Luis Rey* 1944; *Night and Day* 1946; *The Return of Rin Tin Tin* 1947; *The Beast from 20,000 Fathoms* 1953; *Kissin' Cousins* 1964; *True Grit* 1969.

World in Action, The
1942–45 series *prod* NFB. *The World in Action*, made under John Grierson's supervision, is the NFB's most famous wartime series. It was written, directed, and edited by Stuart Legg,* assisted by Tom Daly,* and narrated by Lorne Greene.* The forty films were assembled from existing footage; the events depicted were scripted to add a global perspective and a look forward to the post-war world. These effective propaganda films were shown widely and helped establish Canada's reputation for producing high-quality documentaries.

World Is Watching, The

1988 59m *prod* Investigative Productions, *p* Harold Crooks, Jim Munro, Peter Raymont, *d* Peter Raymont, *sc* Harold Crooks, Peter Raymont, *ph* Jonathan Collinson, Martin Duckworth, Dan Holmberg, *ed* John Kramer, Robert Benson. *The World Is Watching* is focused on Nicaragua in a time of turmoil. However, the scenes shown could take place anywhere that produces the peculiar and ubiquitous by-product of contemporary history known as 'news' – and specifically, the particularly powerful form of news manufactured by American television. This revealing account demonstrates how the raw material of political and historical events are moulded, interpreted, altered, edited, and contextualized in the name of objectivity. **Awards include:** GA: Short Documentary.

Wray, Fay

Actor; b. Cardston Alta., 1900. This almond-eyed beauty raised on her father's ranch, Wrayland, achieved worldwide fame in 1933 as the shrieking heroine in *King Kong*. Wray started in Hollywood almost a decade earlier, during the silent era's golden age, and was one of the few actresses from that period still performing in the late 1950s. One of her early successes was opposite Erich von Stroheim in *The Wedding March*. Like Marlene Dietrich, Wray was paired up with Gary Cooper in a number of star vehicles between 1928 and 1933. Wray also acted on stage throughout her career, and she co-authored a play with Sinclair Lewis. She appeared in her last film, *Dragstrip Riot* in 1958. **Films include:** *Legion of the Condemned* 1928; *The Wedding March* 1928; *The Four Feathers* 1929; *Thunderbolt* 1929; *The Honeymoon* 1931; *Doctor X* 1932; *The Most Dangerous Game* 1932; *Mystery of the Wax Museum* 1933; *King Kong* 1933; *The Bowery* 1933; *Woman in the Dark* 1934; *The Affairs of Cellini* 1934; *This Is the Life* 1944 (sc with Sinclair Lewis); *The Cobweb* 1955; *Dragstrip Riot* 1958.

Z

Zero Patience

1994 110m *prod* Zero Patience Productions, *exp* Alexandra Raffé, *p* Louise Garfield, Anna Stratton, *d/sc* John Greyson, *ph* Miroslaw Baszak, *ed* Miume Jan, *mus* Glenn Schellenberg; *with* John Robinson, Normand Fauteux, Dianne Heatherington, Bernard Behrens, Maria Lukofsky. John Greyson's* first theatrical release is one of his most scathing and strangely hilarious indictments of systematic homophobia. This 'AIDS musical,' as it became known, is also one of his most provocative works – a bold critique of the authorities' handling of the AIDS crisis. Greyson was able to fashion an entertaining fiction and a powerful political statement from elements as diverse as philosophical musings, scientific facts, and musical numbers that would make Busby Berkeley proud. In this engaging mix of sex and science, Greyson imagines an affair between Gaetan Douglas, the infamous 'patient zero,'and Sir Richard Burton, the Victorian explorer and ethnographer who conducted an intensive study of penis size. (V)

Zoo la nuit, Un

1987 116m *prod* Les Productions Oz, NFB, *p* Roger Frappier, Pierre Gendron, *d/sc* Jean-Claude Lauzon, *ph* Guy Dufaux, *ed* Michel Arcand, *mus* Jean Corriveau; *with* Gilles Maheu, Germain Houde, Roger Le Bel, Lynne Adams, Lorne Brass. *Un Zoo la nuit*, one of the most audacious debut features in Canadian film history, is a violent, contemporary story about an ex-con, Marcel (Maheu), who tries to pick up the pieces of his life after a brutal stint in prison. He goes to retrieve the $200,000 he stashed away, but finds everyone, from crooked cops to drug pushers, wants a piece of the action. Struggling to find a sense of equilibrium, he reunites with his dying father (Le Bel) and the pair retreat deep into the woods to fish and hunt, but the respite is only temporary. When his father is hospitalized, Marcel plans one last, bizarre hunting trip. Jean-Claude Lauzon's* direction is remarkably assured, and Guy Dufaux's* vivid cinematography captures the gritty, underworld of Montreal highlighted by neon signs and hot street lights. The film's thirteen Genies set an all-time record. (V) **Awards include:** GA: Picture, Director, Original Screenplay, Actor (Le Bel), Supporting Actor (Houde), Cinematography, Editing, Art Direction, Costumes, Musical Score, Song, Overall Sound, Sound Editing.

Appendix 1
A Chronology of Canadian Film and Television

1894
• April 14, Andrew and George Holland* of Ottawa open the world's first kinetoscope parlour in New York City.

1895
• The Lumière brothers, Auguste and Louis, of France screen the first film for the public in the Salon Indien, Grand Café, Paris, 28 December.

1896
• The first public screening of a film in Canada takes place on 28 June in Montreal. In July the Holland* brothers introduce Edison's Vitascope to the Canadian public in Ottawa's West End Park. Among the scenes shown is *The Kiss*, starring May Irwin,* an actress from Whitby, Ontario. On 31 August the first film screening in Toronto takes place at Robinson's Musée on Yonge Street.

1897
• The first films are shot in Canada. The subject of all three films (for Lumière, Edison, and Biograph) is Niagara Falls.
• Films are screened in vaudeville theatres by travelling showmen who tour them from city to city.

1898
• The Massey-Harris Company of Toronto commissions the Edison Co. to produce films to promote its products. This was the first use of film for advertising purposes.

• In December, John Schuberg presents films in Vancouver for the first time.

1899
• Cameramen for Biograph film a contingent of Canadian volunteers boarding a steamship in Quebec City, bound for South Africa and the Boer War. The film was used to raise patriotic interest in the war.

1901
• Guglielmo Marconi successfully transmits a message via radio signals across the Atlantic from Cornwall in England to St John's, Newfoundland. The technology developed by Marconi to transmit sound over distance by converting radio waves into electrical signals was also applied to the transmission of images – television is radio with pictures.

1902
• The Bioscope Company of Halifax, the first Canadian film production company, produces a series of scenes for Canadian Pacific Railways to encourage British immigration to Canada.

1903
• Joe Rosenthal directs *Hiawatha, The Messiah of the Ojibways* (10m), the first dramatic short to be made in Canada.
• Léo-Ernest Ouimet* establishes Canada's first film exchange in Montreal.
• Adolph Zukor, a Hungarian-born entrepreneur, opens his first penny arcades in

New York and New Jersey. (Zukor became the most influential figure in Canadian film exhibition and distribution.)

1904
• George Scott and Co. make *The Great Fire of Toronto*; this record of the city's worst fire is the first film to be shot in Toronto.
• Zukor opens the first of his palatial movie theatres, the Crystal Hall, in New York City.

1905
• Billy Bitzer shoots two films for Biograph: *Moose Hunt* in New Brunswick and *Salmon Fishing* in Quebec for Biograph. (Bitzer later became D.W. Griffith's main cinematographer.)

1906
• Ouimet* opens his first Ouimetoscope in Montreal, and films the first Canadian newsreels to show in his theatre.
• The American-born Allen* brothers, Jule and Jay, open their first store front theatre in Brantford, Ontario.

1907
• Ouimet* opens North America's largest (1,200-seat) luxury theatre in Montreal.
• *Scientific American* uses the word television to describe the transmission of pictures.

1908
• The Allens* launch their first film exchange, the Allen Amusement Corporation.

1911
• Ontario, Quebec, and Manitoba establish Boards of censors to regulate the content of motion pictures, the first in North America.
• The Allens* open their first luxury theatre – the 800-seat Allen Theatre in Calgary.

1912
• Quebec-born Mack Sennett* releases the first shorts made by his newly formed Keystone Studios in Los Angeles.
• Adolph Zukor forms Famous Players in Famous Plays Film Company in New York.

1913
• *Evangeline,** the first Canadian feature, is shot in Nova Scotia by the Bioscope Company.
• Boards of Censors are established in British Columbia and Alberta.

FILMS INCLUDE:
Battle of the Long Sault, The (Frank Crane)

1914
• At the outbreak of the First World War, the failure of the United States to enter the war results in a swell of anti-Americanism. Provincial censor boards ban or attempt to curtail excessive display of the American flag in American films. (The United States entered the war in 1917.)

FILMS INCLUDE:
Evangeline (E.P. Sullivan and William Cavanaugh)

1915
• Ray Lewis founds the *Canadian Moving Picture Digest*, Canada's first weekly film trade journal. (She remained editor and publisher until her death in 1954.)

1916
• Adolph Zukor joins forces with Jesse Lasky to form Famous Players–Lasky, with the rights to distribute Mary Pickford* films through Paramount Pictures. With a massive loan from the Morgan Bank, Zukor embarks on an ambitious plan to dominate the industry by acquiring motion picture theatres right across North America.
• Minneapolis-born N.L. Nathanson buys his first theatre in Toronto, the Majestic Theatre on Adelaide Street, with the backing of wealthy partners. (Nathanson built Paramount, a theatre chain that soon rivalled that of the Allens.*)

1917
• Ontario establishes the Ontario Motion Picture Bureau, the first public film board in

North America, with a mandate 'to carry out educational work for farmers, school children, factory workers and other classes.'
• Canadian National Features of Toronto opens Canada's first film studio in Trenton, Ontario.

1918
• The federal government follows Ontario's lead and establishes the Canadian Government Motion Picture Bureau (CGMPB).
• The Allens* now own the largest and most modern chain of theatres in Canada, and have exclusive rights to distribute Goldwyn and Famous Players–Lasky films in Canada.

1919
• Nell Shipman,* from Victoria, British Columbia, writes and stars in *Back to God's Country,* the most successful silent Canadian film at the box office.
• Zukor sets his sights on Canada and refuses to renegotiate his distribution agreement with the Allens* unless they take him into partnership. The Allens refuse.
• Toronto-born Mary Pickford* forms United Artists, with Charles Chaplin, D.W. Griffith, and Douglas Fairbanks as partners.

FILMS INCLUDE:
Back to God's Country (David M. Hartford)

1920
• The Canadian Pacific Railways, which has been active in producing films since 1897, incorporates Associated Screen News of Canada (ASN) in Montreal and appoints Ben Norrish, formerly of the CGMPB, as its head. (For the next thirty-eight years ASN was the main Canadian producer of newsreels, shorts, and industrials.)
• Zukor buys a substantial part of Paramount Theatres, the rival Canadian chain operated by Nathanson, and incorporates Famous Players Canadian Corporation (FPCC). The Allens,* however, continue to grow and expand into the United States.

1921
• The Canadian Motion Picture Distributors Association (CMPDA) is formed. (Although Canadian in name, the association consisted of the Canadian offices of the American distribution majors and was in essence a branch of the Motion Picture Producers and Distributors Association of America.)
• American Robert Flaherty films *Nanook of the North* in the Canadian Arctic, one of the most famous and influential films ever shot in Canada.

1922
• The Allen* brothers go bankrupt after an intense bidding war with FPCC.

1923
• FPCC buys all fifty-three Allen theatres at a bargain-basement price.
• Zukor is named in a complaint issued by the U.S. Federal Trade Commission: 'Famous Players–Lasky Corporation now possesses and exercises a dominating control over the motion picture industry [and] is the largest theater owner in the world.'

1924
• The Ontario Motion Picture Bureau purchases the film studios in Trenton (the studios had been closed for four years) in an effort to produce films 'for the purpose of preserving Canadian traditions.' In an opening speech, the provincial treasurer notes: 'Not one per cent of the pictures shown in Canada are made in Great Britain and not one per cent are Canadian made.'

1926
• Scottish engineering genius John L. Baird gives the first public demonstration of a television system in the United Kingdom.
• The Canadian Association of Broadcasters (CAB) is founded by thirteen private radio broadcasters. (CAB became the leading lobby voice for the private broadcasting

industry, and is one of Canada's longest running trade organizations.)

1927
• A fire in the Laurier Palace Theatre in Montreal results in the death of seventy-eight children. The Catholic church in Quebec demands (and gets) a ban on children under 16 from attending cinemas. (This ban remained in place until 1961.)
• Britain passes a bill calling for twenty-five per cent of all films exhibited in Britain to be British-made by 1935; a British film is defined as one 'made by British subjects in a studio in the British Empire.'

1928
• *Carry On, Sergeant!** premieres in Toronto. (It was the most costly film in the history of Canadian silent cinema, but it failed miserably at the box office.)
• Bill Oliver directs and shoots *The Beaver People*,* the first of a series of shorts featuring Grey Owl.

FILMS INCLUDE:
Beaver People, The (Bill Oliver)
Carry On, Sergeant! (Bruce Bairnsfather)

1929
• Sir John Aird, chairman of the Canadian Bank of Commerce, delivers a report to Parliament calling for public ownership of Canadian broadcasting.
• Graham Spry, founder of the Canadian Radio League (an organization that played a major role in the establishment of public broadcasting) issues his famous dictum, 'the state or the States.'
• The Bell Telephone labs in the United States demonstrate colour television transmission.
• Mary Pickford* wins Best Actress at the second annual Academy Awards for her performance in *Coquette*.

1930
• Through his, holding company Paramount Publix, Zukor acquires direct control of FPCC; FPCC, which owns one-third of all the theatres in Canada, is now 100 per cent American owned.
• Under the Federal Combines Investigation Act, Prime Minister Bennett appoints Peter White to investigate more than 100 complaints against American film interests operating in Canada. White's report concludes that FPCC is a combine 'detrimental to the Public Interest.' The provinces of Ontario, Saskatchewan, Alberta, and British Columbia take FPCC and the American distribution cartel to court in Ontario.
• Montreal-born Norma Shearer* wins the Best Actress Academy Award for *The Divorcee*, her brother Douglas Shearer* wins the first-ever Academy Award for sound recording. (This has been the only time in the history of the Academy that a brother and sister have won awards at the same ceremony.)

1931
• Ontario passes the British Film Quota Act, but never enforces its provisions.
• Canadian comedian Marie Dressler* wins an Academy Award for her performance in *Min and Bill*.

1932
• After a lengthy trial, FPCC and other defendants are found not guilty on three counts of conspiracy and combination. A decision against the U.S. cartel would have been a historic turning point for the future of filmmaking in Canada, but it was not to be.
• The Ontario Board of Censors imposes a newsreel quota and insists on the inclusion of a percentage of Canadian and British footage. (This quota remained in force for as long as newsreels were shown in Ontario.)
• Gordon Sparling* directs *The Pathfinder*, his first theatrical short in the *Canadian Cameo* series for ASN.

• The Parliament of Canada passes the first Broadcasting Act, creating the Canadian Radio Broadcasting Commission (CRBC) to engage in broadcasting and to regulate all broadcasting in Canada.
• J. Alphonse Ouimet of Montreal, one of the few Canadian television pioneers, builds a prototype television receiver.

1933
• Fay Wray,* from Cardston, Alberta, finds cinematic immortality screaming atop the Empire State Building in *King Kong*.

1934
• Mitchell Hepburn's Liberal government closes down the Ontario Motion Picture Bureau and the Trenton studios are donated to the city of Trenton for a community hall – a sad end to one of Canada's earliest and busiest film studios.
• J. Alphonse Ouimet joins the CRBC as an engineer. (Ouimet moved up the ranks to become president of the Corporation in 1953.)

FILMS INCLUDE:
Rhapsody in Two Languages (Gordon Sparling)

1935
• Nat Taylor* forms the Independent Theatres Association of Ontario.
• The National Film Society of Canada is founded. (In 1950 this organization became the Canadian Film Institute.)

1936
• Columbia Pictures establishes Central Films in Victoria, British Columbia. (During the late 1930s, this company made fourteen B movies – 'quota quickies' – for the British market with such rising stars as Rita Hayworth.)
• ASN builds Canada's largest sound studio in Montreal.
• The CRBC becomes the Canadian Broadcasting Corporation – Société Radio-Canada (CBC / SRC).

• Vancouver-born Richard Day* wins his first of seven Academy Awards for art direction in *The Dark Angel*.

1937
• Philco demonstrates the first high-resolution television picture, using 411 scan lines. (The current standard is 525 in North America and Japan, and 625 in Europe.)

1938
• Noted documentary filmmaker John Grierson* is invited to Canada from England to study government film production. His report leads to the creation of the NFB.
• The British quota system is revised to exclude films made in the Commonwealth.
• Winnipeg-born Deanna Durbin* shares an Academy Award with Mickey Rooney for 'bringing to the screen the spirit and personification of youth.'

FILMS INCLUDE:
Across the Border (Leon Barsha)

1939
• Parliament passes the National Film Act creating the National Film Board of Canada* (NFB).
• Grierson* becomes Canada's first film commissioner, and the NFB concludes distribution agreements with FPCC and *The March of Time* in the United States. Grierson appoints Stuart Legg* as first director of production.
• Budge and Judith Crawley* shoot their first sponsored film, *Canadian Power*, for the Canadian Geographical Society.
• RCA begins regular television broadcasting in America. Franklin Roosevelt is the first president to appear on American television. (With the advent of war in Europe, virtually all television development was brought to a halt.)

1940
• With the release of *Atlantic Patrol*, the NFB

launches its first theatrical series, *Canada Carries On*.*

• Encouraged by Grierson,* celebrated British director Michael Powell shoots *The 49th Parallel* in Quebec. (This film, which starred Laurence Olivier, Leslie Howard, and Raymond Massey,* was an effective piece of war propaganda and received an Academy Award nomination for Best Picture.)

1941

• The CGMPB is absorbed by the NFB. Scottish animator Norman McLaren* is hired to organize the NFB's animation unit. His first film for the Board is *Mail Early*.
• Quebec establishes Le Service de cinéphotographie de la province de Québec, a central organization to coordinate film activity in the province.
• N.L. Nathanson, a founding board member of FPCC, leaves to form Odeon Theatres, with his son, Paul, as the titular head of the company.
• Exhibitor Nat Taylor* and publisher Hye Bossin launch *The Canadian Film Weekly*.

FILMS INCLUDE:
Churchill's Island (Stuart Legg)

1942

• The NFB launches its second wartime series, *World in Action*.* The Board also creates the department of animation under the direction of Norman McLaren,* and organizes film circuits to bring films to rural areas, factories, and town halls.
• The NFB wins its first Academy Award for *Churchill's Island** in the newly created documentary category.

1943

• The NFB opens offices in London, Chicago, and New York.
• The first dramatic sound feature shot in Quebec, *À la croisée des chemins*,* is released.

FILMS INCLUDE:
À la croisée des chemins (Jean-Marie Poitevin)

Alexis Tremblay: Habitant (Jane Marsh Beveridge)

1944

• The establishment of Renaissance Films in Montreal marks the beginning of commercial feature-film production in Quebec; its first film is *Le Père Chopin*.

1945

• Grierson* resigns his position as Canada's film commissioner.
• Paul Nathanson and the Rank Organization of England open the Queensway Studios outside of Toronto.

1946

• John Grierson's* name appears in Igor Gouzenko's spy papers and he is suspected of having communist sympathies; in the cold-war atmosphere of suspicion, the NFB is also implicated.
• Quebec Productions of St-Hyacinthe, near Montreal, shoots *Whispering City / La Forteresse*,* the first Canadian feature in both English and French.
• Budge and Judith Crawley* incorporate Crawley Films in Ottawa.
• Paul Nathanson retires from Odeon and sells his interest in the company to the Rank Organization. Now both the major exhibition chains in Canada are foreign-owned.
• In the first move to classify films in North America, the Ontario Board of Censors imposes an Adult Entertainment rating.

1947

• Business in Canada booms as wartime industry converts to peace. Everything that is sold to Europe is sold on credit, while Canada must buy U.S. goods with dollars. Liberal finance minister Douglas Abbot asks FPCC and the CMPDA to spend some of their money on Canadian production facilities.
• Ross McLean becomes film commissioner.
• Michael Zahorchak opens Canada's first drive-in theatre, in Stoney Creek, near Hamilton, Ontario.

FILMS INCLUDE:
Bush Pilot (Sterling Campbell)
Whispering City / La Forteresse (Fédor Ozep)

1948
• Clarence D. Howe, minister of trade and commerce, meets with the Motion Picture Association of America and accepts the infamous Canadian Cooperation Project:* Hollywood promises to make films in Canada, distribute more NFB work stateside, export fewer low-toned gangster films to Canada, and make reference to Canada in feature films. FPCC's profits are not restricted and the idea of an exhibition quota is dropped.
• Nat Taylor* opens North America's first twin cinema in Ottawa.
• CBC Radio launches 'This Week at the Movies' with host Gerald Pratley,* the first radio program to deal seriously with film appreciation.
• In August the first television seen in Canada is shown at the Canadian National Exhibition; in October, patrons of the Horseshoe Tavern in downtown Toronto watch the World Series on television via a signal provided by WBEN-TV out of Buffalo, New York.
• The Association of Motion Picture Producers and Laboratories of Canada is created, as is the Toronto Film Society.

FILMS INCLUDE:
Drug Addict (Robert Anderson)
Loon's Necklace, The (Judith and Budge Crawley)

1949
• Allegations concerning the existence of communist cells in the NFB are spearheaded by a red-scare press campaign and the Opposition in Parliament. The Department of National Defence refuses to allow NFB personnel to work on defence films. The Board gives in to pressure and allows the RCMP to secretly review employees files.

• After a distinguished career in film, Toronto-born Walter Huston* wins Best Supporting Actor at the Academy Awards for his performance in *The Treasure of the Sierra Madre*.
• Crawley Films wins Film of the Year for *The Loon's Necklace** at the inaugural Canadian Film Awards held in Ottawa.
• Former NFB animators Jim McKay and George Dunning* establish Graphic Associates, Canada's first private animation studio, in Toronto.
• The Royal Commission on National Development in the Arts, Letters and Sciences (the Massey Commission) is appointed by Parliament.

FILMS INCLUDE:
Begone Dull Care (Norman McLaren and Evelyn Lambart)

1950
• A new National Film Act (replacing the 1939 Act) gives the NFB a mandate 'to interpret Canada to Canadians and to other nations.'
• Ross McLean's NFB contract is not renewed; Arthur Irwin, former editor of *Maclean's* magazine, becomes the new film commissioner.
• The National Film Society becomes the Canadian Film Institute in Ottawa, and creates the first film archives in Canada.
• The Yorkton (Saskatchewan) Film Council holds the inaugural International 16mm Documentary Film Festival – the first film festival in North America.

1951
• The Massey Commission submits its report, calling for the creation of the Canada Council and the establishment of a television system based on the concept of public monopoly with a private component.
• With Mary Pickford* as host, Léo-Ernest Ouimet* is given an award at the third Canadian Film Awards, in recognition of his pio-

neering work in distribution, exhibition, and production.

• Nat Taylor* publishes the first *Film Weekly Yearbook of the Canadian Motion Picture Industry*, edited by Hye Bossin.

FILMS INCLUDE:

Around Is Around (Norman McLaren)
Fight: Science against Cancer, The (Morten Parker)
Now Is the Time (Norman McLaren)
Royal Journey (David Bairstow)

1952

• Canadian television goes on air on 6 September in Montreal (CBFT) and on 8 September in Toronto (CBLT). Each station offers about eighteen hours of programming a week. There are 146,000 households with television sets in Canada.

• *The Big Revue*, the English network's flagship and first variety program, premieres in September. (The series was produced under the supervision of Mavor Moore and directed by Norman Jewison*; the first dramatic production was *Sunshine Sketches*, based on Stephen Leacock's popular *Sunshine Sketches of a Little Town*.)

• *Hockey Night in Canada* / *La Soirée du hockey* goes on air; the first games are broadcast 11 October on the French network (Montreal vs Detroit) and 1 November on the English network (Toronto vs Boston). (This national tradition became the longest running and the most popular show in the history of Canadian television.)

• Alfred Hitchcock shoots *I Confess* with Montgomery Clift and Anne Baxter in Quebec City.

FILMS INCLUDE:

Neighbours (Norman McLaren)

1953

• *Tit-coq** wins Film of the Year and Best Feature Film at the Canadian Film Awards. (This film was the last of a mini-boom of Quebec features which saw twenty theatrical films produced between 1944 and 1953.)

• The Ontario Board of Censors introduces the first x-rating in North America – for people eighteen years and older. (The name of this classification was later changed to Restricted.)

• The CBC / SRC is the first system in North America to broadcast complete coverage of the coronation of Queen Elizabeth, four hours after the ceremony ended in London.

• Roger Lemelin's *La Famille Plouffe*, a hit from radio, goes on air in Montreal and immediately becomes the most popular show on the French television network. (At its peak, Quebec's first téléroman attracted a weekly audience of four million.)

• *Tabloid*, an early public affairs program with interviews and weather forecasts hosted by Percy Saltzman, goes on air in Toronto.

• *General Motors Theatre*, also out of Toronto and produced by Sydney Newman,* presents original Canadian drama, including Ted Allan's *Lies My Father Told Me** (which was later adapted into a feature) and Lister Sinclair's *The Blood Is Strong*.

• CBUT, the CBC film unit in Vancouver, is set up, attracting young filmmakers such as Allan King* and Daryl Duke.*

• McLaren's *Neighbours** wins the NFB its second Academy Award, and *The Romance of Transportation in Canada** wins the Palme d'or for animation at Cannes.

FILMS INCLUDE:

Romance of Transportation in Canada, The (Colin Low)
Tit-coq (René Delacroix and Gratien Gélinas)

1954

• Johnny Wayne and Frank Shuster, long-time favourites on CBC radio, make their television debut. (At the height of their fame Wayne and Shuster topped a North American critics poll as the best television comic act, and they appeared on the *Ed Sullivan*

Show a record sixty-seven times. Their last appearance on CBC-TV was in October 1988. They were masters of ironic, character-based comedy, and their show was a precursor to the sketch comedies of *Saturday Night Live*, *SCTV*, and *The Kids in the Hall*.)
• A fifty per cent capital cost allowance (CCA) is introduced to encourage private investment in Canadian film companies.
• The Duplessis government in Quebec forbids the screening of 'federalist' NFB films in Quebec schools.
• The British Empire Games are broadcast from Vancouver with live coverage of Roger Bannister's historic four-minute mile.
• Dorothy Burritt and Guy L. Coté* found the Canadian Federation of Film Societies.
• Colin Low's *Corral** wins first prize for documentary at the Venice Film Festival.

FILMS INCLUDE:
Corral (Colin Low)
Stratford Adventure, The (Morten Parker)

1955
• Two former NFB filmmakers, Marcel and Réal Racicot, produce Quebec's first animated feature, *Le Village enchanté*.
• Le Centre catholique du cinéma de Montréal publishes the first issue of *Séquences*.
• The opening of Parliament in Ottawa is broadcast live on television for the first time.
• The Royal Commission on Broadcasting is appointed with Robert Fowler as chair.
• McLaren's *Blinkity Blank** wins the Palme d'or for animation at Cannes and the first prize for animation at the British Academy Awards.

FILMS INCLUDE:
Blinkity Blank (Norman McLaren)

1956
• The NFB moves to its new headquarters in Montreal.
• *Anne of Green Gables*, a musical written by

Don Harron and Norman Campbell, is broadcast on the CBC; now fifty per cent of Canadian households have a television set.

1957
• On 1 July a special television program is broadcast to mark the opening of coast-to-coast microwave service. With links from Victoria, British Columbia, to Sydney, Nova Scotia, Canada now has the longest television network in the world.
• In October, CBC / SRC television and radio covers Queen Elizabeth's address to the nation from Ottawa and the first opening of a Canadian Parliament by a reigning monarch.
• *Front Page Challenge* goes on air for the first time. (This show was created by writer John Aylesworth and developed by producer Harvey Hart,* with Fred Davis as moderator. It was originally planned as a summer replacement, but it became one of the most popular and longest-running panel shows in North America.)
• Sidney J. Furie* shoots his first feature, *A Dangerous Age* (originally planned as a CBC production) in Toronto.
• The Canada Council begins operations.
• The *Canadian Moving Picture Digest* ceases publication after forty-two years.
• The NFB's *City of Gold** wins first prize for documentary film at Cannes; *A Chairy Tale** takes top honours for experimental film at Venice and is nominated for an Academy Award.

FILMS INCLUDE:
Chairy Tale, A (Norman McLaren and Claude Jutra)
City of Gold (Colin Low and Wolf Koenig)
Oedipus Rex (Tyrone Guthrie)

1958
• The future cream of Quebec cinema – Gilles Groulx,* Gilles Carle,* Claude Fournier,* Jacques Godbout,* Michel Brault,*

Claude Jutra* – embark on their careers at the new NFB headquarters in Montreal.
• With the release of *Les Raquetteurs*,* Brault* and Groulx* become pioneers in a movement that is known as *cinéma-verité* or direct cinema. (This portable, realistic approach to filmmaking captured the attention of French documentary filmmaker Jean Rouch, influenced the French New Wave, and held sway over the documentary movement in Canada for a generation.)
• *A Dangerous Age* is released theatrically in England, but can't find Canadian distribution. Furie* moves to England and tells the British press: 'I wanted to start a Canadian film industry, but nobody cared.'
• The Fowler Report results in the Broadcasting Act, which establishes the Board of Broadcast Governors (BBG) to regulate all Canadian broadcasting and sets the stage for the licensing of private broadcasters. The BBG requires all television broadcasters to show a minimum of forty-five per cent Canadian content.
• The inaugural Stratford International Film Festival is held in Stratford, Ontario.
• ASN, Canada's longest-running film production company, closes down.
• Al Sens opens his animation studio, the first in Vancouver.

FILMS INCLUDE:
Raquetteurs, Les (Gilles Groulx and Michel Brault)

1959
• Nat Taylor* opens the Toronto International Film Studios in Kleinberg, Ontario, near Toronto, with two of the largest sound stages outside of Hollywood.
• *Candid Eye*,* a series of fourteen direct-cinema documentaries, is broadcast on CBC-TV over two seasons.
• In co-production with the BBC, Crawley Films of Ottawa launches *The RCMP* series in both French and English.
• *Don Messer's Jubilee* goes on air from Hali-

fax. (Over its ten-year lifespan, this show became one of the most beloved programs ever produced by CBC-TV.)
• The microwave CBC / SRC network is extended to Newfoundland.

FILMS INCLUDE:
Back-Breaking Leaf, The (Terence Macartney-Filgate)
Glenn Gould – Off the Record (Wolf Koenig and Roman Kroitor)
Glenn Gould – On the Record (Wolf Koenig and Roman Kroitor)

1960
• The BBG licenses four private broadcasters to compete with the CBC / SRC: Télé-Métropole and CFCF in Montreal; CFTO in Toronto; BCTV in Vancouver.
• *The Nature of Things* premieres. (This program, the flagship of the CBC's science unit, became one of the network's most successful productions in terms of longevity, audience appeal, and international sales.)
• At Cannes, *The Back-Breaking Leaf*,* wins top prize for television documentary and *Universe*,* wins the Jury Prize for animation.

FILMS INCLUDE:
Universe (Roman Kroitor and Colin Low)

1961
• The CTV Network goes on air in October. (CTV, Canada's largest private television network, was set up as a rather unmanageable cooperative. Each owner, no matter how many stations they owned, had a veto and a single vote on the executive board – an arrangement that made for a very unhappy partnership. After decades of corporate machinations, Toronto-based Baton Broadcasting took over ownership in 1997.)
• Nat Taylor* produces *The Mask*. (This 3-D film was the first Canadian feature to be shown extensively in the United States; it was distributed by Warner Bros.)

- Quebec schools are once again allowed to screen NFB films.
- The operations of the Stratford International Film Festival are suspended.

FILMS INCLUDE:
Lutte, La (Michel Brault, Claude Fournier, Claude Jutra, and Marcel Carrière)
Very Nice, Very Nice (Arthur Lipsett)

1962
- Budge Crawley* produces his first feature, *Amanita Pestilens*. (The film was the first screen appearance of Geneviève Bujold,* the first Canadian feature filmed in colour, and the first Canadian film to be shot simultaneously in English and French. It was never released.)
- Crawley Films produces *The Tales of the Wizard of Oz*, the first animated series for television.
- Brian Moore's* play, *The Luck of Ginger Coffey*,* is broadcast on CBC-TV's *Festival*. (In 1964, Moore's play was made into a feature starring Robert Shaw.)

FILMS INCLUDE:
Bûcherons de la Manouane (Arthur Lamothe)
Jour après jour (Clémont Perron)
Lonely Boy (Roman Kroitor and Wolf Koenig)

1963
- The Liberal government in Ottawa establishes an Inter-Departmental Committee on the Possible Development of a Feature Film Industry in Canada with NFB film commissioner Guy Roberge as chair.
- Don Owen* directs *Nobody Waved Good-Bye** for the NFB, the first film to give Toronto a cinematic identity; Claude Jutra* does the same for Montreal with *À tout prendre*.*
- Allan King* and Don Haig* establish Film Arts as an editing and post-production facility in Toronto, with the CBC as their biggest customer.
- *Drylanders*,* the first feature-length English-

language film made at the NFB, is released.
- Pierre Perrault's and Michel Brault's *Pour la suite du monde** is broadcast on SRC and draws an audience of half-a-million.
- The province of Ontario creates the Ontario Arts Council; the Council's mandate includes funding films of an experimental nature.
- Canada signs its first international co-production agreement – with France.
- The Alliance of Canadian Television and Radio Artists (ACTRA) is formed. (In 1984, the organization was restructured under the name Alliance of Canadian Cinema, Television and Radio Artists.)

FILMS INCLUDE:
Anniversary (William Weintraub)
Bitter Ash, The (Larry Kent)
Drylanders (Donald Haldane)
My Financial Career (Gerald Potterton and Grant Munro)
Pour la suite du monde (Pierre Perrault and Michel Brault)

1964
- The theatrical release of *Nobody Waved Good-Bye** in Toronto marks the beginning of an English-Canadian feature film culture. (The film opened first in New York; after favourable reviews the NFB agreed to its release in Canada.)
- *This Hour Has Seven Days* premieres on CBC-TV. (This one-hour weekly show, produced by Douglas Leiterman* and Patrick Watson, became one of the most controversial and influential shows ever run on CBC. Its original mixture of satirical music, investigative film reports, and confrontational and aggressive interviews made it hugely popular. At its peak in March 1966, *This Hour*'s ratings were second only to *Hockey Night in Canada*.)
- Beryl Fox's *Summer in Mississippi* (produced by Douglas Leiterman* and shot by Richard Leiterman*), a direct-cinema documentary about the killing of three civil rights

workers during a voter registration drive, in the southern United States, is broadcast on *This Hour Has Seven Days*.
• The NFB restructures production along linguistic lines. Pierre Juneau is appointed director of French production and Grant McLean director of English production.
• The federal cabinet approves in principle the establishment of a revolving loan to foster and promote the development of a feature-film fund.
• Guy L. Coté* and Michel Patenaude found La Cinémathèque canadienne.
• The Yorkton Short Film Festival begins in Saskatchewan.
• The Committee on Broadcasting, chaired by Robert Fowler, is established.

FILMS INCLUDE:
À tout prendre (Claude Jutra)
Bethune (Donald Brittain)
Chat dans le sac, Le (Gilles Groulx)
Hutterites, The (Colin Low)
Luck of Ginger Coffey, The (Irvin Kershner)
Nobody Waved Good-Bye (Don Owen)
Sweet Substitute (Larry Kent)

1965
• *The Report of Film Distribution: Practices, Problems and Prospects*, by O.J. Firestone, is released. (The *Report* recommended an increase in the CCA allowed for film producers, the initiation of joint international film agreements, and the establishment of a film development corporation. Most of Firestone's recommendations were eventually adopted, but not as a comprehensive package.)
• *The Mills of the Gods: Viet Nam* is broadcast on CBC's *Documentary* series, and wins Film of the Year at the Canadian Film Awards.
• CBC-TV premieres *Seaway*, its most costly Canadian drama to date, at $100,000 per episode. (The show, developed by Abraham Polonsky, the American blacklisted writer and director [*Force of Evil, Body and Soul*], copied the popular American *Route 66*

model. Polonsky also wrote several episodes.)
• The Committee on Broadcasting recommends a new authority to replace the BBG. By now more than ninety per cent of Canadian households have television sets.
• The Ontario Film Association is formed out of the Ontario Association of Film Councils.

FILMS INCLUDE:
Memorandum (Donald Brittain and John Spotton)
Mills of the Gods: Viet Nam, The (Beryl Fox)
Vie heureuse de Léopold Z, La (Gilles Carle)
Winter Kept Us Warm (David Secter)

1966
• The CBC brass cancels *This Hour Has Seven Days*. Patrick Watson is taken off air and his co-host, Laurier LaPierre, is fired for crying over a story about the Stephen Truscott trial. The forerunner to *W5* and *60 Minutes* comes to an abrupt and controversial end.
• CTV launches *W5*. (This program is now the longest-running public-affairs program in North America.)
• *Wojeck*, with John Vernon* as a crusading coroner, runs on the CBC-TV for two seasons. (This series, shot on the streets of Toronto using direct-cinema techniques, set new standards for realistic drama.)
• The original *Take One* magazine, published and edited by Peter Lebensold and Adam Symansky from Montreal, makes its debut. (The magazine later moved to Toronto and continued publishing until 1979.)

FILMS INCLUDE:
Helicopter Canada (Eugene Boyko)
Never a Backward Step (Donald Brittain, Arthur Hammond, and John Spotton)
Paddle to the Sea (Bill Mason)
Things I Cannot Change, The (Tanya Ballantyne)
What on Earth! (Les Drew and Kaj Pindal)

1967
• The NFB presents *Labyrinth*,* a ground-

breaking multi-screen presentation, at Expo 67.

• Christopher Chapman's *A Place to Stand*, a propaganda film for Ontario, is shown on a huge screen (30 by 66 feet) at Expo 67; although shot on 35mm, the film is projected in 70mm.

• The NFB launches the Challenge for Change* program.

• The Canadian Filmmakers Distribution Centre, the first of the alternative distribution cooperatives to spring-up across the country, is established in Toronto.

• CBC-TV begins to broadcast in colour.

• Toronto-born and CBC-trained Norman Jewison* receives an Academy Award nomination for his direction of the groundbreaking U.S. racial drama *In the Heat of the Night*; the film wins five Academy Awards, including Best Picture.

FILMS INCLUDE:
Avec tambours et trompettes (Marcel Carrière)
Flowers on a One-Way Street (Robin Spry)
Labyrinth (Roman Kroitor and Colin Low)
Règne du jour, Le (Pierre Perrault)
Warrendale (Allan King)
Wavelength (Michael Snow)

1968

• The Canadian Film Development Corporation (CFDC) opens for business in February with a budget of $10 million. (However, because no effort was made to affect the distribution and exhibition of films in Canada, the films financed by the CFDC were seen by few Canadians.)

• The 1967–8 Broadcasting Act creates the Canadian Radio-Television Commission (CRTC), with Pierre Juneau as the first chairman. The CRTC exercises almost total judiciary control – although its decisions can be appealed to the cabinet – over broadcasting regulations in Canada. Every broadcaster must renew its licence on a schedule determined by the Commission, and the CRTC has the authority to impose Canadian content regulations on the nation's airwaves.

(In 1976, when the federal government transferred telecommunications from the Canadian Transport Commission to the CRTC, the name was changed to Canadian Radio-Television and Telecommunications Commission.)

• Roman Kroitor,* Graeme Ferguson,* and Robert Kerr form the Multiscreen Corporation to make films in the new IMAX format.

• FPCC is dissolved and replaced by Famous Players Ltd., fifty-one per cent of which is owned by Gulf+Western (Canada) Ltd., which in turn is wholly owned by Gulf+Western in the United States.

• Toronto-born, NFB-trained animator George Dunning* directs *Yellow Submarine*, a feature-length animated film based on the music by the Beatles.

• The Canadian Film Awards are reorganized to include craft and acting awards. Christopher Chapman's *A Place to Stand* wins Film of the Year, and Don Owen's *The Ernie Game*,* a co-production between the NFB and CBC-TV, is named Best Feature Film.

FILMS INCLUDE:
Best Damn Fiddler from Calabogie to Kaladar (Peter Pearson)
Entre la mer et l'eau douce (Michel Brault)
Ernie Game, The (Don Owen)
Isabel (Paul Almond)
Rat Life and Diet in North America (Joyce Wieland)
Walking (Ryan Larkin)

1969

• Donald Shebib* films *Goin' down the Road** on the streets of Toronto with a minuscule budget.

• The Challenge for Change* program is formally established as a studio within the NFB with a specific mandate from the federal Cabinet 'to prepare Canadians for social change' using film, video, and other media.

• *Don Messer's Jubilee* is cancelled, provoking a strong and vocal outrage from loyal viewers across Canada; despite an avalanche of mail in support of the show, the CBC doesn't relent.

• The release of *Valérie*,* directed by Denis Héroux,* launches the mini-boom of sexploitation films in Quebec known as 'maple-syrup porn.'

• The Ontario Board of Censors bans John Hofsess's *The Columbus of Sex* (produced by Ivan Reitman* and Dan Goldberg); it is the first Canadian film to be banned.

• The first Canadian Student Film Festival is held at Sir George Williams University in Montreal.

• Gerald Pratley* founds the Ontario Film Institute.

• Jacques Godbout* is appointed director of French production at the NFB.

• *The Best Damn Fiddler from Calabogie to Kaladar** is named Film of the Year at the Canadian Film Awards. No award is given for best feature film.

FILMS INCLUDE:
Blake (Bill Mason)
Married Couple, A (Allan King)
Reason over Passion (Joyce Wieland)
Valérie (Denis Héroux)
Voitures d'eau, Les (Pierre Perrault)

1970

• Sydney Newman,* is appointed film commissioner. (With events of the October Crisis unfolding, Newman suppresses several films including Denys Arcand's *On est au coton*,* a gritty, realistic exposé of Quebec's garment industry. Arcand's* film was finally released in 1976.)

• *Tiger Child*, the first film to make use of IMAX technology, is projected at the world fair in Osaka, Japan; the film was directed by Donald Brittain.*

• TV Ontario goes on the air, using the first UHF television channel for broadcasting in Canada.

• The animated film *Psychocratie* wins Film of the Year, and *Goin' down the Road** wins Best Feature Film at the Canadian Film Awards.

• Toronto-born director Arthur Hiller* receives an Academy Award nomination for *Love Story*, one of the most popular weepies ever made in Hollywood.

FILMS INCLUDE:
Act of the Heart, The (Paul Almond)
Crimes of the Future (David Cronenberg)
Goin' down the Road (Don Shebib)
Hart of London, The (Jack Chambers)
Pays sans bon sens!, Un / Wake up, Mes bons amis! (Pierre Perrault)
Surfacing on the Thames (David Rimmer)

1971

• *Mon oncle Antoine** wins Best Feature Film at the Canadian Film Awards and the Gold Hugo at the Chicago International Film Festival, establishing Claude Jutra* as Canada's most accomplished director.

• La Cinémathèque canadienne becomes La Cinémathèque québécoise with Robert Daudelin as director.

• The Nelvana Animation Studios* opens in Toronto. (This company, founded by Michael Hirsh, Clive Smith, and Patrick Loubert, grew to become Canada's most successful animation house.)

• L'Association coopérative des productions audio-visuelles (ACPAV) is founded in Montreal, with Marc Daigle as director.

• The first issue of *Cinéma Quebec* is published.

• The Ontario Film Institute revives the Stratford International Film Festival.

• The Toronto Filmmakers' Co-op is established.

• ACTRA initiates the ACTRA Awards for the best in Canadian television.

• Norman Jewison* receives his second Academy Award nomination for *Fiddler on the Roof.*

FILMS INCLUDE:
Acadie, l'Acadie ?!?, L' (Pierre Perault and Michel Brault)
Breathing Together: The Revolution of the Electric Family (Morley Markson)

Evolution (Michael Mills)
Fortune and Men's Eyes (Harvey Hart)
Mon oncle Antoine (Claude Jutra)
North of Superior (Graeme Ferguson)
Région centrale, La (Michael Snow)
Rip-Off (Don Shebib)

1972

• The highlight of the year is 'The Big Broadcast of 1972': the first Canada-Russia hockey series draws a total audience of more than half the population of Canada when Paul Henderson wins the last game and the series with a dramatic last-minute goal.
• The Ontario Ministry of Industry and Tourism appoints producer John Bassett to head a task force to study the Canadian film industry. The conclusion of the Bassett report is that 'a basic film industry exists. It's the audiences that need to be nurtured through theatrical exposure. The optimum method of accomplishing this is to establish a quota system for theatres.'
• The Council of Canadian Filmmakers, an ad-hoc group representing unions, ACTRA, the Directors Guild, and the Toronto Film-makers' Co-op, is formed.
• Kathleen Shannon* begins *Working Mothers*, a series of short films for the NFB's Challenge for Change* program. It is the Board's first commitment to feminist filmmaking.
• The Pacific Cinematheque is formed in Vancouver.
• Anik-1 is launched in November. The orbit of this satellite is such that it can always broadcast to the entire land surface of Canada, providing television and radio service from the forty-ninth parallel to the far North. 'Anik' is the Inuktitut word for 'brother.'
• CBC-TV premieres *The Beachcombers*, starring Bruno Gerussi. (This series was the first to be shot entirely on the West Coast. It became one of CBC's most successful, and longest-running dramas and was sold around the world.)
• Citytv goes on air in Toronto. (With the

launch of *City Pulse News* in the mid-1970s, Citytv began to influence news operations across Canada and abroad. Its portable video eye, open-studio concept was based on the simple notion that television is as much about the people bringing you the story as the story itself.)
• *Cinema Canada* magazine is launched in Toronto by George Csaba Koller and Philip McPhedran.
• John Grierson,* the founder of the NFB, dies in England at age seventy-three.
• Léo-Ernest Ouimet,* a pioneer in Canadian cinema, dies in Montreal.
• William Fruet's *Wedding in White** wins Best Feature Film at the Canadian Film Awards.

FILMS INCLUDE:
Journey (Paul Almond)
Only Thing You Know, The (Clarke Mackey)
Rowdyman, The (Peter Carter)
Temps d'une chasse, Les (Francis Mankiewicz)
Vie rêvée, La (Mireille Dansereau)
Wedding in White (William Fruet)

1973

• The Canadian Film Awards, held in Montreal for the first time, are boycotted by l'Association des réalisateurs et réalisatrices de films du Québec.
• Harold Greenberg* buys Astral Films. (The company later became Astral Bellevue Pathé.)
• The NFB's *Cry of the Wild*,* directed by Bill Mason,* is released theatrically and quickly becomes one of the most successful NFB features.
• Ivan Reitman's* low-budget *Cannibal Girls* is released and turns a huge profit in international sales.
• The Alberta Motion Picture Industries Association is incorporated.
• The International Festival of Women and Film is held in Toronto.
• *Slipstream** wins Best Feature Film at the Canadian Film Awards.

FILMS INCLUDE:
Between Friends (Don Shebib)
Coming Home (Bill Reid)
Cry of the Wild (Bill Mason)
Goodbye Sousa (Tony Ianzelo)
Grierson (Roger Blais)
Hunger (Peter Foldès)
Kamouraska (Claude Jutra)
Paperback Hero (Peter Pearson)
Réjeanne Padovani (Denys Arcand)
Slipstream (David Acomba)

1974

• Ted Kotcheff's *The Apprenticeship of Duddy Kravitz** wins the Golden Bear (first prize) at the Berlin Film Festival – the first Canadian feature to win at a major European film festival – and Mordecai Richler* receives an Academy Award nomination for his screenplay. (There were no Canadian Film Awards in 1974, so *The Apprenticeship* was awarded Best Feature Film for 1974 at the CFA in 1975.)
• The Council of Canadian Filmmakers issues the 'Winnipeg Manifesto,' calling for quotas and for radical and creative solutions to the problem of getting Canadian films shown in Canada.
• The federal government increases the CCA for films to 100 per cent. The concept of certification for a Canadian film is introduced.
• Members of l'Association des réalisateurs et réalisatrices de films du Québec occupy the offices of the Quebec censor board to demand greater provincial support for Quebec cinema.
• The Ontario Film Office is established. The old Association of Motion Picture Producers and Laboratories of Canada becomes the Canadian Film and Television Association.
• The NFB creates Studio D, a unit under the direction of Kathleen Shannon,* with a mandate to focus on production of films for, by, and about women.
• The Atlantic Filmmakers Co-op is founded in Halifax.

• CBC-TV broadcasts *The National Dream*, its most ambitious production to date; this eight-part series is based on Pierre Berton's two-volume best-seller, *The National Dream* and *The Last Spike*.
• Peter Foldès's *Hunger*,* the first NFB animated film to use computer techniques, wins a Special Jury Prize for animation at Cannes.

FILMS INCLUDE:
Action: The October Crisis of 1970 (Robin Spry)
Apprenticeship of Duddy Kravitz, The (Ted Kotcheff)
Black Christmas (Bob Clark)
Canadian Pacific (David Rimmer)
Cree Hunters of Mistassini (Boyce Richardson and Tony Ianzelo)
Hard Part Begins, The (Paul Lynch)
Janis (Howard Alk and Seaton Findlay)
Ordres, Les (Michel Brault)
Quiet Day in Belfast, A (Milad Bessada)
Reaction: A Portrait of a Society in Crisis (Robin Spry)
Why Rock the Boat? (John Howe)

1975

• Secretary of State Hugh Faulkner negotiates a voluntary quota agreement with Famous Players and Odeon Theatres: the chains are to guarantee a minimum of four weeks per theatre per year to Canadian films and invest a minimum of $1.7 million in their production.
• The Newfoundland Independent Filmmakers' Co-op and Winnipeg Film Group are founded.
• The first Grierson Film Seminar, sponsored by the Ontario Film Association, is held.
• Quebec passes legislation creating La Direction générale du cinéma et de l'audiovisuel to stimulate the film industry.
• David Cronenberg's* first feature, *Shivers*,* is released.
• Robert Lantos* and Stephen Roth establish RSL Productions in Montreal; their first production is Gilles Carle's *L'Ange et la femme*.

- In Vancouver, Marv Newland founds International Rocketship.
- CBC-TV's *King of Kensington* debuts, starring Al Waxman* and Fiona Reid. (This conventional situation comedy, one of the most successful shows on the English network, ran for five seasons.)
- Bill C-58 is passed by Parliament; this legislation disallows tax deductions for advertisers who run commercials aimed at Canadian audiences on U.S. programs. Canadian networks are allowed to substitute their signal for U.S. channels on cable.
- *Cinema Canada* magazine moves to Montreal and becomes a monthly edited and published by Connie and Jean-Pierre Tadros.
- Michel Brault* shares the Best Director prize at Cannes for *Les Ordres*,* which also wins Film of the Year and Best Feature Film at the Canadian Film Awards.

FILMS INCLUDE:
Ahô ... au coeur du monde primitif (Daniel Bertolino and François Floquet)
Bar salon (André Forcier)
Gina (Denys Arcand)
Lies My Father Told Me (Ján Kadár)
Man Who Skied down Everest, The (Budge Crawley)
Shivers (David Cronenberg)
Whistling Smith (Michael Scott)

1976

- The Council of Canadian Filmmakers is granted a hearing before the Royal Commission on Corporate Concentration; however, no federal inquiry is called to investigate charges that Famous Players and Odeon work in collusion to block the exhibition of Canadian films. Famous Players responds by attacking the voluntary quota system, claiming that the people of Canada do not appreciate the works of Canadian filmmakers.
- The CMPDA inaugurates the Golden Reel Award, for the producer of the Canadian feature film that achieves the highest box-office gross in Canadian theatres. The first

winner is Ján Kadár's *Lies My Father Told Me*.* This film also wins Best Feature Film at the Canadian Film Awards, as well as a Golden Globe Award for Best Foreign Film, and author Ted Allan* receives an Academy Award nomination for his screenplay.
- CBC-TV launches *For the Record*.*
- The first Toronto Festival of Festivals is held.
- The Moving Image and Sound Archives Division of the Public Archives of Canada in Ottawa is created.
- International Animated Film Festival is held in Ottawa; this is the first time the Festival is held outside of Europe.
- The Film Studies Association of Canada is founded.
- Crawley's *The Man Who Skied down Everest** wins an Academy Award for Best Feature Documentary, and Mary Pickford* receives an Honorary Academy Award.

FILMS INCLUDE:
Blackwood (Tony Ianzelo and Andy Thomson)
Far Shore, The (Joyce Wieland)
Goldenrod (Harvey Hart)
High Grass Circus (Torben Schioier and Tony Ianzelo)
On est au coton (Denys Arcand)
Street, The (Caroline Leaf)
Volcano: An Inquiry into the Life and Death of Malcolm Lowry (Donald Brittain)

1977

- The British-owned Odeon Theatres is bought by Canadian interests headed by Michael Zahorchak, but nothing changes. The federal government gives up on voluntary quotas, which were not working.
- Garth Drabinsky* produces his second feature, Daryl Duke's *The Silent Partner**; this film marks the beginning of the CCA-driven tax-shelter boom years.
- *SCTV* goes on air locally in Toronto on Global TV then moves to Edmonton for the 1979 season. (*SCTV*, one of the funniest paro-

dies of television ever made, was picked up by NBC in 1981 for two seasons in a 90-minute version, a first for an independent Canadian-produced series. The last season was 1983–4.)
• The first World Film Festival is held in Montreal.
• The Saskatchewan Film Pool is formed in Regina.
• Monique Mercure* shares the Best Actress prize at Cannes for her performance in *J.A. Martin photographe.* The film also wins Best Feature Film at the Canadian Film Awards.

FILMS INCLUDE:
Bead Game (Ishu Patel)
Dreamspeaker (Claude Jutra)
J.A. Martin photographe (Jean Beaudin)
Outrageous! (Richard Benner)
Rabid (David Cronenberg)
Special Day, A (Ettore Scola)
Vieux Pays où Rimbaud est mort, Le (Jean Pierre Lefebvre)
Who Has Seen the Wind (Allan King)
Why Shoot the Teacher? (Silvio Narizzano)

1978
• The Ontario Board of Censors bans outright *Pretty Baby*, Louis Malle's controversial film about prostitution in turn-of-the-century New Orleans. (The popular backlash to this ban marked the beginning of the end for Canada's longest-running board of censors.)
• Garth Drabinsky* joins forces with Nat Taylor* to form Pan Canadian Film Distributors.
• Michael MacMillan, Seaton McLean, and Janice Platt form Atlantis Films.
• The Calgary Society of Independent Filmmakers is founded. The Toronto Filmmakers' Co-op ceases operations.
• Ivan Reitman* shoots the low-budget teen comedy *Meatballs* with Bill Murray in Haliburton, Ontario, north of Toronto.
• *The Silent Partner* wins Best Feature Film at the Canadian Film Awards.
• The NFB wins two Academy Awards: for

Co Hoedeman's *The Sand Castle* (Animated Short) and Beverly Shaffer's *I'll Find a Way* (Live-Action Short). These are the first Academy Awards won by the NFB in twenty-five years.

FILMS INCLUDE:
Affaire Bronswik, L' (Robert Awad and André Leblanc)
Afterlife (Ishu Patel)
Blood Relatives (Claude Chabrol)
Champions, Parts I and II, The (Donald Brittain)
I'll Find a Way (Beverly Shaffer)
In Praise of Older Women (George Kaczender)
Silent Partner, The (Daryl Duke)

1979
• *Meatballs* is released and becomes a huge box-office hit in the United States. Its success demonstrates that investment in Canadian films is viable and lucrative. Tax-shelter production peaks, and more feature films are made in Canada than at any other time; many are never released.
• Nat Taylor* and Garth Drabinsky* open Cineplex, an eighteen-theatre complex in Toronto's Eaton's Centre. The theatres are small and play 16mm specialty films, European art film and Hollywood second runs.
• TVO becomes the first North American broadcaster to use direct-satellite technology, transmitting its signal to northern Ontario via the Anik-B satellite.
• Denis Héroux* and John Kemeny* establish International Cinema Corporation in Montreal. Their first film is Louis Malle's *Atlantic City.*
• The Academy of Canadian Cinema is incorporated and takes over the Canadian Film Awards, which are renamed the Genie Awards. (The name comes from the name given by the Academy to the statuette designed for the awards by Sorel Etrog.) No awards are presented this year.
• The New Brunswick Filmmakers' Co-op is founded in Fredericton. The Canadian Film-

makers Distribution West begins operations in Vancouver.

• The Banff Television Foundation is formed and holds the first Banff Television Festival.

• The CRTC orders an extra half-hour of Canadian drama a week from CTV. (CTV fought the CRTC ruling all the way to the Supreme Court, but lost the case in 1982.)

• The first issue of *24 Images* is published.

• Mary Pickford* dies at age eighty-seven.

• The NFB's *Special Delivery* wins an Academy Award for Best Animated Short.

FILMS INCLUDE:
Going the Distance (Paul Cowan)
Meatballs (Ivan Reitman)
Mourir à tue-tête (Anne Claire Poirier)
Murder by Decree (Bob Clark)
Paperland: The Bureaucrat Observed (Donald Brittain)

1980

• The Ontario Board of Censors attempts to ban Volker Schlöndorff's *The Tin Drum*, but backs down in the face of a huge public outcry and agrees to let the film be shown with only minor cuts.

• Montreal producer Rock Demers* establishes Les Productions La Fête to make Tales for All, a series of feature films for children.

• Cineworks opens in Vancouver and the Liaison of Independent Filmmakers opens in Toronto.

• At the first Genies, *The Changeling** wins Best Picture and *Meatballs** wins the Golden Reel Award.

• *Every Child** wins an Academy Award for Best Animated Short; this is the fourth Academy Award won by the NFB in three years.

FILMS INCLUDE:
Atlantic City (Louis Malle)
Bons Débarras, Les (Francis Mankiewicz)
Changeling, The (Peter Medak)
Every Child (Eugene Fedorenko)
Homme à tout faire, L' (Micheline Lanctôt)
Hounds of Notre Dame, The (Zale Dalen)

Prom Night (Paul Lynch)
Sweater, The (Sheldon Cohen)
Tribute (Bob Clarke)

1981

• The Alberta Motion Picture Development Corporation is created.

• The first Atlantic Film Festival is held in St John's, Newfoundland.

• Bonnie Sherr Klein's* controversial *Not a Love Story: A Film about Pornography** becomes one of the most popular feature-length documentaries ever produced by the NFB.

• Bob Clark's *Porky's,** produced by Astral, is released in the United States and becomes the most successful Canadian feature at the box office, worldwide.

• *Les Bons Débarras** wins Best Picture and *The Changeling** wins the Golden Reel Award at the Genies.

FILMS INCLUDE:
After the Axe (Sturla Gunnarsson)
Alligator Shoes (Clay Borris)
First Winter (John N. Smith)
Heartaches (Don Shebib)
Heavy Metal (Gerald Potterton)
Not a Love Story: A Film about Pornography (Bonnie Sherr Klein)
P4W: Prison for Women (Holly Dale and Janis Cole)
Plouffe, Les (Gilles Carle)
Porky's (Bob Clark)
Scanners (David Cronenberg)
Tender Tale of Cinderella Penguin, The (Janet Perlman)
Ticket to Heaven (Ralph Thomas)

1982

• In one of the most important and effective programming decisions in Canadian television history, the CBC moves the national news from 11:00 P.M. to 10:00 P.M. and introduces *The Journal*, a high-profile public-affairs program with former radio host Barbara Frum. This change revitalizes Canadian television news and the CBC gains five hours of prime-time Canadian programming per week.

• The CRTC licenses six pay-TV companies: two national – First Choice Canadian and C Channel – and four regional.

• The first Rendez-vous du cinéma québécois is held. The Vancouver International Film Festival begins.

• The Canadian Independent Film Caucus is created to promote the production of point-of-view documentaries.

• Jean Pierre Lefebvre's *Les Fleurs sauvages* shares the International Film Critics' Prize at Cannes.

• *Ticket to Heaven** wins Best Picture and *Heavy Metal** wins the Golden Reel Award at the Genies.

• *Atlantic City** is the first Canadian dramatic feature to be nominated for an Academy Award, along with its French director, Louis Malle, and American stars, Burt Lancaster and Susan Sarandon.

• Frédéric Back's *Crac!*, produced by SRC, wins the Academy Award for Best Animated Short.

FILMS INCLUDE:
Bête lumineuse, La (Pierre Perrault)
Poetry in Motion (Ron Mann)
Quest for Fire (Jean-Jacques Annaud)
Scissere (Peter Mettler)

1983

• Garth Drabinsky* receives a hearing before the Restrictive Trade Practices Commission, but hours before the hearing begins six major American distributors issue a joint statement saying they will change their practices and ensure competition in the distribution and exhibition of films in Canada.

• C Channel goes on air in February, and six months later goes off the air in major embarrassment, as inexperienced management and poor audience figures kill the first lively-arts channel.

• First Choice Canada causes an immediate uproar by signing a deal with the Playboy Channel. Later in the year, FCC is bought by Harold Greenberg's* Astral Bellevue Pathé with the backing of Bronfman money. (Eventually First Choice Canada became the Movie Network and Astral Communications became one of the largest fully integrated distribution and broadcasting companies in Canada.)

• *Empire, Inc.*, co-directed by Denys Arcand* and Doug Jackson, is broadcast on CBC/SRC. This big-budget CBC / SRC / NFB co-production starring Kenneth Welsh* sets new standards for high-quality Canadian television drama.

• Quebec's new Cinema Act creates La Société générale du cinéma to provide funding for Quebec films.

• The Supreme Court of Ontario rules that the Ontario Board of Censors is operating in violation of the Canadian Charter of Rights and Freedoms.

• The United States Department of Justice labels Terre Nash's *If You Love This Planet** a propaganda film and places restrictions on its distribution.

• *The Grey Fox** wins Best Picture and *Porky's** wins the Golden Reel Award at the Genies.

• The NFB wins its seventh Academy Award for *If You Love This Planet.** *Just Another Missing Kid*, the CBC's *the fifth estate* documentary special on the murder of a Canadian youth in the United States directed by John Zaritsky, wins the Academy Award for Best Feature Documentary.

FILMS INCLUDE:
Au clair de la lune (André Forcier)
Boys and Girls (Don McBrearty)
Grey Fox, The (Phillip Borsos)
If You Love This Planet (Terre Nash)
Maria Chapdelaine (Gilles Carle)
Profession of Arms, The (Michael Bryans and Tina Viljoen)
Raoul Wallenberg: Buried Alive (David Harel)

Stations (William MacGillivray)
Strange Brew (Dave Thomas and Rick Moranis)
Terry Fox Story, The (Ralph L. Thomas)
Videodrome (David Cronenberg)
Wars, The (Robin Phillips)

1984

• Cineplex buys Odeon, and once again the competition for first-run Hollywood movies is effectively reduced to the two major chains. Drabinsky* launches a major buying spree in the United States, setting up Cineplex to become the second largest theatrical chain in North America.
• Francis Fox, the Liberal federal minister of communications, issues the National Film and Video Policy. The CFDC is transformed into Telefilm Canada and a $35-million broadcast fund is initiated.
• The Toronto Festival of Festivals programs the largest retrospective of Canadian films ever held in Canada, and Claude Jutra's *Mon oncle Antoine** is proclaimed the best Canadian film of all time. (This event launched Perspective Canada, the premier showcase for new Canadian cinema, at the Toronto festival.)
• Atom Egoyan* shoots his first feature, *Next of Kin*, marking the beginning of Toronto's new wave.
• *The Dog Who Stopped the War / La Guerre des tuques,** the first film in Rock Demers's* Tales for All series, is released.
• Brian Mulroney's newly elected Conservative government announces a $75 million cut to the CBC / SRC. There are major layoffs in staff and some regional stations are closed. CBC / SRC president Pierre Juneau announces that Canadian programming will move to seventy-five per cent in prime time.
• The CRTC issues more pay-TV licenses, including Citytv's MuchMusic and The Sports Network (TSN).
• *The Terry Fox Story** wins the Best Picture and *Strange Brew** wins the Golden Reel Award at the Genies.

• Atlantis Films wins an Academy Award for *Boys and Girls,** one of six half-hour dramas based on short stories by Canadian authors broadcast on the CBC. The win marks a turning point in Canadian television and heralds the arrival of a major independent television producer.
• Cynthia Scott's *Flamenco at 5:15** wins the Academy Award for Best Documentary Short.

FILMS INCLUDE:
Bay Boy, The (Daniel Petrie)
Dog Who Stopped the War, The / Guerre des tuques, La (André Melançon)
Femme de l'hôtel, La (Léa Pool)
Flamenco at 5:15 (Cynthia Scott)
Louisiana (Philippe de Broca)
Painted Door, The (Bruce Pittman)
Sonatine (Micheline Lanctôt)

1985

• Robert Lantos* and Stephen Roth of RSL Productions join forces with John Kemeny* and Denis Héroux* of International Cinema Corporation to form Alliance Entertainment Corporation.
• After lengthy court appeals, the Ontario Board of Censors is finally disbanded and replaced by the Ontario Film Review Board.
• The CBC broadcasts *Anne of Green Gables* over two nights and draws a record audience of five million viewers. This mini-series, produced and directed by Kevin Sullivan, and starring Megan Follows and Colleen Dewhurst,* is one of the most popular dramas ever shown on the CBC.
• The Academy of Canadian Cinema becomes the Academy of Canadian Cinema and Television.
• *Reel West* magazine begins publishing in Vancouver.
• Ishu Patel's *Paradise** wins the Silver Bear for animation at the Berlin International Film Festival.
• *The Bay Boy** wins Best Picture and *The Dog Who Stopped the War** wins the Golden Reel Award at the Genies.

• *Charade* by John Minnis of Sheridan College wins the Academy Award for Best Animated Short.

FILMS INCLUDE:
Agnes of God (Norman Jewison)
Artie Shaw: Time Is All You've Got (Brigitte Berman)
Big Snit, The (Richard Condie)
Canada's Sweetheart: The Saga of Hal C. Banks (Donald Brittain)
Care Bears Movie, The (Arna Selznick)
Final Offer: Bob White and the Canadian Auto Workers Fight for Independence (Sturla Gunnarsson and Robert Collison)
Joshua Then and Now (Ted Kotcheff)
Masculine Mystique, The (John N. Smith and Giles Walker)
My American Cousin (Sandy Wilson)
One Magic Christmas (Phillip Borsos)
Paradise (Ishu Patel)

1986

• Garth Drabinsky* sells forty-nine per cent of Cineplex Odeon to MCA Inc., the parent company of Universal Studios, effectively putting Cineplex under American control.
• Telefilm Canada announces a $165-million Feature Film Fund over five years to assist in the production and distribution of feature films.
• The MPAA signs an agreement with the province of Quebec (Bill 109) by which only Quebec distributors will be allowed to distribute foreign films in the province. This effectively bars English-Canadian distributors from operating in Quebec.
• The report of the Caplan-Sauvageau task force on broadcasting policy is released; it recommends a new Broadcasting Act, special status for Quebec broadcasting, a revitalized CBC, and guaranteed access to the system for women, minorities, and aboriginal people.
• The ACTRA awards transfer to the Academy of Canadian Cinema and Television and become known as the Gemini Awards / Prix Gémeaux.
• The Ontario Film Development Corporation is established with Wayne Clarkson* as director.
• The National Screen Institute, based in Edmonton, is formed, and the Local Heroes Film Festival begins.
• With the tragic suicide of Claude Jutra,* Canada loses one of its finest film directors.
• The *Film Canada Yearbook*, published by Patricia Thompson, is launched.
• Denys Arcand's *Le Déclin de l'empire américain** wins the International Film Critics' Award at Cannes.
• *My American Cousin** wins the Best Picture and Nelvana's *The Care Bears Movie** wins the Golden Reel Award at the Genies.

FILMS INCLUDE:
Adventure of Faustus Bidgood (Mike and Andy Jones)
Anne Trister (Léa Pool)
Champions, Part III: *The Final Battle, The* (Donald Brittain)
Dancing in the Dark (Leon Marr)
Déclin de l'empire américain, Le (Denys Arcand)
John and the Missus (Gordon Pinsent)
Loyalties (Anne Wheeler)
?O, Zoo! (The Making of a Fictional Film) (Philip Hoffman)
Pouvoir intime (Yves Simoneau)
White Museum (Mike Hoolboom)

1987

• The Canada-Manitoba Cultural Industries Development Office and B.C. Film are established.
• Cinevillage, a major studio and office complex partly financed by Atlantis Films, opens in downtown Toronto.
• Patricia Rozema's *I've Heard the Mermaids Singing** wins the Prix de la Jeunesse at Cannes.
• *Playback*, a bi-weekly trade publication, begins publishing.

• Brigitte Berman's *Artie Shaw: Time Is All You've Got** shares the Academy Award for Best Feature Documentary; Denys Arcand's *Le Déclin de l'empire américain** is nominated for Best Foreign-Language Film; Norman Jewison* receives his third directing nomination for *Moonstruck.**
• *Le Déclin de l'empire américain** wins both the Best Picture and the Golden Reel Award at the Genies.

FILMS INCLUDE:
Candy Mountain (Robert Frank and Rudy Wurlitzer)
Family Viewing (Atom Egoyan)
Gate, The (Tibor Takacs)
George and Rosemary (Alison Snowden and David Fine)
I've Heard the Mermaids Singing (Patricia Rozema)
Life Classes (William MacGillivray)
Zoo la nuit, Un (Jean-Claude Lauzon)

1988
• Federal communications minister Flora MacDonald tables the Film Products Importation Bill. (This bill would have given Canadian distributors some measure of access to films not produced by the Hollywood majors by introducing a licensing system for all film distributors operating in Canada. Eventually it died on the order paper. It was the last serious attempt by the federal government to curtail the activities of major American distributors.)
• La Société générale du cinéma du Québec becomes the film division of La Société générale des industries culturelles du Québec.
• The Canadian Centre for Advance Film Studies, founded by Norman Jewison,* opens in Toronto.
• J. Alphonse Ouimet dies at age eighty. (This early television pioneer was president of the CBC / SRC from 1953 to 1968. He headed a UNESCO conference on satellite technology in broadcasting, and was presi-

dent of Telesat Canada from 1969 to 1980.)
• At the Genies, *Un Zoo la nuit** wins Best Picture (plus twelve other awards, the most in the history of the Genies), and *The Gate** wins the Golden Reel Award.
• Frédéric Back* wins his second Academy Award for the SRC animated short, *The Man Who Planted Trees*.

FILMS INCLUDE:
Alias Will James (Jacques Godbout)
Cat Came Back, The (Cordell Barker)
Comic Book Confidential (Ron Mann)
Dead Ringers (David Cronenberg)
Tadpole and the Whale, The (Jean-Claude Lord)
Tales from the Gimli Hospital (Guy Maddin)
Winter Tan, A (Jackie Burroughs, Louise Clark, John Frizzell, John Walker, and Aerlyn Weissman)
World Is Watching, The (Peter Raymont)

1989
• Newsworld, the first Canadian all-news station, is launched in July.
• Patrick Watson, the former producer of *This Hour Has Seven Days*, is appointed chairman of the CBC board of directors.
• After a lengthy court battle with his original partners, Izzy Asper takes control of the Global Network in Toronto and announces his desire to build a third national network.
• The Canadian Association of Broadcasters initiates the Canadian Broadcast Standards Council, a self-appointed body to oversee a code concerning ethics, sex-role portrayal, and violence – a first in North America.
• Garth Drabinsky* attempts to buy back Cineplex Odeon from his American partners, but loses in a much-publicized corporate struggle.
• The Ontario Film Institute folds into the Toronto International Film Festival Group to become Cinematheque Ontario and The Film Reference Library.
• The NFB receives an Honorary Academy Award in recognition of its fiftieth anniversary. Joan Pennefather is named film com-

missioner; she is the first woman to hold this position.

• *Cinema Canada* ceases publication after eighteen years.

• Arcand's *Jésus de Montréal** wins the Jury Prize at Cannes.

• *Dead Ringers** wins Best Picture and *The Tadpole and the Whale** wins the Golden Reel Award at the Genies.

FILMS INCLUDE:
Bye Bye Blues (Anne Wheeler)
Cold Comfort (Vic Sarin)
Jésus de Montréal (Denys Arcand)
Speaking Parts (Atom Egoyan)
Welcome to Canada (John N. Smith)

1990

• After many months of delay, Phillip Borsos's *Bethune: The Making of a Hero** is finally released to almost universal criticism.

• Francis Mankiewicz's *Love and Hate: The Story of Colin and Joann Thatcher*, produced for the CBC-TV by Bernie Zuckerman and starring Kenneth Welsh* and Kate Nelligan,* is the first Canadian drama to be shown on U.S. prime-time television.

• Johnny Wayne dies at age seventy-two.

• In January, the CBC launches Kevin Sullivan's *Road to Avonlea* series. With an audience of 2.5 million for its first episode, this show receives the highest ratings for an English-Canadian series debut.

• The téléséries *Les Filles de Caleb* sets an all-time record for the SRC with an average audience of 3.2 million.

• CBC / SRC president Gérard Veilleux implements major cuts to take effect over the next three years; more regional stations are closed, all regional programming except for local newscasts is cancelled, and more than 1,000 jobs are eliminated.

• The Nova Scotia Film Development Corporation is formed.

• Denys Arcand's *Jésus de Montréal** sweeps twelve Genies plus the Golden Reel Award.

FILMS INCLUDE:
Archangel (Guy Maddin)
Bethune: The Making of a Hero (Phillip Borsos)
Company of Strangers, The (Cynthia Scott)
Famine Within, The (Katherine Gilday)
Perfectly Normal (Yves Simoneau)
Roadkill (Bruce McDonald)
Strand: Under the Dark Cloth (John Walker)

1991

• Bill C-40, the new Broadcasting Act, is proclaimed after being passed in the Senate.

• The First Nations Filmmakers Alliance is founded in Edmonton.

• L'Institute nationale de l'image et du son, a film school based on Jewison's* Canadian Film Centre, is established in Montreal; Rock Demers* is one of the founders.

• *Jésus de Montréal** is nominated for Best Foreign-Language Film at the Academy Awards.

• The Genies move from March to November. *Black Robe** wins Best Picture, and *Ding et Dong, le film* wins the Golden Reel Award.

FILMS INCLUDE:
Adjuster, The (Atom Egoyan)
Black Robe (Bruce Beresford)
Clearcut (Richard Bugajski)
Deadly Currents (Simcha Jacobovici)
Falls, The (Kevin McMahon)
Making of 'Monsters,' The (John Greyson)
Montréal vu par ... (Patricia Rozema, Jacques Leduc, Michel Brault, Atom Egoyan, Léa Pool, and Denys Arcand)
Rolling Stones at the Max (Julien Temple, Roman Kroitor, David Douglas, and Noel Archambault)

1992

• CBC replaces *The National* and *The Journal* with *Prime Time News* at 9:00 P.M. in a radical move that lasted only two seasons.

• Brian and Terence McKenna's *The Valour and the Horror*, a co-production between the

CBC, the NFB, and Galafilm of Montreal, airs in January; an intense controversy with veterans' groups led to an inquiry by the Senate subcommittee on Veterans Affairs.

• *The Boys of St Vincent,** an NFB / CBC co-production directed by John N. Smith,* is broadcast, but the controversial mini-series is banned in Ontario by the Ontario Court of Appeals on the grounds that the show would prejudice the trial of the Christian Brothers, which is still in process.

• The twenty-hour drama series *Les Filles de Caleb* is sold to the France 3 Network and is shown on French prime-time television.

• CBC staff move into CBC's new state-of-the-art Broadcast Centre in downtown Toronto.

• *North of 60* is the first Canadian prime-time series to be shot in Alberta.

• Le Centre Georges Pompidou in Paris organizes the largest retrospective of Canadian films ever held.

• The first issue of the new *Take One* appears, published and edited by Wyndham Wise.

• *Naked Lunch** wins Best Picture and *Black Robe** wins the Golden Reel Award at the Genies.

FILMS INCLUDE:
Being at Home with Claude (Jean Beaudin)
Boys of St Vincent, The (John N. Smith)
Careful (Guy Maddin)
Grocer's Wife, The (John Pozer)
Highway 61 (Bruce McDonald)
Léolo (Jean-Claude Lauzon)
Manufacturing Consent: Noam Chomsky and the Media (Peter Wintonick and Mark Achbar)
Masala (Srinivas Krishna)
Naked Lunch (David Cronenberg)
Sarrasine, La (Paul Tana)
Titanica (Stephen Low)
Valour and the Horror, The (Brian and Terrence McKenna)

1993

• Robert Lantos* takes Alliance public and creates Alliance Communications Inc. Alliance has become the largest producer and distributor in both film and television in Canada and is a major player in the North American marketplace.

• *Agaguk / Shadow of the Wolf* is released; at a reported cost of $31 million, this Canada / France co-production is the most expensive Canadian film ever made.

• The Feature Film Project is launched at the Canadian Film Centre; the first production is Holly Dale's *Blood and Donuts*.

• Telefilm Canada celebrates its twenty-fifth anniversary.

• *Thirty-Two Short Films about Glenn Gould** wins Best Picture and *La Florida** wins the Golden Reel Award at the Genies.

• The Academy of Canadian Cinema and Television introduces the Claude Jutra Award for first-time directors. The first winner is John Pozer for *The Grocer's Wife.**

FILMS INCLUDE:
Calendar (Atom Egoyan)
Florida, La (George Mihalka)
Forbidden Love: The Unashamed Stories of Lesbian Lives (Lynne Fernie and Aerlyn Weissman)
I Love a Man in Uniform (David Wellington)
In the Gutter and Other Good Places (Cristine Richey)
Kanehsatake: 270 Years of Resistance (Alanis Obomsawin)
Lotus Eaters, The (Paul Shapiro)
Pearl's Diner (Lynn Smith)

1994

• The federal government approves the takeover of the Canadian assets of Paramount Communications Inc. (formerly Gulf+Western) by Viacom Inc. of New York; these assets include the Famous Players theatre chain and Blockbuster Video. In turn, Viacom promises to exhibit more Canadian

films and spend more money in the marketing of Canadian films in Famous Players theatres.
• John Candy,* the most successful of the *SCTV* graduates and one of the most beloved Canadian actors, dies at age forty-three.
• *Due South* goes on air prime time on the CBS network – a first for a Canadian-produced series.
• The CRTC licenses a new tier of speciality channels including Bravo!, The Discovery Channel, and Showcase, which go on air 1 January 1995. However, the use of a negative option billing by cable companies (whereby consumers must cancel the new channels or be charged automatically) creates a customer backlash and public outrage.
• Patrick Watson steps down as chairman of the CBC.
• Nelvana* goes public. Imax Corporation is purchased by American interests and goes public in the United States.
• Atom Egoyan's *Exotica** wins the International Film Critics' Prize at Cannes; this is the first English-Canadian feature to win a major international award since *The Apprenticeship of Duddy Kravitz** won the Golden Bear at the Berlin Film Festival in 1974.
• *Exotica** wins Best Picture and *Louis 19, le roi des ondes** the Golden Reel Award at the Genies.

FILMS INCLUDE:
Exotica (Atom Egoyan)
Louis 19, le roi des ondes (Michel Poulette)
Love and Human Remains (Denys Arcand)
Octobre (Pierre Falardeau)
Paint Cans (Paul Donovan)
Thirty-Two Short Films about Glenn Gould (François Girard)
Whale Music (Richard Lewis)
Zero Patience (John Greyson)

1995

• Through Seagram of Montreal, Edgar Bronfman Jr, buys MCA, owners of Universal Studios, from Matsushita Electric Indus-

trial of Japan for a reported $8 billion Canadian.
• CBC / SRC president Perrin Beatty announces further cuts and pledges to move the network to 100 per cent Canadian content in prime-time viewing.
• *Front Page Challenge* is cancelled after thirty-eight years on air.
• The newly-elected Ontario Tories under Mike Harris cut deeply into the Ontario Film Development Corporation, freezing production funding and slashing the amount of money available for the Ontario Film Investment Program, Ontario's film tax-rebate program.
• La Société générale des enterprises culturelles replaces La Société géneral des industries culturelles du Québec and L'Institut québécois du cinéma, Quebec's film advisory board.
• SRC launches Le Réseau de l'information, the first French-language, all-news network in North America.
• *Due South* is cancelled by CBS after one season but continues on the CTV network and is sold worldwide.
• Disney announces the opening of two new animation studios, one in Vancouver and the other in Toronto.
• A $47 million Cable Production Fund, supported by thirty-nine cable companies across Canada, is launched.
• *Le Confessionnal** wins Best Picture and *Johnny Mnemonic** wins the Golden Reel Award at the Genies. (The ceremonies were held in Montreal in January 1996.)
• The NFB receives its tenth Academy Award – for *Bob's Birthday.**

FILMS INCLUDE:
Bob's Birthday (David Fine and Alison Snowden)
Bones of the Forest (Heather Frise and Velcrow Ripper)
Champagne Safari, The (George Ungar)
Confessionnal, Le (Robert Lepage)
Dance Me Outside (Bruce McDonald)

Double Happiness (Mina Shum)
Eldorado (Charles Binamé)
Johnny Mnemonic (Robert Longo)
Rude (Clement Virgo)
When Night Is Falling (Patricia Rozema)
Who's Counting? Marilyn Waring on Sex, Lies and Global Economics (Terre Nash)

1996

• Harold Greenberg, chairman of the board of Astral Communications, dies 1 July at age sixty-six.
• The Cable Production Fund evolves into the Canadian Television and Cable Production Fund; the Fund consists of $100 million directly from the federal government through the Ministry of Heritage, $50 million from Telefilm Canada, and $50 million from the cable industry.
• The Ontario Film Development Corporation loses its funding for production and marketing, but retains the Ontario Film Investment Program.
• The Alberta Motion Picture Development Corporation ceases operations after fifteen years. B.C. Film cuts its distribution program.
• The NFB responds to federal government budget cuts by reducing its staff by 180, cutting services, and streamlining administration. The renowned laboratory is closed in July and two of the three remaining video libraries are shut down in August.
• Telefilm Canada cuts twenty-four full-time positions and reduces its payroll by $1.1 million.
• David Cronenberg's *Crash** wins a Special Jury Prize at Cannes for 'audacity' after a heated debate that split the jury over the merits of the intensely controversial film.
• *Lilies** wins Best Picture and *Crash** wins the Golden Reel Award at the Genies.

FILMS INCLUDE:
Crash (David Cronenberg)
Hard Core Logo (Bruce McDonald)
Karmina (Gabriel Pelletier)

Lilies (John Greyson)
Long Day's Journey into Night (David Wellington)
Margaret's Museum (Mort Ransen)
Picture of Light (Peter Mettler)
Screamers (Christian Duguay)
Sous-sol (Pierre Gang)

1997

• The National Screen Institute in Edmonton and Telefilm Canada announce the creation of Features First, a feature-film development program for emerging filmmakers outside of Ontario and Quebec.
• Malofilm of Montreal becomes Behaviour Distribution. Norstar Entertainment of Toronto is bought by Alliance Communications. Four senior employees leave Alliance to form Red Sky Entertainment in Vancouver.
• With Ivan Fecan, the former programming chief at CBC-TV at the helm, Baton Broadcasting finally takes control of the CTV network. (The name Baton was formed from the names of the two founding families, the Bassetts and the Eatons.)
• The Toronto Film Critics Association is founded by Wyndham Wise, the publisher of *Take One*.
• A tragic plane crash in Northern Quebec claims the lives of director Jean-Claude Lauzon* (*Un Zoo la nuit,** *Léolo**) and Quebec television star Marie-Soleil Tougas.
• Atom Egoyan's *The Sweet Hereafter** wins the Jury Prize, the International Critics' Prize, and the Ecumenical Award at the Cannes festival, making it the most honoured Canadian film ever to play the festival. The film also wins eight Genies, including Best Picture.
• *Air Bud** wins the Golden Reel Award.

FILMS INCLUDE:
Air Bud (Charles Martin Smith)
Boys, Les (Louis Saïa)
Cosmos (Jennifer Alleyn, Manon Briand, Marie-Julie Dallaire, Arto Paragamian, André Turpin, and Denis Villeneuve)

Guy Maddin: Waiting for Twilight (Noam
  Gonick)
Hanging Garden, The (Thom Fitzgerald)
Hangman's Bride, The (Naomi McCormack)
Kissed (Lynne Stopkewich)
Sweet Hereafter, The (Atom Egoyan)

1998

• The merger of Alliance Communications
and Atlantis Films creates Alliance Atlantis
Communications with Michael MacMillan as
chairman and CEO. Robert Lantos* announces his intention to step aside from the
day-to-day operations of the new company
to concentrate on producing features.
• The chain of U.S. and Canadian Cineplex
Odeon theatres is bought by the Japanese
communications giant Sony. However, the
Canadian distribution division, Cineplex
Odeon Films, is sold to Alliance; it remains
as a stand-alone company, now known as
Odeon Films.
• The CRTC embarks on a complete review
of television policy and the financing system;
broadcasters lobby for direct access to public
funds to produce more of their own prime-
time drama.
• CanWest Global buys the television stations owned by WIC Broadcasting of Vancouver. The purchase completes Global's
ten-year goal to create Canada's third national network.
• John Bassett, newspaper publisher, original owner of CFTO-TV in Toronto and co-
founder of the CTV network, dies at age
eighty-two.
• Joyce Wieland,* considered the mother of
Canadian experimental film, dies at age
sixty-six.
• Veteran Quebec producer, Pierre Lamy,*
dies at age seventy-two.
• Sheila Copps, minister of heritage, announces a federal feature-film policy review.
• Egoyan's *The Sweet Hereafter** is nominated
for two Academy Awards: Best Director and
Adapted Screenplay.

• James Cameron's *Titanic* makes over a
billion dollars at the box office and wins
eleven Academy Awards, including Best
Director – a first for a Canadian-born direc-
tor.
• The Academy of Canadian Cinema and
Television moves the Genie Awards ceremony forward to January 1999. No awards
are presented in 1998.
• The Quebec film industry launches Les
Prix Jutra, an award showcase for features
and documentaries produced in Quebec.
(The first ceremonies were held in February,
1999.)
• Astral Communications announces a
$10 million fund to aid the financing, devel-
opment, and production of French- and
English-speaking documentaries.
• The Canadian Television and Cable Production Fund is renamed the Canadian Television Fund.

FILMS INCLUDE:
Boys II, Les (Louis Saïa)
Coeur au poing, Le (Charles Binamé)
C't'à ton tour, Laura Cadieux (Denise
  Filiatrault)
Cube (Vincenzo Natali)
Last Night (Don McKellar)
Love and Death on Long Island (Richard
  Kwietniowski)
Nô (Robert Lepage)
Red Violin, The (François Girard)
Regeneration (Gillies Mackinnon)
32 août sur terre, Un (Denis Villeneuve)
When Ponds Freeze Over (Mary Lewis)

1999

• American lobbyists and technicians finger
Canada as the main culprit responsible for
runaway film and television productions.
This controversy points to the fact that Canadian locations – especially those in and
around Vancouver, Toronto, and Montreal –
have become popular and less expensive
alternatives for U.S. production companies.

• David Cronenberg's *eXistenZ** wins a Silver Bear for artistic achievement at the Berlin International Film Festival, and Cronenberg* is appointed head of the Cannes Film Festival jury – a first for a Canadian.

• The Quebec and federal governments launch inquires into alleged fraudulent practices in the production sector.

• Alberta introduces the Film Development Program, a new fund to partially offset the loss of business that occurred when the Alberta Motion Picture Development Corporation was closed down in 1996.

• In a decision with far-reaching implications, the CRTC declares it does not have the power to regulate the Internet.

• The Aboriginal Peoples Television Network gets CRTC approval to run as a national network on basic cable systems across the country.

• Wendy Tilby's and Amanda Forbis's *When the Day Breaks** wins the Palme d'or for animation at the Cannes Film Festival and the Grand Prize at Annecy. It also wins the Genie for Best Animated Short and an Academy Award nomination.

• François Girard's *The Red Violin** wins Best Picture at the inaugural presentation of Les Prix Jutra. At the Genies, *The Red Violin** wins Best Picture, and *Les Boys** the Golden Reel Award.

FILMS INCLUDE:
Conquest (Piers Haggard)
Emporte-moi (Léa Pool)
Erreur boréale, L' (Richard Desjardins and Robert Monderies)
eXistenZ (David Cronenberg)
Felicia's Journey (Atom Egoyan)
Five Senses, The (Jeremy Podeswa)
Gypsies of Svinia, The (John Paskievich)
Hemingway: A Portrait (Erick Canuel)
Images of a Dictatorship (Patricio Henriquez)
Just Watch Me: Trudeau and the '70s Generation (Catherine Annau)
Old Man and the Sea, The (Alexandre Petrov)

Place Called Chiapas, A (Nettie Wild)
Post Mortem (Louis Bélanger)
Such a Long Journey (Sturla Gunnarsson)
Sunshine (István Szabó)
When the Day Breaks (Wendy Tilby and Amanda Forbis)

2000

• More than two years after heritage minister Sheila Copps announced the creation of a new feature-film fund, the fund is launched at the Vancouver International Film Festival. The new monies, to be administered by Telefilm Canada, increase feature-film funding to $100 million a year beginning in 2001. Copps declares that the object of the new money is boost the audience for Canadian films, noting that Canadian films account for only two per cent of annual box-office revenue. She sets a target of five per cent in five years.

• BCE Inc. announces its intention to buy the CTV network. The offer is accepted and awaits CRTC approval. The telephone giant views the purchase as means of keeping in step with American Internet and media mega-mergers such as AOL's purchase of Time Warner.

• In March, Cinar founders Ronald Weinberg and Micheline Charest are forced to resign from the company amid reports that $122 million has been invested in an offshore bank without permission of the board of directors. Cinar is also under investigation by the RCMP for fraud resulting from allegations that Cinar's television scripts were written by Americans under Canadian pseudonyms to qualify for Canadian tax credits. The trading of Cinar stocks is halted on the Montreal exchange.

• Corus Entertainment of Toronto, owners of YTV and part-owners of Teletoon, purchase Nelvana* for $530 million.

• In July, the CRTC approves the CanWest Global take over of WIC Communications, which occurred in 1998, making CanWest the third national network and doubling its size. A month later, CanWest announces its intention to buy Conrad Black's Canadian newspaper holdings, including a half-share in the *National Post*.

• *Sunshine** wins the Genie for Best Picture and *Les Boys II** wins the Golden Reel Award. *Post Mortem** wins Best Picture at Les Prix Jutra.

• Les Productions Pascal Blais wins an Academy Award for *The Old Man and the Sea*,* the first animated short shot in IMAX. *The Red Violin** wins the Academy Award for Best Musical Score.

FILMS INCLUDE:
Art of War, The (Christian Duguay)

Cinéma Vérité: Defining the Moment (Peter Wintonick)
Fairy Faith, The (John Walker)
Grass (Ron Mann)
Maelström (Denis Villeneuve)
Moitié gauche du frigo, La (Philippe Falardeau)
Muses orphelines, Les (Robert Favreau)
New Waterford Girl (Allan Moyle)
Possible Worlds (Robert Lepage)
Le P'tit Varius (André Théberge and Alain Jacques)
Stardom (Denys Arcand)
Vie après l'amour, La (Gabriel Pelletier)
Village of Idiots (Eugene Fedorenko and Rose Newlove)
waydowntown (Gary Burns)

Appendix 2
Awards

CANADIAN FILM AWARDS

The Canadian Film Awards were erratic at best. The award categories were never consistent and it wasn't until 1963 that craft categories were acknowledged. The Awards were not held in 1974 or in 1979, the year they were transferred to the Academy of Canadian Cinema (later the Academy of Canadian Cinema and Television) and became known as the Genie Awards. The following list is incomplete: it does not include either television citations or the various sponsored film awards. The Film of the Year and Feature Film awards are followed by the name of the producer.

1949
Film of the Year: *The Loon's Necklace* (Budge Crawley)
Documentary: *The Feeling of Hostility; Drug Addict*
Theatrical Short: *Who Will Teach Your Child?*
Special Award: *Dots; Un Homme et son péché; Loops*

1950
Theatrical Short: *North Shore / La Terre de Cain*
Non-Theatrical Short: *Family Circles*
Special Award: *Begone Dull Care*

1951
Theatrical Short: *After Prison What? / Après le bagne*
Non-Theatrical Short: *Feelings of Depression*
Special Award: *Family Tree; The Fight: Science against Cancer*

1952
Film of the Year: *Newfoundland Scene* (Budge Crawley)
Feature Film: *Royal Journey* (David Bairstow)
Theatrical Short: *Opera School*
Non-Theatrical Short: *Newfoundland Scene*
Special Award: *Around Is Around; Now Is the Time*

1953
Film of the Year: *Tit-coq* (Gratien Gélinas)
Feature Film: *Tit-coq* (Gratien Gélinas)
Theatrical Short: *L'Homme aux oiseaux*
Non-Theatrical Short: *Angotee: Story of an Eskimo Boy*
Special Award: *Age of the Beaver; Neighbours; A Phantasy*

1954
Film of the Year: *The Seasons* (Christopher Chapman)

Theatrical Short: *Farewell Oak Street*
Non-Theatrical Short: *The Seasons*

1955
Film of the Year: *The Stratford Adventure*
(Guy Glover)
Feature Film: *The Stratford Adventure* (Guy
Glover)
Non-Theatrical Short: *Riches of the Earth*

1956
Theatrical Short: *Gold*
Non-Theatrical Short: *The Colour of Life*

1957
Awards were presented only to select individuals and organizations, not to films.

1958
Film of the Year: *City of Gold* (Tom Daly)
Theatrical Short: *The Sceptre and the Mace*
Arts and Experimental: *A Chairy Tale; City of
Gold; Legend of the Raven*

1959
Theatrical Short: *The Quest*

1960
Theatrical Short: *Royal River*
Arts and Experimental: *Les Bateaux de neige*

1961
Film of the Year: *Universe* (Tom Daly)
Theatrical Short: *Universe*
Arts and Experimental: *Lines – Horizontal*

1962
Theatrical Short: *Morning on the Lièvre*

1963
Film of the Year: *Lonely Boy* (Roman Kroitor)
Theatrical Short: *Nahanni*
Arts and Experimental: *Jour après jour*
Cinematography (colour): *Nahanni*
Cinematography (B+W): *Jour après jour*

1964
Film of the Year: *Pour la suite du monde*
(Jacques Bobet)
Feature Film: *À tout prendre* (Claude Jutra)
Theatrical Short: *Anniversary*
Special Award: *Pour la suite du monde*
Cinematography (colour): *Brampton Builds a
Car*
Cinematography (B+W): *The Hutterites*

1965
Feature Film: *The Luck of Ginger Coffey* (Leon
Roth)
Arts and Experimental: *Canon; Le Monde va
nous prendre pour des sauvages*
Special Award: *Sweet Substitute*
Cinematography (colour): *Expedition
Bluenose*
Cinematography (B+W): *Mémoire en fête*

1966
Film of the Year: *The Mills of the Gods: Viet
Nam* (Douglas Leiterman)
Feature Film: *Le Festin des morts* (André
Belleau)
Theatrical Short: *Syrinx*
Cinematography (colour): *60 Cycles*
Cinematography (B+W): *Le Festin des morts*
Direction: *The Gift*
Editing: *High Steel*

1967
Film of the Year: *Warrendale* (Allan King)
Feature Film: *Warrendale* (Allan King)
Arts and Experimental: *Angel*
Special Award: *Helicopter Canada*
Cinematography (colour): *Elément 3*
Cinematography (B+W): *The Last Man in the
World*
Direction: *The Last Man in the World;
Warrendale*
Editing: *Trois hommes au mille carré*

1968
Film of the Year: *A Place to Stand*
(Christopher Chapman)

Feature Film: *The Ernie Game* (Gordon Burwash)
Director: Don Owen, *The Ernie Game*
Actor: Gerard Parkes, *Isabel*
Actress: Geneviève Bujold, *Isabel*
Cinematography (colour): Georges Dufaux, *Isabel*
Cinematography (B+W): Bernard Gosselin, *Le Règne du jour*
Editing: George Appleby, *Isabel*
Sound: *Le Règne du jour*
Feature Documentary: *Never a Backward Step*
Short Documentary: *Avec tambours et trompettes*
Short (under 30m): *Ca n'est pas les temps des romans*
Short (over 30m): *Do Not Fold, Staple, Spindle or Mutilate*

1969

Film of the Year: *The Best Damn Fiddler from Calabogie to Kaladar* (Barrie Howells, John Kemeny)
Director: Peter Pearson, *The Best Damn Fiddler from Calabogie to Kaladar*
Original Screenplay: Joan Finnegan, *The Best Damn Fiddler from Calabogie to Kaladar*
Actor: Chris Wiggins, *The Best Damn Fiddler from Calabogie to Kaladar*
Actress: Jackie Burroughs, *Dulcima*
Supporting Actor: Michael Posner, *And No Birds Sing*
Supporting Actress: Ruth Springford, *Does Anyone Here Know Denny?*
Cinematography (colour): Réo Grégoire, *Là ou ailleurs*
Cinematography (B+W): Tony Ianzelo, *The Best Damn Fiddler from Calabogie to Kaladar*
Editing: Michael Milne, *The Best Damn Fiddler from Calabogie to Kaladar*
Art Direction: *The Best Damn Fiddler from Calabogie to Kaladar*
Sound Recording: *Saul Alinsky Went to War*
Sound Re-recording: *Les Canots de glace*
Sound Editing: *Good Times, Bad Times*
Feature Documentary: *Good Times, Bad Times*
Short Documentary: *Juggernaut*

Animated Short: *Walking*
Short (under 30m): *At Home*
Short (over 30m): *Vertige*

1970

Film of the Year: *Psychocratie* (Robert Verrall, Wolf Koenig)
Feature Film: *Goin' down the Road* (Don Shebib)
Director: Paul Almond, *The Act of the Heart*
Original Screenplay: William Fruet, *Goin' down the Road*
Actor: Doug McGrath and Paul Bradley, *Goin' down the Road*
Actress: Geneviève Bujold, *The Act of the Heart*
Supporting Actor: Gratien Gélinas, *Red*
Supporting Actress: Fernande Giroux, *Red*
Cinematography: Bernard Chentrier, *Red*
Editing: Christopher Cordeaux, *Prologue*
Art Direction: *The Act of the Heart*
Overall Sound: *The Act of the Heart*
Sound Editing: *The Act of the Heart*
Musical Score: *The Act of the Heart*
Feature Documentary: *Wild Africa*
Short Documentary: *KW+*
Animated Short: *Psychocratie*
Arts and Experimental: *Legend*
Short (under 30m): *Blake*
Short (over 30m): *A Matter of Fat*

1971

Feature Film: *Mon oncle Antoine* (Marc Beaudet)
Director: Claude Jutra, *Mon oncle Antoine*
Original Screenplay: Clémont Perron, *Mon oncle Antoine*
Actor: Jean Duceppe, *Mon oncle Antoine*
Actress: Ann Knox, *The Only Thing You Know*
Supporting Actor: Danny Freedman, *Fortune and Men's Eyes*
Supporting Actress: Olivette Thibault, *Mon oncle Antoine*
Cinematography: Michel Brault, *Mon oncle Antoine*
Editing: Douglas Robertson, *Fortune and Men's Eyes*

Musical Score: *Mon oncle Antoine*
Art Direction: *Tiki Tiki*
Overall Sound: *Mon oncle Antoine*
Feature Documentary: *Les Philharmonistes*
Short Documentary: *The Sea*
Theatrical Short: *Don't Knock the Ox*
Animated Short: *Evolution*
Arts and Experimental: *Essai à la mille; Found Sculpture: Victor Tinkl*

1972

Feature Film: *Wedding in White* (John Vidette)
Director: Gilles Carle, *La Vraie Nature de Bernadette*
Original Screenplay: Gilles Carle, *La Vraie Nature de Bernadette*
Actor: Gordon Pinsent, *The Rowdyman*
Actress: Micheline Lanctôt, *La Vraie Nature de Bernadette*
Supporting Actor: Donald Pilon, *La Vraie Nature de Bernadette*
Supporting Actress: Doris Petrie, *Wedding in White*
Cinematography: Michel Brault, *Le Temps d'une chasse*
Editing: Danielle Gagné, *La Vie rêvée*
Art Direction: *Wedding in White*
Overall Sound: *Le Temps d'une chasse; Face-Off*
Sound Editing: *Journey*
Documentary: *Selling Out*
Theatrical Short: *This Is a Photograph*
Animated Short: *Dans la vie*

1973

Due to a last-minute boycott of the 1973 Canadian Film Awards by members of L'Association des réalisateurs et réalisatrices de film du Québec, the ceremony was cancelled; the awards were announced at a press conference held in Montreal.
Feature Film: *Slipstream* (James Margellos)
Director: David Acomba, *Slipstream*
Original Screenplay: Jacques Benoît, Denys Arcand, *Réjeanne Padovani*
Actor: Jacques Godin, *O.K. ... Laliberté*

Actress: Geneviève Bujold, *Kamouraska*
Supporting Actor: Willie Lamothe, *La Mort d'un bûcheron*
Supporting Actress: Camille Bernard, *Kamouraska*
Cinematography: Donald A. Wilder, *Paperback Hero*
Editing: Kirk Jones, *Paperback Hero*
Musical Score: *La Mort d'un bûcheron*
Art Direction: *Kamouraska*
Sound Editing: *Slipstream*
Sound Recording: *L'Infonie inachevée*
Sound Re-recording: *Paperback Hero*
Documentary: *Grierson; Faire hurler les murs*
Theatrical Documentary: *Coming Home*
Theatrical Short: *Goodbye Sousa*
Animated Short: *The Family That Dwelt Apart*
Special Award: *Kamouraska; To War and Back*

1974

No awards were presented.

1975

Film of the Year: *Les Ordres* (Bernard Lalonde)
Film of the Year (1974): *The Apprenticeship of Duddy Kravitz* (John Kemeny)
Feature Film: *Les Ordres* (Bernard Lalonde)
Director: Michel Brault, *Les Ordres*
Original Screenplay: Michel Brault, *Les Ordres*
Adapted Screenplay: William Weintraub, *Why Rock the Boat?*
Actor: Stuart Gillard, *Why Rock the Boat?*
Actress: Margot Kidder, *Black Christmas* and *A Quiet Day in Belfast*
Supporting Actor: Henry Beckman, *Why Rock the Boat?*
Supporting Actress: Lila Kedrova, *Eliza's Horoscope*
Cinematography: Pier van der Linden, *Eliza's Horoscope*
Editing: Stan Cole, *Black Christmas*
Musical Score: *Lions for Breakfast*
Art Direction: *Eliza's Horoscope*
Sound Editing: *Black Christmas*
Sound Recording: *The Apprenticeship of*

Duddy Kravitz
Sound Re-recording: *Eliza's Horoscope*
Theatrical Documentary: *Janis*
Documentary (over 30m): *Cree Hunters of Mistassini*
Documentary (under 30m): *At 99: A Portrait of Louise Tandy Murch*
Theatrical Short: *Along Those Lines*
Animated Short: *The Owl Who Married a Goose*

1976
Feature Film: *Lies My Father Told Me* (Anthony Bedrich, Harry Gulkin)
Director: Harvey Hart, *Goldenrod*
Adapted Screenplay: Ted Allan, *Lies My Father Told Me*
Actor: André Melançon, *Partis pour la gloire*
Actress: Marilyn Lightstone, *Lies My Father Told Me*
Supporting Actor: Frank Moore, *The Far Shore*
Supporting Actress: Tedde Moore, *Second Wind*
Cinematography: Richard Leiterman, *The Far Shore*
Editing: Don Shebib, *Second Wind*
Musical Score: *La Tête de Normande St-Onge*
Art Direction: *The Far Shore*
Sound Recording: *Lies My Father Told Me*
Sound Re-recording: *Lies My Father Told Me*
Documentary: *Volcano: An Inquiry into the Life and Death of Malcolm Lowry*
Theatrical Documentary: *Ahô ... au coeur du monde primitif*
Theatrical Short: *Cooperage*
Animated Short: *The Street*
Arts and Experimental: *Barbara Is a Vision of Loveliness*
Special Award: *The Last Cause*

1977
Feature Film: *J.A. Martin photographe* (Jean-Marc Garand)
Director: Jean Beaudin, *J.A. Martin photographe*
Adapted Screenplay: James DeFelice, *Why Shoot the Teacher?*

Actor: Len Cariou, *One Man*
Actress: Monique Mercure, *J.A. Martin photographe*
Supporting Actor: Jean Lapointe, *One Man*
Supporting Actress: Carole Lazare, *One Man*
Cinematography: Pierre Mignot, *J.A. Martin photographe*
Editing: Jean Beaudin, Hélène Girard, *J.A. Martin photographe*; John Kramer, *One Man*
Musical Score: Paul Hoffert, *Outrageous!*
Art Direction: *J.A. Martin photographe*
Sound Editing: *One Man*
Sound Recording: *One Man*
Sound Re-recording: *J.A. Martin photographe*
Feature Documentary: *The Inquiry Film*
Short Documentary: *Greenpeace: Voyage to Save the Whales*
Theatrical Short: *Spartree*
Animated Short: *Spinnolio*

1978
Feature Film: *The Silent Partner* (Stephen Young)
Director: Daryl Duke, *The Silent Partner*
Original Screenplay: Martyn Burke, *Power Play*
Actor: Richard Gabourie, *Three Card Monte*
Actress: Helen Shaver, *In Praise of Older Women*
Supporting Actor: Henry Beckman, *Blood and Guts*
Supporting Actress: Marilyn Lightstone, *In Praise of Older Women*
Cinematography: Miklos Lente, *In Praise of Older Women*
Editing: George Appleby, *The Silent Partner*
Musical Score: *The Silent Partner*
Art Direction: *In Praise of Older Women*
Sound Editing: *The Silent Partner*
Sound Recording: *The Silent Partner*
Sound Re-recording: *Three Card Monte*
Feature Documentary: *The Champions*, Part III: *The Final Battle*
Short Documentary: *The Hottest Show on Earth*
Theatrical Short: *L'Affaire Bronswik*
Animated Short: *Afterlife*

GENIE AWARDS
These awards are listed according to the year they were presented.

1980
Picture: *The Changeling* (Joel B. Michaels, Garth Drabinsky)
Director: Bob Clark, *Murder by Decree*
Original Screenplay: Len Blum, Dan Goldberg, Janis Allen, Harold Ramis, *Meatballs*
Adapted Screenplay: William Grey, Diana Maddox, *The Changeling*
Actor: Christopher Plummer, *Murder by Decree*
Actress: Kate Lynch, *Meatballs*
Supporting Actor: Gordon Pinsent, *Jack London's Klondike Fever*
Supporting Actress: Geneviève Bujold, *Murder by Decree*
Foreign Actor: George C. Scott, *The Changeling*
Foreign Actress: Trish Van Devere, *The Changeling*
Cinematography: John Coquillon, *The Changeling*
Editing: Stan Cole, *Murder by Decree*
Art Direction: *The Changeling*
Costumes: *Cordélia*
Musical Score: *Murder by Decree*
Sound Editing: *The Changeling*
Overall Sound: *The Changeling*
Feature Documentary: *Paperland: The Bureaucrat Observed*
Short Documentary: *Priory, the Only Home I've Got*
Live-Action Short: *Nails*
Animated Short: *Every Child*

1981
Picture: *Les Bons Débarras* (Claude Godbout, Marcia Couëlle)
Director: Francis Mankiewicz, *Les Bons Débarras*
Original Screenplay: Réjean Ducharme, *Les Bons Débarras*
Adapted Screenplay: Max Fischer, Jack Rosenthal, *The Lucky Star*

Actor: Thomas Peacocke, *The Hounds of Notre Dame*
Actress: Marie Tifo, *Les Bons Débarras*
Supporting Actor: Germain Houde, *Les Bons Débarras*
Supporting Actress: Kate Reid, *Atlantic City*
Foreign Actor: Jack Lemmon, *Tribute*
Foreign Actress: Susan Sarandon, *Atlantic City*
Cinematography: Michel Brault, *Les Bons Débarras*
Editing: André Corriveau, *Les Bons Débarras*
Art Direction: *Atlantic City*
Costumes: *Fantastica*
Musical Score: *The Lucky Star*
Sound Editing: *The Lucky Star*
Overall Sound: *Les Bons Débarras*
Theatrical Documentary: *Plusieurs tombent en amour*
Theatrical Short: *The Strongest Man in the World*

1982
Picture: *Ticket to Heaven* (Vivienne Leebosh)
Director: Gilles Carle, *Les Plouffe*
Original Screenplay: Terry Hefferman, *Heartaches*
Adapted Screenplay: Gilles Carle, Roger Lemelin, *Les Plouffe*
Actor: Nick Mancuso, *Ticket to Heaven*
Actress: Margot Kidder, *Heartaches*
Supporting Actor: Saul Rubinek, *Ticket to Heaven*
Supporting Actress: Denise Filiatrault, *Les Plouffe*
Foreign Actor: Alan Arkin, *Improper Channels*
Foreign Actress: Annie Potts, *Heartaches*
Cinematography: Richard Leiterman, *Silence of the North*
Editing: Ron Wisman, *Ticket to Heaven*
Art Direction: *Les Plouffe*
Costumes: *Les Plouffe*
Musical Score: *Les Plouffe*

Song: *Les Plouffe*
Sound Editing: *Heavy Metal*
Overall Sound: *Heavy Metal*
Feature Documentary: *P4W: Prison for Women*
Live-Action Short: *Zea*

1983
Picture: *The Grey Fox* (Peter O'Brian)
Director: Phillip Borsos, *The Grey Fox*
Original Screenplay: John Hunter, *The Grey Fox*
Adapted Screenplay: Richard Paluk, Robert Guza Jr, *Melanie*
Actor: Donald Sutherland, *Threshold*
Actress: Rae Dawn Chong, *Quest for Fire*
Supporting Actor: R.H. Thomson, *If You Could See What I Hear*
Supporting Actress: Jackie Burroughs, *The Grey Fox*
Foreign Actor: Richard Farnsworth, *The Grey Fox*
Foreign Actress: Glynnis O'Connor, *Melanie*
Cinematography: Michel Brault, *Threshold*
Editing: Yves Langlois, *Quest for Fire*
Art Direction: *The Grey Fox*
Costumes: *Quest for Fire*
Musical Score: *The Grey Fox*
Song: *Melanie*
Sound Editing: *Quest for Fire*
Overall Sound: *Quest for Fire*
Feature Documentary: *The Devil at Your Heels*
Live-Action Short: *Elvis Gratton*

1984
Picture: *The Terry Fox Story* (Robert Cooper)
Director: David Cronenberg, *Videodrome*
Screenplay: Bob Clark, *A Christmas Story*
Actor: Eric Fryer, *The Terry Fox Story*
Actress: Martha Henry, *The Wars*
Supporting Actor: Michael Zelniker, *The Terry Fox Story*
Supporting Actress: Jackie Burroughs, *The Wars*
Cinematography: Pierre Mignot, *Maria Chapdelaine*

Editing: Ron Wisman, *The Terry Fox Story*
Art Direction: *Maria Chapdelaine*
Costumes: *Maria Chapdelaine*
Musical Score: *Maria Chapdelaine*
Song: *Ups and Downs*
Sound Editing: *The Terry Fox Story*
Overall Sound: *The Terry Fox Story*
Feature Documentary: *Pourquoi l'étrange Monsieur Zolock s'intéressait-il tant à la bande dessinée?*
Live-Action Short: *Ted Baryluk's Grocery*

1985
Picture: *The Bay Boy* (John Kemeny, Denis Héroux)
Director: Micheline Lanctôt, *Sonatine*
Original Screenplay: Daniel Petrie, *The Bay Boy*
Actor: Gabriel Arcand, *Le Crime d'Ovide Plouffe*
Actress: Louise Marleau, *La Femme de l'hôtel*
Supporting Actor: Alan Scarfe, *The Bay Boy*
Supporting Actress: Linda Sorensen, *Draw!*
Cinematography: Pierre Mignot, *Mario*
Editing: André Corriveau, *The Dog Who Stopped the War*
Art Direction: *The Bay Boy*
Costumes: *The Bay Boy*
Musical Score: *Mario*
Song: *La Femme de l'hôtel*
Sound Editing: *The Bay Boy*
Overall Sound: *Mario*
Feature Documentary: *Raoul Wallenberg: Buried Alive*
Live-Action Short: *Charade*

1986
Picture: *My American Cousin* (Peter O'Brian)
Director: Sandy Wilson, *My American Cousin*
Original Screenplay: Sandy Wilson, *My American Cousin*
Actor: John Wildman, *My American Cousin*
Actress: Margaret Langrick, *My American Cousin*
Supporting Actor: Alan Arkin, *Joshua Then and Now*
Supporting Actress: Linda Sorensen, *Joshua Then and Now*

Cinematography: François Protat, *Joshua Then and Now*
Editing: Haida Paul, *My American Cousin*
Art Direction: *Joshua Then and Now*
Costumes: *Joshua Then and Now*
Musical Score: *Le Matou*
Original Song: *Night Magic*
Sound Editing: *One Magic Christmas*
Overall Sound: *One Magic Christmas*
Feature Documentary: *Final Offer: Bob White and the Canadian Auto Workers Fight for Independence*
Short Documentary: *No More Hiroshima*
Live-Action Short: *The Edit*
Animated Short: *The Big Snit*

1987
Picture: *Le Déclin de l'empire américain* (René Malo, Roger Frappier)
Director: Denys Arcand, *Le Déclin de l'empire américain*
Original Screenplay: Denys Arcand, *Le Déclin de l'empire américain*
Adapted Screenplay: Leon Marr, *Dancing in the Dark*
Actor: Gordon Pinsent, *John and the Missus*
Actress: Martha Henry, *Dancing in the Dark*
Supporting Actor: Gabriel Arcand, *Le Déclin de l'empire américain*
Supporting Actress: Louise Portal, *Le Déclin de l'empire américain*
Cinematography: Pierre Mignot, *Anne Trister*
Editing: Monique Fortier, *Le Déclin de l'empire américain*
Art Direction: *Dancing in the Dark*
Costumes: *Loyalties*
Musical Score: *John and the Missus*
Sound Editing: *Le Déclin de l'empire américain*
Overall Sound: *Le Déclin de l'empire américain*
Feature Documentary: *Dads and Kids*
Live-Action Short: *I Need a Man Like You to Make My Dreams Come True*
Animated Short: *Get a Job*

1988
Picture: *Un Zoo la nuit* (Roger Frappier, Pierre Gendron)

Director: Jean-Claude Lauzon, *Un Zoo la nuit*
Original Screenplay: Jean-Claude Lauzon, *Un Zoo la nuit*
Actor: Roger Le Bel, *Un Zoo la nuit*
Actress: Sheila McCarthy, *I've Heard the Mermaids Singing*
Supporting Actor: Germain Houde, *Un Zoo la nuit*
Supporting Actress: Paule Baillargeon, *I've Heard the Mermaids Singing*
Cinematography: Guy Dufaux, *Un Zoo la nuit*
Editing: Michel Arcand, *Un Zoo la nuit*
Art Direction: *Un Zoo la nuit*
Costume Design: *Un Zoo la nuit*
Musical Score: *Un Zoo la nuit*
Song: *Un Zoo la nuit*
Sound Editing: *Un Zoo la nuit*
Overall Sound: *Un Zoo la nuit*
Feature Documentary: *God Rides a Harley*
Live-Action Short: *George and Rosemary*

1989
Picture: *Dead Ringers* (David Cronenberg, Marc Boyman)
Director: David Cronenberg, *Dead Ringers*
Original Screenplay: Trevor Rhone, Glen Salzman, *Milk and Honey*
Adapted Screenplay: David Cronenberg, Norman Snider, *Dead Ringers*
Actor: Jeremy Irons, *Dead Ringers*
Actress: Jackie Burroughs, *A Winter Tan*
Supporting Actor: Rémy Girard, *Les Portes tournantes*
Supporting Actress: Colleen Dewhurst, *Obsessed*
Cinematography: Peter Suschitzky, *Dead Ringers*
Editing: Ronald Sanders, *Dead Ringers*
Art Direction: *Dead Ringers*
Costumes: *Les Portes tournantes*
Musical Score: *Dead Ringers*
Song: *Cowboys Don't Cry*
Sound Editing: *Dead Ringers*
Overall Sound: *Dead Ringers*
Feature Documentary: *Comic Book Confidential*
Short Documentary: *The World Is Watching*

Live-Action Short: *The Mysterious Moon Men of Canada*
Animated Short: *The Cat Came Back*

1990
Picture: *Jésus de Montréal* (Roger Frappier, Pierre Gendron)
Director: Denys Arcand, *Jésus de Montréal*
Original Screenplay: Denys Arcand, *Jésus de Montréal*
Adapted Screenplay: Richard Beattie, L. Elliot Simms, *Cold Comfort*
Actor: Lothaire Bluteau, *Jésus de Montréal*
Actress: Rebecca Jenkins, *Bye Bye Blues*
Supporting Actor: Rémy Girard, *Jésus de Montréal*
Supporting Actress: Robyn Stevan, *Bye Bye Blues*
Cinematography: Guy Dufaux, *Jésus de Montréal*
Editing: Isabelle Dedieu, *Jésus de Montréal*
Art Direction: *Jésus de Montréal*
Costumes: *Jésus de Montréal*
Musical Score: *Jésus de Montréal*
Song: *Bye Bye Blues*
Sound Editing: *Jésus de Montréal*
Overall Sound: *Jésus de Montréal*
Feature Documentary: *Strand: Under the Dark Cloth*
Short Documentary: *Stunt People*
Live-Action Short: *In Search of the Last Good Man*
Animated Short: *Juke Bar*

1991
Picture: *Black Robe* (Robert Lantos, Stéphane Reichel, Sue Milliken)
Director: Bruce Beresford, *Black Robe*
Original Screenplay: Eugene Lipinski, Paul Quarrington, *Perfectly Normal*
Adapted Screenplay: Brian Moore, *Black Robe*
Actor: Rémy Girard, *Amoureux fou*
Actress: Pascale Montpetit, *H*
Supporting Actor: August Schellenberg, *Black Robe*
Supporting Actress: Danielle Proulx, *Amoureux fou*

Cinematography: Peter James, *Black Robe*
Editing: David Wilson, *The Company of Strangers*
Art Direction: *Black Robe*
Costumes: *Bethune: The Making of a Hero*
Musical Score: *La Damoiselle sauvage*
Song: *Angel Square*
Sound Editing: *Angel Square*
Overall Sound: *Angel Square*
Feature Documentary: *The Famine Within*
Short Documentary: *The Colours of My Father*
Live-Action Short: *Saeed*

1992
Picture: *Naked Lunch* (Jeremy Thomas, Gabriella Martinelli)
Director: David Cronenberg, *Naked Lunch*
Original Screenplay: Jean-Claude Lauzon, *Léolo*
Adapted Screenplay: David Cronenberg, *Naked Lunch*
Actor: Tony Nardi, *La Sarrasine*
Actress: Janet Wright, *Bordertown Café*
Supporting Actor: Michael Hogan, *Solitaire*
Supporting Actress: Monique Mercure, *Naked Lunch*
Cinematography: Peter Suschitzky, *Naked Lunch*
Editing: Michel Arcand, *Léolo*
Art Direction: *Naked Lunch*
Costumes: *Léolo*
Musical Score: *Being at Home with Claude*
Song: *Secret Nation*
Sound Editing: *Naked Lunch*
Overall Sound: *Naked Lunch*
Feature Documentary: *Deadly Currents*
Short Documentary: *A Song for Tibet*
Live-Action Short: *The Battle of the Bulge*
Animated Short: *Strings*

1993
Picture: *Thirty-Two Short Films about Glenn Gould* (Niv Fichman)
Director: François Girard, *Thirty-Two Short Films about Glenn Gould*
Original Screenplay: Peggy Thompson, *The Lotus Eaters*

Actor: Tom McCamus, *I Love a Man in Uniform*

Actress: Sheila McCarthy, *The Lotus Eaters*

Supporting Actor: Kevin Tighe, *I Love a Man in Uniform*

Supporting Actress: Nicola Cavendish, *The Grocer's Wife*

Cinematography: Alain Dostie, *Thirty-Two Short Films about Glenn Gould*

Editing: Gaétan Huot, *Thirty-Two Short Films about Glenn Gould*

Art Direction: *Agaguk / Shadow of the Wolf*

Costumes: *Agaguk / Shadow of the Wolf*

Musical Score: *Cadillac Girls*

Sound Editing: *The Lotus Eaters*

Overall Sound: *Le Sexe des étoiles*

Feature Documentary: *Forbidden Love: The Unashamed Stories of Lesbian Lives*

Short Documentary: *Le Singe bleu*

Live-Action Short: *The Fairy Who Didn't Want to Be a Fairy Anymore*

Animated Short: *Pearl's Diner*

Claude Jutra Award: John Pozer, *The Grocer's Wife*

1994

Picture: *Exotica* (Atom Egoyan, Camelia Frieberg)

Director: Atom Egoyan, *Exotica*

Original Screenplay: Atom Egoyan, *Exotica*

Adapted Screenplay: Brad Fraser, *Love and Human Remains*

Actor: Maury Chaykin, *Whale Music*

Actress: Sandra Oh, *Double Happiness*

Supporting Actor: Don McKellar, *Exotica*

Supporting Actress: Martha Henry, *Mustard Bath*

Cinematography: Paul Sarossy, *Exotica*

Editing: Alison Grace, *Double Happiness*

Art Direction: *Exotica*

Costumes: *Exotica*

Musical Score: *Exotica*

Song: *Whale Music*

Sound Editing: *Whale Music*

Overall Sound: *Whale Music*

Feature Documentary: *In the Gutter and Other Good Places*

Live-Action Short: *Arrowhead*

Claude Jutra Award: Michel Poulette, *Louis 19, le roi des ondes*

1995

Picture: *Le Confessionnal* (Denise Robert, David Puttman, Philippe Carcassonne, Steve Norris)

Director: Robert Lepage, *Le Confessionnal*

Adapted Screenplay: Gerry Wexler, Mort Ransen, *Margaret's Museum*

Actor: David La Haye, *L'Enfant d'eau*

Actress: Helena Bonham Carter, *Margaret's Museum*

Supporting Actor: Kenneth Welsh, *Margaret's Museum*

Supporting Actress: Kate Nelligan, *Margaret's Museum*

Cinematography: Tom Burstyn, *Magic in the Water*

Editing: Michael Pacek, *Dance Me Outside*

Art Direction: *Le Confessionnal*

Costumes: *Margaret's Museum*

Musical Score: *Margaret's Museum*

Sound Editing: *Dance Me Outside*

Overall Sound: *Magic in the Water*

Feature Documentary: *The Champagne Safari*

Short Documentary: *Fiction and Other Truths: A Film about Jane Rule*

Live-Action Short: *Les Fleurs magiques*

Claude Jutra Award: Robert Lepage, *Le Confessionnal*

1996

Picture: *Lilies* (Anna Stratton, Robin Cass, Arnie Gelbart)

Director: David Cronenberg, *Crash*

Original Screenplay: Pierre Gang, *Sous-sol*

Adapted Screenplay: David Cronenberg, *Crash*

Actor: William Hutt, *Long Day's Journey into Night*

Actress: Martha Henry, *Long Day's Journey into Night*

Supporting Actor: Peter Donaldson, *Long Day's Journey into Night*

Supporting Actress: Martha Burns, *Long Day's Journey into Night*

Cinematography: Peter Suschitzky, *Crash*
Editing: Ronald Sanders, *Crash*
Art Direction: *Lilies*
Costumes: *Lilies*
Musical Score: *Curtis's Charm*
Song: *Hard Core Logo*
Sound Editing: *Crash*
Overall Sound: *Lilies*
Feature Documentary: *Bones of the Forest*
Short Documentary: *Maman et Eve*
Live-Action Short: *The Home for Blind Women*
Claude Jutra Award: Peter Wellington, *Joe's So Mean to Josephine*

1997

Picture: *The Sweet Hereafter* (Atom Egoyan, Camelia Frieberg)
Director: Atom Egoyan, *The Sweet Hereafter*
Original Screenplay: Thom Fitzgerald, *The Hanging Garden*
Actor: Ian Holm, *The Sweet Hereafter*
Actress: Molly Parker, *Kissed*
Supporting Actor: Peter MacNeill, *The Hanging Garden*
Supporting Actress: Seana McKenna, *The Hanging Garden*
Cinematography: Paul Sarossy, *The Sweet Hereafter*
Editing: Susan Shipman, *The Sweet Hereafter*
Art Direction: *Karmina*
Costumes: *Karmina*
Musical Score: *The Sweet Hereafter*
Song: *L'Homme idéal*
Sound Editing: *The Sweet Hereafter*
Overall Sound: *The Sweet Hereafter*
Feature Documentary: *Tu as crié Let Me Go*
Short Documentary: *Unveiled: The Mother / Daughter Relationship*
Live-Action Short: *The Hangman's Bride*
Animated Short: *The Old Lady and the Pigeons*
Claude Jutra Award: Thom Fitzgerald, *The Hanging Garden*

1998

No awards were presented in 1998; the Genie Awards ceremony was held in January 1999.

1999

Picture: *The Red Violin* (Niv Fichman)
Director: François Girard, *The Red Violin*
Original Screenplay: François Girard, Don McKellar, *The Red Violin*
Actor: Roshan Seth, *Such a Long Journey*
Actress: Sandra Oh, *Last Night*
Supporting Actor: Callum Keith Rennie, *Last Night*
Supporting Actress: Monique Mercure, *Conquest*
Cinematography: Alain Dostie, *The Red Violin*
Editing: Jeff Warren, *Such a Long Journey*
Art Direction: *The Red Violin*
Costumes: *The Red Violin*
Musical Score: *The Red Violin*
Song: *The Fishing Trip*
Sound Editing: *Such a Long Journey*
Overall Sound: *The Red Violin*
Feature Documentary: *A Place Called Chiapas*
Short Documentary: *Shadow Maker: Gwendolyn MacEwen, Poet*
Live-Action Short: *When Ponds Freeze Over*
Animated Short: *Bingo*
Claude Jutra Award: Don McKellar, *Last Night*

2000

Picture: *Sunshine* (Robert Lantos, Andras Hamori)
Director: Jeremy Podeswa, *The Five Senses*
Original Screenplay: Louis Bélanger, *Post Mortem*
Adapted Screenplay: Atom Egoyan, *Felicia's Journey*
Actor: Bob Hoskins, *Felicia's Journey*
Actress: Sylvie Moreau, *Post Mortem*
Supporting Actor: Mark McKinney, *Dog Park*
Supporting Actress: Catherine O'Hara, *The Life before This*
Cinematography: Paul Sarossy, *Felicia's Journey*

Editing: Ronald Sanders, *eXistenZ*
Art Direction: *Souvenirs intimes*
Costumes: *Grey Owl*
Musical Score: *Felicia's Journey*
Song: *Jacob Two-Two Meets the Hooded Fang*
Sound Editing: *Sunshine*
Overall Sound: *Sunshine*
Feature Documentary: *Just Watch Me: Trudeau and the '70s Generation*
Short Documentary: *Hemingway: A Portrait*
Live-Action Short: *Moving Day*
Animated Short: *When the Day Breaks*
Claude Jutra Award: Louis Bélanger, *Post Mortem*

2001
Picture: *Maelström* (Roger Frappier, Luc Vandal)
Director: Denis Villeneuve, *Maelström*
Original Screenplay: Denis Villeneuve, *Maelström*

Actor: Tony Nardi, *My Father's Angel*
Actress: Marie-Josée Croze, *Maelström*
Supporting Actor: Martin Cummins, *Love Come Down*
Supporting Actress: Helen Shaver, *We All Fall Down*
Cinematography: André Turpin, *Maelström*
Editing: Susan Shipton, *Possible Words*
Art Direction: *Possible Words*
Costumes: *Stardom*
Musical Score: *Here's to Life!*
Song: *Laura Cadieux ... la suite*
Sound Editing: *Love Come Down*
Overall Sound: *Love Come Down*
Feature Documentary: *Grass*
Live-Action Short: *Le P'tit Varius*
Animated Short: *Village of Idiots*
Claude Jutra Award: Philippe Falardeau, *La Moitié gauche du frigo*

LES PRIX JUTRA

These Quebec film awards are listed according to the year they were presented.

1999
Picture: *The Red Violin* (Niv Fichman)
Director: François Girard, *The Red Violin*
Screenplay: François Girard, Don McKellar, *The Red Violin*
Actor: Alexis Martin, *Un 32 aôut sur la terre*
Actress: Pascale Montpetit, *Le Coeur au poing*
Supporting Actor: Colm Feore, *The Red Violin*
Supporting Actress: Anne-Marie Cadieux, *Le Coeur au poing*
Cinematography: Alain Dostie, *The Red Violin*
Editing: Gaétan Huot, *The Red Violin*
Art Direction: *The Red Violin*
Sound: *The Red Violin*
Musical Score: *The Red Violin*
Documentary: *L'Erreur boréale*
Short Film: *Les Mots magiques*

2000
Picture: *Post Mortem* (Lorraine Dufour)
Director: Louis Bélanger, *Post Mortem*
Screenplay: Louis Bélanger, *Post Mortem*
Actor: Gabriel Arcand, *Post Mortem*
Actress: Karine Vanasse, *Emporte-moi*
Supporting Actor: Julien Poulin, *Le Dernier Souffle*
Supporting Actress: Pascale Bussières, *Emporte-moi*
Cinematography: Pierre Gill, *Souvenirs intimes*
Editing: Lorraine Dufour, *Post Mortem*
Art Direction: *Emporte-moi*
Sound: *Histoires d'hiver*
Musical Score: *Alegria*
Documentary: *Images d'une dictature*
Short Film: *Atomic Sake*
Animated Short: *The Old Man and the Sea*

Golden Reel Award

The Golden Reel Award was established in 1977 by the Canadian Motion Picture Distributors Association to recognize the producer of the Canadian feature film that achieved the highest box-office gross in Canadian theatres. Since 1980, the Award has been presented at the Genie Awards ceremony. The winning producers and films are listed below according to the year the award was presented.

1977
Anthony Bedrich and Harry Gulkin: *Lies My Father Told Me*

1978
Lawrence Hertzog: *Why Shoot the Teacher?*

1979
Allan King: *Who Has Seen the Wind*

1980
Dan Goldberg and Ivan Reitman: *Meatballs*

1981
Joel Michaels and Garth Drabinsky: *The Changeling*

1982
Ivan Reitman: *Heavy Metal*

1983
Harold Greenberg and Melvin Simon: *Porky's*

1984
Louis Silverstein: *Strange Brew*

1985
Rock Demers and Nicole Robert: *The Dog Who Stopped the War / La Guerre des tuques*

1986
Michael Hirsh, Patrick Loubert, and Clive Smith: *The Care Bears Movie*

1987
Roger Frappier and René Malo: *Le Déclin de l'empire américain*

1988
John Kemeny and Andras Hamori: *The Gate*

1989
Rock Demers: *The Tadpole and the Whale*

1990
Roger Frappier and Pierre Gendron: *Jésus de Montréal*

1991
Roger Frappier: *Ding et Dong, le film*

1992
Robert Lantos, Stéphane Reichel, and Sue Milliken: *Black Robe*

1993
Claude Bonin and Pierre Sarrazin: *La Florida*

1994
Richard Sadler and Jacques Dorfman: *Louis 19, le roi des ondes*

1995
Don Carmody: *Johnny Mnemonic*

1996
Robert Lantos, Jeremy Thomas, and David Cronenberg: *Crash*

1997
Michael Strange and Robert Vince: *Air Bud*

1998
No award was given.

1999
Richard Goudreau: *Les Boys*

2000
Richard Goudreau: *Les Boys II*

2001
Nicholas Clermont: *The Art of War*

ACADEMY AWARDS

This list includes only Academy Awards presented to Canadian-produced films. The awards are listed according to the year they were presented.

1941
Documentary: *Churchill's Island*, Stuart Legg (p/d)

1953
Short Documentary: *Neighbours*, Norman McLaren (p/d/an)

1976
Feature Documentary: *The Man Who Skied down Everest*, Budge Crawley (p/d)

1978
Animated Short: *The Sand Castle*, Gaston Sarault (p), Co Hoedeman (d/an)
Live-Action Short: *I'll Find a Way*, Yuki Yoshida (p), Beverly Shaffer (d)

1979
Animated Short: *Special Delivery*, Derek Lamb (p), John Weldon and Eunice Macauley (d/an)

1980
Animated Short: *Every Child*, Derek Lamb (p), Eugene Fedorenko (d/an)

1982
Animated Short: *Crac!*, Frédéric Back (d/an)

1983
Feature Documentary: *Just Another Missing Kid*, John Zaritsky (d)
Make-up: *Quest for Fire*
Short Documentary: *If You Love This Planet*, Edward Le Lorrain (p), Terre Nash (d)

1984
Live-Action Short: *Boys and Girls*, Seaton McLean (p), Don McBrearty (d)
Short Documentary: *Flamenco at 5:15*, Adam Symansky and Cynthia Scott (p), Cynthia Scott (d)

1985
Animated Short: *Charade,* John Minnis (an)

1987
Feature Documentary: *Artie Shaw: Time Is All You've Got*, Brigitte Berman (p/d)

1988
Animated Short: *The Man Who Planted Trees*, Frédéric Back (d/an)

1989
Honorary Academy Award: National Film Board of Canada, in recognition of its fiftieth anniversary

1995
Animated Short: *Bob's Birthday*, David Fine and Alison Snowden (d/an)

2000
Animated Short: *The Old Man and the Sea*, Alexandre Petrov (d/an)
Musical Score: *The Red Violin*